The Microelectronics Revolution

D0120733

By the same author

The Labour Party and the Working Class (1976)

The Microelectronics Revolution

THE COMPLETE GUIDE
TO THE NEW TECHNOLOGY
AND ITS IMPACT ON SOCIETY

Edited and Introduced by
Tom Forester

Basil Blackwell · Oxford

First published 1980 by
Basil Blackwell Publisher
5 Alfred Street
Oxford OX1 4HB
England
Fourth Impression 1982

British Library Cataloguing in Publication Data

The microelectronics revolution.
  1. Computers and civilization
  2. Microcomputers – Social aspects
  I. Forester, Tom
301.24'3   QA76.9.C66

  ISBN 0-631-11651-6
  ISBN 0-631-12572-8 Pbk

Filmset by Vantage Photosetting Co. Ltd.
Southampton and London
Printed in Great Britain by
Billing and Sons Ltd.

Contents

Chapter 3   Applications of the New Technology

PART TWO: ECONOMIC AND SOCIAL IMPLICATIONS

Chapter 4   The Impact in Industry

Chapter 5   The Revolution in the Office

Chapter 6   The Consequences for Employment

Contents   vii

Preface

It is now two years since the "silicon chip" burst on to the public stage in Europe. "The Chips Are Down", "Chips With Everything", "Britain Has Had Its Chips" – the headline writers had a field day as newspapers, magazines and TV documentary makers rushed to cover the "mini marvel" and the "tiny terror". What was a little-known invention only months before became firmly implanted in the public consciousness overnight. Silicon-spiced asides became commonplace in everyday conversations. Politicians wrote worthy references to microprocessors into their speeches. Indeed (and in keeping with the pun tradition), we can report that the chip in Europe has become a hot political potato.

Contrast the situation in North America. Ask Americans for their views on the "job destroyer" and they respond with a blank stare. Even though the original automation and unemployment debate began in America in the 1950s, the less fanciful and more believable projections about the social impact of the new microelectronic technology have not been so widely reported. Perhaps it is because in the more mobile, risk-taking society of America people have become acclimatized to rapid technological and social change. Certainly unemployment, though just as high, is not the burning issue it is in the older, less adaptable nations of Europe. But as the United States plunges into recession in the 1980s, all that may change.

For this anthology, I have included what I regard as the best that is available on both sides of the Atlantic on the technology of the microprocessor and its social implications. The likely impact on the factory floor, the office and on society as a whole is examined, with special reference to the consequences for employment and industrial relations. I make no apology for the fact that the style of each piece varies: such is the nature of a reader which has also been designed to form the basis of a comprehensive course on society and the new technology.

At the end of each chapter there is a guide to further reading. The items described or listed have mostly been looked at with a view to inclusion in this collection – and have, for various reasons, been rejected. However, many are well worth following up, as the commentary will make clear.

The editorial consultants on this project were Professor Ernest Braun of the Technology Policy Unit at the University of Aston in Birmingham; Professor Christopher Freeman of the Science Policy Research Unit at Sussex University; and members of the Electronics Applications Division of the Department of Industry, London.

For additional inspiration and assistance, I would like to thank Ray Curnow, formerly of Sussex University; Keith Dickson of the University of Aston; Tom Hinkelman of the Semiconductor Industries Association, Santa Clara, California; Ed Zuckerman of Cambridge, Massachusetts; John Davey of Basil Blackwell; and most important of all, my wife Delia.

Tom Forester

Acknowledgements

The editor and the publisher are grateful to the following:

Business Week, for A. A. Perlowski, "The 'Smart' Machine Revolution", reprinted from the 5 July 1976 issue of *Business Week* by special permission © 1976 McGraw-Hill, Inc., New York, N.Y. 10020, all rights reserved;

Control Engineering, for Neil P. Ruzic, "The Automated Factory", reprinted from *Control Engineering*, April 1978, by permission of *Control Engineering*, 1301 S. Grove Avenue, Barrington, Ill. 60010;

Data Processing, for *EDP Analyzer*, "The Experience of Word Processing" in *Data Processing*, May 1978, condensed from the February 1977 issue of *EDP Analyzer* (a monthly report designed to keep data processing management abreast of new approaches to application, of ways to improve productivity, of development of staff, and of the day-to-day running of the installation: further details may be obtained from Canning Publications, Inc., 925 Anza Ave., Vista, Calif. 92083);

Datamation, for J. Christopher Burns, "The Automated Office", originally appearing as "The Evolution of Office Information Systems", in *Datamation*, April 1977, and for Joe Weizenbaum, "Where Are We Going? Questions for Simon", orginally appearing as "Controversies and Responsibilities" in *Datamation*, 15 November 1978, both reprinted with permission of *Datamation*® magazine, © copyright by Technical Publishing Company, a Dun & Bradstreet Company, 1977, 1978 – all rights reserved;

John Garrett and Geoff Wright, for John Garrett and Geoff Wright, "Micro is Beautiful", reproduced from *Undercurrents*, No. 27,

April/May 1978, © John Garrett and Geoff Wright by permission;

The MIT Press, for Daniel Bell, "The Social Framework of the Information Society", and "A Reply to Weizenbaum", and for Joe Weizenbaum, "Once More, the Computer Revolution", reprinted from *The Computer Age: A Twenty-Year View*, Michael Dertouzos and Joel Moses, eds., by permission of the MIT Press, Cambridge, Massachusetts, copyright © 1979 The Massachusetts Institute of Technology;

New Society, for Tom Forester, "The Jelly Bean People of Silicon Valley", reproduced from *New Society*, 27 July 1978, © New Society, by permission;

Online Conferences Ltd, for Tom Stonier, "The Impact of Microprocessors on Employment", reprinted by permission of Online Conferences Ltd, Cleveland Road, Uxbridge, Mddx;

Science, for Philip H. Abelson and Allen L. Hammond, "The Electronics Revolution", Lawrence B. Evans, "Industrial Uses of the Microprocessor", originally appearing as "Impact of the Electronics Revolution on Industrial Process Control", Arthur L. Robinson, "Electronics and Employment: Displacement Effects", originally "Impact of Electronics on Employment and Displacement Effects", and for Herbert A. Simon, "What Computers Mean for Man and Society", all from *Science*, vol. 195, 18 March 1977, pp. 1087–94, and 1186–91 © 1977 the American Association for the Advancement of Science;

Scientific American, for Robert N. Noyce, "Microelectronics", and William G. Oldham, "The Fabrication of Microelectronic Circuits", both from *Scientific American*, vol. 237, no. 3, September 1977, reprinted with permission, copyright © 1977 Scientific American, Inc., all rights reserved;

The Times, for Philip Venning, "Microcomputers in the Classroom", originally appearing as "Snoring Robot in Commercial Assault on the Home-Learning Market", reproduced from *The Times Educational Supplement*, 20 October 1978, by permission;

and Unesco, for Bruno Lefèvre, "The Impact of Microelectronics on Town Planning", reproduced from *Impact of Science on Society*, vol. 27, no. 2, April–June 1977, p. 227 © Unesco 1977, by permission of Unesco.

Editor's Introduction

"The most remarkable technology ever to confront mankind" was the verdict of Sir Ieuan Maddock, former British government Chief Scientist, when he addressed a 1978 conference on microelectronics in London. It was prompting by Sir Ieuan and other key figures that forced the British government to wake up in 1978 to the significance of the microelectronics revolution. Reports were hastily commissioned on the state of the British electronics industry, the degree of awareness about the new technology in backward British industry, and the implications for British society.

Other nations hurried to study microelectronics: Australia, Canada, Denmark, Finland, France, Germany, Holland, Italy, Japan and Sweden all launched major investigations in 1978. In France, a characteristically weighty and intellectual government report by M. Simon Nora on "The Information Society" caused shock waves across the continent. In Germany, leaks of a secret study carried out for the multinational firm Siemens, which predicted that forty per cent of office jobs would go, created a national sensation. In Holland, the leader of the opposition party even called for a new tax on automation.

But most government initiatives were more constructive. The British government introduced a series of measures that were typical of what was happening in other countries: steps were taken to encourage the domestic microelectronics industry, through the formation of INMOS, a technology company, INSAC (computer software) and NEXOS (office equipment), under the auspices of the National Enterprise Board; a crash programme was launched to increase awareness about microelectronic technology in industry; grants were made available to encourage investment in new technology; universities were asked to train more electronic engineers; schools were told to introduce minicomputers into the classroom, and to schedule discussions about the new microelectronic age into the timetable. The trade unions, already very active with their own studies, were further encouraged to spread awareness of microelectronics and the shape of things to come among their members – something made seemingly more urgent by the absence of *The Times* from the streets of London owing to a long-running dispute over the introduction of new microelectronic technology.

All this uncharacteristic haste on the part of governments was further enhanced by the realization that changes in microelectronic technology happen very quickly. The pace of the microelectronics revolution has been exceptionally rapid, with the introduction of new devices being immediately followed by dramatic *reductions* in price. For example, the market leader among chip producers, Texas Instruments, calmly announced in late 1978 that the price of their new 64K dynamic RAM (for explanation, see glossary) would fall from $55 at introduction, to $38 by the end of 1979, $18 in 1980, $8 in 1983 and $4 in 1985.

In addition, the sales of microprocessors and microprocessor-based products have been going up by leaps and bounds. The international consultancy firms like Arthur D. Little are predicting a massive expansion in the markets for such things as industrial robots and word processors. All the indications are that the predicted pervasiveness of the chip is indeed proving correct and that it is infiltrating every sector of our social life.

A whole variety of products incorporating microprocessors are already available. There are chip-controlled automatic machine tools for industry, and all kinds of new office equipment, like sophisticated photocopiers, which have chips inside. Apart from the better-known microprocessor-based consumer goods such as electronic calculators, digital watches, electronic toys and TV games, larger consumer durables like the TV itself, washing machines, music centres, video recorders and microwave ovens all incorporate numbers of chips which provide control and memory functions and constant digital readouts. There are chip-based thermometers and weighing machines, chip-controlled warehouses, multistorey car parks and church organs, even an "electronic waiter" for direct-dialling your order to the restaurant kitchen.

Chips have already invaded the supermarket, in the form of "point-of-sale terminals" and the Universal Product Code. They are poised to invade labour-intensive banks (electronic funds transfer), people's homes (home computers) and the family car (electronic ignition, timing and dashboard instrumentation). There are even plans for them to invade the female bra: a Scottish firm recently announced a chip that will predict a woman's "safe" and "unsafe" periods by monitoring temperature variations from its strategic position inside the bra. Information would then be conveyed either by suitably-positioned digital readout or by two bra-mounted lights, one showing red, the other showing green.

But the greatest impact of the microprocessor will be felt at our places of work. Offices, in particular, are ripe for technological revolution: a 1974 US survey revealed that labour accounted for eighty-four per cent of office costs. While each factory worker was backed by an estimated $25,000 of capital investment, office workers had just $2000 behind them. While productivity in American industry had increased by eighty-three per cent in the 1960s, office productivity had crept up at just four per cent per annum. Poor productivity in the offices of the service sector was seen as a major reason for the failure of advanced industrial societies to sustain economic growth.

Earlier this year, another survey found that America spent $27 billion on data processing in 1978, $46 billion on office equipment, but $373 billion on the wages of office staff. No wonder some of the biggest multinational companies in the world are converging on the office equipment market, which is predicted to become *the* growth industry of the 1980s. The potential for labour shedding is enormous: as Victor A. Vyssotsky, an executive director at Bell Laboratories, recently pointed out, a two per cent per annum reduction in office staffs in America would displace twenty-five million workers by the year 2000.

Of course, offices have been getting less labour-intensive for years. While central London, for instance, lost 50,000 clerical jobs between 1966 and 1971, the amount of office space available grew by sixteen million square feet. But there seems little doubt that the pace of labour-substitution will increase substantially in the near future with the rapid reduction in costs and the growing sophistication of products that only microelectronics can provide. There was a recognition of this in a British government report published in April 1979, which predicted, in effect, that employment growth in Britain's civil service would soon cease.

In industry, the employment impact may not be so severe overall, but it will vary greatly from sector to sector. Rather than creating new products or completely displacing old ones, the introduction of micro-electronic technology will mean that it will take less time to produce existing products. This is partly because production lines can be auto-mated or speeded up, but mainly because the number of components in a product – and thus the time taken to assemble it – can be greatly reduced by the incorporation of chips. A colour TV once contained 1200 components. Now, with chips, it only contains 450. One of the new electronic telex machines takes eleven hours to assemble, compared with seventy-five hours for the old electromechanical ones. A semi-automated textile mill incorporating microelectronic technology was opened in August 1978 at Atherton, Manchester. It covers 8500 square metres and employs ninety-five people. The first new mill to be built in this old industrial area for fifty years, it replaced three mills covering 45,000 square metres and employing 435 people.

Some say that new jobs will be created for people engaged in the production of the new microelectronic devices. It once seemed likely that employment would grow in the short term in the electronic components industry itself, although in the medium term many more jobs would be lost elsewhere as microelectronic technology became more and more widely applied. But now it appears that, taking employment in the electronic components industry as a whole, the number of jobs available is already falling. A British report from the National Economic Development Council in February 1979 revealed that the number of new jobs created in the microelectronics industry will be tiny compared with the number lost from old-fashioned electronics. Even on the most optimistic trading assumptions, high productivity in the manufacture of microelectronic devices will ensure that employment in the British electronic components industry will fall from 129,000 to 114,000 – and that includes the 15,000 to 18,000 jobs that will be created as a result of public and private sector investments now planned.

Microelectronics makes possible all kinds of innovations hitherto relegated to the realms of science fiction: cash transactions can now be eliminated by electronic funds transfer (EFT); electronic mail will be able to replace the surface carriage of documents; sophisticated teaching machines incorporating voice processors will soon be available; telecommunications will be revolutionized by the greater use of satellites, one effect of which will be to aid communication with, and technology transfer to, the Third World.

Some of these developments are already further advanced than many realize – indeed, many companies are loath to trumpet their new systems for fear of encouraging hostile trade union reaction. But the Friends' Provident insurance company in England now has an "electronic mail" policy-issuing system that has cut the time taken to issue a policy from a customer's proposal from three weeks to three minutes. The microelectronic technology being used enables the proposal form to be checked and the premium calculated by a computer in Dorking, Surrey. The policy document is then composed in the local branch office almost instantaneously, thus eliminating mounds of paperwork and numerous transitional stages involving the use of surface mail. On the teletext front, the British Post Office introduced the world's first computerized information service, Prestel, early in 1979.

Concrete examples such as this may help to demonstrate that microelectronics really will have a major impact on society. The sceptics point to the "automation" debate of the late 1950s and the early 1960s, when wild predictions were made about the capabilities of mainframe computers. But that debate was premature: the early computers were clumsy great installations, they were extraordinarily expensive to buy and to run, and they needed armies of data processors to run them. The chip, on the other hand, is tiny, costs virtually nothing to produce, and is more reliable, more powerful and more versatile than any of the huge 1950s computers.

The new "automation" debate therefore differs from the 1950s debate in two crucial respects. First, the chip is a genuinely revolutionary device. Second, it has appeared at a time when economic growth in the industrial societies can no longer be taken for granted. Deindustrialization and rising unemployment, now affecting Europe, North America and Japan, has given this debate about the future shape of society an added sense of urgency.

The following papers, I hope, will convince you that the chip is here to stay and that we must give serious thought to our microelectronic future.

PART ONE: THE MICRO-ELECTRONICS REVOLUTION

1 The New Technology

Here Comes the Second Computer Revolution

Gene Bylinsky

The first full-length feature on the microelectronics revolution to appear in a nonspecialist publication, this article was published in the US magazine Fortune *in November 1975. Others picked up the story (see the guide to further reading), but it was not until 1978 that the silicon chip became big news.*

Less than thirty years ago, electrical engineer J. Presper Eckert Jr. and physicist John W. Mauchly, at times assisted by as many as fifty helpers, laboriously built the world's first electronic digital computer. Their ENIAC (Electronic Numerical Integrator and Computer) was a fickle monster that weighed thirty tons and ran on 18,000 vacuum tubes – when it ran. But it started the computer revolution.

Now under way is a new expansion of electronics into our lives, a second computer revolution that will transform ordinary products and create many new ones. The instrument of change is an electronic data-processing machine so tiny that it could easily have been lost in the pocket of one of those ENIAC tubes. This remarkable device is the microcomputer, also known as the computer-on-a-chip. In its basic configuration, it consists of just that – a complex of circuits on a chip of silicon about the size of the first three letters in the word ENIAC as printed here. Yet even a medium-strength microcomputer can perform 100,000 calculations a second, twenty times as many as ENIAC could.

This smallest of all data-processing machines was invented six years ago, but its mass applications are just beginning to explode, setting off reverberations that will affect work and play, the profitability and productivity of corporations, and the nature of the computer industry

3

itself. For the microcomputer provides an awesome amount of computer power in a package that in its simplest form costs less than $10 bought in quantity and easily fits inside a matchbox. Accessory devices bring microcomputer prices to between $50 and $250 apiece, to be sure, but that's still a lot less than the thousands of dollars in minicomputer costs.

And unlike the familiar older computers that come in their own boxes, the microcomputer is mounted on a small board that can be made to fit easily and unobtrusively into a corner of an electric typewriter, a butcher's scale, a cash register, a microwave oven, a gas pump, a traffic light, a complex scientific instrument such as a gas chromatograph, and any of a myriad other devices whose capabilities already are being enhanced by these slices of electronic brainpower. Soon microcomputers will start replacing wheels, gears, and mechanical relays in a wide variety of control applications, because it's much more efficient to move electrons around than mechanical parts.

To cite these applications and capabilities, as well as many other uses to come in the home, the factory, and the automobile, is to do only pale justice to this marvellous invention. What sets any computer apart from every other kind of machine is its stored and alterable program, which allows one computer to perform many different tasks in response to simple program changes. Now the microcomputer can impart this power, in a compact form and at a low price, to many other machines and devices.

In the most common form of microcomputer, furthermore, a user can change the program simply by unplugging a tiny memory chip and putting a new one in its place. To show off this versatility, Pro-Log Corp. of Monterey, California, built a demonstration apparatus that in its original version is a digital clock; when a program chip that runs the clock is removed and another is put in its place, the thing suddenly starts belting out a tinny version of the theme from *The Sting*. With still another memory chip, it becomes a rudimentary piano.

Besides providing versatility for users, the microcomputer makes possible large economies in manufacturing. Now a manufacturer can buy a standard microcomputer system for many different products and use a different program chip with each. By doing so, the manufacturer can save substantial amounts of money since a single microcomputer can replace as many as 200 individual logic chips, which cost about $3 each.

The use of microcomputers, moreover, can substantially reduce service and warranty costs because the reliability of the electronic portion of a device is increased up to tenfold. A microcomputer that replaces, say, fifty integrated circuits does away with about 1800 interconnections – where most failures occur in electronics. The microcomputer, in other words, is one of those rare innovations that at the same time reduce the cost of manufacturing *and* enhance the capabilities and value of the product. Thus the microcomputer may be the best technological antidote for inflation in quite a while.

Even the men who make and use microcomputers say that they haven't yet grasped the device's full implications, but they know the implications are large and far-reaching. Fairly typical is the comment of Edward L. Gelbach, senior vice president at Intel Corp., the Santa Clara, California, semiconductor company where the tiny computer was invented. "The microcomputer," he says, "is almost too good to be true."

The microcomputer is the logical end result of the electronics industry's headlong drive to miniaturize. The industry has galloped through three generations of components in as many decades. In the late 1950s, the transistor replaced the vacuum tube. Within a few years the transistor itself gave way to "large-scale integration", or LSI, the technique that now places thousands of micro-miniaturized transistors – an integrated circuit – on a sliver of silicon only a fraction of an inch thick. LSI made possible the suitcase-sized minicomputer.

The semiconductor logic circuit, of course, contained the seed of the microcomputer, since the chip had logic elements on it – the transistors. But the individual chips were designed to perform limited tasks. Accordingly, the central processing units of large computers were made up of hundreds, or thousands, of integrated circuits.

Logic chips were also employed for control or arithmetic functions in specialized applications. In what became known as "hardwired logic" systems, chips and other individual components were soldered into a rigid pattern on a so-called printed-circuit board. The fixed interconnections served as the program. Curiously, it was even less flexible than ENIAC's primitive array of plug-in wires that could be moved around to change the program.

The electronic calculator, in all but the latest versions, uses hardwired logic. The arithmetic functions, or the operating program instructions, are embedded in the chips, while the application program is in the user's head – his instructions yield the desired calculations.

A young Intel engineer, M. E. Hoff Jr, envisaged a different way of employing the new electronic capabilities. He had received a Ph.D. in electronics from Stanford University, where he had become accustomed to solving problems with general purpose data-processing machines. In 1969 he found himself in charge of a project that Intel took on for Busicom, a Japanese calculator company. Busicom wanted Intel to produce calculator chips of Japanese design. The logic circuits were spread around eleven chips and the complexity of the design would have taxed Intel's capabilities – it was then a small company.

Hoff saw a way to improve on the Japanese design by making a bold technological leap. Intel had pioneered in the development of semiconductor memory chips to be used in large computers. (See "How Intel Won Its Bet on Memory Chips", *Fortune*, November 1973.) In the intricate innards of a memory chip, Hoff knew, it was possible to store a program to run a minuscule computing circuit.

In his preliminary design, Hoff condensed the layout onto three chips. He put the computer's "brain", its central processing unit, on a single chip of silicon. That was possible because the semiconductor industry had developed a means of inscribing very complex circuits on tiny surfaces. A master drawing, usually 500 times as large as the actual chip, is reduced photographically to microminiature size. The photo images are then transferred to the chip by a technique similar to photoengraving.

Hoff's CPU on a chip became known as the microprocessor. To the microprocessor, he attached two memory chips, one to move data in and out of the CPU and one to provide the program to drive the CPU. Hoff now had in hand a rudimentary general-purpose computer that not only could run a complex calculator but also could control an elevator or a set of traffic lights, and perform many other tasks, depending on its program. The microcomputer was slower than minicomputers, but it could be mass-produced as a component, on the same high-volume lines where Intel made memory chips – a surprising development that would suddenly put the semiconductor company into the computer business.

Hoff had strong backers in Intel's top executives: President Gordon E. Moore and Chairman Robert N. Noyce, the co-inventor of the integrated circuit. Unlike many other specialists, Noyce and Moore had sensed the potential of the microcomputer early on, and they lent enthusiastic support to Hoff's project. Most others had visualized a computer-on-a-chip as being something extremely expensive and far in the future. When in the late 1960s Noyce suggested at a conference that the next decade would see the development of a computer-on-a-chip, one of his fellow panellists typically remarked in all seriousness: "Gee, I certainly wouldn't want to lose my whole computer through a crack in the floor." Noyce told the man: "You have it all wrong, because you'll have 100 more sitting on your desk, so it won't matter if you lose one."

After other Intel engineers who took over the detailed design work got through with it, Hoff's invention contained 2250 microminiaturized transistors on a chip slightly less than one sixth of an inch long and one eighth of an inch wide, and each of those microscopic transistors was roughly equal to an ENIAC vacuum tube. Intel labelled the microprocessor chip 4004, and the whole microcomputer MCS-4 (microcomputer system 4). "The 4004 will probably be as famous as the ENIAC," says an admiring Motorola executive. Despite its small size, the 4004 just about matched ENIAC's computational power. It also matched the capability of an IBM machine of the early 1960s that sold for $30,000 and whose central processing unit took up the space of an office desk. If any had suggested in the days of ENIAC that this kind of advance would take place so soon, says Presper Eckert, now a vice-president at Sperry Univac, the idea would have struck him as "outlandish".

For logic and systems designers the appearance of the microcomputer brought with it a dramatic change in the way they employed electronics. They could now replace all those rigid hardwired logic systems with microcomputers, because they could store program sequences in the labyrinthine circuits of the memory chip instead of using individual logic chips and discrete components to implement the program. Engineers thus could substitute program code words for hardware parts.

For the semiconductor industry the arrival of the microprocessor on a chip signalled the end of a costly search for ways to reduce the complicated technology to more generalized applications. "The problem," says Moore of Intel, "was that as the technology got more complex you couldn't find any generality to the circuit functions. What customers wanted was one of this circuit, one of that circuit, to build a system." Such demands threw monkey wrenches into the industry's efforts to hold down costs through mass production.

The industry kept flailing and groping for ways to master the problem. Texas Instruments, for instance, had a big project aimed at using computer-guided design to make production of integrated logic components more flexible. Fairchild Semiconductor talked about turning out as many as 500 different logic components a week to suit the requirements of different customers. In these attempts, engineers were trying to force the technology to become more flexible. Ted Hoff's solution, to make the internal design itself more flexible, was far more elegant and more powerful. Says Moore: "Now we can make a single microprocessor chip and sell it for several thousand different applications."

At first the semiconductor industry showed surprisingly little interest in this great leap in its technology. Robert Noyce recalls that when Intel introduced the microcomputer late in 1971, the industry's reaction was "ho hum". Semiconductor manufacturers had made so many extravagant promises in the past that the industry seemed to have become immune to claims of real advances. Besides, the big semiconductor companies – Texas Instruments, Motorola, and Fairchild – were preoccupied with their large current business, integrated circuits and calculator chips. "Looking back," says J. Fred Bucy, TI's executive vice-

Ted Hoff's miracle
chip shown here is a
little more
convenient in shape
and size than TREAC,
an equivalent 1953
computer developed
by Britain's
Telecommunications
Research
Establishment.
*Above courtesy of
Intel Corporation;
below courtesy of
Professor
A. M. Uttley*

president and chief operating officer, "we probably should have started on microcomputers earlier."

Only Rockwell International and National Semiconductor got into the field early on, about a year after Intel. Fairchild came out with a microprocessor chip that it sold primarily to calculator manufacturers. It took another six months or so before the new economics of the microcomputer stung the other giants into action. By that time, hardly anyone could have missed the message: a microprocessor and its memory could replace a lot of individual logic chips – anywhere from ten to 200. To speed the adoption of microcomputers, Intel undertook to recast the thinking of industrial-design engineers – the company taught 5000 engineers the use of the microcomputer in the early 1970s and another 5000 or so later on. Once these engineers started ordering the tiny computers in some quantity, the big companies, as Noyce puts it, said: "We've got to get on board here."

They rushed to get on board by "second-sourcing" – that is copying – Intel's microcomputers. Second-sourcing is a common practice in the semiconductor industry. More often than not, it is done without the original manufacturer's permission or cooperation, but the practice is nonetheless widely accepted by the companies involved. It works to the benefit of the user in establishing a competitive source for the component as well as a backup for the original manufacturer. In fact, users normally demand second-sourcing.

Second-sourcing microcomputers proved to be a complex task, however. What's more, Intel kept moving. It followed up the 4004 with a more capacious 8008 model in 1972, and towards the end of 1973 brought out its second-generation microcomputer, the 8080. This was twenty times faster than the 4004. Even then most competitors had no microcomputers of their own to offer. The first real competition to the 8080 was Motorola's 6800, which came a year afterward. The late starters began to catch up this year (1975) when Texas Instruments, General Instrument, and others announced microcomputer models of their own. TI also introduced its copy of the 8080.

To paper over the gap, some nimble competitors upgraded calculator chips and started calling them computers-on-a-chip. With memory on the same square of silicon, these basic units can perform simple and even medium-complexity control functions – running washing machines or microwave ovens, for instance. TI, Rockwell, and others now offer such chips. The TI product, TMS 1000, sells for as little as $4 in large quantities.

All these companies, and many others, are battling for a market that so far is fairly small – this year it will amount to only about $50m. But it is expected to expand to $150m next year, and to reach $450m by 1980.

In these estimates, the microprocessor chips account for only fifteen to twenty per cent of the dollar total, with memories and other components making up the bulk of the new business.

Applications of microcomputers today are tilted heavily towards data-processing equipment of various kinds, including computer terminals and other accessories. The other major market is retailing equipment – electronic cash registers and point-of-sale terminals. But the picture is expected to change drastically in a few years as microcomputers invade consumer products in force. TI estimates that consumer product uses will account for about one third of the predicted $450m-a-year market for microprocessors in 1980.

In their capabilities, microcomputers cover quite a range of applications. A simple microcomputer can act as a miniature controller, replacing an electromechanical relay or hardwired logic systems. A more powerful model, such as the 8080, can control a computer printer, or a whole series of them. Still more powerful models begin to match – and some already exceed – minicomputers in their computational speeds.

The tiny computer is beginning to generate not only new products but new companies as well. Says Gordon Hoffman, an executive at Mostek, a Dallas semiconductor house: "A lot of big companies are going to be improperly prepared to take advantage of the microcomputer. If they don't take advantage of it, they may find themselves out in the cold when a little upstart comes along and says: 'I can do it better with a microcomputer.'"

That kind of competition has already begun, with many fast-moving small companies taking advantage of the microcomputer's mighty power. A few examples:

> Chemetrics Corp. of Burlingame, California, only two years old, has brought out an advanced blood-chemistry analyser.
> Electro Units Corp. of San Jose has developed an electronic control system for bars; it doles out precisely measured drinks and serves as an attentive inventory controller too.
> Telesensory System Inc. of Palo Alto is introducing this autumn a "talking" calculator for the blind, with a recorded vocabulary of twenty-four words for spoken verification of calculation steps and results.

Large companies, of course, are also using the capabilities of the computer-on-a-chip to turn out new products. Among them:

> General Electric, which is looking into many possible applications, recently introduced a robot industrial tool run by a tiny computer.
> AMF, with the aid of Motorola, developed an automatic scorer now being demonstrated in bowling alleys.

Tappan Co. is designing a microwave oven with "touch-and-cook" controls; it uses the single-chip microcomputer made by Texas Instruments.

For companies large and small, instrumentation is proving to be one of the most rewarding areas of microprocessor applications. Because of its powerful data-processing capacity, a computer-on-a-chip can not only impart brand-new capabilities to an instrument but also make it much easier to operate. With the microcomputer helping out, an unskilled person can operate a complex instrument, because, as one Perkin-Elmer engineer puts it: "The skill now resides in the microcomputer." Perkin-Elmer has already introduced two different spectrophotometers incorporating the microcomputer and is working on other uses in scientific instruments.

Microcomputers will also make a lot of laboratory-type analytical equipment more readily applicable to process control. Leeds & Northrup has already produced one such instrument, a particle analyser that uses a laser beam to measure particles and a microcomputer to figure out their size distribution. The device is being tested in a taconite (iron ore) plant, but it can be adapted to other customers' needs through a change in its program.

Semiconductor manufacturers are also looking for applications of microcomputers to appliances such as washing machines and refrigerators. The current recession has delayed new-product introduction in this field, but microcomputers are being designed into models that are expected to start showing up in about two years.

The automobile may prove to be a big user of electronics in years to come. Some electronic components are already being employed in cars to supervise ignition, measure voltages, and so on. Microcomputers are expected to start appearing in automobiles towards the end of this decade. Ford Motor Co. has found that microcomputer-run controls can cut fuel consumption by as much as twenty per cent under test conditions. The company plans to introduce the tiny computers in a 1979 car. Other auto-makers have similar plans.

In many other areas, microcomputers promise spectacular advances. In the home, microcomputer controls could result in savings on electric and heating bills. For the military, the tiny computers promise the evolution of more versatile weapons. In medical electronics, they open up possibilities for compact and less costly diagnostic instruments. There are indications that in conjunction with complex optical and mechanical devices, microcomputers could help restore vision for some of the blind. In one project, a microprocessor chip will be embedded in an eyeglass frame to decode visual information from artificial "eyes" and send it to the brain.

As is true with any other computer, the largest costs – and most problems – arise in writing application programs for microcomputers. Basically, a digital computer runs in response to instructions written in the binary code of ones and zeros. That's how the first computers were programmed – with the complex instructions written out painstakingly by hand. To ease the programmers' task, the industry has over the years developed high-level computer languages in which abbreviations or even words substitute for whole series of numbers. Along with the languages came such programming aids as assemblers and compilers.

The semiconductor industry makes such aids available to micro-computer users. The machines are, in effect, small computers that utilize microprocessors. They sell for $2500 to $10,000. Motorola calls its device the Exorciser; Intel's is called the Intellec.

Problems arise when design engineers who have previously dealt with electromechanical relays, or even hardwired logic, and are untutored in computer programming, suddenly face the complex accoutrements of data processing. For some, says one specialist, the experience is like "going from wood burning to nuclear fuel". As a result, something of an occupational obsolescence has temporarily developed in the design field because the engineers who are most skilled in product design usually have little or no experience with microprocessors and their applications.

Trying to fill the educational gap, MIT and some other universities have begun intensive courses for both students and industry representatives. Reports MIT Professor H. M. D. Toong: "Students go right from here out into industry and get jobs first thing heading microcomputer development and applications departments." Some specialists think that the applications of microcomputers will start expanding manyfold when the new graduates begin to enter the work force in large numbers.

For semiconductor companies, the microcomputer opens another broad avenue for growth. With phenomenal price declines a way of life, the industry is a voracious consumer of new markets. Industry executives like to note that the price of an electronic function such as a transistor dropped 99.9 per cent from 1960 to 1970 and is still declining. As one man puts it: "It's like putting an $8 price tag on an $8000 Cadillac."

At the same time, each new advance in technology has brought with it a widening use of electronics. Texas Instruments calculates that during the vacuum-tube era, digital-electronic sales rose on a slope of about ten per cent a year. In the days of the transistor, the slope steepened to an eighteen per cent annual increase. Integrated circuits increased the sales growth rate to thirty-eight per cent. Now TI expects another upward tilt in the curve in the late 1970s, thanks chiefly to the microcomputer. The company anticipates that for the foreseeable future sales of electronic components will climb at a dizzying rate of fifty to sixty per cent a year.

There seems to be little disagreement that the microcomputer is close to being an ultimate semiconductor circuit and that it now sets the direction for semiconductor technology. On the face of it, the principal beneficiary of this trend would appear to be Intel. The company now dominates the microcomputer market. What's more, it mainly makes semiconductor memories of the kind that go into microcomputers and does not make the integrated circuits that microcomputers replace. The principal losers would seem to be Texas Instruments, Fairchild, Motorola, and National Semiconductor, which are big in what is called transistor-transistor logic (TTL), the mainstay of the integrated-circuit business today – precisely the circuits the microcomputer replaces.

But that's not how top executives of some of those companies see the future. TI's Fred Bucy envisages his company emerging as a major force in microcomputers. So does Charles E. Sporck, president of National Semiconductor. And both are probably right. Bucy stresses, and others agree, that the microcomputer's biggest use will be in applications where electronic devices have never been employed before. New applications thus will be far more important than replacement of TTL logic. Bucy also notes that TI is the only semiconductor company "that has lived through all the generations of electronic components. We've successfully moved from one horse to the next." Few executives in the industry would dispute TI's obvious strengths as a $1.5-billion company even if it has been late in microcomputers. National Semiconductor, too, is an exceedingly clever marketer.

Everyone agrees, furthermore, that there will be a whole spectrum of microcomputers aimed at different applications, with many companies sharing the anticipated big market. And it is generally agreed that the most successful makers of microcomputers will be those that supply the best operating programs. The need to generate software to go with the tiny computers is a new activity for semiconductor companies, with the exception of TI, which for years now has been making both mini-computers and very large machines.

Bucy and other TI executives feel that's another plus for their company. To keep its computers tied together, and to ease the task of users who want to employ microcomputers in conjunction with bigger machines, TI early in 1975 introduced a powerful microcomputer whose software is compatible with that of the company's minis. TI sees a big competitive advantage in this approach, since the software of most other microcomputers does not directly match that of bigger computers.

The ability of users to operate a whole hierarchy of computers, from a big host machine to the microcomputer far down in the organization, will speed the trend towards "distributed" computer power. Bucy sees as a result a computer world polarized into giant machines and huge numbers of microcomputers, with medium-sized computers diminishing in importance.

Other specialists see computers of the future evolving into modular processor systems based on microcomputers, with many of their programs embedded in microcomputer memories, replacing expensive software. Frederick G. Withington, of Arthur D. Little, Inc., predicts that ten years from now, as a result of the semiconductor industry's nonstop price erosion, the cost of even the largest CPU may come down to about $30,000.

Manufacturers of bigger mainframes are indeed beginning to incorporate microcomputers not only into terminals and minicomputers but also into their large machines, to control such functions as input and output of data. A vice-president of NCR says that his company is "going to concentrate on the use of microprocessors in microcomputers, minis, and on up the line". NCR buys microcomputers from semiconductor manufacturers but it also plans to make its own. Burroughs already manufactures its own microcomputers and uses them in a variety of devices, including a small business computer. Control Data buys from Intel. IBM and Honeywell do not yet make a microprocessor on a chip.

For manufacturers of big mainframes, then, the microcomputer has so far been a new component rather than a competitor. But for manufacturers of minicomputers, the arrival of the microcomputer has created a competitive danger – the micros are encroaching on the minis. To counter the threat, Digital Equipment Corp., No. 1 in minis, has made arrangements with a semiconductor company, Western Digital Corp., under which Western makes microprocessors and associated components. Digital Equipment then puts the devices on circuit boards and sells the microcomputers in direct competition with the semiconductor houses.

Some semiconductor companies, in turn, have come out with microcomputers that run on programs written by Digital Equipment and Data General Corp. for their minicomputers. These microcomputers do essentially the same job, but sell for a lot less than the original minis. This blurring of dividing lines between computer and semiconductor manufacturers is expected to continue. Only half in jest, Noyce already calls Intel "the world's largest computer manufacturer".

In its impact, the microcomputer promises to rival its illustrious predecessors, the vacuum tube, the transistor, and the integrated-circuit logic chip. So far, probably no more than ten per cent of the tiny computer's potential applications have reached production stage. Today, nearly thirty years after the debut of the ENIAC, there are about 200,000 digital computers in the world. Ten years from now, thanks to the microcomputer, there may be twenty million.

The Electronics Revolution

Philip H. Abelson and Allen L. Hammond

Written by the editor and a staff member of Science *magazine, this article sets the microelectronic revolution in historical perspective and surveys the areas of social life it will affect. It formed the introduction to a special issue of* Science *magazine on 18 March 1977 (vol. 195, No. 4283).*

Earlier in the century, the United States experienced a long era of sustained growth in many aspects. There was a steady increase in level of education, life expectancy, and standard of living. Growth of all kinds was welcomed, including industrial expansion and population increase. A feeling of progress, of achievement, of well-being was everywhere. As a corollary, a striving for excellence and the search for understanding were widely admired.

Today the mood of America has turned pessimistic and negative. Those who are so inclined can find much evidence to support these views. Growth in the use of energy in the form of oil was suddenly curtailed in 1974. Growth in consumption of the kind seen in the 1950s and 1960s will not occur again. That part of the standard of living which is based on large-scale consumption of energy is not likely to improve during this century.

However, those who prefer optimism have reason for hope. Human ingenuity in solving problems is great. And native intelligence has been amplified enormously by the use of knowledge accumulated through research. An important product of research and a basis for hoping for a bright new future is the vitality of the electronics revolution. This revolution has been in progress for about sixty years. Lately its tempo has increased greatly. Until recently, its importance was overshadowed by changes due to the large-scale expansion in the use of energy. But it

16

promises to be more important, of more enduring consequence, than the earlier industrial revolution.

Some of the great changes brought about by the electronics revolution have gone comparatively unnoticed; at the start they were evolutionary rather than sudden and drastic. The telephone, which we take for granted, was invented one hundred years ago. Nearly every decade since then the quality and scope of service have steadily improved, and the cost (measured in constant dollars) is now a tiny fraction of what it was fifty years ago.

Numerous applications of electronics gradually affected individuals and almost every component and activity of society. Radio was a marvellous toy and a source of wonderment when it was introduced fifty years ago. Now Americans listen to commercial radio an average of nearly four hours daily, and radio is accepted as practically a natural phenomenon. Television, which created a stir twenty-five years ago, is likewise commonplace.

During the last few years the impact of electronics on society has increased greatly. Examples are the rapid growth in popularity of citizens band radio, the worldwide use of the telephone, and the current astonishingly low prices at which handheld calculators and electronic watches are being sold. Less evident to the individual but in total more important to society are other applications of electronics that affect nearly every sector of our economy.

This revolution, which is destined to have great long-term consequences, is quite different in nature from the industrial revolution. The industrial revolution was based on a profligate use of energy (mainly fossil fuels). Much of its technology was crude, with only a modest scientific or theoretical base. In large measure what the industrial revolution did was to make available and to employ large amounts of mechanical energy.

In contrast, the electronics revolution represents one of the greatest intellectual achievements of mankind. Its development has been the product of the most advanced science, technology, and management. In many applications, electronics requires little energy. Indeed, one of the factors that guarantee enduring impact for the electronics revolution is that it is sparing of energy and materials.

With electronics one can control the disposition of large amounts of energy and force, but much in the way the brain is used in directing the action of muscles. In some aspects, electronics can be more subtle, more nimble, more dependable than the brain. In other applications, electronics serves as a great extender of human capabilities by rapidly carrying out routine but complex calculations, thus freeing the mind to make intuitive judgements and find shortcuts to new insights.

The industrial revolution, dependent on energy and materials, will be slowed and limited by the paucity of these necessary ingredients. The electronics revolution, fuelled by intellectual achievements, is destined for long-continued growth as its knowledge base inevitably increases. Obviously, the current rapid rate of evolution of electronics cannot persist indefinitely, but significant change is likely to continue for a long time.

One of the factors contributing to this dynamism is that in laboratories devoted to extending the electronics revolution the use of powerful investigative tools based on electronics is speeding new developments. Moreover, the body of knowledge that is being accumulated in the natural sciences continues to grow, and its growth has been fostered by the new tools that electronics has provided. There are few laboratories devoted to studies on the frontiers of the natural sciences that are not dependent on one or many items of electronic-based equipment. Two examples indicate the extent of the impact. A human's speed of reaction is about one fifth of a second. Measurements can now be made in times as short as 10^{-12} second. More important is the overall effect of electronic devices on quantitative determinations of many kinds. In some instances, sensitivities have been increased by orders of magnitude while the times required for measurement have been diminished to a hundredth or less of those needed in earlier methods.

One of the factors favouring the development of electronics has been a comparatively high degree of social acceptance. There have been sporadic attacks on various electronic devices such as computers and there is continuing concern about privacy, but the intensity of criticism has diminished. In comparison to the number of objections raised to chemical products, to the environmental concerns associated with nuclear and fossil fuel energy, or to fears of recombinant DNA, objections to electronics have been few.

The average citizen is fearful of air pollution, for example, and is frustrated by a feeling that there is little an individual can do about it. In contrast, if a television programme is offensive, it can be summarily dispensed with. Items that have recently become broadly available, such as the handheld computer, electronic watch, and citizens band radio, enhance the public's feeling of participating in the benefits of electronics while not bringing with them discernible side effects. In future, electronics will provide many new tools useful to the general public.

Three major themes are worth stressing: the tempo of the revolution, its magnitude, and the changing driving forces that have spurred it.

Until 1940, developments in electronics took place at a comparatively moderate pace. As was true with many scientific and technological matters, the pace quickened during World War Two and was further maintained during the Cold War. Two major developments occurred independently during the late 1940s and later fused to give enormous impetus to electronics. One was the construction of programmable electronic computers. The second was the invention of the transistor. Subsequent developments in solid state physics led to the present-day silicon chip with its large-scale integrated circuits. One such circuit can contain more active elements than the most complex equipment of twenty-five years ago.

After about 1960, when solid-state devices were incorporated in computers, there was a rapid development in the capabilities of computers and a steady reduction in the costs of calculations. An important effect of integrated circuits has been a reduction in the size and power requirements of electronic equipment that has made possible, for example, a Viking lander. Other advantages include reproducibility, maintainability, and reliability. Especially helpful is a sharp decrease in the need for making interconnections.

The tempo of change has been impressive. In 1959, a chip that was commercially available contained one component of a circuit. By 1964, the number of components per chip had risen to ten, by 1970 to about 1000, and by 1976 to about 32,000. The cost per chip advanced only modestly. Thus, the cost per function has dropped drastically. It is this great change in the cost-effectiveness ratio that has made possible inexpensive handheld calculators and related microprocessors and minicomputers. One of the key individuals who have been pushing the development of large-scale integrated circuits is Robert Noyce, the co-founder of Intel Corp. He argues that further advances can be expected. Theoretical considerations show that physical limits have not been approached. He is so bold as to state that "if the present rate of increase of complexity were to continue, integrated circuits with 10^9 elements would be available in twenty years."

All of us have seen examples of the sudden termination of exponential growth, so perhaps Noyce's figure will never be attained. But substantial advances toward his goal are already in progress. He seems justified in the view that "the potential for developing inexpensive processing power is truly awesome." He projects that with low-cost processing many new tasks will be undertaken that are uneconomical today.

Another way of glimpsing the tempo and magnitude of the electronics revolution is to focus on what has been happening in computers. In the early 1950s, almost all computers were owned by or devoted to tasks of the federal government. Computers were procured for use in such applications as defence and nuclear reactor design. By the mid-1950s there were about 1000 large-scale computers, and the tendency was toward increasing computational power. By the mid-1960s, there were 30,000 computers, and the generally accepted view was that costs of computation decreased with size; that is, the larger the better. At the end of 1976 there were about 220,000 computers in the United States. Of these, forty per cent were medium or large computers; the remainder were minicomputers which are small and by definition cost less than $50,000. At the same time, there were 750,000 of the microprocessors that form the heart of microcomputers. Ruth Davis has estimated that by 1980 the number of minicomputers will reach 750,000, while the number of microprocessors will increase to more than 10 million.

As the number of computers in service grew, the uses and the organizations involved broadened. The current distribution of ownership of conventional computers, with the percentages in the major categories, are: manufacturing industry, 31; miscellaneous business, 13.3; financial institutions, 13.4; wholesale and retail trade, 13.1; educational institutions, 5.7; state and local government, 5.7; and federal government, 3.4. There is further scattering of ownership throughout virtually every kind of organized activity. Thus it may seem that an enormous shift in the nature of the market for large computers has occurred. Beyond that is the larger market for minicomputers and the much larger mass demand for microprocessors.

Coincident with the expansion in the number of computers has been an increase in the number of computer professionals. During the past twenty years the total number of analysts, designers, programmers and operators has increased from 100,000 to 2.5 million. The number of students having some degree of familiarity with computers is much greater. This reservoir of people familiar with applications of computers is certain to facilitate additional applications of electronics. The emergence of computer hobby shops is bringing additional enthusiasts and imagination into the field. One group that is likely to make substantial contributions is the working scientists in the natural sciences. Often their progress and ability to tackle problems are limited by their equipment. Having experienced the advantages of incorporation of microprocessors in measuring devices, they will be looking for novel kinds of electronic sensors that can be coupled with the current data processors.

Because many of the new major applications involve various kinds of computers, one might have the impression that the electronics revolution and computers are synonymous. It is easy to lose sight of the importance of the noncomputer aspects of electronics. Key to many applications are the transducers or sensors. For example, computers would have a limited role in process control if electronic devices for sensing temperature, pressure, and concentrations of components were not available.

The potential applications of electronic technologies are so numerous and so provocative as to give free rein to futurologists and science-fiction writers. The domestic robot, the wired city, the global electronic village – none of these can be dismissed as being beyond the bounds of technical feasibility. But it is not necessary to look so far afield to see how pervasive the impact of electronics is, how many areas of human endeavour and how large a portion of the country's economic activity may be substantially altered. Indeed, it is probable that reality will outstrip fiction in the rate of introduction of new and often unexpected applications of electronics in coming years. Witness, for example, the incredible growth in popularity of citizens band radio. It is clear that the capability of some electronic devices, particularly microprocessor circuits and memory units on single silicon chips, is developing more rapidly than applications can be conceived of and introduced.

The markets for kitchen appliances, office equipment and leisure games, to mention just a few, are ready to be revolutionized or at least substantially modified by the addition of logic and memory to yield "smart stoves" and similar products, the first of which are already available.

The driving force behind many of the commercial applications is the extremely low prices for sophisticated electronic circuits, which in turn derive from mass production. The key innovation allowing such large markets is the microprocessor, a general-purpose logical unit that can be programmed to perform an unlimited number of tasks, thus eliminating the necessity of designing new circuitry for each new application. Among other applications, microprocessors are making it possible to extend computer control to mechanical and electrical equipment of every description, from consumer appliances and automobile engines to milling machines and industrial boilers. In the past, automation of manufacturing and process control has moved slowly because of fear of dependence on a central computer and the cost of the controlling units. The first process control computers introduced in the late 1950s, for example, cost about $300,000; minicomputers reduced this to less than $100,000 by the late 1960s; now microprocessor controllers are available for $3000, cheap enough to automate control and data collection for even small process steps. What seems to be evolving is a linked, hierarchical arrangement in which microprocessors are used to control individual pieces of equipment; minicomputers collect and process management information from the microprocessors for an entire factory; and large central computers use the resulting data in compiling corporate financial reports.

But the impact will not be confined merely to consumer products or isolated devices. The application of electronics is already having a pervasive effect on the entire economy and on our way of life, one that

promises to intensify in coming years. Consider the following areas –
medicine, education, national defence, banking and retail sales, postal
and other communications, and the research process itself.

The practice of medicine, for example, has already begun to change in
such areas as the handling of patient records, billing and other administrative chores, and computer-controlled examinations in response to
conventional data-processing equipment. Even more fundamental extensions of the physician's skill are resulting from the application of
compact integrated circuitry to diagnostic and monitoring equipment.
The potential of medical electronics is indicated by the unprecedented
demand for tomographic X-ray scanning equipment, which by computer
processing and synthesis is able to distinguish different tissues with a
sensitivity fifty times that of ordinary X-ray techniques; hundreds of
these new diagnostic tools have been ordered. Another new and
non-invasive diagnostic approach, the use of acoustic waves in such
devices as ultrasound cameras, is also beginning to be widely applied;
here the key role of electronics is to translate the acoustic information
into visual and analytical data. Perhaps the most striking illustration of
the unique power of electronic circuits in medicine is their potential use
as prostheses to supplement or replace damaged neural tissue, a circumstance that is only possible because modern circuits now approach the
size, power consumption, and logical capability of the natural tissue.
The cardiac pacemaker is an early example of such a prosthesis and the
development of far more complicated devices such as an implantable
electronic ear for the deaf is well under way.

Potentially, electronics and electronic media could have an important
impact on education, as almost anyone who has observed children
watching Sesame Street could confirm. Despite a few such successes,
however, there seems to be general agreement that television and
computer-assisted instruction have not yet lived up to that potential.
But educational innovators have not yet given up. There is another
sense, however, in which electronics is certain to affect education for
better or for worse, and that concerns the prospective flood of inexpensive electronic devices of which the handheld calculator is only the first.
Calculators have substantially altered the character of the traditional
"problem sets" in science and engineering courses at the university
level, they are becoming common in high school courses, and they are
already creeping into use in primary schools. Some parents and
educators are trying to stem this growing tide on the grounds that it will
only add to the reasons "why Johnny can't add". Others see the trend as
inevitable and point out that how computation is performed is irrelevant, what really counts is whether the students learn the underlying
concepts, and in this respect the impact of the calculator is still uncer-

tain. In any case, the ubiquity of the calculator seems to guarantee that electronic arithmetic will become the language of the real "new maths", and these developments suggest the potential of the more elaborate calculator-based games and educational devices that are beginning to appear either alone or as attachments to the home television set.

It is difficult to imagine a modern military force without heavy dependence on electronics. Aircraft instrumentation, missile guidance systems, radar and other surveillance sensors, tactical computers – all depend on electronic components. But electronics plays more than a passive role in military systems; in recent years, advances in electronics have been perhaps the most important factor guiding the evolution of new weapons and new strategies. One example is the emergence of "smart bombs" and other unpiloted weapons, which can evaluate guidance information to track themselves to target or make use of pre-programmed instructions to manoeuvre evasively. Carried to its logical conclusion, this trend might eliminate the need for many manned aircraft and is at the core of the current debates over the B-1 bomber and the cruise missile. A second example is the NAVSTAR satellite system, for which prototypes are now being tested. These navigational satellites are designed to allow any military vehicle carrying an inexpensive receiver and computer to instantaneously determine its position anywhere in the world with an accuracy of better than ten metres in horizontal and vertical coordinates; civilian aircraft and ships will also be able to use these satellites, but with somewhat less accuracy. This phenomenal accuracy is expected by many defence analysts to revolutionize navigation, weapons targeting, battlefield management, and other aspects of warfare; this is especially true for fixed targets, since the coordinates of any such target can be readily determined. The system also may supplant many of the commercial navigation systems now in use.

In twenty years, the role of computers in research has been transformed from what W. O. Baker has described as "a minor annex of mathematics research" to a major and often dominant role characterized by the proliferation of minicomputers and timeshared terminals in most research institutions. He asserts that computers have transformed the research process from conceptualization to experimentation to publication. Baker should know, since his organization has been in the forefront of actually putting computers to work in research – Bell Laboratories now have an average of one dedicated minicomputer and five interactive terminals for every fifteen professional staff members. Electronics has also transformed other instruments of scientific research, from the electron microscope to vidicon astronomical cameras, and the process is accelerating as more and more "smart instruments" are designed around microprocessors.

Nowhere is the potential impact of electronics greater than in the banking industry and the postal service, both of which face the prospect of converting from moving pieces of paper around to using electronic transfers for at least part of their business. These changes will certainly not come overnight and will raise a host of social problems; how does one protect against theft when most retail transactions are done electronically rather than by cheque, or guarantee privacy if much first-class mail travels by wire? But electronic transfers of money, of messages, and of documents are already established features of our society. The US government, for example, makes some five million social security payments each month by sending banks magnetic tapes that the bank computers are able to use to credit depositors' accounts directly. Pre-authorized, nonpaper payments are estimated to account for ten per cent of bank transactions in some areas of the country. Point-of-sale electronic terminals are now becoming common in retail stores, although their role is presently restricted to credit verification and inventory control, not direct transfer of funds from the customer's account to the store's. But with twenty-six billion cheques a year passing through the banking system and the likelihood that the volume will double by 1985, there is ample incentive for banks to move towards electronic transfer and chequeless banking. Such a move will change the boundaries between the retail trade and the banking system, possibly resulting in more decentralized but far more complex financial networks.

Chequeless banking, if and when it does occur, will intensify the economic pressures on the postal service, since nearly forty per cent of the mail consists of cheques and other financial transactions. Diversion of this mail will reduce revenue but will not noticeably lower costs. But that is not the only threat. As complaints about lost or delayed mail increase, many large businesses are looking towards electronic mail systems. One prototype of such a system is the Department of Defence's ARPA computer network, which is routinely used by researchers all across the country to exchange messages and information. New optical scanning and electronic printing techniques are being developed by many companies that would allow users to transmit documents or whole pages of text. The postal service may be forced to embrace electronic mail or face the future as an obsolete, increasingly expensive system serving fewer and fewer people.

Postal communications are not the only form of communications facing new challenges. Not long ago radio and marine cable telephone circuits were the principal means for rapid intercontinental communications. Now an international satellite communications system is well established and carrying a growing volume of traffic. Domestic satellite systems are just getting under way in the United States, but they seem certain to expand the options for voice, television, and digital data communications. The transmission of digital information is the most rapidly growing area of electronic communications and reflects the increasing need for computers and other intelligent machines to "talk" with each other. Indeed computer and communications technologies have become so similar and intertwined that they are difficult to distinguish. More and more communications are transmitted in digital form, even within the telephone system. And more and more information in the communications systems is processed both before and after transmission; voice signals are compacted and compressed to put more calls on a channel, for example, or the output of the intelligent terminal on one end of the phone line becomes the input for a computer or a display device on the other end. Distributed processing – essentially networks of small and medium-sized computers connected by communications links – is clearly going to be one of the major forms in which computers are used.

These developments clearly pose a major problem for those, such as government regulators, who must decide where communications – a regulated activity – ends and where the unregulated computer market begins. There are a number of public policy issues involved in this intensifying conflict, and among the principal contenders are some of the giants of American industry, AT&T and IBM. It promises to be a multibillion-dollar fight and one of the thorniest technological policy problems the government must face in the coming decade.

The evolution of computers to the point where communications is a major part of their activity is also reflected in other changes. The traditional use of computers as calculating engines for numerical work is rapidly being replaced by a new principal role, that of managing, storing, retrieving, and distributing information. A search for new computer architectures that better reflect this new role is under way and includes experiments with such things as augmented sets of instructions for the computer's own control program, specialized subcomputers or processors to manage data-bases, and multiprocessor machines. The generation of computer programs – all too often a bottleneck to effective use of computers – is increasingly being put on a firm mathematical basis. The way information is stored in computer systems is changing too, as researchers look for more efficient search routines, new methods of combining memory devices, and new computer languages adapted for information processing. S. E. Madnick believes that what is emerging is the goal of an information utility that can serve many users for many purposes. Prototype experiments with information utilities are actually under way in Britain, where the British Broadcasting Corporation is testing a small decoder attached to television sets that can, on demand, deliver current information on a variety of subjects; the British Post Office, which runs the telephone network, is also experimenting with a telephone-based information utility that would combine the functions of a daily newspaper with the resources of a library.

We are increasingly an information-based society. Economically, for example, information industries ranging from broadcast television to book publishing to computer services contribute a large part of the US gross national product and employ nearly half of the work force. The information sector of the economy is also among the more rapidly growing. Moreover, information is a resource that greatly enhances individual capabilities and opportunities and is not depleted by use. H. A. Simon argues that the development of the ability to process and manipulate information on a large scale has a significance, on the scale of human evolution, equivalent to the development of written language or the invention of the printed book. In any case, it is clear that the information revolution will accelerate as more persons acquire their own computers and as these computers are able to make use of larger and larger information resources.

The conventional economic wisdom is that the expanding opportunities in information-related activities will more than offset jobs lost to more productive electronic equipment. Recent experience in the electronic manufacturing industries would seem to bear this out, although substantial layoffs in some companies have been avoided only by a commitment to large retraining schemes. In the coming decade automated electronic equipment is likely to make inroads into the service sectors of the economy as well. The nature of secretarial and other office support jobs may change, for example, as may that of mail clerks and bank tellers. Whether any of these changes will result in displacing large numbers of people from these traditionally labour-intensive occupations is not clear, but the process of change is certain to be uncomfortable for the individual whose job is involved and maybe for society as a whole. Consider the impact of converting the postal service, one of the largest employers of unskilled and semi-skilled labour, to an electronic mail system.

Despite such problems, the electronics revolution is not likely to slow down anytime soon, if only because the research base is broad and vigorous and is already producing a host of new ideas and new concepts that are certain to be translated into new products and services in coming years. One trend that can be identified is the incorporation of magnetic, acoustical and optical phenomena into electronic devices, giving rise to a host of new effects that can be put to use. Examples include magnetic bubbles in memory devices, surface acoustic-wave filters in signal processing equipment, and optical fibres in communications. Particularly fascinating in this regard is the push towards optical communications.

The concept of transmitting information on a light wave dates back at least to Alexander Graham Bell, who in the 1870s demonstrated a wireless telephone based on light that could transmit sound for more than a kilometre. A hundred years later, optical communication is on the verge of becoming a reality. The principal advantage of communicating with light waves is their high frequency, compared with radio waves, which gives them a superior capacity to transmit information. A single optical fibre, for example, can carry hundreds of times as many bits of information per second as a copper wire. The Bell system is already experimenting with an optical link for interstation connections in areas with a high volume of calls, and others are looking at applications ranging from computers to military vehicles. As large-scale production of fibres and other components gets under way, cost reductions as dramatic as those in electronic calculators are expected.

In its modern configuration, optical communications relies on such components as lasers or light-emitting diodes for light sources and glass fibres for the transmission medium. It is, in fact, the dramatic improvement in these components that has brought the technology to the verge of utility. Optical fibres have been produced with losses less than 1 decibel per kilometre – less than the loss in light passing through a single windowpane. But, just as solid-state technology progressed from individual devices to integrated circuits, integrated optical circuits incorporating lasers, amplifiers and detectors on a single chip are already being developed. Many semiconductor materials, it turns out, are optically as well as electrically active, thus permitting the intimate interplay of both kinds of circuits. This activity is leading to an era in which the electron, long the workhorse of the electronics revolution, will be supplemented by the even greater potential of the photon.

The range of phenomena and the indications of still-to-be-exploited potential to be found in electronics research are convincing evidence that we have not yet seen the limits of what is possible. Still less are most of us and most of our institutions prepared to decide what we should do with our new capabilities or even how to cope with the speed at which electronics technology is changing the ground rules under which we operate. In business the price of being unprepared is often high, as many white goods (cookers, fridges, freezers, washing machines, etc) manufacturers found out when one of their competitors introduced an electronically controlled microwave oven that has rapidly become the best-selling product in its field. For governments and individuals alike the stakes are arguably lower at present, but the continuing electronics revolution promises to be so pervasive as to compel the attention of even the most unobservant.

Microelectronics

Robert N. Noyce

Perhaps the most famous of all statements on microelectronics, by a founder of the most famous of all microprocessor manufacturers, Intel Corp., this paper appeared in a special issue of Scientific American *in September 1977 (vol. 237, No. 3). Noyce's graphs illustrating the basic "laws" of microelectronics have been widely copied and quoted, testifying to the fact that this is indeed a definitive article.*

The evolution of electronic technology over the past decade has been so rapid that it is sometimes called a revolution. Is this large claim justified? I believe the answer is yes. It is true that what we have seen has been to some extent a steady quantitative evolution: smaller and smaller electronic components performing increasingly complex electronic functions at ever higher speeds and at ever lower cost. And yet there has also been a true revolution: a qualitative change in technology, the integrated microelectronic circuit, has given rise to a qualitative change in human capabilities.

It is not an exaggeration to say that most of the technological achievements of the past decade have depended on microelectronics. Small and reliable sensing and control devices are the essential elements in the complex systems that have landed men on the moon and explored Mars, not to speak of their similar role in the intercontinental weapons that dominate world politics. Microelectronic devices are also the essence of new products ranging from communications satellites to handheld calculators and digital watches. Somewhat subtler, but perhaps eventually more significant, is the effect of microelectronics on the computer. The capacity of the computer for storing, processing and displaying information has been greatly enhanced. Moreover, for many purposes the computer is being dispersed to the sites where it is

29

operated or where its output is applied: to the "smart" typewriter or instrument or industrial control device.

The microelectronics revolution is far from having run its course. We are still learning how to exploit the potential of the integrated circuit by developing new theories and designing new circuits whose performance may yet be improved by another order of magnitude. And we are only slowly perceiving the intellectual and social implications of the personal computer, which will give the individual access to vast stores of information and the ability to learn from it, add to it and communicate with others concerning it.

Here I want primarily to show how the evolution of microelectronics illustrates the constant interaction of technology and economics. The small size of microelectronic devices has been important in many applications, but the major impact of this new technology has been to make electronic functions more reproducible, more reliable and much less expensive. With each technical development costs have decreased, and the ever lower costs have promoted a widening range of applications; the quest for technical advances has been required by economic competition and compensated by economic reward.

It all began with the development thirty years ago of the transistor: a small, low-power amplifier that replaced the large, power-hungry vacuum tube. The advent almost simultaneously of the stored-program digital computer provided a large potential market for the transistor. The synergy between a new component and a new application generated an explosive growth of both. The computer was the ideal market for the transistor and for the solid-state integrated circuits the transistor spawned, a much larger market than could have been provided by the traditional applications of electronics in communications. The reason is that digital systems require very large numbers of active circuits compared with systems having analog amplification, such as radios. In digital electronics a given element is either on or off, depending on the input. Even when a large number of elements are connected, their output will still be simply on or off; the gain of the individual stage is unity, so that even cascading several stages leaves the gain still unity. Analog circuits, on the other hand, typically require amplification of the input. Since the gain of each amplifier may typically be ten, only a few stages can be cascaded before the practical limit of voltage levels for microelectronic elements is reached. An analog system therefore cannot handle large numbers of microcircuits, whereas a digital system requires them; a pocket calculator contains one hundred times as many transistors as a radio or a television receiver.

In spite of the inherent compatibility of microelectronics and the computer, the historical fact is that early efforts to miniaturize electronic components were not motivated by computer engineers. Indeed, the tremendous potential of the digital computer was not quickly appreciated; even the developers of the first computer felt that four computers, more or less, would satisfy the world's computation needs! Various missile and satellite programs, however, called for complex electronic systems to be installed in equipment in which size, weight and power requirements were severely constrained, and so the effort to miniaturize was promoted by military and space agencies.

The initial approach was an attempt to miniaturize conventional components. One program was "Project Tinkertoy" of the National Bureau of Standards, whose object was to package the various electronic components in a standard shape: a rectangular form that could be closely packed rather than the traditional cylindrical form. Another approach was "molecular engineering". The example of the transistor as a substitute for the vacuum tube suggested that similar substitutes could be devised: that new materials could be discovered or developed that would, by their solid-state nature, allow electronic functions other than amplification to be performed within a monolithic solid. These attempts were largely unsuccessful, but they publicised the demand for miniaturisation and the potential rewards for the successful development of some form of microelectronics. A large segment of the technical community was on the lookout for a solution of the problem because it was clear that a ready market awaited the successful inventor.

What ultimately provided the solution was the semiconductor integrated circuit, the concept of which had begun to take shape only a few years after the invention of the transistor. Several investigators saw that one might further exploit the characteristics of semiconductors such as germanium and silicon that had been exploited to make the transistor. The body resistance of the semiconductor itself and the capacitance of the junctions between the positive (p) and negative (n) regions that could be created in it could be combined with transistors in the same material to realize a complete circuit of resistors, capacitors and amplifiers. In 1953 Harwick Johnson of the Radio Corporation of America applied for a patent on a phase-shift oscillator fashioned in a single piece of germanium by such a technique. The concept was extended by G. W. A. Dummer of the Royal Radar Establishment in England, Jack S. Kilby of Texas Instruments Incorporated and Jay W. Lathrop of the Diamond Ordnance Fuze Laboratories.

Several key developments were required, however, before the exciting potential of integrated circuits could be realised. In the mid-1950s engineers learned how to define the surface configuration of transistors by means of photolithography and developed the method of solid-state diffusion for introducing the impurities that create *p* and *n* regions. Batch processing of many transistors on a thin "wafer" sliced from a large crystal of germanium or silicon began to displace the earlier technique of processing individual transistors. The hundreds or thousands of precisely registered transistors that could be fabricated on a single wafer still had to be separated physically, assembled individually with tiny wires inside a protective housing and subsequently assembled into electronic circuits.

The integrated circuit, as we conceived and developed it at Fairchild Semiconductor in 1959, accomplishes the separation and interconnection of transistors and other circuit elements electrically rather than physically. The separation is accomplished by introducing *pn* diodes, or rectifiers, which allow current to flow in only one direction. The technique was patented by Kurt Lehovec at the Sprague Electric Company. The circuit elements are interconnected by a conducting film of evaporated metal that is photoengraved to leave the appropriate pattern of connections. An insulating layer is required to separate the underlying semiconductor from the metal film except where contact is desired. The process that accomplishes this insulation had been developed by Jean Hoerni at Fairchild in 1958, when he invented the planar transistor: a thin layer of silicon dioxide, one of the best insulators known, is formed on the surface of the wafer after the wafer has been processed and before the conducting metal is evaporated onto it.

Since then additional techniques have been devised that give the designer of integrated circuits more flexibility, but the basic methods were available by 1960, and the era of the integrated circuit was inaugurated. Progress since then has been astonishing, even to those of us who have been intimately engaged in the evolving technology. An individual integrated circuit on a chip perhaps a quarter of an inch square can now embrace more electronic elements than the most complex piece of electronic equipment that could be built in 1950. Today's microcomputer, at a cost of perhaps $300, has more computing capacity than the first large electronic computer, ENIAC. It is twenty times faster, has a larger memory, is thousands of times more reliable, consumes the power of a light bulb rather than that of a locomotive, occupies 1/30,000 the volume and costs 1/10,000 as much. It is available by mail order or at your local hobby shop.

In 1964, noting that since the production of the planar transistor in 1959 the number of elements in advanced integrated circuits had been doubling every year, Gordon E. Moore, who was then director of research at Fairchild, was the first to predict the future progress of the

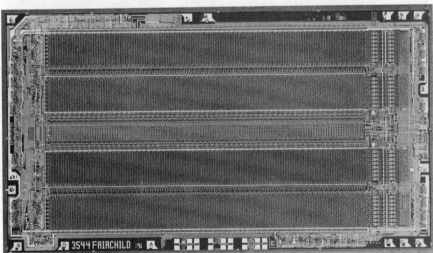

(Above) A blow-up of a large-scale integrated circuit made by Intel, which includes a memory and central processing unit. *Photo courtesy of Intel Corporation*

(Below) Another large-scale integrated circuit made by Fairchild, which consists entirely of memory. *Photo courtesy of Fairchild Camera and Instrument Corporation, 464 Ellis Street, Mountain View, California*

This IMSAI minicomputer measures 8 by 10 inches. The microprocessor is the square chip in the light grey package in the middle of the board array. *Photo by Ben Rose Photography, Inc., New York*

integrated circuit. He suggested that its complexity would continue to double every year. Today, with circuits containing 2^{18} (262,144) elements available, we have not yet seen any significant departure from Moore's law. Nor are there any signs that the process is slowing down, although a deviation from exponential growth is ultimately inevitable. The technology is still far from the fundamental limits imposed by the laws of physics: further miniaturisation is less likely to be limited by the laws of physics than by the laws of economics.

The growth of the microelectronics industry illustrates the extent to which investment in research can create entrepreneurial opportunity, jobs and a major export market for the US. After the introduction of the integrated circuit in the early 1960s the total world consumption of integrated circuits rose rapidly, reaching a value of nearly $1 billion in 1970. By 1976, world consumption had more than tripled, to $3·5 billion. Of this total, US-based companies produced more than $2·5 billion, or some seventy per cent, about $1 billion of which was exported to foreign customers. The impact on the electronics industry is far greater than is implied by these figures. In electronic equipment less

The familiar "caterpillar" profile of the packaged chip. *Photo courtesy of Ferranti Electronics Limited*

than ten per cent of the value is in the integrated circuits themselves: a $10,000 minicomputer contains less than $1000 worth of integrated circuits, and a $300 television set contains less than $30 worth. Today most of the world's $80 billion electronics industry depends in some way on integrated circuits.

The substitution of microelectronic devices for discrete components reduces costs not only because the devices themselves are cheaper but for a variety of other reasons. First, the integrated circuit contains many of the interconnections that were previously required, and that saves labour and materials. The interconnections of the integrated circuit are much more reliable than solder joints or connectors, which makes for savings in maintenance. Since integrated circuits are much smaller and consume much less power than the components they have displaced, they make savings possible in such support structures as cabinets and racks as well as in power transformers and cooling fans. Less intermediate testing is needed in the course of production because the correct functioning of the complex integrated circuits has already been ensured. Finally, the end user needs to provide less floor space, less operating power and less air conditioning for the equipment. All of this is by way of saying that even if integrated circuits were only equivalent in cost to the components they have displaced, other savings would motivate the use of fewer, more complex integrated circuits as they became available.

The most striking characteristic of the microelectronics industry has been a persistent and rapid decline in the cost of a given electronic function. The handheld calculator provides a dramatic example. Its cost has declined by a factor of one hundred in the past decade. A portion of the rapid decline in cost can be accounted for in terms of a "learning curve": the more experience an industry has, the more efficient it becomes. Most industries reduce their costs (in constant dollars) by twenty to thirty per cent each time their cumulative output doubles. Examining data for the semiconductor industry, we find that integrated-circuit costs have declined twenty-eight per cent with each doubling of the industry's experience. Because of the rapid growth of this young industry these cost reductions have come at a much more rapid pace than in mature industries; the electronics industry's experience has been doubling nearly every year. The cost of a given electronic function has been declining even more rapidly than the cost of integrated circuits, since the complexity of the circuits has been increasing as their price has decreased. For example, the cost per bit (binary digit) of random-access memory has declined an average of thirty-five per cent per year since 1970, when the major growth in the adoption of semiconductor memory elements got under way. These cost declines were accomplished not only by the traditional learning process but also by the integration of more bits into each integrated circuit: in 1970 a change was made from 256 bits to 1024 bits per circuit and now the number of bits is in the process of jumping from 4096 per circuit to 16,384.

The hundredfold decline in prices for electronic components since the development of the integrated circuit is unique because, although other industries have shown similar experience curves, the integrated-circuit industry has been unique in its annual doubling of output over an extended number of years. Rather than serving a market that grows only in pace with the gross national product or the population, the industry has served a proliferating market of ever-broadening applications. As each new application consumes more microelectronic devices more experience has been gained, leading to further cost reductions, which in turn have opened up even wider markets for the devices. In 1960, before any production of integrated circuits, about 500 million transistors were made. Assuming that each transistor represents one circuit function, which can be equated to a logic "gate" or to one bit of memory in an integrated circuit, annual usage has increased by 2000 times, or has doubled eleven times, in the past seventeen years. This stunning increase promotes continual cost reductions.

The primary means of cost reduction has been the development of increasingly complex circuits that lower the cost per function for both the circuit producer and the equipment manufacturer. The main technical barrier to achieving more functions per circuit is production yield. More complex circuits result in larger devices and a growing probability of defects, so that a higher percentage of the total number of devices must be scrapped. When the cost of scrapping exceeds the cost saving in subsequent assembly and test operations, the cost per function increases rather than decreases. The most cost-efficient design is a compromise between high assembly costs (which are incurred at low levels of integration) and high scrapping costs (which are incurred at high levels of integration).

Technological developments have concentrated primarily on increasing the production "yield", either by reducing the density of defects or by reducing dimensions. Meticulous attention to process control and

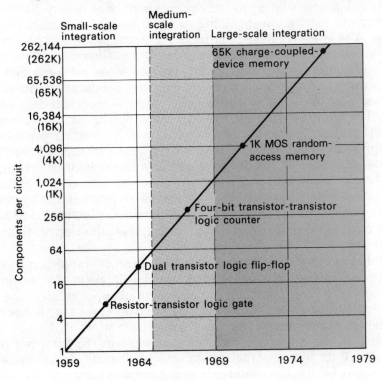

Fig. 1.1 Number of components per circuit

cleanliness has been necessary to reduce defect density. A dust particle in any critical process is enough to make a device worthless, so that most operations must be carried out in "clean rooms". Reduction of the dimensions of the basic circuit elements, which enables one to crowd more complex circuits within a given area, has been accomplished by improving the resolution of the photoengraving processes. Now optical limits are being reached as dimensions in the circuit patterns enter the range of only a few wavelengths of light, and methods in which electron beams or X-rays are substituted for visible light are being developed in order to reduce the dimensions even further (see William G. Oldham, below).

The reduction in size of the circuit elements not only reduces the cost but also improves the basic performance of the device. Delay times are directly proportional to the dimensions of circuit elements, so that the circuit becomes faster as it becomes smaller. Similarly, the power is reduced with the area of the circuits. The linear dimensions of the circuit elements can probably be reduced to about a fifth of the current size before any fundamental limits are encountered.

In an industry whose product declines in price by twenty-five per cent a year the motivation for doing research and development is clearly high. A year's advantage in introducing a new product or new process can give a company a twenty-five per cent cost advantage over competing companies: conversely, a year's lag puts a company at a significant disadvantage with respect to its competitors. Product development is a critical part of company strategy and product obsolescence is a fact of life. The return on successful investment in research and development is great, and so is the penalty for failure. The leading producers of integrated circuits spend approximately ten per cent of their sales income on research and development. In a constant-price environment one could say that investment for research and development buys an annuity paying $2·50 per year for each dollar invested! Clearly most of this annuity is either paid out to the purchasers of integrated circuits or reflected in price reductions that are necessary to develop new markets.

In this environment of rapid growth in market, rapid technological change and high returns on the successful development of a new product or process, a great number of entrepreneurial opportunities have been created and exploited. It is interesting that whereas the US has led in both the development and the commercialization of the new technology, it was not the companies that were in the forefront of the vacuum tube business that proceeded to develop its successor, the transistor. Of the ten leading US producers of vacuum tubes in 1955, only two are among today's top ten US semiconductor producers: four of

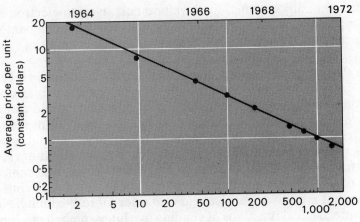

Fig. 1.2 Prices of integrated circuits

the top ten semiconductor companies were formed after 1955, and those four represent only a small fraction of the successful new ventures in the field. Time and time again the rapid growth of the market has found existing companies too busy expanding markets or product lines to which they were already committed to explore some of the more speculative new markets or technologies. And so the door was left open for new ventures, typically headed (originally at least) by an entrepreneur with a research or marketing background who had enough faith in the new market and technology to gamble. Fortunately for the US economy capital was readily available in the late 1950s and the 1960s to finance these ventures, and approximately a hundred new companies were formed to produce semiconductor devices; many of them made significant contributions to the development of microelectronics. Two such contributions in which I was directly involved were the development of the planar transistor and planar integrated circuit at Fairchild when that organisation was only two years old, and the development of the microprocessor at the Intel Corporation only two years after that company was founded. There are many more examples. The environment for entrepreneurial innovation in the US is not matched in other industrialized nations and it has been a major contributor to America's leadership in the field.

The growth of microelectronics has in turn created other opportunities. A host of companies have been established to serve the needs of the integrated-circuit producers. These companies supply everything from single-crystal silicon to computer-controlled design aids to automatic test equipment and special tooling. Often the novel consumer products that are spawned by developments in microelectronics have been manufactured and marketed initially by new companies. The digital watch and the television game are familiar examples.

When the integrated circuit was still an infant, Patrick E. Haggerty of Texas Instruments called attention to the increasing pervasiveness of electronics and predicted that electronic techniques would continue to displace other modes of control, reaching into nearly all aspects of our lives. Just such a displacement has been taking place, primarily because the microelectronics industry has been able to make ever more sophisticated functional elements at ever decreasing costs. Mechanical elements of the calculator and the watch have been displaced by integrated circuits that are less expensive and also offer more flexibility. Now the electromechanical functions of vending machines, pinball machines and traffic signals are being displaced. In the near future the automobile

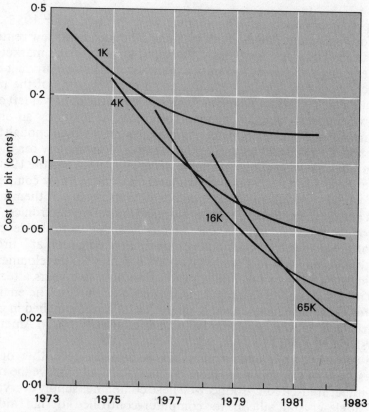

Fig. 1.3   Cost per bit of computer memory

engine will be controlled by a computer, with a consequent improvement in efficiency and reduction of pollutants. All these applications are simply extensions of the traditional applications of electronics to the task of handling information in measurement, communication and data manipulation. It has often been said that just as the industrial revolution enabled man to apply and control greater physical power than his own muscle could provide, so electronics has extended his intellectual power. Microelectronics extends that power still further.

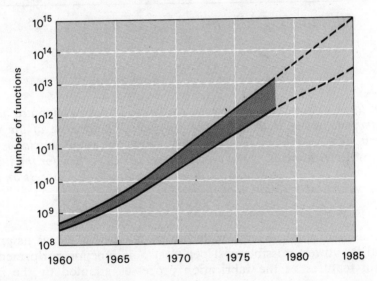

Fig. 1.4 Annual utilization of electronic functions

By 1986 the number of electronic functions incorporated into a wide range of products each year can be expected to be one hundred times greater than it is today. The experience curve predicts that the cost per function will have declined by then to a twentieth of the 1976 cost, a reduction of twenty-five per cent per year. At such prices electronic devices will be exploited even more widely, augmenting mail service, expanding the library and making its contents more accessible, providing entertainment, disseminating knowledge for educational purposes and performing many more of the routine tasks in the home and office. It is in the exponential proliferation of products and services dependent on microelectronics that the real microelectronic revolution will be manifested.

The Fabrication of Microelectronic Circuits

William G. Oldham

An understanding of what chips really are and how they are made is important if one is to grasp the enormous significance of the micro-electronics revolution. This account, from the same special issue of Scientific American *as the previous essay, was written for the layman. Although a little technical in places, it remains the clearest and most comprehensive description of chipmaking.*

The manufacture of large-scale integrated circuits has as its primary goal the lowest possible cost per electronic function performed. The main features of the fabrication processes adopted by the micro-electronics industry can be best understood in terms of this goal. These features include the fabrication of many circuits at a time (an extraordinary example of mass production), the reduction of the circuits to the smallest possible size and the maximum simplification of the processing technology.

The dramatic reduction in the cost of microelectronic circuits achieved in the past few years has not resulted from any major new breakthrough in fabrication technology. Indeed, most of the basic manufacturing processes involved have been widely adopted in the industry for five years or more. The recent sharp drop in fabrication cost has been achieved during a period of general economic inflation. The cost of processing a "wafer" of silicon, the substrate on which the microelectronic circuits are made, has risen moderately, but the area of the wafers has increased more rapidly, approximately doubling every four years. Thus the processing cost per unit area has actually decreased. Meanwhile the space required for a given electronic function has shrunk by a factor of two every eighteen months or so. This reduction in size has come not only from great ingenuity in designing simple circuits and simple technological processes for making them but also from the continuing miniaturization of the circuit elements and their interconnections. Moreover, the gradual elimination of defects in various manufacturing steps has resulted in a significant decrease in the net cost of fabrication. With a lower frequency of defects the yield of good circuits on a given wafer increases.

The current pace of developments in the manufacturing of micro-electronic circuits suggests that the progress in reducing production costs will continue. Virtually every stage of fabrication – from photo-lithography to packaging – is either in the midst of a significant advance or on the verge of one.

A large-scale integrated circuit contains tens of thousands of elements, yet each element is so small that the complete circuit is typically less than a quarter of an inch on a side. The pure, single-crystal silicon wafers that bear the circuits are much larger: currently three or four inches in diameter. One of the key economies in the manufacture of microelectronic circuits is the simultaneous fabrication of hundreds of circuits side by side on a single wafer. An even greater scale of mass production is attained in several stages of manufacture by processing as many as one hundred wafers together in a batch. Hence the cost of labour and equipment is shared by thousands of circuits, making possible the extremely low per-circuit cost that is characteristic of microelectronics.

After a wafer has passed through the fabrication stage (see Figure 1.5) it is sectioned into individual dice, or chips, each of which is a complete microelectronic circuit. Not all the circuits will work. Defects in a wafer cannot be avoided, and a single defect can ruin an entire circuit. For example, a scratch only a few micrometres long can break an electrical connection. It is impossible both physically and economically to repair the defective circuits; they are simply discarded.

As one might expect, the larger the die, the greater the chance for a defect to appear and render the circuit inoperative. The yield (the number of good circuits per wafer) decreases with the size of the dice, both because there are fewer places on a wafer for larger dice and because the larger circuits are more likely to incorporate a defect.

At first it might appear most economical to build very simple, and therefore very small, circuits on the grounds that more of them would be likely to be good ones. It is true that small circuits are inexpensive; simple logic circuits are available for as little as ten cents each. The costs of testing, packaging and assembling the completed circuits into an electronic system, however, must also be taken into account. Once the circuits are separated by breaking the wafer into dice, each die must be handled individually. From that point on the cost of any process such as packaging or testing is not shared by hundreds or thousands of circuits. In fact, for medium-scale integrated circuits packaging and testing costs often dominate the other production costs.

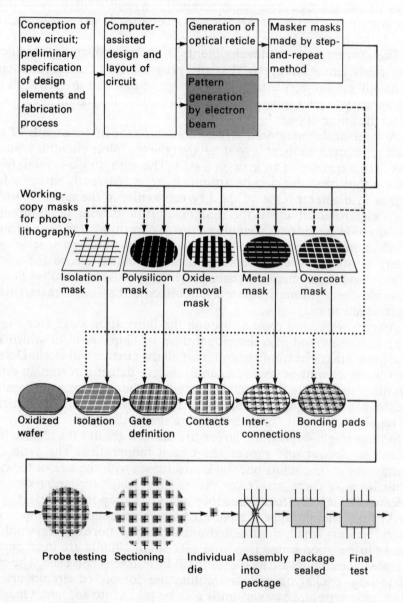

Fig. 1.5 An outline of the manufacture of a large-scale integrated circuit

A typical microelectronic system contains both large-scale and medium-scale integrated circuits, and the cost of designing and constructing the system rises rapidly as the number of circuits increases. To minimize the total cost of the system one would like ideally to use either a small number of very powerful circuits (requiring that each circuit be large) or a large number of very cheap circuits (requiring that each circuit be small). In many complex systems the minimum total cost is achieved with the more expensive, larger circuits: ones costing closer to $10 each than to $1. If less powerful, cheaper circuits were to be used, many more would be needed for constructing the system, and testing and assembly costs would tend to build up. On the other hand, if too much electronic function is packed into a circuit, the large size of the die would result in such a low yield per wafer that the cost per circuit would become prohibitive.

Assuming a typical selling price of $10 for a large-scale integrated circuit, one can work backward and estimate optimum die sizes. (The selling price of the circuit must of course be high enough to recover not only the direct costs of manufacture but also the costs of research and development, marketing and general overheads; thus it is reasonable to assume that the direct manufacturing cost is a good deal less, say about $5.) It costs roughly $100 just to process a silicon wafer, regardless of the size of the dice; when testing and packaging are included, the total manufacturing cost is perhaps doubled. Hence if the manufacturing cost of the particular integrated circuit in question is assumed to be $5, the optimum die size is one that yields about forty good circuits per wafer. At present it is possible to achieve such a yield for dice that measure approximately five millimetres on a side. It is interesting to note that in this example a rather low percentage of the circuits on the wafer are good. The yield is only forty good circuits out of the 250 that can be fabricated in a single wafer 100 millimetres in diameter.

The structure of an integrated circuit is complex both in the topography of its surface and in its internal composition. Each element of such a device has an intricate three-dimensional architecture that must be reproduced exactly in every circuit. The structure is made up of many layers, each of which is a detailed pattern. Some of the layers lie within the silicon wafer and others are stacked on the top. The manufacturing process consists in forming this sequence of layers precisely in accordance with the plan of the circuit designer.

Before examining how these layers are formed, it will be helpful to take an overall look at the procedure by which an integrated circuit is transformed from a conception of the circuit designer to a physical reality. In the first stage of the development of a new microelectronic circuit the designers who conceive of the new product work at specifying the functional characteristics of the device. They also select the processing steps that will be required to manufacture it. In the next stage the actual design of the device begins: the size and approximate location of every circuit element are estimated. Much of this preliminary design work is done with the aid of computers.

A computer can simulate the operation of the circuit in much the same way that electronic television games simulate the action of a table-tennis game or a space war. The circuit designer monitors the behaviour of the circuit voltages and adjusts the circuit elements until the desired behaviour is achieved. Computer simulation is less expensive than assembling and testing a "breadboard" circuit made up of discrete circuit elements; it is also more accurate. The main advantage of simulation, however, lies in the fact that the designer can change a circuit element merely by typing in a correction on a keyboard, and he can immediately observe the effect of the modification on the behaviour of the circuit.

The final layout giving the precise positions of the various circuit elements is also made with the aid of a computer. The layout designer works at a computer terminal, placing and moving the circuit elements while observing the layout magnified several hundred times on a cathode-ray-tube display. The layout specifies the pattern of each layer of the integrated circuit. The goal of the layout is to achieve the desired function of each circuit in the smallest possible space. The older method of drawing circuit layouts by hand has not been entirely replaced by the computer. Many parts of a large-scale integrated circuit are still drawn by hand before being submitted to the computer.

At each stage of this process, including the final stage when the entire circuit is completed, the layout is checked by means of detailed computer-drawn plots. Since the individual circuit elements can be as small as a few micrometres across, the checking points must be greatly magnified; usually the plots are 500 times larger than the final size of the circuit.

The time required to complete the task of circuit design and layout varies greatly with the nature of the circuit. The most difficult circuits to design are microprocessors, and here the design and layout can take several years. Other devices, such as static memories with a largely repetitive pattern, can be designed and laid out more quickly, in some cases in only a few months.

When the design and layout of a new circuit is complete, the computer memory contains a list of the exact position of every element in the circuit. From that description in the computer memory a set of plates, called photomasks, is prepared. Each mask holds the pattern for a single layer of the circuit. Since the circuits are so small, many can be fabricated side by side simultaneously on a single wafer of silicon. Thus each photomask, typically a glass plate about five inches on a side, has a single pattern repeated many times over its surface.

The manufacture of the photomasks is an interesting story in itself. Typically the process consists in first generating from the computer memory a complete pattern for each layer of the circuit. That is done by scanning a computer-controlled light spot across a photographic plate in the appropriate pattern. This primary pattern, called the reticle, is checked for errors and corrected or regenerated until it is perfect. Typically the reticle is ten times the final size of the circuit. An image of the reticle that is one tenth its original size is then projected optically on the final mask. The image is reproduced side by side hundreds of times in a process called "step and repeat". The constraints on both the mechanical system and the photographic system are demanding; each element must be correct in size and position to within about one micrometre. The original plate created by the step-and-repeat camera is copied by direct contact printing to produce a series of submasters. Each submaster serves in turn to produce a large number of replicas, called working plates, that will serve for the actual fabrication process. The working plate may be either a fixed image in an ordinary photographic emulsion or a much more durable pattern etched in a chromium film on a glass substrate.

A complete set of correct masks is the culmination of the design phase of the development of the microelectronic circuit. The plates are delivered to the wafer-fabrication facility, where they will be used to produce the desired sequence of patterns in a physical structure. This manufacturing facility receives silicon wafers, process chemicals and photomasks. A typical small facility employing a hundred people can process several thousand wafers per week. Assuming that there are fifty working circuits per wafer, such a plant can produce five million circuits per year.

The inside of a wafer-fabrication facility must be extremely clean and orderly. Because of the smallness of the structures being manufactured even the tiniest dust particles cannot be tolerated. A single dust particle can cause a defect that will result in the malfunction of a circuit. Special clothing is worn to protect the manufacturing environment from dust carried by the human operators. The air is continuously filtered and recirculated to keep the dust level at a minimum. Counting all the dust particles that are a micrometre or more in diameter, a typical wafer-fabrication plant harbours fewer than one hundred particles per cubic foot. For the purpose of comparison, the dust level in a modern hospital is on the order of 10,000 particles per cubic foot.

The circuit manufacturer often buys prepared wafers of silicon ready for the first manufacturing step. The low price (less than $10) of a prepared wafer belies the difficulties encountered in its manufacture. Raw silicon is first reduced from its oxide, the main constituent of common sand. A series of chemical steps are taken to purify it until the purity level reaches 99.9999999 per cent. A charge of purified silicon, say ten kilograms, is placed in a crucible and brought up to the the melting point of silicon: 1420 degrees Celsius. It is necessary to maintain an atmosphere of purified inert gas over the silicon while it is melted, both to prevent oxidation and to keep out unwanted impurities. The desired impurities, known as dopants, are added to the silicon to produce a specific type of conductivity, characterized by either positive (*p* type) charge carriers or negative (*n* type) ones.

A large single crystal is grown from the melt by inserting a perfect single-crystal "seed" and slowly turning and withdrawing it. Single crystals three to four inches in diameter and several feet long can be pulled from the melt. The uneven surface of a crystal as it is grown is ground to produce a cylinder of standard diameter, typically either three inches or one hundred millimetres (about four inches). The crystal is mounted in a fixture and cut into wafers with a thin high-speed diamond saw. In the finishing step the wafers are first smoothed on both sides by grinding and then are highly polished on one side. The final wafer is typically about half a millimetre thick. The final steps must also be carried out in an absolutely clean environment. There can be no defects, polishing damage, scratches or even chemical impurities on the finished surface.

The dominant role of silicon as the material for microelectronic circuits is attributable in large part to the properties of its oxide. Silicon dioxide is a clear glass with a softening point higher than 1400 degrees C. It plays a major role both in the fabrication of silicon devices and in their operation. If a wafer of silicon is heated in an atmosphere of oxygen or water vapour, a film of silicon dioxide forms on its surface. The film is hard and durable and adheres well. It makes an excellent insulator. The silicon dioxide is particularly important in the fabrication of integrated circuits because it can act as a mask for the selective introduction of dopants. Convenient thicknesses of silicon dioxide can be grown at temperatures in the range between 1000 and 1200 degrees C. The exact thickness can be accurately controlled by selecting the appropriate time and temperature of oxidation. For example, a layer of oxide one tenth of a micrometre thick will grow in one hour at a temperature of 1050 degrees C in an atmosphere of pure oxygen. A layer five times thicker will grow in the same time and at the same temperature in steam.

An important aspect of the oxidation process is its low cost. Several hundred wafers can be oxidized simultaneously in a single operation. The wafers are loaded into slots in a quartz "boat", separated by only a few millimetres. The high-temperature furnace has a cylindrical heating element surrounding a long quartz tube. A purified stream of an oxygen-containing gas passes through the tube. The boats of wafers are loaded into the open end and slowly pushed into the hottest part of the furnace. The temperature in the process zone is controlled to an accuracy of better than one degree C. Often the entire procedure is supervised by a computer. A small process-control computer monitors the temperature, directs the insertion and withdrawal of the wafers and controls the internal environment of the furnace.

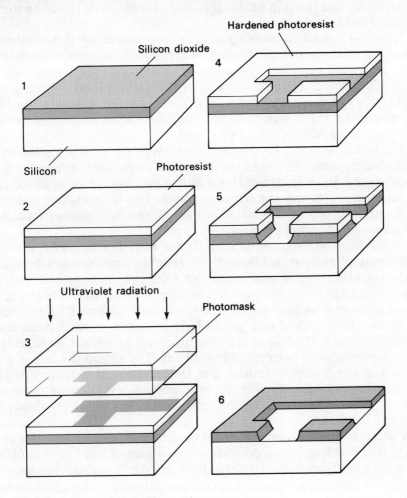

Fig. 1.6 The process of photolithography

The fabrication of integrated circuits requires a method for accurately forming patterns on the wafer. The microelectronic circuit is built up layer by layer, each layer receiving a pattern from a mask prescribed in the circuit design. The photoengraving process known as photo-lithography, or simply masking, is employed for the purpose.

The most basic masking step involves the etching of a pattern into an oxide. An oxidized wafer is first coated with photoresist, a light-sensitive polymeric material. The coating is laid down by placing a drop of the photoresist dissolved in a solvent on the wafer and then rapidly spinning the wafer. A thin liquid film spreads over the surface and the solvent evaporates, leaving the polymeric film. A mild heat treatment is given to dry out the film thoroughly and to enhance its adhesion to the silicon dioxide layer under it.

The most important property of the photoresist is that its solubility in certain solvents is greatly affected by exposure to ultraviolet radiation. For example, a negative photoresist cross-links and polymerizes wher-ever it is exposed. Thus exposure through a mask followed by develop-ment (washing in the selective solvent) results in the removal of the film wherever the mask was opaque. The photoresist pattern is further hardened after development by heating.

The wafer, with its photoresist pattern, is now placed in a solution of hydrofluoric acid. The acid dissolves the oxide layer wherever it is unprotected, but it does not attack either the photoresist or the silicon wafer itself. After the acid has removed all the silicon dioxide from the exposed areas the wafer is rinsed and dried, and the photoresist pattern is removed by another chemical treatment.

Other films are patterned in a similar way. For example, a warm solution of phosphoric acid selectively attacks aluminium and therefore can serve to pattern an aluminium film. Often an intermediate masking layer is needed when the photoresist cannot stand up to the attack of some particular etching solution. For example, polycrystalline silicon films are often etched in a particularly corrosive mixture containing nitric acid and hydrofluoric acid. In this case a film of silicon dioxide is first grown on the polycrystalline silicon. The silicon dioxide is pat-terned in the standard fashion and the photoresist is removed. The pattern in the silicon dioxide can now serve as a mask for etching the silicon film under it, because the oxide is attacked only very slowly by the acid mixture.

Photolithography is in many ways the key to microelectronic techno-logy. It is involved repeatedly in the processing of any device, at least once for each layer in the finished structure. An important requirement of the lithographic process is that each pattern be positioned accurately with respect to the layers under them. One technique is to hold the mask

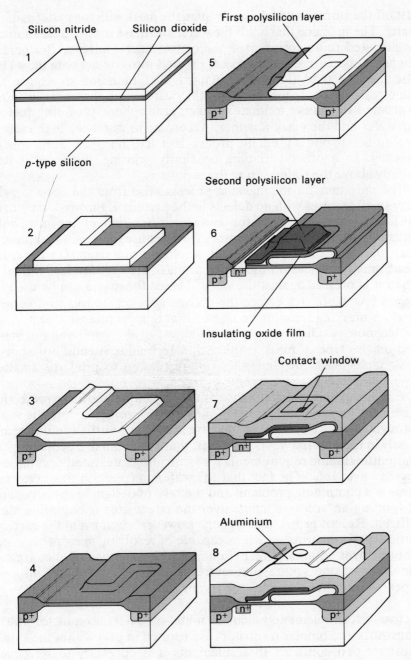

Silicon nitride   Silicon dioxide

First polysilicon layer

p-type silicon

Second polysilicon layer

Insulating oxide film

Contact window

Aluminium

Fig. 1.7 The complete fabrication sequence for a two-level *n*-channel polysilicon-gate MOS circuit element

just off the surface and to visually align the mask with the patterns in the wafer. The machine that holds the wafer and mask for this operation can be adjusted to an accuracy of one or two micrometres. After perfect alignment is achieved, the mask is pressed into contact with the wafer. The mask is then flooded with ultraviolet radiation to expose the photoresist. The space between the wafer and the mask is often evacuated to achieve intimate contact; atmospheric pressure squeezes the wafer and the mask together. According to whether a high vacuum or a moderate one is used, the process is called "hard" or "soft" contact printing. In another variation, proximity printing, the mask is held slightly above the wafer during the exposure.

The variations in the masking process arise from the need to print very small features with no defects in the pattern. If the mask were to be positioned very far from the surface, diffraction of the ultraviolet radiation passing through the mask would cause the smaller features to blur together. Thus hard contact would be preferred. On the other hand, small particles on the wafer or mask are abraded into the mask when it is pressed against the wafer. Hence the masks can be used for only a few exposures before the defects accumulate to an intolerable level. A masking technique is chosen that is appropriate to the particular technology. Depending on the flatness of the wafer and the mask, and on the type of mask employed, a technique is chosen that gives reasonable mask life and sufficient resolution to print the smallest circuit elements in the device.

A recent trend has been towards the technique known as projection alignment, in which the image of the mask is projected onto the wafer through an optical system. In this case mask life is virtually unlimited. It is only in the past few years, however, that optics capable of meeting the photolithographic requirements for fabricating integrated circuits have become available. The fact that the wafers increase in size every few years is a continuing problem, and the task of designing optics capable of forming an accurate image over the larger area is becoming more difficult. Recent projection aligners, however, circumvent the extreme difficulty of constructing a lens capable of resolving micrometre-sized features over an area of many square inches. A much smaller area, of the order of one square centimetre, is exposed, and the exposure is repeated by either stepping or scanning the image over the wafer.

Active circuit elements such as metal-oxide-semiconductor (MOS) transistors and bipolar transistors are formed in part within the silicon substrate. To construct these elements it is necessary to selectively introduce impurities, that is, to create localized *n*-type and *p*-type regions by adding the appropriate dopant atoms. There are two

The microcircuit is laid out with the aid of a computer. Sections of the large-scale integrated circuit can be scrutinized and modified with a light pen on a visual display unit. *Photo courtesy of Applicon*

The chip layout is laboriously checked on a light table by the minute examination of each photomask image. The blow-up is 500 times normal size. *Photo by Jon Brenneis*

A typical wafer fabrication plant is kept spotlessly clean and the air continuously filtered to avoid even the tiniest of dust particles interfering with the manufacturing process. *Photo by Jon Brenneis*

This ingot of doped silicon is ready for slicing into thin wafers by a diamond-edged circular saw. *Photo by Jon Brenneis*

Once sliced, the wafers are sent in a glass "boat" for "cooking" in an oxidation furnace. *Photo courtesy of NCR Corporation*

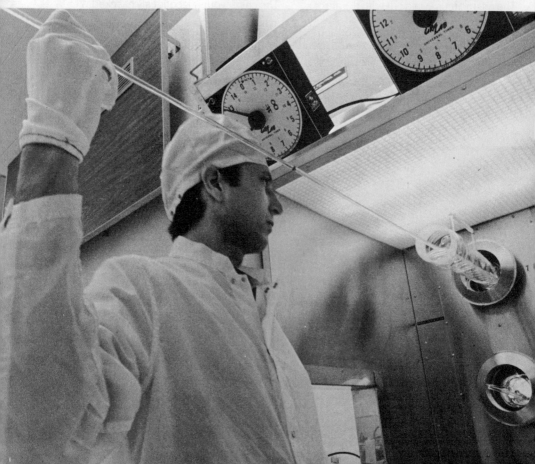

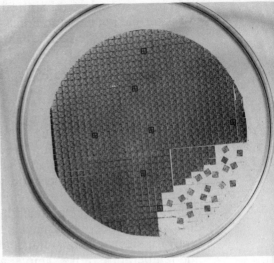

When the chips have been built up on the wafer, grooves are cut into the surface, prior to breaking the wafer into individual dice. *Photo by Jon Brenneis*

Each of these dice contains a complete large-scale integrated circuit. Around two hundred are snapped off the average wafer. *Photo courtesy of British Information Services, Central Office of Information*

The chips are individually tested prior to packaging to see if their circuitry is defective. The long contact needles are directed on to the probe pads whilst viewing down a microscope. *Photo courtesy of Ferranti Electronics Limited*

techniques for selectively introducing dopants into the silicon crystal: diffusion and ion implantation.

If silicon is heated to a high temperature, say 1000 degrees C, the impurity atoms begin to move slowly through the crystal. Certain key impurities (boron and phosphorus) move much more slowly through silicon dioxide than they do through silicon itself. This important fact enables one to employ thin oxide patterns as impurity masks. For example, a boat of wafers can be placed in a furnace at 1000 degrees in an atmosphere containing phosphorus. The phosphorus enters the silicon wherever it is unprotected, diffusing slowly into the bulk of the wafer. After enough impurity atoms have accumulated the wafers are removed from the furnace, and solid-state diffusion effectively ceases. Of course, every time the wafer is reheated the impurities again begin to diffuse; hence all the planned heat treatments must be considered in designing a process to achieve a specific depth of diffusion. The important variables controlling the depth to which impurities diffuse are time and temperature. For example, a layer of phosphorus one micrometre deep can be diffused in about an hour at 1100 degrees.

To achieve maximum control most diffusions are performed in two steps. The predeposit, or first, step takes place in a furnace whose temperature is selected to achieve the best control of the amount of impurity introduced. The temperature determines the solubility of the dopant in the silicon, just as the temperature of warm water determines the solubility of an impurity such as salt. After a comparatively short predeposit treatment the wafer is placed in a second furnace, usually at a higher temperature. This second heat treatment, the "diffusion drive-in" step, is selected to achieve the desired depth of diffusion.

In the formation of *pn* junctions by solid-state diffusion the impurities diffuse laterally under the oxide mask about the same distance as the depth of the junction. The edge of the *pn* junction is therefore protected by a layer of silicon dioxide. This is an important feature of the technique, because silicon dioxide is a nearly ideal insulator, and many of the electronic devices will not tolerate any leakage at the edge of the junction.

Another selective doping process, ion implantation, has been developed as a means of introducing impurities at room temperature. The dopant atoms are ionized (stripped of one or more of their electrons) and are accelerated to a high energy by passing them through a potential difference of tens of thousands of volts. At the end of their path they strike the silicon wafer and are embedded at various depths depending on their mass and their energy. The wafer can be selectively masked against the ions either by a patterned oxide layer, as in conventional diffusion, or by a photoresist pattern. For example, phosphorus ions

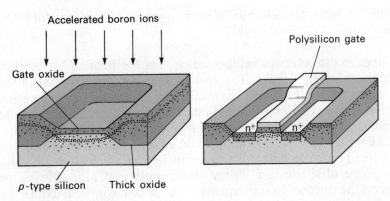

Fig. 1.8 Ion implantation

accelerated through a potential of 100,000 volts will penetrate the photoresist to a depth of less than half a micrometre. Wherever they strike bare silicon they penetrate to an average depth of a tenth of a micrometre. Thus even a one-micrometre layer of photoresist can serve as a mask for the selective implantation of phosphorus.

As the accelerated ions plough their way into the silicon crystal they cause considerable damage to the crystal lattice. It is possible to heal most of the damage, however, by annealing the crystal at a moderate temperature. Little diffusion takes place at the annealing temperature, so that the ion-implantation conditions can be chosen to obtain the desired distribution. For example, a very shallow, high concentration of dopant can be conveniently achieved by ion implantation. A more significant feature of the technique is the possibility of accurately controlling the concentration of the dopant. The ions bombarding the crystal each carry a charge, and by measuring the total charge that accumulates the number of impurities can be precisely determined. Hence ion implantation is used whenever the doping level must be very accurately controlled. Often ion implantation simply replaces the pre-deposit step of a diffusion process. Ion implantation is also used to introduce impurities that are difficult to predeposit from a high-temperature vapour. For example, the current exploration of the use of arsenic as a shallow *n*-type dopant in MOS devices coincides with the availability of suitable ion-implantation equipment.

A unique feature of ion implantation is its ability to introduce impurities through a thin oxide. This technique is particularly advantageous in adjusting the threshold voltage of MOS transistors. Either *n*-type or *p*-type dopants can be implanted through the gate oxide, resulting in either a decrease or an increase of the threshold voltage of the device. Thus by means of the ion implantation technique it is possible to fabricate several different types of MOS transistors on the same wafer.

The uppermost layers of integrated circuits are formed by depositing and patterning thin films. The two most important processes for the deposition of thin films are chemical-vapour deposition and evaporation. The polycrystalline silicon film in the important silicon-gate MOS technology is usually laid down by means of chemical-vapour deposition. Silane gas (SiH_4) decomposes when it is heated, releasing silicon and hydrogen. Accordingly, when the wafers are heated in a dilute atmosphere of silane, a uniform film of polycrystalline silicon slowly forms on the surface. In subsequent steps the film is doped, oxidized and patterned.

It is also possible to deposit insulating films such as silicon dioxide or silicon nitride by means of chemical-vapour deposition. If a source of oxygen such as carbon dioxide is present during the decomposition of silane, silicon dioxide is formed. Similarly, silicon nitride is grown by decomposing silane in the presence of a nitrogen compound such as ammonia.

Evaporation is perhaps the simplest method of all for depositing a thin film, and it is commonly employed to lay down the metallic conducting layer in most integrated circuits. The metallic charge to be evaporated, usually aluminium, is placed in a crucible, and the wafers to be coated are placed above the crucible in a movable fixture called a planetary. During evaporation the wafers are rotated in order to ensure the maximum uniformity of the layer. The motion of the planetary also wobbles the wafers with respect to the source in order to obtain a continuous aluminium film over the steps and bumps on the surface created by the preceding photolithographic steps. After a glass bell jar is lowered over the planetary device and a high vacuum is established the aluminium charge is heated by direct bombardment with high-energy electrons. A pure aluminium film, typically about a micrometre thick, is deposited on the wafer.

In the fabrication of a typical large-scale integrated circuit there are more thin-film steps than diffusion steps. Therefore thin-film technology is probably more critical to the overall yield and performance of the circuits than the diffusion and oxidation steps are. In a recent development a thin film is even employed to select the areas on a wafer that are to be oxidized. The compound silicon nitride has the property that it oxidizes much more slowly than silicon. A layer of silicon nitride can be vapour-deposited, patterned and used as an oxidation mask. The surface that results is much flatter than the surface if the thick oxide is grown everywhere and selectively removed. For *n*-channel MOS devices there is the additional advantage that an ion-implantation step involving boron can be added just before the oxidation step, relying on the nitride pattern as a mask. This procedure results in a heavily doped *p*-type region located precisely under the oxide, which acts as an obstacle to the formation of channels from adjacent elements in the device.

This "channel stopper" diffusion step is necessary in high-performance *n*-channel MOS technology. Without selective oxidation a special masking step would have to be added. The spacing between elements would then necessarily be larger; hence selective oxidation leads to greater circuit density. Bipolar integrated circuits also benefit greatly from the use of selective oxidation. By replacing the conventional diffused isolation with oxide isolation the space taken up by one bipolar transistor is reduced by more than a factor of four.

The wafer-fabrication phase of manufacture ends with an electrical test. Each die on the wafer is probed to determine whether it functions correctly. The defective dice are marked with an ink spot to indicate that they should be discarded. A computer-controlled testing machine quickly tests each circuit, steps to the next one and performs the inking without human intervention. It can also keep accurate statistics on the number of good circuits per wafer, their location and the relative incidence of various types of failure. Such information is helpful in finding new ways to improve the yield of good circuits.

The completed circuit must undergo one last operation: packaging. It must be placed in some kind of protective housing and have connections with the outside world. There are many types of packages, but all have in common the fact that they are much larger and stronger than the silicon dice themselves. First the wafer is sectioned to separate the individual chips, usually by simply scribing between the chips and breaking the wafer along the scribe lines. The good circuits are bonded into packages, and they are connected to the electrodes leading out of the package by fine wires. The package is then sealed, and the device is ready for final testing. The packaged circuit goes through an exhaustive series of electrical tests to make sure that it functions perfectly and will continue to do so reliably for many years.

After the individual chips are obtained from the wafer the cost per manufacturing step rises enormously. No longer is the cost shared among many circuits. Accordingly automatic handling during packaging and testing must be introduced wherever possible. The traditional cost-saving technique has been to employ less expensive overseas labour for the labour-intensive packaging operation. As the cost of overseas labour rises and improved packaging technology becomes available, overseas hand labour is gradually being supplanted by highly automated domestic assembly.

A number of advanced processing techniques are now under development. For example, the simple wet-etching process in which films of aluminium or polycrystalline silicon are selectively removed is already being supplanted by dry-etching processes. Polycrystalline silicon can be "plasma-etched" in electrically excited gas of carbon tetrafluoride molecules (Freon). A high-frequency electric discharge at low pressure breaks the Freon molecule down into a variety of ions and free radicals (such as atomic fluorine). The free radicals attack the film but do not react with the photoresist mask. In addition to being a more controllable method for the selective removal of silicon, plasma-etching promises to be much less harmful to the environment. Instead of yielding large quantities of corrosive acids, the reaction products are very small quantities of fluorine and fluorides of silicon, which are easily trapped from the output of the system.

The technology of photolithography, which was stable for about ten years, is also undergoing several changes. First, as projection lithography replaces contact lithography, the number of defects is decreasing. Second, the availability of masks of higher quality is steadily reducing the size and cost of microelectronic devices. Third, new methods of lithography are being developed that could result in a tenfold reduction in the size of individual circuit elements and a hundredfold reduction in circuit area.

The smallest features that can be formed by the conventional photolithographic process are ultimately limited by the wavelength of light. Present technology can routinely reproduce elements a few micrometres across, and it appears possible to reduce the smallest features to about one micrometre. Electronic beams and X-rays, however, have wavelengths measured in nanometres (thousandths of a micrometre) and smaller; hence they are capable of producing extremely fine features.

X-ray lithography is simply a form of contact photolithography in which soft X-rays are substituted for ultraviolet radiation. The X-ray technique does indeed offer high resolution; simple structures less than a tenth of a micrometre across have already been produced. Because the entire wafer is exposed the process is also potentially quick and cheap. There are still many unsolved problems, however. X-ray masks, which consist of a heavy metallic pattern on a thin membrane such as Mylar, are fragile and difficult to make. It is also hard to align the mask with respect to the pattern on the wafer. Because of the attenuation of X-rays in air, the wafer must be exposed in a vacuum or in an atmosphere of helium. Present-day X-ray sources are comparatively weak, and long exposures are required. As a result no commercial integrated circuits have yet been manufactured with the aid of X-ray lithography.

Electron-beam lithography is an older and maturer technology, having its basis in electron microscopy. Actually a system for electron-beam lithography is much like a scanning electron microscope. A fine beam of electrons scans the wafer to expose an electron-sensitive resist in the desired areas. Although impressive results have been demonstrated, the application of electron-beam lithography is limited by its present high cost. The machines are expensive (roughly $1m per machine), and because the electron beam must scan the wafer rather than exposing it all at once the time needed to put the pattern on the wafer is quite long. The rate of progress in this area is rapid, however, and more practical systems are clearly on the way.

Although electron-beam lithography is currently too expensive to be part of the wafer-fabrication process, it is already a routine production technique for the making of photolithographic masks. With the aid of the electron-beam method it is possible to eliminate two photographic-reduction steps and write the pattern directly on the mask from the information stored in the computer memory. Masks can thereby be created in a few hours after the design is finished. The advantages of higher resolution, simplicity of manufacture and shorter production time may well result in the complete conversion of the industry to electron-beam mask-making. Gradually, as the cost decreases, electron-beam lithography will be introduced directly into the fabrication of wafers, and a new generation of even more complex microelectronic circuits will be born.

Guide to Further Reading

General

Following on from *Fortune* magazine, *Newsweek* carried an introductory article on "Computers: A New Wave" on 23 February 1976. Kenneth Lamott wrote a very simple account of "The Impudent, Magical Silicon Chip" in the magazine *Horizon* in July 1977.

Apart from the *Science* and *Scientific American* collections, which are strongly recommended (the latter being better on the actual technology, the former better on the social implications), an excellent description of "The Computer Society" appeared in *Time* magazine on 20 February 1978.

In the US, *Popular Science* also had special issues on "Microprocessors" in March 1977, and on "Microelectronics" in January 1978. In Britain, *Design* contained an introductory article by James Woudhuysen, "What Shall We Do With Microprocessors?" in September 1977; *Management Today* carried an authoritative acount of "The Micro-Revolution" in March 1978 by Philip Hughes and Trevor Armstrong of the British software firm Logica; and the editor of this volume contributed "The Microelectronic Revolution" and "Society With Chips – And Without Jobs" in *New Society*, 9 and 16 November 1978. The *Financial Times* had a special supplement on "Microelectronics" on 29 March 1979, as did *The Economist* on 1 March 1980.

By far the most important single event – and the one that really sparked widespread interest in the new technology in Britain – was the screening by the BBC of Ed Goldwyn's TV documentary "Now The Chips Are Down" in April 1978. This film has been widely acclaimed and it became a BBC worldwide bestseller. A shortened version of the script appears in chapter 6 of this book.

More recent introductions to the microelectronics revolution are:

"The Microprocessor: A Revolution for Growth", *Business Week*, 19 March 1979, which is recommended.

Adam Osborne, *Running Wild: The Next Industrial Revolution* (Osborne, Berkeley, 1979). Authoritative.

Ray Curnow and Susan Curran, *The Silicon Factor: Living with the Microprocessor* (National Extension College, Cambridge, 1979).

W. H. Mayall, *The Challenge of the Chip* (HMSO for Science Museum, London, 1980). Profusely illustrated.

Technology

The simplest introduction to microcomputing can be found in Adam Osborne, *An Introduction to Microcomputers* (Osborne, Berkeley, 1977), which consists of three volumes, Vol. 0, *The Beginner's Book*, Vol. 1, *Basic Concepts*, and Vol. 2, *Some Real Products*.

The best textbooks are generally reckoned to be:

Edwin E. Klingman, *Microprocessor Systems Design* (Prentice-Hall, Englewood Cliffs, New Jersey, 1977).

John B. Peatman, *Microcomputer-Based Design* (McGraw-Hill, New York, 1977).

But the following are widely used:

D. D. Givone and R. P. Roesser, *Microprocessors/Microcomputers: An Introduction* (McGraw-Hill, New York, 1980).

Daniel R. McGlynn, *Microprocessors: Technology, Architecture and Applications* (John Wiley, New York, 1976).

Carol Anne Ogdin, *Microcomputer Design* (Prentice-Hall, Englewood Cliffs, New Jersey, 1978).

G. W. Rao, *Microprocessors and Microcomputer Systems* (Van Nostrand Reinhold, 1978).

D. Roddy, *Introduction to Microelectronics* (Ontario, Canada, 1978).

Dwight H. Sawin, *Microprocessors and Microcomputer Systems* (Lexington Books, Lexington, Mass., 1977).

Charles J. Sippl, *The Microcomputer Handbook* (Petrocelli/Charter, New York, 1977).

M. E. Sloan, *Introduction to Minicomputers and Microcomputers* (Addison Wesley, London, 1980).

J. Watson, *Semiconductor Circuit Design* (Adam Hilger, Bristol, 1977).

Edward S. Young, *Fundamentals of Semiconductor Devices* (McGraw-Hill, New York, 1978).

In addition, there are two books in the *Electronics* magazine book series, *Microprocessors* and *Large-Scale Integration* (both McGraw-Hill, New York, 1976). "Primers" on the microprocessor have also appeared in the personal computer magazines, *Creative Computing* (Sept./Oct. 1977) and *Personal Computing* (June 1978).

A good technical account of the microprocessor by the co-founder of Intel can be found in Gordon E. Moore, "Microprocessors and Integrated Electronic Technology", *Proceedings of the IEEE*, Vol. 64, No. 6 (June 1976). Another neat introduction is "The Microprocessor In Control", a paper delivered to the Institution of Electrical Engineers in London on 10 October 1978, by H. A. Barker.

Christine Sutton, "Taking The Mystery Out Of Micro", *New Scientist*, 17 May 1979, explains how junction transistors, semiconductors and bubble memories actually work.

Infotech, *Microelectronics* (Maidenhead, UK, and Auerbach Publications, Pennsauken, New Jersey, 1980). The 58th Infotech state of the art report. This 650-page two-volume study is notable for the prediction that gallium arsenide will soon displace silicon as the base component of microprocessors.

2 The Microelectronics Industry

The Jelly Bean People of Silicon Valley

Tom Forester

The Santa Clara valley in California – "Silicon Valley" – is the home of the microelectronic revolution and remains the key location in the world microelectronics industry. This account of life in that extraordinary part of the world was the result of a short visit in June 1978. It appeared in New Society *on 27 July 1978.*

At the flat and marshy south end of San Francisco Bay, some fifty miles from downtown San Francisco, highway 101 veers east around Moffett naval airfield just past Palo Alto, then plunges south at San Jose through the super-fertile flatlands of the Santa Clara valley. On one side, Pacific mist hangs loose around the damp green wooded slopes way up on the coastal Monte Bello ridge. On the inland side, arid Mount Misery, Poverty Ridge and the Diablo range wobble in the shimmering haze.

Luscious fruit orchards covered the flat valley floor until recently, but now timber apartment blocks march towards the horizon. Snazzy rows of brand-new, low-rise factory units, all bronze glass and black plastic, line highway 101 and the grid iron road system on either side. Weird names on them proclaim "Signetics", "Aqueonics" and "General Devices". A huge half-built spaghetti junction in a field stands ready for further expansion. A small airport comes up on the right, its tarmac packed with executive jets. A black Mercedes scorches past, its driver shouting into a radio telephone.

The cars, the planes, the bustle, above all the evident explosion in real estate: the Santa Clara valley has boom written all over it – which isn't surprising, because this strip between Palo Alto and San Jose is the backbone of the world's microelectronics industry, the spectacular growth industry that will figure in just about everybody's future. In particular, it is the home of the revolutionary minicomputer, computer "chip" or "jelly bean", the remarkable ten-year-old invention that the British government, through the NEB, is at last waking up to. You may still not know the way to San Jose, but by now you've probably heard of this place by its nickname: "Silicon Valley".

Silicon Valley is where they serve up chips with everything and chips for everything. What Silicon Valley develops today (and new innovations do come almost daily) the world will be using in a multitude of applications tomorrow. In the appliances in our homes, in our cars, in the office, in the shops and all over industry we will be punching those buttons and reading those digital dials as never before. Thanks to the Silicon Integrated Circuit (SIC) and similar devices like the bubble memory, which can cost as little as $4 to produce yet can outperform a roomful of early 1960s equipment, some say we are on the verge of a second industrial revolution.

As if to underline their faith in this vision of the future, the conventional computer giant IBM has just completed its very own university campus in Silicon Valley, down the south end on the old cottonwood slopes at Santa Teresa. Inside the silver blocks of this fortified monastery, twentieth-century monks will dedicate themselves to the study and refinement of computer programming techniques; 2000 lone researchers will meditate and worship in individual rooms, in space-age structures of aluminium and mirror glass. I don't want to labour the religious bit, but most of the IBM buildings *are* shaped like a cross.

With its hegemony in computers threatened by the fast-growing chip specialists, like the market leader Intel Corp., IBM's decision to locate a major research facility in the area is a belated recognition of Silicon Valley's unique ability to foster innovations in electronics over the past twenty years. Nobody quite knows why the Valley is so good at it, or why microelectronics began here in the first place (though the proximity of four universities, especially the high-technology Stanford University at Palo Alto, was no doubt important). But ever since William Shockley, co-inventor of the transistor, founded the Shockley Transistor Corp. there in 1956, growth and innovation has preceded at a bewildering pace – thanks largely to the availability of venture capital, the benefits of near-perfect competition, the existence of an infrastructure of firms able to carry out specialist tasks and, perhaps most crucial of all, the advantages of staying small but beautiful.

For unlike most industries, the microelectronic firms of Silicon Valley have demonstrated, until now, a remarkable ability to split up regularly rather than combine – and the freedom of bright engineering teams to go off and set up their own companies has been a vital precondition to innovation. It has also created the unique vitality of the Valley.

As Rob Walker, market communications manager of Intel Corp., explains, even in the early 1950s it was apparent that big firms like Westinghouse and General Electric were unable to produce good transistors. So key engineers left to spawn a new generation of companies like Texas Instruments, Motorola and Fairchild Semiconductor. Of key importance were eight engineers who left Shockley to form Fairchild. They included a Robert Noyce and a Gordon Moore, later to become multimillionaire bosses of Intel Corp. "It was something to do with the nine to five attitude and not feeling a part of a team in the big corporations." But though the new firms were good at transistors, they in turn weren't making much progress with SICs. So *another* new generation of companies began to be formed in the late 1960s.

Intel became the first to really develop the miracle chip. Since 1968, its growth has been nothing short of astonishing: revenues have leapt from nothing to nearly $300m per annum, they employ over 8000 people in ten plants worldwide, their return on capital is about thirty per cent, they have no debts but instead have huge cash reserves. In fact Intel has got dangerouly big, so Noyce and Moore and their chief operating officer, Hungarian brain-drainer Andy Grove, have split it up into five autonomous divisions. They have also started to create research "fellows", like the brilliant Ted Hoff, who are allowed complete freedom. These fellows are sometimes called "individual contributors".

But Intel, like National Semiconductor, Signetics, Siliconix, Advanced Micro Devices and the other star firms in the Valley, is run by expert electronic engineers. There is no administrative class or layer of know-nothing bureaucrats. As Andy Grove of Intel points out: "A manufacturer of high-technology jelly beans needs a different breed of people. The wild-eyed, bushy-haired boy geniuses that dominate the think tanks and the solely technology-orientated companies will never take that technology to the jelly-bean stage [the mass market]. Likewise, the other stereotype, the strait-laced, crewcut, sideburn and moustache-free manufacturing operators of conventional industry, will never generate the technology in the first place. Our needs dictated that we fill our senior ranks with a group of highly competent technical specialists who were willing to adapt to a structured and disciplined environment."

And adapt they did. While Intel and other small outfits were leaping ahead in the 1970s, the corporate giants like Honeywell, Philips, Siemens and Bosch were all trying to develop viable SICs – but without success. The only way they managed to get into chips was by buying out small firms for their knowledge. Rob Walker says: "In a small-team setup, it's something to do with not having to refer things to some goddamn committee all the time. You just get right on with the job yourself. We get English guys coming out here all the time saying they can't take the bureaucracy. That and wasting their time tooling around in some crummy undercapitalized lab with an obsolete product.''

More than forty firms in Silicon Valley can, like Intel, trace their roots to Fairchild. Add to that all the other firms competing in the same field and you've got intense competition. A US Federal Trade Commission report on the semiconductor industry in fact said that the industry in January 1977 was as perfectly competitive as any industry could get. Success or failure usually comes swiftly, but there appears to have been venture capital ready to take high risks.

Nowhere is competition more acute than in the job market. Skills are in short supply and local house prices have gone through the roof. In consequence, firms fall over themselves to steal each other's labour. Every Saturday, the San Jose *Mercury News* has no fewer than forty or fifty pages of small ads for jobs, more than any paper in the US apart from one in Los Angeles. Firms not only offer high salaries, they offer thirty-hour three-day weeks, cars, housing subsidies, long holidays, stock options and flying lessons. They also offer courtesy and free-and-easy working conditions. Many employees come and go as they please – though, as Ralph Shattuck, a $36,000 a-year data-processing auditor points out; ''Although we're pretty free, most guys will work on into the evening. Even so, if your employer is a bastard, you just go right on down the road to another firm. You just take another exit off highway 101 in the morning.''

In fact, Ralph had tried job-hopping: the previous Friday, he had tired of firm A and their $30,000 a year salary. On Monday he joined firm B on $34,000, but they were a bit stuffy and made him wear a tie. Tuesday was a bank holiday but on Wednesday he was back with firm A – on $36,000 plus stock options. As we set off down the freeway to go eat, a Siliconix Inc. advertisement hoarding screamed at us: ''Have FUN on July 4! Join US on July 5!''

At the Marriott Hotel, just off highway 101, near the screaming rollercoaster of Great America Park, two English guys prop the bar. On business for a UK firm, they came over in a group of three. One joined a US firm immediately, but they are giving it more thought: ''I don't want to live here, but Britain *is* going down the drain. In our field, electronics, the British firms are hopeless – they are large, monolithic and inflexible. They've got no imagination. The NEB is right to ignore them and set up their own outfit. But whether it will work without the Silicon Valley infrastructure, I doubt it. And look where they're going to put it! In the north of England. Where would you rather be? Sunny Halifax or sunny California?''

Around the bar, a favourite with the Valley's silicon merchants,

An idea of the competition for the silicon superstars is given by this ad from a Silicon Valley recruitment agency

people talk chips. I pick up snatches: "Listen Harvey, people-wise we're thirty per cent down. We just can't get them. Last week we only recruited eight new guys. We just ain't gonna get them wafers to you in time."

Harvey's friend may not have to worry much longer. Or he may. It all depends on the performance of the new high-powered recruitment agencies coming into the valley. Typical of these is Upward Mobility, who have a hectic office in Santa Clara. The co-founder, Don Roy, says: "Our main target are kids fresh out of college or with a couple of years' experience. We can get them for $25,000 or less. Hopefully, the firm will get four or five years out of them before they move on. But the average engineer changes every two years. It's a real seller's market. We're having a hell of a lot of trouble recruiting right now. The housing situation is terrible. Tell them English engineers we can get the best deal for their skills."

Don was not exaggerating. So good are the deals now being negotiated by some highly gifted engineers that people are talking about electronics superstars – people who can earn in excess of $80,000 a year. Above *them* are the silicon millionaires. Nobody knows how many of them exist, but there must be quite a few. And those who succeed tend to do so at a young age. Like Gerry Sanders, aged 37, boss of Advanced Micro Devices and driver of a white Rolls-Royce. There's Zeev Drori, an Israeli in his mid-thirties running Monolithic Memories. Liverpudlian Wilf Corrigan is boss of Fairchild at forty, while his Scottish No. 2, George Wells, is younger. Many of them live in nearby Los Altos Hills, where three-acre wooded lots and a large pool are *de rigueur*.

Tom Hinkelman's job is to develop an objective picture of what is happening in this bizarre and fast-moving Valley. From his desk at the Semiconductor Industries Association office in nearby Cupertino, he collects statistics and monitors the industry's performance for its thirty-five members. No long-established bureaucracy this – the association was only started last year, a main aim being to represent the manufacturers at national level. But there is also concern, perhaps premature but nevertheless real, about the future of the industry – especially in view of possible Japanese competition.

"The Valley is under pressure in a number of interesting ways," Hinkelman says. "Some companies have found it most difficult lately to raise venture capital. We have this capital gains tax which has made the risk/reward ratio of high technology far less favourable than real estate." So firms have sold out interests or sold out completely to the laggardly giants. In the past two years, Philips have bought out Signetics, Siemens have a stake in Advanced Micro Devices and also own Litronix outright. Bosch have just bought into Advanced Micro Systems, and so on.

Might this not endanger the vitality of the Valley which, after all, was based on the ability of engineers to raise capital to start their own firms? "Yes, it could, and so are rising costs, especially housing, which are preventing people from coming here."

Are there any other clouds in Silicon Valley? "Yes. The main threat we perceive is from foreign government-coordinated and directed efforts to establish their own home-based industries. The main one being the Japanese, who we've been studying this past six months, but we are also very interested in this British proposal. It's very political. For years the amount of investment in industry has been zilch in your country. Now, in a sense, we're catching the British disease. There's too little attention being given here to basics. Microelectronics is *the* foundation technology. If you're not in it, you're not going to be in almost any industrial process in the future. The world leader in microelectronics will lead the world in everything else."

From Transistor to Microprocessor

Ernest Braun

For the next piece, a paper specially commissioned for this volume, Professor Braun goes back to the beginning of the microelectronic revolution – which was in fact 1945, although nobody realized it at the time. The author describes the major scientific breakthroughs and the key commercial developments in the historical evolution of the microprocessor, and also points up the essential characteristics of the microelectronics industry.

Early developments

The development of microelectronics really started at the end of World War Two in the Bell Laboratories in the United States. In the summer of 1945, the vice-president for research at Bell, Mervin Kelly, signed the authorization to start work with the aim of producing devices useful in telecommunications. A group of very able scientists, mostly just returned from wartime research, was put together to perform this task. Three of the men in the group have become well-known names: Bardeen, Brattain and Shockley. The kind of devices they were searching for were switches to replace cumbersome mechanical relays in telephone exchanges and amplifiers to replace the bulky and energy-consuming valve.

The efforts of the Bell group were, of course, not the first. The solid-state amplifier had been invented many times before, ever since crystals were first used to detect radio and, much later, radar waves. But all previous inventions had failed to work and the prize was still there to grasp. The Bell group had three major advantages, probably all indispensable: first of all, a great deal of knowledge about semiconductor materials, especially germanium, had been accumulated in wartime research on radar detectors; secondly, the group consisted of very able

72

men from several scientific disciplines who were looking for a particular device but who at the same time were interested in the fundamental properties of the materials. Theirs was not a blind empirical fumbling. They really tried to understand the electronic processes in solids and yet keep their eyes open for practical applications. This blend of fundamental research with applications in mind proved highly successful and was just what was needed. Third, and a very important third it was, the Bell group had luck on its side.

Armed with these three advantages and after a good deal of hard, painstaking and clever work, the first fruit of their labours was announced to the world in June 1948. This was the point contact transistor. The device consisted of a small piece of germanium – the original chip – with two closely spaced wire contacts made on one of its surfaces. The voltage across one of these contacts, that is the voltage between the germanium base and one wire, influenced the current which flowed between the base and the other contact. The reason for this influence is the injection or extraction of carriers of electricity – electrons or holes – from the vicinity of the contact, thus modifying the conductivity in that region. If the voltage between two terminals of a device causes a change of current between a second pair of terminals, then we have an amplifier. The point contact transistor is rather like two point contact rectifiers in very close proximity, but the result is the long-dreamed-of crystal amplifier.

The point contact transistor was announced to the world, but the world took little notice at first. Perhaps this is not surprising, as the initial device was not very effective. It amplified, but only a little and only over a very limited range of frequencies. Its stability and reproducibility were poor and it was extremely difficult to manufacture and therefore quite expensive. It required a considerable amount of foresight to see in the point contact transistor the forerunner of the microelectronic revolution. Certainly neither the press nor most electronic engineers had this foresight. The researchers in the world's electronic industry did see immediately that there was something important here and began their own programmes of research and development on semiconductor electronics. Nobody, however, could or did foresee just how far the development would go and how enormous its total impact would be.

The point contact diode, or rectifier, became a well-established product and was really just a modern version of the wartime radar detector and the even earlier "cat's whisker" radio detector. The point contact transistor also became commercially available and it found a small number of applications, especially in hearing aids where the small size and low power consumption were particularly advantageous. But by the time the first applications became available, its successor device had already been announced by Bell – the junction transistor. This became typical of the semiconductor industry. In the early years, virtually everything that worked was at best obsolescent and at worst obsolete.

The junction transistor was also made of a germanium chip, though this was mostly replaced later by silicon. The chip had three electrically different layers in which the current was carried by different charge carriers. The crystal was a kind of sandwich with the two outer, and thicker, layers consisting of material of one conductivity and the middle, the thin base, of another conductivity. The current in the outer layers was carried by electrons, negative charge carriers, and the current in the base was carried by holes, in effect positively-charged carriers. The device came to be called *n-p-n*.

No sooner was the junction transistor announced than the battle began for suitable technologies to manufacture it. The basic material in all transistors has to be an extremely pure single crystal of germanium or silicon, and the different conducting regions are obtained by the inclusion of minute amounts of suitable impurities – donors for *n*–type material and acceptors for *p*-type. But great difficulty was soon experienced in making sharp junctions and a sufficiently thin base region – both conditions for successful amplification at high frequencies. In fact, even at that stage it became clear that improvements in the quality of the product went hand in hand with improvements in the economic viability of manufacture. Both were almost entirely dependent upon manufacturing technique.

In the next few years, developments of manufacturing technology were very rapid and innovation chased innovation. The performance of transistors increased sharply and prices fell dramatically. In this period (the mid-1950s) there was also an enormous upsurge in scientific activity, and learned article followed learned article. And while all this was going on in the large electronics firms and the research laboratories of the world, a new breed of person emerged in the United States: the scientific entrepreneur.

Men with knowledge in semiconductor physics and technology began their own small manufacturing operations. At a time of rapid change there was a premium on knowledge, ideas and flexibility. From 1951 to 1956, the number of firms manufacturing transistors in the US increased from four to twenty-six. By 1957 the new firms, firms with no experience in the valve industry, had captured sixty-four per cent of the total semiconductor market.

In the early and mid-1950s, most of the innovations emerged from Bell Laboratories or from the other large valve companies. Even in

1956 the new firms were only producing twenty per cent of the patents in the industry. Yet what turned out to be the truly crucial innovations for the 1960s and 1970s emerged mostly from the newer firms which had attracted men of ability and had concentrated on the development of production technology. It was process technology that determined the winners in the semiconductor race. As early as 1954, Texas Instruments, who had no experience of electronics before 1949 and did not establish a research laboratory until January 1953, produced the first silicon transistor. In the same year, Texas Instruments also collaborated in the production of the first commercial transistor radio. Fairchild Semiconductor, a company started in 1957, produced the first transistors by the planar technique.

The planar technique, which consists of a sequence of three processes – oxidation, photo-etching and diffusion – very quickly became the dominant technique throughout the industry. A wafer of silicon is oxidized and then coated with a photosensitive polymer, a photoresist. A suitable pattern is photographed onto the resist which becomes vulnerable to some chemicals when exposed to light. The photographed pattern can therefore be etched through the resist and through the silicon oxide underneath it. The resist is then washed off and the desired impurities are allowed to diffuse into the exposed parts of the silicon wafer, while the rest is protected by the remaining oxide layer. This process can be repeated at will, and in this way intricate patterns of diverse conducting layers can be built up.

Initially the process was used just to produce a large number of transistors on a silicon wafer. The wafer was then sliced into individual chips, each containing one transistor, and these were eventually wired into electronic circuits. The great advantages of the process were that it improved manufacturing yield and produced reliable products relatively cheaply. The planar process was devised in 1958 and went into commercial production in 1959.

Thus it took approximately one decade from the first tentative postwar steps to a large, sophisticated industry producing, in 1959, $228.5m worth of transistors and $166.5m worth of diodes and rectifiers in the US alone. By then there were twenty-seven firms in the US making transistors and fifty-seven firms making diodes and rectifiers. However, with hindsight we may say that this first decade of the semiconductor industry really only set the stage for the next decade.

The first applications of semiconductor electronics had been in the telephone industry and in hearing aids. This was rapidly followed, in 1954, by the first transistor radios. Television cameras, but not receivers, soon followed and what was to emerge as one of the major applications, computers, began to use transistors in 1955. In that year

IBM marketed a computer in which 1250 valves had been replaced by 2200 transistors, reducing the power consumption of the computer by ninety-five per cent. Military purchases of transistors, for communication and other electronic equipment, also increased rapidly and in 1955 the government was buying twenty-two per cent of all semiconductor devices made. This accounted for thirty-five per cent of the US market in money terms. By 1963 the total US transistor market had increased to over $252m and of this, government purchases accounted for $119m.

Prices of devices dropped rapidly as companies progressed along the so-called learning curve: in the early stages of manufacturing a new device all sorts of technical difficulties arise and thus manufacturing costs are high. To make matters worse, development costs have to be recouped. As manufacturing experience increases, yields increase and the price drops. Eventually competition forces the price down even further and finally the device bows out as obsolete: for example, the average price of silicon transistors dropped from $17.81 in 1957 to $2.65 in 1963.

The arrival of the integrated circuit

The crucial importance of the planar process lay not only in its ability to improve the manufacture of transistors, but also in the fact that it facilitated the next step in microelectronic developments – the integrated circuit. The idea that whole circuits, consisting of several transistors and their interconnections, as well as resistors and capacitors, should be made in a single chip had been talked about for some time. Perhaps it was first articulated by Professor Dummer of Royal Radar Establishment, Malvern, but the final technical steps were taken by Jack Kilby of Texas Instruments and by Robert Noyce of Fairchild.

The first integrated circuits were manufactured at high cost in the early 1960s. The manufacturing processes had not been fully mastered, but military purchases helped the firms to move along the learning curve towards prices which commercial customers were willing to pay. The role of early purchaser of expensive new devices was arguably the most important role the US military played in the development of the microelectronics industry.

In the 1960s, transistors and integrated circuits were commercially mass-produced. Sales of transistors overtook those of valves in 1959. Between 1963 and 1971 shipments of transistors from the US semiconductor industry rose from 303 million to 881 million, while the number of transistor equivalents in integrated circuits rose from 108 million to 40,653 million. During the same period, the average price of the integrated circuit fell from over $30 to about $1. The role of the military as a purchaser declined accordingly. The number of discrete components incorporated in each integrated circuit also increased by leaps and bounds, from twenty-four in 1963 to sixty-four in 1971. By the mid-1970s world sales of semiconductor products had risen to about $4000m. The packing density of integrated circuits continued to rise until today chips containing 100,000 components are perfectly feasible.

Apart from integrated circuits manufactured by the planar process, similar manufacturing techniques made it possible to realize the idea of solid-state amplification which had failed many times before. The idea was to induce additional charge carriers into a slab of semiconductor by making it one plate of a capacitor. As the conduction of electricity in a semiconductor is limited by the availability of charge carriers, the induction of additional carriers should cause the resistance of the slab to change. A sandwich consisting of a semiconductor coated by its insulating oxide and having a metallic electrode evaporated on top of the oxide (metal-oxide-semiconductor or MOS) can act as an amplifier in that the voltage between semiconductor and metal alters the current between two contacts applied to the semiconductor. Today, most integrated circuits are based either on the planar transistor system or on the MOS system.

As the number of components per chip increased and correspondingly the price per component decreased, a shift in the mode of designing electronic circuits occurred. In the past, operations were predominantly carried out in the "analogue" mode, that is the output of the electronic circuit was proportional to the intensity of the property being represented. An example is the audio-amplifier: at any instant of time the voltage at the output terminals is proportional to the amplitude of the sound being amplified and reproduced. The modern trend for more and more applications is the "digital" mode of operation. In this mode, the input signal is first converted into a binary number, or a sequence of numbers, and the output signal consists of another sequence of numbers logically related to the input signal. The final output can, of course, be amplified to actuate various devices, such as servomotors or loud-speakers, if numerical display is not the desired end result.

The trend towards digital operations is symptomatic of the very close relationship between computers and microelectronics. It may be said that the development of modern computers was entirely dependent upon developments in integrated circuits, but also that modern integrated circuits developed in directions largely determined by computers. Thus even the original Bell intention of using transistors for switching purposes in telephone exchanges has, after very long delays, now finally led to digital transmissions of speech on the telephone, and exchanges which are in effect computers.

As the density of active components on a chip increased with better

VACUUM TUBE AEG
MID 1950s

TRANSISTOR AEG
EARLY 1960s

IC AEG*
1978 LSI

1 AEG

*Magnified 1000X

Area=4 sq. in.

Area=¾ sq. in.

Area=2½ Millionths sq. in.

The shape and size of the electronics revolution as seen through the eyes of market leader, Texas Instruments. *Photo courtesy of Texas Instruments Incorporated*

manufacturing technology and better design of circuits, so the capability of a chip obtainable for a given sum of money increased. The culmination of all these developments was the microprocessor, which has become virtually synonymous with microelectronics, but should not be confused with it. The microprocessor is an integrated circuit which has the properties, and fulfils the role, of a complete central processing unit of a computer. This means that the circuit does not just react in a fixed, pre-programmed way to an input signal to produce an output signal. The main feature of the microprocessor is that its response, its logic, can be altered. In other words, the microprocessor can be programmed in different ways rather than react in one pre-programmed way only.

The microprocessor was first invented by Hoff at Intel in 1971 – another example of a major innovation originating in a small, new company. It took about three years before the first devices reached the market, but in the meantime about a hundred different microprocessors had become available, though only a few types sold in large quantities. As with all microelectronic products, the capabilities of microprocessors advanced rapidly and the sophistication of the circuits increased almost day by day. Even the elusive aim of a complete computer on a single chip has been achieved.

The semiconductor industry

The electronics industry has become dominated by semiconductors, and several other major industries, such as aerospace, computers and telecommunications, have become entirely dependent upon the electronics industry. The semiconductor industry originated in the United States, and the US industry is still both the largest and the most advanced. A large number of European microelectronics manufacturers are, in fact, subsidiaries of American firms. On the other hand, there is now considerable activity by European firms acquiring American subsidiaries or starting joint ventures. It seems that the early character of the industry, with its diversity and its many new ventures, is beginning to disappear. A consolidated mature industry of a few large advanced firms, surrounded by some satellite ancillary suppliers, is emerging.

World consumption of semiconductor products rose from $2217m in 1969 to $4846m in 1976, while the US share of world production remained fairly stable around fifty-five per cent. In thirty years the industry has gone full circle. It started in the large valve companies, but it allowed many new semiconductor firms to enter the market. It is now an industry dominated by a few large semiconductor firms. The scientific entrepreneur was characteristic of the industry, given the dominant role of expertise and the small scale at which ventures could be started. The Americans always had the advantage: they started the industry, and they also have an economic system and an outlook which fosters the entrepreneur. The US still has the lead, but only because its firms are established as leaders and because of the very large domestic market. The entrepreneurial advantage has gone. This has been handed over to users of the new electronics. It remains to be seen what Europeans can make of these opportunities.

It is easy to think of the American semiconductor industry as being located entirely in Silicon Valley. In fact, the Santa Clara valley near San Francisco is neither the original home of semiconductors, nor is it today the only location of the microelectronics industry. The industry started on the East Coast, where most of the old valve companies, including Bell, were located. The first of the new companies remained on the East Coast, and both Long Island and the Boston area proved attractive. The main attractions were the availability of ancillary industries and the availability of risk capital. Also, many of the founders of the new companies had their roots in either or both the old companies and the East Coast universities.

The move to the West started when William Shockley decided to leave Bell Laboratories and go it alone in 1955. Shockley Semiconductor Laboratories was established in Palo Alto, Shockley's home town. The company changed hands several times and completely changed its nature over the years, with Shockley eventually pulling out and the Palo Alto factory closing. However, Shockley had attracted several other experts to work with him and some of these founded a new company, Fairchild Semiconductor. Dozens of further companies were eventually founded by employees of Fairchild – sometimes referred to as *The Fairchildren* – and not surprisingly most of these remained in the same vicinity. The area is also favoured because it has many modern industries, excellent educational and cultural facilities, and pleasant living conditions. The close proximity of companies to each other facilitated the sharing of ancillary services, not least financial services, and it helped the exchange of information. A certain bar in Silicon Valley was called the "fountainhead' of the semiconductor industry, as this was where semiconductor men drank, exchanged information and hired employees. The informal exchanges of information and the rapid movement of employees probably caused a much more rapid general growth than strict and paranoic commercial secrecy and immobility would have allowed.

Despite the great fame of the Santa Clara Valley, many of the most important firms in the industry are located elsewhere. Some of the older firms have remained on the East Coast and have retained their importance. The largest microelectronics firm selling on the open market, Texas Instruments, is surviving very happily in Dallas, Texas, and Motorola in Phoenix, Arizona, is also doing very well. These two companies are large enough to have created their own satellite supply industries and they do not need the close proximity of like-minded companies.

Licensing arrangements are very common in the industry and are often made necessary because large customers need a second source of supply. Any truly large-scale production of a newly patented device therefore becomes possible only if at least one other supplier has been granted a licence to produce the same device. Customers gain security of supply and the industry gains by a reasonable flow of information within it. Bell set the tone early on with an open attitude to licences, possibly under some legal pressure as a public service corporation, but also with the intention of helping to create a flourishing industry. All this is not to say that industrial secrecy does not exist – there is still a premium on being first in a field – but that secrecy is not obsessive and does not, on the whole, hamper progress.

As well as supplying the first licences, Bell supplied the first experts. At a time when universities had not started courses on solid-state physics, Bell were practically the only source of experts in the new field. Soon other valve companies and the universities produced experts as a result of their researches. Eventually the new companies, often founded and staffed by people trained in the older firms, started to provide a flow of experts to the newer firms. The American semiconductor industry, unlike its British counterpart, was characterized by great mobility of personnel. The best experts achieved rapid advancement, large salaries, and large stakes in companies by accepting offers they couldn't refuse.

The most successful people in the industry are those who combine commercial acumen with sound scientific and engineering knowhow. As one of them put it: "Many of us start out as technologists or engineers and then become more and more interested in the business or economic aspects of the corporation. Semiconductors allow you to do both."

Although the industry was undoubtedly based on science and many firms in the early 1950s invested heavily in fundamental scientific research, it soon became apparent that success came to those who harnessed scientific principles to the needs of production and of engineering. Many firms reacted to the initial invention of the transistor by large increases in their fundamental research budgets. Gradually their enthusiasm waned, as success became increasingly a matter of good engineering. The research budgets were soon trimmed, in many cases severely. In 1972, the total budget for fundamental research and development in the US industry was $36m, and of this about eighty per cent was spent by Bell and IBM, both firms producing microelectronic devices only for their own needs.

As the industry has matured, its relationship with the universities, never overwhelmingly strong, has grown weaker. The dependence of the industry upon military markets has decreased markedly. While in 1960 about half the total US semiconductor purchases were made by the military, this proportion had fallen to twenty-four per cent in 1972. In Western Europe, the proportion of military purchases in 1972 was fourteen per cent, while in Japan it was zero.

Britain, France, Germany and Japan quickly developed semiconductor industries of their own in the wake of America. The average timelag for the introduction of major American innovations into these countries varied from about 1.2 to 3.4 years. Not only have the Americans never lost the initiative in new products, they also have a considerable stake in the European market by a combination of direct imports and manufacturing facilities in Europe. The American share of the British market was fifty-eight per cent in 1972, while their share of the French and German markets was ninety-five per cent and fifty-one per cent respectively. Only the Japanese effectively prevented American penetration and kept it to twelve per cent of their market.

In the 1950s, British scientists and engineers had been quick to pick up the challenge of the new electronics and many became highly expert in the field. Alas, the research effort of the large and cumbersome British firms was largely ineffectual and many of their scientists joined the Brain Drain to the United States. This phenomenon largely came to an end in the late 1960s and the 1970s, but the research and development effort in British industry had by then declined to a level well below its peak. Some British products, however, are fully competitive in world markets and with the recent government initiatives – if they are maintained – there is every hope that the British and European industries will become more equal partners in the worldwide microelectronics industry.

Micros: The Coming World War

Ian M. Mackintosh

Formerly with Bell Laboratories, Westinghouse and Elliot Automation, and now chairman of the British consultants Mackintosh International, Professor Mackintosh is well placed to analyse international trends in the microelectronics industry. In this paper he argues that American global domination will soon be seriously threatened by Japan. It formed the keynote address to the 1978 International Solid-State Circuits Conference in San Francisco and is reprinted from the Microelectronics Journal *(vol. 9, No. 2, 1978).*

The popular but simplistic view – widely held outside the United States – is that the American domination of this industry has been based primarily on very substantial and continuous financial support from the US government. Whereas this funding has obviously been important, the real foundations of the American success are far more complex and need to be understood in detail before the outcome of the impending intercontinental battle can be correctly forecast.

Indeed, any prognosis of future structural developments in this industry must begin with an understanding of the principal historical forces which have moulded the industry into its present form. The reason, quite obviously, is that whereas important new strategic influences are now emerging, these historical forces will continue to have a significant effect for the foreseeable future.

This paper therefore comprises two main parts. The first looks briefly at some aspects of the historical development of the semiconductor industry in general, and integrated circuits (ICs) in particular, in the US, Europe and Japan, giving due attention to the various factors which produced the different pace and direction of development in each

83

geographical region. It is then possible to identify a number of key factors which have led to the current American domination of world IC markets.

From this foundation, the second part goes on to examine the relevance of these factors, plus the new strategic forces now gathering momentum, to the future chances of success of IC producers in each geographical region, and to offer a prognosis of the future capabilities of each of these regions to compete in the Very Large Scale Integration (VLSI) era.

The origins of the semiconductor industry

It is well known that the 1950s were characterized by the germanium transistor first going into high-volume production. Its most immediate application was in cheap portable radios, and the nation which seized this opportunity most effectively was Japan, possessing at that time the considerable advantage of low labour costs. However, Europe (in particular, Philips) was not left far behind.

In the US, however, the gleam in the electronic industry's collective eye was not caused by radios, largely because of the high American labour costs (the idea of moving labour-intensive assembly operations off-shore had not yet been tried). Instead, the greatest *need* (what we might call the "user-pull", as distinct from the "maker-push" effect) for the transistor was mainly in the defence and aerospace sectors – 1957 being the year of the Sputnik – and in the infant computer industry. The demands of these military and industrial sectors for devices of higher performance and reliability thus led in time to the emergence of the silicon transistor and later to integrated circuits – both developed, of course, by American companies.

The final effects of these original, basic reactions to the advent of the transistor were as follows:

(1)   The Europeans and Japanese became strong in germanium technology *and* in the main types of equipment (i.e. consumer electronic products) which were based at that time on germanium transistors.
(2)   The Americans became pre-eminent in silicon technology *and* in the main types of equipment (military, computers, communications, etc) based on this technology.
(3)   These distinctive postures, originally taken up fifteen to twenty years ago, still pertain today, with the Europeans and Japanese leading by a significant margin in most aspects of consumer electronics and the Americans continuing to dominate every other sector of the electronics industry.

What can be learned, therefore, from this brief historical review is that industrial synergism – the mutual interdependence of different industrial sectors and, in particular, of the equipment and components sectors of the electronics industry – has been a significant factor in shaping the development of the electronics industry in different geographic regions. This is explored later.

With the advantage of this historical perspective, the principal strategic factors which have affected – and in most cases will continue to affect – the development of the global IC industry can be identified.

There are, obviously, many such strategic factors, and considerable analysis of data, case histories, etc, is necessary if their relative importance is to be correctly assessed. This allows certain principal conclusions to be drawn, although it is obviously impossible to present the mass of detailed evidence on which these conclusions are based.

The main strategic factors which need to be discussed are:

Government Support
Industrial Synergism
Technological Innovation
Market Factors
Industrial Structure
Management and People

(1) *The role of governments.* It is beyond question that, almost from its beginning, the American semiconductor industry as a whole has received substantial and broadly-based support from various US government agencies. It has been estimated that this totalled about $900m for R & D alone between 1958 and 1974, representing a subsidy of the cost of American semiconductor innovation to the tune of about $55m per

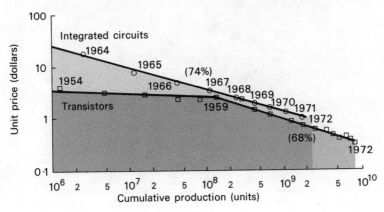

Fig. 2.1   Learning curve

annum (in the terms of, say, 1965 average dollar values). Now, it is clear
that financial support from public funds on such a large scale has grossly
distorted normal competitive conditions and commercial criteria in this
industry, and it is difficult to imagine, therefore, how any non-American
nation could succeed without providing support to its own indigenous
industry on a comparable scale.

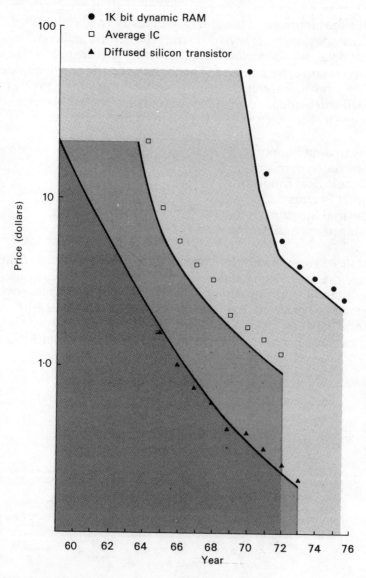

Fig. 2.2 Typical price trends of silicon devices

(2) *The benefits of industrial synergism.* The general, theoretical benefits of industrial synergism are familiar. However, in a paper of this type it could be useful to emphasize the particular importance of synergism in

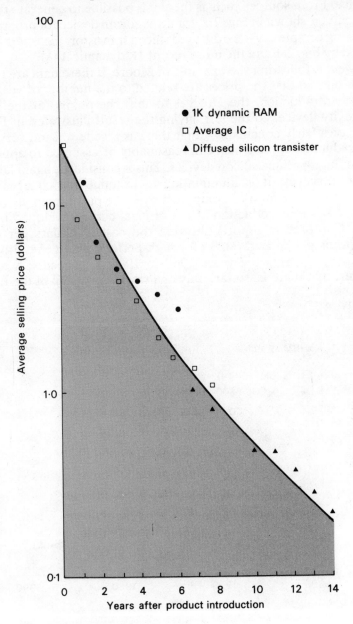

Fig. 2.3 Normalized silicon device price trends

the development of the global IC industry. Figure 2.1 represents the well-known learning curves for silicon transistors and ICs, showing the systematic relationship between price and cumulative production experience. From sources such as these it is possible to generate the price trend curves, shown in Fig. 2.2, for three silicon devices of progressively increasing complexity – the diffused silicon transistor, the 'average' IC as defined by Fig. 2.1 and the more recent 1K dynamic RAM.

However, following the example of Moore, if these data are normalized in time so that the prices are related to the number of years since product introduction, the effect is to shift the points for the higher-complexity devices to the left, giving the result illustrated in Fig. 2.3. This shows fairly conclusively that there is a general (and very steep) price-reduction curve which can reasonably be assumed to apply to all kinds of high-volume silicon devices. This is considered again later.

First, however, it is illuminating to examine the changes in the performance/cost ratio of computers over the past fifteen years or so. Figure 2.4 is a reproduction of the original curve developed by Turn (Rand Corporation report) showing the cost in dollars per million instructions per second (MIPs) for high-performance general-purpose computers, covering the years 1960 to 1990. It is necessary to note, however, that there is, so far, only one working version of the Illiac IV

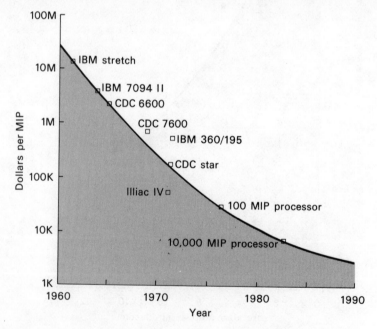

Fig. 2.4 Cost trends in high-performance, general-application computers

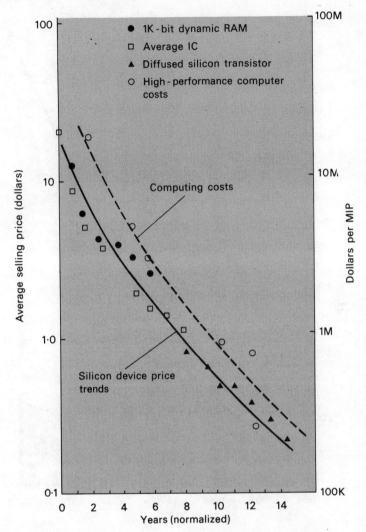

Fig. 2.5 Comparison of computing costs and silicon device costs

computer, and the 1000 MIP and 10,000 MIP processors have yet to be developed.

Figure 2.5 shows Turn's curve re-drawn to give greatest weight to actual, well-documented cost data, and this is compared with the device price curve shown earlier in Fig. 2.3. The correlation is striking and seems to prove what every IC engineer has always instinctively believed: that the computer industry's spectacular growth has been due mainly to its ability to produce equipment which could compute at ever-

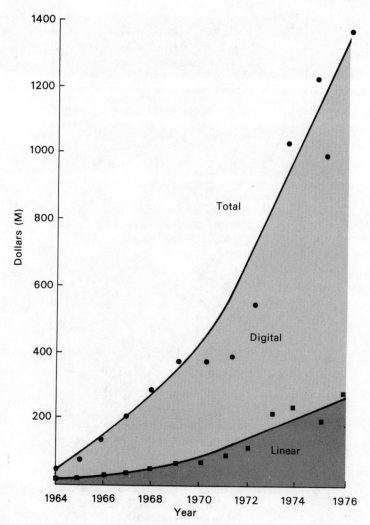

Fig. 2.6 US consumption of monolithic integrated circuits

increasing speeds and reliability levels, and ever-decreasing cost and size, and that essentially *all* of these attributes have stemmed from advances in silicon technology.

However, there is another side to the coin. Figure 2.6 shows the growth of the total US consumption of monolithic silicon ICs over the period 1964 to 1976, with digital ICs indicated separately. Since most of these digital ICs, needless to say, were necessarily used in computing equipment of all kinds (including military), the conclusion is inescapable. Just as the American computer industry's growth has been critically dependent on the availability of ever-increasing numbers of ever-improving ICs, so has the spectacular growth of the American IC industry depended to a very high degree on having a large, innovative and "local" computer market avid to make use of its rapidly-developing semiconductor capabilities.

This must be regarded as a particularly convincing example of the benefits of industrial synergism and leaves no doubt that the simultaneous American domination of the integrated circuit, computer and professional electronics sectors are all part of the same basic phenomenon, and that this is the main – not the only, but the *main* – reason for today's domination by the United States of the worldwide IC business.

And the corollary, of course, is that the absence until recently of such synergetic user industries outside America has been the principal reason for the early lack of success of the European and Japanese IC producers.

(3) *The impact of technological innovation.* It is clear that innovation has been, and will for the foreseeable future remain, a major strategic factor in the growth of the international semiconductor industry. Analysis of case histories shows, however, that the key elements in the total process of innovation are development and marketing – not basic research. In fact, there has been no correlation whatsoever in the US between the commercial success of an IC company and the quality of its basic research programme, an ability to recruit key personnel having usually been much more important. Nevertheless, disciplined in-house development of processes and products has been, and will remain, a key factor in any semiconductor company's success, but for product development work to be relevant it is essential for the company to compete actively in the world's most innovative markets – wherever they may be – for those products.

In Europe and Japan, however, the process of innovation in the field of advanced semiconductor components has been hindered by the relative absence until recently of innovative "user-pull" markets and, especially in Europe, by too much emphasis on basic research and too little on development and marketing.

A recent development of enormous significance, and an excellent example of the innovative strengths of the American IC industry, is the microprocessor. Its strategic importance stems mainly from its great commonality of application, as illustrated in Fig. 2.7, thus allowing LSI products the opportunity to break out of the vicious circle of greater complexity: fewer applications: higher cost. It is clear that the microprocessor offers as big a step forward for digital systems as did the original integrated circuit, and it is symptomatic that in this product area

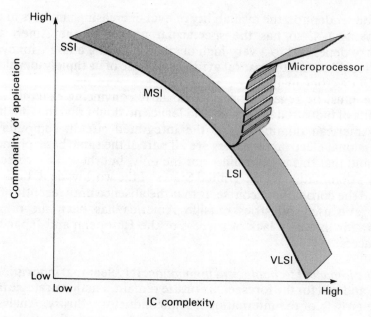

Fig. 2.7 Complexity versus commonality

Europe as yet has an almost insignificant capability, whereas Japan is already beginning to produce microprocessors, albeit on a modest scale.

(4) *Market factors.* In the light of the earlier comments on industrial synergism, it is clear that access to large, innovative markets is a key factor influencing success in the IC business. Today, both Japan and Europe have finally developed large and innovative markets in the consumer electronics sector, but not yet in other industrial sectors, and hence these non-American producers have no choice but to aim for the maximum possible degree of penetration of export markets appropriate to their product spectrum. By and large, this means attacking the US

Table 2.1 Comparison of IC usage trends

	Total IC consumption ($m)			Per capita IC consumption ($)		
	1965	**1975**	**1985**	**1965**	**1975**	**1985**
USA	c 60	c 1200	c 3500	0.3	5.7	15.9
EEC	4	c 480	c 2200	—	1.9	8.5
JAPAN	c 7	c 480	c 1900	—	4.4	16.2

market – which is already giving cause for concern to some US IC producers.

By way of comparison, Table 2.1 shows my organization's estimates of the 1965, 1975 and 1985 total markets for ICs in Europe, Japan and the United States, in both absolute and per capita terms. The much larger future rate of growth of the Japanese and European markets is worth noting. It will be understood, of course, that the high per capita usage in Japan is related to the high production of electronic goods containing ICs.

(5) *Industrial structure.* Major differences exist between the structure of non-American and American IC companies. In both Europe and Japan, the bulk of the current IC capability resides within vertically integrated and highly structured companies, whereas in the US – with the exception of organizations such as IBM and Western Electric – most of the IC capability resides in companies in which the semiconductor activity is a major part of its total industrial commitment. Some blurring of these historically sharp differences has recently occurred, however, through the various vertical integration moves which several US component and equipment companies have made. Clearly, the whole question of vertical integration is of great importance, but it is, however, a topic of enormous complexity. All that can be included here is to offer a brief summary of certain overall conclusions which are relevant to the main theme of this paper.

In general, it is my view that the vogue for vertical integration is an irrelevant diversion in the long-term development of the electronics industry. We live in an age of specialization, and it has for a long time been difficult to accept that IC companies can sell watches, for example, better than the established specialists, or that the minicomputer companies, as another example, will succeed in establishing and maintaining a cost-effective semicondutor capability over the long term. Of course, there are the notable exceptions of IBM, Texas Instruments and one or two others which seem to disprove the Mackintosh General Theory of Vertical Disintegration, i.e. the general hypothesis that vertical integration, by and large, is a snare and a delusion. However, apart from some special circumstances mainly centred on the microprocessor, I believe that of all the vertical integration activities – upwards and downwards – now going on in many parts of the world, only a few will turn out to be successful in the long term.

(6) *Management and people.* Anyone who has worked extensively in the electronics industry both inside and outside the United States will recognize that there often exists in other countries a real sense of

inferiority about American management skills. It is not just the general aura of infallibility surrounding a Harvard MBA, for example, but the sheer bewilderment with which the typical non-American electronics executive compares his apparent performance with that of his American counterpart. This, however, is a misconception and to support this view Table 2.2 shows a listing of the top ten American companies: (a) in the electron tube and transistor businesses in 1955; (b) in the semiconductor business in 1960 and 1965; (c) in the IC business in 1975.

Table 2.2 The leading US manufacturers

	1955 Tubes	1955 Transistors	1960 Semi-conductors	1965 Semi-conductors	1975 Integrated Circuits
1	RCA	Hughes	TI	TI	TI
2	Sylvania	Transitron	Transitron	Motorola	Fairchild
3	GE	Philco	Philco	Fairchild	NSC
4	Raytheon	Sylvania	GE	GI	Intel
5	Westinghouse	TI	RCA	GE	Motorola
6	Amperex	GE	Motorola	RCA	Rockwell
7	National Video	RCA	Clevite	Sprague	GI
8	Ranland	Westinghouse	Fairchild	Philco/Ford	RCA
9	Eimac	Motorola	Hughes	Transitron	Signetics (Philips)
10	Lansdale Tube	Clevite	Sylvania	Raytheon	AMI

This table, by and large, reflects the abilities of US managements to bridge the gap between radically different technologies (i.e. vacuum tubes to germanium; germanium to silicon) and, in fact, only *one* of the leading ten US tube manufacturers in 1955 has survived as a significant IC producer today (RCA). The inescapable conclusion is that (popular opinion sometimes to the contrary) American companies in general do not have a good track record in the management of electronics technology. A few, however, have obviously exhibited very impressive skills, and it is these *successful* managements, of course, on which the US domination (and reputation) is based.

What it all adds up to is that America's overwhelming success in the IC business has been, not surprisingly, something of a statistical phenomenon. With so many companies starting up, in such favourable conditions, some at least were likely to succeed in a big way. And they certainly did.

There are some other advantages which American managements have enjoyed. The distinguishing organizational feature of the *successful* US semiconductor companies is that they are geared to react swiftly to new developments. They are also, in many cases, led by an impressive new breed of technical entrepreneurs who are skilled at this particular trade. By comparison, European and Japanese semiconductor companies have often been too ponderous in their decision-making and have sometimes been managed by individuals whose understanding of the complexities of the semiconductor industry was sometimes less than perfect.

In the last analysis, the IC industry – like every other – depends on the right people being motivated in the right way to do the right job. In this sense, America has so far had most of the advantage, since the evidence is very strong that entrepreneurial drive and freedom are essential conditions for success in the IC industry, and these are qualities that seem to thrive preferentially in America's relatively laissez-faire economy.

The United States has also had a major advantage in the fortuitous combination of a high rate of personnel mobility with the existence of several large and highly capable research laboratories which have acted as national generators of technology and technologists. Thus, in America the diffusion of technology has occurred mainly through the diffusion of people, and the commercial exploitation of new techniques has rarely been inhibited for long because the possessor of knowhow and the would-be exploiter could not make common cause. By comparison, both Europe and Japan exhibit a considerably lower degree of personnel mobility, with the result that companies must rely on – and pay for – a proportionately much larger in-house programme of research and development.

Another, indirect consequence of America's high personnel mobility – particularly of technical and managerial personnel – has been the emergence of what can be called "skill clusters". So far as electronics is concerned, this can be applied to centres such as Boston's Route 128 and, of particular reference today, to areas of semiconductor expertise such as "Silicon Valley" in California. It is abundantly clear that the existence of Silicon Valley confers important advantages on the IC companies which operate within it, particularly in regard to the high (but informal) level of localized communication and debate, and to the availability of the strong common-services industry which has developed in that area.

(7) *The present state of the industry.* Summarizing the present state of the worldwide IC industry, including one or two strategic points in addition

to those discussed above, it can be concluded that the American domination has so far been founded on the following ten inherent advantages.

(1) Critically important synergism with major user industries.
(2) Large and innovative domestic markets.
(3) Substantial government support over many years.
(4) Business climate suitable for entrepreneurs.
(5) Availability of substantial amounts of venture capital.
(6) Enough good management in enough good companies.
(7) Existence of large, capable research laboratories.
(8) High mobility of technical and managerial personnel.
(9) Skill clusters (e.g. Silicon Valley).
(10) Good fortune – including cheap energy and enormous international economic strength.

The future importance of these factors will obviously have an important bearing on any changes which may occur in the competitiveness of the American IC industry.

Future prospects

It is not the aim here to provide a detailed forecast of IC technology per se, but it is clear, nevertheless, that future technological developments will profoundly influence any strategic forecast of the IC industry. To this end, the evidence is now strong that a new high-resolution lithographic technology will emerge within the next few years, probably based on electron beam techniques, which will be very expensive to establish. This VLSI technology will find application first in circuits requiring vast numbers of components (principally, of course, memory, microcomputers and imaging), but will later be used also for numerically more mundane applications since by then the production economics will strongly favour VLSI against more classical technologies.

One major change which will therefore occur within a few years is a substantial increase in the investment required to compete at the "leading edge". Thus the industry will begin to move into an era in which the sheer size of the initial financial commitment will provide a stabilizing feedback effect. There will therefore be reduced opportunities for spinoffs to leapfrog into prominence by means of some astute technical, marketing or economic stratagem.

With this general scenario, then, the probable future changes in the ten key strategic factors already identified can be considered (Fig. 2.8). Taking the first two together (Industrial Synergism and Market Availability), much of the future growth in the world's markets for electronic functions is likely to be in domestic and personal product sectors, not

	US	Japan	Europe
1 Industrial synergism	A	B	B
2 Market availability	A	B	B
3 Government support	A	B	C
4 Business climate	B	C	C
5 Venture capital	C	C	C
6 Management qualities	A	A	A
7 Research capability	A	A	B
8 Personnel mobility	A	C	D
9 Skill clusters	A	A	D
10 Economic conditions	A	A	D

A – Very good   B – Good   C – Fair   D – Poor

Fig. 2.8 Future prospects in LSI/VLSI

industrial. Despite the maker-push effect which the American IC industry has so far exerted in products such as calculators, electronic watches and video games, the fact is that it is in just these areas of consumer, automotive and personal electronics that Europe and Japan are strong. Their budding IC industries therefore have the prospect of the kind of critically important synergistic relationship with major user industries which the American IC industry has so far enjoyed with its data-processing customers.

In addition, there is certain to be substantial growth, in both Europe and Japan, in "protected" applications such as telecommunications and the "national" computer industries. Overall, therefore, there will be selective growth of the IC markets in Japan and Europe and much of this growth will be in user companies which, by corporate inclination or national preference, will tend to select "local" suppliers, all other things being equal. For these first two items, therefore, in the future Japan and Europe will enjoy much greater parity with the US than in the past.

So far as government support is concerned, it seems that until quite recently the importance of this factor had not been understood properly by the governments of many advanced nations, although things are now changing rapidly. In Europe, for example, the British, French, German and Italian governments are all beginning to talk about – and in some cases activate – plans to provide support typically in the range

$50–$100m spread over four to five years. And in Japan, there is, of course, the famous VLSI programme, about which it is very difficult to obtain hard facts. Our own estimate in Mackintosh International is that the purely government funding for this VLSI project is running at an annual rate of about $65m (in 1978 dollars) and there is little doubt that it will continue at about this level well into the 1980s. In any event, several non-American governments are now beginning to support their indigenous IC industries with meaningful sums of money and, therefore, the long-standing American advantage in this respect will diminish, although substantial support of the US industry can be expected to continue.

Taking the fourth and fifth factors together (i.e. Business Climate and Venture Capital), so far as the business climate is concerned, despite the probable stabilizing influence of the advent of VLSI technology, the entrepreneurial touch will remain an important ingredient of success in the IC industry in which long-term success will only go to him who can afford, has control of, and knows how to fully exploit the most complex industrial technology man has yet devised. The multi-sector conglomerate, therefore, with too many of its eggs *not* in the semiconductor basket, will tend to lack the total commitment to success of the entrepreneurially-led specialist IC companies.

Thus America will continue to have the edge over both Japan and Europe, where the large corporations are unlikely to allow their semiconductor managers the same freedom of decision which their American counterparts will enjoy. Nevertheless, the opportunities for *new* American entrepreneurs will diminish as the size of the risks exceeds acceptable limits for conventional American venture capitalists. (Indeed, the diminution of classical US venture capital has already been observable for some time, with a sharp reduction in the number of new semiconductor start-up companies.)

In both Japan and Europe, the financial community has historically been markedly unadventurous about providing venture capital, and this situation is unlikely to change in the foreseeable future. On the other hand, the fact that the IC capability in these countries is mainly controlled by large companies could turn out to be an advantage from this point of view, since most of these will be capable of funding VLSI technology – especially with the aforementioned government support. The resource question, therefore, seems likely to become fairly evenly balanced in the future between the US, Europe and Japan.

The question of the Quality of Management can be dealt with very briefly. In my assessment there is no significant difference between the inherent capabilities of executives in these different countries. Moreover, evidence has been offered already which strongly suggests that Americans do not have a monopoly of competence when it comes to the management of technology. The conclusion can be drawn that the managements in all of the relevant countries are, within experimental accuracy, about equally skilful (or incompetent) at creating commercial success from this esoteric semiconductor technology.

The next three factors – Research Capability, Personnel Mobility and Skill Clusters – can also conveniently be discussed together, since they are interrelated. Taking the US first, it is unlikely that any significant diminution in its strength will occur in any of these areas. While there may well be some reduction in the amount of basic research carried out, this will be more than offset by increases in applied research in areas such as VLSI techniques, product testing and software problems. Personnel mobility will certainly remain high, and it is very unlikely that any of the important American skill clusters – whether they are called Silicon Valley, TI, IBM, Bell Labs or whatever – will disappear.

By and large, therefore, America can be expected to continue to enjoy great strength in all three of these areas.

Turning to Japan, a systematic build-up of the national research capability has been under way for many years and this process will undoubtedly continue. For reasons which are well-known, personnel mobility is low in Japan, due primarily to the high level of loyalty which tends to exist between company and employee. However, there will be some increase in mobility as joint ventures, company mergers and government policies slowly blur individual corporate identities, and increasingly permeate the Japanese way of life. On the question of skill clusters, Japan also enjoys a strong position since the Japanese electronics industry is already mainly confined to the two metropolitan areas of Tokyo and Osaka. This clustering will be reinforced by an increasing number of cooperative industrial R & D activities, such as can already be seen in the VLSI program. Overall, therefore, Japan is either already strong, or will soon become so, in each of these three strategic areas.

In Europe, however, things look distinctly worse. In the first place, although it is a fact so patently obvious as to seem hardly worth mentioning, it is nevertheless sometimes forgotten that whereas the US and Japan are single nations, each with a single language, national sense of commitment, set of laws, customs and cultural attitudes, etc, Europe represents a set of highly individualistic nations, each with its own language, national objectives and way of doing things. The net result – hardly surprisingly – is that there is not yet such a thing as a truly "Common Market". Thus even neighbouring markets (e.g. France in relation to West Germany) can often represent as great a problem as a far-distant market such as the United States. Echoing this general situation, the European semiconductor industry basically consists (with the exception of Philips) of a number of predominantly national producers, each organized principally to serve the needs of its own national markets.

One of the consequent liabilities is that Europe has nothing remotely to compare with America's Silicon Valley, nor is it likely that any meaningful geographical skill clusters will ever develop in the European IC industry. For the same general reasons, personnel mobility in Europe is also low, inhibited both by employment traditions and national boundaries, and is unlikely to increase significantly. The European research capability in solid-state electronics has always been high, although often commercially ineffective through an inability to bridge the gap between science and sales. However, this research capability will improve due to increasing government support, and increasing cooperation both between European laboratories and outside Europe. Overall, therefore, in these three categories Europe comes behind Japan which, in turn, will be deficient in relation to America only in respect of personnel mobility.

The final category – Economic Conditions – really warrants a complete paper in its own right if its relative importance is to be accurately assessed. Some aspects have already been covered earlier in this report, but with regard to the relationship of the USA with other world nations the key points can very briefly be summarized as follows. In the years since the end of World War Two, America has dominated the economic state of health of the OECD nations. This strength has primarily been founded on cheap energy, abundant natural resources and a large enough population for the producers of manufactured goods to enjoy the benefits of considerable economies of scale. Meanwhile, however, other nations – in particular Germany and Japan – have been recovering from the ravages of war and one of the pillars of American economic strength has eroded as the dramatic increase of oil prices has coincided with the gradual depletion of America's oil resources. For the future, therefore, there is likely to be much more balance of economic strength between the US, Europe and Japan, which is the situation reflected in Fig. 2.8.

Conclusions
As a summary of the foregoing discussion Fig. 2.9 shows the changes which will probably take place in the principal strategic factors on which America's ascendancy in the integrated circuits industry has so far been based, and on which the future domination of VLSI technology may depend.

In brief, even allowing for the many remaining strengths of the

	The past			The future		
	US	Japan	Europe	US	Japan	Europe
1 Industrial synergism	A	D	D	A	B	B
2 Market availability	A	D	D	A	B	B
3 Government support	A	D	D	A	B	C
4 Business climate	A	D	D	B	C	C
5 Venture capital	A	D	D	C	C	C
6 Management qualities	A	A	A	A	A	A
7 Research capability	A	C	C	A	A	A
8 Personnel mobility	A	D	D	A	C	D
9 Skill clusters	A	C	D	A	A	D
10 Economic conditions	A	C	C	B	B	B

A – Very good   B – Good   C – Fair   D – Poor

Fig. 2.9 Summary – the shifting balance of advantage

American IC industry – such as its immensely strong technological base, its position on the learning curve, management-in-depth, etc – and the fact that the European and Japanese managements will still suffer from important liabilities such as the relative absence of entrepreneurial freedom, there can be no doubt that the balance of advantage is now beginning to swing away from the United States. For this reason, in the VLSI era American producers will face problems of daunting magnitude in maintaining their global market share and innovatory lead against escalating transatlantic and transpacific competition, and the most probable prognosis is that the US domination of this critically important industrial sector will eventually disappear, to be replaced first by a condition of approximate parity between America and Japan, who will possibly be joined somewhat later by Europe.

It hardly needs to be said that the effects of these changes – on both component and equipment companies – will be immense and will need to be understood in detail if the changing competitive circumstances are to be digested without acute corporate discomfort.

Postscript

Since 14 February 1978, the day on which this paper was originally delivered to the International Solid-State Circuits Conference in San

Francisco, there has been considerable new activity in the IC sector in Europe, particularly by the UK government. In brief, over a period of approximately three months, announcements have been made about an investment of £25-50m by a UK government agency (National Enterprise Board) in a new transatlantic LSI company, Inmos Ltd; a £70m Microelectronics Industry Support Program, designed to enhance the capabilities of both British national IC producers and also the UK-based activities of certain multinationals; and a £15m Microelectronics Applications Program designed to encourage and accelerate the use of leading-edge ICs such as microprocessors. Another relevant development in the UK has been the announcement of a joint venture between GEC and Fairchild which, if successful, could lead to a major growth of Britain's production capability in MOS LSI.

In addition, at the time of going to press there are strong indications that similar developments are about to take place in France. In particular, it is highly probable that there will be a major increase in the financial support by the French government for its indigenous IC industry.

Thus, although many of Europe's relative disadvantages, as described in the paper, will remain, these recent events strongly suggest that the third criterion for success (Government Support) will be much more nearly met than seemed possible early in 1978. For these reasons, if I were now to redraft Fig. 2.9, I would assess future government support in Europe as being "very good" (A) rather than "fair" (C), as presently shown.

Guide to Further Reading

Professor Braun's section is based largely on his book, written jointly with Stuart MacDonald, *Revolution in Miniature: The History and Impact of Semiconductor Electronics* (Cambridge University Press, 1978).

George A. Champine, "Microprocessors Present and Future", is a memorable paper consisting entirely of graphs, charts and diagrams, which was presented to a conference in Nice, France, in September 1978. The conference was arranged by Sperry Univac, of which Dr Champine is the Director of Advanced Systems. The paper charts the trends in microelectronics outlined above.

"Microprocessing Means 'Macro' Profits" was the unambiguous title given to an article by John C. von Koschembahr in the American publication *Financial World* of 15 February 1978. The author reviews the growth of two market leaders, Intel and Motorola.

"New Leaders in Semiconductors" in *Business Week*, 1 March 1976, is a very readable extended profile of Charles Sporck of National Semiconductor and Robert Noyce of Intel, with general observations about the industry.

The San Jose *Mercury News*, especially the *Sunday Mercury News*, is a good source of stories about goings on in Silicon Valley. Revealing interviews with Noyce, Moore and Grove of Intel form the basis of "Vision at the Top Makes Intel a Giant" in the *Sunday Mercury News* of 22 January 1978, while the same paper on 28 January 1979 had a special supplement on working in the Valley.

More strait-laced accounts of developments in electronics include:

K. J. Dean and G. White, "The semiconductor story", in *Wireless World*, vol. 79 (1973), p. 1447.

Charles Weiner, "How the transistor emerged", *IEEE Spectrum* (January 1973).

M. F. Wolff, "The genesis of the integrated circuit", *IEEE Spectrum* (January 1976).

An important socio-economic study is:

Ed Sciberras, *Multinational Electronics Companies and National Economic Policies* (Jai Press, Connecticut, 1977).

103

There is an interesting profile of market leader, Texas Instruments, in *Business Week*, 18 September 1978. That firm has managed to escape the fate of others featured in "Mostek and the Vanishing Pioneers: Takeovers Shrink the List of Semiconductor Companies", also in *Business Week*, 15 October 1979.

The Japanese challenge is dealt with in:

Gene Bylinsky, "The Japanese Spies in Silicon Valley", *Fortune*, 27 February 1978.

Bro Uttal, "Japan's Big Push in Computers", Parts 1 & 2 in *Fortune*, 25 September 1978 and 9 October 1978.

Gene Gregory, "The March of the Japanese Micro", *New Scientist*, 11 October 1979.

The French government's moves are detailed in "French Chase Micros For Freedom". *New Scientist*, 15 November 1979, while the Pentagon's recent decision to fund development of VHSIC (Very High Speed Integrated Circuits) with major semiconductor manufacturers, reported in the *Financial Times*, 26 September 1979, is also discussed at greater length in Louise Kehoe, "Super Chip Joins the Army", *New Scientist*, 7 February 1980.

3 Applications of the New Technology

The "Smart" Machine Revolution

A. A. Perlowski

Most people will have come across microelectronics through their daily use of calculators, digital watches and other microprocessor-based consumer products. This survey, which appeared in Business Week *on 5 July 1976, correctly predicted that microprocessors would be incorporated into more and more products and machines. By providing them with brainpower at low cost, machines could be made "smart". This is a solid piece of research based on interviews with key figures in firms busy finding new uses for chips.*

"This is the second industrial revolution", says J. Sidney Webb, executive vice-president of TRW Inc. "It multiplies man's brainpower with the same force that the first industrial revolution multiplied man's muscle power."

The engine of the revolution is the microprocessor, or computer-on-a-chip, a tiny slice of silicon that is the arithmetic and logic heart of a computer. The first surge of products with microprocessor brains is just now starting to reach the marketplace, and this is demonstrating that never before has there been a more powerful tool for building "smart" machines – machines that can add decision-making, arithmetic, and memory to their usual functions. Included in the first wave of smart machines are:

The "Smart" Watch: One digital model now in final development permits the wearer to enter a date – such as his wedding anniversary – in his watch computer, and months later the watch will flash a reminder on its screen in time for him to rush out and buy an anniversary present.

The "Smart" Scale: Its microcomputer brain, programmed with postage rates, zip codes, and the location of the scale itself, weighs a package and

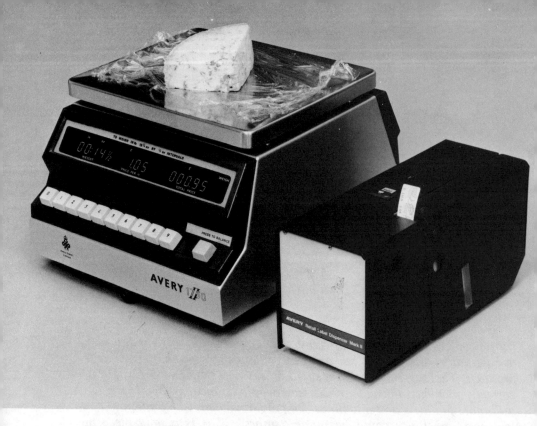

The "smart" machine revolution at perhaps its most familiar: one of the new generation of shop scales from the British firm, W. & T. Avery, which gives an instantaneous readout of weight and price. *Photo courtesy of W. & T. Avery Limited*

computes the postage when the operator keys in the zip code of the destination.

The "Smart" Mobile Phone: It stores as many as ten different phone numbers and automatically dials any one of them when the caller pushes the send button. If the line is busy or if the radio channels are loaded, it automatically re-dials at a touch of the button.

The "Smart" Can-making System: Microcomputers direct the metal-cutting and welding machines and feed data on the number of good and bad cans produced to a computer that generates production reports for management.

The "Smart" Video Game: The microcomputer, connected to a TV set, has a memory that can be programmed to play as many as 200 different games. Instructions for each game are contained in a separate cassette. The microcomputer pulls the game information out of the cassette and sends it to a video processor chip, which puts the game on the TV screen.

A tidal wave of smart products such as these is on the way. They will dramatically change the marketplace for consumer, commercial, and industrial products. The computer-on-a-chip, powering the brains of smart products, will spawn new industries and thousands of new companies. And in the process it will wipe out some existing companies and even some industries.

As recently as two years ago it would have been difficult to back up such sweeping forecasts. Only a handful of microprocessors were in production, and few smart machines had got beyond the design stage. Computer specialists and other major users of electronic logic were about the only ones who understood what was happening.

Now the growth rate in microprocessor production and applications is breathtaking. "We have several typical customers who used only a handful of microprocessors in 1975, but they'll buy 100 systems this year and 5000 next year," says Ernest P. Barbaro, a sales manager for Motorola Inc, a major producer. "The industry pretty much agrees," says Barbaro, "that microprocessor sales next year will jump tenfold and will hit one million systems." And this excludes the many smaller MPUs (microprocessors) going into calculators.

The key to the sudden surge in the sales of microprocessors and to the wave of new smart machines they will power is simply price. C. Lester Hogan, vice-chairman of Fairchild Camera & Instrument Corp., demonstrated this element dramatically at a Boston convention a few weeks ago. He pulled eighteen microprocessors from his pocket and tossed them out to his audience. "That's $18 million worth of computer power – or it was twenty years ago," he said. Hogan explained that his $20 microprocessor is as powerful as International Business Machines' first commercial computer, which cost $1 million in the early 1950s. "The point I'm making," Hogan said, "is that computer power today is essentially free."

Even a year ago, those $20 microprocessors cost more than $100 and the sudden slash in price led designers to start work on the beginnings of the flood of smart products. Switching from conventional electronic parts, such as integrated circuits (ICs), to the MPU cuts design time and manufacturing costs because it replaces hundreds of ICs and other parts. Once the MPU is designed into a product, it can provide tremendous marketing advantages; a product's functions can be altered not by a costly redesign of its electronics but simply by changing the instructions, or software, stored in the MPU's memory. New features can be added with little increase in cost, and the new smart machines can handle work that could not be done economically before. Today's smart products already are demonstrating the strategies that manufacturers are following. Some companies are adding intelligence to existing "dumb" products to obtain growth in a mature market or to penetrate it for the first time.

National Controls Inc.'s smart postal scale – costing $5000 and up –

has won 300 sales in a mature market. The payout for the purchase comes from eliminating the excessive postage that the company says is put on 8% of all outgoing commercial mail. Union Bank in Los Angeles saves about $8000 annually with one of the smart scales and believes it saves more in labour because bank employees do not now have to learn or use the complex postal rates.

Bru-Der Instrument Corp. is "undercutting the mechanical taxi meter makers at their own game" with its lower-priced, $305 smart taxi meter, says James Bruce-Sanders, the company's 33-year-old president. He shipped more than 700 of the meters, which have many features that could not have been offered without the MPU. The meter will keep track of and display the fare of each of five passengers boarding at different locations.

One of the riskier marketing strategies is to use the microprocessor to create totally new products, and this is where the most significant innovations will occur and the payoffs will be higher. "The MPU will create a host of new products that even our most imaginative people cannot conceive of today," predicts James Hillier, executive vice-president of RCA Corp. Threshold Technology Inc. installed a microcomputer-based microphone on the floor of the Chicago Mercantile Exchange. The instrument converts a spoken quote into digital information. Now, when a price reporter in the trading pit hears the quote, he writes it down and hands the slip to a runner. The exchange hopes to cut the fifteen seconds it now takes to display price quotes to around five seconds. The microcomputer compares what it "hears" with its thirty-two-word vocabulary, translates it, and transmits it to a computer, which displays the price and sends it out over the ticker. The unit has just gone back to the shop, however, for modifications. It seems that as trading got frantic in the pit, the strain caused the reporter's voice to change, and the computer could not understand a word he was saying.

Trans World Airlines will begin commercial flight-testing this year a "performance advisory system" that promises to be the pilot's best friend. The "black box" will take flight information such as altitude, weight, outside air temperature, and engine pressure ratios and tell the pilot what his altitude should be. By more accurately selecting the proper altitude for the aircraft's weight, the smart system should save from 2% to 5% of the total fuel burned. The only way that a pilot can establish his most efficient altitude now is to use a suitcase full of charts and his cockpit gauges.

Over the past few years, conventional electronic circuits were built into a wide spectrum of products. But while this hardwired logic, or minicomputer in some cases, did a good job, it simply cost too much. Now a growing number of smart products, built around the micro-

Now on trial in Britain, a new electronic payphone, incorporates a microprocessor. It features push-button dialling, digital display of charges and a fault-finding capability. *Photo courtesy of the Post Office (London)*

processor, are doing the job for a lot less money and are making some of these markets "real" for the first time.

Way back in 1973, optical character recognition (OCR) had a limited market because it was a "half-million-dollar solution". So Jay Rodney Reese, president of Recognition Equipment Inc., and others set out to do something about it. The result is an OCR data entry device with a price tag as low as $1500 – thanks to the microprocessor. The handheld wand, which an operator moves manually across a line of type, can read the data more than five times as fast as the fastest operator can keyboard it. Recognition Equipment has shipped 2000 wands to retailers such as Penney's and Sears, which use them to read sales tags automatically. The company expects to sell 10,000 more wands this year. A Spokane company, Key Tronic Corp., is selling another handheld OCR wand for such scanner applications as time cards, invoices, laundry tags, airline tickets, and bank documents. "OCR is driven by the buck, and without the MPU the wand would have been too expensive to be used," says Frank E. Seestrom, Recognition's OCR wand engineering manager.

Controlling traffic signals by computer was another market going nowhere until the MPU came along. Using the minicomputer was overkill because it "spent 93% of its time waiting," said John S. Strance, head of Eagle Signal Corp.'s transportation division, the market leader, with 1000 MPU-backed traffic controllers installed. The minicomputer also needed an expensive insulated cabinet and an air conditioner for its street-corner location. The MPU model sells for $5000 and up, less than half the cost of a minicomputer installation. And because of its flexibility there will be new jobs in monitoring the number of passing cars, their speed, and the number of occupants and in collecting tolls.

Consumer products

The most exciting new products to come from the computer-on-a-chip will be for the consumer. Microprocessors will go into homes, autos, appliances and other consumer goods in far greater numbers than into other products. "Between seven and ten microprocessors will be in each home by 1980," predicts Andrew A. Perlowski who heads microprocessor activities at Honeywell Inc. His company is already hard at work on energy management and security systems for the home.

So far only a handful of smart consumer products are on sale, but many more are on their way. Amana Refrigeration Incs.'s pioneering microwave oven is running away with the market, but competitors will soon be introducing their own smart ovens. This month Fairchild Camera is introducing its "home entertainment centre," the first of the smart video games. Later this summer Oldsmobile will introduce the

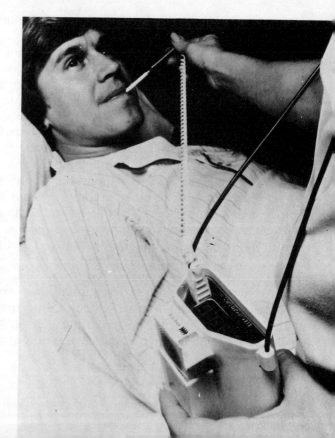

This microprocessor-based thermometer made by Electromedics Inc. in the US claims to give a quicker, more accurate temperature "readout". According to the manufacturers it "eliminates patient impatience". *Photo courtesy of Texas Instruments*

Less fanciful than the thermometer and in common use in Britain and elsewhere is this Timtronic microprocessor-based bus fare calculating and ticket-issuing machine. *Photo courtesy of EMI Industrial Electronics Limited*

1977 Toronado, the first car to employ a microprocessor – a Rockwell MPU will control the engine spark advance. Fairchild's smart video game will sell for about $120, a higher price than that of the games now on the market. But current models are made of conventional circuitry, which limits each model to a small number of games. Fairchild's first game cartridge, priced at about $20, will contain Tic-Tac-Toe, a shooting gallery game, and a program that allows a person to doodle on the TV screen. The company plans to introduce one multigame cartridge a month and to have 34 games on sale by Christmas. In addition to the 200 games or more that can be played with its entertainment centre, Fairchild is also looking at the possibility of putting out scientific calculator and education modules for it. But even that is just the beginning.

"What will grow out of the game is more exciting than the game itself," says Fairchild's Hogan. He believes that the game will be the entry into the home for the long-predicted home computer centre. "Every home has a display – the TV set – and a 10-digit keyboard – the pushbutton phone," he says, and coupling these two instruments with a microcomputer provides a rudimentary home computer. Fairchild is just one of many companies that are working toward the home computer centre. There are the computer makers, of course. The Sperry Univac Div. of Sperry Rand Corp. predicts that the home computer may be a standard feature in many homes by 1985. But Univac sees it more as a general-purpose MPU system, also controlling such things as heat and air conditioning. The home computer would "store printed news items from press services and show the ones you wish to see on a computerized television set," says Earl Joseph, Univac staff scientist. "You could even program the processor to call your attention to all stories on a certain topic." Television makers are interested in the home computer, too, RCA Laboratories has already developed several prototypes it believes could sell for only a few hundred dollars late in this decade. One such system includes an RCA microprocessor, a memory circuit, an interface device to drive the display – the TV set, a calculator-like keyboard for data input, and an audio tape cassette player for loading programs.

The biggest single customer for MPUs will be the auto industry, but even though the first smart cars will roll off the line this year, it will be the 1980s before use is widespread. The MPU's job will be solely in engine controls and not in running glamorous new features such as dashboard displays. This is because it is government legislation that is pushing Detroit into the electronics age. "The probability is very low that you would see widespread introduction of MPU engine controls if we remained at present emission levels," says Robert S. Oswald, manager of electronic engine controls at Ford Motor Co. Chrysler Corp. seems the most committed. "If I had my hardware today, I'd use microprocessors," says Earl W. Meyer, assistant chief engineer for the number three auto maker. "We believe MPUs give us benefits immediately, and there can only be greater benefits with time. It wouldn't surprise me to see MPUs on Chrysler cars in 1979 or 1980."

Until recently, the slow-moving appliance industry was an even more ethereal customer for the microprocessor than the auto makers. But the picture has suddenly changed. Just one year ago Amana introduced the first MPU-controlled appliance and the industry will never be the same. "The microwave oven was the ticket for the MPU to get in – many more people now see the potential for the MPU than did a year ago," says Dan R. McConnell, vice-president for planning at Amana. "People who do things conventionally from now on are going to drop out. Nothing in the appliance industry has ever taken off like the Touchmatic," says Richard D. Maxwell, Amana senior vice-president. "We're still back-ordered in every market in the country." Microwave ovens had timers before, of course, but they were limited in function and tended to be inaccurate over long time settings. They normally operate for only up to fifteen minutes – not nearly time to cook a roast, for example. The MPU

Typical of the vast number of multi-function digital watches now on the market is this one from National Semiconductor, offering many features such as a calendar and snooze alarm. *Photo courtesy of National Semiconductor Corporation*

Apart from microwave ovens, many other items of kitchen equipment, like this Hamilton-Beach blender, are susceptible to microprocessor control. *Photo courtesy of Texas Instruments*

replaced the buttons and knobs with an electronic touch keyboard and digital display that provided the precise timing accuracy to cook anything. For the first time an oven can be programmed to perform in a series – for example, defrosting, pausing to equalize the temperature, then cooking.

Amana has picked up market share with the new oven and expects to account for one-third of the $650 million microwave oven business this year. The Touchmatic is now the number one selling model at the high-priced end of the market – something that even Amana did not anticipate. Its microwave oven sales were up 62% in 1975 and are expected to double this year. Amana will soon have company. "Every significant competitor is moving full speed ahead to come out with a product," says McConnell. Some of them are now field-testing smart microwave ovens, and at least two – Tappan and Litton – are expected to introduce MPU controlled models this year. Turned on by Amana's success, design activity in white goods appliances has picked up speed this year. Most of the efforts are concentrated on developing microprocessor controllers for microwave ovens, washing machines, and conventional range-oven combinations. But at least one dishwasher is also being tested now with an MPU controller. "The white goods people would like to be more like the auto industry, with more new models and features," says Harvey G. Cragon, MPU strategy manager at Texas Instruments Inc. "Nothing new has happened in washing machines or refrigerators for years." On a dryer, for example, the MPU could look up data, do some calculations using humidity and temperature as inputs, and decide the right time and speed of the drying cycle.

It probably will be at least two more years before MPU controllers start showing up in major appliances beyond the microwave oven. "It will take three to five years for such products as dishwashers, dryers, and washing machines," says William H. Slavik, director of advanced R&D at Rockwell International Corp.'s Admiral Group. Making this happen will be lower MPU prices – $1.50 or less for a one-chip appliance MPU. "Two years off, there will be enormous amounts of power available, so it becomes a matter of applying it," says Amana's McConnell. But applying microprocessor power will not be easy for an industry that has little electronics capability. For Amana, a Raytheon Co. subsidiary, it took four years to move from concept to production on the Touchmatic. "It took longer than usual because we were ploughing new ground," says McConnell. Says a senior executive at one major appliance maker: "The appliance industry is still a metal-bending business, so it generally has been unaware of what is going on, or what is going to happen because of the microprocessor." The appliance industry also thinks of the microprocessor as primarily a replacement for mechanical controls.

Another American firm, Recognition Products, has on the market a microprocessor-controlled wand optical character recognition (OCR) reading and recording system, which is used for keeping track of stock in large stores.
Photo courtesy of Texas Instruments

This is not taking advantage of what the MPU really has to offer. Even Arthur D. Little Inc. got caught in this trap when it concluded a year-and-a-half ago that consumer appliances were not a good MPU application "because they weren't complex enough."

Time may be running out on at least one group of these traditional producers, the clock makers. "With the emergence of the low-cost MPU and the digital display, the clock could easily be the calculator all over again," one appliance maker says, referring to the way mechanical calculators lost out in the consumer calculator business. "Making a clock alone is a terrible application for an MPU," says Admiral's Slavik. "Once you've got the MPU built in, you've got power to add features that won't quit. The people who add the right features will be the winners." For example, in a clock-radio, the MPU can turn on a coffee pot five minutes before turning on the alarm or the radio. When the radio comes on in the morning, the MPU could increase the volume after five minutes.

In the factory

In the factory, the computer-on-a-chip is dropping the cost of electronic intelligence so low that it is turning the smallest production units into smart machines. And it is speeding the day of the automated factory by linking the smart production machines, sensors, and other instruments into distributed data acquisition and control systems.

Factory automation has moved slowly, partly because manufacturers did not want an entire plant shut down because one big computer failed. "The advantage of the MPU is that it chops up the control job in smaller pieces, and an individual MPU won't pull down a whole network if it fails," says Sheldon G. Lloyd, engineering vice-president at Fisher Controls Co. "The microprocessor makes it economically possible to develop and build hierarchical systems."

In a hierarchy, the microprocessors in the smart production machines are linked to supervisory minicomputers that collect and send management reports and status information to a central factory computer. At the top is the big corporate computer, which when linked to the factory system, will be able to generate up-to-the-second financial reports for the entire company. No one has quite reached that point yet, but computer hierarchies are in various stages of development at a growing number of factories. RCA, for example, is putting in a discrete manufacturing system at its Somerville (NJ) Solid State Div. plant. MPUs will be

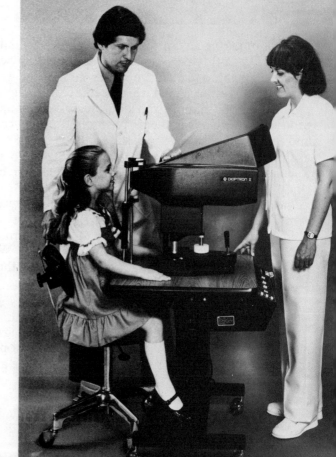

An example of the many medical applications of the microprocessor is the Dioptron, a microprocessor-based eye-testing machine. *Photo courtesy of Coherent Medical Division*

spotted throughout semiconductor wafer fabrication, device assembly, and testing, with the data link moving through supervisory minicomputers up to a central IBM 370 system. "What we are doing here has real impact on the rest of the company since it can be adapted for similar jobs at other RCA plants," says Robert O. Winder, RCA's director of MPU products.

Comparing microcomputer controller prices with earlier systems shows the dramatic decline still going on in industrial control costs. In 1958 the first process control computers cost as much as $300,000 installed. By the late 1960s, minicomputers had brought the price to less than $100,000. And now the MPU controllers start at $3000.

One job where MPUs are pushing out both hardwired logic and minicomputers is in numerical control. It is doing it for both cost and reliability reasons. At Ex-Cell-O Corp.'s Work Center Div., 90% of the NC systems being turned out use microcomputer controllers now. An earlier hard-wired system required eighty-five circuit boards to run a boring, tapping, drilling, and milling machine. "Our new microprocessor runs the same machine with ten boards," says Douglas J. Foreman, chief control engineer. "And," he adds, "it does the job better and faster."

The overwhelming advantages in replacing relays with a microprocessor controller are demonstrated by a smart paint-mixing machine now being built. The MPU controls 36 pumps and also helps the central computer by keeping track of gallons mixed and the total cost of the operation. "In the past, if you lost one pump in a relay-controlled system, you lost the whole batch," says William W. Huppert, general manager of Eagle Signal's Industrial Control Div. Now the MPU keeps track of the pump strokes so that in case of failure, the job can be finished manually instead of throwing the batch away. The Eagle Signal MPU controller costs only $5500. "There are not any minis that you could put in and program for $5500," Huppert says.

Testing products is a natural for microprocessors, and this will help reduce factory labour costs. Fever thermometers, for example, have to be carefully graded by hand now because each one reacts slightly differently to the same temperature. Honeywell is now completing final tests on a grading system that automatically sorts thermometers into 48 chutes. Each grade specifies a different location for the temperature scale that will be painted on the tube. The Honeywell system will replace 34 workers when it is shipped to the customer.

Many jobs now being done by microprocessors were too small to automate before. Dow Chemical Co. is considering MPUs for a variety of jobs "where computations are required that aren't quite complex enough to justify a minicomputer," says Charles R. Honea, process instrument manager at Dow's Texas Div. For instance, Dow uses microprocessors to calculate the flow of ethylene piped into the plant. The information was charted manually and required half a dozen people. "And it was always a day behind," Honea says. "You had no way of knowing how much ethylene you used today."

The process industries are a conservative lot, partly because of the reliability needed in control gear to keep their plants running continuously. It usually takes five to six years for a major technology breakthrough to find widespread use in the process control industries. "Microprocessors will be no different," says Nicholas P. Scallon, vice-president for marketing at Fisher Controls. "But the microprocessor will speed up automation," he says, "by breaking up control loops into smaller segments. Instead of trying to control the whole system, we will use a dedicated microprocessor to control such things as a boiler, an evaporator, or a catalytic conversion."

In data processing

Today's microprocessors are slow and limited in what they can do as a general-purpose computer system, but they already are playing a fast-growing role in the most important trend in data processing today – – distributed processing. In this, minicomputers and remote terminals are tied together into communications networks to perform the work of a single giant computer. Computer terminals, which originally were nothing more than the lowly teletypewriter for talking to the central computer, are rapidly becoming more powerful with the aid of the microprocessor. This intelligent terminal is really a computer itself now and is doing more data processing locally and communicating less with the central mainframe system.

The intelligent terminal is the fastest-growing segment of the terminal business. About 124,000 intelligent terminals are currently installed, says Creative Strategies Inc., a San Jose (Calif.) market research firm, and it predicts that installations will double by 1977. NCR says that all intelligent terminals will soon be using the microprocessor. "The MPU has only one-fourth to one-third of the performance and power, but the minicomputer engine was never run at full throttle in terminals," says C. William Kessler, NCR Corp.'s assistant vice-president for engineering and development. Many more microprocessors will be used in data processing as dedicated controllers, however, than for general-purpose computer applications. "We are using gobs of microprocessors in our new terminal lines," says Kessler. There will be as many as seven or eight microprocessors in each NCR terminal, each controlling a key part such as the display, the printer, communications, and the cassette memory.

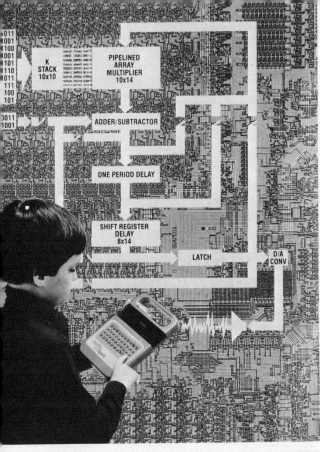

K STACK 10x10

PIPELINED ARRAY MULTIPLIER 10x14

ADDER/SUBTRACTOR

ONE PERIOD DELAY

SHIFT REGISTER DELAY 8x14

LATCH

D/A CONV

011
1001
1 100
1001
1 101
1110
1011
111
100
101

0011
1001

A montage shows the technology that lies behind Texas Instruments' educational toy, Speak and Spell. This learning aid can speak 200 words and the child is trained to spell them correctly. *Photo courtesy of Texas Instruments*

Once the computer-on-a-chip is designed into the NCR terminal, or any product for that matter, it internally becomes the answer to a product designer's dream. The MPU gives him the ability to make changes in a product quickly or add features by simply changing the software rather than having to redesign the electronic hardware. This flexibility not only saves the designer time and money but also makes it possible for him to do things that he could never have done before. There is always the customer, for example, who wants changes made in a standard product. One customer of Axiom Corp. needed a foreign character font on the smart computer printer that he was buying. "We made the software changes almost overnight and shipped the production unit at a cost only nominally above our standard price," says Simon J. Harrison, Axiom's vice-president. Without the MPU, the printer's price would have tripled, and it would have taken several weeks to get in production, he says. Pertec Corp. was already in production on a smart data-entry terminal for Singer Co. when Singer asked for several design changes. "We handled them inexpensively without messing up our whole production line," says Alan K. Jennings, manager for advanced business systems. For the same reasons, Pertec was able to design the original terminal faster. "Two months after we decided to go ahead, we had a prototype built," Jennings says.

As easy as designing with MPUs might seem, the unsophisticated can be trapped by the difficulties of programming. "The hardware part is easy for even a half-witted design guy – the problem is the software," says William H. Hunscher, president of Fasfax Corp., who builds smart point-of-sale systems for fast-food companies, such as Burger Chef and Burger King. Says NCR's Kessler: "It's hard to understand the stored-program concept and doing everything sequentially instead of just figuring how to reach a solution." So far, users do not get much software help from microprocessor vendors. "The microcomputer is following the general trend of minicomputers 10 years ago," says David Curtis, electronic systems manager at Arthur D. Little. "At that time, minis had limited software and limited capabilities. It took some time before minicomputer makers were able to provide sophisticated software packages," he adds. Software is not only the biggest problem now for MPU users, but it is also where most of the costs are. "Software costs are actually even more for a microcomputer than for a minicomputer," says Richard Marley, a New Hampshire consultant who has designed smart products for several small companies. He says that he spends up to $100,000 on every software design, while the cost of hardware designs is down to around $20,000.

The effects on companies

Though this microcomputer revolution is just starting, it already is having a profound effect on user companies that jumped on the bandwagon early. Dramatic changes are occurring in such areas as personnel, hiring, procurement, the rate of new product development, and the organisation of the engineering department.

Raytheon is using its microcomputer in seventeen different programmes throughout five divisions. NCR has designed ten products – two are announced – around an Intel microcomputer. At Texas Instruments, Cragon whips out a list of sixty-seven different company-funded programmes in which microprocessors are being designed into such customer products as Tappan's new microwave oven, into military systems that TI is bidding on, and, of course, into its own products. "Microprocessors are making a tremendous impact at Honeywell," says Perlowski, who runs a corporate MPU evaluation centre. "It has allowed us to introduce a bunch of new products and to penetrate new markets we've never been in before." And because the MPU is reducing development costs, he sees new products coming out at a faster rate from Honeywell.

The microprocessor is probably affecting no other single industry as much as the instruments business. In the next two years, predicts technology consultant Lynwood O. Eikrem, analytical instruments using microprocessors will rise from 2 per cent to 50 per cent of the market. "Companies are rushing into microprocessors, and those who don't move fast will lose market," he says. So far the biggest MPU effort is coming in digital test instruments, such as voltmeters, counters, and frequency synthesizers, and in such analytical instruments as spectrometers and chromatographs. "Probably 90 per cent of digital instruments selling for $2000 or more will use microprocessors by 1980," says industry analyst Galen W. Wampler.

Cutting costs is a major incentive, of course, but MPU technology already is creating instruments with a new range of capabilities. A Tektronix Inc. spectrum analyser automatically sets itself up to locate a particular frequency – a tricky chore that taxes even experienced engineers. And a Hewlett-Packard Co. distance-measuring device computes and displays angles, heights, and distances that previously had to be measured separately or worked out after measurements were taken. "Until recently, most instruments were designed just to make fundamental measurements like time and frequency," says Marco R. Negrete, engineering manager for H-P's instrument group. "But what the user really is interested in are quantities like distortion or power that are the function of more than one variable. "Thanks to microprocessor technology," he says, "our instruments will be able in every case to talk to the user in language he can understand."

Last September, Eagle Signal's Industrial Controls Div. launched a programmable logic controller aimed at the petrochemical, auto, and process control industries, and was quickly overwhelmed. The 600-odd employees at the Davenport (Iowa) division are now rushing to reorganise the engineering department, set up a software operation, open a training school for dealers and new customers, and start a major sales promotion campaign. With nearly one hundred end-equipment makers already buying the controller, Eagle Signal's factory is desperately trying to boost production to meet orders. "We are unable to react as fast as we want," says division manager Huppert, "so now we are trying to hire as fast as we can before competition moves in." For many companies, the changes can be all-encompassing. "The MPU means a major change in every aspect of the way in which our company does business," says J. David Forney Jr., vice-president for R&D at Codex Corp. The Newton (Mass.) company has just developed a line of intelligent network processors – "a product we just couldn't have built before," he says. "There are implications on the factory floor in how you build your machines, implications in how you service them, and in how you market them," he says. "We were already a high-technology company, but moving to the MPU meant developing new skills and new tools."

The microprocessor has created a far different kind of engineering organization at many companies. To MSI Data Corp., a data entry terminal maker, the scarcity of people forced it to teach engineers how to be programmers. "What it means is taking engineers who spent years in school learning how to design logic and digital circuits and teaching them to do with software what they'd previously done with hardware," says MSI's president, William J. Bowers. The company has gone through at least five design changes to improve the software. "It's been like teaching ourselves to do brain surgery by trial and error," he says.

For all the smart-product activity going on now, it is not difficult to find the critics. Among them, the process control companies say it is too slow, the appliance people say it is too expensive, the auto makers say it is unreliable, and the data-processing equipment makers gripe about the lack of software. But the same things were being said ten years ago about today's highly successful minicomputer.

The future

Over the next several years, smart products and machines will spread at an ever-increasing rate. Software will become available so that anyone will be able to program a microcomputer. Schools will be turning out a flood of young people familiar with microprocessors and eager to build products with them. The semiconductor industry will continue to develop more powerful parts. "In the next five to ten years we will be able to turn out one million devices on a single chip," predicts Richard L. Petritz, vice-president of New Business Resources, a venture capital company. This will mean that the power either of a large mainframe computer or of a complete minicomputer with large amounts of memory will be available on a single chip. By 1980 the worldwide market for microprocessor systems will grow to $1.1 billion, up from only $60 million last year, predicts William D. Baker, MPU group head at National Semiconductor Corp. "And $400 million worth of this," he adds, "will come from people who don't know yet that they are going to buy MPUs." There are an estimated 25,000 potential applications, but "active designs are being pursued in only about 10 per cent of them," says Robert N. Noyce, chairman of Intel.

Development time is so short for a smart product now and the entry costs are so low that there will be "myriad examples of new companies spawning, with bright, young fellows developing MPU-based products," says Fairchild's Hogan. Petritz says: "The MPU will reduce the application of electronics essentially to that of writing a computer program, and the average person can be educated to program a computer." That spells danger for the established companies. Already, manufacturers have to be looking at microprocessors "or somebody will come along

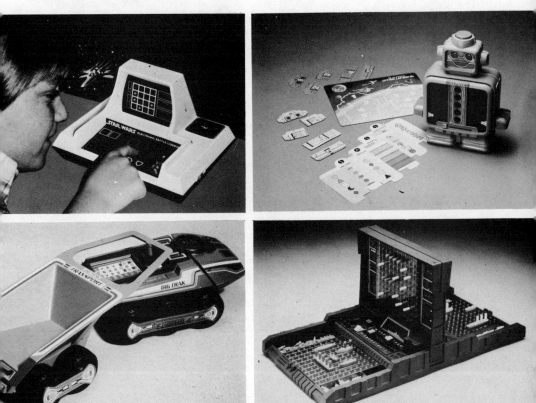

Four examples from the avalanche of microprocessor-based electronic toys now on the market. Some have succeeded and some have failed, but there is no denying that chips have extended the ingenuity of the toymakers. *Photos courtesy of Texas Instruments*

and obsolete their product," warns Donald V. Kleffman, a marketing manager at Ampex Corp. Says Kessler of NCR: "There will be many new companies coming in with MPU technology, and they will replace some of the old companies. A lot of companies will be beaten down."

When that time comes, microprocessors will be everywhere – from the smart machines of the factory and the office to the handheld, personal microcomputers costing less than $100, and the personal mobile telephone. "Each individual will have his own personal phone with him at all times," says RCA's Hillier. "And it will automatically keep the phone system informed as to where he is located." Consultant Marley believes that an individual will be able to run cash flow problems or his own econometric model on his microcomputer. The more complex microprocessors, Marley predicts, will enable "smaller and smaller, and more and more pervasive microprocessor-based machines to do whatever the big mainframe computers are doing today."

An Overview of Microprocessor Applications

A. J. Nichols

This short but neat paper summarizes the advantages of using the microprocessor in products and predicts future trends in their application. It appeared in the US publication, Proceedings of the IEEE *(Institute of Electrical and Electronic Engineers), in June 1976. The author is with the Intel Corporation.*

When the first microprocessor was introduced a little over four years ago, it was largely ignored by the electronics industry. However, since that inauspicious beginning, this new device has become the hottest topic in current technology. Of course, many technological breakthroughs have started out as hot topics only to fade into obscurity when practical application problems could not be solved. What is unique about microcomputers is that their application is limited less by the technology than by the imagination of the designers who use them. Consequently, as more and more product designers become familiar with the capabilities of microcomputers, the number of new applications increases geometrically.

This is perhaps the most exciting aspect of the microcomputer revolution. In a very few years, we have gone from a laboratory curiosity to volume use in thousands of products. In most of these applications, the new technology has been used to replace designs which were formerly implemented with TTL (transistor – transistor logic). However, an increasing number of products are surfacing which would have been impractical prior to the microcomputer era.

Microprocessor advantages

Why are microcomputers making such a diversity of new applications possible? Why are they altering previous limitations on size, weight,

125

power consumption and price? How do they make possible increased sophistication in the functions of new products?

First of all, microprocessors are the result of the semiconductor industry's ability to place an ever-greater number of transistors in a single integrated circuit. The complexity of integrated circuits has approximately doubled every year. Since microprocessors are relatively new devices, we would expect them to concentrate great functional power in a few small pieces of silicon. Hence, simply by being based on the latest technology, microprocessors should be able to implement a given function with a smaller number of chips than older devices.

Added to this is the fact that microprocessors substitute programmed logic for hardwired logic. The programmed logic can be placed into semiconductor read-only memories (ROMs) which have a very regular structure and hence offer even greater functional capability per chip. It has been shown that a ROM can replace a large number of standard logic gates. For example, a single 16,384-bit ROM is equivalent in logic power to a hundred or more TTL integrated circuits. Thus once the basic microprocessor module is built, enormous logic power can be added with only a few additional integrated circuits. The cost for a microprocessor-based system grows at about fifteen per cent of the rate of growth for TTL systems. With today's costs and circuit complexity, the crossover point is in the range of thirty to fifty TTL circuits. This point is being lowered due to the rapid decrease in the cost of a basic micro-processor module as the volume for the products builds up and as ever more function is added to a single integrated circuit.

Important as the cost advantages are, the most significant change that microprocessors have brought to the design function is a substantial shift in the philosophy of electronic design. The older technique of implementing the logic of a product in the interconnection of standard logic gates has been replaced by standard interconnection of standard hardware with the logic stored in a ROM. This has permitted the designer to place nearly all of his product logic in a very small portion of the total design. That is, the logic is in a few integrated circuits rather than diffused throughout the design in wiring. With the logic concentrated in only a few components, a high degree of design flexibility is possible.

All of this gives rise, then, to the seven primary advantages of microprocessor-based architectures over their random logic counter-parts.

(1) The manufacturing costs of the product are generally lower. Typical microprocessor-based designs cost twenty to sixty per cent of their TTL equivalents.

(2) The time and cost for the original development can be substan-

tially lowered. An accomplished design team can cut the design time by about two thirds. As support tools improve, the design cycle will continue to decrease.

(3) As a consequence, products can be brought to the market faster and in closer correlation with market needs. This can provide a significant edge in obtaining or increasing market share.

(4) The inherent flexibility makes possible a quicker response to competitive pressures in the market place with consequent increases in product lifetimes.

(5) Greater functional capability can be provided at reasonable cost. This permits the realization of better products for the same or lower prices.

(6) The smaller number of components in a microprocessor system increases the reliability of the final product.

(7) Should failure still occur, the computational capability of a microprocessor can be used to perform self-diagnosing of the product to provide substantial reductions in service charges.

Current applications
One way of looking at the variety of microprocessor applications is by industrial category. We find that instrumentation, industrial control and aerospace lead the list. However, many of the actual applications are common across industrial boundaries. It is more informative to look at the type of function to be performed and its relation to past implementation methods.

The replacement of TTL circuitry and under-utilized minicomputers accounts for sixty to seventy per cent of the current applications of microcomputers. Thus we find them concentrated in such products as data collection terminals, office equipment, business machines, calculators, point-of-sale terminals, and various kinds of data communications equipment. Even in many of these replacement applications we are finding product changes. The incremental cost for additional functions is very small in a microprocessor-based system. Thus there is an increasing tendency to add greater functional capability than would have been practical with previous design techniques. This tendency is most noticeable in the area of instrumentation, where increasingly sophisticated products are finding their way to market in growing numbers. For example, instrument manufacturers are finding it practical to add such features as remote control, programmability, improved readout and peripheral interfaces with little impact on product price. This tendency is true of all types of instruments including those for the electronics lab, medicine, physical analysis and a myriad of other scientific requirements.

Microcomputers are also finding their way into products where electronics were not used before because the job could be done through electromechanical means. For example, microprocessors are being used to control traffic lights, appliances, elevators, and the mixing of cocktails. It is expected that an increasing number of functions that are currently realized with electromechanical techniques will yield to microprocessors as their prices decline into the $5 and $10 range. Devices in this price category will be available by the end of this decade.

Finally, this technology is making possible an increasing number of applications which were totally impractical scant months ago. For example, a decompression computer now exists to increase the safety of deepsea divers. An automatic eye examiner can analyse a reflected laser pattern and determine various eye abnormalities. A number of projects exist to assist handicapped persons, including a microcomputer-controlled system which can synthesize words typed in on a keyboard by the vocally retarded. Finally, there is at least one top class dragster in the world whose fuel mixture of nitromethane and alcohol is dynamically controlled, as are other motor functions such as multiple spark ignition. The microprocessor also controls the complete shutdown sequence which replaces the fuel mixture with inert gases to prevent the motor from exploding.

Application trends
Considering current applications and recent events, a number of future trends are clear.

(1) As new microprocessor-based products come into being, there will be a rapid tendency to add increasing sophistication to the initial product.

(2) The number of analytical instruments based on microcomputer technology will explode. The sophistication of these instruments will increase tremendously while at the same time simplifying their operator control.

(3) There will certainly be microprocessors in the home. They will control many aspects of our lives, such as appliances, temperature, lighting and security.

(4) Entertainment will become a major area for microprocessors, with sophisticated real-time participation games moving into the living room.

(5) Significant inroads will be made into the area of transportation. Microprocessor control will appear in most transportation units such as automobiles, trains, airplanes and boats. In addition, control of the flow of units in traffic control and freight car identification will come to rely more and more on this new technology.

(6) A significant revolution will take place in process control, as well as in other manufacturing functions such as inventory management and data collection.

(7) The use of microcomputers in communication modules will continue to increase. They will make possible more sophisticated switching systems, multiplexers, error detection and correction circuits, and encryption equipment.

Simply put, microprocessors will spread into an ever-increasing number of new products. Although it has just been four years since their introduction, microprocessors now appear in thousands of products. In not too many more years, these thousands will grow to millions.

Furthermore, as we can easily see, the microcomputer is quickly moving out of purely technical applications and is swiftly moving into the everyday life of the layman. By the end of this decade, it is evident that microprocessors will be involved in such ordinary daily tasks as the purchasing of goods, the treatment of medical ailments, the performance of household tasks, the driving of an automobile, and the use of leisure time. In fact, the potential applications of microcomputers are so numerous as to make it impossible to accurately predict the new applications we shall see in the future. For perspective, consider that the microprocessor has been compared to the fractional horsepower motor in terms of its use in widely diverse product lines. At the time the fractional horsepower motor was in its early days of application, it is extremely doubtful that anyone realized that some day we would be brushing our teeth with these devices.

We may not brush our teeth with microprocessors, but applications which are even more inconceivable today are waiting for tomorrow.

Microprocessors in Consumer Products

Paul M. Russo, Chih-Chung Wang, Philip K. Baltzer and Joseph A. Weisbecker

A little technical this one, but the general reader may just about get through with the help of the glossary at the back of the book. It is taken from another Proceedings of the IEEE *overview which appeared in February 1978. The authors are with the* RCA *Laboratories, which might explain their terse American computer men's jargon.*

The large-scale integration (LSI) revolution, and in particular the microprocessor revolution, is having an ever-increasing impact on the consumer market. The proliferation and extreme low cost of such products as calculators and digital watches were only the beginning, and would simply never have taken place without a sophisticated, rapidly evolving semiconductor manufacturing base. This semiconductor manufacturing technology is producing circuits with both exponentially increasing complexity and exponentially decreasing costs, as a function of time. The impact of LSI microprocessors and memories on a vast array of consumer products, from washing machines to microwave ovens, from automobiles to sophisticated programmable video games, is the leading edge of what is surely becoming the consumer microprocessor revolution.

This paper will explore a few aspects of that revolution and discuss some of the design tradeoffs associated with the development of intelligent consumer products. Microprocessor applications that only vicariously impact the consumer, such as intelligent gasoline pumps, arcade games and portable encryption devices will not be discussed in this paper.

This paper begins with a brief examination of the uses of dedicated microcomputers, single-chip devices containing all the basic elements of a computer system, in a variety of applications. It then briefly explores the potential impact of LSI and microprocessors on two-way cable television (CATV) systems, and on dedicated nonvideo games. Following that, an overview of metal-oxide-semiconductor (MOS) LSI technology trends is presented, especially as it impacts digital video game display architectures. Finally, an overview of existing microprocessor-based video game products is discussed and a detailed description of the system architectural tradeoffs associated with the RCA Studio II product is presented.

Microprocessors and microcomputers

Before we can begin to explore consumer applications of microprocessors and microcomputers, the distinguishing features of these two classes of device should be clearly delineated. Any single-processor computer system, from the simplest microwave oven controller to a sophisticated data-processing system, consists of three classes of subsystems – the central processing unit (CPU), direct memory, which can be read/write (RAM) or read-only (ROM), and input/output (I/O) interfaces. The CPU subsystem performs all the classical arithmetic, logic and control functions. The direct memory contains both the program (instructions to be executed by the CPU) and the currently active data on which the CPU is operating. The I/O interfaces represent the critical communication links between the internal computer operations and the external world (I/O devices including mass memory, human operators, etc).

Microprocessors are single-chip realizations of the CPU function of a computer system. Microcomputers, in the context of this paper, are single-chip realizations of the entire computer system function, i.e., CPU, RAM and ROM, and enough I/O capability to permit the single-chip implementation of desired control functions. Additionally, many microcomputers sport an option of having either mask-programmed ROM (low-cost for high-volume applications) or EPROM (UV light-erasable, reprogrammable for low-volume applications). From the above, it appears that minimal configurations for microprocessor-based systems require three chips. This is usually true, although in some architectures the I/O functions are shared between custom CPU and memory chips resulting in two-chip minimal configurations. Other system architectures may require the use of multiple CPUs to achieve desired objectives. The design of microprocessor-based system architectures will not be discussed below, since considerable literature exists on the subject.

Microcomputers and microprocessors in control

As described above, microcomputers are single-chip realizations of entire small-scale computer systems. They come in different varieties with instruction sets, memory organizations, word sizes and I/O capabilities optimized to varying classes of applications. Micro-computers range from relatively simple (and low-cost) four-bit devices to more powerful eight-bit units. Additionally, custom microcomputers exist with features uniquely tailored to the volume application at hand.

Low-cost microcomputers are already impacting a host of consumer products. From exercise and coffee machines to electric ranges, from sewing machines to microwave ovens, a whole new generation of intelligent consumer products is emerging. The technological wonders of these developments are rarely apparent to the consumer. He or she buys a product with new or preferred features at costs that would have been prohibitive but a few years ago. Additionally, these new products have more reliable controls and sport features clearly intended to add flair, if not true functionality.

Advantages of programmable single-chip controller implementa-tions are many. Less board area, an overall lower systems parts count and less power consumption reduce manufacturing costs and tend to improve reliability. In addition, servicing is usually simple and is accomplished by replacing an appropriate circuit module. Most home appliances typically need only relatively simple controls. For that reason four-bit devices, with their low costs, are being shipped by the millions. Various RAM and ROM size combinations and various tech-nologies are usually available so that a specific control function can be implemented at minimal cost.

(1) *Standard versus custom parts.* Is it always desirable to use standard microcomputers such as the TI TMS 1000, or the Mostek 3870? Or are custom microcontrollers preferable? The answer is not simple and a host of home product manufacturers are supporting both approaches. For example, Litton's Model 460 Memorymatic microwave oven uses a TMS 1000 series part, whereas the Amana RR-9 Radarange uses a custom chip developed by General Instrument Corporation. Other examples abound. The Singer Athena sewing machine uses a custom PMOS part to minimize mechanical control and hence improve the human interface and product reliability simultaneously. The basic questions put forth cannot be simply answered. About all that is fair to say is that very large volume applications, or those requiring unique I/O capability, will tend to be custom. However, most typical applications would be more economically implemented via standard parts both because of reduced product turnaround times, and the ease of product updates via software changes.

The products discussed above were predominantly examples where electronics have replaced mechanical controls in consumer applications. More interesting, however, are the host of new consumer products spawned by the ongoing revolution in LSI.

(2) *Intelligent turntable.* The Accutrac 4000 is an ultrasonically remotely controlled microcomputer-based high-quality audio turntable. A remote keyboard can program the turntable to sequence through the tracks in any order, repeat favourite selections, reject to the next record, or turn the device on or off. Here is a product that would have been unthinkable on a cost basis before the 1970s. It provides desirable features and represents, in effect, a new type of consumer product.

(3) *Nonvideo intelligent games.* Nonvideo microcomputer-based games are just beginning to appear, but already most of the major toy manufacturers are getting heavily involved. From action games such as Parker Brothers "Code Name: Sector", a one-player submarine chase game, and Milton Bradley's "Battleship", a missile-firing two-player naval warfare game, to more cerebral games such as Mattel Inc.'s "Football", future toys will never be the same again.

(4) *LSI impact on colour television.* The full impact of LSI and, hence, microprocessor technology would not be complete without at least a brief examination of its impact on colour television, usually the consumer's single largest investment in electronics. To date, LSI technology has primarily affected the design of the classical TV subsystems, i.e., tuning, signal processing and colour correction circuitry. However, many new functions such as remote random-access channel selection are now possible. Systems of this type may also offer the consumer such amenities as on-screen display of channel number and time of day. The RCA system, in addition, allows the consumer to remotely adjust colour and tint. Other LSI developments, such as the metal-nitride-oxide-silicon (MNOS) nonvolatile memory, have obviated the need for backup power in digital tuning address systems. In addition LSI is making possible new colour correction approaches, such as the vertical-interval reference (VIR), which makes use of colour information on line 19 which is often transmitted by the broadcaster. The most visible LSI impacts on colour TV, however, will be in the area of new functions. Domestically, Magnavox is retailing a 19-in. colour receiver with a built-in game system. Heath has a microprocessor-based TV programmer. Both Sylvania and Quasar have announced microcomputer-based tuning systems.

In Europe, a host of new TV functions have been unveiled. Two British systems, Teletext and Viewdata, are adding alphanumeric (ordering by letters and numbers) capability to TV receivers – Teletext via a special decoder within the receiver, and Viewdata via a telephone link to a central data bank. Several West German receivers sport the ability to insert a small black and white picture of another channel onto the colour picture of the viewed channel. These include AEG-Telefunken, Saba and Grundig. Grundig has also demonstrated a receiver with built-in programmable games. Finally, Blaupunkt has begun marketing a receiver that can be "programmed" remotely to turn itself on and off automatically, at pre-selected times.

The bulk of applications discussed so far in this section were simple enough to permit microcomputer control. In subsequent sections, more complex applications such as programmable video games will be described, most of which require the use of more powerful microprocessors. Another example of a consumer product requiring the computational capability of an eight-bit microprocessor is Fidelity Electronics Ltd's "Chess Challenger", which uses a Nippon Electric CPU.

LSI impacts on CATV

During the late 1960s and early 1970s, cable TV manufacturers were gearing up for what was supposed to be a major increase in the use of two-way CATV systems. In the "wired-city" concepts espoused during that era, planned uses of two-way CATV were limited only by one's imagination. Unfortunately, two factors dominated in slowing down this potentially rapid growth – technical problems in two-way transmission and the high costs of putting specialized control centres in consumer homes.

A two-way CATV system consists basically of head-end (headquarters) equipment, usually computer controlled, a cable network connecting all the users with the head-end, and control centres or terminals at each user installation. The frequency spectrum is typically divided into bands for forward (head-end to subscriber) and reverse (subscriber to head-end) transmission. The bulk of the frequency spectrum is assigned to the forward band, most of which is utilized for broadcast TV signals, with a small band reserved for data. In addition, a small part of the spectrum is used for data transmission from subscribers to the head-end. The types of two-way functions achievable cover such applications as home security, interactive shopping, weather information, remote electronic fund transfer including banking, and message services (electronic mail). Additional proposed functions include remote game playing, information retrieval and wake-up services.

The impact of LSI in home terminal design and in computer-based head-end equipment needs no comment. The microprocessor, however, is only beginning to impact the two-way CATV business. Under design are microprocessor-based pay-TV systems for hotels and motels, which can provide additional communication services, such as room and message status, room service requests, and security. It will not be long before microprocessors impact home two-way CATV terminals, since many new functions and expanded flexibility will be made possible at incremental cost.

LSI technology trends
It is evident from the above discussions that the LSI revolution is having a strong impact on the consumer market. The technology provides the means to realize new functions and products to satisfy the cost-conscious consumer. It seems appropriate at this point to examine the historical evolution of LSI technology and extrapolate its future impacts on logic and memory costs. This understanding will provide the background for discussion on consumer digital video display architectures.

(1) *Technology evolution.* For the past decade, we have witnessed the explosive development of integrated-circuit technology. Since the development of planar transistors in 1959, the growth rate amounts to doubling the complexity every year. This growth rate and its future trend can be understood from the contributing elements: larger die size, higher density due to finer microstructure, and advanced device and circuit design. The annual doubling law has been based on the exponential growth in each of these elements. For the next few years, however, the trend towards finer dimensions and larger die size are expected to continue, but packing density improvement through clever design will become more and more difficult. The diminished contribution from packing efficiency improvement will change the growth rate to doubling every two years.

(2) *Estimating cost.* The growth in complexity has a direct effect on the cost of integrated circuits. The cost of integrated circuits consists of two major components: silicon chip cost and assembly/test cost. Based on the available design techniques and process technology, silicon chip cost is roughly an exponential function of complexity. On the other hand, the assembly/test cost, as a first approximation, can be treated as independent of complexity. This leads to the inverse relationship between assembly/test cost per function and complexity. By combining these two components, the cost per function will have a minimum corresponding to the optimum complexity for the state-of-the-art design technique and process technology. As time goes on, the silicon chip cost will decrease due to improving density, processing technology, and material. This will result in the optimum cost per function decreasing with time.

For the bulk of future consumer-oriented video display systems under development, the cost of static RAM will play a dominant role. Since the storage element for static RAM continues to be some form of flip-flop (a half-shift register), price reductions will continue, but the real price breakthrough, relative to dynamic RAM, will not occur until a new storage element is developed. Based on the per bit price of 200 millicents for static RAM in 1977, the price will drop with an annual reduction factor between 0.7 and 0.8 resulting in per bit costs between 48 and 82 millicents by 1981.

The bulk of the data presented above pertains mainly to NMOS technology, but from all indications, a new generation of semiconductor technologies, high-performance MOS (HMOS), double-diffusion MOS (DMOS), V-notch MOS (VMOS), silicon on sapphire (SOS) and integrated injection logic are ready for commercial use. The increases in LSI performance promised by these new technologies will certainly make possible many new areas of applications in consumer products.

Programmable video games

The explosive growth of the general video game market has been nothing short of phenomenal. Unit sales grew from a few hundred thousand in 1975 to 3.5 million in 1976 and are expected to top six million in 1977, with a market value exceeding $400m. This impressive growth will be achieved despite publicity given to problems that have occurred in isolated instances. The video game revolution began in the early 1970s on two fronts: Atari pioneered the development of video arcade games with the 1972 introduction of PONG, a TV tennis-type game sporting on-screen scoring and minimal sound capability. During the same year, Magnavox introduced Odyssey, a consumer ball and paddle game based on circuitry patented by Sanders Associates. Both systems were well received, but it was not until 1975 that the market began to grow rapidly. Current projections indicate that the market will soon go in two radically different directions – complex, dedicated games based on increasingly sophisticated chip sets, and microprocessor-based programmable games. Dedicated games based on a very few custom chips will increase in importance, even as their costs follow patterns established by calculators and digital watches. Their sophistication will increase, but the ease with which small companies can enter the business will result in fierce competition. The resulting aggressive pricing will inevitably bring about severe price erosion.

Programmable games represent a new breed of consumer product, somewhat akin to the audio turntable. A consumer purchases a basic system for a relatively high price ($130 – $190), but can then add game capability by the purchase of relatively inexpensive ($10–$20) plug-ins, which are usually ROM-based. The basic game units, usually microprocessor-based, may be viewed as specialized computer systems that can be reprogrammed via plug-in cartridges.

This class of product requires extensive software support in the form of a large selection of plug-ins to remain competitive. Hence, substantial front-end investments are required to enter this business. Thus, the competition should not be so severe, and an additional money-making business, that of the plug-ins, will evolve simultaneously. However, unlike the audio standards for the record business, no display architecture standards have yet emerged. Nor will any such standards be established in the foreseeable future. This is due to the rapid evolution of LSI capability, which will result in new product generations every few years. Only when LSI costs reach the point where display resolution and colour capability approach the NTSC bandwidth limit will the possibility of "standards", and plug-compatible units, emerge. At that time, plug-in sales will become a dominant and highly competitive business, requiring significant innovation and software investment to remain competitive. Estimated annual plug-in sales of $170m are projected for 1980.

Conclusions

The impact of LSI and microprocessor technology is having on the consumer market has been overviewed. With regard to the future, we perceive the emergence of two types of markets – control and entertainment/education/information. In the control area, the use of microcomputers in appliance control, energy management and home security systems will continue to expand rapidly. In the entertainment/education/information area, programmable video games will continue to improve, offering ever higher display resolution, and colour and sound capability. A software plug-in market will grow in parallel presenting the consumer with a wide variety of program selections.

Further in the future, stand-alone systems will emerge with mass storage (most likely bubble memories) capability. Future two-way CATV or telephone-based systems may well become the focal points for these developments. The major hurdles to be overcome do not appear to be technical, but rather consumer-oriented. What functions do consumers really want and how much are they willing to pay for these capabilities? It is clear that the rapid evolution of LSI will soon make available powerful computing and memory subsystems at low cost. The applications for which these subsystems are put to use will be the determining factors in the products' success.

Industrial Uses of the Microprocessor

Lawrence B. Evans

The "process industries" – such as chemicals, pulp paper and food – have tended to be the growth industries in recent years. They have also been in the forefront of developments in automation, especially new control technology. Here the Professor of Chemical Engineering at the Massachusetts Institute of Technology shows how the revolutionary advances in electronics will greatly accelerate evolutionary change in industrial process control. The article comes from Science *magazine, 18 March 1977.*

The first computer control system went on-line in an industrial plant in 1959. Since then, there have been remarkable advances in our ability to acquire, process and transmit information electronically. Developments in the technology of digital hardware, software, basic sensors and all forms of communication offer the potential for industrial process control systems that are highly automated and provide improved operating performance.

The role of process control in industrial plants

The focus in this article is on the "process industries" as opposed to the manufacturing industries. Products of the process industries include chemicals, petroleum, metals, electric power, pulp and paper, food, cement and textiles. Their plants manipulate the composition of materials by chemical reaction, purification and blending of components to convert raw materials and energy into more valuable products. The earliest applications of computer control were in the process industries, where instruments were available to monitor the continuous flow of a product and to send the data to the computer, which could then direct changes in the process by adjusting valves and switches.

Automation in the manufacturing industries – automobiles, appliances, electronics – is beyond the scope of this article. These industries manipulate the geometries of their raw materials so that discrete parts are assembled to form products. Computers are being used on the factory floor to run machine tools, track the contents of a warehouse, test products, and so forth, but the methods of measurement and control are basically different from those used in the process industries, and the problems of automation are greater.

Industrial processes are designed to operate in either a continuous or a batch mode. In the first, materials flow continuously through the plant from one processing unit to the next. At each stage, different operations are performed, such as heating, cooling, mixing, chemical reaction, distillation, drying and pressurization. For most operations there are optimum conditions of temperature, pressure and residence time at each stage.

In the batch mode, the material being processed stays in one place (such as in a reaction vessel), and the process steps are carried out over time during the batch cycle. There is an optimum schedule of such factors as temperature and pressure. For large-scale production, engineers have traditionally tried to develop continuous processes, because they are easier to instrument and control, require less labour, and do not waste time in emptying, cleaning, and refilling vessels between batch cycles.

Flow rate is by far the most common variable manipulated, whether by adjusting a valve, turning a pump on or off, or by other means. The measured variables in addition to flow rate are normally temperature, pressure, chemical composition and liquid level. A typical plant, such as one for manufacture of ethylene or ammonia, will have several hundred control valves and more than a thousand measured variables. Changes are made in the operation of the process on a time scale ranging from a few seconds to a few hours.

The elements of a control system are shown in Fig. 3.1. The important functions are measurement, control, actuation and communication. Measurement refers to the sensing of variables such as flow rate, temperature, pressure, level, and chemical composition, and the transmission of the measurement to the controller. Control is the decision-making operation; it compares the measured state of the process with the desired conditions and decides how the variables should be manipulated. Actuation is the means by which the operating variables are manipulated; typical actuators are valves, rheostats, switches and relays. Communication includes the display of information to the plant operators as well as the transmission of important variables to the plant management.

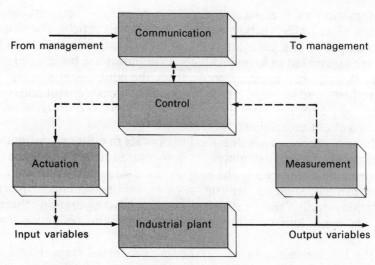

Fig. 3.1 Schematic diagram of an industrial control system

The organization of a plant control system in the hierarchical structure is shown in Fig. 3.2. The lowest level is occupied by the control
computer that regulates a single process unit to hold it to the desired
operating conditions and move the unit to a safe condition in emergen-
cies. The next step is a computer responsible for coordinating several
units, for scheduling operations, and for optimizing the plant's performance. At the top level is the corporate control computer, which makes
available to management current information about its manufacturing
operations. The operations at the lowest level (of regulating the process
and watching for system failures) are the simplest, but they must be
done frequently. The optimizing and scheduling tasks at the higher
levels are much more complex but are done less frequently. An advanced automation system is concerned not only with the physical
control of the process but also with its management (the gathering and
application of both process and business information for decision
making).

There are four basic objectives of plant operation that an advanced
management and control system can help achieve:

(1) To perform the primary mission of the plant. The plant must
produce products of the required quantity and quality and be available
and operating when needed. If it doesn't perform its primary mission,
the plant is a failure even if succeeding objectives are met.

(2) To maintain safe operating conditions. The control system should
constrain processing to safe operating conditions, such as allowable

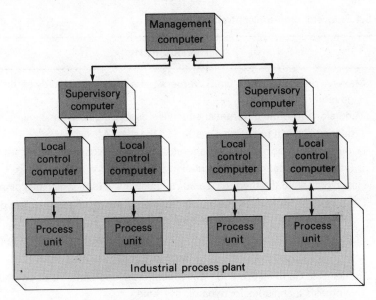

Fig. 3.2 Hierarchical organization of an advanced control system

temperatures and pressures, and should be able to shut the system down safely in an emergency.

(3) To comply with government requirements. Society imposes restrictions on the operation of most industrial plants in the form of government regulations. These restrictions require the control of environmental emissions to acceptable levels, control over the exposure of workers to toxic materials, the keeping of records required by law, and so forth.

(4) To improve productivity. This can be achieved by increasing the yield of products, reducing requirements for raw materials, energy and labour, and reducing capital investment. The greatest opportunities for advances in the application of modern control technology are in those situations that provide obvious benefits in meeting one or more of these objectives.

Advances in control technology
There have been significant advances in control theory, in industrial applications of control, and in hardware and software available for control. Each of these areas will be reviewed.

Almost all of the early control systems, such as the flyball governor developed by James Watt in 1788 for controlling the speed of a steam engine, were developed empirically. Maxwell in 1868 wrote the first theoretical paper on control with his analysis of the stability of the

Table 3.1 Developments in control theory

Date	Developments
1868	Maxwell read his paper, "On Governors", the first analytic study of the flyball governor.
1922	Minorsky wrote the differential equations describing automatic ship-steering gear and used it to design a system on the *New Mexico*.
1932	Nyquist presented his basic regeneration theory, which established him as the father of feedback control technology.
1934	Hazen published the theory of servomechanisms, a term which he coined.
1936	Callender, Porter and Hartree published an early study of the transient performance of a valve-controlled process.
1938	Philbrick developed the electronic analog computer at the Foxboro Company.
1953	Mason introduced the signal-flow diagram techniques.
1956	Boltyanskii, Gamkrelidze and Pontryagin introduced generalized optimization synthesis techniques for dynamic systems.
1958	Kalman and Bertram pointed out the utility of state-space representation of the dynamics of control systems.
1961	Kalman and Bucy presented a new approach to filtering and prediction for linear systems.

flyball governor. Since that time there have been rapid advances in the mathematical theory of control. These have led to improved understanding of the behaviour of complex feedback control systems and to the development of mathematical and computational techniques for their design. Major developments in control theory are listed in Table 3.1. Advances in the application of control technology to industrial processes are summarized in Table 3.2.

When continuous processes began replacing batch stills in the oil industry in 1910, most processes were controlled manually with use of local temperature and pressure measurements. In the late 1920s the pneumatic controller was developed with proportional and integral (reset) modes that could be tuned in the field. A few years later the derivative mode was added to form the so-called PID (proportional-integral-derivative) three-term controller. This was a turning point in process instrumentation and led to a tremendous extension of the use of automatic control to processes previously difficult or impossible to control except manually. Pneumatic transmitters were developed in the mid-1930s and led in the 1940s to centralized control rooms with large control panels (see accompanying photograph). Electronic controllers became available in the 1950s. Since installation of the first computer-controlled system in 1959, there has been a steady growth in the number of computers installed in process plants. An important historic observation is that significant developments took place essentially at plants. The development of the three-term pneumatic controller in essentially its modern configuration was completed in 1942 without the a priori support of any theory.

Table 3.2   Major advances in industrial process control

Era	Measurement	Control	Communication and display
1900 to 1915	Indicating thermometers and pressure gauges	Manual control; off-on controllers; pneumatic valve actuators	Local indicators
1915 to 1930	Orifice plate used for flow measurement	Pneumatic proportional controller; reset mode added	Field-mounted recorders
1930 to 1945	Laboratory analysis of product quality; recording viscometer	Adjustable controller gain; derivative action added	Pneumatic transmission; centralized control rooms beginning to be used
1945 to 1960	On-line analytical measurements; pH measurement; gas analysers	Electronic controllers; first computer control system installed	Miniaturized instruments; graphic panels introduced; electronic transmission used
1960 to present	Specialized sensors; on-line chromatograph	Feedforward control; direct digital control; supervisory control	Cathode-ray-tube console for display; computer hierarchies

Among the recent developments in hardware and software for control are decreased cost of electronic hardware, improved communications capabilities, techniques for producing less expensive software of better quality, and the development of specialized sensors.

The cost of complex electronic circuitry continues to decrease exponentially (by a factor of about 1/2 each year) due to large-scale integration (LSI) semiconductor technology. Such technology has led to more powerful microprocessors with greater memory and speed and smaller cost per unit. The real cost of a system is in the hardware for communication between man and that system (displays, keys, typewriters) and this cost is a function of the way the system is packaged. Thus, automation functions and data processing become economic if they can be done blindly, without the need for human communication.

Improvements in cathode-ray-tube (CRT) displays are continuing to permit displays of higher quality with greater flexibility at lower costs. Colour displays are becoming much less expensive. The problem will be to determine how to present information to the operator so that it will be most useful.

Improved communications are making it possible to use systems in which elements of the control system are dispersed throughout the plant and communicate with each other through networks. New technologies for communication based on the use of coaxial cable, fibre optics and other carriers are emerging. Communication over these networks is by a digital rather than an analog signal.

The major cost of a computer control system is in the engineering and programming of the system. A new technology for producing computer programs, known as "software engineering", is becoming established. Instead of programmers writing their programs in whatever way they think best, software is designed and produced by engineers who use proven techniques. This approach reduces software costs, errors and implementation time while improving reliability and maintainability.

Analytical instruments are increasingly used to measure stream composition and condition at the output of a process for on-line control. Sensors are being developed to measure all sorts of specialized compositions, such as flue gas, sulphur in oil, and brightness. Frequently the availability of such a sensor is the key to developing an advanced control system for a particular process.

Trends in process plants

The use of advanced control technology has been influenced by developments in industrial processes and in the constraints imposed by society on their operation. The search in industry is for plants that produce more valuable products in greater quantity at lower cost. Plants are consequently becoming larger and more complex and must be operated to closer tolerances. To achieve economies of scale in the production of chemicals that are important commodities, such as ammonia and ethylene, plants of enormous size have been developed in which the processes are designed as a single train. The cost of a malfunction that stops production for any length of time is prohibitive. The need to reduce pollution and to conserve energy has led to increased recycling and exchange of heat between process streams. Plants are becoming more tightly integrated so that changes in one part of the process have an effect in many other places. The control system must account for the resulting interaction.

Processes are being developed that involve more complex sequences of chemical operations requiring precise conditions of temperature and pressure. The increased use of catalytic processes requires controls to maintain conditions that will preclude catalyst degradation and poisoning. The production of more sophisticated and valuable products requires closer control of product specifications. To manufacture Polaroid's new colour film, nine layers of chemicals no more than a few 10,000ths of an inch thick are deposited on the film as it passes through a large coating machine. As the layers are applied, the sheet of film must be alternately dried, heated, and cooled under extremely precise computer control of temperature and humidity.

All these trends in major industrial processes lead to requirements of more sophisticated control. Social and political considerations affect the way industrial plants are designed and operated. Important long-term forces are the needs for protection of the environment, conservation of energy and resources, safety and good working conditions. Because of the need to reduce emissions, it is now economical (in fact essential) to control the contents of waste streams. In the past, plant effluents have been the only streams not placed on automatic control. The energy crisis has caused many companies to re-evaluate their processes. New ground rules for designing plants favour tighter energy integration and the corresponding need for more sophisticated control.

Concern for safety works both for and against automation. Arguments are raised that it is not safe to run a plant without operators present and that an unattended plant would never get past a safety review board of the Office of Safety and Health Administration. However, sophisticated, properly designed systems can get people out of noisy, dirty environments, and this favours automation. In some parts of the country, there are simply not enough skilled people available to serve as operators. People are less willing to devote their lives to the same employer and geographic region. Thus, industry can no longer depend on having an operator with years of experience available to assume responsibility. This encourages the use of more automated processes that are easier to operate.

Advanced automation affects job enrichment in two ways. On the one hand, it eliminates some drudgery, but, on the other, operators tend to get bored with computer systems. A highly automated system must be carefully designed if it is to enrich the job.

Industrial policies on the proper role of the operator in running plants vary, and there is corresponding variation in practice. There are two extreme approaches: (1) to automate the process as much as possible and use a relatively unskilled operator who could do little more than shut the plant down in case of an emergency, and (2) to use a better trained, perhaps college educated, operator who would also serve as a manager. The ultimate direction industry will take is not clear at this time.

On balance, the social and political forces for environmental protection, energy conservation, safety and better working conditions favour greater automation.

Rate of acceptance
In recent years there have been some striking successes in the application of advanced digital communication and control systems in industrial plants. Computers have become commonplace in refineries, steel mills, chemical plants and most process industries. They are no longer considered revolutionary or glamorous but have become an accepted part of the process control.

Each year the *Oil and Gas Journal* publishes a list of the computer control systems in operation, being installed, or contracted to be installed worldwide in refineries, petrochemical plants, pipelines and producing plants. There has been a steady increase with a growth rate of about twenty-five per cent per year (Fig. 3.3). These figures include only a portion of the process industries, and many computer control projects are kept secret for proprietary reasons. But they indicate a trend. A recent estimate states that today there are well over 200,000 digital computers worldwide in on-line industrial control applications (not just in the process industries) with the number increasing by sixty-seven per cent annually.

Despite the successes and the large number of process control computers that have been installed, there is still a great untapped potential for the introduction of advanced computer-based automation systems into the industrial plant. Most observers in the industry agree that the acceptance of advanced technology is far less than the state of the art would permit.

In the late 1950s and early 1960s there was a burst of enthusiasm and

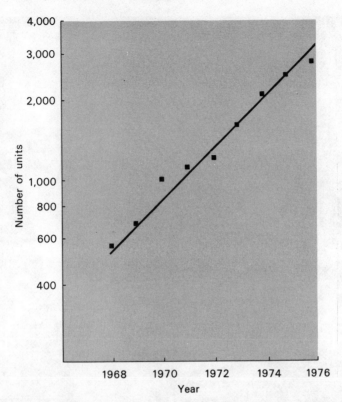

Fig. 3.3 Total number (cumulative) of computer control applications in the petroleum and petrochemical industry

a feeling that process control was about to enter a new era. Vannah and Slater observed: "Process control today is at the start of a new era – an era of analysis, introspection, and basic improvement." Yoxall remarked: "We stand upon the threshold of a new decade and there is a general feeling that we shall see, during these next ten years, significant developments in the specialized field of instrumentation." It was visualized that there would be computers connected to processes, that these processes would be optimized, that there would be improved techniques for measurement.

The new technology has not been accepted at anything approaching the rate forecast. McMillan in 1966, writing a review of on-line computer control in the process industry, noted: "It is clear that the explosion never came and probably never will. Real progress has been made, but, as always, it continues to be hard-won."

While the practitioners in the field were lamenting the lack of use of advanced computer hardware, the control theorists were also complain-

The finishing mill of a large steel plant is typical of the many industrial processes that are amenable to computer control. There is not a man or woman in sight. *Photo courtesy of the British Steel Corporation*

ing that modern control theory was not being used to its potential. A number of papers sought to explain the gap between theory and practice.

Blocks to acceptance of new technology
A major stumbling block to the application of advanced control systems has been our lack of understanding of the processes to be controlled. To apply single-loop controllers, one needed to know only the direction of a change. (If the fuel supply to the boiler is increased, the steam pressure rises.) The application of advanced control, however, requires refined process knowledge and mathematical models.

The control room of another modern steel plant shows copious use of microelectronic technology and the new style of work in this traditionally mucky industry. *Photo courtesy of the British Steel Corporation*

Another block has been a shortage of trained people who both understand the industrial processes and also have knowledge of and sophistication in computer control. A third limitation is the inertia and conservatism in the industry. The heavy process industries with large capital investments are hesitant to take technical risks because the penalty for failure is so large. Some companies had bad experiences with systems installed in the early days of computer control that failed to deliver as promised; it may take a generation to overcome this resistance.

Part of the resistance to advanced control systems is technological. It is economically difficult to provide systems that are reliable and maintainable. It may well be technically feasible to achieve the required degree of reliability, but for some applications such systems are so expensive they are no longer practical. The lack of standardization in control systems and plant designs poses yet another problem. Because each control system is custom designed, it is difficult to automate design. Great engineering talent, for instance, is often wasted making routine decisions on matters such as the size of valves. If some of these routine decisions could be automated, the productivity of a systems engineering team could be increased substantially.

The lack of key sensors can prevent the installation of advanced control systems. We need better, more reliable, fundamental measurements of the composition and condition of material being processed. We need direct measurements of the quality of final products. For every achievement of an unattended industrial plant, suitable solutions have been available to the problem of directly measuring the quality of the final product. Another factor that slows acceptance of advanced control systems is the availability of other ways for plants to solve their problems. The company that makes a product is concerned primarily with making enough material that meets the specifications and satisfying its customers: it often has a number of options for solving these problems, only one of which is more automation.

The factors that influence acceptance of advanced automation can be explained by means of a model based on an analogy to the flow of a fluid through two branches in a flow network (Fig. 3.4). The model mimics

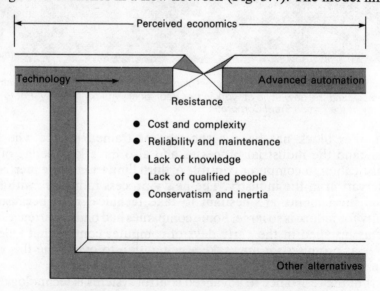

Fig. 3.4 Model of factors influencing acceptance of advanced automation

the application of resources to solve process problems. These resources may flow along the path towards advanced automation, or they may flow towards other alternatives.

The driving force is the economic perceptions of the industry. The resistance to the application of advanced automation involves such perceived risk factors as the cost and complexity of control, the lack of systems that are reliable and maintainable, the lack of understanding of the process to be controlled, the lack of qualified, experienced technical people, and the conservatism and inertia of the industry. The other alternatives towards which resources may be directed include adopting a different process, using a new raw material, changing the business plan, finding an alternative market for a product, and negotiating a revised labour contract.

Conclusions and future directions
The major driving force for acceptance of advanced automation will continue to be the perception of economic benefits by the users. As the cost of control hardware decreases, the economic forces increase. The resistance is steadily being reduced by new technology and by education. Therefore we can expect a continued evolutionary introduction of advanced control in industry but no revolutionary change.

Research and development should focus on reduction of the resistance. Work should be aimed at systems that have increased reliability and maintainability, reduced cost and complexity, require less expertise to implement, are explainable to users with limited sophistication and knowledge, and can be implemented in an evolutionary fashion. There is need for education of potential users and for increased standardization whenever possible.

These are exciting times for workers in the field of industrial process control. There are great opportunities for improved operation of industrial plants by means of advanced automation. The revolutionary developments in electronics now becoming commercially established are apt to greatly accelerate the evolutionary change in process control in the next five to ten years.

Microcomputers in the Classroom

Philip Venning

Early attempts to introduce computerized educational technology into the classroom met with little success, but the cheaper, more reliable and more versatile microelectronic gadgetry stands a much better chance. However, as Philip Venning points out in this report, which first appeared in The Times Educational Supplement *of 20 October 1978, it seems unlikely that many teachers will lose their jobs over it.*

Electronics are about to transform our whole way of life, but Britain could miss out on many of the benefits if our education and training system fails to produce enough skilled people.

In the next twenty-five years virtually everything we do – from the way we work to the goods we buy – will be blessed or blighted (depending on your viewpoint) by the microprocessor, a component so small and so cheap as to be almost insignificant, but with the power and versatility of an old-fashioned computer. The potential of the micro-processor, a tiny silicon chip on which thousands of circuits are etched, lies in the fact that it can control almost anything.

The technological ostriches admit its wizardry but doubt its effects. They expect its progress to be slow, its influence to be no wider than any other specialized technological advance. So far its impact has been in trivial fields. Calculators, digital watches and television games may be little more than frippery, but they are the heralds of a trend – already planned in factories throughout the developed world – to include it in a vast range of normal consumer products.

But its real importance is in its power to make automation – that mirage of the 1950s and 1960s – an almost immediate reality. The Cabinet is now seriously worried about the danger of mass unemployment resulting from the rapid introduction of "chips" to manufacturing processes. The alternative is even less attractive. Japan, the United States and leading European countries are already so far committed to microelectronics that British industry must either follow or perish. We can go forward or back, but we cannot stay where we are. If we do decide to join the race, and the government has accepted that we have no option, we have urgent ground to make up.

Education has been singled out as one of the crucial areas for attention, and the Department of Education and Science has already set up three working groups to look into short, medium and long-term effects on education of the micro revolution.

There is, of course, a danger that once again too much may be expected of education. But there is no doubt that among the main things that will hold us back are a shortage of skilled designers, technicians, technologists and engineers to install the new automated machinery, and antiquated attitudes to the new hardware among management.

But, just because the most obvious areas for action are in the further, higher and adult education system, the schools should not be sitting back. Their pupils will increasingly be entering a world where traditional skills and attitudes are inappropriate. The answer is not simply a matter of shoving one new lesson on microelectronics into the general studies slot. Some fairly substantial changes in school, university and college teaching methods and syllabuses will be needed, and planning for these must begin without delay. The education system works too slowly to allow it time to wait and see.

Indeed the new technology may have an effect on schooling itself. Programmed learning may suddenly find a new acceptability in the home as the consumer market is increasingly flooded with cheap do-it-yourself learning toys, games and gadgets; while in the long term, as industry dispenses with labour, public services such as education may be expanded substantially and class sizes of half a dozen might become quite normal.

Within the next few months a surge of amazing new gadgets will herald the most dramatic revolution in home learning since the invention of the book. Or so the chipmakers hope to convince us. For to survive they have to be on permanent lookout for products where demand is likely to be in millions or hundreds of millions. With world demand for simple calculators sated, an obvious next step is to move more explicitly into education.

Many of the imminent devices are merely calculators adapted for different uses, often including an A to Z keyboard instead of or as well as the familiar numerals. Later this year Texas Instruments, the American giant, will be launching an English version of a speaking machine known as Speak and Spell. Aimed at children aged seven to twelve, it is designed to teach them how to spell and pronounce more than 200 basic words. "They include words most frequently mis-spelled from kindergarten days into adulthood – words like anxious, ocean, language, obey and learn."

The machine, the size of a large book, randomly pronounces a word. In the version on sale in the United States this is, not surprisingly, in standard American English – hence the need for the British adaptation. The child then tries to spell the word by typing the spelling on to the screen (limited at the moment to eight-letter words). Right answers earn verbal and visual praise. A wrong answer and the child is encouraged to try again. A Speak and Spell student progresses through four levels of more than fifty words each, working at his own pace.

Now this is nothing more nor less than a simple version of good old-fashioned programmed learning. But with a huge difference. The machine sells in the United States for only £25 (and is likely to come down further as sales take off) and is clearly intended to be as common in the home as power tools or food mixers. And with more sophisticated versions of the idea almost certainly in preparation, the big chipmakers will have a vast financial incentive to make sure the software – the actual educational content – is fun and effective. No parent is going to shell out for each new improvement (imagine the traditional toy cupboard full of discarded electronic gadgets once the novelty has worn off) unless they do the job.

Texas Instruments, whose power to shape our spending and leisure patterns in the future is vast, are so convinced of the home study uses of the chip that they have organized a Learning Centre to supervise their five educational machines. As well as Speak and Spell, another spelling device known as Spelling Bee should soon be in the shops.

In the same tradition as calculators, which replaced slide rules overnight, electronics may soon take over from dictionaries. The Lexington Corporation of Miami, Florida, for example, will shortly be launching a calculator-like machine which will translate 1500 commonly-used words or phrases from one language to another from a choice of twelve. Although it is mainly intended for businessmen travelling abroad, some development of the idea for classroom use seems inevitable. Wisely, the manufacturers realized early on that only a dedicated minority would pay for, and force their children to use, a machine that was purely educational in a narrow, formal way. So to guarantee the mass market, they are busy disguising new hardware as educational games or toys (keeps the children happy and the educational content helps parents justify spending the money).

The Mego Corporation of New York, for example, has produced

something known as 2-XL, that looks like a talking robot. Though using microprocessors, it is not a relation of the calculator, but a glorified eight-track tape recorder. Pre-programmed tracks give the machine a personality, and it asks the user simple educational questions in a multiple-choice format. When no answer is attempted, the machine becomes "bored" and snores out loud, and it also sings songs and tells jokes.

Ingenious though all these devices are, they tend to be restricted by the size of their memories and, in the case of the calculator-based machines, by the amount of information they can process and display on their screens. If programmed learning in the home is to become anything more than next year's minor fad, it needs something a great deal more powerful. Which is where the domestic television and the home computer come in.

Everyone will be aware of the television games now on the market – by plugging a special unit into a normal television it is possible to play table tennis and a host of simulated sports. These, too, are probably only in their infancy. More complicated types come regularly on to the market. In Britain the imported Fairchild Grandstand offers a choice of twenty-four programs, two of which are elementary maths quizzes. More elaborate hardware and software are on sale in the United States and are under further development in laboratories throughout the industrial world.

But the real impact of the chip on home learning is probably still anything from a year to three years off, when the complete home computer – a logical extension of television game systems – will start appearing in more prosperous homes throughout the country.

The objections are immediately obvious. Who on earth wants a household computer that initially at least can do little more than work out household accounts, remember birthdays, and perhaps control the central heating? Though no one expected pretty useless machines like calculators and digital watches to catch on the way they did, household computers are likely to be expensive enough to be beyond the reach of casual fashion to start with, at least. Nevertheless, the home computer revolution is virtually unavoidable. It is already well established in the United States, where the market is likely to be worth nearly £200m a year by 1980. And Texas Instruments, amid great secrecy, is pouring huge sums into the development of its own home computer.

For nearly ten years the industrialized countries have been looking for a new generation of mass consumer products to succeed the car, washing machine, refrigerator, TV and similar industries which gave the rapid postwar economic growth. These markets are now stable – what use is a second fridge? – and real wages are rising. Rather than choosing overtime, people seem unwilling to shift from the traditional pattern of spending more and more on material goods, however questionable their utility. The microcomputer is clearly the first of the new generation.

At well under £1000 (the price of a foreign holiday for a family) there are bound to be prosperous households keen to try the latest hardware. And education will be an important rationale. The manufacturers will be keen to show the value of the computers in presenting relatively sophisticated programmed learning, suitable for all age groups. And as more development goes into the production of program learning material (a new source of employment for teachers?), it will become increasingly common for parents to see the computer as just another educational expense such as a school trip or musical instrument. With inflation and the falling price of chip-based technology, the costs should quickly be much the same.

Another technological advance which also professes value in home education is teletext, the use of the TV screen to show "pages" of printed information. The two systems which use broadcast information, BBC's Ceefax and ITV's Oracle, appear to be too limited to have much direct instructional use.

By contrast the Post Office system Prestel (formerly Viewdata), which links the user's own TV set with a central mainframe computer via the telephone, looks more possible. In due course the person at home should be able to "interact" with the computer and this may allow some form of programmed learning. This might enable educational entrepreneurs to sell educational courses of a fairly simple nature, linked in some cases to normal educational television programmes. But the costs and the technology are still too unclear to indicate whether this could be educationally significant.

If we are going to be offered all these splendid chances to learn at home, what role does this leave for the schools? Should the schools themselves be buying all this new hardware? Was the huge National Development Programme in Computer-Assisted Learning, which reached cautious conclusions about the value of computer-assisted learning in the classroom, really ten years too early?

It would be dangerous to assume that because technology will eventually provide better opportunities for certain types of study, everyone will suddenly give up their spare time to become swots, however attractively the learning is packaged. A whole range of aids to home study already exist – foreign language record systems, educational broadcasts, and perhaps the most efficient of do-it-yourself learning devices, the book. But we are not as a whole a nation of home study freaks.

What seems likely is that children from homes where they are encouraged to use the machines, presumably the same homes where books will be found, may arrive at school better versed in some aspects of their subjects. But like all home study, such as exam coaching in the holidays, there may well be a conflict between the educational programme available on the microcomputer at home and the teaching methods and syllabus used by the school.

Are the schools then the real place to benefit from the new, possibly improved and certainly cheaper teaching machines? Is it time to reinstate the long-discarded vision of a happy classroom presided over by a creative caring teacher where all the educational drudgery is done by machine?

One of the main conclusions of the NDPCAL study was that cost was a substantial obstacle to the wider use of computer-based instruction. But Richard Hooper, former director of the project, does not believe that chips will bring about the long-awaited revolution. "The experience of educational broadcasting here and in America is not encouraging. Educational broadcasting is cheap but it has not brought the revolution."

While recognizing the likelihood of a big increase in informal education and distance learning, he is sceptical about the willingness of schools to use the new equipment. If there was any suggestion that machines might replace teachers – the old 1950s prophecy – it would be strongly opposed by the unions at a time of teacher surplus. And as the chip brings automation to industry, labour-intensive services such as education would be likely to expand. He thinks the trend is likely to be greater public spending on more teachers rather than on hardware.

Computers would play an increasing part in many subjects, particularly in the upper forms of secondary schools, but their value would be as an aid. Schools would undoubtedly buy the microcomputers, but the weakness of direct teaching by machine would remain the software. The danger was that schools would see the price of micros falling to £600 and go ahead and buy. As with language laboratories, the school was then likely to discover it had not the staff capable of writing the programs.

If programmed learning does become a reality either in the home or classroom there will be a vital need not to leave the software production to the American hardware makers. American programmed learning material to date is of very dubious quality. Britain does seem to have some expertise in software fields, and educational publishers and academic institutions will no doubt be quick to produce their own transferable packages. Some moves are already being made in this direction. But this will depend on the extent to which the different systems available to schools are compatible. Richard Hooper fears that huge sums may be wasted by local authorities on hardware that remains in the cupboard for want of transferable software.

But if programmed learning is not strictly suitable for conventional academic education, it has a clear and obvious job to do in industrial and vocational training. Computer simulations are ideally suited to some kinds of training and the widespread use of the micros in further education colleges, on employers' premises and in Skillcentres is inevitable.

The new technology also has a highly significant job to do in educating the handicapped or those with special learning difficulties – ranging from programmed learning down to devices that aid a child overcome its physical handicap.

Guide to Further Reading

The paper by Russo *et al.* reprinted in part above appears in a volume of IEEE papers – *Proceedings of the IEEE*, vol. 66, No. 2 (February 1978) – which includes John Marley of Motorola on the use of microprocessors in cars and William C. Randle and Norm Kerth of Tektronix on their application to instrumentation. Dan C. Stanzione of Bell Laboratories looks at the use of microprocessors in the fast-growing telecommunications industry and new products like the transaction telephone.

The Applications of Semiconductor Technology is the famous report of the British government's Advisory Council for Applied Research and Development (Cabinet Office, HMSO, London, September 1978), which revealed to many people for the first time the impact that microelectronics will have on industry. It chronicled Britain's lack of readiness and urged an immediate campaign to promote the application of MOS technology in British products and to spread awareness of the changes to come.

But the thing to really get hold of is *Microprocessor Applications – Cases and Observations*, by Robert T. Lund, Marvin A. Sirbu Jr, James M. Utterback and others from the Massachusetts Institute of Technology. This lengthy report was prepared for the Office of the Chief Scientist and Engineer at the Department of Industry, London, and delivered in June 1979. It remains unpublished. The MIT researchers looked at eight products, ranging from sewing machines and hydraulic cranes to fuel injection systems for cars and heating and ventilation controls, and examined the process by which the firms involved introduced microelectronics to their products to make them "smart". Apart from the design and development phases of each project, the report gives special attention to the marketing strategies employed by the companies. The report concludes that firms which do not innovate by plunging into microelectronics will not maintain their market position and in the long term will probably not survive.

An early piece on the same theme, and something of a little classic, is "How Microprocessors Boost Profits" by William Davidow, which appeared in *Electronics* magazine, 11 July 1974. W. Harding, "Microprocessors Beyond

159

the Price Tag", *Machine Design*, 49, No. 10 (1977), also outlines the advantages of microprocessor-based products.

"The Application of Microprocessors" was the title of a (so far unpublished) paper given to the Royal Society in London in February 1979 by Professor John Westcott, Head of the Department of Computing and Control at London's Imperial College. Westcott emphasizes in particular the role of the microprocessor in manufacturing, process control and instrumentation, arguing that their rapid incorporation into products and production processes is the key to future industrial efficiency.

An interesting paper by Malcolm Peltu, former editor of the British *Computer Weekly*, delivered to a conference at South Bank Polytechnic, London, in July 1978, argued that the big companies will determine needs and the rate of absorption of chip-based products. Market forces and the marketing men are "the decisive influences in shaping the future".

This was a point not lost on the Stanford Research Institute, whose *Microprocessor Applications in Western Europe* is paper no. 1027 in their "Business Intelligence Programme" (February 1978).

Other useful articles or books on microprocessor applications include:

D. Aspinall (ed.), *The Microprocessor and Its Application* (Cambridge University Press, London, 1978).

"Computer-Aided Design" by anonymous authors at the Computer-Aided Design Centre in *Computer Technology and Employment* (National Computing Centre Publications, Manchester, UK, 1979).

J. Crudele, "Consumer Electronics", *Electronic Engineering Times*, 4 April 1977.

M. Hessey, "The Application of Microprocessors to Materials Handling", in *Management Services* (December 1978).

P. J. Klass, "Major Impact Seen in Microprocessors", *Aviation Weekly*, 31 May 1976.

B. Le Boss, "Microprocessor Sparks a Quiet Revolution in Instrumentation", *Electronics News*, 4 August 1975.

Daniel McGlynn, *Personal Computing* (Wiley, New York, 1980).

D. Moberg, "Medical Applications of Microcomputers", *Interface Age*, 3, No. 7 (July 1978).

"Video Games: A Struggle for High Stakes", author anonymous, *Business Week*, 17 January 1977.

The *Financial Times* has annual supplements on Mobile Communications, Viewdata and Video Systems.

Three useful articles appeared in *Electronics*: "LSI Chips Taking Over More Household Chores" by G. M. Walker (28 October 1976); "LSI Controls Gaining in Home Appliances" by the same author (14 April 1977); and "Electronic Games No Longer Need TV" by A. Rosenblatt (18 August 1977).

A personal favourite is "Beer Blending With Microprocessors" by E. Valentine, *Electronics and Power* (March 1978). The author demonstrates how chips can be used to brew a better beer, a revelation that will surely win over any remaining sceptics.

On educational applications, it may be worth consulting Tom Whiston, Peter Senker and Petrine Macdonald, *An Annotated Bibliography on the Relationship Between Technological Change and Educational Development* (Science Policy Research Unit, Sussex University, December 1978). But more readable introductions may be found in "The Micros Take to the Classroom", *Business Week*, 23 July 1979, C. Doerr, *Microcomputers and the 3Rs: A Guide for Teachers* (Hayden, Rochelle Park, New Jersey, 1979) and Peter Marsh, "Rise of the Teaching Machine", *New Scientist*, 3 May 1979.

The laser scanning revolution in supermarkets – sometimes referred to as the "counter revolution" – is dealt with in Amanda Spake, "The Real Supermarket Sweepstakes", *Mother Jones* (San Francisco, June 1978); in a pamphlet by Donald Harris, *Retailing in the Eighties – The Challenge of the Chip* (Tesco Stores, Cheshunt, Herts, December 1979); and by the editor of this volume in *Labour Weekly*, 21 March 1980.

Automobile applications are particularly well described in "How the Car Computer is Changing Detroit", *Business Week*, 22 October 1979, and Peter Marsh, "The Making of the Computerised Car", in *New Scientist*, 6 December 1979.

PART TWO: ECONOMIC AND SOCIAL IMPLICATIONS

4 The Impact in Industry

The Automated Factory

Neil P. Ruzic

We begin this chapter with a look into the future – or rather with a look at an experimental "unmanned" aircraft parts factory in St Louis, Missouri, an example of the shape of things to come. The author, who is director of the National Space Institute in Washington, argues that the acceleration of developments in microelectronics means that the completely automated manufacturing plant may not now be far off. The Japanese are in the lead and look like beating everyone else. This article first appeared in the US publication Control Engineering *in April 1978.*

Your first impression when you view the McDonnell Douglas parts fabrication plant in St Louis is the sheer size and loneliness of it all. Some two dozen acres of milling machines noisily grind grooves, slots and intricate patterns in airframe parts to a tolerance of 0·0025 inch. The machines, for the most part, work alone – watched by only a few men who glance occasionally at a control panel or sweep the cuttings.

Nor are these men in charge here. The machine tools are directed by numerical controllers, which in turn are directed by a whole hierarchy of computers presided over by a master computer. This 750,000 sq. ft aircraft parts plant is among the most advanced computer-aided manufacturing factories in the world. But it is far from unusual. Highly automated plants elsewhere in the US, Japan, and Europe turn out automobiles, engines, earth movers, oilwell equipment, elevators, electrical products and machine tools. These plants – especially in Japan – are well on their way to evolving into what had been a dream for two decades: the automated factory.

165

The space contribution
"Unmanned manufacturing" may be a logical contradiction since "manufacturing" literally means "making by hand". But it is a perfect description of the goal of many companies throughout the world. The concept had its beginnings some twenty-five years ago when numerical control tapes and computer graphics using light-pens first entered the manufacturing process. These rudimentary automatons were given a powerful stimulus throughout the 1960s as we entered the space age full force.

The sudden acceleration in the reliability and sophistication of all kinds of machines, especially computers and adaptive controllers, was a direct offshoot of NASA's zero-defects philosophy required by manned space flight. The forcing function of stringent space requirements imposed computers on American industry, and in the process they increased not just reliability of machines but efficiency and economy as well. As one measure of their success, computers today are growing at the rate of forty per cent a year (seventy per cent a year in industrial control). Within a few years, we will have a million installed in industrial control alone. US computer exports increased 1400 per cent in the first decade of the space age and virtually every major computer in the world is American-made.

All that was just the beginning of the transfer of space technology to the automated factory. Since then the space agency had been deliberately applying its technology to industrial processes. A group within NASA called the Technology Utilisation Branch is charged with carrying out part of the Congressional mandate imposed when the agency was established, namely to transfer space technology to industry. In that way, the government attempts to derive double benefit from tax-paid R&D money.

The emergence of computers was a response to our need to derive complex systems for space travel and at the same time was a result of technical information transferred. Take it a step further and you can see how the elaborate advances in computers now have magnified productivity throughout the world in all industries that use computers – and that means just about all industries.

Three breakthroughs
In the slow but inexorable evolution of the unmanned factory, the first segment of the manufacturing process to become computer-aided was the fabrication machines that mill, drill, tap and otherwise form intricate parts from castings or forgings. The breakthrough responsible was direct numerical control, in which a general-purpose computer is connected directly to several numerically controlled machine tools. At

McDonnell Douglas, about a hundred machine tools are under direct control, or soon will be. These machines range from very large multi-spindle multi-axis profilers to point-to-point drills.

Soon thereafter came computer-assisted design engineering. Both CRT (cathode-ray tube) light-pens and sophisticated flexible computer programs adaptable to a variety of design problems made it possible. Engineers now could draw their modifications directly on the tube. And programs such as NASRAN (NASA Structural Analysis – which is designed to analyse the behaviour of dynamic or static structures of any size, shape, or purpose – began to save millions of engineering design dollars each year.

The third entrant to computer-aided manufacturing was the adaptive control system. Here both the speed and feed of a cutting tool are adjusted automatically from the environmental cutting conditions such as deflection torque, and heat generated. In other words, environmental conditions feed back to the controller to determine what action is to be taken.

Planning the process
With these breakthroughs you now could design by computer and produce parts by computer. The large step in between – process planning – was next to undergo the rigorous definitions and thought disciplines inherent in computerization.

"Companies make or lose money on the effectiveness of their process planning," according to Louis N. Mogavero, chief of NASA's Technology Utilization Branch. Mogavero should know. Prior to coming to the space agency he was in charge of process planning at Vertol Corp. (a Boeing subsidiary) in Morton, PA. An entire floor of engineers and technicians he directed now have had their jobs upgraded as computers have largely taken over the process planning function.

In order to help push the state of the art and help transfer space-derived computer technology to industry, Mogavero's office last year supported a project at McDonnell Douglas Automation Co. in St Louis. NASA invested funds and expertise that were matched by a unique organization called Computer Aided Manufacturing International. CAMI is a nonprofit R&D association based in Arlington, Texas, with 106 company and university members throughout the world concerned with applying computers to manufacturing.

Success stories involving computerized manufacturing have over-simplified the difficulties in achieving such successes. Thus CAMI both creates and disseminates information in an attempt to solve many fundamental problems in automating the various plants of its members. For instance, the NASA-CAMI-funded project at McDonnell Douglas sought to automate the process planning phase in such a way that it could serve as a model for other manufacturers across diverse industries.

Today, as a result of that and similar projects, the entire spectrum of planning and producing a manufactured part is automated at McDonnell, both for greater economy and higher reliability. In fact, the Department of Defence credits computer-aided design and manufacturing here as being mostly responsible for the air superiority of the F-15 Eagle.

The automation of process planning is considerably easier in plants that produce parts in great volume such as for automobiles. However, through the ingenuity of computer experts this technology also now can be used in small-volume plants. The complex fighter planes that cost $10m or more each require relatively low-volume production, for instance. In fact, seventy-five per cent of all parts made in the US are made in quantities of fifty or less. The emphasis thus has had to be on flexible methods of planning batch manufacturing. One approach is to program machine tools to carry out different operations on a variety of parts with minimum human supervision.

Another is to redesign the part so it will fit existing machines. When engineers in an aircraft or other plant design a new machine, they invariably call for a host of entirely new parts. Then the process planners (who used to be called production engineers) redesign the part so it can be made faster or more simply, perhaps on available machine tools, or in combination with other parts. They establish a plan by which the part is made. The "process plan", for instance, specifies whether the part is to be made of titanium rather than aluminium, how it will be milled, which fixtures and jigs will accept it, how it is to be heat-treated and how, where, and when it will be sent for assembly.

Finding common denominators

To automate that process, planners seek the common denominator among different parts. "You would be surprised," says Mogavero, "at the tremendous similarity among parts, even from one complex modern aircraft to another." Mogavero, who helped develop the idea of reproducibility in the early 1950s, simply extended the mass production premise that "You have to make a lot of the same part to make money."

Today, where process planning is automated, all parts that have been made for any product are defined and stored in the computer. The size, function, and other parameters of any part can be recalled and modified if necessary to fit the new requirement.

Yet reproducibility is only one ingredient in commercializing a product. Even if you can reproduce machined parts like a biological organism – by the millions – you still need to examine the market, the capital investment required, and other economic factors. "Engineers are notorious for tunnel vision," according to Mogavero, who himself is an engineer. "We normally think about *how* you can make something – not how you can make it *profitably*."

McDonnell Douglas' system

Process planning is the key to intricate manufacturing procedures. An example of how process planning integrates various manufacturing operations is offered by J. H. Schulz, director of industrial engineering at the McDonnell St Louis plant. Here parts fabrication is housed in a 750,000 sq. ft building. Major and final assembly buildings containing another million sq. ft each are nearby. In recent years the plant has turned out about 5000 F-4 Phantom airplanes, lesser numbers of F-3H Banshees and F-101 Voodoos in the 1950s and 1960s and, currently, F-15 Eagles.

Schulz explains that computer-aided manufacturing has resulted in greater design freedom, better management control, shorter lead time, greater operating flexibility, improved reliability, reduced maintenance, reduced scrap and rework, and – as a result – increased productivity.

Design freedom. It doesn't do much good to design a complex part if it cannot be made efficiently. Graphic numerical control, in which the mathematical representation is stored in the computer's memory, allows process planners to produce the part.

The parts programmer accesses this same data to design the required fixturing, and then uses graphics to create the part programs to fabricate the tooling. Finally, the quality assurance programmer, also using a CRT terminal, accesses the data to create a program for inspecting the part. Thus, computer graphics not only allows more complex parts design, but also reduces costs and time.

Adaptive control provides better part tolerances and guarantees that a given accuracy will be met, thus reducing rejects. Since the human machinist cannot override the feed rate, adaptive control also improves part run time. Another system, fondly called "IRS" for "Improved Reliability System", assures that part tolerances are not violated. These systems result in twenty per cent more production.

Shorter lead times. Two factors shorten lead times: the design and programming of the part, and actual time required to fabricate the product. Time to produce a good parts program is substantially shortened through both the graphic numerical control and a remote processing system called "RAPID". RAPID is a tortured acronym containing an acronym: "Remote APT (Automatically Programmed Tools) Processing via Interactive Devices". Parts programs are created with coding manuscripts and the jobs are submitted to the computer in batch mode.

The parts program is stored in an on-line data-base for retrieval through a CRT display. The parts program is viewed, modified, and processed. Its output is reviewed and placed in a retrieval queue, all interactively from the display. When the programmer is satisfied with his program, he transmits it to the large computer for plotting. These systems facilitate the incorporation of engineering changes to existing parts, eliminating the confusion and sometimes panic of pre-automated times.

Greater operating flexibility is achieved by having the computer in the loop. A job can be transferred from one machine to another in minutes using direct numerical control. Changes can be made in programs and the machining cycle restarted in minutes. The tedious task of book-keeping parts programs is handled automatically by the computer assuring that only the properly updated command information is delivered to the shop floor.

Improved reliability is effected through several programs, of which the conversion to direct numerical control is the most significant. A recent analysis revealed a fifty-five per cent improvement in scrap rate on those machines converted to direct numerical control. It is the mission of the direct numerical controller and the improved reliability system to ensure that the programmed data reliably cut the part once the information arrives at the machine tool.

Redundant data checks are built into the master computer (IBM 370), through the process-control computer (IBM 1800), down to the controller on the floor, thus increasing reliability. An information-management system upgrades the reliability of the initial data used to produce the part. This system assures that a valid parts program, with no unexpected changes, is being sent to the machine tool.

Reduced maintenance is the result of many factors. Direct numerical control entirely eliminates the high-maintenance tape reader of a conventional numerically controlled machine. Integrated circuits in the controllers have fewer malfunctions. And since most of the logic functions are accomplished in the minicomputer, less hardware is employed in the controller.

Less scrap. A machine tool run by a direct numerical controller and integrated into the improved reliability system virtually eliminates all scrap and rework. During the first month of operating a profiler watchdogged by the improved reliability system, two events took place that would have scrapped three F-15 titanium bulkheads and two DC-10 flap hinge fittings if the system had not shut down the machine. Value of the parts was $80,000. Cost of installing the improved reliability system was $20,000 per machine.

Higher productivity. The pressure to deliver reliable, highly sophisticated fighting-flying machines mandates objectives of increased productivity. Of course, in a broad sense, increased productivity is the goal of all manufacturing efforts. At McDonnell Douglas, it is attained with adaptive control because the machines can cut metal faster and more efficiently. And parts programs are optimized even further using the RAPID system.

But another way of increasing productivity is to reduce "dead time": the time a machine is not working, caused by controllable factors such as lack of cutters, fixtures, or materials. Dead time at McDonnell was seven per cent before a management data-reporting system was automated. Devices for manually entering information were provided on the direct numerical controller console and provisions made to sense certain machine conditions automatically. The result is series of management reports indicating production bottlenecks – which still occur now, but considerably less frequently than before.

Progress by the centimetre
The McDonnell Douglas progression towards the automated factory is fairly typical, although more advanced, than at the average airplane, car parts, or machinery producers. Such manufacturers as Otis Engineering, Caterpillar Tractor, Ingersoll-Rand, Sundstrand and Allis-Chalmers have automated their batch manufacturing processes quite ingeniously. Computers select parts from a transfer line and feed them to the cutting machines that mill, bore, turn, tap, and drill – all automatically.

Yet, all of these operations are experienced-based. They must be programmed for a specific task and so can't be transferred directly to other situations without modifications. While these factories are relatively lonely places, they are not unmanned.

You get the feeling that a dramatic breakthrough is required, a fundamental change. If the machines were alive, you would say they need a dose of intelligence, a mutation into a higher being. Intelligent machines that sense, recognize, remember, learn by experience, and respond like a rudimentary human brain, the robots of tomorrow, are theoretically feasible. Self-organizing systems that learn from their environment and their experience have been demonstrated repeatedly for two decades in research laboratories. But there they remain, curiosities, unapplied to automated manufacturing.

The fact is that the United States – despite its enviable technological lead and despite a necessity mothered of high labour costs - is not pushing the unmanned factory any faster than other countries. The consensus at CAMI seems to be that Europe and the US are on a par, and that Japan is forging somewhat ahead.

The Japanese edge

Japan's fast-growing industrial capacity not only supplies an enlarged domestic market but makes it possible to compete in most other countries. Perhaps the incentive to boost productivity is greater in this single-minded island nation. Japan Inc. truly is an alliance of manufacturers and government, as opposed to the often antagonistic government–industry relationship in the more diversified United States.

Whatever the reason, unmanned manufacturing plants seem closer to achievement in Japan than in the rest of the world, according to several CAMI members. The Japanese Ministry of International Trade and Industry announced last year that the basic methodology for the unmanned factory has been completed. The statement implies utilization of a universal principle, which is to be demonstrated by 1980, with the first factories operational by 1990.

The unmanned plant the Japanese are considering need employ only one per cent of a conventional plant's labour force. Twenty people would operate a factory that employed 2000 workers in pre-automation days. Not only will such a plant automate the design, process planning, and fabrication functions, but it also will bring the entire assembly operation under computer control.

Already at several factories operated by the $6-billion-a-year Hitachi Ltd, and by the Honda Motor Co., subassemblies are brought together on a conveyor line and held to each other by clamps. When the parts – electric machines or car body panels, for instance – reach a welding machine, hundreds of welding heats are aligned automatically and the parts are welded. Other conveyors and staging areas converge to put together many of the subassemblies. Direct numerical controlled machines are more commonplace than in the US or Europe. The whole country seems to be moving together towards a national goal of complete automation. First the tooling machines themselves are automated, then a group of machines, and finally the whole plant.

In the United States and Western Europe, a few sophisticated industries such as aircraft, car engines, farm equipment, electrical equipment or machine tools have highly automated plants. But other companies that make ships, homes, steel, textiles, or scientific instruments seem to employ almost as many people as they did in the days of Charles Dickens.

Despite that possibly exaggerated commentary, the automated factory continues its inexorable evolution. The trend is set. It simply may take longer in the United States and Europe. Some have predicted the first completely automated factories in the US by the mid-1990s, soon after the Japanese forecast.

Factors contributing to the trend towards unmanned manufacturing are everywhere evident:

Economic forces such as inflation and higher labour rates, along with increased governmental regulation per employee.

New generations of faster computers and more flexible software.

The spread of automation from industry to industry, such as the recent entry of computer-aided manufacturing in chemical processing.

Closer supervision of processes through the use of improved man/process interfaces.

Upgrading of numerically controlled machines to direct numerical controls.

The influx of microprocessors and chip technology.

A greater emphasis on the transfer of money-saving, often advanced, space technologies to a variety of industrial processes.

That these trendlines are converging towards unmanned manufacturing – the most dramatic breakthrough since Henry Ford first harnessed a conveyor belt – is unmistakable. Only the timetable is in dispute.

Petfoods by Computer: A Case Study of Automation

Keith Dickson

Specially written for this volume, the following account shows what happens when a factory goes over to minicomputer-controlled production. The installation was a success in terms of productivity, but the impact on management, maintenance staff and in particular on the employment of non-unionized, hourly-paid unskilled production line workers was considerable. The author, who is with the Technology Policy Unit at the University of Aston, describes the progress of a "Manpower Reduction Programme" which aimed at reducing the number of jobs at the plant by 500.

This paper summarizes the findings of a four-month study into the strategy and impact of the introduction of automated food processing and canning facilities in the Pedigree Petfoods factory at Melton Mowbray, Leicestershire.*

The factory is by far the major source of employment in this small market town and the surrounding rural area. A medium-sized, privately owned company with 2500 employees, Pedigree Petfoods is totally concerned with the manufacture of petfoods, including a wide variety of both canned and dry products (dog biscuits, bird seed, and so on). With an annual growth rate of about ten per cent (in terms of output), it currently holds over sixty per cent of the total UK canned petfood market – a market, incidentally, which is forecast to continue expanding for many years. Such a situation permits both an expansionist and an innovative approach to company operations, so that a heavy investment programme involving capital-intensive and novel technology, as was the

* Acknowledgement of their cooperation and permission to publish is gratefully extended.

174

case with the introduction of automation in 1978, clearly becomes feasible.

Petfood manufacture is essentially a "simple" process of preparing the raw materials (offal, fish, cereals, gravy, and so on), combining them according to a formula and canning the mixture. The sealed cans are then sterilized, labelled and packed. Once canned, processing of the product is relatively straightforward and has been automated for years. It is the weighing, handling and mixing of the raw materials, the "pre-can" stages of production, that have only recently been automated.

Technically, the major differences between the old and the new systems are the mechanized materials-handling system and the computerized control system. With the latter, all aspects of the process are controlled by the minicomputer system, ranging from the automatic periodic "feeding" of specified quantitities of each raw material into the bunkers and mixers, to the recording and analysis of all relevant production data. Eventually, it is envisaged that the whole organization will be connected by a network of computers so that sales figures, production details, storage data and so on will be continuously and interactively analysed and acted upon.

In terms of production, the new automated system offers further advantages in, for example, production capacity, where the mixers now handle twice the load, and in line speeds, where the automated line is able to process over 1000 cans per minute compared with the previous limit of around 800. In design concept, however, there is a more fundamental difference, for whereas the former, conventional system consisted of discrete units of equipment brought together, the new line is completely integrated. This new holistic approach is an example of the trend towards "systems" thinking in production.

Motivation and justification for automation

Two central themes seemed to have dominated the motivation for introducing automated facilities – the desire for modernization and the need for a long-term site development strategy. During the previous fifteen or so years, the factory had grown rapidly but haphazardly, with a labour force which had been continuously increasing in numbers. Inevitably, the factory environment suffered. Modernization was seen as offering a solution by upgrading the production facilities, improving the working conditions and, with a long-term view to automation, reducing labour numbers and so improving productivity. Site development would rationalize and integrate the layout, enable the modernization plans to progress efficiently, and significantly increase the potential for further site expansion. These two themes were articulated in proposals for the five-year Capital Investment Programme (1976–81), which put forward the initial proposal to build automated canning lines, the first of which was to be completed in 1978 with another possible three new lines to follow.

Though automation was "sold" as part of this modernization programme, it also had to be seen as a commercially viable venture in its own right, as well as being politically acceptable within the parent organization. Commercial justification alone was not sufficient either, for it was dominated by the other two factors just mentioned, so that the factory management had to primarily demonstrate to Head Office their commitment and confidence in the long-term site development strategy, and that automation was a necessary, integral part of that strategy. As one manager remembered it: "The figures weren't really that important, they can always be bent in so many ways. A project is much more subjective than that."

While these figures did eventually turn out to be inaccurate, due to a drastic underestimation of inflation among other things, the commercial justification remained, though somewhat undermined to the extent that management had to seek Head Office approval for further project modifications in order to meet the cash ceiling limits for the project. Nevertheless, there were still strong manufacturing reasons for automated production. For example, factory capacity with the existing facilities was near its limit, unsatisfactory working conditions could only have been improved through dramatic modernization, and, most importantly, the labour-saving potential of automated production with its long-term implications for manpower levels were all put forward as major justifications. Interestingly, the stronger commercial option of a greenfield development was not chosen because of the personnel problems it would have created in "running down" the Melton site – further evidence, clearly, of the commitment to that site.

Technological sophistication and elegance did not feature as strong influences other than as necessary adjuncts to the modernization programme (arising, for example, from the priority for human food standards in production demanded by senior management). However, the electronic controls and the computer systems were seen as something akin to "magic black boxes".

Strategy
The period of time from initial approval to completion of the project was unusually short, so that a high degree of organization and coordination was crucial. Computerized network analyses and design simulations, innovations in themselves, were aids in this respect, but very deliberate efforts were also made to publicize the project in the best light in order to ensure the support and participation of all personnel,

thereby minimizing any resistance. At management level, therefore, the project's viability was emphasized in terms of increased productivity (a potent argument, since remuneration is related to company performance) and long-term development, while at shopfloor level emphasis was placed more on the potential for improved working conditions and continuing company prosperity. Resistance to development, stemming mainly from the Manpower Reduction Programme which had begun in 1974 and to which the automation project was to make a significant contribution, was defused by strong reassurances from management to the effect that labour reductions would only occur through natural wastage and voluntary redundancies.

A more positive strategy for overcoming resistance was the commitment that the new jobs created on the automated lines would be "better"(that is, more varied, less strenuous, cleaner, more stimulating, more highly paid and so on) than the existing positions. Upgrading of the jobs would lead, it was thought (correctly), to less indifference among the factory workers. General conservatism among employees, related in part to the large technological "jump" being made, also had to be overcome, particularly from maintenance and production managers who were sceptical of the viability of a wholly automated production system. By way of a compromise, the incorporation of a manual control option within the system overcame such resistance. Interestingly, it has been subsequently agreed that the second automated line presently under construction will not contain any manual control panels.

Another obstacle that occurred during the implementation period concerned contractors, particularly those associated with the electronic control systems and computer software, who readily "oversold" themselves in terms of their technical capability of producing the specified goods in the required time. Only with continual prodding of such people, full-time attention to coordination and an almost obsessive commitment to the timetable, was the initial project completed on time so that the first automated processing and canning line was fully operational by the end of 1978.

The impact on the organization and management

The automation project stimulated a series of reappraisals of the company's activities which generated a much more analytical approach to management and a greater confidence in sophisticated management systems. Given that the project's approval was an indication of commitment to that site and to company development in general, it is not surprising therefore that as the project progressed, more innovative activities were generated.

The company's organization is very flexible and dynamic, so that role demarcations are not rigid. Manager mobility between positions is a notable feature. Such organizational flexibility facilitated the response to the demands of the new technology, particularly in the maintenance and production departments, where the organizational structure became more functionally based rather than geographically based. Flexibility within the organization is also promoted by the frequent reliance on interdepartmental working parties, all the more noticeable since the inception of this project. Such a phenomenon has given rise to greater integration within the organization and tends to discourage tendencies towards overspecialization, rigid role definitions and hierarchical attitudes. Such working parties tended to aid the company's attempts towards participative management, and it did appear that their existence, and the participative management practices used, facilitated the introduction of the new technology, both physically and psychologically.

The influx of computer technology and its associated sophisticated electronics systems and techniques have resulted in a rise in the numbers of graduate managers and specialists in OR, systems analysis, and so on. While this has served to permanently introduce these new techniques into the company in such a manner that their practitioners are now having considerable influence in decision-making and planning, it has also tended to highlight the problem of "hierarchical estrangement" for the older, "shop-floor" managers and supervisors who have to increasingly deal with complex technology and with younger superiors and who, perhaps, have less inclination to accept new management techniques.

The computer technology has of course spread rapidly through the company, so that, for example, a computerized quality control information system and a computerized maintenance schedule are now used. It is this increased sophistication in management techniques that is the most significant organizational consequence, since much of it is irrevocable (the new technology, itself, being dependent on it), whereas other effects – the integration of functions or participative practices, for example – are dynamic features and may only be transitory.

Impact on production
Production management needed to make considerable adjustments in the face of the introduction of automated production lines. A line management structure was introduced (necessitated by the integrated nature of automated lines), a redistribution of manufacturing personnel occurred and is continuing to occur, and production planning methods were comprehensively re-evaluated. In this latter respect, much longer production runs were established (to maximize the utilization of the

facilities), thereby radically affecting both raw materials and finished goods storage policies. While this indicates the high priority and commitment to automation (since minimum stock levels had previously been a sacrosanct principle within the company), it also increased the predictability of production and the time horizon for planning, but at the same time reduced its flexibility. An example of this latter point may be seen in the manipulation of product formulations that had occurred in the past to accommodate raw material variations but which are no longer so possible with the automated equipment. This constraint on production flexibility must be seen as an important disadvantage of automation.

As a result of the expansive layout of the automated facilities and the relatively small numbers of employees in attendance, it was thought that general communications and employee interactions would be significantly impaired. To rectify this, an extensive intercom system as well as a video system have been installed.

Many of the new demands made upon production arise from the dramatic increases in output and line speeds resulting from automation. Meeting these demands (for example, can supply and accumulation problems, product consistency), has resulted in a general raising of efficiency not immediately associated with the advent of automation. In terms of product quality, for example, improvement occurred owing to less handling of raw materials and to more consistency in production, while more effective quality control was achieved with the introduction of new techniques and electronic equipment which gave greater control over production variances. On the other hand, the faster line speeds could threaten quality, since quicker response time to any deviation is required, while the degree of segregation of materials inside the can and the frequency of can seam defects appear to be functions of canning speed. Moreover, with much less opportunity for visual checking, quality control needs to be especially rigorous.

The first automated line will account for nearly twenty-five per cent of total production this year (1979) and will produce at least fifteen per cent more than any one of the conventional lines. But of course the really important difference is in productivity, since the new line produces its larger output with fewer operators (thus accelerating the already increasing productivity trend). On a direct line-to-line comparison, the automated line doubles the direct manufacturing labour productivity figure in terms of product weight per man-hour. Though the investment cost needed to achieve these increases was heavy, the production costs of the new line per unit weight of output are lower than those of the conventional lines, so that the total company manufacturing costs per unit weight of output are expected to decline as more of the production becomes automated.

Impact on employment

The company's emphasis on employee participation, combined with a generous, paternalistic approach to employees, has resulted in a strong loyalty and a predominant attitude among both managers and employees that there is no need for any externally organized collective representation.* The absence of unions is significant in view of the rapidity of the recent technological changes, their consequential effects on manpower and the flexible attitude of workers towards their introduction. Such flexibility has permitted, for example, considerable use of temporary labour during the introductory period of the new automated facilities. Interestingly, a recent increase in union activity has been noticed, because the introduction of automation and the Manpower Reduction Programme (MRP) have given the unions more opportunity and leverage in attracting members based on the issue of future job security.

The MRP, initiated about the same time as the automation project, called for a reduction of 500 employees during the five-year period 1976–81. A large contribution to this programme would be made by new technology, particularly the automated facilities. By 1981, when production would have increased substantially if current growth trends continue, the level of employment in manufacturing would be seventy-five per cent of the 1976 level. However, to separate from this general trend the impact of the first automated line would be a complex task, since it would be difficult to assess the line's effect on indirect labour or the effect it has had in avoiding recruitment of those personnel otherwise needed to produce the extra output now produced by the new line. Its direct impact can, however, be seen in a comparison of line crew numbers (eight for the former canning lines, five for the automated line) which signifies an overall ten per cent reduction in the canning department workforce. (Two other major projects for new production facilities exhibit even greater manpower reduction, one being new automated packing facilities. These projects were not, however, part of this case study.)

The labour force in the factory is made up predominantly of unskilled, hourly-paid workers, and it is this group, rather than managerial and non-manufacturing personnel which has been most affected by the manpower reductions. This has resulted in significant changes, so that, for example, the ratio of managers to manufacturing workers will increase from 1 : 5 (in 1976) to an estimated 1 : 4 (in 1980). Similarly,

---

* A government Advisory, Conciliation and Arbitration Service survey concerning union recognition within Pedigree Petfoods, which had just been completed at the time of this case study, found a nine to one vote against union recognition by employees.

the proportion of manufacturing personnel in the total company work-force will decrease from over seventy-six per cent in 1976 to less than seventy per cent in 1980. Even within the manufacturing division there has been a redistribution of labour, indicated by a trend away from direct line production jobs into support services. This trend is also discernible at the "white collar" level, with a rapid increase in design and project personnel, accompanied by only a small increase in direct production management numbers.

Training and management development techniques have also been influenced by the technological change: a more conscious effort has been directed towards generating an anticipatory style of management (as distinct from a reactive style) which is thought to better serve the demands of long-term planning associated with automated technology. A spinoff from this new training approach, arising largely from the widespread publicity given to the project, has been a much greater awareness among workers of what is happening around them. This has resulted in more questions being asked, an increased propensity to absorb technical and commercial data, and a greater inclination to make formal suggestions. Training has also brought about a general upgrad-ing of skills for some groups, so that technicians now incorporate more complex diagnostic skills in their repertoire, while the new line workers carry out quality control activities in addition to their production duties.

The selection of technically unsophisticated supervisors to operate the automated line served to de-emphasize the technological "gap" between the old and the new lines – an important factor in the acceptance of the new situation, especially for the older workers. Nevertheless, the supervisors' responsibilities have increased, in terms of the amount of new equipment and the timespan of production under their control. In contrast, the ratio of supervisors to operators has decreased from about 1 : 25 to under 1 : 10.

For the production line workers selected, the new jobs represented a considerable promotion, since the new job specifications had been upgraded to include extra skills and variety of work. As a result of their special training and the publicity, the motivation and expectations of these workers were particularly high, so much so that there was a danger of creating an elite group within the workforce. In an attitudinal survey conducted during their training, they expressed great confidence in the new equipment, offered few negative opinions towards the new tech-nology, and, interestingly, thought that they would be more involved in decision-making over line operation, and that their control over the work rate would be increased.

To an outsider, these benefits are much less apparent than the vast improvement in the working environment. Since this was a major justification, this is how it should be. Such an improvement has also produced a much wider appreciation of the benefits of a safe and healthy environment, so much so that managers and designers now pay more than lip service to these aspects.

Impact on the maintenance function

Reorganization of the maintenance department was carried out in direct response to the new technology, for it was recognized that there were greater differences between the types of maintenance required for automated technology (repair maintenance and planned maintenance having become quite distinct activities) than between the different technologies and equipment on the various factory sites (computerized systems, for example, having been installed in various departments). Thus a change from geographical to functional organization was effected. The growing sophistication of maintenance activities (for example, the increasing use of vulnerability analyses and computerized maintenance schedules) is reflected in a comment by one maintenance manager that: "We're out of the era of intuitive maintenance now and into the era of analytical maintenance."

The shift towards more planned maintenance activities is such an analytical approach, brought about partly by the invasion of complex electronic equipment. Such a shift can be associated with the trend towards the increased predictability of production mentioned earlier.

As techniques have become more complex, employment in the maintenance department has intensified, so that the ratio of maintenance to production workers is steadily increasing (from 1 : 11 in 1978 to at least 1 : 9 in 1981). However, the categories of maintenance skills are changing, with the demise of refrigeration fitters' and machinists' posts and an increase in jobs for electricians and skilled electronics workers. Thus the balance between mechanical fitters on the one hand and electrical fitters and electronics workers on the other is gradually favouring the latter. Perhaps the most important change will result from the management's attempts to encourage multi-skilled, dual-role fitters who will combine both electrical and mechanical activities. In contrast, the demand for specialised expertise has been satisfied by the creation of more highly-graded electrical/electronics technician positions.

The attitudes of the various maintenance groups to the new technology appeared quite distinct: while the mechanical fitters exhibited general indifference (their side of the technology not being radically affected), the electrical fitters were particularly interested, for they perceived the introduction of electronics and of the automation technology as an opportunity for extending their role, and thus securing their future with the company. This perception of increased status is reflected in the lack of resistance to the transfer of simple, routine maintenance activities from themselves to the new line operators, an event which previously would have encountered strong resistance, no matter how insignificant the encroachment.

Summary
The success of the introduction of automated technology was clearly due to its timeliness, the intense commitment given to the project by management and its widespread positive publicity. This success can be gauged by the fact that such a dramatic technological "jump" occurred with few signs of resistance from employees. To continue in this vein will be a stern test for the future. The timeliness of the innovation arose from its immediate and complete integration into the company's long-term strategy. It was apparent from less successful projects, or at least from those that were not so quickly realized, that such strategic relevance becomes almost a prerequisite for the long-term success of an innovation such as this.

An indication of the effect of publicity can be seen in the way in which the automation project became a focal point and a motivating force for many other innovative activities. It was, so to speak, a catalyst for development or as one employee put it "a sort of coathanger on which other projects were hung for justification".

In conclusion, we may note several of the more important results (both intended and unforeseen) of automating production. These include a tendency towards greater production inflexibility, an increased dependence on quality control, a stronger emphasis on the "systems approach" to management, a greater predictability in production, longer time horizons in planning, and, perhaps most socially beneficial, a trend towards multi-skilled production and maintenance workers.

The Robots are Coming – Slowly

Ricardo Zermeno, Russell Moseley and Ernest Braun

Developments in microelectronics make possible the increasing use of industrial robots. But it is not all plain sailing, as is made clear by the authors of this hitherto unpublished study, also from the Aston Technology Policy Unit. The paper describes developments in robot technology and discusses their potential uses in industry. It examines the international diffusion of robots and seeks to explain why Britain has been particularly slow in adopting them. From a look at a number of case studies, the authors analyse the motives behind the introduction of robots and their impact once they have been installed. They conclude that robotization is coming, but because of the problems, it will not happen overnight.

Karel Capek first used the word "robot" in his play *RUR* (*Rossum's Universal Robots*) published in 1920. Capek's robots – the word is derived from a Czech expression for work, implying drudgery or serf labour – were androids, made by a secret process. They were living, intelligent creatures, totally devoid of feelings and the ability to make value judgements. Their purpose was to provide cheap, flexible, undemanding labour, willing and able to work for long hours. In Capek's novel things went badly wrong and robots thus acquired an undesirable reputation which has not been improved by subsequent generations of science fiction novels. This paper will concentrate on the more earthly aspects of robots, and, in particular, their use in manufacturing industry.

The modern concept of the industrial robot revolves around the notion of a "general purpose" or "universal" machine. This has recently been given a considerable boost by the ability of microelectronics to provide control and memory devices of unprecedented capacity and flexibility. In the past, automation has been applied to industrial

184

processes in a variety of ways, although this has usually been achieved through the saving of labour by technology designed to perform a job in a manner not necessarily similar to the one used by humans. By contrast, a robotic approach to automation follows human performance much more closely, since it reflects a move away from "purpose-built" machines towards "universality". However, since the technical and economic obstacles littering this path are numerous, development has been directed towards dextrous machines. Dexterity depends upon the ability to move the robotic tool through different points in space and the ability to actuate the tool. To achieve maximum dexterity, it is essential to have extensive command ability: to follow a particular sequence of actuation events; to memorize different sets of sequences; and to communicate with the outside world in order to modify a sequence of events. Finally, and possibly most important, dexterity is dependent upon the ability to sense changes in the environment and to adapt behaviour accordingly.

A robotic approach to automation is intended to exploit advantages which become more apparent as the dexterity of the machine increases, because a highly flexible machine would be suitable for many applications. The possibility of buying highly developed off-the-shelf robots will facilitate the introduction of automation. With a potentially large market for standard machines, the design and development costs can be spread; robot automation can be applied to smaller batch production and short-life product design because robots are versatile; and finally the maintenance and setting functions become less diversified and therefore simpler to carry out.

The extent to which these features are exploited depends on the type of applications and robots used. A highly versatile robot, for example, would be more expensive than a purpose-built automatic device when applied to simple, common jobs. Less sophistication generally means less cost, while simplicity may also mean a greater speed of application accompanied by fewer teething troubles. Thus if the environment is static, hard automation rather than robot automation may become more appropriate.

Classification of robots

A classification of robots may help to clarify certain aspects of the technology. A robot consists basically of three elements: the mechanical structure, the power unit and the control system.

The mechanical structure consists of a series of mechanical linkages and joints capable of movements in various axes. These movements are supplemented by others present in the tool located at the end point of the structure. When the tool takes the form of a wrist and gripper it usually adds three more axes of motion. The total number of axes is identified as the number of degrees of freedom. This can be considered as indicative of the degree of versatility. Another indicator of the degree of versatility is the volume of the robot's working space.

Both the power unit and control system provide a basis for robot classification. The power used for actuation of the mechanical structure can be of three kinds – hydraulic, pneumatic or electrical. In terms of the control system, classification becomes particularly interesting, since the control element is the most dynamic as far as technological development is concerned. In recent years, development of the control system has greatly increased the versatility and adaptability of robots. There is a wide range of controllers: pneumatic logic systems, diode matrix boards, electronic sequencers, microprocessors and minicomputers. According to Tanner (1977), robots can be classified as non-servo and servo-controlled. Non-servo robots have mechanical stops (which can be fixed or variable) and limit switches for positioning and informing the controller, whereas servo-controlled robots use sophisticated feedback devices (encoders, potentiometers, and so on) and monitor the state of the variables until they reach a desired value, at which point the controller stops actuating the robot member. In the latter case, robots can be further classified as either point-to-point (PTP) or continuous path (CP) controlled: PTP systems do not control the path between the points to be reached whereas CP systems do, and achieve a smooth continuous movement.

All the above criteria for robot classification are basically "static" and compare the elements of a robot structure, power or control. Other criteria, more concerned with the actual behaviour or performance of a robot (Engelberger, 1976), can be used to classify robot technology. These are "dynamic" characteristics and include, for example, load capacity, acceleration, deceleration, speed, coordination, operational conditions, manipulative power, ease of programming, reliability, sensory perception and self-diagnosis.

Robot applications
Robots have been used in a large variety of applications since their invention, reflecting the concept of universality. However, it must be emphasized that each application, at least for the present generation, demands, to a greater or lesser degree, the development of peripheral technology. This is especially true of the tool which performs the manipulative functions. In fact many suppliers do not provide such a tool and it has had to be developed by the user (often in conjunction with the manufacturer), although some offer standard grippers.

When studying the diffusion and adoption of this technology, the variety of applications presents a major problem. Studying robot applications in general can result in gross overgeneralizations and disguise

Table 4.1 Simple classification of robot applications

1 *Workpiece gripped by robot*
  1.1 Transfer
    1.1.1 Simple transport operation
    For example:
    From fixed position to fixed position

    1.1.2 Complex transfer
    For example:
    From conveyor to conveyor
    Palletizing
    Stacking
    Packing
    Sorting

    1.1.3 Loading/unloading of equipment
    For example:
    Casting
    Pressure die casting
    Injection moulding
    Metal working
    Cold/hot pressing
    Heat treatment (furnaces)
    Glass cutting
    Soldering
    Brazing

  1.2 Manipulation and process
    For example:
    Forging
    Fettling
    Investment casting

2 *Tool handled by robot*
  2.1 Metal working
    For example:
    Flame cutting
    Grinding
    Pneumatic chipping

  2.2 Joining
    For example:
    Spot welding
    Arc welding
    Stud welding

  2.3 Surface treatment
    For example:
    Paint spraying
    Enamel spraying
    Glass fibre and resin spraying
    Sprinkling enamel powder
    Ceramic ware finishing
    Water jet cleaning
    Applying sealing compounds

  2.4 Inspection
    For example:
    Dimensional checks

  2.5 Others
    For example:
    Glass gathering
    Marking

3 *Assembly by robot*
    (still in development stage)
    For example:
    Automobile alternators
    Electric motors
    Electric sub-assemblies

some of the basic characteristics of the technology itself. Building general purposeness into the technology means increasing the variety of applications and therefore the range of environments into which the technology is introduced. Table 4.1 shows a range of robot applications in manufacturing industry.

The diffusion of robot technology
The invention, innovation and diffusion of industrial robots illustrate the dynamic nature of these processes. As the diffusion of robots takes place, invention and innovation activities continue. When studying the early stages of robot innovation, several general points emerge: first, it illustrates the validity of both a technology-push and demand-pull model of innovation. On the one hand, the early history of robotics reveals individual inventor/entrepreneurs with a firm belief in the market potential of the technology; on the other, it is possible to identify firms which developed robots in response to a perceived need. Those innovators who have stayed in business all reveal a common characteristic: their products have not only increased in reliability and dexterity but their range has diversified both in terms of models and possible applications. These changes have had a significant influence on diffusion rates.

As the innovation process has advanced, robot dexterity, or general purposeness, has come more and more to be seen in terms of specific applications and environments: what we might call dextrous machines with specialist scope. It has become important for users to introduce the technology with as little effort as possible, so that, for example, the gripper or special tool and other peripheral equipment have now been developed and standardized to a greater extent. Emphasis has changed as the diffusion of robots progressed from the supply of "robots without hands" towards the supply of "robot systems" – a turnkey approach where the user needs to expend less and less development effort.

The American Unimate (Unimation Inc.) and Versatran (AMF Inc.) robots were the first to penetrate the UK market. By the end of 1967, two British companies had bought licences from Unimation and AMF and started to market their machines in the UK and in Europe. The background of the two British companies revealed significant differences: one was in the aerospace industry, the other in general metal working. Despite the expertise in hydraulics and electronics of the first, and the experience in the field of applications of the second, both firms dropped the licence before 1974. By this time, the first fully British teachable robot (RAMP) had been developed by Hall Automation, an entrepreneurial firm employing some of the personnel formerly working in the company which had bought the Versatran licence.

The multi-purpose character of the Versatran and Unimate robots made the process of introduction an inherently difficult business. As each application demanded some degree of special development, and the variety of applications was large, the demands on the technical expertise of the suppliers were considerable. Moreover, this large variety of applications involved robot suppliers in dealing with many different manufacturing processes and industrial environments. As a result, demands on marketing and managerial skills were also high.

By 1974, the robot "Trallfa" was well-established in the field of spraying. This "specialist" robot, designed to satisfy a particular need in a Norwegian firm, stimulated a rapid growth in spraying applications and the first UK robot was introduced to this market.

A German survey (Warnecke and Schraft, 1974) estimated a European robot population of 800. This survey analysed the distribution of robots according to applications. The most common uses were: coating (20.8 per cent), welding (20 per cent), pressing (15.4 per cent), and injection moulding (11.2 per cent). By the beginning of the 1970s, coating and welding (mostly spot welding for assembly of motor car bodies) were becoming important areas for the diffusion of robot technology. Another trend was apparent in robot innovation in the first half of this decade: the introduction of numerous robots making use of medium to simple technology, that is, non-servo controlled robots of the fixed and variable sequence kinds. These machines have been directed at such areas as diecasting and injection moulding, where a simple device could be used for the automation of a large proportion of the market. The past few years have also seen the consolidation of Unimate robots in the spot welding field. In 1977, for example, of 1400 Unimate robots in operation approximately fifty-five per cent were in the spot welding area.

Some estimates of the actual extent of robot diffusion are given in Tables 4.2 and 4.3, on an international and a European basis. Since we are dealing only with estimated numbers, we should point out that any conclusions drawn from figures such as these must necessarily be tentative. This makes studying diffusion patterns even more difficult: there are problems of definition; reported figures often include unsuccessful trials and possible orders; some companies producing medium-technology robots do not classify them as robots; and large companies may have developed robots for internal use in significant numbers about which we unfortunately know little.

Despite these difficulties, Tables 4.2 and 4.3 can be used to illustrate several diffusion trends. As has been frequently pointed out, the UK has been relatively slow in introducing robot technology – "relatively" because diffusion has nowhere been rapid in view of the technology's likely potential. In other industrial countries, the first half of the 1970s

Table 4.2   Estimates of the international diffusion of robots

	1970	1974[b]	1978[d]
Japan	161[a]	1500	3000
USA	200[b]	1200	2500
Europe	—	800	2000
Worldwide	<1000[c]	3500	8000

Sources: a Yonemoto and Shiino, 1977 (variable sequence and playback only)
b Frost and Sullivan, 1974
c Ghali, 1972
d Shah, 1978

Table 4.3   Estimates of the European diffusion of robots

	1974[a]	1975[b]	1978
Sweden	164	445	>600[c]
United Kingdom	136	166	70[d]
West Germany	133	243	600[d]
Italy	93	362	300–400[d]
France	30	144	—
All Europe	839	1697	2000[e]

Sources: a Warnecke and Schraft, 1974
b Frost and Sullivan, 1975
c Hartley, 1978
d British Robot Association, 1978
e Shah, 1978

saw a more widespread adoption, and differences between Japan, the USA and Europe have become less marked.

Apart from Sweden, which has remained Europe's largest user of robots – if anything the Swedish figures are underestimates: see Rooks (1977) – all the other countries referred to in Table 4.4 have changed places in the ranking of users. Both Germany and Italy have increased their use of robots after a slow start, while France has remained a low-level user. There is, however, evidence that France is now making more of the technology than the UK is.

The *decline* of the UK as a user of robots is clearly seen in Table 4.4 and is confirmed by other evidence. This has occurred despite the fact that UK firms were early adopters of robots, and that the technology, transferred from the USA, was being used to supply the European as well as the home market. Moreover, British universities have since the early

Table 4.4 Relative diffusion of industrial robots*

	Measure 1[1]	Measure 2[2]
Sweden	1.00	1.00
Japan	0.41	0.39
Italy	0.19	0.12
USA	0.14	0.20
West Germany	0.09	0.10
UK	0.03	0.02

* No estimates are available for France. However conversations with several suppliers reveal that the extent of diffusion is similar to that in the UK.
[1] At 1978 prices, converted at current exchange rates
[2] Industrial workforce in 1975

Source: Tables 4.2 and 4.3, and Carr (1978)

1970s carried out considerably more robotics research than their European counterparts; the first two international symposia on industrial robot technology were held in England in 1971 and 1972; the only international robotics journal is published in Britain. Nonetheless, British industry remains indifferent to the claims of the technology, and not only has there been a relative decline in the adoption of robots, but also the number of innovators in the field is very small. Indeed, if one compares for each country the number of firms supplying robots then a similar ranking is obtained to that concerning robot use.

The most appropriate comparison that can be made of the use of robots in various countries must include a measure of the potential market for robots, and a useful indicator in this respect is the size of industry on a national basis. Consider two measures of industrial size: the share of combined industrial production (measure 1) and the share of the combined workforce (measure 2). Thus we can obtain a ratio of the share of combined robot usage to each of our two measures. The results, in normalized form, are shown in Table 4.4.

Because of the imprecision of the data, the conclusions from this comparison must be limited, although it is clear that Japan and Sweden have been the principal adopters of robots, and that the UK has lagged far behind. For the other countries the picture is less clear-cut, although it appears that West Germany has also been a slow adopter. It is interesting to note that the order of ranking revealed in Table 4.4 remains much the same when innovation in robotics is considered: Sweden, Japan and the USA are the most innovative nations, and are followed by Italy, West Germany and France, which have recently become increasingly involved in robot manufacture, reflecting their accumulated experience in certain key applications.*

Since robots are intended to replace human labour it might be expected that unit labour costs would play an important part in determining the rate of diffusion. However, this factor alone will not provide an explanation. Other factors such as unemployment, rates of investment, export dependence and social attitudes to work have a considerable effect.

The adoption of robot technology

The general diffusion trends we have discussed above may be further illuminated by studying adoption at the level of the individual firm. Our research in this area has involved a series of case studies of robot usage, supplemented by interviews with manufacturers, suppliers of robots, and university research workers. This section contains a very brief summary of some of our findings so far, concentrating on only one class of applications of robots in the UK, that of coating.† In practice, this means mostly either paint or enamel spraying – the most common uses to which robots are put in the UK. Coating by robots takes place in a variety of industrial sectors, and worldwide there is a notable concentration in the domestic appliances and automobile industries. It is interesting to note that in Britain the latter industry makes little use of robots for spraying.

A total of fourteen robots introduced for coating work have been studied, nine in vitreous enamel spraying and five in paint spraying. Thirteen were installed in firms manufacturing consumer goods (electrical domestic appliances, sanitary ware, furniture) and one in a firm producing plastic components for the industry. Table 4.5 summarizes some of the motives influencing the adoption of robot technology in the case of coating applications.

In general, the type of incentives for automation outlined in Table 4.5 are also reflected in the adoption of robots for other applications. Problems of labour recruitment, labour supervision and so on are frequently offered as reasons underlying the decision to use a robot, while environmental factors appear to be of particular significance. This reflects both the strengthening of health and safety legislation and a

---

* This is especially true of spot welding in the automobile industry. American car manufacturers set the trend in the early 1970s by introducing multi-machine installations for resistance-welding of car panels. European firms followed suit: by 1977 Volvo had a total of fifty-eight robots; Fiat had 180; and Renault thirty. British Leyland recently announced plans for installing thirty robots, to be commissioned in late 1979.

† Coating applications include paint spraying, enamel spraying, glass fibre and resin spraying and dry enamel sprinkling.

Table 4.5 Motives influencing the adoption of robots in coating applications

	Case study					
Factors	**1**	**2**	**3**	**4**	**5**	**6**
LABOUR						
Job and working conditions unattractive	X	X	X	X	X	X
Job is particularly unpleasant		X			X	X
Frequent breaks	X		X			
Absenteeism	X	X	X	X	X	
High labour turnover	X		X	X	X	X
Difficulty of recruitment	X	X	X	X		
Shortage of sprayers	X		X	X		
ECONOMIC						
Increase in economic efficiency	X	X	X	X	X	X
Need to reduce rejection levels or increase quality/ consistency	X	X		X		
MANAGERIAL						
Easier supervision, control and planning of production	X	X	X		X	

realization that young workers are less willing to undertake particularly unpleasant jobs.

Although motives for introducing robots reveal some common themes, the results of adoption tend to be much more varied and relate to the application in question. As an illustration, Table 4.6 gives some of the main results following the introduction of robots into spraying operations in six firms. The economic returns depended on the number of shifts worked, the labour saved, and the output per shift. Although in some cases robot cycle times were faster than for human operators, usually they were the same. It was more common for increased output to result from increases in the utilization of the spraying equipment once robots were introduced. In some cases the number of shifts was reduced, which indicates the potential of robots in terms of rationalization.

Other results worth noting include improvements in the quality of production, with rejection levels generally reduced. Saving of materials was an important though less notable feature of spraying by robot, while the one case for which material use was increased revealed the need for

Table 4.6   General results of the introduction of robots in spraying applications

	Case study					
Results	**1**	**2**	**3**	**4**	**5**	**6**
ECONOMIC						
Cycle time faster	X	X				
Increased levels of utilization	X	X	X			
Increased output per shift	X	X	X			
Rejection levels reduced	X	X	X			
Material savings achieved	X	X				
Satisfactory payback period	X	X	X		X	X
MANAGERIAL AND TECHNICAL						
Difficulty of matching maintenance skills to robot requirements		X	X	X	X	X
Poor reliability				X		
Long time to repair			X		X	
Control unit is vulnerable	X	X	X	X		
LABOUR						
Positive acceptance of the technology	X	X	X	X		
Reduction of skill requirements for spraying	X	X	X			
Unpleasant spraying is now totally allocated to the robots	X	X				
Approximate ratio of people displaced per robot	6	1	1	0	1	

a more dextrous robot system to cope with the wide variety of parts being sprayed.

Problems associated with robot introduction often included faults in the control system caused by dust or dirt. An unwelcome reliance on external services for maintenance, particularly when electronics was involved, was also a feature of robot adoption. To some extent problems of reliability are being lessened by contemporary developments in electronics, which enable magnetic tape memories to be replaced by floppy discs or by solid-state memory devices.* These developments

---

* In only one case was poor reliability the reason for abandoning the use of a robot.

will reduce – but not eliminate – reliance on external expertise for maintenance, particularly as electronic technicians are few and far between and the creation of in-house skills is not economic when robot use is small.

The limited extent of the introduction of robots makes the study of labour implications difficult. The fact that in a majority of cases labour resistance was not encountered, for instance, does not mean that a more widespread use of the technology would be equally unproblematic. It is clear, however, that robot spraying systems result in a reduction of demand for "skilled" sprayers. This, and the elimination of "unpleasant" jobs, depends not only on the extent of robot use but also on the way in which the entire system is designed. In the one case where robot and conveyor systems were introduced at the same time (in all the others conveyors existed before robots), a larger proportion of people were displaced per robot and a more dramatic shift of skill requirements was evident.

The transformation of the labour task is one of the most important issues to consider when adopting robot technology, the more so as those tasks left for humans can be extremely monotonous. A different organization of labour might avoid this: for instance, the combination of programming and setting functions with the remaining monotonous tasks is a possibility, although it would require considerable training. Since the introduction of robots demands a heavy involvement from managers and engineers, adoption is very much affected by managerial skill and incentives. Not only is the choice of robot system crucial, but management has to cooperate in finding the best labour organization and way of sharing the benefits of investment. At the same time they must overcome the technical problems which arise.

Conclusions
Largely thanks to developments in microelectronics, the evolution of robots has resulted in a wide range of machines, most of which are highly dextrous yet specialized in a particular area of application. Spot welding and spraying have been particularly successful and new firms, eager to win a share in these expanding markets, have recently entered the fray. The invention, innovation and diffusion of robots have been prominent in the automobile and machine tool industries – and the reason for the slow diffusion of robots in the UK is partly to be found in the poor performance of these sectors. In addition, premature introduction of robots in a variety of applications resulted in numerous failures in the early 1970s and these experiences have acted as a disincentive to further adoption.

Studying the adoption process sheds light on the factors affecting the

UK's performance. The use of robots in spraying, one of the most common applications, is encouraged by the need to improve working conditions. Legislation on health and safety may indeed partially explain international differences in robot diffusion. More generally, social attitudes and living standards have a considerable bearing upon the speed of adoption. At this relatively early stage in the diffusion of robots, the policy of the firm towards innovation can be identified as a more important factor than pure economics, and this is reflected in the high concentration of robots in some firms. In these cases a strong belief in the future of this technology has been an important driving force.

At present, unemployment levels are more easily identified as a brake upon the diffusion of robots than as a consequence of such diffusion. Skill shortages may also affect the rate of introduction, and this effect can be either positive or negative.

Economic benefits in terms of productivity and quality gains by the use of robots are potentially great, but depend upon the type of robot system introduced. The effects on work also depend critically upon the type of system introduced and the method of its introduction. Management policy on consultation and workers' participation in technological change are important issues which may help to explain international differences in diffusion rates.

Government support under the "humanization of work" banner has stimulated research, innovation and diffusion of robot technology in Germany, Japan, Sweden and the USA. In the UK, the British Robot Association (BRA), formed at the beginning of 1978, has succeeded in attracting government and industrial interest, as became apparent at the Second Annual Industrial Robot Conference held in March 1979. A high attendance at this event supported the BRA view that the British robot population would soon double.

However, a more widespread use of robots is unlikely to occur overnight. The introduction of this technology demands radical changes in manufacturing systems, organization, and the control of production and distribution. This is especially true of small and medium batch production, an area with the biggest potential for flexible automation. The widespread diffusion of industrial robots will only come about through the coordinated activity of management, workers and outside agencies. Despite the revolutionary changes in electronics, the switch-over to robots is, on present evidence, unlikely to be dramatic.

References

British Robot Association, "Robot Association Aims To Educate Potential Users", *Machinery and Production Engineering*, 27 September 1978.

J. Carr, "The West German 'Economic Miracle'. The High Price of Productivity", *Financial Times*, 15 August 1978.

J. F. Engelberger, "Performance Evaluation of Industrial Robots", in *Proceedings of the 3rd Conference of Industrial Robot Technology and the 6th International Symposium on Industrial Robots* (1976), pp. 51–64.

Frost and Sullivan, *The U.S. Industrial Robot Market* (Frost and Sullivan Inc., New York, 1974).

Frost and Sullivan, *The Industrial Robot Market in Europe*, Report N.E125 (Frost and Sullivan Inc., New York, 1975).

X. B. Ghali, "Robotology and An Overview of the International Robot Situation", in *Proceedings of the 2nd International Symposium on Industrial Robots* (Chicago, 1972), pp. 1–7.

J. R. Hartley (ed.), *British Robot Association Newsletter*, Number 2 (1978), pp. 1–4.

R. Shah, "Growth Is the Word For Robots", *Iron Age Metalwork Int.* (vol. 7, 1978), pp. 19–21.

W. R. Tanner, "Basics of Robotics", *SME Technical Paper* MS77–734 (1977), pp. 1–10.

H. J. Warnecke and R. D. Schraft, "The Gap Between Required and Realised Properties of Industrial Robots", in *Proceedings of the 4th International Symposium on Industrial Robots* (Tokyo, 1974), pp. 101–12.

K. Yonemoto and K. Shiino, "Present State and Future Outlook of Industrial Robots in Japan", *The Industrial Robot*, vol. 4, Part 4 (1977), pp. 171–9.

Microelectronics in Manufacturing Industry: The Rate of Diffusion

John Bessant, Ernest Braun and Russell Moseley

The third piece prepared specially for this volume by the Technology Policy Unit at Aston University is a major summary paper. It provides an overview of the impact and diffusion of microelectronics in industry, with microelectronics being regarded as an example of a labour-saving technology. From a number of case studies, the authors show that the advantages of microelectronics in terms of cost, size, flexibility and reliability are less straightforward than would appear at first sight. Social factors, such as the fear of unemployment and the state of management/labour relations, are also very important in determining both the rate of take-up and government policies toward the new technology. The paper concludes with a review of the policy options.

The impact of microelectronics will be felt in three main ways. First, some entirely new or considerably modified products are made possible only by microelectronics: new types of car parking controls, word processors, microcomputers, new controls for domestic machinery, and so on. Second, the new technology will have a considerable influence on the provision of services. In the newspaper industry, for example, the use of microelectronics can eliminate or modify many traditional tasks, while in the office a typewriter may be replaced by a word processor – essentially a typewriter associated with a small computer and a video display unit – increasing the efficiency of the typist and providing new editing possibilities. Third, microelectronics will be used in the manufacture of traditional goods, and it is this area with which the present paper is concerned.

The manufacture of goods is a diverse activity which ranges from the volume production of basic chemicals, through the mass production of motor cars, to the small batch production of ships or airplanes. At first sight, these processes have little in common other than the conversion of raw materials into some product and the use of energy for the purpose. All manufacturing processes, however, include a number of basic tasks which can be undertaken by microelectronics in conjunction with other devices. Among the most important of these tasks we might include:

(1) The controlled movement of materials, components and products.

(2) The control of process variables such as temperature, pressure and humidity.

(3) The shaping, cutting, mixing and moulding of materials.

(4) The assembly of components into sub-assemblies and finished products.

(5) The control of the quality of products at all stages of manufacture by inspection, testing or analysis.

(6) The organization of the manufacturing process, including design, stock-keeping, dispatch, machine maintenance, invoicing and the allocation of tasks.

The word control appears several times in this list, and even where it does not appear some form of sequencing and orderly arrangement is required, since manufacturing is essentially concerned with bringing together materials and ordering them, by the use of energy and intelligence, into desired forms.

This provides a key to understanding the use of microelectronics in manufacture, for microelectronics can perform tasks associated with "intelligence" or processed information. The essential feature of microelectronics is that it performs tasks of logic – a given input of information is transformed, in a predetermined way, into an output. The input may be a number – as in a calculator – or a letter, or the reading of any kind of meter. In the final analysis, all inputs are converted into a suitable sequence of electrical pulses and it is the function of transducers and input circuitry – often microelectronic itself – to achieve the desired input in the required form.

The transformation of an input signal into an output is carried out according to a set of suitable instructions which are determined by the operator from time to time. With a calculator, the operator instructs the machine how to process the number he or she has put in – for example, the machine can be instructed to obtain the square root of the number. In a computer, the instructions can be much more complex and involve the use of a program, that is a series of instructions to the machine. In control devices, the machine can be instructed to process the input signal in such a way as to obtain the desired control function – for instance, it might adjust the current through a heater to obtain constant temperature.

The output of the microelectronic circuit consists of an electrical signal, and this can be used to activate any desired display unit, such as a video display or a typewriter, or alternatively the signal may be further processed to determine mechanical movement, heater current or any other manufacturing variable. Thus microelectronics can be used either for the pure processing of information and the display of the result, or it can be used for the processing of information and the transformation of the result into some action, such as the closing or opening of valves.

Control systems can be arranged hierarchically so that small microprocessor units interact with larger computers. For example, individual machines controlled by microprocessors can feed information to a minicomputer controlling an entire production unit, which in turn can feed a large mainframe computer. The latter, taking account of other operations and external factors, for example, stock levels and market demands, feeds back scheduling and production control information down the line.

In order to obtain the full benefit of the capabilities of microelectronic devices, they have to be able to store items of information, either permanently or temporarily, and hence we speak of memories and memory devices. The memories store instructions, such as computer programs or inputs to be processed, or simply serve as convenient filing systems for libraries. Since all microelectronic circuits make use of small silicon chips, that containing a memory device will be known as a memory chip; if it serves the function of a complete programmable information processor, say in a small computer, the chip will be known as a microprocessor. Other microelectronic devices, serving a variety of functions, have not acquired such well-known names; among these are chips which process information in a fixed, nonprogrammable manner.

One of the chief reasons for the microprocessor's widespread fame (perhaps notoriety) is its flexibility coupled with extremely low cost. As we shall see, in practice these advantages are not as straightforward as they might appear. Nonetheless, it is in theory now possible for microprocessors to perform cheaply and reliably many logic functions which previously required the use of either very expensive electronics or the use of human logic. When the purchase price of an item of logic in a microprocessor became cheaper than the hire of an item of logic from a worker, talk about the impact of microprocessors upon the labour market became serious. We shall return briefly to these questions later, after examining in more detail the role that microprocessors are beginning to play in manufacturing industry and those factors determining their introduction and acceptance.

When a microelectronic device is used solely for the processing, storage, transmission and display of information – such as in a computer or a word processor – its importance lies mainly in the performance of administrative and service tasks. In such cases the impact is potentially greatest in the service sector of the economy, for instance in banking, insurance, distribution and public administration. Of course, the impact of information processing in manufacturing industry can also be considerable, since a substantial proportion of total effort is concerned with administration and organization.

Nevertheless, in what follows we shall concentrate on aspects of microelectronics which are primarily important for manufacture, that is, the use of microelectronics for the processing of information to control or activate manufacturing operations directly. We shall thus concentrate on the first five of our list of manufacturing activities and neglect the sixth.

Microelectronics and manufacturing industry

The potential benefits of microelectronics make this technology extremely attractive to manufacturing industry. Since microelectronics can play a prominent part in controlling the movement of materials and goods we might, for example, use a flow-meter and a simple controller to actuate valves to control the flow of a liquid or, at an extremely sophisticated level, we might have a large warehouse in which all necessary components for the manufacture of, say, motor cars are automatically stored and retrieved at the press of a button. In the latter case, the operator need only indicate the model number and the required components will be retrieved from the automated warehouse and delivered in the correct sequence at the correct places on the production line.

Control of process variables has been achieved by electrical means for some time. Microelectronics, however, can add dimensions of sophistication and reliability which significantly increase the scope for automated control functions. For example, a device using microelectronics can control a large number of variables in such a way as to achieve optimum operational conditions for the system as a whole. It is possible to ensure that each variable will be adjusted in accordance with some external or internal conditions – such as the particular characteristics of a batch of raw material. As a result, very complex cycles of operations are possible – for example, heating and cooling at specified rates and maintaining fixed temperatures for specified times or until some measurement indicates that the temperature should be changed.

The potential impact of microelectronics is just as great in the areas of shaping, cutting, mixing and moulding of materials. Numerically controlled machine tools, for example, have been in existence for some while. Future generations of such equipment incorporating the new technology will offer considerable advantages in terms of flexibility and ease of programming. Similarly, the use of robots is already making some impact on such tasks as welding, paint spraying and the assembly of parts into finished or intermediate products, and in those cases where robots offer an unnecessarily high degree of sophistication, special purpose assembly machines using microelectronics can be custom built.

Finally, we should note the possibilities of automatic testing, sampling and inspection that microelectronics provides. In chemical processes, metallurgy and food processing, where there is a need for sampling the product continuously, it becomes possible to fully automate analysis, while in the manufacture of components – whether machined, cast, or extruded – weighing, measuring and flaw detection can be carried out automatically. In a related context, the potential for monitoring the factory environment (both internally and externally) is enormously increased: the air of a factory can be continuously sampled for smoke or toxic hazards and the results of effluent analysis can be constantly fed back to the production process.

In view of this diverse range of microelectronics applications, a number of questions are immediately raised. Why, given these apparently obvious advantages, is manufacturing industry in Britain reacting so slowly to the technology? Should the rate of diffusion be increased? If so, how? In what ways can an awareness of the wider social implications of microelectronics be effectively integrated into those policies designed to effect this diffusion? In a paper such as this, based upon work which is still taking place, it would be presumptuous to offer definitive answers to these questions. Rather we will attempt to provide some information and insights into the adoption and diffusion of microelectronics in manufacturing industry in the belief that questions of policy will be best answered with as full a knowledge as possible of such processes.

The diffusion of microelectronics

Much of the literature concerned with the diffusion of innovations concentrates upon product, and, to a lesser extent, process innovation. For our present purposes, it is more useful to define a class of "manufacturing innovations", which can be defined as new ways and procedures of making established products by established methods.* Since microelectronics applications in manufacturing industry are likely to fall by and large into this category, it is useful to distinguish it from the more

* The substitution of a robot for a human operator in a traditional paint-spraying operation is an example of a manufacturing innovation.

general class of process innovation. This section then looks at the diffusion of microelectronics, chiefly in the form of manufacturing innovations, drawing upon a wide-ranging set of case studies, chosen to include actual users of microelectronics, potential users, and those seeking to introduce the innovation. Since these case studies are at present being extended in both depth and range, this section is not intended to provide a comprehensive list of factors influencing the diffusion of microelectronics, but rather to suggest areas which appear to be of importance.

There are a number of general points that our case studies have raised, particularly in relation to existing accounts of innovation. In certain respects the case studies confirm previous findings, notably those concerning the importance for innovation of technically competent management, and of the role played by "champions" within the firm. On the latter point it is clear that "champions" – or, more accurately, "promoters" – become of greater significance when the technology in question is perceived as radical, and this has important implications for the adoption of microelectronics.

On the other hand, the case studies have revealed certain features of the innovation process which either differ from previous accounts or have received little attention. In the former case, the most striking example concerns management motives for introducing manufacturing innovations. Since such innovations are all potentially labour-saving, conventional wisdom would suggest that a desire to save on labour costs is the most important (if not the only) factor influencing the decision to innovate. In fact the picture is much more complex. In a majority of cases potential labour savings were not a *prime* motive for innovating: of far more importance were such factors as the need to expand output; to increase the quality of output or the consistency of production; to improve safety by the elimination of hazardous or physically strenuous operations; to improve the working environment by automating unpleasant tasks; to economize on stocks of intermediate products by improving the flow of production; to save on materials, and so on.

An aspect of innovation that has received little attention in the past, and which our case studies have revealed to be of crucial importance, concerns the strategies of both management and labour towards the adoption of an innovation. Clearly, detailed adoption strategies remain specific to an individual firm and the response of the workforce will be similarly unique. Nonetheless, there are some aspects which bear generalization. Consultation, for example, emerges as a key factor in the successful adoption of new manufacturing methods, and those firms which seek simply to impose an innovation can expect to encounter difficulties which might otherwise have been avoided. A frequently observed variant of consultation is the "marketing" approach. Here attempts are made to "sell" the new technology to the workforce, which still has no direct involvement in design or implementation. Later on, after a honeymoon period of acceptance, there may well be resistance and hostility as problems show up.

Two broad approaches on the part of management towards the introduction of an innovation may be identified. The first we may call the gradual approach, in which innovation takes place slowly and which frequently sees a mixture of old and new production methods, the balance being adjusted in favour of the latter. It should be pointed out that this slow introduction of an innovation has as much to do with a learning process as with management/labour confrontations. The second, less common, approach involves separating the old and new production facilities, described by one manager as the "out of sight out of mind approach". Since the innovation is physically separated from the old line, management believe that it is perceived as less of a threat by the workforce. While this enables the new production methods to be made operational, the problem for management of phasing out the old still remains. It was noticeable from the case studies that this approach

This Unimate industrial robot is being used for heavy forging work at a fire extinguisher factory in Chesterfield, England. It has eliminated a dirty, noisy, backbreaking job previously done by a man. *Photo courtesy of Unimation*

The inside of the Fiat factory in Turin, Italy, where they build the Fiat Ritmo/Strada. Unlike the famous TV advertisement, there *are* a couple of people in the picture, checking computer printout. *Photo courtesy of Fiat Auto*

was most commonly adopted in firms where labour relations were poor. An extreme variation of this which appeared in several case studies is the decision to introduce new production methods on a new site – the so-called "green field approach" – either in addition to existing plant or following its closure.

General issues such as these all have a bearing upon the adoption and rate of diffusion of manufacturing innovations – including those which do not make use of microelectronics. However, in order to identify some of the more specific factors influencing the introduction of microelectronics it is useful to focus attention on the innovation itself, on the innovators, and on the users of the technology.

Innovation characteristics. The decision to adopt any innovation is largely conditioned by the degree to which it is perceived as being better in some way than whatever it is intended to replace. As we have seen, in the case of microelectronics the advantages at first sight seem overwhelming but certain problems can complicate such a simple judgement. Certainly, microelectronic devices are very cheap to produce and assemble, and the average cost of processing information has decreased significantly. The scale of this fall is one of the main reasons for the current interest in their application. However, the costs of devices suitable for industrial uses can only be reduced by taking advantage of mass production economies (as has been the case with calculators, watches and TV games), and industrial applications tend to be user-specific and often have to include programming and development costs in their overall price. Inevitably, this makes them more expensive. Attempts are being made to overcome this obstacle in a number of ways, notably by fitting microelectronics as standard on original equipment. The cost of such additions is small (perhaps £500-£1000 on machinery costing from £10,000 to £100,000), but evidence suggests that the UK is reluctant to take up this option at present. Standardization problems can be overcome by using modular design, where standard circuit boards are offered to make up microcomputers according to user requirements. Developments in this area still require simplification of the programming step, since even high-level languages need highly skilled programmers who are in short supply. A third option consists of selling complete functional systems, controlling temperature or flow for example, which will find application in a large number of industries. However, the range of generally applicable systems is small, and costs rise as developments become more specific.

The size of microelectronics is an attractive feature where space saving is an important determinant, such as in watches or similar applications. Where accessibility is a problem, there are clear advantages in size reduction, and the limitations of many production layouts make any change of control system dependent upon space and configuration. Most industrial users are unlikely to require this level of space reduction, and any savings in functional component space requirements will have to be balanced against the need for stronger casings to accommodate sensitive and fragile microelectronic systems. The great advantage of microelectronics is its flexibility of application. However, much of this flexibility relies on the development of software, and on hardware which supports ease of programmability and application. Most microcomputers are now built on the basis of "mother and daughter" boards, in which a central linking board can be used to plug in the relevant components for a particular application (power supply, memory boards, central processor unit, input/output devices and so on). Fixed and erasable/reprogrammable memory means that users have the option of using standard routines or programming their own instructions.

The lack of moving parts and the low operating demands give microelectronics exceptional reliability characteristics. Typically, microprocessor chips have reliability indices close to unity. Maintenance is also simplified with built-in diagnostics and indicators which identify the source of failure; repair is often a simple replacement of a whole board. This means that spares must be carried, but this expense is offset by lower maintenance costs. However, the devices are highly complex and until diagnostic facilities become a standard feature, an element of dependence on suppliers' after-sales service remains a problem. This is a particularly important issue in large firms, since it implies a radical change in maintenance skill patterns and demands.

Thus the considerable advantages of cost, size, flexibility and reliability of microelectronics can be seen as less straightforward than they appear at first sight. Other characteristics of the technology raise potentially more serious obstacles to its adoption. Consider the question of compatibility: the degree to which the innovation "fits in" – not only with existing technology but with all other aspects of the user organization.* Here, attention has to be paid to technological isolation: industrial applications are limited considerably at present by the fact that microelectronics has developed at a faster rate than the peripheral sensing and actuating technologies. Until it is possible to measure variables and convert this information to a suitable signal and, at the other end of the process, actuate a suitably responsive controlling device, applications will not fully benefit from the use of microelectronics. However, new developments in transducers and fluidics are signs of a catching-up process.

Compatibility with the physical environment can also present problems. Microelectronics components are highly sensitive and fragile, and many users report having had problems with electrical noise, dirt and dust, on-line interference and direct physical damage to their systems. Incompatibility of this kind may be minimized by attention to the design of the system as a whole, although for potential users wishing to make only limited use of microelectronics the problem remains. The issue of compatibility may also become important when the organizational environment is considered. Evidence suggests that introducing microelectronics into organizations where such a change is seen as radical is accompanied by major difficulties. Despite their modular design and "idiot-proof" nature, such systems depend on suitable operators and maintenance, and their effectiveness can be considerably reduced if such personnel are not present.

Finally, before leaving the characteristics of the innovation itself, two further features deserve mention: complexity and observability. The former relates to the fact that the extent to which an innovation can be understood will also determine the rate at which it is adopted. In the

---

* An industry is unlikely to adopt a technology which has a rate of obsolescence incompatible with that of its own products or production facilities. A case in point is the late adoption of electronics by the car industry.

case of microelectronics this is particularly true, since the technology involved is highly complex and sophisticated. Programmers and electronic engineers are in great demand as a result, and fear of dependence on specialists is a commonly reported resistance to adoption. "Failsafe" options are a key requirement specified by users who cannot risk production stoppages, especially on continuous operations. Reservations have been expressed about the difficulty of testing chips: this leads to reluctance to entrust important operations to them.

Observability is closely related to complexity, referring to how "visible" the innovation is. Since its functional operation is completely invisible, this is one of the central psychological problems associated with the use of microelectronics. It is this "black box" nature which is responsible for much hesitation on behalf of potential adopters and reflects the difficulty in accepting that it is no longer necessary to see (or know) what goes on within a system in order to reap its benefits. That people watch television without understanding the technology involved does not alter the fact that they wish to understand what they are supposed to control.

Innovator characteristics. The person trying to market new microelectronic capital products to manufacturers finds a number of problems. After initial failures by companies trying to include component manufacture and assembly in their operations, most firms are now content to buy in hardware and assemble and program it according to specific applications. Attempts are being made to simplify programming languages, and diagnostics have also developed considerably, thus reducing after-sales commitment. One problem here is that in "idiotproofing" a system, knowledge of all possible sources of failure needs to be programmed in, and this information is clearly never completely available. Cooperation with the user is necessary to monitor problems and continually update this feature.* Indeed, close contact at all stages appears to be of considerable importance: for example, innovators frequently report problems in obtaining suitably detailed specifications of user needs. This is, of course, just the usual requirement for successful product innovation: efficient market coupling. In view of high programming and development charges, a major problem facing innovators in microelectronics is that of cost reduction. One option is to sell to production machinery manufacturers, where high volume and reproducibility of sales is possible, although there appears to be resis-

---

* A problem with close user cooperation is that development of a system to suit the needs of one customer may involve licensing and confidentiality agreements to exclude the possibility of selling competitors similar systems. This is another factor influential in keeping specificity, and therefore costs, high.

tance in this sector to joint ventures. Original equipment markets also have the problem of being linked to investment cycles, and although the cost of the microelectronics involved may be small, the overall unit has high capital costs and thus long working life before replacement. Several industries report having missed the microelectronics boat on their last investment round and are now committed to several years' operation before replacement with more sophisticated plant. Selling into existing production layouts depends upon the flexibility of the device and its compatibility: in almost every case where problems were reported, both user and innovator indicated that the "green field option", which we referred to earlier, would have eliminated them.

Finally, the innovator is faced with the question of service: here reputation counts for a great deal and most user organizations need to have confidence in their suppliers in the introduction of what is often a radical and complex technology. Close user/innovator coupling before, during and after introduction is strongly associated with success, while there are numerous warning tales of incompatibility, poor design and unmaintainable equipment associated with bad relationships.

Adopter characteristics. Despite the wide-ranging advantages associated with microelectronics, it is clear that they are not the answer to every organization's prayer. Table 4.7 indicates the pattern of factors favouring and retarding the introduction of microelectronics across a number of industrial sectors: from this it can be seen that take-up is likely to be varied.*

Within different sectors, the size of organization is an important variable. The most direct way in which size determines adoption is in internal organizational capability. Large organizations can usually afford research into long-term technological options and often have internal resources to devote to them (in the form of R&D, OR, and similar groups). Small firms usually have to go outside for their technology and, unless they can afford it, will have to rely on standard rather than user-specific systems. The MAPCON† scheme is one attempt at redressing this balance and should prove particularly attractive to small firms.

Size is also related to "innovative inertia" in a technology such as microelectronics: to introduce it on a small scale requires limited commitment, but in large-scale operations major strategic decisions are involved and occupy long time-scales for both decision making and implementation. Thus many large organizations report interest and

---

* This table is intended to provide only a rough indication of factors affecting adoption. Within each sector there are, of course, wide variations.

† MAPCON is the Microprocessor Application Project Consultancy Scheme, sponsored by the Department of Industry.

Table 4.7 Factors in the diffusion of microelectronics for some industrial sectors

Sector	Factors favouring the adoption of microelectronics	Factors retarding the introduction of microelectronics
1 Chemicals	Improvements in process and quality control – accuracy, reproducibility, safety New options for automated and/or continuous operation, including on-line optimization Some saving of labour Savings in energy and raw materials through better controls (especially on high throughput processes, as in petrochemicals) Improved production management by better information and monitoring systems Automation in packaging and improved stock-keeping and distribution Reduced need for work in hostile environments Improved pollution controls	Capital-intensive industry with plants of long life Tradition of incremental process innovation Tradition of low-technology process controls (except in petrochemicals) Low labour intensity. Shortages of maintenance workers and especially instrument and electronic technicians Inadequate development of sensors and actuators for some processes and vulnerability of microelectronics in hostile environments
2 Pharmaceuticals	Improvement in accuracy and reproducibility of process control Improved quality control Reduction of hazards Improved efficiency in automated weighing, packaging and distribution Some labour saving Some move from batch production to automated continuous production	Research-intensive industry with little emphasis on production efficiency and much emphasis on product innovation High profit margins even with low production technology
3 Paper and allied products	Possibility of fully automated production Improved control of processes and quality	Highly capital-intensive industry subject to trade cycles and low profit margins

Sector	Factors favouring the adoption of microelectronics	Factors retarding the introduction of microelectronics
	Savings in energy and in materials, especially in additives Improved materials handling and distribution systems, better waste recycling facilities Possibility of wider range of products through finer control of composition	Low labour usage even with low technology Lack of suitable sensors and actuators No tradition of innovation
4 Food and Drink	Shift towards continuous automated production Improvements in mechanical handling of fragile products Improved process and quality control Improved control over additives in response to public pressure Automation of packaging and distribution Improved stockholding Some labour saving Savings in energy and materials Shift to process improvement as alternative to product innovation to remain competitive	Slow rate of plant renewal in relatively capital-intensive and low-profit industry High cost of materials Intense competition and pressure from legislation Labour cost relatively small portion of total costs Highly specialized process and quality variables for which no adequate sensors and actuators exist No tradition of process innovation Large-volume operations, (for instance, biscuit manufacture), already highly mechanized
5 Plastics and Rubber	Improvements in process control offering savings in energy and materials Improved monitoring and control of production process, e.g. improved scheduling Automated and integrated operations, continuous or semi-continuous, with self-feeding and optimization Handling machines for feeding	Industry has to wait for suitable modernized machinery to come on the market Low labour intensity Much of the industry composed of very small plants with very short production runs Prices determined mainly by costs of raw materials

Sector	Factors favouring the adoption of microelectronics	Factors retarding the introduction of microelectronics
	moulding presses Improved safety Some labour saving	Profit margins depressed by intense competition
6 Motor Vehicles and Accessories	Automated warehousing improving stock control Improvement over wide range of production controls, e.g. automated assembly, spot welding robots, paint spraying robots, automated machining, press transfer machinery Considerable labour saving, skilled and unskilled Some saving of materials Opportunities for computer-aided design Improved flow of production Possibility of working to finer tolerances leading to improved product quality Improved products incorporating microelectronics	Severe industrial relations problems Shortages of labour with required skills Large investment in existing production facilities Shortage of investment capital because of squeezed profit margins owing to severe competition
7 Metals Manufacture	Process control and monitoring remote from hostile environment Improved quality and reproducibility of products Savings in energy and materials Extensive labour saving in some cases Improved safety Improved working environment	Fragmented capital-intensive industry with a few large and many small firms Small firms have low level of technical awareness in management, strong traditional orientation, and shortage of risk capital Overcapacity: fierce competition forcing industry into recession Poor industrial relations Technical limitations of microelectronics in hostile environments
8 Metals Fabrication	Automated welding, handling, painting	Large diversity of products often with very small batch

Sector	Factors favouring the adoption of microelectronics	Factors retarding the introduction of microelectronics
	Computer-controlled machining Production controls, warehousing Savings in materials, energy and some labour Automated handling by robotic devices in mass production	production Retention of highly skilled labour necessary, automation in less skilled areas only Capital cost of automated machinery high
9 Textiles	Automated manufacture and continuous operations Control of manufacture, including stockholding and distribution Materials handling Weaving, printing and dyeing can be made very flexible by computer control Improved speeds and quality control Extensive savings on labour Tradition of programmable operations	Shortage of capital because of intense pressure from (mainly foreign) competition Industrial relations problems and severe problems of regional unemployment Strong commitment to existing (often outdated) plant; high capital cost of new plant
10 Electrical and Electronic Products	Improved production control Automated machining, assembly and wiring Extensive labour saving (at least in some sectors, notably telecommunications) Extensive knowhow available Product innovation and manufacturing innovation go hand in hand as many mechanical linkages are replaced by electronic logic Semiconductor industry requires adequate environmental and process control which are only possible by use of electronics	Industrial relations problems Severe competition and considerable import penetration, especially in some components Low capital availability and overcapacity in certain parts of the industry (such as consumer goods) Certain areas fragmented and not highly automated Shortage of skills in certain areas (such as electronic technicians)

activity in the area of microelectronics applications, but it may well take two years or longer to see the fruits of their involvement on a large scale.

The basic experience and level of technology practised by the organization and its competitors will be a significant determinant of applicability and compatibility: thus differences in adoption patterns will be apparent between high and low technology sectors (for instance petrochemicals and refractories) and "leader"/"follower" organizations. Whatever the sector, an important condition for the adoption of new technology will be the availability of technically competent personnel, particularly in managerial positions within the adopting firm.

Related to the size of the organization and its use of sophisticated technology is the question of general awareness. This factor is particularly significant in small and traditional organizations. Most people have heard the term microprocessor, but understanding of the overall concept and, more importantly, its possible applications is far less developed. In many respects it represents a parallel to the "not invented here" problem – firms may believe microelectronics is "not applicable here", without adequate investigation of the state of the art and its possibilities. "Gatekeeper" figures within the organization can often play an important part in calling attention to the potential of microelectronics.

In the case of large organizations implementing major schemes, the internal structure may well be modified by the adoption of microelectronics and there is evidence that such structural alterations are by no means welcome in all cases. Information flow rearrangement and the rise of specialist skill groups modify the balance of power and control at all levels. This requires suitable new structures for activities from shop floor to senior management level, at the same time integrating their efforts more closely according to systems principles. Defensive reactions to these changes can be an important contributory factor to slow take-up.

With smaller, more specific applications there remains the problem of alterations to work patterns This may take the form of replacement of labour, displacement (e.g. from operator to machine minder), or "expansion", where the content of the job increases (such as one man taking responsibility for several automated machines). In turn this may reduce or eliminate the need for supervisory staff, since monitoring and control can take place directly. Microelectronics can, of course, be applied in single isolated cases by virtue of its cost and flexibility; in this instance there will be little effect on the organization.

In general, though, microelectronics alters existing production patterns, and this has implications for both management and labour. The possibility of labour-saving replacement of scarce skills, improvements in flexibility, mobility and the like through the use of microelectronics must be set in the context of industrial relations. Examples of success and failure in this area reinforce the importance of staff consultation. Similarly, making more information available for all concerned via monitoring and display systems has improved cooperation in a number of cases.

Training is another area in which changes in production patterns have significant implications. Provision of enough skilled and experienced personnel to cope with operating and servicing microelectronics largely depends on internal development schemes, since demand on the open market for such staff is high. The problem of retaining trained personnel is also commonly reported; pay restrictions within firms tend to stimulate high mobility of this group.

Before leaving the users of the new technology, it is necessary to point to some of the more significant economic factors involved. Mention has already been made of the problem of capital commitment and investment cycles, which makes the *timing* of microelectronics adoption an important factor. Further, the attractive investment characteristics which are associated with microelectronics (such as rate of return and payback time) do not hold for capital equipment in general. Investment patterns are depressed and some sectors have over-capacity, so technological expansion rates are often slow. The exception to this is, of course, the electronics industry itself.

This section has attempted to outline some of the more important factors involved in the take-up of microelectronics by manufacturing industry. Of course, simply focusing attention on the characteristics of the innovation, the innovators and the users themselves, cannot provide a complete picture of developments. We must also take account of more general environmental factors. For example, it is important to point out the significance of current trends and fashions. Whether market-led or stimulated as a result of campaigning and publicity, evidence suggests that interest in microelectronics is high at present. However, in many cases this is not supported by an understanding of what microelectronics is or what it can be applied to, and there are many examples of inappropriate applications of fashionable technology when a simpler alternative was available and more appropriate. Unfortunate experiences such as these may well act as a deterrent to adoption if they become widespread and well-known.

Finally, the environment within which debates surrounding microelectronics are taking place is heavily influenced both by public opinion and by government. The former, rightly concerned with the effects of the new technology on employment, may act to slow the rate of diffusion, while the policies of government are explicitly designed to increase it. It is in reconciling these conflicting interests that the most immediate challenge for policy lies, and to this we now turn.

Some policy considerations
Earlier we looked at the wide range of motives influencing the decision
to innovate in production methods. We suggested that despite the
potentially labour-saving nature of such changes the desire to reduce
labour was by no means the only factor determining the introduction
of the innovation. Other requirements were equally important: for
example, the desire to increase output; the need to achieve greater consistency and/or quality of production; and the requirements imposed by
health and safety considerations. If an innovation is undertaken in
response to these pressures, then clearly labour-saving plays a less
important part and indeed need not occur at all. This is not, of course,
intended to imply that questions of employment (whether loss of jobs or
de-skilling) are unimportant.

Although our case studies have not revealed major redundancies, it is
generally true that the studies have only been concerned with the use of
microelectronics on a limited scale. Thus it may be the case that
redundancies have been avoided by management for strategic reasons,
and that with a more widespread adoption of the technology the picture
might change markedly.

Increasing productivity resulting from innovation, particularly in an
expanding market, can enable employment levels to be maintained
within an innovating firm. It may also be the case that reductions in the
labour force can be partially compensated by increased labour demand
in those industries supplying equipment using microelectronics. But this
clearly depends on the extent to which these industries are themselves
subject to manufacturing innovations, and on the degree of foreign
competition. On this latter point, there is a clear need for British
industry to develop a capacity not only in the production of microelectronics itself but also in a diverse range of capital equipment using the
new technology.

Other prescriptions for alleviating technological unemployment are
by now familiar: shorter hours, earlier retirement, an expansion of
services, and encouragement of new products of all kinds, capital and
consumer. The last two of these remedies require mobility of labour
both in terms of geographical location and in terms of crossing skill
boundaries. The shift in employment from manufacture to services is
likely to continue and might even accelerate. Despite the loss of jobs
following the introduction of microelectronics in certain areas of the
service sector, other areas will benefit from the new technology through
increased efficiency and therefore increased demand.*

* Services internal to manufacturing industry will be subject to similar trends.

In general, it is essential that Britain's record in the realms of technological innovation should be rapidly improved. Incremental innovation and improvement are important to keep existing products and processes competitive and new products are vital to create opportunities by satisfying both existing and new demands. Of course, the problem of encouraging innovation is not a new one and much government activity is directed towards this goal. The real difficulty is not perhaps the total level of activity – although it has been shown that Britain is falling behind its competitors in R&D effort – but rather the choice of projects and the effectiveness of the coupling between R&D and innovation. For example, the employment potential of the small firm is important because some innovations take place most readily in entrepreneurial firms. Also, changes in technology in large organizations often require the services and goods supplied by small firms surrounding the large one in a symbiotic relationship.

The extent to which labour displaced from traditional areas of manufacturing industry can be absorbed by a shift of employment to services and the manufacture of new products, whether in large or small firms, remains an open question. What is clear is that these (and many other) policy options need to be fully explored if unemployment resulting from the introduction of new technology is to be minimized, if Britain is to remain competitive in international markets, and if a national capability in a radical new technology is to be fostered. Achieving these aims poses some fundamental problems, and attempts to frame relevant policies to date have tended to focus largely on stimulating the adoption and diffusion of microelectronics rather than on reconciling widespread use of the new technology with wider social objectives.

The arguments that have encouraged concentration on the use of microelectronics are by now familiar: in a world of relatively free trade, British industry must do everything in its power to be internationally competitive, and one of the things that can be done is to increase productivity by using microelectronics. While this will reduce the number of employees required to produce the present range and quantity of goods, thereby creating – other things being equal – technological unemployment, it is nonetheless essential if Britain is to remain internationally competitive and job losses are not to become yet more severe in future. Moreover, every historical period has one or more "leading edges" of technological change, and the current leading edge is associated with microelectronics. Thus if Britain is to remain a technologically advanced country it must advance along the leading edge by making use of microelectronics.

While these arguments must command our attention, they are, by themselves, not sufficient. Technology policy has to mean more than a concern for the rapid diffusion of new technologies at all costs, and there is an urgent need to work towards an integration of technical and social policies on the understanding that neither are effective by themselves. This can only be accomplished if the problem is attacked at a variety of levels. It will be necessary to continue detailed studies of the adoption of microelectronics in individual firms in order to avoid mere speculation as to what *might* happen with its introduction. At the same time, the debates have to be widened to include not only those who might introduce the new technology but also those who will be most affected by it. Wide-ranging discussion, consultation and investigation are required. The issues are too important for policy to be solely the province of government.

Guide to Further Reading

Two papers from the Science Policy Research Unit at Sussex University are worth looking out: the first, by Ray Curnow and Chris Freeman, is called *Product and Process Change Arising From the Microprocessor Revolution and Some of the Economic and Social Issues*, and is available from SPRU. It takes a broad-brush look at the impact of microelectronics on the manufacturing process and goes on to discuss the possible employment impact against a background of low economic growth and energy crisis. The perilous position of UK industry is highlighted. Mick McLean and Howard Rush, *The Impact of Microelectronics on the UK: A Suggested Classification and Illustrative Case Studies* (SPRU Occasional Paper No. 7), is a well-written analysis of international trends in the adoption of microelectronic technology and the poor performance of the UK with reference to four industries: materials handling (forklift trucks); textile machinery; automobiles and office products.

Two general articles are:

R. Allan, "Electronics Boost Productivity", *IEEE Spectrum*, vol. 15, No. 1 (January 1978).

M. E. Merchant, "Technology Assessment of the Computer-Integrated Automatic Factory", Final Report, *CIRP Annals*, vol. 25, No. 2 (1976).

On robots, two highly readable pieces are:

Caroline Weinstein, "Robots in Industry – Too Few or Too Many?" *Electronics and Power* (May 1978). A lively introduction to robots and interviews with academics, trade unionists and employers on reasons for their low take-up in the UK.

James Woudhuysen, "Look, No Hands", *Design* 339 (March 1977), an account of eight Japanese factories using robots on production lines.

Two "think" pieces are:

M. E. Merchant, "Social Effects of Automation in Manufacturing", in *Proceedings of the 1976 Joint Automatic Control Conference, West Lafayette, Indiana* (American Society of Mechanical Engineers, New York, 1976).

M. Zinkin, "The Impact of Social Change on Industry", *Technology and Society*, vol. 6 (May 1976).

5 The Revolution in the Office

The Automated Office

J. Christopher Burns

The author of this introductory article, who is a researcher with international consultants Arthur D. Little Inc., sets the scene on the "office revolution" with a sober account of the new technology available and the scope for office managers to improve efficiency. While some dramatic changes in offices are on the cards, he cautions that there are many problems to overcome yet. This article first appeared in the US publication Datamation, *in April 1977.*

Over the past few years we have seen a dramatic increase in the number of new products aimed at simplifying the task of writing memos, letters and reports. Under the banner of "Word Processing" (WP) or "Office of the Future", businesses are experimenting with the long evolutionary process that promises to streamline information exchange in the office and stem the rising tide of paper. To get a sense of where this evolution is taking us, and at what speed, let's look back briefly at the changes which have already occurred.

Twenty-five years ago a letter was written by hand or dictated to one's secretary who transcribed it later from her own shorthand. A draft was typed, revised, and retyped with several carbon copies – one for the file and one to be circulated or "routed" across the desks of all interested parties. There was an art to routing a carbon, and a cost. The pecking order was occasionally violated; a junior staffer sometimes missed a useful lesson; and people often arrived for meetings who had not seen the memo and were unprepared.

In time, dictation equipment eliminated the need for shorthand skills and made possible a central typing pool, though even now there are organizations which cannot afford the work separation and queueing implied. While several million dictation machines are in use today – 600,000 shipped in 1975 alone – there remains a significant resistance to the device. The overwhelming majority of letters, memos, reports and contracts are still drafted by hand.

At least the carbon paper is gone. We estimate that while sixty-five billion copies were still made on conventional spirit and stencil duplicators during 1976, about seventy-eight billion copies were made on convenience copiers in the office – about 5000 made for *each* of the

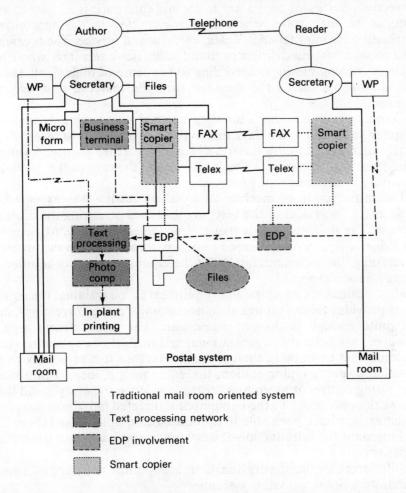

Fig. 5.1 First text processing and photocomposition are added to the traditional "mail room oriented" office information structure. As soon as communications capability is added, existing computerized business systems immediately become involved. (We're just experimenting at that level now.) Future products, like smart copiers, will help to tie the mix together

fifteen million secretaries, stenographers, typists, and clerical workers employed in the US during that year. The photocopy machine is as close to a revolution as we are likely to see in the growth of business communications systems, and it single-handedly raised the office mail room to the stature of a major information switch.

Consider the office information system as it operates today (Fig. 5.1). The author of a message (a memo, report, letter or contract) drafts it with his secretary, revises the draft, corrects the revision and reviews the correction. Sufficient copies are made and then each is addressed and sent to the mail room where it is transmitted to the appropriate destination via internal mail, Telex, or the postal service. The receiving mail room sorts and distributes to the addressee's secretary who sorts again, screening messages according to her sense of their significance, and then supplements the message with file material that may be appropriate.

Communications within a building can take a day; going through the postal system takes two days under the best of circumstances – and nearly all messages follow this route regardless of their nature. An angry blast from the boss will take as long to make the tour as the quarterly inventory listing from data processing.

The introduction of mechanical word processing was expected to eliminate a good deal of the retyping that goes on during the drafting process. The ability to store text on a removable medium (card, cassette, cartridge or floppy disc) seemed to be a natural answer to the problem of retyping the document, but so far the equipment has not resulted in the revolution expected.

Most designs are complex and require extended training; the equipment provides more features than necessary to make corrections, and not quite enough to do major revisions. The most difficult aspect, however, has been the organizational and work flow implications of a machine that costs more than $10,000. Because it is too costly to be installed at every typing station, the equipment is located in a word processing centre, or given to a "correspondence secretary", and then the work appropriate to the equipment is directed into the queue. Few organizations have been able to optimize the equipment and the work, and for many the introduction of word processing has been a frustrating experience.

Still, forces are driving organizations to experiment further with more elaborate office information systems:

(1) The scope of management has broadened over the last decade. Organizations grow more complex and data processing brings in rapid measurement of performance from diverse corners of the manager's

field of responsibility; he is arguing now that he has a commensurate need to communicate.

(2) Certain kinds of operating information lose their value over time, and a delay in assembling the right proposal, the complete answer or the appropriate files can mean a missed opportunity. If managers are to be made more effective, they need better information systems.

(3) There is a sincere desire in some quarters to eliminate the tedious aspects of the secretary's job, thereby "enriching" it. This is, in part, a self-serving goal: a secretary who isn't retyping the report for the fourth time can be gainfully employed at other tasks. But there is also the hope that a revised secretarial role which minimizes the typing, the sorting and the message switching might ease the way for talented women whose progress has so far been blocked by the rigid clerical/ management caste system.

Finally, there is an urge to try new office systems because new systems are possible. In the last few years we have seen several technological developments that may support some of the bolder approaches:

- The cost of microprocessors is dropping sharply, even as their power and flexibility increase. An 8K processor capable of performing text editing is expected to drop in cost from $200 to $50 over the next ten years.
- The cost of solid-state memory will fall even more rapidly. We estimate that by 1986 a typewriter could be equipped with 256K memory for less than $100.
- Telephone technology is expected to make important progress in the near future, allowing faster and simpler management of digital data.
- New imaging devices may replace the electro-mechanical impact print mechanisms that dominate the office. Ink jet is already available. Low-power lasers may be used in the near future to image the photoconductor of an office copier, painting the characters directly from a distant computer's memory.
- Further developments are expected in microform technology, and in the physical storage and retrieval systems which manage these important image files. We expect to see a continued growth of computer output microfilm technology, particularly as computer systems begin to manage correspondence and other text files in addition to their data processing (DP) chores.
- Distributed systems based on minicomputers are already successfully dealing with the problem of supporting more than one hundred special terminals, printers and other peripherals in a text

processing environment. The newspaper industry has been working with such systems for more than five years.

- We expect future software offerings to support the need for far-flung peripherals accessing the system on dial-up lines for the purpose of storing, retrieving and editing text. Existing text-editing software packages like ATMS and STAIRS are practically obsolete in the face of demands for far more sophisticated capabilities.

Out of this ferment we expect to see several classes of products arise, each helping to define the evolution of office information systems. For example, while mechanical word processing equipment (word processors without video display) will continue to be sold by IBM, Xerox, Redactron, and others, there is growing evidence to suggest that display word processors will overtake their predecessors – certainly in the rate of market acceptance. Users appear to be selecting display devices not as supplements to, but as replacements for mechanical word processing.

From the beginning of WP development there has been a class of shared-logic word processing products. A similar class of systems has arisen in the printing and publishing industry, designed to handle the text-processing requirements of newspapers, though some of these have been sold to support the most formal of office messages: reports, manuals and proposals. The distinction between these product classes – if ever there was one – is growing blurred. Together they define an important evolutionary stage.

A document destined for this system is typically drafted by the secretary in an optically scannable font (modified Courier, for example) with a minimum of coding. The document is scanned into the system, proofs are generated on a high-speed printer, and revisions are made as required in the central editing facility. Ultimately the document, supplemented by boilerplate or other frequently used material, is composed on an impact printing device, or on a photocomposer capable of setting type in several faces and in many different sizes. Such systems appear to offer several advantages: revisions are far easier to accomplish and can be done in the context of a substantial software environment; any ten-pitch typewriter can become an "input station" by snapping in a different typing element ($18); and photocomposition is often able to assemble more text on a page while retaining – even enhancing – legibility. Paper savings of twenty-five per cent are not unusual. (See Figs. 5.2 and 5.3.)

As more word processors are equipped with communications capability, some of the initial output and much of the editing can be done remotely. Word processors communicating in a dial-up mode can establish a network allowing a draft to be "routed" for review and comment before being delivered to a central facility for final composition. The Federal Trade Commission has set out to build such a network, nationwide, using Dacronics (Xerox) display word processors. Commercial firms, including Arthur D. Little, Inc., hope to develop such networks to link branch and international offices in an early electronic mail system.

The existing business systems are likely to become involved fairly quickly after the establishment of a word processing network. In most installations a digital data network has already been set up to meet business related demands, and word processing users may seek this switching capability.

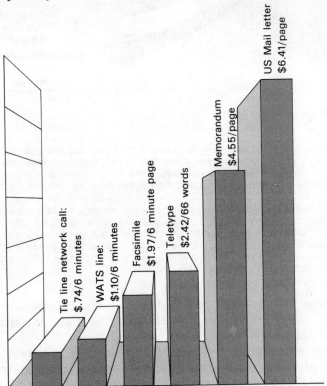

Fig. 5.2 What does it cost to communicate?
In surveying its competition, the US Post Office recently reported that business communications costs were heavily in favour of digital data transmission. On the basis of this information, at least one major corporation urged its staff to use facsimile and Telex whenever possible. A memorandum to that effect was mailed to all 10,000 employees

The display word processors equipped with communications capability can begin to resemble the universal office terminal so frequently predicted, and we expect that in many situations there will be one more

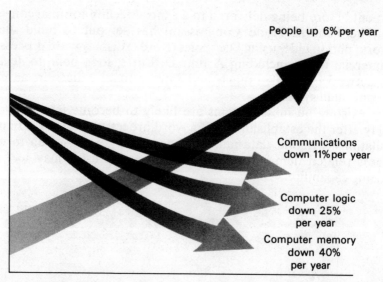

People up 6% per year

Communications
down 11% per year

Computer logic
down 25%
per year

Computer memory
down 40%
per year

Fig. 5.3 What will it cost tomorrow?
Although the rate of change varies among specific technologies, certain general trends can be identified among the elements which will determine the cost of business communications over the next ten years. One public utility installed a central word processing system and saved more than $200,000 in labour the first year. They expect to save more than $1m each year when the full program is implemented. A large manufacturer installed an electronic mail system on the offpeak hours of a private telephone network and saved $200,000 on postage for intra-company mail. He also got overnight delivery around the world. A major computer manufacturer uses text editing equipment and photocomposition to prepare documentation and manuals, and expects to save several hundred thousand dollars each year in paper and warehousing. He gets more text on the page and the manual is easier to read. A large bank converted its letter of credit file to updatable microfiche and now has a faster update cycle and better control over the records

persuasive argument for adding dial-up communications management facilities to the mainframe, thereby bringing it into the growing office systems network.

The main computer system may also be linked to the text processing system, providing large, long-term storage of contracts and reports, and annexing that photocomposition capability as an alternative computer output device.

File management. The remote business terminal, a traditional and successful alternative for providing conventional data processing services, may take on an interesting new role in conjunction with recent innovations in image storage and retrieval. Central to most office information systems is an image file. It may contain the actual hardcopy files of orders, shipping and accounting actions, personnel records, etc, or have the same information recorded on microfilm or microfiche, or be built on the newer, updatable microfiche systems.

In many cases these files cannot be replaced by digital storage; signatures have legal significance, and paper or silver-based films have archival qualities essential to many kinds of files. Nonetheless, serious efforts have been made in the past few years to use data processing as an aid in managing these files. A capsule summary of the hardcopy record, for example, may be digitally stored in a companion file in the computer. In many situations the majority of questions can be answered using the digital file, thus avoiding the arduous task of pulling a folder (and putting it back).

At the office of the Secretary of the Army, one gets a fascinating glimpse of what some of this new technology can mean in managing a flood of office documents. There, each letter, report, memorandum, and contract is recorded on updatable microfiche as soon as it arrives in the mail room. A companion record is made in a digital file, noting the origin, destination, date, and nature of the document. Thereafter, the images that have been selected for this control can be quickly retrieved by one or more of a dozen variable terms. The digital system identifies the microfiche – and the panel – on which each image is stored and the information can be then viewed on a reader, or reconstituted as a full-sized hard copy. Other government agencies use the same system to manage massive personnel files, and still others are exploring the system's potential for managing a complex library of technical documentation.

As word processing and microform systems evolve, it is likely that the existing DP facilities will be called upon to assist in the management of large files; contracts, memoranda, reports, documentation, correspondence, and perhaps reference data frequently used.

One of the major issues concerning organizations moving in this direction is the availability of software to manage files whose primary relationship is not sequential but contextual. Given a subject, an author, an approximate date, a contract number, or an employee's name, the system may be asked to report an index of documents on a digital (or image) file and must be prepared to deliver that index at a remote terminal or facility.

This is not to suggest that a new level of data-base management tools will herald the paperless (or even less-paper) office, but that such tools would materially assist the organization in preparing, consulting and distributing documents considered to be significant.

Electronic mail. In time, the main computer system – or a subordinate processor – might take on the characteristics of a protected message switch capable of distributing a document to multiple terminals (both video and hardcopy) simultaneously. Such a system would include such standard features as store and forward, format for Telex, redial and/or retransmit, and journalize. Many corporations already have rudimentary electronic mail systems, and it would seem logical to incorporate this transmission capability into an overall system which supports preparation, composition, and retrieval.

One of the more serious obstacles to software products in this area is the variety of message formats employed in office communications. Though apparently simple, they present the user with a complex variety of ways in which to transmit his message: the memo (multiple copies or routed), the sealed envelope, the authorized message (signed), the letter (with copies to . . .), the broadcast announcement to all staff, the handwritten blast, the marginal comment. Replicating these formats in a protected switch implies several levels of confidentiality, several levels of priority, the ability to chain messages together and incorporate comment, as well as a very advanced mailbox capability.

Finally, it is logical to expect that such a fully formed central DP facility would find enormous advantage in developing communications capabilities with other branches of the organization, thus completing the network from word processor to word processor, from universal terminal to a distant microfiche file, from one portion of the organization's data-base to another. There is nothing blue-sky about this. Since the late 1960s such linked-processor, linked-file systems have been used by various branches of the government and by some large corporations to manage inventory, order processing, and highly structured communications. The innovation is merely a shift from fixed-field, numerical records to an admittedly more complex format containing text. In the process, though, the DP facility has assumed the role once performed by the mail room; it is now the primary information switch in the organization.

There are more new products to be announced. It is axiomatic that continued reduction in the cost of electronics, plus further development in the power and flexibility of microprocessors, will have a major influence on the shape of word processing equipment over the next few years. New displays are possible, new storage media feasible and very different approaches can be made to the operator/function interface. Beyond this, we can expect those suppliers of text-editing systems for the newspaper industry to announce products for the office market. This would simply be a normal outgrowth of existing product classes.

More dramatic announcements are possible. We expect to see a new class of typewriters announced with minimal display and correction capabilities at prices far closer to the $800 cost of a typical office typewriter. We expect to see important improvements in microform technology, taking advantage of the new vesicular microfilms.

The "smart copier". The most interesting of these new products is likely to be the "smart copier", a combination of traditional electrostatic copying technology with a low-power laser character generator and a communications interface. The ability to form sharply imaged letters with a laser has been part of phototypesetting technology for several years; the letter shape is typically called from memory in response to a single code and imaged by a modulated laser on to dry silver paper at speeds of up to 1000 characters per second. It is at least theoretically possible to image the photoconductor of an office copier in the same way with the effect of turning the copier into a silent, reasonably high-speed printer/duplicator.

Such a device, on-line to the kind of DP office information facility described above, would be a natural adjunct to word processing, electronic mail, and even remote business applications. The quality of the letter shape could exceed the impact print quality now standard in most offices. Furthermore, both the IBM 4640 Ink Jet printer and Kodak's Ektaprint Copier/Duplicator demonstrate important improvements in paper handling technology that would presumably be incorporated into a new design. The 4640 even addresses envelopes.

In the distant future lies the now famous "terminal on every desk", though it is more likely to be part of the telephone than the kind of monitor we know today, probably a 3-inch × 5-inch screen or panel with a simple thirty-character key pad not very different from the sort used in a pocket calculator (and by the way, the phone will *include* a calculator). Whether the telephone system will ultimately replace large portions of our ingeniously designed DP office information system is a debate we can confidently anticipate, even if we can't set the date. Evolutions take time. After all, it took ten years to add the shift key to the early typewriter.

Technology over common sense?
Just because the system can be built doesn't mean it will be, or even that it ought to be. The obstacles to a logical evolution of office information systems are enormous. The relationship between management and clerical staff in an office, for example, is built on years of experience and habits not easily changed. In the technical area, communications protocols already introduced into the office via word processing, text editing, remote business terminals, facsimile transmission, teletype networks, and distributed data processing are inconsistent and defy integration.

Even the suppliers can't get their act together. The floppy disc used by IBM's System/32 is not compatible with the floppy disc used in the System 6; Digital Equipment's word processor cannot communicate with Digital Equipment's text processor; Harris's text processing systems cannot be linked to Harris's switching systems, and so it goes.

Although many of these components will find their way into the office independently of any plan, they must sooner or later be connected and rationalized. Who will do that, and when? The office manager who bought the magnetic card typewriters? The Report Centre manager who bought the text editing system? The Record Systems manager who bought the shared-logic microfiche system? The telecommunications manager who just leased an electronic mail system? No, in all probability it will be the DP manager, because he has the budget to do "systems maintenance" and the staff to evaluate the user's needs across the corporation, and because – quite correctly – information is his business.

Information networks constitute the nervous system of an organization, and if they cannot be planned together, they should at least be supervised under a common management objective. Many DP managers already experience some of this problem: the organization maintains a business system (typically batch processing), the rudiments of a message switching system, and a timeshared system for engineering and program development, while simultaneously supporting a legion of faceless APL terminals on a dozen different outside machines. Office information systems are likely to aggravate that complex situation, even while they process memos about fixing it.

Johnny still can't read

Finally, there is the sobering question of who will use the system, and how? Persons writing and reading documents in the office today have measurably lower reading and writing skills than the generation that preceded them. One of the "advantages" often cited for the dictation machine is that it is quicker. "I don't have to worry so much about the wording," the user admits. "I just say what I mean." As a matter of fact, he typically says it several times; after one boils down the message and adds up the cost, dictated letters and memos have a marked tendency to be longer and less efficient than hand drafted versions of the same message. When the message is formed and revised it is copied several times for the benefit of all interested parties, each of whom must now work his way through a higher stack of less efficient messages to do the same day's work.

There is serious evidence to support the argument that the next generation of managers will be even less skilled than the present. According to the Educational Testing Service in Princeton, New Jersey, reading comprehension scores achieved by college-bound high school students have dropped ten per cent over the past fifteen years. According to Dr Mel Levine of the Children's Medical Centre in Boston, writing disabilities among teenage children are "rampant".

It cannot be substantiated that television, or new teaching methods, or the habits of parents have damaged the reading and writing abilities of our children, but it is certainly clear that the *average* office worker and middle manager is less articulate than the average office worker of the preceding generation. For whatever reason, the probable user of office information systems is likely to be less competent in constructing and interpreting messages. He will talk longer, say less, make more copies of what he says, and not read his mail as quickly or comprehend it as well.

One can imagine that compensating filters will be erected to knock "junk mail" out of the queue, and that important messages will travel over a privileged network in a curt, staccato shorthand like the one which evolved on the Department of Defence's ARPA computer network. The critical signals will be delivered verbally, and the rationale behind decisions will be lost in the noise. But messages occupying the middle ground on the length/priority scale will swell to fill the available system, and join the growing tide of printout that already includes everything you always wanted to know but don't have the time to read.

Office information systems *will* evolve, many of the components are already available, and users are reporting that the benefits increase as the systems grow. The efficiency of our messages may decline as their number rises, but the technology contains the promise for new, more structured formats, far faster transmissions, lower costs, and easier access to complex files. After years of using computer technology to measure the work performed, we may soon be able to apply it to the communications process on which that work is based.

The Experience of Word Processing

EDP Analyzer

Plenty has been written about the potential of word processors, while little is known about the experience of those actually using them. The following is taken from a two-part analysis of the new office technology which appeared in the US publication EDP Analyzer *in early 1977. This condensed version comes from the British magazine* Data Processing *(May 1978) and uses two case studies to illustrate different ways of handling the new technology. A guide to the successful installation and operation of word processors is the main feature of the article.*

Some organizations have found that word processing has been accepted rather well by employees, while others have encountered considerable resistance. Let us consider two experiences that illustrate this.

The Federal Aviation Administration is the agency that regulates air commerce and traffic within the United States. It oversees a national system of airports and a common system of air traffic control. We visited one of the twelve regional offices of the FAA, located in Lawndale, a suburb of Los Angeles. There are about 500 employees at this office, working on such functions as air traffic, flight standards, air transportation security, airports, law, and aircraft engineering.

In mid-1975, this FAA office decided to investigate WP by first surveying the typing workload in two of the divisions – air transportation security and airports – as a sample of the total workload that a WP centre would have to handle. There were thirty "principals" in these two divisions; a principal (or author or word originator), in WP terminology, is any person in the office who originates written business communications. This initial study determined that the workload could be

232

handled by one correspondence secretary using the office's existing equipment – a stand-alone display text editor.

The next step in the study was a three-month test. During the test, all typing work from the two divisions was sent to the secretary at the WP centre. As so often happens when a WP centre is started, a lot of "hidden" work began appearing. This is work that should be done but has never been done due to a lack of enough secretarial support. This work most often comes from the lower levels of management and from other persons who receive "leftover" secretarial support in a traditional secretarial arrangement.

At the end of the test period, the WP study group had a good idea of the workload that a WP centre would have to handle. The next step was to investigate the various types of WP equipment on the market. So for several months, the WP study group visited numerous other WP centres. Based on its findings, the study group recommended that the FAA procure a shared-logic system with multiple terminals. Such a system would allow them to have a central file and would give them extensive editing capabilities. In addition, the existing stand-alone system was to be retained for use by offices not served by the new WP centre.

Preparation of the new WP centre then got under way. A user manual was developed for the two divisions to be served by the centre. A site was chosen, dictation training for principals was arranged, and a study was made of the workload for the *next* office whose work would be brought into the centre.

In mid-1976, the centre began operation. The first step was to enter and store some 200 frequently used "documents" for the divisions to be serviced. These included general forms, special-purpose forms and specified formats, and standard letters. Each principal received a user's manual which contained a copy of this commonly used information, plus a dictionary of words frequently misspelled and sound-alike words, a phonetic alphabet, tips on good dictation methods, and procedures for submitting work to the centre.

In one of the divisions served by the WP centre, fifteen principals previously had secretarial support from one typist and one secretary/specialist. The principals had to do some of their own typing and filing. When the WP centre was installed, these two secretaries became administrative secretaries and the non-typing work of the division was distributed between them. The decision on who would handle the various jobs was made by the secretaries themselves, based on their preferences and skills. They now handle the telephones, filing, mail, directives, small typing jobs, dictation, and so on. The new arrangement has also, to a large extent, freed the principals for their primary duties. All in all, the FAA is pleased with the new WP centre. It is gradually taking over the typing functions within the various divisions. But not all WP installations go in as easily. Sometimes considerable employee resistance is encountered. Consider the experience of Jewel Companies.

Jewel Companies is a diversified retailer with headquarters in Chicago, Illinois. Jewel consists of nine autonomous companies which operate supermarkets, drug stores, sandwich shops, self-service mass merchandising stores, and an in-home shopping service. Jewel has sales in excess of $2.8 billion a year and employs 21,500 full-time and 30,500 part-time employees.

In late 1972, a WP system was planned at the Jewel corporate office, using IBM magnetic card equipment. There were at that time eighty-three principals and thirty-four secretaries in the corporate office. But the idea of being a correspondence secretary in a WP centre (rather than dealing with the principals themselves, as an administrative secretary or a regular secretary) was not well received by many of these secretaries. So any secretary wishing to work in the traditional one-for-one environment was offered a transfer to another Jewel company.

The WP centre opened in February 1973, with a supervisor, twelve correspondence secretaries, and a work coordinator. The secretaries who remained in the various departments as administrative secretaries were reorganized into cluster groups. But they continued to report to the principals, rather than to an office supervisor.

The WP operation had top management support from the beginning – but it did not have middle management support. And from the beginning, employee resistance arose. Work turnaround from the WP centre was not fast enough to please users. The paperwork load on the administrative secretaries was "horrendous". Cooperation among the administrative secretaries was "limited". Communication between the administrative secretaries and the correspondence secretaries in the WP centre was "strained". In short, the WP management team felt that they had some real problems to resolve.

So Jewel tried another approach, where the administrative secretaries worked in a task-oriented manner. One secretary did filing for several principals, another handled the telephone for several principals, and so on. They found that this approach did not work well either, because no one secretary had a total picture of a principal's work. And the principals did not like having to deal with several different secretaries.

In mid-1973, principal-oriented secretarial teams were formed. Each principal dealt mainly with one secretary, but the secretaries in a team kept each other informed about their work and substituted for one another when necessary. A manager of secretarial services was selected. She, along with the WP manager, began working on the turnround problem and the communications with the WP centre. With this arrangement, things started to straighten out.

Jewel now has four secretarial grades and four salary levels, with the same grades and salary levels for the administrative secretaries and correspondence secretaries. So most secretaries see a career path ahead of them. The more complex the work of a principal, the higher the level of the secretary assigned.

The people at Jewel have learned a number of things from their experiences. Primarily, they learned that fitting the word processing and administrative support operation into their organization was an evolutionary process; they had to find out what worked for them. They are pleased with their current operation because it provides better office cost control; there is now a total of thirty-one secretaries, a coordinator, and two supervisors serving 110 principals where previously they had thirty-four secretaries to serve eighty-three principals. The department managers have been relieved of the secretarial management task. Further, Jewel has found that principals now prefer to talk to the administrative supervisor when there is a problem, rather than with the secretary.

Jewel has also found that there is a better workload distribution within the administrative teams; as productivity increased, so did job satisfaction. And some secretaries, seeing career paths ahead of them, are developing new skills and becoming specialists in their own areas of interest. Jewel believes that the administrative secretary is the key interface between principals and the WP centre. The administrative secretaries can either smooth things out or cause irritation and thus can make or break the operation. The Jewel Companies corporate headquarters is now much more satisfied with what word processing and administrative support is doing for them.

History of word processing

During its rather short existence (less than fifteen years), word processing has developed several branches and offshoots.

It all began in 1964 with the introduction of the IBM magnetic tape Selectric, an editing typewriter. The main claimed advantages were two: typists could type at rough draft speed (because changes could be made easily) and only the changes needed to be re-entered and proofread. But these two benefits did not really materialize. Editing typewriters required typists to enter editing codes along with the text, thus slowing down the typing speed. And the easy changes were limited to correcting typographical errors and one-word changes. A real jump forward occurred for word processing when the typewriter was tied to the computer, in the early 1970s.

Stand-alone display text editors. This popular type of word processing system typically consists of a minicomputer or microcomputer tied to a CRT (cathode-ray tube) display, a keyboard, a printer, and a storage device (usually a floppy disc or cassette recorder). The CRT display makes it easier to change the text and to see the effects of a change. The computer provides much greater power for making insertions, deletions, moving of text, and so on. Most systems use function keys for these actions but some still require the secretary to enter editing codes.

Shared-logic systems. The next obvious step was to use a somewhat more powerful (dedicated) computer for serving a cluster of input and output devices. It can serve several CRT input terminals, perhaps an optical character recognition (OCR) reader, and perhaps a high-speed (but correspondence quality) printer. Other options include photocomposition interface units and computer output microfilm interface units. Because the computer is larger than is normally found in stand-alone units, the capabilities generally are greater. Large amounts of text can be entered, accessed, edited, and merged by a number of typists at one time. With an OCR input option, documents typed on typewriters equipped with OCR font can be read into the system; secretaries at the display terminals can then edit the material, as needed. It is not too likely that manufacturers of word processing systems will push this option however, because it reduces the amount of word processing equipment needed.

Some of these systems also provide the global editing feature. With global editing, one command can initiate repetitive operations such as replacing all occurrences of a specific word. Some also provide a dictionary of abbreviations; the typist enters the abbreviation and the system expands it. Also, some manufacturers are now providing systems that will do both word *and* data processing.

Time-shared systems. These systems are the next logical step up the line from the shared-logic systems. Either the in-house central CPU or an outside time-sharing service can be used. The advantages are more extensive logic, faster output speeds, and other such benefits that typically come with larger computers.

There is a real problem, though, that is faced with many in-house CPUs. The majority of the CPUs in the field were developed for batch processing and do not handle interactive processing particularly well. Further, additional equipment (discs, memory, printers with both upper and lower case characters, etc) may be required. And word processing users will probably demand access to the system during all normal working hours, plus overtime hours for urgent work. Outside time-sharing companies offer word processing services. There are, however, wide differences in the capabilities and ease of use of these services.

The benefits of word processing and administrative support fall into three areas: (1) increasing the productivity of correspondence secretaries by replacing their typewriters with WP equipment, (2) increasing the productivity of administrative secretaries by taking their typing load from them and by reorganizing and expanding their responsibilities, and (3) increasing the productivity of principals by giving them an improved range of secretarial support. These benefits can be obtained if the solution fits well within the company environment.

When word processing was first starting, the "ideal" solution that users sought was (a) one WP centre combined with (b) departmental clusters of administrative secretaries. But by the early 1970s, it became apparent that this solution was far less than ideal; in fact, it was causing many attempts to fail.

Should you consider word processing? The answer we have heard from many authorities is: "Yes, *provided* that you can find an approach that fits your company's environment."

Possibly the best approach is to find one or two departments in which the managers are keenly interested in considering word processing. Then get top management to set the ground rules, such as what might happen and what will not be allowed to happen to the secretaries. And then perform a feasibility study.

An evaluation of the existing workflow needs to be performed to discover what will work best. Robert Burk believes that a three-part study is most effective. This study consists of: obtaining secretarial job descriptions, studying the documents, and taking a random sampling of what the secretaries are actually working on.

The secretarial job description study should develop the functions secretaries perform and the estimated time requirements for each function. For example, for each document type, the study should determine the time spent in original typing, the amount of revision normally required, and the required turnround time. This will help determine the cost of producing this document, for future reference and comparison. The non-typing jobs need to be described similarly.

The documents study discovers the types and volume of work done. In this study, documents can be catalogued into generic forms, such as text pages (as found in manuals), correspondence pages (as found in letters and memos), and statistical pages. Other categories could be used, such as commonly used formats, form letters, periodically updated manuals, and documents requiring high-quality lettering or multi-fonts. This information will be used to select the correct equipment for the various jobs, as well as the types of secretaries that will be needed. There are week-long, month-long or longer documents studies. It all depends on what time period constitutes the typical workload of the department, to make sure that all document types are considered.

The random sampling estimates the actual workloads and the secretarial inefficiencies, such as away-from-desk time, waiting time, "go-for" time, etc. It acts as a double-check for the two previous parts of the study.

Once the study has been completed, the equipment best suited to meet the applications must be selected. Not only should the various word processing systems on the market (both equipment and services) be investigated but also users of the most appropriate ones should be visited. It is hard to say which step should come first and which second in all cases when planning a word processing and administrative support operation. Some companies perform a cursory feasibility study before deciding whether to consider WP at all.

Once management has made this decision, then a second, more in-depth, study should be made. The central people who will run the operation should be selected as soon as possible. The prospective WP centre and administrative supervisors should be involved in the feasibility study. The success of the entire programme will ultimately rest on them, so they should be involved in the early decision-making.

Likely impact
Probably the most important consideration in deciding on a WP and administrative support operation is its likely impact on the organization.

The corporate view. The current trend is to put WP in the administrative services department, along with the mail room, the print shop, and the copying services. This view is probably only a short-term solution. In the near future, when WP is incorporated into the "office of the future", many diverse technologies will interconnect, making separation of authority difficult. The WP system will interact on-line with the corporate data-base, with the in-house print shop, with branch offices, and with public communication networks.

Harvey Poppel discusses putting all of a company's "information resources" in one organizational component. He proposes creating a new division to handle these resources. He defines information resources as the communication process and its resources, including non-electronic communication forms (such as paper, travel and meetings) and electronic forms (such as data processing, telecommunications and word processing).

He reports that there is a trend towards combining responsibility for data processing and telecommunications. A recent study done by his company, Booz, Allen and Hamilton, of sixty midwestern manufacturing companies showed that forty per cent have now combined responsibility for the computing and telecommunications functions. Poppel states that only a few companies, however, have attempted to consolidate responsibility for the full range of information resources. But the trend towards a more global management of information resources is accelerating, he adds.

The department view. Word processing actually involves two separate functions: the word processing function and the administrative support function. A secretary who works in the WP function is called a correspondence secretary. She is responsible for transcribing dictation, typing documents, editing revisions, producing final copies, and possibly filing master records. The secretary who works in the other function is called an administrative secretary. She is responsible for all other non-typing secretarial work.

The word processing function. John Brennan describes four organization structures for the WP function. One is the centrally administered, single WP centre operation, where the WP centre is under the administrative services department. All correspondence secretaries are located at the centre and all typing and dictation transcription from the other departments in the company are sent there.

The arguments for this approach seem to be the same that we have heard for centralization of computer equipment: concentrate the expensive text-editing equipment and trained personnel in one location for the most efficient operation, say the advocates. However, if this centre gets unmanageably large or if portions of it become too specialized, another approach is satellite centres within the departments but under central administration. This is the second of Brennan's approaches. Accounting might have a satellite centre with people trained in statistical typing. Sales might have another satellite centre, and so on. These centres may house only correspondence secretaries or may have both correspondence and administrative secretaries. For a large organization, there might be both satellite centres plus a central centre.

The third organizational structure that Brennan describes is the central support WP centre. In this arrangement, instead of doing all the typing and transcription for a company, the WP centre does only specific jobs. It is a backup to the traditional secretary. For example, all legal briefs or all reports over ten pages or all purchase orders could be performed at the centre. Brennan states that this approach is the easiest to implement, because it does not require secretaries to change their roles. One problem that often arises in this arrangement is that this centre becomes the "leftovers" centre. If the departmental secretaries make the decisions on what work to send to the centre, they will undoubtedly send the most undesirable work. To guard against this, jobs to be done at the centre must be clearly defined.

The fourth organizational structure is the departmental WP centre. We have also heard this called the "work group" approach. In this approach the department manager retains control over the centre. This approach can achieve productivity increases, but it does not facilitate interfacing WP with other components of the information resources.

The argument for having a WP centre at all is that it allows the correspondence secretaries to concentrate on typing, instead of having the numerous interruptions that the traditional secretary has. David Swett states that employees typing in supervised, specialized areas are usually twice as productive as the unsupervised, unspecialized secretary, regardless of the equipment used.

The organization within the centre is another question. How specialized should each secretary become? Should she (sic) do only typing and no proofing? Should she deliver the finished work or should a messenger do this? Should she do work from all departments or work only for one department? These questions are important for the morale of the centre. Overspecialization is not good; it leads to morale problems. Some people do like to type all day, but their work needs to be varied to keep it interesting.

The administrative support function. The administrative support function can be performed in two ways, or a combination of these two. The first is called "principal-oriented" administrative support.

In this approach, an administrative secretary does all of the non-typing secretarial work for one or a few principals. She may serve only one principal if the workload warrants it, particularly if she is raised to para-professional status. She is located close to her principals in an office with one or more other secretaries, forming a cluster or team. In this approach, she may report to a supervisor, who reports to the administrative services department manager or to the functional department manager. Or she may report directly to one of the principals whom she serves.*

The second approach is called "functional or task-oriented". Here, an administrative secretary does one or more jobs for many principals. For example, she may handle travel and meeting arrangements for an entire department. She may be located in the department or in the WP

---

* Editor's Note: This assumption that secretarial staff will always be female is discussed by Hazel Downing, pages 275–87.

centre. In this arrangement, the secretary normally reports to a supervisor rather than to a principal whom she serves. The supervisor may report to the functional department manager or to the administrative services department manager.

Other considerations
A combination of these two approaches can be taken, with some secretaries doing a few of the more specialized jobs, while the others perform all of the other jobs for their principals. Robert La Due has pointed out that an administrative secretary should not be overspecialized in areas where principals require dedicated support.

There are several other important factors to consider when planning the installation of a WP and administrative support operation:

Top management commitment. For a successful installation, top management commitment is essential. Management must make a clear statement of the objectives of the project and the support to be given. Perhaps even more important, top management itself must use the WP and administrative support function, rather than continuing to use one-for-one secretaries. (This proposal, of course, will demonstrate just how much support top management is giving to the project.) Also, management must be patient. It can take months or even years to get the kinks straightened out of a new operation. Careful planning and phased implementation, such as we are discussing, should help to minimize the difficulties. But problems can occur.

Staffing and training. Secretarial hostility to a WP and administrative support operation is to be expected, unless the groundwork has been carefully laid. Some secretaries fear that they will lose their jobs. Some do not want to do just typing all day. Some have worked for the same bosses for years and do not want to change. Others know their jobs and do not want to have to learn new skills. Also, many managers will resist the changes. Private secretaries are status symbols and "office wives". Some have developed effective working relationships with their secretaries which they fear would be disrupted with word processing.

A suggested approach is for the WP and administrative support project to include career paths for secretaries (several levels each for both correspondence and administrative secretaries). The personnel department should then devise job descriptions. Note that these are *new* jobs and have different skill requirements from those of the traditional secretarial jobs. These career paths can provide benefits to the secretaries. The job descriptions can indicate to the managers just what levels of support each should receive.

Facilities. Traditionally, no one pays much attention to the secretary's working environment. Her office is just an extension of her boss's office. With word processing, this is not the case. The working environment for both correspondence and administrative secretaries should be planned.

Randy Goldfield has proposed four elements to consider in designing the WP centre. These are: acoustics, colour, privacy, and workstations. Printing devices in WP equipment are noisy, so particular attention should be paid to soundproofing the centre via carpeting, curtains, and a special ceiling. Attractive colours are not costly; their use helps counteract the negative connotation of a "typing pool". Decorative accessories help humanize a WP centre. Individual "offices" help provide privacy, make the secretaries feel more secure, and help improve the productivity. Finally, the workstations should be designed with the typing function in mind, be attractive, hold adequate supplies, and have sufficient desk space.

For administrative secretaries, Burk recommends creating mini-offices instead of "parking them in the hallway". These secretaries should be at the hub of the offices they serve. The phone system may need to be revised to allow each secretary to answer other secretaries' phones in their absence without leaving their desks. And a portable typewriter should be provided for each group of secretaries, for handling small typing jobs. The WP people we talked to stressed the importance of having the physical facilities in place before putting the function into operation.

Procedures and manuals. One strongly recommended procedure is to schedule formally the new workloads for the WP centre, by having written agreements with each department head on what work will be done by the centre. Some work is just not appropriate.

Principals should be required to attend training sessions on the types of work to submit to the WP centre, how to submit it, how to use dictation equipment (and how to dictate properly), and how to submit revisions. For instance, one centre encourages original work to be dictated but revisions must be marked on the hardcopy printouts.

Administrative secretaries must also be trained in what types of work to submit, how to submit it, filing, and the other procedures they will be responsible for performing.

Few companies today, after hearing the horror stories of past word processing implementations, are rushing into a pure WP and administrative support operation. Instead, they are going application by application and department by department.

The people at the successful WP centres say this approach whets the appetite of other departments. One department that is using word processing well and getting benefits from it is the best publicity possible. Getting that first user department operating successfully as quickly as possible should be achieved easily by following the steps that we have outlined.

Forces Controlling the Paperless Revolution

A. E. Cawkell

Offices are not isolated units. They must communicate with other offices and information sources. This article, by the director of research at the Institute for Scientific Information, 132 High St., Uxbridge, Middx., spells out what is meant when people talk about the "information revolution" brought about by the "convergence" of developments in electronics, computing and telecommunications. The author provides a comprehensive review of the technological forces and social factors shaping the new electronic office information systems, and takes a look at things like Prestel, teleconferencing and electronic mail. He ends with an appeal for a new breed of "sociotechnologists" – "There ought to be some sociologists who are able to master the technology, and some engineers who are prepared to study the social issues and politics" – which is a gratifying observation, for bridging the yawning gap between the social and natural sciences is a major aim of this book. Dare I say we are on the same wavelength? The article first appeared in Wireless World, *July and August 1978 issues.*

The rate at which electronic information systems will take over from paper depends on various technological and social factors. This article looks first at developments in the technology and the rapid fall in the price of devices; also at input and output methods and the control, cost and future of communications channels. European and American politics are contrasted and the conditions for innovation described. Electronic information systems are expected to develop more quickly in non-domestic areas where the incentives and economics are more favourable. Social forces, such as unemployment, disruption of social activity, and fears about intrusion, secrecy, the control of information

244

sources and "the machines taking over", will slow down the introduction of the technology. Engineers should make it their business to understand the issues and publicize the accumulating evidence about trends in this revolution.

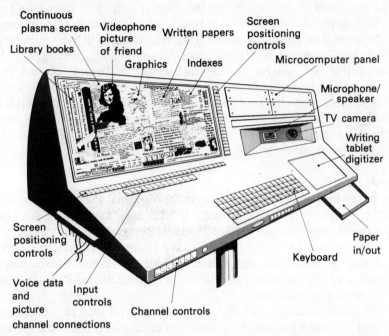

Fig. 5.4 The "consumersole", an information console that could be in use in the home or at work by the end of the century

Fig. 5.4 represents an information console as it may exist in any home, or with slight modifications, in any office or workplace in the year 2000. This all-purpose communication/information facility is based, in nearly every detail, on currently feasible technology. Many human activities involve information processing, and nearly all of them could be performed without leaving the console.

This report is a review of the forces which will control the rate of widespread introduction of such a facility. Of course, all the systems shown in the drawing will not come into existence suddenly. Various devices and alternative channels will be introduced, improved, varied in price, etc, in an evolutionary way, not necessarily in the home first; the several channels shown may be eventually unified into, say, an all-satellite system – but these are details in the sweep of events. Factors controlling these events will be the technology and the vested interests tending to force a sometimes premature introduction of new devices.

They will have to do with market forces which will encourage new developments; availability of communication channels and the politics of their control and pricing; resistance to change by those people likely to be displaced and organizations with an interest in preserving the status quo; and resistance by an informed public and later by a better informed general public who will find it difficult to distinguish between beneficial and harmful changes. This resistance will be concentrated against developments which provoke profound social changes or those considered to be intrusive or of a "big brother" nature. Economic forces will be very important and the gap between information-rich and information-deprived people will probably widen. For instance it seems unlikely that the thirty million people in Cairo and Tehran will benefit much; neither city has a telephone directory; hotels in Athens are used by Cairo businessmen who fly there to place international calls.[1]

New device technology
The basis for much of the new technology is the development of semiconductor chips and large-scale integrated (LSI) circuits. An assembly of these devices can enable extremely complex data processing and control functions to be reliably carried out at high speed while occupying a very small space and consuming little power. Basic material research and production knowhow owe much to military and space exploration requirements.

Microprocessors are already being introduced into cars experimentally and will soon be used as a matter of course in domestic appliances. Do-it-yourself computer kits are available for a few hundred dollars and software – always the main problem – is catching up with new languages like Micro-Cobol.

Projections based on what has already happened in this field and in developments in storage devices can be made with some confidence. The first four- and eight-bit word microprocessors – the 4004 and 8008 – were introduced in 1972 by Intel; sixteen-bit microprocessors are now available. Developments in MOS semiconductor devices and PMOS/NMOS combinations known as CMOS (complementary metal oxide silicon) now seem to be of importance. Since 1960 minimum integrated circuit dimensions have halved every five years to about $4\mu m$ with correspondingly reduced capacitances and time-delays because of shorter circuit paths and interconnections; optical limits are being approached. At this rate, internal delays of one nanosecond and complexity increases of 2000 times would be achieved in fifteen years. The cost of including redundancy for greater reliability will drop; error correction for an eight-bit word requires four bits, but for a sixty-four-bit word only seven bits are needed. Arrays of 250,000 gates at 0.04cent per gate are foreseeable (see Fig. 5.5 for a graphic representation).[2]

The rate of development and cost reduction of storage has also been very rapid. In five years' time 250K chips costing $100 may be available,[3] but this forecast may already be out of date since 16K RAM chips at $25 have just been announced.

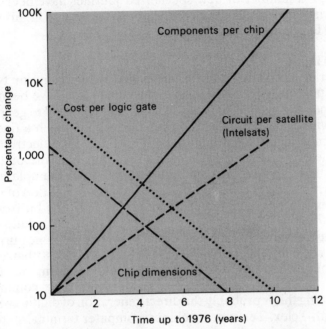

Fig. 5.5   Rates of change in integrated circuit and other technology up to 1976

Work is in progress on a whole range of new storage technologies including charge-couple devices (CCD), magnetic bubbles, electron-beam accessed semiconductor memories, and optical memories.[4] Magnetic bubble memories first became available commercially in 1977 as a 92,000-bit storage chip; the 1978 quantity price is expected to be $75; these devices look like a powerful competitor for microcomputer storage, versus, say, the floppy disc, since they are more reliable and the cost per bit is about 0.08cent compared with about 0.3cent (1977) for the floppy.[5]

Complete instruments embodying holographic storage have been described; one such has been designed for textual information storage and retrieval using film for holographically stored text with associated graphics stored on microfiche frames.[6] In another a terminal is available commercially, capable of retrieving information stored on a 4-inch × 6-inch strip.[7] The film carries 200Mbit in the form of holograms. The information is read out by a laser which projects the image on to a photodetector array from which an electrical output is available to drive, say, a CRT display.

The rate of progress is so fast that keeping up with current work and deciding which of the new companies will endure is extremely difficult, even although a number of new specialized journals have been introduced covering the various fields. Sufficient has been said in this rather brief review to convey the flavour of the technology.

Information input

The transfer of nonverbal information starts with writing or typing; since many people cannot type, some ingenious ideas have been tried out to enhance the writing process. In one, digital codes are generated by writing with a magnetic stylus on a tablet within which a fine wire matrix is embedded.[8] Coordinates of induced EMFs (electromotive forces) formed by character patterns are read out. The wire pattern is arranged so that Gray not binary code is generated; for example, eleven not 1024 terminating connections are needed for a resolution of one in 1024, and since a one-position error differs by only one bit from the desired position the effect of errors in the writing process is quite small. This idea illustrates one of many methods all having the same purpose – the second stage of the information transfer process – that is, the conversion of information from the human-generated form into a form suitable for machine processing or transmission. The commonest method of doing this is probably the direct generation of digital codes by keying as with Telex, Teletype machines, computer terminals, etc; the codes are then stored on disc, tape, or other media by direct connection between keyboard and storage device, or by transmission and storage remotely on similar devices.

Since the paperless revolution is at an early stage, a huge fund of already keyed or typeset information exists as print on paper. Optical character recognition (OCR) machines, usually requiring preferred fonts to make the machine's pattern recognition task easier, have been developed for converting print to digital codes. Advances in pattern recognition, typified in the Kurzweil reading machine,[9] enable almost any printed text to be recognized. In this machine, scanning is carried out by a 500-element CCD device, with a 2ms sampling period; a "split analysis" module isolates character entities, and a character is then recognized and transformed into the appropriate digital code by a "minimal invariable property extraction" process, followed by a "disambiguator" module which makes a final decision; the phonemes formed by character sequences are determined by rule look-up associated with an exception dictionary; a syntax analyser adds prosody across sentences so that the emitted sounds will not emerge as a monotone; finally, control signals actuate a set of electronic synthesizers which generate speech sounds. The machine was developed to enable blind people to read a variety of printed material, and acceptable speech is generated.

This brief description of the Kurzweil machine has necessarily overlapped into another area of this subject – information output. However, this particular technology – speech communication with machines, in which intensive research has been carried out – certainly merits inclusion in this section.

It is important to distinguish between word recognition and speech-machine communication. Machine recognition of speech uttered by any person may or may not be achieved early in the next century; nevertheless there has already been some substantial progress. Speaker verification systems have been developed, to operate over the dial telephone system, which are capable of an identification accuracy of ninety-one per cent on a set of one hundred persons with several thousand impostors (Bell Telephone). Of more interest here is the state of the art of speech-machine communication. One current system uses adaptive differential pulse code modulation (ADPCM) for carrying out a machine-prompted standardized-phrase dialogue – for instance in a flight booking system.[10] In the design of such a system decisions must be made about the size of the stored vocabulary which the machine will be required to recognize and the analysing resources which are needed to extract sufficient information from the speech to enable it to be correctly matched against the stored vocabulary. In the flight booking system a 24K-bit/s rate is generated from the incoming speech, compared with a rate of about 60K-bit/s normally used for good quality PCM speech transmission. This is achieved by generating, say, three bits per quantized speech sample, with a sampling frequency of 8kHz. With ADPCM the quantizer step size is continuously adjusted to follow changing speech characteristics. The codes generated are then matched against the stored vocabulary. In the flight booking system, the machine utters questions like "Where would you like to fly to?" and recognizes replies like "Washington" from a trained speaker. It will recognize dates, times, destinations, classes, number of seats required, etc. Research continues into more sophisticated systems in which a detailed computer analysis of the characteristics of the actual speech is made – a requirement for comprehensive speech recognition.[11, 12] Quite recently a speech-recognizing microcomputer, selling for $249, has been put on the market in the USA by Speechlab.[13] It stores sixty-four different words, each word being stored as sixty-four bytes, and it also embodies the software for speech analysis and matching. Ninety-five per cent recognition accuracy is claimed after machine "training" by a particular speaker.

Information output

Again it is only possible to highlight here some current developments in order to show that most of the technology is available or being developed for the "information console" shown earlier.

There are two ways of composing textual information displays, although the distinction between them is blurred. A display can be built up character by character, or by words, sentences, etc, which are individually called up from computer store, processed, ordered, and displayed in some desired way. Alternatively the smallest available element can be a complete page – as in the viewdata system – although of course pages are received as a character by character bit-stream in this case; a microfiche image is another example based on a page-at-a-time display.

The conception of an all-purpose information machine was put forward by Vannevar Bush in an often quoted 1945 article.[14] This machine – the "Memex" – would embody various input facilities, a large store, associative indexing of the stored information, and a comprehensive display system. Bush was of course well aware of cathode-ray-tube displays which received an enormous development effort during the war. Twenty-five years later he reviewed the situation and concluded: "... a long time from now, I fear, will come the personal machine."[15] Insofar as displays are concerned, Bush's remarks still hold good.

Although CRT terminals have received enormous development and the electronics can be contained on a microprocessor chip,[16] today's CRTs are not greatly different, at least in their capacity for displaying textual information. A good terminal – say a Tektronix 4006-1 – can display about 2600 characters at a time, assuming that the user knows what he wants. In reality, information requirements for forming successive sets of mental images often cannot be precisely specified in advance. A convenient arrangement is a very large display of ordered information, in anticipation of the general need, from which a specific selection can be made by using the extremely rapid scanning and information-processing power of the eye-brain. A set of preselected papers on a desk can present at least a quarter of a million characters; adjust the papers and a new set of a quarter of a million characters is presented. Two volumes of an index, opened to display four pages of 6-point characters – admittedly rather small – can alone present 180,000 characters at one time.

The contrast between the CRT and the print-on-paper "windows" presenting 2600 characters and one hundred times that number respectively, is very marked. What is needed is a window of the size represented by the papers, served by the full power of an on-line information retrieval system in which all the information likely to be needed is stored. High-speed computer selection then replaces the laborious business of assembling the right collection of papers for each requirement. In a practical arrangement a screen would be required for the display of whole pages, notes, illustration, ordered lists, etc – at least 50,000 characters at a time – which could be called up from store, scanned, noted in a voice-controlled computer, rearranged, etc. As with papers and indexes on a desk, the power of the eye-brain may then freely be utilized to scan and absorb what is required from a mass of material.

The screen would need to be at least 4ft × 2ft with light-pen or touch control of discrete areas enabling information in various formats to be displayed, repositioned, expanded, contracted, etc. This screen size would accommodate about 150 rows of 12-point characters; since about twelve lines or dots are needed to resolve a character satisfactorily, and allowing for space between rows, this screen would require at least 24000 × 5000 dots for matrix addressing. Facilities of this kind have been suggested in at least two cases, one using a conventional CRT[17] and the other a so-called plasma display 8.5 inches square.[18] However, the "window" size in both cases is quite inadequate for the purpose and the requirements made above do not seem to have been recognized.

New display technology under development includes piezo-electric ceramic storage, magnetic particle, banks of LEDs or LCDs, electrophoretic and electroluminiscent displays. Of the so-called "plasma" displays, a promising development is a 3ft square bank of neon-filled capillary tubes controlled by an electrode matrix. Resolution is at present 33 lines/inch.[19] The driving electronics is manageable, and a light-pen controlled cursor for area manipulations is described. A device of this kind coupled to a microprocessor-controlled trackball/cursor facility[20] might, one day, be available at the right price for the "consumersole".

Small window displays are adequate for the more limited requirements of reading page-by-page sequences, look-ups in specific lists, displays of information in response to specific questions demanding relatively short answers and so on. Such displays could form a part of a larger panel, perhaps being projected onto it. Currently available displays are usually based on the cathode-ray tube or on enlarged projections of a film image. Microfilm and microfiche (multi-image film cards) and associated equipment are of particular interest. Their advantage lies in cheap storage of an enormous quantity of information in a very small space; one application has been for archival storage, as in libraries. However, microforms of this type have never taken off, primarily because of user resistance to inconvenient microform reading equipment of poor quality. The low-priced reader which can successfully compete with the convenience, portability, clarity, and resolution of print on paper is as yet unavailable.[21] A reader like the new book-sized Izon machine, which incorporates 500 micro-lenses and a fibreoptics lighting system from a 12-volt lamp may be the answer.[22]

A more recent development is the production of microform from machine-readable information (computer output microfilm or COM), as opposed to the photo-reduction of print on paper, and the introduction of computer controlled equipment for mechanically retrieving and projecting one frame out of tens of thousands carried on film strip or fiche cards. In the Marconi automated microfiche terminal[23] one hundred and twenty fiche cards, each containing 3500 size A4 page images are carried in a magazine – a total of 420,000 pages; magazines can be quickly changed. An indexing and fiche-selection program is held in a minicomputer connected to the terminal and controlled by the terminal user with a keyboard. A desired fiche is selected and projected on to the terminal's screen in a few seconds after typing the appropriate indexing terms. A typical Marconi system consists of a number of terminals with locally updated fiche, each connected by telephone line to a common timeshared minicomputer which performs the selection operation for all terminals.

Stabletron,[24] on the other hand, offers a system in which there is one central fiche-selecting machine with a timeshared mini beside it. Terminals, connected by lines to the central facility, consist of keyboard and a CRT screen with local page storage. A user's commands are received by the machine and the desired image is despatched down the line, where it is stored locally and viewed at leisure on the terminal. Since the central facility embodies a queueing buffer and in any case takes only about 1.8 seconds to select a fiche and transmit it, and as most users spend most of the time reading or thinking, response time is normally quite adequate. An advantage of this system is that only one central update is needed, and since the system is television based, urgent updating may be achieved by overlaying part or all of a given fiche image with keyed characters inserted at the central facility. The disadvantage is that, unlike the Marconi, the terminal to central facility connection has to be a wideband channel, or a narrowband channel with slow scan equipment at either end. Stabletron use a 15MHz 875-line system for transmission of small typeface. The facilities for quickly changing part of the fiche provided by Stabletron are reminiscent of another new development, computer input microfilm (CIM), which enables film or fiche to be quickly changed. All material is stored in machine readable form and can be selectively viewed and modified from a

CRT terminal. New material is rephotographed and added to the file.[25]

Turning from nonverbal to verbal machine-man communication, one sophisticated way of doing this was discussed earlier in connection with the Kurzweil machine. In general, the problem consists of applying digitally coded representations of speech to a speech synthesizer. For example, in the commercially available Votrax multi-lingual synthesizer[26] one of 122 phonemes at one of eight pitches and one of four durations is selected by a twelve-bit command word. When fed with appropriate driving information – for example ASCII code at a rate as low as 300 bit/s – usable audio output is generated. The driving code is pulled from some external storage media, such as disc, by appropriate computer software. Less sophisticated microprocessor speech synthesizers for home computers requiring an appropriate microprocessor CPU and storage,[13] are already available in the US for $400.

Communications channels – the politics

For communication at a distance, human-generated information is changed into a form suitable for transmission through a communication channel operating within the frequency bands shown on the spectrum in Fig. 5.6. To avoid chaos, national and international control has been organized for orderly use of the available communication channels within the frequency bands which it is physically possible to use. More information demands more channels and technological developments have provided them – for example, by satellite communication at EHF – but there is a limit. Once it becomes feasible to use a channel the question arises, by whom should it be controlled and used? Because transmission of information is of such vital importance the politics of communication channel control is equally vital. I am referring here to the higher-order politics – for example, governmental versus private

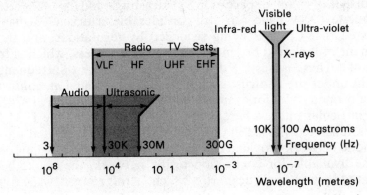

Fig. 5.6 Spectrum of sound, ultrasound and electromagnetic waves, showing where various information transmission systems fit in

control – rather than to the politics of channel allocation for broadcast-ing, radio communication, etc, which is agreed internationally through the International Telecommunication Union (ITU).

Telecommunications history started with telephone systems, organ-ized in most countries as public services with the object of providing a universal service at minimum cost; heavy R&D costs and investment are involved in the setting up of plant with a working life of decades. Telephone organizations are usually large bureaucratic monopolies which change slowly. As radio communication developed, channel allocation in the electromagnetic spectrum was reasonably well man-aged, but conflict soon arose about public and private control of communications generally, including telephone voice and data trans-mission, radio and television broadcasting, cable television, computer communications and satellite networks. Ownership and government control is arranged on the basis of mutually exclusive applications, whereas in reality there are now no sharp divisions – for example, computer data communications may be established along analog tele-phone lines where ownership and tariffs are geared to universal voice communication requirements.

In this situation the contrast in the styles of change as between the USA and Europe is very marked. The "freedom of speech or of the press" referred to in the First Amendment in the US Constitution extends to broadcasting, cable, etc (*Winters v. New York*, 1948, when it was held that one person's entertainment is another's doctrine). Furth-ermore, although the early activities of the Federal Communications Commission in broadcasting appeared to be restrictive, its regulations were later considered to support the First Amendment by ensuring the expression of diverse views (e.g. *NBC v. US*, 1943). Freedom of choice issues do not arise in the same way in cable television (CATV) – there is no shortage of channel space as in broadcasting – and the FCC's attempts to regulate CATV have run into considerable criticism.[27] It has been suggested that CATV is being strangled by regulations, and that the treatment of it should be similar to that of the press, which is free of restraint.[28] These issues are discussed openly in the US; frequent suits brought under the antitrust laws, with lengthy discussion, confirm this generally open style (for example MCI's suit against AT & T, 1974).

Of particular interest here are the events following the 1934 Com-munications Act, passed in order to establish an integrated universal telephone network provided by controlled monopolies. As new devices became available for connection to the network, the public became frustrated by monopolistic inertia, which, in this respect, was broken in 1968. In that year an antitrust suit was brought against AT&T, the largest US telephone company (it includes Bell R & D and Western Electric manufacturing associates). The FCC established a precedent for the connection of competitive devices to the telephone system by allowing connection of Carterphone equipment via acoustic or inductive coupling. In 1975 the principle was extended when the FCC ruled against preferential tariffs offered by the telephone companies when their own equipment was used.[29]

Meanwhile communication technology was developing in the area of microwave and satellite communication, packet-switched networks, etc, accompanied by the formation of new innovative companies. In 1968 MCI applied to the FCC to operate a microwave link using local telephone lines for distribution; the FCC agreed (with support in a later legal appeal "the Specialized Common Carrier" decision 1971), on the grounds that the public interest would best be served by communication innovations. In consequence of this a number of "Value Added Network Services" (VANS) now operate in the United States (or, to use the current jargon, Resale and Sharing Carriers). The FCC took the same viewpoint in 1972 with its "open skies" satellite communications policies. A rash of appeals followed and in 1976 (Docket 20097) the FCC produced rules which are an attempt to encourage innovative services. They do not permit the degree of "cream-skimming" which would affect the revenue of the telephone companies to the extent of endangering universal service.

During 1976/77 discussions started about reforming the 1934 Act; proposals are (at the time of writing) before Congress committees. Major issues include the effect of competitive equipment and private line services on the national telephone network, and whether groups such as large businesses, are likely to benefit at the expense of low-income users.[30] These issues, particularly the last, are of course as relevant in Europe as in the US. While the US system of discussion before regulatory commissions, followed by appeals, court rulings, etc, is laborious, costly, and time-consuming, it seems to me that the outcome will be a relatively free flow of information. It should also be remembered that the flow of information generally is subject to the beneficial effect of the Freedom of Information Act.

I am unable to report comparable progress in Europe, or in the UK in particular. Here the climate is symbolized by the suffocating effect of the Official Secrets Act, passed on the nod after a half-hour debate in 1911 during a spy scare.[31] (In the US the 1973 Federal Advisory Committee Act requires that some 2000 committees should meet in public.)

In the UK communications are provided by the Post Office (PO), a Corporation whose Board is accountable to the Secretary of State for Industry, a member of the government. The Secretary presents the PO's annual report before parliament; although he has the right to issue directives he seldom does. "Without the stimulus of regular public hearings there is relatively little public debate, consequently the community of informed commentators who can act as advisers or write about policy is relatively small."[32] The main discussion forum is, therefore, parliament, the supreme institution, whose supremacy is an expression of custom and is nowhere defined. This is certainly not the place to discuss the unwritten British constitution, but it is the place to discuss briefly the prospects for the free flow of information through electrical channels vis-à-vis the PO.

Post Office activities were reviewed in the "Carter Report" presented to the Secretary of State in 1975; separate corporations for postal and telecommunications services were recommended. In 1977 a government committee made proposals (the "Bullock Report") about trade union representation on boards, and proposals about the constitution of the PO's board have been made; in consequence the Carter proposals have been shelved. Attempts to extend the very limited liability of the Post Office have also failed.

The title of a recent article (by a member of the Post Office staff), "Uncertainty and Inertia",[33] summarizes the situation in which the Post Office finds itself. "The size of the system . . . complexity . . . plant with a life of 40 years . . . 237,000 staff with 11,112 multi-page telecommunication page instructions . . . all militate against rapid changes . . . any change will tend to benefit some at the expense of others." Elsewhere similar points have been put more strongly, with suggestions that overconservatism about telephone-connected devices and excessive charges compared with the US are a constraint to information flow.[34] However the Post Office may consider, rightly or wrongly, that the funds, investment policy and resources available to it are insufficient to provide the digital channels and equipment on a scale appropriate to the information age. They may feel that their traffic forecasts do not justify the investment; if they did make that investment the information-deprived might become more deprived. Unfortunately there seems very little possibility, because of the monopolistic UK communications policy, that any other organization disposed to incur the risk and make the investment for entering the field will be allowed to do so; nor is it likely that the degree of prior consultation and public discussion, appropriate to the importance of this issue, will be allowed to occur. The inevitable conclusion must be that the UK, and probably most of Europe, will only very slowly introduce an appropriate mix of communication channels. The general climate will dampen an already rather low propensity to innovate.

However, the Post Office, given sufficient incentive, can and does innovate. Presumably the development of Viewdata (to be discussed later) is considered to be justifiable socially and financially by reason of the traffic it will generate in the existing network. This praiseworthy enterprise is somewhat tarnished by the cynical change of a monopolistic rule – hitherto rigidly enforced – to permit within-receiver signal conversion devices, simply because without such a change the system would be less likely to take off. The rule still applies to the community at large.

The current Europe-US scene is particularly interesting; US carriers have provided special services which have generated new traffic by the penetration of low-cost networked digital communication networks set up by commercial organizations like Tymshare and Telenet.[35] One reason for this has been the growth of on-line usage from Europe of large data-bases spinning on multi-port timeshared US computers.

Europeans have woken up to the realization that it would be undesirable, in view of the predicted large increase in the flow of all kinds of information along electrical channels, for this flow to be along foreign-controlled channels, however cheap and efficient. At the end of 1975 nine European PTTs agreed to cooperate and implement a network for accessing computers via packet-mode interfaces from various kinds of terminals including those connected to the switched telephone network. One major type of traffic – users to scientific and other information data-bases on network "host" computers – will be administered by EURONET, organized by the EEC Committee for Information and Documentation of Science and Technology (CDST).[36] EURONET may be operational in 1978/79.

By contrast, in the United States the FCC attitude of encouraging innovation whilst protecting public service has resulted in intensive activity by small and medium-sized companies, and some actual or planned large-scale risk and investment by large companies. This has encouraged the monopolies to become more venturesome, for example AT&T's 96-city Dataphone proposals (1974), which raised another question: was Dataphone created to oust the competition by operating at a loss that AT&T could easily afford? On the other hand some private companies have been taking advantage by "innovations" which are in fact duplications of message services already handled quite well by the monopolies. The FCC's handling of these issues is described in the literature.[37]

Communication channels and systems – the next few years
Terrestrial microwave and satellite communication channels are being further developed and new kinds of channels at an early stage of development include waveguide and fibreoptic channels. Table 5.1

Table 5.1 Capacities of channels (approximate)

Channel	Bit/s	Number of phone circuits	Cost per phone circuit	Number of TV channels
Paired cable	5M	500	$200	1
Coaxial cable	300M	30,000	$30	30
Terrestrial-microwave	10^9	10^5	$15	100
Satellite – (Intelsat 5)	10^9	10^5	$30	100
Waveguide (TEO1)	10^9	10^5	$1	100
Fibreoptics	10^{12}	10^8	?	10^5

shows some details and capacities of various kinds of communication channels.

In the US, interest is currently centred on the activities of IBM and the specialized common carriers (e.g. MCI, Telenet. and at least a dozen others) versus AT&T, and the degree to which the proposed systems would be a complementary whole, improving the flow of information, or a fragmented structure with different organizations offering profitable *crème de la crème* specialized services not necessarily in the overall public interest.[38] Thus the Satellite Business System (owned by IBM, AETNA and COMSAT subsidiaries) will offer a transmission network in the 12–14 GHz band with speeds of up to 6.3M-bit/s available to users. AT&T lines will be unnecessary since communication will be via rooftop aerials[39] with stations rented at $135 a month or less.

A Business Satellite System would further improve information-flow. Companies could fit their various offices with rooftop aerials and their communication costs would drop substantially, governments and PTTs permitting. Unquestionably satellite circuits do reduce costs: US transpacific satellite circuits cost $4000 a month today compared with $15,000 a few years ago. Satellite technology based on space-shuttle launchings will result in further reductions; NASA predictions include personal ground-stations operating at fractions of a milliwatt costing around $10.[40] As yet, international discussions on direct television broadcasting from satellites, planned for the 12GHz band, with all the implications for interference, programme control, etc, have hardly started; it seems unlikely that there will be much impact on the man in the street for many years. Meanwhile public service experiments, such as those with ATS-6 for remote communities in Canada and Alaska, and common carrier communications via Comstar will continue.

Fibreoptic and waveguide channels are likely to be used mainly by major carriers to improve their networks – the Post Office is connecting its electronic telephone exchange at Martlesham to the trunk network via a fibreoptic link to Ipswich as a first step.[41]

Most broad-impact new developments during the next five to ten years are likely to occur within the existing telephone and television channels. The development of cable television in the United States offers a salutary example as to the constraints of current political and economic issues even when the technology is available and the situation seems ready to take off. Although there are at least eleven million subscribers in the US and the growth rate of CATV has been about sixteen per cent per annum since 1970, the ebullient future, confidently forecast as "cable in forty to sixty per cent of American homes by 1980" has not materialized. This seems to be due to a combination of unsatisfactory FCC regulations, cost of entry, and lack of standardization.[42] A comprehensive series of NSF-funded studies for CATV social services, including interactive systems, did not produce any firm guidelines because of doubt about content and "critical-mass" audiences, lack of standardization, and financial doubts.[43] A *Wall Street Journal* headline "talking to the tube" describes a "new interactive system" apparently limited to yes-no responses by viewers;[44] perhaps this item should have been entitled "back to the drawing board".

Paradoxically, the monopolistic structure and a classic combination of circumstances for innovation have given rise to home services with a potentially wide impact in the UK. These circumstances include several or all of the following factors:

- Recent developments in LSIS.
- Monopolistic control and so quick agreement about standardization.
- Ease of distribution over existing geographically concentrated networks.
- Relatively low R&D costs and no essentially new technology for transmission.
- Low costs of collecting revenue by suppliers.
- Increased revenue incentive for carriers by increased usage of existing channels.
- Common low-cost entertainment/information TV "all-purpose" terminals.
- Development of simple retrieval procedures for accessing large files.
- Capacity of, and attraction for a static TV industry for "terminal" manufacture.

These services are the teletext systems Ceefax (BBC), Oracle (IBA), and the Post Office's Viewdata, now called Prestel.[45] In all of these systems, a "page" of information, filling the screen, consists of up to about 960 characters of text, or graphics. Ceefax and Oracle are receive-only page-capture systems. Data is transmitted in bursts of 7M-bit/s on spare TV lines. A viewer sets a counter on his receiver to capture one out of, say, one hundred sequentially transmitted pages; the picture is displayed 12.5 seconds later on average.

In the Viewdata system (see *Wireless World*, Feb.–May 1977 and April–June 1978) the user dials a computer, in which page data are stored, and "orders" a page by pressing numerical keys. These command data are transmitted from a keypad at 75 bit/s through the switched telephone network. In response, page data are received at 1200 bit/s. The number of pages available is limited mainly by economic considerations and could be many millions. Page information will be fed into a network of local computers by a variety of different organizations, operating independently from the Post Office; because of the nature of the system the information will tend to be less time-dependent and more archival than Ceefax/Oracle. A Viewdata page is selected by viewing ten broad choices, choosing one by depressing a button, choosing one out of ten subsets of the first choice then displayed, and so on; the user proceeds from the general to the specific; one out of one million pages could be selected by six successive choices in this manner. This procedure escapes most of the intellectual indexing problems and the need to store inverted files, concerned solely with indexing, which consume as much storage space as the information itself in most computer-based systems.

A combined entertainment TV/teletext/Viewdata receiver will contain individual front-end modules, selected by a switch, according to the service desired. The rest of the receiver is common to teletext/Viewdata; the heart of it is a programmed read-only memory (ROM) matrix within which characters and shapes (for graphics) are permanently stored. Selected characters are "switched on" by the incoming data and continuously displayed. In Viewdata each page, whether a "routing" page or a final information page, starts to be viewable as soon as a button is depressed. At an incoming data rate of 1200 bit/s a complete picture is formed in a few seconds.

The implementation of national teletext and Viewdata systems will depend upon the progress of trials of increasing scope and the ability of information suppliers to anticipate demand. The expansion rate will depend primarily upon economic and social factors. The cost of terminals is expected to diminish as LSI modules are manufactured in larger and larger quantities until a terminal costs perhaps only ten per cent more than a colour TV set. With Viewdata the public will incur local telephone time costs and information supplier charges depending on the material supplied. Social factors will be discussed later. The indexing and page arrangement of ISI's Viewdata service called SCITEL is shown in Fig. 5.7.

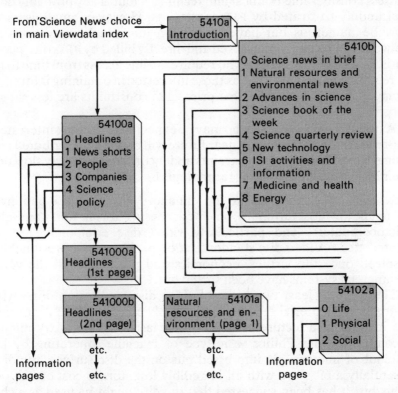

Fig. 5.7 Indexing and page arrangement of Scitel scientific information service for Viewdata/Prestel provided by the Institute for Scientific Information

Near-future activities

Teletext and Viewdata may be the precursors of a wider integration of information processing systems and channels culminating in the "Consumersole" type of facility within the next two or three decades. Various kinds of electronic systems will be introduced sooner in fields where information transfer ranks higher as an occupational necessity and economic pressures are greater. For example, efficient information flow in business, particularly time-dependent information as in stockbroking, is vital, and quite sophisticated networks exist already, such as Reuter's Manhattan cable system using video display units (VDU), the Bunker-Ramo business information system and Datastream in England.

When traffic is substantial and private lines can be leased from PTTs on a national or international scale – for example, as with the banking (Swift) and airline reservation (Sita) systems – the system operators possess considerable political and technical clout. They probably do not feel unduly frustrated by PTT constraints. However, small users who may be numerous but have to rely on individual connections to a network can be easily monitored and directly billed by PTTs on a per-use basis. For example, people who require on-line access from time to time to remote computers – such as those interested in obtaining information from US data-bases – find that prices and constraints are less satisfactory.

A number of the people who may be expected to become interested in paperless information in the near future will be widely distributed and it seems likely that prices, constraints and inconveniences may slow down their rate of adoption of new technologies.

Education. The possibilities for enhanced teaching via nationwide channels, low-cost terminals, on-line access to information, stand-alone microcomputers, and particularly video disc equipment are well appreciated.[46] Video disc standardization problems will presumably be resolved once the virtues, economics and production of the various commercial systems have been sorted out.

There are at least two kinds of video disc application. First, visual instructional material may be continuously played into a TV monitor in the manner of a lecture – current discs last for about sixty minutes; second, with the Philips/MCA type of machine, operating by laser readout of microscopic impressed pits on the disc surface, the disc is essentially a bit store with an incredibly low storage cost of 0.000012 cents/bit; it has been suggested that the disc might be used as a cheap read-only memory.[47] However, the primary purpose, at present, would be to use the MCA machine's possibilities for digitally-controlled selection of one out of the 54,000 disc tracks. By stepping back the reading head once per revolution, one TV frame may be viewed continuously. The National Library of Medicine in the US is currently considering this system for the storage, delivery and dissemination of audiovisual information.

Another technique which has been tested in prototype form is the VIDAC audiovisual educational distribution system for still pictures with a commentary. In essence the scheme consists of transmitting 1/30th second single still-picture TV frames, using disc storage at a central receiving point for refreshing locally connected TV monitors at the frame repetition rate. The same disc also stores audio information which has been transmitted as a video signal for the remaining 29/30th of a second. A US 4.2MHz TV channel can accommodate an enormous amount of 15kHz audio information once the audio is converted into video, due to a "time compression factor" of 280 times (ignoring the occupancy by sync signals). This information is distributed to local TV monitors as "real-time" audio commentary. Nine hundred fifteen-minute programmes may be transmitted from a video tape running for one hour.[48]

However, it has to be said that applications of well-established technology are not in widespread use in US education. What is in use now was in use twenty or more years ago. The average teacher does not like "teaching technology".[49]

Teleconferences. If a telecommunications link were to be as satisfactory for the exchange of information as a direct face-to-face meeting between two or more people, then the implications for human behaviour would be profound. According to Short *et al*: "The supposed benefits of remote working include improvements in the quality of life through a reduction in time wasted travelling and the greater efficiency in the use of office space and travel facilities."[50] This would fulfil one of the major conditions necessary for the late Peter Goldmark's "rural society".[51] On the other hand, is travelling itself a change or a relaxation, and would a video link replace informality with stress? What is the importance of "social presence" at a face-to-face meeting, and what subtle forms of information are lost in any electrical link? Some quite elaborate experiments have been carried out to try and answer these questions, including a video conference between a Congressman in Washington and 150 people in his North Carolina district via the CTS satellite.[52]

In work done by the Post Office (Confravision), Bell Canada, University of Quebec, and the UK Civil Service, similar conclusions were reached. Comprehensive TV facilities with an expensive wideband channel were much more costly than a narrowband telephone conference but not proportionately more acceptable. The choice of media for certain tasks was less important than the imperative to travel – for instance in order to get to know someone by face-to-face social presence. The opportunities for social etiquette are lost if the meeting is conducted via a communication channel (the "coffee and biscuits" syndrome). However, the difficulty of measuring such intangibles makes conclusions hard to reach; more experiments and further development of lower cost video facilities are needed.

Electronic journals and on-line information. The economic pressures on commercial, learned society, and other publishers of scientific journals, are heavy. Individual subscriptions are rapidly disappearing as journal prices rise; libraries respond to budget cuts by reducing subscriptions. The function of journals, which is to provide rapid information about current research and a record for the archives, has become less satisfactory as the number of journal titles has risen to tens of thousands. In 1975 about 327,000 articles were published in 4175 scientific and technical journals in the US,[53] so probably at least one million articles were published throughout the world. Fifty-five per cent of US journals had fewer than 3000 subscribers; the price of the average journal has increased fourfold between 1960 and 1974.

There have been various responses to this situation; photocomposition is increasingly used as the cost of equipment decreases and sophistication increases. Equipment is becoming available for text preparation with minimum rekeying; text may be prepared on a word-processing machine and the final format stored on floppy disc. The disc can be used to transfer the text to the photocomposer's display and the operator simply enters command codes. The possibilities for using these facilities in mitigation of the above-mentioned journal problems prompted a cost-reducing resource-sharing system called "an editorial processing centre".[54] An advanced form of this idea is shown in Fig. 5.8. It can be seen that various paperwork operations are replaced by a movement of manuscripts by digital transmission. Such a facility might be shared for the publication of a number of journals.

After fairly comprehensive investigations the funding organization (NSF) considered it had done enough to demonstrate feasibility;[55] it

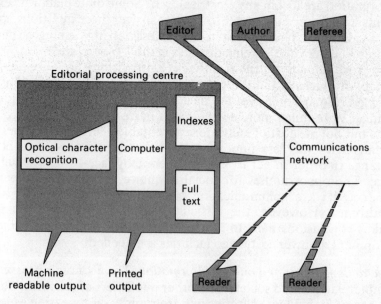

Fig. 5.8 Proposed editorial processing centre for an electronic journal. Movement of paper is replaced by digital transmission

remains to be seen whether any publishers will take it up. If readers were to be connected to this network, then we have, in effect, an "electronic journal" (the dotted extensions in Fig. 5.8). So the question arises: when will this happen? According to Senders it is almost imminent.[56] Certainly something like it – an "electronic information exchange" – is under consideration. This exchange would take place using minicomputers with substantial disc storage accessed through thirty-two Telenet ports at the New Jersey Institute of Technology. Authors in a particular research community would be able to exchange information and "publish" work in electronic form.

A more important question than the one posed above is "when will electronic journals replace existing journals to any significant degree?" According to Garfield, not in the next decade; even then the "electronic journal" will still fulfil the functions that it does today.[57] A reasonable discussion of what may – and may not – happen has been given by Woodward.[58] It seems likely that research communities will use existing networks much more: the ARPA network is already widely used for author information exchange in the US. Existing publishers will, in due course, possess articles in machine-readable form as part of their journal production processes. Access to these electronically, if made available, will erode subscriptions to the printed version.

It is hard to visualize the changeover mechanics of a print-on-paper corpus of readers, to a corpus of terminal viewers. Conventional publishing requires little capital; a replacement electronic journal requires a great deal. In a specific case, an appreciable fraction of readers of a particular journal might also possess terminals connected to some communications network. Collective action by these readers would enable the electronic journal function to ride on existing functions, but in how many cases would this opportunity arise and could it be suitably organized? All in all it seems likely that the impact upon conventional journal publication will be gradual unless a government injects very substantial launching capital.

Meanwhile a different kind of activity impinges upon the publication scene. I refer to the on-line secondary information services which are being increasingly used to locate a published item of interest out of the total mass.[59] Organizations like the Institute for Scientific Information, Chemical Abstracts and Biological Abstracts, maintain machine-readable indexes which are available from dial-up computer centres such as Lockheed and SDC via international networks like Tymnet and Telenet, and soon via Euronet. This activity impinges upon publication to the extent that centralized photocopying of articles located by these services may be reducing journal subscriptions. If a cheap "relevant article selected from the world's literature" on-demand service exists, it is less necessary to subscribe to and browse through journals in the hope of finding relevant articles. Theoretically, at least, it is absurd to "broadcast" an article in a journal in order to reach a relatively small number of interested persons, and then set up elaborate secondary services to enable those persons to find the article. This brings us back full circle to a notion of a more direct author – reader connection with an "electronic journal" as already discussed.

Electronic funds transfer. Credit transfer between banks is already carried out on a large scale using the Society for World Wide Interbank Financial Telecommunication (SWIFT) network. This private data network interconnects a number of banks in the US, Canada and Europe. Banks were also among the first to use data transmission between offices and branches. A recent development is the transatlantic credit rating system between VISA/Barclaycard using PDP11/45s at Northampton and VISA in San Mateo, California. It takes only a few seconds to put through an inquiry. According to an A. D. Little spokesman there will be a steady move towards a cashless society as magnetic "transaction cards" become widely used for payments via special cash-registers at points of sale. The rate of adoption will depend on the rate of development of the necessary communication networks, but these cards are expected to be widely used in the US by 1985.

Electronic mail. A form of electronic mail is starting up in the UK; it will be possible for Viewdata users to send messages to each other experimentally during the 1978 market trial, and more widely when the national network becomes established.* This will of course affect the postal service, but as the Post Office also run Viewdata they are in a position, through pricing policies, to control relative usage; their intentions in this respect are unknown.

In the US, "computer mail" over the ARPANET government-controlled computer network is well established;[60] as many people with common interests and the facilities for message exchange are interconnected via this network, it is hardly surprising that a message exchange system has been established.

Current prices for electronic mail in the US are difficult to establish. Commercial computer mail services are being offered at around $1 for a short message, and this may soon be reduced to 50c. Studies undertaken by the National Research Council ended with the strong recommendation that the US postal service should provide electronic mail services, since its basic business is likely to be seriously threatened.[61] Already operating at a loss, the service is steadily losing revenue from the switch

---

* Editor's Note: In fact the Post Office's Viewdata system, *Prestel*, went on stream in the London area in mid-1979.

by business – an estimated eighty per cent of first-class mail is business related – to telecommunications. It will lose more from the growth of electronic funds transfer. The computer-mail services mentioned above are illegal; to operate computer mail, legally onerous FCC common carrier regulations have to be adhered to, so US operators conduct their services under cover. Like other services the reality of channel requirements is one thing and outdated regulations, drafted for mutually exclusive use, are another.

With the possible exception of business communication, electronic mail seems likely to grow slowly in the UK since appropriate equipment and a channel connection are beyond the means of most people: nearly half of private houses do not have telephones and virtually none a computer terminal. Electronic mail will start to ride upon multi-function systems such as Viewdata and although postal services in the UK and elsewhere have deteriorated and become much more costly they will still represent the most satisfactory method for most people's intermittent communication needs for many years. However, low-price, convenient facsimile systems are a form of electronic mail, and it seems likely that a new generation of fast equipment, capable of transmitting an A4-size page of text in one minute or less, will soon be available. Until now transmission time has been five or more minutes. It remains to be seen whether the new equipment, which incorporates data-reducing coding, will be available at a price which will encourage wide use.

Social forces
Much of the above discussion has been about technology, although it has been hard to treat social issues separately and impossible not to discuss politics. It would be a bold man who would attempt to provide any kind of timetable for the paperless revolution, since the expected changes are without precedent and the rate of acceptability is impossible to predict.

Some people think the changes brought about by the increasing use of electronics, computers, microcomputers and so on in industry, education, the professions and at home, will proceed at a rate which may cause concern but not alarm. Others feel that a revolution without precedent is upon us, demanding immediate attention particularly in its likely effects upon employment.

Those inclined towards a moderate view use data from the past to provide reassurances about the future. They point out that dire predictions about the effects of automation turned out to be unfounded. One notable authority[62] suggests that: ". . . computers are simply one of the many labour-saving devices that have been appearing since the begin-

ning of the industrial revolution . . . a large body of empirical evidence
demonstrates that there is no relation, positive or negative, between the
technological sophistication of an economy and the level of employment that it maintains." In another review[63] opinion is more mixed:
"The volume of pocket calculators produced has probably more than
made up for the number of displaced slide-rule manufacturers and their
employees"; in another case, the telephone industry, there has been a
wholesale changeover from electromechanical to electronic and
computer-controlled switched lines between 1962 and 1976, and the
number of employees in Western Electric's switching division has not
changed much. But in the *operating* telephone companies, less than half
the number of people are now needed to administer and maintain the
new exchanges; generally "if speculation turns out to be anywhere near
the mark . . . the impact on employment could dwarf earlier concern
about automation." Continuing on an alarmist note, a recent newspaper
article, speculating about breakdowns in communication channels,
started with the headline "Computerised chaos feared for 2002 AD."[64]

Intrusion and secrecy have probably received more attention than
any other social matter, centred mainly upon the abuse of personal
information held in computer storage. In Sweden – with the early
Swedish Data Act – privacy protection is ranked higher than social care
for children and the aged.[65] Similar concern has been expressed in other
countries; in the US, the Privacy Act was passed in 1974. This gives the
individual the right to go to any federal agency, check his record, and
have it corrected if it is erroneous; furthermore a commission is
currently considering extension into the private sector, together with
the right to make comprehensive error corrections propagated back-
wards and forwards to other information which may contain related
errors.[66] In the UK secrecy has received the tortoise-like speed of
consideration that might be expected. A White Paper was published in
1975 about the subject, and in September 1977 the following comment
was made: "We hope to report in the next few months but I cannot say
what our recommendations will be."[67] Another controversial issue is
possible European protectionism against US data processing; Swedish
trade unions are alleged to have exerted strong pressure against the
export of data for foreign processing.

In addition to the ease of integrating and communicating personal
data via large interconnected computer networks to presumably
authorized persons, there is the question of unauthorized reception of
data in transmission or called up from computer storage. Many cases of
sophisticated in-transit eavesdropping and in-house computer frauds
have been reported. One remedy is to scramble data using a code which
is secure and convenient to use. Machines for this purpose were devised

during the last war but messages using the supposedly secure Type X (US) and Enigma (German) coding machines were successfully decoded. Another well-known method is to use a so-called "one-time pad" which is reasonably secure but inconvenient. A system has recently been introduced in the US by the National Bureau of Standards (NBS) called the Data Encryption Standard (DES); the system and algorithm may be accommodated on chips attached to a computer for encoding and decoding data. Each device has its own fifty-six-bit key. The code is said to be unbreakable, but the matter is controversial and surrounded by cloak-and-dagger activity.[68] Whether or not the code is unbreakable, the key has to be sent to authorized users to enable them to decode messages. It could be changed as necessary by substituting a new set of randomly chosen digits, but earlier recorded messages could be decoded at leisure if the old key became known. Even so some banks believe that this is a considerable advance over other methods and plan to use it.

People have in their minds another future image of computers – that the machines may become too clever by half and take over as masters. There is no doubt that chess-playing machines, progressing towards the grandmaster level, have caught the imagination of the public; in a recent contest two international masters were unable to beat a machine. Artificial intelligence research and machines capable of executing 100 million instructions per second reinforce a feeling of uneasiness. Real problems would start, according to one researcher, if programs, already extremely complex, became inscrutable. There may be a real need to guard against this with an "open box" rather than a "black box" approach in the next few years.[69]

After unemployment and secrecy, a third, possibly a very insidious effect, might accompany the paperless revolution. Will Viewdata-like systems ". . . buttressed by the superficial impartiality of the computer and dominated by the awesome authority of the box . . . distort the process of debate and persuasion that holds a democratic society together?" (as one observer eloquently puts it).[70] If events take a turn in this direction it will be because people are spending more time communicating by electronic media at the office and at home and there is a general drift towards receiving a higher proportion of information in this way. At best people will be at arm's length instead of face-to-face. At worst they will become conditioned passive listeners or viewers. This in turn could result in a further reduction in conversation, a tendency to watch potted digests at the expense of more general reading, and a general lessening of social contacts, discussion and controversy.

Associated with this possible trend there could be a reduction in the number of information sources; the number of newspapers is steadily diminishing and it is easy to visualize the influence, by information selection, suppression, or distortion, that could be exerted should there ever be only one national newspaper. Pursuing such a trend, if ever information reception by electronic media became overwhelmingly attractive in economic and Zipfian* terms, the power possessed by the providers would be immense.

Next the question of copyright, designed for print-on-paper, has yet to be resolved. In the United States steps have been taken to alleviate the effects of photocopying by setting up an agency for royalty collection when a defined quantity is exceeded, and copyright is under consideration in many other countries. Problems raised by property rights in electronically disseminated information have yet to be clarified.

It is impossible to say when or if some of the suggested unpleasant consequences of the paperless revolution which I have discussed will be with us. The technology per se is neutral – it's the purpose to which it is put that matters. Governments of whatever complexion will intervene, but the complaint of "too little too late" will be increasingly heard, particularly in democracies, because the mechanics are too slow to respond to an ever-increasing rate of change.

It seems just as likely that "progress" will be achieved by confrontation rather than by smooth transition. If labour-intensive activities are going to be reduced at an unexpectedly rapid rate, the only way in which those displaced can be re-employed is by utilization of the new wealth created by the value added to the new knowledge-intensive products and services. I am not aware of any convincing argument which suggests that sufficient wealth can be produced in this manner.

It is unreasonable to expect that technologists in a technology of increasing complexity will take time off to develop a collective social conscience and use it to influence the course of events. There might be an advance in "socially-clandestine technology" – social consequences, privacy, privacy intrusion, etc, would be played down until eventually the public would find that it had drifted into a highly unpleasant situation brought about by a series of apparently innocuous small steps. There could then be a violent overreaction in which a whole range of services and activities would be labelled as bad, including those which are in fact beneficial. This situation could arise because of the difficulty of connecting a particular event with a particular social consequence; for example, it is difficult to correlate a percentage increase in unemployment with particular events.

Since hard evidence of forthcoming widespread unemployment or

---

* Zipf's Law concerns the human tendency to select minimum-effort solutions to a problem.

behavioural changes is not available, it is unlikely that governments or other bodies are going to pay any attention to mere prophets of doom. Such people are likely to exaggerate in order to get a hearing, and their pleas will be discounted. However, considering the sum total of the issues, it seems to me that when a whole spectrum of events are changing at an ever-increasing rate, some combination of them is likely to add up to Future Shock for a good many people. This shock could be alleviated by the continuous monitoring of events, observation of trends, and accumulation of evidence. If this information was widely publicized as an early warning perhaps planning or action would follow – surely a better way of doing things than by ad hoc emergency action.

There ought to be some sociologists who are able to master the technology, and some engineers who are prepared to study the social issues and politics. An articulate group of sociotechnologists, as I will call them, might be able to command as much attention from government and public as does Ralph Nader for other areas of consumption. The formation and funding of a body of this kind is worthy of consideration.

Notes

1   W. I. Guzzardi, "The great world telephone war", *Fortune*, 96(2) (1977), pp. 142–54.
2   R. N. Noyce, "Large scale integration; what is yet to come?" *Science*, 195(4283) (1977), pp. 1102–6.
3   D. A. Hodges, "Review and projection of semiconductor components for digital storage", *PIEEE*, 63(8), (1975), pp. 1136–47.
4   J. A. Rajchman, "New memory technologies", *Science*, 195(4283), (1977), pp. 1223–7.
5   J. E. Juliussen, D. M. Lee & G. M. Cox, "Bubbles appearing first as microprocessor mass storage", *Electronics*, 50(16), (1977), pp. 81–6.
6   Anon, "Holography microfiche retriever", *Laser & Electro-optik*, 2 (1976), pp. 14–15.
7   See "Holofile" brochure from Holofile Industries Ltd, 10850 Wiltshire Boulevard, Los Angeles, USA.
8   J. A. Gordon, "Digital X-y position indicator using Walsh functions", *Electron Letts.* 11(1), (1975), pp. 5–6.
9   R. Kurzweil, "The Kurzweil reading machine – a technical overview", paper presented at "Science Technology and Handicapped" symposium (1976), AAAS Annual Meeting, Washington D.C.
10 J. L. Flanagan, "Computers that talk and listen; man-machine communication by voice", *PIEEE*, 64(4), (1976), pp. 405–15.
11 M. J. Underwood, "Machines that understand speech", *Radio & Electronic Eng.* 47(819), (1977), pp. 368–76.
12 D. R. Reddy, "Speech recognition by machine – a review", *PIEEE*, 64(4), (1976), pp. 501–31.
13 H. Wiener, "For hobbyists – computers that talk and listen", *Computer Weekly*, (13 Oct. 1977), p. 16.

14 V. Bush, "As we may think", *Atlantic Monthly*, 176, (1945), p. 101.

15 V. Bush, "Memex revisited", in *Science is not enough* (Apollo Editions, New York, 1969).

16 M. S. Miller, "Design a low-cost CRT terminal around a single chip microprocessor", *Electronic Design News*, 22(9), (1977), pp. 88–94.

17 A. C. Kay, "Microelectronics and the personal computer", *Scientific American*, 237(3), (1977), pp. 231–44.

18 Anon, "The GCC-1 graphic communication console", 1977 report from Science Applications Inc., Arlington, Va., USA.

19 R. K. Jurgen, "Competing display technologies struggle for superiority", *IEEE Spectrum*. 11(10), (1974), pp. 90–5. R. A. Strom, "High-speed low cost selection circuitry for large-area plasma displays", *Proc. SID*, 18(1), (1977), pp. 94–9.

20 J. Adams, & R. Wallis, "New concepts in display technology", *Computer*, 10(8), (1977), pp. 61–9.

21 C. M. Spauling, "The fifty dollar reading machine", *Library J.* 10(18), (1976), pp. 2133–8.

22 W. L. Wallace, "Developing a book size reader system", *J. Micrographics*, 10(4), (1977), pp. 161–5.

23 F. Duerden, "Automated microfiche terminal", *GEC J. Sci. & Tech.* 43(2), (1976), pp. 51–60.

24 See brochure "The Stabletron integrated display system" from Stabletron Ltd, Fareham, Hants., England.

25 A. K. Griffith, "From Gutenberg to Grafix 1 – new directions in OCR", *J. Micrographics*, 9(2), (1975), pp. 81–9.

26 See brochure "The Voltrax ML-I multi-lingual voice system" from Dicoll Electronics, Basingstoke, Hants, England.

27 B. L. Kenney, "The future of cable communications in libraries", *J. Library Aut.*, 9(4), (1976), pp. 299–317.

28 Anon, "Cable television and content regulations; FCC, the first amendment, and electronic newspapers", *New York Univ. Law Rev.*, 51, (1976), pp. 133–47.

29 For a review of events see R. E. Wiley, "The U.S. communications consumer and the monopoly supply", *Telecomms. Policy*, 1(2), (1977), pp. 99–111.

30 L. L. Johnson, "A review of the FCC and AT&T position", *Telecomms. Policy*, 1(2), (1977), pp. 119–24.

31 A. E. Cawkell, "Information and privacy", *Financial Times* (20 October 1977).

32 R. Pye, "The British Post Office – an extensive monopoly", *Telecomms. Policy*, 1(4), (1977), pp. 356–9.

33 A. A. L. Reid, "Uncertainty & Inertia", *Telecomms. Policy*, 1(3), (1977), pp. 207–11.

34 J. G. Thompson, "The free flow of information", *Proc. Eusidic Conf.* (Oslo, 1975), pp. 92–100, G. Pratt & S. Harvey (eds.), Aslib, London, 1976.

35 A. Tomberg, "On-line services in Europe", *On-line Review*, 1(3), (1977), pp. 177–93.

36 *Euronet – The European on-line information network*. Booklet from Directorate General, STI management, Luxembourg, June 1976.

37 D. N. Hatfield, "Communications or data processing? A regulatory dilemma", *Bull. Amer. Soc. Info. Sci.* 3(5), (1977), pp. 13–14.

38 For an excellent discussion of the issues see D. Farber & P. Baran, "The convergence of computing and telecommunication systems", *Science*, 195(4283), (1977), pp. 1166–70, and M. R. Irwin & S. C. Johnson, "The information economy and public policy", *Science*, 195(4283), (1977), pp. 1170–4.

39 S. Caswell, "Satellite business systems; the start of something big", *Computer Decisions*, 9(3), (1977), pp. 16–21.

40 J. C. Fletcher, "Remarks by J. C. Fletcher at the conference on satellite communications", *Information Hotline*, 8(5), (1977), pp. 3–4.

41 L. A. Jackson, & J. R. Stern, "Optical fibre systems for the civil communications network", *Optics & Laser Technol*, 9(5), (1977), pp. 233–40.

42 B. L. Kenney, "The future of cable communication in libraries", *J. Libr. Automat*, 9(4), (1976), pp. 299–317.
    P. Baran, "Broadband interactive communication services to the home – part 2 impasse", *IEEE Trans. Com.* COM23(1), (1975), pp.178–84.

43 "Social services and cable TV". Report prepared for NSF by RANN, NSF/RA 761061, July 1976, NSF, Washington.

44 "Talking to the tube – Columbus viewers will take part in programs when two-way TV service begins late in year", *The Wall Street Journal* (10 August 1977).

45 P. L. Mothersole, *et al*, in "Broadcast and wired Teletext systems – Ceefax, Oracle, Viewdata", *IEE, London, colloquium digest no. 1976/3.* A. E. Cawkell, "Developments in interactive on-line television systems and teletext information services in the home", *On-line Review*, 1(1), (1977), pp. 31–8. S. Fedida, "Viewdata", *Wireless World*, (Feb.–May 1977), commencing issue No. 1494, and April–June 1978, in seven parts.

46 R. J. Seidel, "Introduction, summary, and implications"; p. 17 in R. J. Seidel and M. Rubins (eds.), *Computers & Communications; implications for education* (Academic Press, New York, 1977).

47 E. W. Schneider, "Applications of videodisc technology to individualized instruction", ibid, pp. 313.

48 H. M. Diambra, & N. L. Gulliford, "A report and demonstration of a new technology for improving the effectiveness of television distribution networks", ibid, p. 189.

49 D. H. Ahl, "Does education want what technology can deliver?", ibid, p. 157.

50 J. Short, E. Williams, & B. Christie, *The Social Psychology of Telecommunications*, John Wiley, New York, 1976.

51 P. C. Goldmark, B. Kray, & A. Egerton, "Communications for survival; perspective and proposed programs", *Habitat*, 2(1/2), (1977), pp. 13–35.

52 L. J. Carter, "Videoconferences via satellite; opening congress to the people?" *Science*, 197(4298), (1977), pp. 31–3.

53 D. W. King, "Systemic and economic interdependence in journal publication", *IEEE Trans.* PC-20(2), (1977), pp. 106–13.

54 L. H. Berul, & B. I. Krevitt, "Innovative editorial procedure; the editorial processing centre concept", in P. Zunde (ed.), *Proc. 37th ASIS meeting*, vol. 11 (American Society for Information Science, Washington, 1974), pp. 98–102.

55 S. N. Rhodes, "Editorial processing centre-prelude to phase 3", *IEEE Trans.* PC-20(2), (1977), 102–5.

56 J. Senders, "An on-line scientist journal", *The Information Scientific.* 11(1), (1977), pp. 3–9.

57 E. Garfield, "Is there a future for the scientific journal?", *Sci-Tech. News*, 29(2), (1975), pp. 42–4.

58 A. M. Woodward, "The electronic journal – an assessment", Aslib R&D Department (London, 1976), BL R&D report No. 5322.

59 C. E. Wilmot, "On-line opportunity; a comparison of activities in America and the United Kingdom", *Aslib Proc.* 28(4), (1976), pp. 134–43.

60 R. R. Panko, "The outlook for computer mail", *Telecomms. Policy*, 1(3), (1977), pp. 242–53.

61　W. A. McLean, "Three US electronic mail studies", *Telecomms. Policy*, 1(5), (1977), pp. 422–3.

62　H. A. Simon, "What computers mean for man and society", *Science*, 195(4283), (1977), pp. 1186–91.

63　A. L. Robinson, "Impact of electronics on employment; productivity and displacement effects", *Science*, 195(4283), (1977), pp. 1179–84.

64　A. Berry, in *The Daily Telegraph* (10 Nov. 1977).

65　J.Freese, "Preserving the open flow of information across borders", Paper TDF2 in *Symp. Trans-border Data Flow and Protection of Privacy* (OECD, Vienna, Sept. 1977).

66　W. H. Ware, "Computers and personal privacy", *Proc. Am. Philos. Soc.* 121(5), (1977), pp. 355–9.

67　Sir Norman Lindop, Contribution to the panel discussion in *Symp. Trans-border Data Flow and Protection of Privacy* (OECD, Vienna, Sept. 1977).

68　G. B. Kolata, "Computer encryption and the national security agency connection", *Science*, 197(4302), (1977), pp. 438–40. G. B. Kolata, "Cryptography; on the brink of a revolution?" *Science*, 197(4305), (1977), pp. 747–8.

69　D. Michie, "What if the machines become inscrutable?" *Computer Weekly*, (27 Oct. 1977), p. 6.

70　Anon ("The listeners"), "Information technology for the home", *The Information Scientist*, 11(4), (1977), pp. 146–8.

Word Processors and the Oppression of Women

Hazel Downing

And now for something completely different: a radical analysis of the office revolution direct from the shop floor – or should I say the word processing centre. The author, an ex-graduate student, was employed as a temporary secretary or "temp" when she wrote the following paper for this volume. The introduction of new technology into the office is set firmly in the context of the evolution of capitalism. Of particular interest is the analysis of social relations in the office and the predicted end of the "social office". There are also some acute observations on the role of women.

Seventy per cent of clerical workers and 98.6 per cent of secretaries and typists in the UK are women. The choice of paid work for working-class women is largely limited to the lowest-paid jobs in offices, factories, shops and industrial and private cleaning. For many women, office work stands out as perhaps the cream of the choice, offering clean, comfortable, respectable work with the possibility of promotion up through the secretarial hierarchy. In contrast to factory work, office hours are generally more relaxed with little or no clocking on and off, and work is rarely paced or subject to the intense control resulting from time and motion studies. Perhaps most important of all, the office has traditionally been an area where the working relationship between the boss and the typist/secretary has been personal in nature.

The reproduction of the capitalist mode of production depends crucially on the continued accumulation of capital. The current economic climate, which has produced a period of nonprofitability, challenges this accumulation process and demands that capital find ways of stabilizing its position. Historically, this drive for accumulation has depended in large part on the constant reorganization of the labour

275

process: this is done to cheapen the price of labour and to take control over the labour process out of the hands of the individual worker and transfer it into the hands of management. It is within this context that we must view the introduction of new technology – not as part of some inexorable law of technological progress, but as part of capital's strategy to continually realize itself.

The office, however, stands out as an anomaly, and one which exists precisely because of the contradiction between capital's need for optimum efficiency and the inefficiency of the social relations in the office. In contrast to many other sectors of employment which discipline their labour force through direct "naked" economic forms, the office operates a form of control which can be defined as gender-specific in its direct reflection of the relations of male domination and female subordination which permeate the whole of society. In addition, the typewriter, the essential tool of the secretarial worker, has changed very little since its invention in 1873. The impact of the electric typewriter, which did no more than replace the mechanical motor by electrical impulses, was simply to speed up the process; fundamentally, control over the machine has always remained in the hands of the typist.

The impact of word processing on the office will be to radically restructure its social relations. It will also, significantly, divest secretarial workers of the control they have over their own labour process. By becoming paced by the machine, they will in effect be rendered machine minders.

But the initial effect of the application of microelectronic technology on the office will be the displacement of large numbers of workers. One word processor, boasts its manufacturers, can do the work of from two and a half to five typists on conventional typewriters and increase productivity by 150–400 per cent. This is no empty sales talk. In those offices where word processors have been introduced, office staffs have been cut by one third to one half.* Many of these jobs have been lost peaceably with no resistance from the workers involved – the one exception being Bradford Metropolitan Council, which despite opposition from some staff, introduced word processing into its Jacob's Well office in May 1977.† The traditionally high turnover in office personnel

---

* Examples include: Bradford Metropolitan Council where sixteen word processors reduced staff in one section from forty-four to twenty-two. The Central Electricity Generating Board in Bristol reduced their "girls" from fifty-plus to twenty-six. The National Coal Board Western Area reduced staff from twenty to fourteen.

† In February 1979, eighteen typists at Bradford went on strike when the Council announced the introduction of more word processors. The strike ended with a decision to set up a working party to look into the new technology. Both sides later signed a New Technology Agreement.

has permitted managements to reduce their staffs by natural wastage or redeployment to other departments, thus avoiding the necessity of paying redundancy money and possible confrontations with the workforce.

The application of office automation on its own, however, does not necessarily increase productivity, nor does it eliminate the social office. I shall, therefore, look in some detail at the nature of the secretarial labour process in order to bring out what word processing will and won't do. But first I wish to underline the importance of seeing the introduction of word processors as part of the logic of capitalist development.

Developments in the capitalist labour process

The entry of women into the office coincided with a massive expansion in that sector broadly described as clerical/administrative, but which, historically, can be seen as the beginning of "management" – a process which involved the separation of conception and execution, or the mental/manual division of labour.* The "putting-out" system had predominated in early factories, restricting the extent to which the individual capitalist could ascertain the amount of labour he required and the extent to which he could regulate the production and purchase of raw materials, ensure production schedules and make reasonably accurate forecasts of profits. The need to render the production process as efficient and profitable as possible required the owner of the factory to take control over the labour process.

Taylorism, or "scientific management", developed in the latter part of the nineteenth century by Frederick Taylor, provided a major impetus to the sophistication of management techniques. This system involved the fragmentation of the task in question. Each subdivided task was then timed and paced, permitting management to guarantee the time the job would take and hence labour costs. The division of labour and the application of advanced technology are part of the process of rendering labour functions quantifiable and of stripping the individual worker of knowledge of the labour process as a totality. The application of machinery to the production process is used not simply to secure increased productivity, but to divest workers of control over their own labour and to discipline them by pacing them to the machine.

Early applications of Taylorism to the manufacturing process contributed to the growth of the white-collar sector. The process of the subordination of a worker's skills to production and control depends on the acquisition of knowledge about each human action within any given

* For a fuller discussion see Harry Braverman, *Labour and Monopoly Capital: The Degradation of Labour in the 20th Century* (Monthly Review Press, New York and London, 1974).

labour process, so that the job can be paced or replaced by machinery. The process of acquisition and control created more jobs in the acquisition, storage, presentation and transmission of this information, alongside a relatively declining number actually working at the point of production. This "information sector" is concerned, therefore, not just with the accounting of surplus, but with the control and putting into motion of the actual production process. It is concerned with a "paper replica of production" (Braverman, 1974).

Since World War Two, the proportion of office workers in the UK workforce has been growing. From thirty per cent in 1964, it is estimated that this sector now accounts for about forty-five per cent of the total. The cost, in both the public and the private sectors, of employing a large number of essentially "nonproductive" people is proving very high. Yet as early as 1925, in a book dedicated to the Taylor Society, William Henry Leffingwell had unequivocally attacked what he termed the "private secretary evil". The private secretary, he argued, was essential to important executives but there was a growing tendency "for persons of lesser importance . . . to surround themselves with the atmosphere of a great man, and whether or not there is any need for it, they insist upon having a private secretary." This could only

This Commodore PET wordprocessing system handles mailings and accountancy at an advertising agency. The memory and printer stand either side of the keyboard and VDU. *Photo courtesy of PCD Ltd*

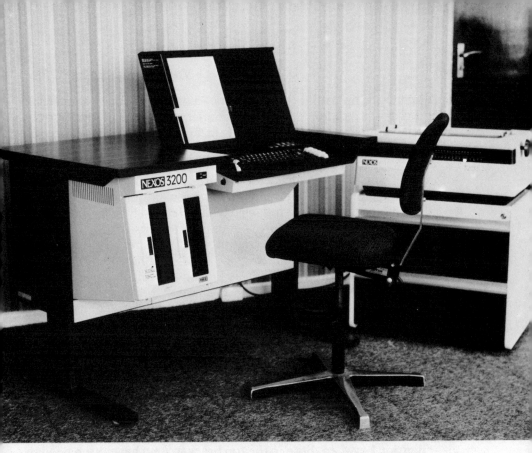

This thin window display word processor has been developed by Nexos, a British government-backed office equipment firm. *Photo courtesy of Nexos Office Systems*

result in "a sub-executive with an exaggerated ego and a spoiled stenographer – two very expensive and superfluous luxuries" (Leffingwell, 1925).

Despite Leffingwell's exhortations to eliminate the "social office" and fully Taylorize office organization, this has not occurred. Early attempts at mechanization through the use of adding machines, dictaphones, and later mainframe computers, certainly effected some rationalization of office organization. But, despite the subdivision of offices into separate departments – accounts, wages, sales, customer service, reprographics, post room, etc – in which each clerical worker has his or her specific job to check and process, the backwardness of office technology coupled with unregulated forms of labour discipline has meant the retention of costly periods of nonproductive time.

Social relations in the office
The mythology of the secretary, and her designation as the "office wife" has its basis in the reality of office social relations. Historically, we can view the early male clerks of the nineteenth century as in an almost

feudal relationship with their employers – a working relationship which relied for its smooth functioning on a gentlemanly sense of loyalty, duty and obligation of a strongly paternalistic nature (Lockwood, 1958). In today's office, this paternalism is reflected in the closely personal nature of the male boss/female secretary relationship. But the entry of women into office work had involved the transformation of this paternalism into a relationship of male domination and female subordination. The social relations of the office today are characterized by gender-specific forms of control. It is, therefore, impossible to consider the nature of office work without regard to gender specificity. As we have seen, 98.6 per cent of secretaries are women.*

Secretarial work presents itself as having a straightforward career structure, which provides the same promotion prospects to all who enter, even at the lowest rungs. The illusion of this career structure is maintained in secretarial manuals, commercial colleges, and by career teachers. "A top secretarial position is an excellent stepping stone to many interesting and remunerative careers in various fields" (Bosticco, 1975). But despite the fact that the hierarchy is deceptive, ensuring that for working-class girls in particular there is no guaranteed move from one rung to the next, many girls still leave school armed with typing and shorthand certificates with the hope that they will one day make it to the anteroom of the managing director's office. The reality is that there is a clear division between those in the top bracket, who have often been to public schools or finishing schools, and those in the bottom bracket of low-paid routine jobs.

Generally, the status and position of a secretary is dependent not so much on her skills – her speeds in shorthand and typing, her ability to work to a high degree of efficiency – but on the status of her boss. The secretary to the managing director is guaranteed a much higher place in the organization. She is given her own office, she probably has more modern equipment and she is often allowed greater flexibility than the secretary or shorthand typist of a lower manager. While the essential skills of any secretarial worker are shorthand and typing, the proportion of the job which relates to these paper qualifications decreases as one ascends the hierarchy to a point at which the secretary is called upon to demonstrate other qualities which are specifically "feminine" and which can only be learned through an apprenticeship in womanhood.

Significantly, job descriptions are a rare feature in advertisements for

* The following story from the *Daily Mirror* (1 March 1979) illustrates this. Under the headline WHY SECRETARY GOT THE NEEDLE, it reported: "A secretary got shirty when asked to sew a button on for the boss. For the £3500 a year shorthand typist was . . . a man. He also refused to make coffee or help the boss on with his coat – complaining that these were 'domestic chores'. He was fired."

secretaries. If they are included they usually specify shorthand, typing (or audiotyping) and general office duties, and tagged on to the end is an "etc". It is this etcetera which assumes the naturalness of women performing specifically feminine tasks which involve caring and servicing. This is stated quite explicitly in secretarial manuals:

> In order to stay in the battle and reap a victory in the form of a top job, other far more intangible qualities are required ... These qualities are mainly concerned with dealing with people. They include poise, good manners, tact, sensitivity, and adaptability. They also include good personal habits and the ability to speak well. In short, the top secretary should look the part, sound the part, and act the part. (Bosticco, 1975)

While the working-class girl can be trained at school in shorthand and typing and reach high speeds, she will rarely if ever make the heights of Secretary to the Director, particularly in a large company, to say nothing of using her typing as a stepping stone, "a magic carpet, an open sesame, to a life full of interest – a life with complete fulfilment" (Hardwick-Smith and Rowe, 1958). Promotion does not depend on high speeds, but on the successful manipulation of modes of femininity which are class-specific. To move up the hierarchy with any degree of ease, the working-class girl must develop specifically middle-class modes of femininity, in particular a "tasteful" dress sense, a "natural" telephone voice and "perfect grooming" – in other words, she must "look the part, sound the part, and act the part". In addition, she must learn to isolate herself from her workmates and distance herself from the "girls".

But for many women, especially married women, it is rarely the content of the job which keeps them there, but the company of other women. Given the largely boring and impersonal content of their work, resulting from the rationalization of information processing, the cosy atmosphere of a group of women is generally preferred to the isolation of an office with only the boss to talk to: here the mental/manual division of labour mediated by gender relations precludes the possibility of an equal relationship based upon shared experience and culture. In reply to the argument, "Well, it's their own fault if they're not ambitious and get stuck in low-paid jobs", I would argue that women are realistic and recognize that the hierarchy is deceptive. They therefore engage in an implicit form of resistance by imbuing their working lives outside the home with concerns which relate to the family and domestic responsibilities.

Women are seen and see themselves primarily in relation to the family, always as wives and mothers or potential wives and mothers. The work they do outside the home is almost always seen as peripheral to their lives, despite the fact that most women do work almost continuously in paid employment, which is only interrupted by a spell of childcare. Their "nonworking" hours are more often spent on their other unpaid job – housework. Yet married women's incomes provide the sole economic support for about two million UK households and keep millions of families who would otherwise be in poverty above the poverty line (Royal Commission on the Distribution of Income and Wealth, 1977). While I would argue that women do see themselves as wage workers, this view of themselves is strongly mediated by their domestic responsibilities. Because of the "loyalty" which is built up around the personal working relationship between boss and secretary, the "naked" economic control of the wage packet becomes subsumed under a massive sense of duty and obligation.

Conversations in offices reflect this: married women talk about their families and children; women about to be married talk about wedding plans, purchases for the new home, colour schemes; young unmarried women talk about their social lives and their boyfriends. The office also becomes the perfect environment for showing off new clothes. A large proportion of the wages of young women office workers is employed specifically to reproduce their femininity through the massive consumption of clothes and make-up in order to perfect what are superficially personal attributes into marketable commodities. This transference of the home, family and femininity into the workplace can be seen as a way in which women develop an informal work culture which cannot be penetrated by "masculine" work standards.

Resistance in the form of industrial sabotage, absenteeism, lateness and high labour turnover is almost always regarded as the preserve of men. From my experience of secretarial work, however, I would emphasize that despite or perhaps because of the gender-specific nature of office discipline, women have a certain degree of control which has enabled them to develop a *culture of resistance*. Because conventional typewriters rely on the control of the typist, she can adopt any number of methods to cease working: she can pretend to look busy yet have a chat; she can drop a paperclip in the basket of her typewriter and wait around for the mechanic to come; she can run out of stationery and meet someone on the way back from the stationery office; if the work is late, then "the ribbon got stuck" or she had to phone a company to get Mr So-and-So's correct title and "it took ages getting through". Duties which are auxiliary to typing, such as filing, also enable her not to be tied to the typewriter all day.

She thus has a certain amount of control over her space and movements. She can go off to the loo, or visit someone in another office for a chat. In addition, there are those extra little jobs which women are expected to perform just because they are women, such as making the tea, watering the plants, organizing leaving/wedding/birthday presents, going out of the office on errands for the boss, all of which, while on the one hand they reinforce their ideological role as "office wife", can also be *used to create space* and time away from the routine of typing.

The automation of the office can and will change this in very radical ways, as Braverman notes:

> Among the subsidiary benefits management expects to derive from (office automation) is the reduction and thus cheapening of the skills of administrative employees, and *not least the squeezing out of the minutes and hours of labour power lost in the personal relations and contacts among secretaries and between secretaries and their "principals"* – which is what they mean when they speak of the "end of the social office". (Braverman, op cit)

Word processing and the "end of the social office"

The move to word processing effectively transfers the control which the typist has over a conventional typewriter on to the machine itself. Word processors are designed with supervisory and monitoring elements built into them. In addition, the word processor can perform all the elementary functions of typing which take a person years to perfect.

Briefly, a word processor consists of a keyboard, a visual display unit (VDU), a memory, a mini- or microcomputer, plus printout facilities. The image of what is "typed" or keyboarded into the memory (not on to paper) is displayed on the VDU and only when the document is displayed in its correct form is it printed on to paper. It can indent, centre, justify margins, tabulate, store and retrieve standard paragraphs and letters, removing the need for the skill in producing well set-out work. The application of word processors thus removes one of the important areas of control which the typist has over her work. Through choosing how to lay out a particular document, the typist is telling the machine what to do: her skills are guiding the typewriter through its various functions. Control over a word processor is limited to pressing the appropriate button. Fast, accurate typing becomes redundant with the easy correction facilities which enable the typist to simply backspace and type over. As one of the manufacturers, WANG, states:

> System 30, a visual word processor, requires minimum operator training for maximum productivity. Such operational features as an operator screen prompts and the automatic word wraparound assist the operator in producing final documents in one quarter of the time that it would take with most conventional typewriters.

The "minimum operator training" is an important aspect of the de-skilling process. Once trained to operate the word processor, in the words of the supervisor of the Central Electricity Generating Board in Bristol: "A less experienced typist is able to produce the same quality of work as a really skilled girl and almost as quickly" – thus enabling cheaper labour to be employed.

The decision regarding which type of word processing system to install depends on a study of the workflow, so for the first time many office workers will find themselves subject to time and motion studies. In order to achieve maximum productivity and return on the initial capital outlay (from £5000 plus), the office must be completely reorganized and the typist's job becomes further fragmented, so that she can work, in theory, continuously in front of the machine. With the storage of documents in the memory she no longer needs to leave her seat to look up documents in a filing cabinet. The possibility of continuous working is reinforced by the built-in monitoring elements. WANG again:

> Monitor your workload: And finally a built-in reporting system helps you monitor your work flow. It automatically gives the author's and typist's names, the document's number, the date and time of origin of last revision, the required editing time, and the length of the document.

In addition, Dictaphone Corporation have recently developed two systems designed to measure performance and increase productivity of word processor centres. They are called, appropriately, "Timemaster" and "Mastermind" with the latter providing "complete information on the status of up to 200 active dictation and transcription jobs in the centre. A disc memory offers a permanent, unlimited archive of the completed work. A companion report printer provides detailed, daily, weekly or monthly summaries of input and output activity." As one spokesperson for the company said: "They give all that a good supervisor would know – but now electronically. You couldn't fail to get to work on time."

Fragmentation is further increased by having the printing out done elsewhere. With shared logic systems, the printing out process can take place in a separate room, so that the typist doesn't even see what she has keyboarded in its finished state. By reorganizing their typing system around a shared logic system, Bradford Council were able to employ a school-leaver print controller with no previous experience – at a lower rate than they would otherwise have had to pay a shorthand typist. As WANG observes:

> Input and output at the same time . . . simultaneous input and output allows your typist to continue creating or editing work in the work station, while the printer automatically plays out completed documents. Your typists become more efficient and productive.

The need for shorthand – the one area where personal contact with the boss could be maintained even for those working in a pool – has been gradually eroded since the first dictaphone machine appeared at the beginning of the century. Its replacement by that most dehumanizing task, audiotyping, has been first on the checklist of most efficiency-minded managements, anxious to save the extra wasted time which dictation involves. Word processing centres work more efficiently with the use of audiotyping, which means for the typist involved being plugged in from head to toe. London Transport have a centre where the operators are allocated their work via an automatic tandem dictation system. This operates through the internal telephone network and permits executives to dictate letters and reports over the telephone for recording. Personal contact between operator and "originator" is reduced to a minimum and only occurs during extreme situations. According to a spokesperson for London Transport: ". . . if the typist wishes to clarify a particular passage, it can be replayed over the telephone to the person originating it. The possibility of personal contact minimizes the extent to which the job is dehumanized."

Perhaps the most insidious impact is that which comes loosely under the rubric "health and safety". Although no data are available on the long-term effects of working with visual display units, tests have shown that the VDU can have hazardous effects on the eyes, causing fatigue, irritation and tension. Fatigue, a medically defined condition, occurs as a result of, for instance, waiting for an image to appear on the VDU and being forced to sit continuously in front of the screen , without being able to move around, thus inducing "spatial alienation". Tests in France showed an increase in shortsightedness amongst VDU operators, and Dr Gary Busch, who carried out extensive research among people operating VDUs in the American banking and insurance industries, isolates what he calls "visual fatigue" or eyestrain. This is a direct consequence of VDU operation, rendering the eyes dry and uncomfortable, burning and tender, and producing a feeling of "grittiness". Operators also reported bad focus, double vision, blurred edges on figures as well as headaches and muscular pains in the neck and arms. An additional problem he noted was that because of the boredom of the work, many VDU operators attempt to combat their stress and fatigue through the use of drugs – such as Valium and Librium – and alcohol, which exacerbates the problems of eyestrain. Perhaps it would be more effective to let this £33/forty-hour-week VDU operator speak for herself:

> When you get home you feel tired and tense and irritable. All the girls here complain about headaches and waking up in the morning with puffy eyes. Sometimes when you're working you get very dizzy and have to

have a break. A friend of mine went to have her eyes tested because the
headaches were getting so bad. The optician said she had long vision so
it's very bad for her to be working so near the screen (it's about eighteen
inches away). He said she would have to wear glasses if she went on
working under these conditions. He'd been getting people in practically
every day from working with these things. (*TUCRIC Bulletin* No. 4
Sept/Oct 1978)

Conclusion

A woman I spoke to in Bradford who is being threatened with word
processing commented: "They picked on us because they thought we
were the weakest." With the ideological notion of the family wage
which always sees the man as the breadwinner, it has, historically, been
relatively easy to pull women in and out of paid work as the economy
demands. The same woman in Bradford reported a conversation she
had had with a management representative who, somewhat confused at
the typists' resistance to word processing, responded: "Well you're all
going to leave and have children anyway."

The application of word processing is part of capital's attempt to pull
itself out of the current period of nonprofitability, by the reorganization
of the labour process in order to maximize productivity. While other
sectors of employment are equally vulnerable to this type of reorganization through microelectronic technology, the scale of the possible
impact on the office is enormous. The office has so far been relatively
relaxed in terms of labour discipline. But office costs have soared since
World War Two to the extent that seventy-eight per cent of office
expenditure is on people and very little is on office equipment. As
Braverman noted with reference to the USA: "Top managers watched
this multiplication of secretaries with nothing more than amusement,
until it grew to dimensions which threatened the balance sheet." The
question for management is, however, not simply one of saving money
through reducing the payroll, but clearly one of securing the maximum
control over the labour process in pursuit of maximum profitability.

My reasons for stressing the class nature of secretarial work can now
be made clearer. I emphasized the fact that the notion of a secretarial
career structure is in fact illusory. Now it is likely that the need for
people with traditional secretarial skills will not disappear; there are
always letters to type which cannot be standardized and the contents of
which are so secret that the typist's loyalty to the company must be
ensured. However, thinking back to the pyramidal structure of secretarial work, in order for word processing systems to prove themselves a
complete restructuring of the hierarchy will be inevitable. As secretarial
work becomes more fragmented, the repetitive, standardized typing

will go to the word processing centres and the cream of the secretarial workforce will hang on to those few jobs at the top – the two extremes of the structure becoming increasingly polarized. The loss of skills which word processing effects will make it almost impossible to bridge the gap between the two extremes.

This will not mean, however, that promotion prospects for women office workers will become limited, but that the limitations which exist already, for working-class girls in particular, will become more visible. In becoming tied to, paced and controlled by machine, typists will not simply become de-skilled, but will become increasingly subject to forms of control whose real nature will no longer be masked by the social relations of the "social office".

Over the past few years there have been increasing manifestations of discontent among previously weak sections of the white collar workforce. The introduction of word processing may lead to an increase in conflict in this area.

Bibliography

Benet, Mary Kathleen, *Secretary: An Enquiry into the Female Ghetto* (Sidgwick & Jackson, London, 1972).

Bosticco, Mary, *How to Be a Top Secretary* (New English Library, London, 1975).

Braverman, Harry, *Labour and Monopoly Capital* (Monthly Review Press, New York and London, 1974).

Davies, Margery, "Woman's Place is at the Typewriter: The Feminization of the Clerical Labour Force", *Radical America*, vol. 18, No. 4 (July-August 1974).

Hardwick-Smith, S. & Rowe, B. *The Private Secretary* (Museum Press, London, 1958).

Harman, Chris, *New Technology and the Struggle for Socialism* (SWP Industrial Department, London, 1979).

Klingender, F. D. *The Condition of Clerical Labour in Britain* (Martin Lawrence, London, 1935).

Leffingwell, William Henry, *Office Management: Principles and Practice* (A. W. Shaw, London, 1925).

Lockwood, David, *The Blackcoated Worker* (Allen & Unwin, London, 1958).

Silverstone, R. "Office Work for Women: An Historical Review", *Business History*, vol. 18, Part 1 (January 1976).

Tepperman, Jean, *Not Servants, Not Machines: Office Workers Speak Out* (Beacon Press, Boston, 1976).

TUCRIC *Bulletin* (September/October 1978) No. 4, Leeds Trade Union Community Resources and Information Centre.

Guide to Further Reading

The full version of the *EDP Analyzer* report may be found in *EDP Analyzer*, vol. 15, Nos 2 & 3 (February and March 1977). An early article worth looking at, with a realistic assessment of the trends that might lead to the "office of the future", was "Toward the Automated Office" by Edward K. Yasaki, *Datamation* (February 1975).

The APEX report, *Office Technology: The Trade Union Response*, features in chapter 7 – but only from the industrial relations point of view. A second instalment has now been added to this excellent pamphlet, *Automation and the Office Worker* (APEX, London, April 1980).

A brief summary of the advantages of word processing can be found in "Word Processing Primer" by Frank Greenwood in the *Journal of Systems Management*, vol. 29, No. 5 (May 1978). Another introductory – and fairly sceptical – piece by Elizabeth deAtley appeared in *Computers and People* (September 1975).

"Computing's Youngest Grandchild – An Accident" by Ivan Berenyi in *Data Processing*, vol. 19, No. 4 (April 1977), details how IBM failed to spot the potential of its 1964 Selectric typewriter that was being used for text editing. The rest of the article is mostly a review of companies in the field and their products.

The well-known writer on this subject Amy D. Wohl explains why the automated office hasn't arrived yet in "Communicating Word Processors", *Datamation*, vol. 24, No. 3 (March 1978). But, she concludes: "The current situation in communicating word processors and in the entire field of electronic mail is somewhat similar to the situation of television in the 1940s: until many people could receive TV programmes, no one wanted to spend money on programming; but until there were programmes to receive, there was little incentive to buy a TV. Now the situation is that everyone will watch to see who else is buying word processing communications capabilities (and what types they are, remembering the compatibility question). Fortunately, the experience with TV suggests there will be a point when a 'critical mass' is reached and many firms will almost simultaneously begin broad use of the new technology."

A sceptical view of the productivity increases claimed by word processor manufacturers can be found in Ray Oman, "Cost/Productivity of Automatic/Conventional Typewriters", *Journal of Systems Management*, vol. 29, No. 7 (July 1978).

"Word Processing by Computer: Report of a Pilot Project at the Department of Education and Science, Darlington", Central Computing Agency, London (November 1978), assesses the cost-effectiveness and productivity gains achieved for different "mixes" of typing work.

H. A. Rhee, *Office Automation in Social Perspective* (Basil Blackwell, Oxford, 1968), contains an interesting discussion (pp. 158–88) of the 1950s/1960s debate on automation, with some amusing quotations from some of the wilder prophets. Rhee was concerned with the new-fangled "electronic data processing" and concluded: "Studies of the immediate and direct effects of EDP on office employment leave us in no doubt . . . that by and large it has resulted in little, if any, serious large-scale or chronic unemployment of office employees, up to the present."

The Future with Microelectronics: Forecasting the Effects of Information Technology by Iann Barron and Ray Curnow, was a report for the Department of Industry, London, which was felt not to merit publication (Frances Pinter, London, 1979).

Also worth checking out are:

"The Office of the Future", *Business Week*, 30 June 1975.

"The Office of the Future is Here Today!" – a *Time* magazine advertisement supplement, 18 September 1978.

The *Financial Times* annual supplements on "Word Processing" and "Office Equipment".

A down-to-earth review of the problems of installing and using microcomputers in local government was contained in "Your Next Computer", *Local Government Chronicle*, 26 January 1979.

A supplement to *Management Services in Government*, vol. 34, No. 2 (May 1979), a journal produced by the Civil Service Department, contains a full list of computer installations in UK government departments.

Finally, Victor A. Vyssotsky, "The Use of Computers for Business Functions", in Michael L. Dertouzos and Joel Moses, *The Computer Age: A Twenty-Year View* (MIT Press, Cambridge, Mass; 1980) provides an overview of the office revolution.

6 The Consequences for Employment

Welcome Back to the "Automation" Debate

Philip Sadler

Analysts of the employment impact of the new technology fall roughly into two camps: the optimists and the pessimists. The optimists argue that labour-saving technology is nothing new. It has never, by itself, increased unemployment in the long term. The application of microelectronics will create new wealth which will be spent on new products and services, thus creating new jobs. The pessimists take a dimmer view, arguing that the microprocessor is a genuinely revolutionary device and that the threat of unemployment from "computers" and "automation" twenty years ago (postponed for various reasons) is now about to be realized in the microcomputer. Low economic growth, de-industrialization and public expenditure cuts make matters much worse.

Both the optimists and the pessimists obviously claim to have the correct perspective – though what they base their predictions on is always a little vague. For the layman, it is probably safe to assume that the truth lies somewhere in the middle, a position taken up by Philip Sadler, whom I invited to open the debate with the following scene-setting paper. Philip Sadler, author of Social Research on Automation *(1968) and now Principal of Ashridge Management College, has been studying the impact of technology on employment for many years. His paper is followed by contributions from three "pessimists" and three authors who might be described as "cautiously optimistic".*

In the early 1960s, long before the microprocessor had even been invented, there was already widespread concern about the future impact of information processing technology on employment. In 1965, the Organization for Economic Cooperation and Development (OECD) called a conference in Washington on the theme "The Requirements of

290

Automated Jobs".[1] The participants included representatives of government, industry, labour unions and the academic world in the US and Canada, together with delegates from European countries, including a nominee of the British Employers' Confederation (a forerunner of the CBI).

Fig. 6.1 A glimpse into the future? *Courtesy of* New Scientist *David Austin*

The question of the impact of automation on employment emerged as the central issue of the conference, and a wide range of opinions emerged in the debate. At one extreme lay the prediction of Professor Crossman, then of Oxford University: "There seems to the writer little doubt that unemployment due to automation will grow steadily over the next few decades, perhaps centuries, and in the end it is likely to reach a very high figure, say ninety per cent of the labour force, unless radical changes are made in the present pattern of working." At the other end of the spectrum were those who were inclined to doubt that automation itself could be considered a basic cause of unemployment.

Although opinions differed concerning the future levels of unemployment that could be expected as a consequence of information processing technology, there was more or less unanimous agreement on three propositions which have formed part of the debate on automation and employment ever since:

(1) The impact of automation on employment will vary considerably in relation to the underlying growth rate of the economy. Economies with high growth rates, like Japan, have less reason to be fearful of mass unemployment than low growth economies, like Britain.

(2) Similarly, the impact of automation on employment will be related to the rate of growth of the labour force. Countries with rapidly growing labour forces are, of course, more likely to experience mass unemployment (particularly among school-leavers), as a consequence of a given rate of technological innovation, than countries with stable or slowly increasing labour forces.

(3) Technological change inevitably creates transitional unemployment. New jobs occur in new places and may be radically different from the old jobs. Thus, retraining, re-education and steps to encourage the mobility of labour are vitally important.

The 1965 conference was followed by a major European symposium in Zurich in 1966, also arranged by the OECD, entitled "Manpower Aspects of Automation and Technical Change".[2] This meeting took place in the context of quite severe manpower shortages in the major European countries. In consequence there was less concern about the spectre of mass unemployment, with rather more attention being paid to such effects of automation as changes in occupational structure, job content, the location of industry and the role of education and training.

Case study evidence presented at the conference was reassuring in that it did not indicate that applications of automation were leading to wholesale redundancies. For example, one survey of UK experience in office automation showed an average increase of eight per cent in the total number of office employees following the introduction of data processing systems. More widespread investigations such as the International Labour Office (ILO) report on "Automation and Non-Manual Workers",[3] published in 1967, confirmed these general findings.

Anxieties about the employment effects of automation were reduced even further by a series of studies and reports in the late 1960s and early 1970s. An International Labour Office report, "Labour and Social

Implications of Automation and other Technological Developments",[4] published in 1972, pointed out that many of the forecasts made in the 1950s and early 1960s had been clearly disproved by the course of events. The report quoted Norbert Wiener's prediction, made in 1950, that automation would result, within twenty-five years, in a depression that would make that of the 1930s seem like a pleasant joke. It concluded: "Twenty-two years later it does not seem likely that his prophecy will come true either by 1975 or fortunately even during the following twenty-five years." This optimistic conclusion killed any remaining enthusiasm for continuing the debate about automation and employment.

Interest has since revived, however, for two main reasons. First, there has been a major and widespread increase in unemployment ever since 1975, and the generally accepted opinion is that this is likely to persist or get worse in the foreseeable future. Second, although the increase in unemployment coincided with the world economic recession (after 1973) rather than with any measurable acceleration in the rate of technological change, the recent spectacular advances in information technology, in particular microelectronics, carry very important implications for future employment. Therefore, with the high level of anxiety already existing over employment prospects, attention is once again being focused on the relationship between employment and technological change.

Unemployment did not grow significantly in the period up to 1973, and this masked considerable changes in the pattern of employment in the advanced industrial societies. Two long-term trends – the decline in employment in agriculture and the growth of white-collar employment relative to employment in manual work – continued to affect occupational structures in many countries. A third and novel development appeared, however, in the second half of the 1960s. This was the decline in the proportion of employment accounted for by secondary industries – manufacturing, construction and the utilities. In some countries this relative decline has become absolute.

This process of structural change in the pattern of employment has become known as "De-industrialization". A simplistic view sees it as the transfer of employment from producing industries, particularly manufacturing, to the service industries. This is an oversimplified view, since the decline in employment has not been uniform across all producing industries, nor has employment increased in all service industries. The main falls in employment in the UK, for example, have been in coalmining and in such production industries as construction, locomotives, cutlery, cotton weaving, motorcycles, woollens and worsteds, electrical machinery and branches of footwear and clothing. The decline can be attributed in varying proportions to a drop in demand for an industry's products (hatmaking is often quoted as an obvious example); the growth of foreign competition (for example, motorcycles or cutlery); and increases in productivity, the causes of which include rationalization, the removal of restrictive practices and other factors besides the adoption of labour-saving technology, which has tended to play a minor part. Employment has also declined in two major service industries: transport and distribution. Here also the principal factors are to do with demand (for public transport, for example) and rationalization (as with supermarkets), rather than the adoption of new technology.

Before 1975 the loss of jobs in such industries was to a considerable extent offset by growth in employment opportunities elsewhere – mainly in the service sector, but also in some production industries. In the service sector, the main gains in numbers of jobs until very recently were in the public services, particularly health and education, and among private sector industries, in banking and financial services and leisure industries. Among these, the financial services sector is the one most likely to become an industry of declining employment opportunities as a result of technological advance.

De-industrialization is occurring, therefore, but it appears to have resulted so far mainly from changes in demand and competition. However, it is a process likely to accelerate under the impact of new labour-saving technology. In consequence, the main hopes of European countries for employment must inevitably focus on those service industries likely to remain labour-intensive in the context of expanding demand. Such a definition excludes such large providers of jobs as distribution, banking, insurance, finance, transport and communications. It leaves, apart from leisure industries and professional and scientific services, largely those services which tend increasingly to be located in the public sector – health, education and social services.

A further and most important conclusion from this analysis is that present levels of unemployment reflect the recent acceleration of the process of long-term decline in manufacturing employment, together with a slowing down of the rate of job creation in the service sector – more a function of loss of economic confidence than the increased impact of new technology.

The main factors which will affect employment opportunities and the level of unemployment in Europe in the future include:

(1) Underlying rates of economic growth and the associated demand for manpower.

(2) Rates of change in the productivity of labour resulting from the

rationalization of production, the quality of industrial relations and the adoption of new technology.

(3) The extent to which European industries remain competitive in both exports and import substitution in the face of growing competition from Japan, the developing countries and the Eastern bloc.

(4) The success with which European countries are able to restructure their economic activities, in relation both to changes in patterns of demand and the growth of competition from other countries.

(5) The extent to which the supply of manpower changes in relation to such factors as changes in the female participation rate, in the hours of work, and in the length of the working life.

(6) The extent to which there is a good fit between the skills and qualifications of the workforce and the nature of the demand for manpower.

The relationship between technology and employment opportunities most commonly considered and discussed is, of course, the tendency for technology to be labour-saving and thus eliminate employment opportunities – if not actual jobs. Technological change exercises its influence, however, in other ways which are less obvious and less direct, but which are increasingly important from the standpoint of policy making. European industries face a stark choice – adopt new technology and lose some jobs, or fail to remain competitive and lose most or all of your jobs.

The conclusion arising from this analysis is that the threat to employment opportunities from the new technology in Europe may even today be in danger of being overemphasized. I believe that a greater danger is posed by increasing industrialization in other (less developed) parts of the world and that technology is useful in answering this threat.

Future employment prospects in Europe will depend, in consequence, on four main factors, given reasonably stable, if undramatic, economic growth. These factors are, first, the extent to which the restructuring of economies towards more advanced technology-based industries can be achieved. This will increasingly call for European-scale rather than purely national ventures. Second, the extent to which employment opportunities will develop in the service sector. The third factor affecting employment prospects will be the extent to which education and training provision matches up to job opportunities. Finally, and not least in importance, there is the question of the factors which will affect the future supply of labour.

In the last analysis, the labour supply is a function of three influences: the number of people of working age, the proportion of such people needing or desiring employment, and government action which effectively decreases the labour supply by raising the school leaving age or lowering the retirement age. Consequently, public policies required in the next ten years will include the encouragement of investment in new technologies like microelectronics, and efforts to aid the growth of employment opportunities in the service sector.

But this will only happen if people in positions of power and influence can be convinced that European countries have a future as well as a past. In particular, they need to be convinced that there is no way ahead to be found by turning back – either to the comfortable postwar period characterized by the rapid increase in the output of manufactured goods and employment in manufacturing industry, or even less to some earlier cottage industry type of economic activity.

The gravest threat to the employment opportunities for our young people lies not so much in technology as in the slowness of our political and social institutions to recognize and adjust to changed circumstances.

Notes

1   *The Requirements of Automated Jobs,* North American Joint Conference, Washington DC, 8–10 December 1964, Final Report and Supplement (Organization for Economic Cooperation and Development, Paris, 1965).
2   *Manpower Aspects of Automation and Technical Change,* European Conference, Zurich, 1–4 February 1966, Final Report (Organization for Economic Cooperation and Development, Paris, 1966).
3   *Automation and Non-manual Workers,* Labour and Automation Bulletin No. 5 (International Labour Office, Geneva, 1967).
4   *Labour and Social Implications of Automation and Other Technological Development,* International Labour Conference, 57th Session, Geneva, 1972 (International Labour Office, Geneva, 1972).

Now the Chips are Down

Ed Goldwyn

This is a condensed version of the script of the famous BBC 2 television documentary "Now the Chips are Down". It appeared in The Listener *on 6 April 1978. First screened in March 1978, the film was written and ⧗ produced by Ed Goldwyn, and it went on to win awards and become a BBC world bestseller.*

A computer can read an ordinary book to a blind man, speaking aloud in its own artificial voice. A man can talk, and a computer obey; the man's voice being understood by a machine. At the heart of both such machines are tiny computers built around the new technology of silicon chips – as powerful as the biggest computer of only a few years ago, but 1000 times cheaper. Such chips are the reason why Japan is abandoning its shipbuilding – and why our children will grow up without jobs to go to.

Their story began only thirty years ago. In the early 1950s, the switches in computers were valves. Each one was hand-made and expensive – around £5 each at today's prices – and the world market was dominated by huge American manufacturers. But in 1948 William Shockley invented the transistor, for which he was to get a Nobel prize. It murdered the valve industry with a rapidity that was brutal: the US valve makers had been slow to see the importance of transistors, and Japan quickly took advantage of the breakthrough. They became the major transistor makers in the world, but they did not keep the lead. In 1955, Shockley left Bell Telephone Laboratories, where he had invented the transistor, for Stanford University, where "Shockley semiconductors" began.

Shockley had chosen a team of eight brilliant scientists to help him

297

create a transistor of a new material – silicon. But after two years they left him and persuaded the Fairchild Camera Corporation to set them up as a new company, with Robert Noyce as general manager.

Noyce developed the technique (first suggested by an Englishman) of making several transistors at once. Insulated conductor bars were printed on a chip of silicon; three more layers of conducting material were printed on top, and square holes punched through, so that each layer could make contact with any of the others. In each hole, the touching layers formed a transistor. The final metal layer wired them together.

The knowhow of getting more transistors onto a chip evolved fast. The single transistor was made in 1957; in 1963, it was eight on a chip. Today, the figure is a quarter of a million.

What fuelled these developments was that an enormous number of circuits was needed to beat the Russians to the moon and to the second generation of guided missiles – money for defence and space really made the industry boom. The industry grew in a valley at the south end of San Francisco Bay, where Shockley's eight were running Fairchild. But senior staff from Fairchild left to set up one company after another; the valley is now filled with huge industrial parks, all in the silicon chip business.

Five years ago, a whole computer was put on to a single chip: the "£5 computer", the microprocessor. It was supervised by Robert Noyce. From microprocessors, he has made a personal fortune of $50m; and among the staff of his factory, he admits there are as many as thirty millionaires.

Production begins by taking the designer's drawings and recording the position of each part into a computer, which will reduce the scale 10,000 times, to create a photographic printing mask. That is used to print the circuits on to wafers of silicon, 200 chips at a time. The lines are no more than two ten-thousandths of an inch wide. Layer upon layer, each is placed upon the next to an accuracy of one ten-thousandth of an inch. One layer is etched on the wafers and, in the oven, with the right temperature and the right gases flowing past, the second layer forms a translucent film over the pattern already there.

The next stage removes all of this second coat, except a cobweb of fine lines, fitted into the first layer. Each wafer is given a coat of photographic emulsion, and spun, to spread it evenly. Where this coat is exposed to ultraviolet light, it goes hard; where it is unexposed, it dissolves easily. The pattern to be projected onto the wafer is in a mask which is aligned with the pattern already on the wafer. Then, after a flash of ultraviolet light, the unexposed parts of the emulsion dissolve away and strong acids reach through to etch off the unwanted parts of the second coat. And so the whole complex circuit is built up, layer after layer.

But completing the wafer is not even half the cost of the process; there are many more people, more equipment, and more money spent on testing the circuits than actually making them. Each computer chip is tested with a full run-through of every possible instruction it can obey. Each test takes less than a quarter of a second. And most chips fail. In fact, they are doing extremely well if as few as one-quarter of the circuits work.

After the wafers have been tested, they are shipped to the Far East by air – all the manufacturers send their chips to be mounted where labour is cheap. Good chips are worth about 50p each, and making connections to a chip adds another 30p.

Miniaturization is not an end in itself, it is simply the best way to make the cheapest circuits. And yet, the smallness is impressive. A human brain has about 1000 billion electrical connections. To have built that with valves (if we knew how) would have resulted in a machine the size of Greater London. Built out of 1960s transistors, it would have been the size of the Albert Hall. With the present-day integrated circuits, and including power supplies, wiring and everything, we could fit it into a single dressing-room. And by 1980, with the next generation of integrated circuits (already in the laboratory), it could actually be smaller than the human brain; if it were not for the necessity of mounting the chips, that would already be true today.

It is now feasible to replace defective nervous tissue with synthetic brain. At Stanford University, John Freitras, who is totally deaf, will soon have a small circuit (a microprocessor and three other chips) embedded in his skull. It will pick up power and sound through aerial coils, as it lies buried. The microprocessor will convert speech into patterns of electric pulses, and send these to his brain along four fine wires, which have already been permanently implanted and connected to his brain.

Temporarily, those four wires come out through a plug. The level in each can be adjusted until they all feel equally loud to him. John Freitras will not hear words; he will feel inside himself patterns of a quite new kind, and will have to learn the meaning of each sensation that the buried microprocessor sends to his brain.

The device is a good example of what is to come. Electronics pervades almost all manufacturing techniques, and when key components become a thousand times cheaper, through the use of silicon chips, there will be a dramatic effect. Some changes we have already seen. At least twenty manufacturers rushed in to make calculators, using about £100m worth of chips a year. The existing mechanical calculator industry did not know what had hit them. They were out of business.

The next idea was to sell chips in watches. The effect on the Swiss watch industry was shattering. They used to make half the watch movements in the world, but the electronic watch – at its cheapest below £10 – has put seventeen firms out of business. There was widespread unemployment, and Europe lost a £200m industry to the Americans.

Now there is a new war. It may seem trivial, but making games around chips that control TV screens is an industry worth a quarter of a billion pounds a year.

But the significance of the chip does not lie in gadgets. The way we will live, the work we will do will be different. For example, the new supermarket checkout terminals have microprocessors inside them. Besides totalling the bill, such a terminal can check up on the validity of a credit card – which is just a step from the terminal actually ringing a person's bank's computer and transferring funds to the shop's bank's computer.

As each item is checked out, the terminals remember what has been sold, so, automatically, a total list of what has to be ordered to restock the shop is built up. In the future, that re-order will be issued quite automatically, and will be responded to by a completely automatic warehouse.

Automatic warehouses are working now. Loads are delivered by lorry, a camera reads the label and a computer automatically decides where the load will be stored. No one needs to know where anything is stored, and no one cares. When the goods are needed the computer will know where to find them.

Few people realize how automated some industries have already become. At Fiat in Italy, twenty robots "man" the production line by themselves. The United States government is financing robot research projects, though keeping a low profile, for fear of attracting union hostility.

But automation is not just for blue-collar jobs. It is going to affect lawyers, businessmen, teachers – everyone. One of the most eminent consultants in internal medicine in the USA, Dr. Jack Myers, has been building his skill into a machine for the past seven years. A junior hospital doctor, using Myers's automatic consultant, can make a diagnosis that would normally require the experience of several qualified consultants. Jack Myers feels that the computer is now more competent than he is in the diseases he has taught it.

Automation can affect everyone. It is coming in every farm, office, factory and shop. The people involved in the technology are concerned about the future. Mike Cooley, past president of the white collar section (TASS) of the engineering union (AUEW) said: "We must expect that many of the big electrical companies, such as General Electric and Philips, will reduce their total employment by up to thirty per cent in the early 1980s, even though their total production may be double what it is now. It may improve the profit for the corporations, but it's going to cause massive problems in this country. And, if necessary, we should protect ourselves against the introduction of this kind of equipment. I think we fail to understand just how important work is to human beings. If you ask anybody what they are, they never say, 'I'm a Beethoven lover', or 'a Bob Dylan fan', or 'a James Joyce reader', they say, 'I'm a teacher', 'an engineer'. People relate to society through their work."

But the use of the equipment is already growing fast in Japan, Germany and the USA. If we don't automate as fast as they do, won't this only further disadvantage the UK? Won't the sheer cheapness and volume of their production kill our industries? So won't the jobs be lost anyway?

The future is not necessarily bleak. We do have companies which are booming on the products of Silicon Valley. In one key industry, we are world leaders – software, the instructions that make a computer do its job.

At the Chase Manhattan Bank in New York, when the dealers trade, they don't know how much currency the bank has already bought at any given moment – the figures they work to are usually several hours old. The bank is installing an information system to give a real-time display of the bank's position, which will be updated within seconds of each deal. Such a system is relatively difficult to build, and Chase Manhattan have bought their software package from a British company, called Logica. It took thirty man-years to write, and the customer pays $100,000 for it. The tailoring – the work needed to modify the package for the particular bank – costs another $150,000.

There is nothing physically being exported, yet this is our booming industry: software is a major cost in computers – often as much as forty per cent of any new application. Some people believe that we should stake our future on the chips, not by making them, but by programming them, and that we should use our software skills to develop high-technology industries around them. The example of such "industry creation" which is much quoted is the EMI body scanner – an idea that didn't exist six years ago has now sold two million pounds' worth of equipment.

Is our future, then, the creation of more industries like that? One can hope so – but, so far, there are no other examples to point to.

What will happen to the men in today's jobs? Can we all live on the wealth of automatic factories and the earnings of an elite band of 60,000 software engineers?

It is time to think about the future. The questions are these. In the long term, when the only plentiful resource is going to be people, is automation the wrong road to take?

But, in the short term, can we afford not to automate? If we do not, won't our industry be disadvantaged by the automated industries abroad? And if we do automate, will we be able to cope with the problems of large-scale unemployment? Perhaps the survival of a nation depends upon its people finding meaningful lives.

The questions shout. The government seems totally unaware of the effects that this technology is going to create. The silence is terrifying.

The Impact of Microprocessors on Employment

Tom Stonier

Some of the boldest predictions about future trends in employment have come from Professor Stonier, an American currently at the University of Bradford, England. In this paper, delivered in January 1979 to a conference at Middlesex Polytechnic on technical change and the future of work, Tom Stonier suggests that by early next century we will require only ten per cent of today's labour force to provide all our material needs. He goes on to argue that the best way to tackle the problem is through a massive expansion of the education system.

The last few years have seen the appearance of a new form of information technology referred to as the microprocessor, or often more popularly as "the miracle chip". The microprocessor is the latest in a series of technological developments based largely on earlier scientific discoveries emerging from solid-state physics. Originally modern information machines emerged during World War Two, and because such information machines were put to the task of mathematical calculations or "computations" they came to be referred to as computers. The microprocessors of today do not do anything very different from what more sophisticated computers were able to do, but they are able to do it much faster, more reliably and, more importantly, much cheaper. Compared with the world's first large computer, ENIAC, microprocessors in the late 1970s were a thousand times more reliable, consumed a millionth the amount of energy, were twenty times faster, had a larger memory, occupied only one thirty-thousandth the volume, and perhaps most important, cost only one ten-thousandth of ENIAC.

A new technology displaces an older technology as a function of how much better it is. Better means superior in terms of any of the qualities mentioned above, including being more durable, more resistant to damage and so on. If a new technology is only ten per cent better it displaces existing technology very slowly, or may not do so at all – it just isn't worth the bother. If it is fifty per cent better then it begins to make inroads, although the process may take decades. When it is ten times better, as the new microprocessor technology is, then it moves very rapidly indeed. It takes only a matter of months, certainly less than a year, to displace an entire industry, as was witnessed in the shift from manual mechanical calculators to electronic cash registers. Similarly the Swiss watch industry found themselves in dire straits once the electronic watches began to hit the market.

Among other new technologies emerging are industrial and office robots. Such robots do not look like science fiction robots with large eyes, clumsy walk and muttering "It does not compute" kind of nonsense. Rather, industrial robots look like any other piece of industrial machinery except that they have, in addition, control panels. Let us take, for example, a welding robot put in an assembly line to weld a wing onto a car coming down the assembly line. Such a robot is instructed very simply by flicking a switch which activates its memory circuits, and having the best welder in the plant "show" the robot how to weld the wing on; that is, the welder must very carefully trace out the motions that the machine must make in order to achieve its task successfully. If this is done properly the machine needs to be shown only once. It is the perfect apprentice. After that, the input switch is pressed, the "operate" button is pushed, and from here on in that robot will continue to carry out its function twenty-four hours a day, 365 days a year, never stop for a tea break, never go on strike, never report sick (unless it has been designed badly), and will not be perturbed if it is put on "hold" for an indefinite period while production schedules are reworked. Such a robot when priced at ten times a welder's annual wage is too expensive to be considered in anything but highly specialized situations. When, however, it has come down to three years' wages most companies believe that they will get their money back in about a year and a half, because after all this robot can work three shifts, and increase productivity even if it works only two.

A robot that we have just described is fairly stupid, because if the automobile is not lined up properly it will end up welding the wing to the window. But other robots can be designed to ensure a proper lining-up and to monitor the entire assembly line. Such automated systems not only correct for faults but if the fault cannot be corrected will shut down the system or bypass it, alerting the human engineer monitor to check out the difficulty and adjust the system accordingly. In addition, robots can be used to keep track of stocks needed for making the automobiles and to inform the office as certain stocks become depleted. However, it will not be necessary to have such robots report to a manager in the office; rather one could link the terminals directly to the suppliers and inform them of the need to re-order, while at the other end of the assembly line robots monitoring the inventories can be connected not to the head office but directly to the retailers all over the world, the way an airline is connected to travel agents all around the world. Thus the cars may be manufactured in accordance to specifications of individual customers. A man in Bradford, for example, might order his next mini to be purple and have two wing mirrors – a piece of information transmitted from the retailer directly to the factory, where the robots in charge of painting and final accessory additions would be informed that the next car coming down the line ought to be painted purple and have two wing mirrors.

We can see, therefore, that displacement of labour will involve not only the man on the shop floor but line management as well. Furthermore, computers can probably come out with much better programs for optimum cash flow strategies, payroll policies and so on, and therefore some middle-line management will be obviated as well. Equally startling will be the displacement in offices in the City of Bradford. In one section of the Corporation employing microprocessors it was found that they were able to cut their temporary typing pool in half, yet achieve an increase in output such that overall there was a 300 per cent increase. Interestingly enough, once the girls got used to it they loved working with microprocessors, and employment turnover has dropped to virtually nil, while at the same time the costs to the Corporation were zero, since the microprocessors were bought on time out of the savings of reduced labour costs.

At the beginning of the eighteenth century, ninety-two per cent of the labour force worked on farms to feed the other eight per cent. Today it needs only two or three per cent to feed the rest. That process, which occurred largely over the last hundred years or so, is now happening in the manufacturing industries, has been going on for some time, but will probably be completed over the next two or so decades. It is highly probable that by early in the next century it will require no more than ten per cent of the labour force to provide us with all our material needs – that is, all the food we eat, all the clothing we wear, all the textiles and furnishings in our houses, the houses themselves, the appliances, the automobiles, and so on. In the near future, the vast majority of labour will be engaged as information operatives. The dominant form of labour in the eighteenth and well into the nineteenth century involved farm operatives. From the nineteenth and well into the twentieth century it was machine operatives. Today it is information operatives.

One reason for this shift is that modern productive systems no longer depend on land, labour and capital as their primary input; rather they require information. The displacement of labour by knowledge in the form of technology has been already referred to. Similarly land, either for agricultural purposes or for home space requirements, also becomes obviated in part by advancing technology. About ten times as many people live on Manhattan Island in New York as do in a traditional nineteenth-century city such as Bradford, even though the area involved is about the same. This reflects the technology which allows building skyscrapers. A modern chicken farm factory uses a quarter of an acre site instead of the hundreds of acres it would take to feed a comparable number of chickens. Similarly with the advent of tractors, millions of acres dedicated to growing oats for horses became available for other purposes. This process will be dramatically extended with the advent of single-cell protein to displace the need for growing huge quantities of cattle feed.

Capital today exists largely in terms of credit information. Banks no longer ship around large quantities of cash; instead they transmit credit information. Any time someone has a good idea that looks as though it is going to be a money maker there is no problem making available capital, often involving sums exceeding the entire national budget of major countries. In modern postindustrial society, where the labour requirements are beginning to shrink dramatically (as they did in industrial society for agricultural activities), the primary input is knowledge and the most important single resource the postindustrial society has is its human capital. It is no longer the material and mineral resources, or the rich farmland, but rather it is the skills and knowledge of its people. We all know that the British economy has been greatly helped by North Sea Oil. That North Sea Oil was not a resource until technology made it so.

Similarly, a thousand years ago Northern Europe was just coming out of its Dark Ages. What historians generally do not tell us is why. The reason is the emergence of a new technology centred on the deep plough, which at last made the fertile plains of Northern Europe highly productive, and a poor, backward part of the world became affluent and blossomed during the subsequent Middle Ages. Again, the wealth of the Lowlands in the seventeenth century was preceded by draining polders to produce some of Europe's most fertile lands. In each of these instances, "nonresources" became converted into resources through knowledge. This process is accelerating and will continue to accelerate as the new emerging electronic information devices make problem solving easier and create modern productive systems which allow the rest of us to live off the backs of robots.

The new employment patterns, therefore, will be in the knowledge industries, and the biggest problem confronting British society at the moment is how to transfer labour from the manufacturing industries, where jobs are shrinking at an alarming rate, into the knowledge industries which need to be subsidized by the government. The most sensible and logical way to do this is through a massive expansion of the education system, because the education system is, first of all, labour-intensive in its own right, and could produce hundreds of thousands (if need be millions) of jobs; secondly it would help keep many of the young people who comprise the bulk of the unemployed off the labour market, or draw them back into the education system; and thirdly the upgrading of the UK's knowledge base would allow it to devise new industries which would produce the wealth from which the government could draw its revenues to pay for the whole thing. Think in terms of North Sea Oil for a moment, and then extend the possibility to cheap oil from coal, to wave-power-generated electricity, to coastal fish farming, and to a substantial expansion of single-cell protein production in this country. The successful solution of these four technologies alone could mean that Britain remains energy independent after the oil runs out, therefore avoiding serious balance of payment problems, and could even become a net exporter of food! Thus an expanded education base, coupled to government-subsidized research and development, would not only provide productive employment opportunities for millions of people, but would provide the knowledge from which would emerge new productive technologies making nonresources, such as an excess of coal, or waves, into valuable resources to increase the wealth of the nation.

Unemployment and Government

Chris Freeman

This sober analysis of the problem of technological change and employ-ment mirrors Philip Sadler's paper, except that Professor Freeman appears more of a "pessimist". He highlights the dilemma of a nation like Britain, facing the choice of whether or not to invest heavily in microelectronic technology, and argues that the British government has failed to ap-preciate the importance of the microelectronic revolution. The author is head of the Science Policy Research Unit at Sussex University and this paper formed the basis of the J. D. Bernal Memorial Lecture delivered at Birkbeck College, University of London, in May 1978.

Perhaps more than any other scientist of his generation, J. D. Bernal was concerned with the social and economic context of science and technology. His book *The Social Function of Science** was the first systematic attempt to analyse and measure the total resources com-mitted to organized scientific research and experimental development (R & D) in this country, and to discuss the problem of their allocation in terms of social goals. Characteristically, there were two main themes in this book, "What Science Does" and "What Science Could Do", reflecting Bernal's consistent preoccupation with policy problems.

Most of the topics which he discussed are still relevant to this day, and here I shall be concerned with three of them. The first is the problem of technical change and unemployment. When Bernal wrote his book in the 1930s, unemployment was of course one of the biggest social problems and it is so again today. The second is the problem of the standard of living of the British people and the performance of the

* John Desmond Bernal, *The Social Function of Science*, Routledge, London 1939; 2nd Edn. 1940 and The MIT Press, Cambridge, Mass, 1967.

British economy. The third is the means of mobilizing and organizing our scientific and technical resources to contribute to the solution of these problems.

Bernal was optimistic, some would say superoptimistic, about the potential of science and technology for the resolution of these problems, provided that fairly fundamental social changes permitted this potential to be realized. In a long-term sense I share his optimism, but it is no use pretending that the problems confronting Britain and other industrialized societies in the 1980s will be easy to solve.

Take first the question of unemployment. When it first reached the present levels in 1975 there was a tendency to dismiss it as being essentially transitory and the result of the OPEC crisis. But it is now fairly generally agreed not only that the problem is more severe than at any time since the war, but also that it is likely to get worse. All the major international organizations – the ILO, IMF, OECD, EEC and others – now accept the importance of policies designed to reduce the level of unemployment, and the topic has moved to the top of the agenda at various international summit meetings.

The level of unemployment is high in almost all European countries, except Norway and Sweden and the Communist bloc. In most countries it is between four and eight per cent of the labour force, compared with levels of one or two per cent over much of the postwar period in Europe, and rather higher levels in North America. This level of unemployment has hardly fallen at all, outside the United States, during the period of recovery from the 1974–5 recession, in spite of the introduction of many job-creation and temporary employment schemes, and the return of many migrant workers, especially from Germany and Switzerland.

In the United Kingdom the level of unemployment has been higher than in most European countries, although Denmark, Italy and Belgium have experienced similar high rates. The problem is likely to become still more severe during the 1980s, for three main reasons: demographic trends, the relatively weak competitive performance of the UK economy, and the slower growth of the world economy as a whole. A fourth factor which might make the problem still more difficult is the rate and direction of technical change. This last point is an extremely controversial one, and I want first of all to show that the unemployment problem is serious enough, even if we disregard technical change and return to consider this later.

The demographic trends are fairly clear-cut. After a period of rather slow growth of the available labour force, there will be a much more rapid increase up till 1985. This is because the number of young people entering the labour force is increasing while the number of people reaching retirement age will temporarily fall. After that there will be a fairly sharp fall in the rate of increase because of the falling birthrate in the 1970s and the increased number of people reaching retirement age. Another continuing source of increase in the size of the available labour force is the rise in female "participation rates" which has been a major social change in all industrialized countries. The combination of labour-saving household equipment, falling birthrates and the far-reaching changes in women's attitudes makes it probable that the female participation rate will continue to rise, although at a slower rate as it approaches the level of male participation.

This increase in the size of the available labour force is taking place at a time when registered unemployment has been persistently high for several years at about 1½ million and when "unregistered unemployment" has also been increasing. The level of "unregistered unemployment" is very hard to estimate, as it consists in large part of women who experience difficulties in re-entering the labour force after a period of child-bearing. In a period of labour shortage it is highly probable that many more of them would be encouraged to register and take jobs. The Cambridge University Department of Applied Economics (DAE) has estimated "unregistered unemployment" at one million, and the increase over the past few years at half a million.

Thus to get back to a "full employment" situation in the 1980s would require the creation of rather more than three million new jobs – nearly two million to absorb the increase in the available labour force, plus a million to bring registered unemployment down to half a million (about two per cent of the labour force) and perhaps nearly half a million to reduce unregistered unemployment to a similar level. Total employment today in the UK is no greater than it was in 1968, which gives some idea of the magnitude of the task. Whereas the number of jobs has not increased at all in the last decade, it must now increase by more than ten per cent.

Before continuing with the main line of this argument I must digress slightly to deal with two subsidiary issues which sometimes cloud this discussion. It is sometimes suggested that the rise in unemployment is largely, or even entirely, a "voluntary" phenomenon, due to "scrounging" or the erosion of the Protestant work ethic. My memory is long enough to recall the same kind of thing being said in the 1930s, yet it only took a year or two of high demand for labour for almost all of this unemployment to disappear like the melting snow, not to return for thirty years. It is true of course that the ratio of unemployment benefit to earnings is mercifully much higher than it was in the 1930s, and to that extent the hardship of unemployment is diminished. The acceptable period of search for a new job is probably a little longer; nevertheless it is my view that unemployment is overwhelmingly involuntary and that as before it would largely disappear in the event of a strong and sustained demand for labour.

Another source of confusion is the view that even if unemployment is not "voluntary" then it ought to be. We should learn to live with it and like it and discard the inhibitions of the "Protestant work ethic". I would not deny the desirability of reduced working hours and longer holidays in the formal sector of the economy, nor the desirability of phasing out many boring, dangerous and unpleasant occupations. Nevertheless I share the view of Marie Jahoda, Freud and Marx on this question: the psychological as well as the economic consequences of unemployment can be devastating for individuals and for societies, because work, both formal and informal, is the main means by which people in most different cultures relate to each other and to the world, and acquire a sense of dignity and purpose, even though many jobs are boring and hard. (Incidentally, I don't know how many Protestants there are in Japan, China or Korea!) I now return to the main thread of my argument.

Apart from demographic changes, a second reason for believing that unemployment in Britain may be a particularly difficult problem in the 1980s is the disappointing competitive performance of the UK economy in international trade. The Cambridge DAE analysis, even though it explicitly discounts any increase in the rate of labour-displacing technical change, nevertheless projected a serious possibility of five million unemployed by 1990. This level would in their view result from the pursuit of "orthodox" economic policies, that is excluding either import restrictions or major and continuing devaluation of the currency. This dismal forecast results from the Cambridge view that the chronic weakness of the British balance of payments is so serious that even with generous estimates of the benefits of North Sea oil, sustained rapid growth and the resulting higher levels of employment will be impossible without a long period of protection for British industry.

The Cambridge Report has been heavily attacked for its advocacy of protection, and the critics may be right about some of the negative effects that this could entail. Nevertheless the Cambridge analysis has not met with a refutation of anything like comparable logical force and intellectual rigour.

The Cambridge analysis is by no means the only one which comes up with depressingly high possibilities on the level of unemployment in the 1980s. For example, Colin Leicester at the Institute of Manpower Studies in my own university calculated that unemployment would reach five million by the year 2001 if the British economy continued to grow in the future at the same rate as in the past twenty years, unless there were substantial reductions in working hours, and an increase in part-time work.

In a crude sense the dilemma confronting British economic policy can be simply stated. If the growth rate of the economy goes above three per cent, then even with the benefits of North Sea oil, all past experience indicates the high probability of renewed balance of payments difficulties, *unless* there is a marked improvement in the relative efficiency of the UK economy by comparison with the EEC, Japan, the USA and other industrial countries. If, however, the rate of growth remains much below three per cent, then there is no real prospect of reducing the rate of unemployment. If it is as low as two per cent or less, then unemployment will tend to creep up to three or four million during the 1980s. Even with North Sea oil, the UK economy is still on a familiar tightrope.

Obviously much depends on the future performance of the world economy. All past evidence suggests that only if the world economy grows at an annual rate of five per cent can the British economy hope to grow at three or four per cent. This is of course why the British government has been pressing strongly for international measures to stimulate world economic growth. But there are a good many reasons for believing that the world economy is very unlikely to grow in the fourth quarter of this century as rapidly as it did in the third quarter. Among these are the changing pattern of investment from capacity extension to rationalization, the loss of impetus and overcapacity in several key sectors of the world economy, the falling rate of profit in several major industrial countries, the instability in foreign exchange markets, the high priority assigned to countering inflation by monetarist policies, and diminishing returns to formal R&D.

If the world economy grows at only two or three per cent, then it would be extraordinarily difficult for Britain to achieve a return to full employment, and indeed several other countries, including France, Germany and the USA, would also experience severe unemployment problems. All of this is on the assumption that past relationships between the growth of output and the growth of employment continue to hold. But as I aim to show, these relationships may become less favourable for employment. Even if this is not the case generally, then it is nevertheless true for Britain that an improvement in our relative positions would require a higher than average growth of labour productivity. Obviously it would be highly desirable for the British economy to grow for a while much faster than the rest of the EEC, so that we could catch up in living standards and overcome some of our structural weaknesses. High rates of productivity growth are generally associated with overall high rates of economic growth, but if the world economy grows more slowly, the UK would be in the extraordinarily difficult situation of trying to achieve the one without the other.

George Ray, of the National Institute of Economic and Social Research, has calculated that if the UK were to achieve average EEC rates of labour productivity growth in the next decade, then unemployment could increase to fifteen per cent of the labour force by 1991, that is, over four million unemployed. According to his estimates, the increased unemployment would occur mainly in the services, rather than in manufacturing, which is important when we come to consider where new jobs might be available in the 1980s. This means that if we are to combine the two goals of high productivity growth and balance of payments equilibrium, then that growth must partly be attained by labour displacement in the services and in manufacturing. Ultimately, of course, this might lead to such an improvement in the relative performance of the British economy that the balance of payments constraint on our rate of growth could be somewhat relaxed. But the timelag could be substantial and that day still seems a long way off.

Thus for all three reasons – the demographic trends, the weak competitive position of the UK and the slower growth of the world economy – we face a very difficult unemployment problem in the 1980s. The only escape from the growth/trade dilemma, if we remain in a competitive market situation, is to produce exports which are competitive not so much because of low cost, but because of design and technical features which make them less sensitive to the ordinary forces of price competition. Technical innovation, so far from being a peripheral problem, is actually central to the entire British economic dilemma. In so far as Britain is involved in world price competition with standardized products like steel, cars, TV sets and textiles, British goods must compete on high productivity, which involves factor-saving technical change, including labour-saving technical change. In so far as we are involved in new product and new service competition, as with many engineering products, instruments, microelectronics, fine chemicals and consultancy work, we have to establish very high technical standards and ideally, technical leadership.

If we fail, then in either case we shall have to pay the price in increased imports and faltering exports. If it takes twice as many people to produce a ton of steel or a car in Britain as in Japan or Korea, then in a competitive trading system the ultimate penalty is inevitable. Either they must work for much lower wages or many of them will be unemployed. If German engineering exports have a value/weight ratio twice as high as our own, then they may be able to afford living standards twice as high, because they are competing on product quality, design and technical leadership as well as on efficient production, and not on low wage costs.

This leads directly to the fourth factor which I mentioned – the direction of technical change and its implications for employment. Technical change is a two-edged process. On the one hand it leads to the creation of completely new industries and occupations, such as the electronics industry or in its day the automobile industry. On the other hand it can lead to the displacement of labour through increases in efficiency in existing processes of producing and delivering the goods and services, if they are not compensated by adequate increase in total demand for these goods and services. Sometimes people tend to assume that these processes are automatically in balance, but it could be dangerous to oversimplify the process by which this balance is achieved. This is especially true of the major technical change now confronting us – the microprocessor revolution – which will both create many jobs and also destroy many jobs.

In a paper which I contributed to an OECD conference on structural unemployment last year I suggested that with the big technological revolutions like the introduction of railways, electricity and electronic computers, there are two phases which may be associated with long-term fluctuations in the growth of the world economy. In the first phase, which may last about a quarter of a century, the effects of the new technology are predominantly employment-generating. Much new investment takes place throughout the economy and many new products are manufactured and new services introduced. In the later phase, when the technology has matured and economies of scale can be fully exploited, labour-displacing effects become more widespread and predominate over job-creating effects.

I would be the first to agree that this is largely speculation and that the employment effects of the microprocessor revolution cannot be forecast on the basis of such a speculation. What is needed is very careful empirical work in every sector of application and development to assess the probable employment consequences over the next ten years. We have started this work on a very small scale in the Science Policy Research Unit, but it needs to be done much more extensively and much more thoroughly. But even from the small amount of work we have done we know that many of the labour-displacing effects are not speculation but reality.

The importance of this technological revolution is still completely underestimated in Britain both in terms of its employment consequences and in terms of its overall economic consequences. This is, I believe, partly because the "automation scare" of the 1950s did not materialize or materialized rather slowly and in a much less dramatic way than had been predicted by some of the early prophets of computerization.

For a major new technology like electricity or the automobile or the computer to reach its full social and economic impact takes a fairly long period of gestation. In the early days, even when the technical potential is clearly established there are still major problems of relatively high cost, lack of standard designs, unreliability in performance, lack of trained people familiar with the new technology and widespread distrust both by management and the public in general. It takes a generation, rather than a few years, to prepare the way for a really far-reaching change in technology. The early computers were huge, expensive, clumsy, unfamiliar and often unwelcome. It is remarkable that they diffused in the 1950s and 1960s as rapidly as they did.

Microprocessors are extremely small, extremely reliable and extraordinarily cheap. Moreover they are coming in at a time when there now exists a fairly large pool of skilled people (although not large enough) already familiar with electronic computer technology and systems analysis.

Of course I would agree with the Cambridge DAE that the scale of applications in the UK has so far been too small to have perceptible effects on the aggregate employment trend. I am talking about the impact in the 1980s and 1990s rather than the 1970s, and it will take a new cycle of investment in manufacturing and the services before the full consequences are felt. But what has happened on a small scale already in the 1970s seems to me sufficiently indicative to warrant serious concern. If you take such areas as telecommunications, machine shops, automobile assembly, automated warehousing, printing and publishing, clocks and watches, then there is already sufficient evidence available in Europe, Japan and the USA to show that the labour-displacing consequences may be very severe indeed. There are cases of the labour force being halved despite a substantial increase in production.

Probably the most important question for research is the impact of microelectronics in the service sector of the economy. I have already quoted George Ray's estimate of fifteen per cent unemployment in the UK service sector by 1991 if we attain EEC rates of productivity increase, and this could be a reality if the full potential of the computerization of office and distribution employment is unleashed in the 1980s with the large-scale displacement of secretaries, filing clerks, typists and paperwork generally. Much of this still sounds like science fiction, but I think we have to take it seriously.

According to the estimates of Machlup and Porat more than half of all service sector employees in the United States are "information workers" and in all countries of the EEC a large part of the service sector is concerned with generating, recording, processing, reproducing and transmitting information in numbers or in words. So far computers have affected only a small part of this vast system, mainly that part concerned with the storage and processing of routine statistics. But the new developments in electronic technology mean that textual information and its transmission will now be increasingly affected, with all the immense consequences for office work, for printing and publishing, for telecommunications, and for postal services.

We thus have a stark dilemma facing us. If we do not keep up with the international race in the use of microprocessor technology, then we risk becoming even more uncompetitive in terms of world trade, so that even before North Sea oil expires, the problem of growth and levels of employment in the British economy would be even more severe than it is today. If we adopt this revolution enthusiastically in every branch of our economy and make it the cornerstone of our industrial strategy, then we also risk accelerating the scale of labour displacement through the very success of this technical revolution, although this might ultimately be offset by some relaxation of the balance of payments constraint, by the job-generating effects of new technologies, and by an increase in total demand through cost and price reductions.

In the face of this dilemma there are four possible solutions.

The first is a "Burmese strategy" of isolating the UK from the world economy and to some extent also from world political and cultural trends, and pursuing purely national values and goals on an increasingly autarchic basis, and striving for national self-sufficiency in energy, food and even materials supplies.

The second is a full-blooded socialist strategy, involving a state monopoly of foreign trade, long-term planning agreements with other socialist or Communist countries, and dealing with lack of competitive power by direct control of imports.

The third is the "Cambridge" strategy of a fairly long period of protection for British manufacturing industry in an attempt to secure a much higher rate of growth behind a protective wall, and thereby the long-run improvement in productivity.

The fourth is to continue as a full EEC partner, accepting a high degree of international competition, striving for a major relative improvement in the performance of the British economy, and using the small benefits of the North Sea oil to try and bring about this improvement. The faster growth, if it could be attained, would then be partly a result of productivity improvements.

In my view the success of any of these strategies of medium-term economic policy, with the exception of the Burmese strategy, would require a major planned national effort to develop and adopt micro-processor technology on a large scale. I say "planned national effort" because the speed and effectiveness of this technical revolution depends on major changes in our infrastructure which cannot by their nature occur spontaneously.

If we were to be successful in such a planned national effort, then the employment-generating consequences of the microelectronic revolution might be more substantial, and a deliberate aim of national policy should indeed be to maximize such employment benefits, not by preserving unnecessary inefficient jobs but by creating new ones, with social as well as more narrowly defined economic objectives.

The microelectronic revolution is not just "one more step" in the process of technical change or one more new product. It is far more significant for the entire British economy than aircraft development or nuclear power, which at present constitute the largest part of government-financed R&D activities. It is more important than the future of the car industry, which at present has the greatest press coverage of any major industry. It is far more crucial to our future than the drug industry, which makes the biggest profits, or the steel industry, which makes the biggest losses. All of these activities are of course important and none of them should be neglected. We need to improve economic performance in every branch of the economy and a strategy of "picking winners" will not help us. But to achieve an improvement throughout the economy we need to recognize which are the "heart-land" technologies – those which can give leverage over the whole system and raise its level of performance. Steam power and electric power were such key technologies in their time. Today electronic information technology represents this "heartland" technology critical for our entire future. The capacity to handle, process, store and transmit information is now the critical technology for advanced industrial countries both for industry and for services. Without wishing to belittle what has been done, in general this finds no recognition in our govern-ment structures, in our R&D priorities, in our investment priorities, in our industrial strategy, in our education system or in our national thinking. It must find such recognition.

Electronics and Employment: Displacement Effects

Arthur L. Robinson

A rare American contribution to the employment debate, from a member of staff on the US magazine Science, *in which this article first appeared (vol. 195, 18 March 1977). The author provides a well-documented review of what is known about the employment impact so far in certain key industries, and although his perspective is basically "optimistic", he ends up adding a questionmark.*

Structural unemployment is the technical name for the loss of jobs when changing technology makes currently held skills obsolete. If the question asked is "What impact will advances in electronics have on structural unemployment?", the answer is "Very little", according to most government economists and industry executives.

None the less, individual workers will continue to feel substantial and sometimes traumatic impacts, including the need to learn new skills for jobs with different responsibilities and the necessity of relocating to other plants or to other parts of the country. Not only will the requirements for some old talents disappear and new ones be created, but, somewhat contrary to intuition, the electronics "revolution" may also open up opportunities for the relatively unskilled. In fact, the upcoming labour force may be structured into large numbers of relatively unskilled workers at one end and highly trained managers and engineers at the other, with very few medium-skilled individuals in between. And, as technological change continues at a rapid rate, a pattern of lifelong education and multiple careers will replace the tradition of training for one lifetime vocation.

According to some observers, the changes to be brought about by solid-state electronics will, in the final analysis, be comparable to Henry

Ford's move from custom to mass production. Since the invention of the transistor, the electronics industry has undergone a profound transition, and the changes of the last twenty-five years exceed those of the preceding seventy-five. Moreover, there may be social impacts that even now are not fully appreciated. Some of these impacts most likely will involve the kinds of jobs that people work at and how many persons are needed for those jobs. If speculation about the electronics-dominated society of tomorrow turns out to be anywhere near the mark, then the impact of advances in electronics on employment could dwarf earlier concerns about automation, such as those typical of the early 1960s.

Hard numbers reflecting the impact of advances in electronics on employment are for the most part unavailable, in part because the problem is not yet of interest to manpower economists. Says one manpower specialist: "Displacement due to changing technology is now only a small part of the total job deficit, but the situation could change in the next two years if the recovery from the recession is slow and if technological change and competition from overseas increase." Technological change is also extremely difficult to separate from other influences, thus making its study unsatisfying.

One effect that can be documented is the large growth in the number of workers making and using electronics technology in the form of computers and communications equipment. Marc Porat of the Department of Commerce's Office of Telecommunications has chronicled the rise of what some are calling the information economy.[1] Included in the information economy are all jobs that involve the manufacturing of information machines, and the production, processing, transmission, distribution, or selling of knowledge or information. Also included are various information activities of both public and private bureaucracies, such as managing, planning, monitoring, marketing and coordinating.

Not every occupation in the information economy depends, either directly or indirectly, on the existence of electronics technology, but a substantial fraction does. Porat's data show that, in about 1955, a rising percentage of information jobs surpassed a declining percentage of industrial jobs, and that information activities became the dominant sector in the US economy. From about 1965, the now dominant information sector accounted for about forty-five per cent of all employment (Fig. 6.2). Furthermore, as computers and information machines made their appearances in the late 1950s, exacerbating the trend towards large bureaucracies that began to build up in private industry and in government in the years after World War Two, the percentage of the total national income earned by those in information occupations rose to more than fifty-three per cent (Fig. 6.3).

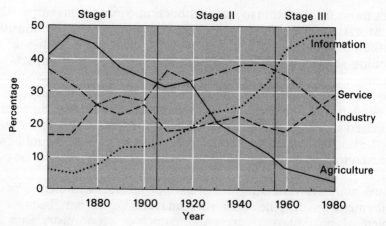

Fig. 6.2 Changing composition of US workforce by per cent from 1860 to 1980. Stage I is a primarily agricultural economy; stage II is an industrial economy; and stage III is the information economy

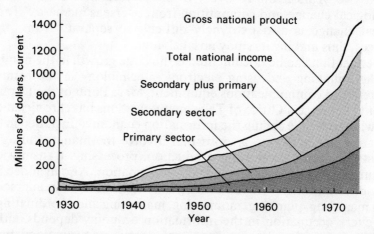

Fig. 6.3 Portion of total national income originating in the information sector, 1929 to 1974. The information sector comprises a primary (manufacturing, information producing, information processing and transmission, and information selling) sector and a secondary (information services produced and consumed internally by industries and government) sector. (Source: M. U. Porat, Office of Telecommunications)

Porat thinks that these trends offer considerable solace to those fearful of job displacements from electronics. In his view, every new computer or information machine introduced in an odfice, for example, leads to many more jobs than it displaces: in a more complex environment people are needed to gather information for the machine to process and to interpret what it puts out. A scenario of this type does, however, imply a steadily growing bureaucracy, and Porat worries how long society can support an increasing number of less and less productive individuals.

A more conventional viewpoint is that increased productivity arising from technological innovation will, given a reasonably healthy economy, create an increased demand for labour and raise real wages.[2] C. Lester Hogan, vice-chairman of Fairchild Camera and Instrument Corporation, the third largest producer of semiconductor devices in 1976, says bluntly: "Advancing technology never reduces employment in the long run."

John Kendrick, chief economist of the Department of Commerce, pretty much echoes these sentiments. Kendrick, who has made a career of following the effect of technological change on labour productivity, recently told an IBM-sponsored seminar on this subject that "There is a significant positive correlation between industry rates of change in productivity and in output. . . . Thus, despite temporary problems of labour displacement, it would appear that technologically progressive industries create more jobs on net balance than the backward industries which are more vulnerable to dynamic change."[3]

Jerome Mark, assistant commissioner for productivity and technology of the Department of Labour's Bureau of Labour Statistics, explains why this might be so. Over all industries in the United States, there has been a relatively small spread in the hourly wage increases granted to labour, but there has been a much larger range in the growth of productivity. Thus, prices of goods are much more sensitive to productivity than to wages, and an edge in labour costs goes to the industry with the better growth in productivity. Reduced costs lead to more sales and ultimately more employment. Kendrick told *Science* that, far from causing displacements, technological change may even be having a smaller impact than it did fifteen years ago because of a reduced research and development investment that has caused the rate of productivity increase to decline in the United States. Productivity advance is now lower in the United States than in some European countries and Japan, according to a recent article by economist Lester Thurow of the Massachusetts Institute of Technology.[4]

The electronics industry has been on the front line of those feeling the effects of technological change, as well as being the source of the changes that affect the rest of the economy. It is perhaps also an exemplar of the innovation-increased productivity-lower costs-increased sales-more jobs scenario. During the period from 1960 to 1976, for example, about 664,000 jobs were added to electronics out of a total of 2,130,000 new jobs in all manufacturing industries, according to statistics provided by L. M. Rice, Jr, a vice-president at Texas Instruments, the largest US semiconductor device producer.

Most spectacular of all has been the rise of the US semiconductor industry. From its beginnings in the early 1950s, the industry mushroomed to sales of about $520m in 1961 (the era of the discrete transistor) and to 1976 sales of about $2.4 billion (the era of the integrated circuit). The worldwide industry (excluding the Communist bloc) sales were about $5.4 billion (see Fig. 6.4).

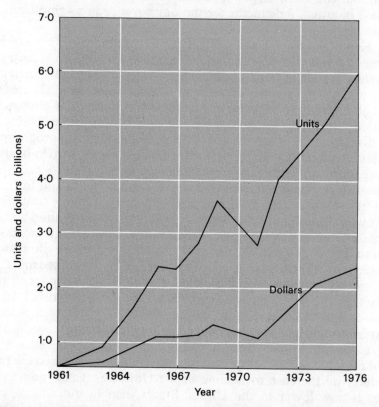

Fig. 6.4 Semiconductor industry sales by year for the period 1961 through 1976. A unit is the semiconductor device defined in the text. Over the period graphed, the average price per unit sold declined from $1 to about $0.32. Since the average number of transistors per unit increased from one to about fifty, the cost per transistor plummeted by a factor of 150. (Source: C. L. Hogan, Fairchild Camera and Instrument Corporation)

In 1961, between 10,000 and 15,000 employees produced about 520 million devices, nearly all of which were discrete transistors, diodes and the like. By 1976, about 120,000 workers made a total of about six billion devices. (A device could be a discrete transistor or a complex integrated circuit containing 20,000 transistors; but, on the average, according to Fairchild's Hogan, who supplied the figures, a device contained about fifty transistors.) Thus, while the average labour productivity measured in devices per employee did not change greatly, measured in transistors per employee, the average labour productivity skyrocketed. And the increased sales stimulated by the resulting lower cost were the foundation for the more than a tenfold increase in employment during those fifteen years.

At Fairchild, experience with manufacturing silicon diodes provides another perspective of the effect of productivity. In 1966, Fairchild sold $87m worth of these devices with about 200 employees to make them. By 1976, sales had decreased somewhat – to $50m; but the number of employees had increased slightly to 225. The startling statistic is that the number of labour hours required to manufacture 1000 diodes had decreased by a factor of ten. Therefore, the increased productivity had stimulated sales to about ten times the number of diodes sold previously. In this instance, however, increased productivity did not greatly increase the level of employment, but did perhaps postpone the demise of a device that is being supplanted by other types.

Not everyone is quite so euphoric. One who is not is J. A. Haddad, vice-president for engineering programming and technology at IBM. Haddad feels that careful and detailed econometric studies are necessary before expansive projections become anything other than speculation. The IBM executive points to two examples, one of which vividly backs up the productivity and growth argument and one of which does not.

In the former category is the well-trodden example, of the handheld calculator, which was made possible by the development of inexpensive but computationally powerful general purpose integrated circuits. While makers of sliderules may have taken a beating, relatively few persons ever bought sliderules in the first place. The handheld calculator, on the other hand, has so caught the public fancy that practically every child has one now. The volume of calculators produced has probably more than made up for the number of displaced sliderule manufacturers and their employees.

Digital watches are a different story. Mechanical watches were already pervasive among all groups of society and probably not that many people own more than one or two. Since relatively few man-hours are needed to make a first-class digital watch, Haddad guesses that the net effect of electronics in this case may be to decrease employment.

A concern of many nowadays, including Haddad, involves the question of how much longer society can continue to rely on unlimited economic growth. "Sooner or later, continuing economic growth will no longer be sustainable because of dwindling natural resources and supplies of energy," Haddad insists. "We will be as big as we can get." At this point, the question will be one of finding how to improve the standard of living without further growth. Other industry executives would counter Haddad's argument by saying that they never meant that growth is the same as increasing consumption. Says William Hittinger, executive vice-president for research and engineering at RCA, it is a matter of "growth by new concepts, not just consuming more".

Whatever the outcome of debates about economic growth, it is clear that within the electronics industry, changing technology has already effected major changes in employment of a qualitative nature in addition to the quantitative one already discussed. From a different viewpoint, RCA's Hittinger restated some of Porat's conclusions about technology leading to increased bureaucratic activities. According to the RCA research director, solid-state technology of all types, not just silicon integrated circuit technology, has caused an expanding demand for people of many backgrounds and skills.

After World War Two when vacuum tubes were still the dominant active devices, electronics companies mainly provided an off-the-shelf catalogue service for discrete devices that other companies used to build their products, and most employees had physical science backgrounds. Today there is a full spectrum of practitioners of basic sciences (physics, chemistry, metallurgy) and applied sciences (electrical and mechanical engineering, statistics), and there is, as well, a great demand for the "softer" sciences (sociology, economics).

The need for the softer science practitioners has arisen because semiconductor houses are now marketing products and systems of their own, and must therefore engage in such market research activities as demographics, consumer preference testing, and input-output studies. If your company's microprocessor is the essential ingredient of a pocket calculator, why sell the microprocessor to someone else to package? Sell the complete product yourself.

There has also been change within the manufacturing divisions of semiconductor companies, as the transition from discrete devices to integrated circuits transpired. Hollis Caswell, director of applied research at IBM's Yorktown Heights laboratory, describes some of these changes. Fifteen years ago, an engineer designed a silicon transistor with a sliderule (chose the vertical dimensions, the specific impurities and their doping levels, and the geometry needed to give the desired characteristics); he had the transistor fabricated; and he tested it. He could do this and not be overly concerned with the interactions of the transistor with other discrete components of his circuit.

Now with silicon integrated circuit technology, building individual transistors and designing logic or memory circuits merge into the same task. Furthermore, the engineer will design the circuit with the help of a computer with which he can interact by way of a light-pen and a cathode-ray-tube display. He will simulate the circuit performance on the computer, a process known as software bread-boarding, in contrast to the previous practice of wiring transistors together into a circuit to see how the assembly worked.

Similarly, the process of making the series of masks used in the integrated circuit fabrication process has been computerized. Where once the engineer would actually draw patterns on a piece of paper, the patterns being photographically reduced after being manually transferred to a suitable working material, today the engineer and his interactive computer can bypass much of the manual labour. In fact, according to Hogan at Fairchild, much of the work can be carried out by technicians trained to use the computer once the basic logic design for the circuit has been worked out.

As does IBM, the Western Electric Company, which is the manufacturing arm of the Bell System, itself makes a substantial fraction of the electronic devices needed for its products: telephones, switching machines for branch and for long-distance (toll) offices, and other equipment. The pervasiveness of advanced electronics in the telephone system was the subject of a recent speech to Bell Laboratories officials by Joseph West, vice-president and chief operating officer of Western Electric. The theme of West's presentation was that, although advancing technology is the lifeblood of the Bell System, it is not without certain problems for those managing its implementation.

Western Electric experience with the transition from discrete semiconductor devices to integrated circuits has paralleled that of the semiconductor industry. But because Western Electric is primarily concerned with the manufacture of end products, there have been other effects. The manufacturing of devices, for example, has taken on a substantial portion of the manufacturing effort that was formerly carried out in the final assembly operation. This has occurred because so much of the circuit interconnections are incorporated as an essential part of the integrated circuits now being manufactured. Thus, says West, "where historically the task of interconnecting circuit elements has been very labour-intensive, as we move more and more into large-scale integration, we see an interconnect cost trend which closely tracks that of the cost per equivalent transistor" (Fig. 6.5).

Switching machines to route telephone calls through branch exchanges and long-distance toll offices are a major product of Western Electric and indeed are central to the telephone business. They also provide some excellent illustrations of the impacts of technology.

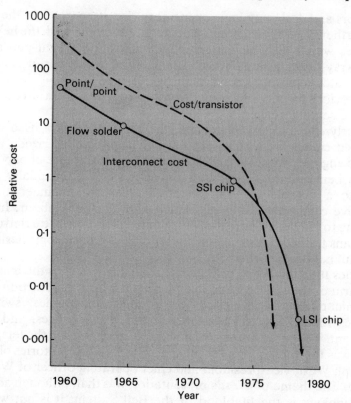

Fig. 6.5 Cost trends of transistors and interconnections at Western Electric. Point/point refers to connecting discrete transistors on a panel. Flow solder refers to connecting a transistor into a circuit on a printed circuit board. SSI dip refers to an estimated cost for the interconnection between transistors in an early small-scale integrated circuit. LSI chip refers to the same cost for a contemporary large-scale integrated circuit. (Source: J. T. West, Western Electric Company)

Shown in Table 6.1 are some statistics for production and employment in Western Electric's Switching Division over the last fifteen years.

At the start of this period, the dominant switching technology was an electromechanical one generally known as crossbar. In 1962, the first all-electronic switches were manufactured under the appellation ESS. The most recent versions make extensive use of integrated circuitry and are heavily computerized – that is, their functions are determined by stored programs rather than by fixed or "hardwired" circuits.

West told the Bell Laboratories officials: "An unglamorous way of describing your new designs in manufacturing terms is to point out that you have designed for us a switching machine that in terms of lines switched weighs one-sixth as much as [crossbar], has one-fifth the

Table 6.1   Impact of changing technology upon the Switching Division of the Western Electric Company

| | Employees at year end | | Switching lines shipped | |
Year	Total corporation	Switching division	ESS	Total
1962	144,874	26,962	1000	2,723,100
1963	141,468		5000	2,734,100
1970	178,000	39,000	1,728,000	5,400,000
1975	147,651		3,386,000	4,358,200
1976	144,123	27,172	4,683,000	5,473,000

(*Source:* Western Electric Company)

connections, takes one-third the floor space to make, and somewhat surprisingly, takes one-third the capital and substantially less installation and engineering. Direct impact can be seen on Western's need for wiremen – installers – standards engineers."

But the impact on Western Electric's need for switching division employees has been more qualitative than quantitative. Twenty-five years ago, according to Western Electric officials, a typical communications equipment factory comprised three categories of operations: (1) materials working using punch presses, moulding presses, and automatic screw machines; (2) apparatus assembly and adjusting; and (3) equipment assembly, wiring, and testing. Cable forming and manufacture of vacuum tubes were also part of the factory.

None the less, displacement effects due to the changeover to integrated circuit technology with more chemically based processes and more computer-aided processes were not large. From 1962 to 1976, the number of workers there did not change greatly; indeed total Western Electric employment did not change much, but the total number of switching lines doubled. Furthermore, a projection further into the future reveals that the demand for switching lines may continue to rise but without a need for additional division employees.

As compared to switching division employment in 1970, the lower numbers of employees in 1976 would seem to indicate dramatic displacement effects. But for various reasons company officials regard employment that year as anomalously high. Also to be borne in mind is that not all division employees are directly involved in manufacturing switches.

That the qualitative nature of jobs will change with different skills, different levels of training and different responsibilities being involved has other repercussions. In addition to a forty-four per cent decrease in employment in the Switching Division between 1970 and 1976, there was, according to Western Electric officials, a marked shift in the distribution of personnel over grade levels. Where once there had been a smooth distribution in hourly skills, gradually decreasing in numbers at higher skill levels, now the curve shows two pronounced peaks. The first occurs at high grade levels and reflects the need for highly trained testers and analysts. The second peak occurs at the lower end of the range of skills. A rather large valley corresponding to decreased requirements for middle-level skills rests between the two peaks.

At IBM, Haddad, who more or less seconds this perception, points out that the thrust of technological advance is generally to "take out the middle". Sophisticated levels of training are needed to design and less training is needed to "make things happen". Haddad philosophizes that this trend is part of an overall drift in society that is taking away from the concept of the whole, self-sufficient man. Everyone, whatever the skill and level of training, is becoming more interdependent.

Most of the individuals who will feel the impact of the advances in electronics, no doubt, do not work for the semiconductor industry or for companies like IBM and Western Electric. Thus, the effects of electronics on employment in these industries may not be entirely representative; they just happen to be the easiest to document for the present. One example, possibly more representative, resides in the experience of the operating telephone companies, those which use the switching equipment manufactured by Western Electric. The data in Table 6.2 show that the introduction of the all-electronic switching equipment in long-distance toll offices is estimated to have reduced the need for administration and maintenance people to from less than one half to less than one third, depending on the size of the office. The reduction is due in part to the availability of computerized diagnostic and testing systems for use in administration and maintenance. Where once an administrator was needed to order maintenance work after detection of a malfunction, now detection and decision-making can be done electronically.

The mail,[5] banking,[6] offices,[7] schools,[8] factories,[9] and communications industries,[10] are some of the places where electronics will change employment patterns both qualitatively and quantitatively, although in most cases the impact is as yet more speculation than fact.

At the Bureau of Labour Statistics, however, two studies were made in the early 1970s of the effects of computerization, one on electronic data processing machine makers and users[11] and one on process control in factories.[12] According to Mark at the bureau, there was no dramatic evidence for widespread displacements in either area, although both studies were completed before minicomputers had become as pervasive as they are now. Mark did, however, support the observations made at Western Electric and IBM as to the changing distribution of skills needed. He added the further observation that the grade levels comprising the lower peak of the distribution approximately corresponded to semiskilled, not unskilled, personnel. In addition, there was some demand for mid-level skills in the form of repair and maintenance people.

Martin Ernst of Arthur D. Little Inc thinks that retail store automation systems will be among the first to have significant employment effects. Point-of-sale terminals in retail and grocery stores have the potential of enabling automatic checkout and inventory management with the consequent lessening need of labour for these functions. Connection of terminals in stores directly to computers in banks and other financial institutions and of computers in financial institutions to one another may also lead to a less cash-oriented society with less need for persons to process financial paperwork. Ernst guesses, however, that what personnel reductions do occur will be by attrition – failure to rehire – rather than by firing or layoffs.

Table 6.2 Estimated impact of changing technology on the operating telephone companies of the Bell System

Type office	Administration and maintenance people required	
	ESS	Crossbar
Small toll (20,000 trunks)	32	68
Large toll (100,000 trunks)	60	200

(*Source:* Western Electric Company)

The United States Postal Service is another likely candidate for large-scale impact by electronics. With about 650,000 employees, the Postal Service is the third largest nongovernment employer in the United States. Currently, it is in big trouble, as rising costs and decreasing revenues are leading to larger and larger deficits ($1.2 billion in fiscal year 1976) and the prospect of poorer and poorer service. (Surpluses in the second half of 1976 are regarded as unreliable indicators of the long-term situation.) Both the public and the US Congress, which supports the mail organization with subsidies, are screaming for change. At present a congressionally established Postal Service Commission is feverishly putting together a set of recommendations on what should be done; its report is due by the end of the month.

One of the reasons for decreased revenues – a reason that most likely will become ever more important if postal service declines further – is that electronic technologies are permitting users to find alternative ways to send first-class mail. Electronic transmission of messages, electronic transmission of funds, and data transmission systems will soon be able to service most of the needs of commerce; and business mail accounts for seventy-four per cent of the nation's letter mail. A just completed National Research Council study on electronic message systems for the US Postal Service estimated "as much as thirty per cent of all government and business mail may be amenable to transmissions as electronic messages".[13]

Interestingly enough, in the Postal Service's six-year life, this is the fifth report recommending the adoption of electronic message transmission by the Postal Service (a sixth is still under way), yet practically no planning in this direction has begun. In this case, even the labour unions are clamouring for the Postal Service to adopt electronics technology. J. Joseph Vacca, president-elect of the 230,000-member National Association of Letter Carriers, testified to the Commission on Postal Service: "I am firmly convinced, though, that if we do not soon become ... comfortable with the language of Electronic Message, Fund and Data Transmission, we will be literally out of business."[14]

Vyra Imondi, director of electronics communications studies on the commission, points out that approximately half of the current Postal Service employees will be eligible for retirement in the next ten years. If the Postal Service adopts the new technology, many will be hired with new skills to fill in for those retiring. But the failure to adopt electronic mail technology made possible by advancing electronics could be the driving force for the further deterioration of postal service and the concomitant loss of jobs.

From the point of view of the individual who is impacted by advancing electronics technology, the most immediate questions are personal. Will I lose my job? What provisions are there for me to retrain into another job in the company? Will I be transferred to another location? To the individual faced with these and other uncertainties, euphoric pronouncements about productivity, multiplier effects on employment, better standards of living and the like are pretty irrelevant.

Economists and some industry executives view the problem as one easily solved by retraining. Says the Office of Telecommunication's Porat: "Displacements are important to economists only if people are not retrainable and if phasing out of occupations is not anticipated. One wants labour resources to shift as soon as possible because it is inefficient for them to be idle." Furthermore, the very technology that may cause temporary displacements can be used to ameliorate their effects. For example, two-way computer-aided instruction sent into the home or neighbourhood learning centres by way of satellites or broadband cables could be one vehicle for retraining. Porat underscores the desirability of the now developing enthusiasm for lifelong learning as being especially important for times of low population growth, when lateral mobility will be the major kind.

Retraining has become a big business at Western Electric. In the next several years, the company will put into service some 800 electronic switching systems. About twenty per cent of the company's installation efforts are now in this area, but this figure will increase as more telephone systems become all-electronic. In former years, Western Electric would generally not retrain installers experienced in electromechanical technology, but would start from scratch by training new personnel. Now, as crossbar demand slackens, the company has a near-crash programme under way to retrain electromechanical people to proficiency in ESS installation. Since 1975, about 1000 such people have received some ESS instruction.[15]

Widespread retraining is not always needed. Says a company official: "Displacement effects in the Switching Division were small because attrition was such in the crossbar operations that limited hiring was required to maintain a crossbar workforce" in the 1960s. Retraining was necessary, however, to "develop electronics diagnostic capabilities in the testers. This was accomplished in a number of ways, including in-hours classroom training, after-hours company sponsored schools and on-the-job training."

Priding itself on not having to lay off employees, IBM also has extensive retraining programmes. But, points out Caswell, "of those having skills needed fifteen years ago but no longer needed, many are retrained into sales, sales support and service jobs, not other manufacturing jobs." Haddad observes that retraining is very effective, but its usefulness varies with skill level. People with Ph.D.s are generally flexible and can do many jobs from the start, so retraining needs are minimal. On the other end of the skill curve, retraining is very effective because there is not that much skill to be learned. Even unskilled people off the street can be quickly trained for many electronics manufacturing jobs. It is the mid-level people who are hardest to change. A person with a lifetime devoted to mechanical skills just does not pick up electronics the way a younger person raised in the era of calculators does, according to the IBM executive.

For precisely this reason, as well as for many others, labour union officials do not regard retraining as the panacea for all displacement due to technological change. According to Markely Roberts, an economist in the department of research of the AFL-CIO, there is "no single solution, but a whole variety of approaches. Which is best depends on the industry and the quality of the labour-management relationship." Roberts has summarized some of the possible strategies for dealing with displacement effects.[16] In addition to retraining, he included prior notice, attrition, seniority rights, early retirement, transfer and relocation rights and severance pay as possible mechanisms to cushion labour from the effects of change. In all cases, the labour philosophy is that the companies should regard the costs of cushioning labour as one of the expenses of introducing new technology, and these costs should be just as important in deciding upon the economic viability of new technology as any other. Roberts concluded, however, that the best protection for labour resided in a full-employment economy.

Another tactic will be tried by the Communications Workers of America in its upcoming negotiations with the American Telephone and Telegraph Company (AT&T). Since 1974, AT&T has reduced its work force by almost 100,000 to a current total of about 900,000 employees. The communications workers want the Bell System to spread the available work by reducing each person's work hours without a cut in pay.[17]

Few of those who ought to be concerned with the effect of electronics on employment seem to think of it as other than one more step in the evolution of technology. Such phenomena as the rise of bureaucracies, simultaneously made necessary and possible by communications technology, and the lumping of worker skills at the ends of what was once a smooth distribution would seem to indicate that more than evolution is going on. The evolution not revolution viewpoint may well be correct. But if it is wrong, a long line of unemployed may find themselves with the wrong skills for the wrong job.

Notes

1 M. U. Porat, *The Information Economy*, vol. I, thesis. Program in Information Technology and Telecommunications, Centre for Interdisciplinary Research (Stanford University, 1976).
2 H. A. Simon, *Science*, 195 (1977), p. 1186.
3 N. Valéry, *New Sci.*, 73 (1034), (1976), p. 70.
4 L. C. Thurow, *Newsweek*, 14 February 1977, p. 11.
5 R. J. Potter, *Science*, 195 (1977), p. 1160.
6 F. E. Balderston, J. M. Carman, A. C. Hoggatt, *Science*, 195 (1977), p. 1155.
7 M. Shepherd, Jr, speech at *Trends and Applications Symposium: Micro and Mini Systems*, National Bureau of Standards, Gaithersburg, Maryland, 27 May 1976.
8 J. F. Gibbons, *Science*, 195 (1977), p. 1139.

9 N. H. Cook, *Sci. Am.*, 232 (2) (1975), p. 23; L. B. Evans, *Science*, 195 (1977), p. 1145.

10 D. Farber and P. Baran, *Science*, 195 (1977), p. 1166; M. R. Irwin and S. C. Johnson, ibid., p. 1170.

11 US Department of Labour, Bureau of Labour Statistics, *Computer Manpower Outlook*, Bulletin 1826 (Government Printing Office, Washington, DC, 1974).

12 US Department of Labour, Bureau of Labour Statistics, *Outlook for Computer Process Control*, Bulletin 1658 (Government Printing Office, Washington, DC, 1970).

13 National Academy of Sciences, *Electronic Message Systems for the U.S. Postal Service* (National Technical Information Service, Springfield, Virginia, 1976).

14 Testimony given before the Commission on Postal Service, 28 January 1977, Washington, DC.

15 T. Dau, *WE*, 28 (6) (1976), p. 2.

16 M. Roberts, *American Federationist*, 80 (1973), p. 13.

17 "Union to Demand Job-Security Provisions in AT&T Pact to Spread Available Work", *Wall Street Journal*, 16 February 1977, p. 7.

The Computer Revolution, Industry and People

Duncan S. Davies

Someone else "inclined to be optimistic" is Dr Duncan Davies, the Chief Scientist and Engineer at the Department of Industry, London. Top government officials don't often put their thoughts down on paper – at least not on paper destined for public consumption – and they certainly don't like to commit themselves on a matter as contentious as the employment impact of the microprocessor. Dr Davies's comments are therefore interesting. He ends up asking a lot of questions. This paper first appeared in Chartered Mechanical Engineer *(June 1978).*

This symposium will raise a wide variety of important questions for a large number of industries and social processes. To catalogue them would be an impossible task, for every case is different. But the state of the opportunity and the problem is the same in every case, and it may be as well to state these basic facts in the simplest possible terms, and provide a standard series of questions to pose. For the ease of using microelectronics varies greatly from activity to activity, and the impact on market expansion and on manpower productivity also varies greatly. Some changes will affect only a limited range of activity; others will start domino effects that will cause changes to run through a much wider range of markets and habits. Thus, some effects will come quickly and some much more slowly – taking perhaps decades. Some will promote innovation and some, oddly enough, may inhibit it. A given change will be seen very differently by the consumer, the worker in the manufacturing industry, and workers in related industries – to some it will be welcome and others threatening. It would be good to be able to say quite clearly whether we have an Aladdin's lamp or a Pandora's box.

Unfortunately, we don't know. I personally am inclined to think that it is neither, but I can't be confident. However, of one thing we can be sure. The UK is not in command of the situation, and those who lead the technology – USA and Japan – will use the processes of the free market to the full, for both have key imports to pay for and foreign exchange to create, whatever their political stance. Short of adopting a self-sufficient siege economy, which would require a restraint on consumption beyond the powers of a democratic government, a country like the UK has no option but to face the technological facts and seek to develop a selective and determined policy, possibly in association with others such as EEC. Whether the prospect is seen as daunting or exciting, major changes are inevitable. But we will do best if we neither wildly exaggerate the likely pace of events, nor complacently engage in ostrich-like hopes that much of the problem will go away, and that it will be all right on the night. And we are speaking of processes that will take from five to a hundred years to complete, with many big ones taking twenty.

The human and social dimensions
Put briefly, signal processing, arithmetic, and information processing and storage are becoming so cheap and reliable that we can assume that the cost of the physical equipment for their conduct is becoming almost negligible in relation to the cost of the equipment for the overall processes being affected or controlled. Further, the compactness of the equipment makes it of almost negligible size and weight, and its power consumption is almost negligibly small, so much so as to be within the compass of very small primary or secondary batteries. The cost of the means for human programming or questioning, and of display for human eyes (the peripherals) is often more than the total cost of the processors and stores, so that it is cheapest to take the input directly from sensors such as thermocouples or cameras, and feed the output directly to control systems such as valves or gates, without any display at all. The cost of the hardware is also becoming less – and in due course negligibly less – than the cost of analysing the system so as to describe its behaviour in the logical software. Accordingly, once a programmable operation has been adequately and logically defined, it can be repeated almost infinitely using a very cheap black box. It is possible to make the black box digitize and mimic many kinds of programmable human operations, and especially those of limb movements (for example during welding or painting). The black box can learn from its successes or mistakes, provided that it has clear criteria of both, and that a clear and logical program can be written for the learning operation that is required. The learning will obviously increase in subtlety as time goes by.

Man (and animals) provided a significant amount of power for mechanical systems no more than a few decades ago: they pushed handcarts and trucks, lifted all of the bricks into place in a building, and so forth. The efficiency of the process of food conversion for this purpose was low – yet man has not given up walking, lifting, or bicycling or is likely to do so, even though in principle he could. He needs a certain amount of exercise, and has now taken to jogging to fulfil the physiological needs that were once fulfilled by walking to work and at work, and by other effort during the working day. But when the effort can be rationalized or aggregated, the machine is better and of course can do far more, even though it is at present using fossil fuel at a nonsustainable rate. Man, assisted by machines, has turned increasingly to their second function – that of a programmable and programmed servosystem for turning signals (for example, the arrival of parts on an assembly line) into action (for example, subassembly by welding, bolting, screwing and so on). Those with the opportunity, craftsmen, for example, can and do change the operation and the product, according to a process apparently more complex than that of programmable learning. We could build random caprice into a robot, but human caprice seems to be different. Men did not like hoeing turnips in fields, where turnips are now grown using mechanical cultivation: with some of the time and effort so saved, men grow prize vegetables competitively in their allotments or gardens. Men in affluent developed nations do not like assembling vehicles; presumably the job will now be done using machines plus microprocessors: with some of the time so saved, some men will build machines by hand, to their own design. The overall process seems to be the escape not from effort, but from routine, repetition and predictability (if vegetable growing were totally predictable, there could be no shows and competitions). Accordingly, man will continue to use himself both as a prime mover and as a servomechanism; if he does not, he will probably lose essential physiological function. But he wants choice and caprice.

Had anyone asked the question in 1800: "Where will the heat engine lead?" he might have visualized a grim prospect of static man doing nothing but think, talk, hear, see and touch, or a limited prospect held back by Luddites. Some – Jules Verne, for instance – saw flying machines and space travel, but none saw the complex equilibria that, for example, led to the private motor car but to very few private airplanes or nonpleasure boats – and correspondingly, to the possible rejection of the videophone alongside the acceptance of the telephone. It is in these sort of terms that it seems fruitful to look at microprocessors. Outline perceptions may be helpful.

On this view, the social effects of computer technology become the exercise of a new set of human options, and not the inexorable advance of an army of threatening robots. The trouble is that these options call for some philosophical adjustments, and create the possibility of serious conflict between those (for instance, systems analysts whose circumstances encourage them to move into the new philosophies) and those (for instance, factory employees) whose circumstances make such movement more difficult. Each side in this conflict will see success by the other as being antihuman – the systems man thinking forward into the longer term, and the operator thinking of the present and immediate future. Thus it can be seen that the likelihood of social upheaval depends, more than anything else, on the rate of the computer revolution. Its speed will be determined by what can be achieved in the society which best balances the social and technical factors, and not by the technological possibilities alone. If there are large disparities between the more and less adaptive there may be serious trouble. If, however, it turns out that though some of the process may be quick, other parts of it are slow enough to allow general adaptation, then all may be well. But it can be argued that the wars of 1918 and 1939 arose partly from disparities of performance in the mechanical revolution. Clearly, we cannot afford disorder on this scale as part of the microelectronic revolution. I am inclined to be optimistic, and to see a wide range of rates of change in different activities – some excitingly, dangerously and inevitably fast, and some irritatingly, safely and equally inevitably slow. Does the whole process fail safe? It seems well worth detailed examination of likely overall rates of change.

In passing, it as well to take a sidelong glance out of the window. While the microelectronic revolution is in progress, man is also very busy interfering physiologically with himself in quite new ways, and may well bring about genetic and other interference which, while also possibly not catastrophic, may interact strongly with activities of the electronic, control and robotic engineers. Six years ago, an SRC-sponsored study on Artificial Intelligence by Sir James Lighthill showed that there was a big gap between the activities of the mathematically inclined psychologists and the physiologically inclined control engineers. This gap may be closing: if it does, then watch out for trouble!

The technical dimension
Some people will feel that what I have just said is too remote and speculative to be useful. I would of course disagree with them and say that far more trouble has been caused in the past by disregard of the philosophical boundary conditions and the basic assumptions, than by imperfection of the machine or the calculus. But I must agree and get down to brass tacks and hard economics.

The first computer revolution was based on the transistor, then the commodity chip, and the printed circuit board. The new situation is based on the combination of specially designed chips with such boards (in reduced numbers, and sometimes in their absence). The chip embodying Large-Scale Integration (LSI) or Very Large-Scale Integration (VLSI) enjoys two separate kinds of economies of scale. First, its cost is much more sensitive to the number made. Secondly, the cost per gate or element (for a given scale of production) comes down very sharply with the number of gates on the chip. If a basic circuit involves (say) 1000 elements, and the production and design system can put 100,000 elements on a chip, then extra circuitry can be added at very little cost beyond that of the initial extra design work. On the first point, some typical numbers for a typical present-day 1000-element assembly might be as shown in Table 6.3. Further, at the 10,000 production scale,

Table 6.3

Type of assembly	Cost per 1000-gate assembly		
	100 off	1000 off	10,000 off
Board, made up from commodity chips accepting 70–80 per cent redundancy	£100	£70	£50
Special Chip	£200	£70	£25

an extra 1000 or more gates could be added at virtually zero extra assembly cost, because of the spread of the modest extra design overhead.

It is this sort of situation that leads to predictions that the average microprocessor chip, by 1990, will be able, at very little additional cost, to have the processing capability of a 1970 mainframe computer, and (on average) have direct access to 128K or so of store – the same amount as for the 1970 machine. By comparison, the power of the average chip at present is smaller by two orders of magnitude, and accesses on average perhaps 8K of store.

What, then, will be the utility of this great and cheap power process and store? Roughly this: that any system can be simulated in the form of cheap hardware that a designer can satisfactorily reduce to circuit logic, visualizing all the extra capability that may be needed, and putting it in as a precaution. The critical step becomes the designer's appreciation of the present and likely future system characteristics. For, if he fails to foresee a possible eventuality, the modification or redesign may well be expensive. It may be even necessary to start again at the beginning.

The capability is at its best in long-life systems involving little or no assumption, in the simulation about human behaviour. There are two underlying reasons. First, a simulation or model is as good (or as bad) as the builder's skill in seeing how the problems may change over time. If a system of microelectronic hardware has been built for simulation, without foreseeing the kind of changes that might lie ahead, then its existence as a control mechanism may in due course provide a harmful straitjacket. Often, it is the human element in a simulation that is hardest to predict. Inventory systems are seriously upset by market changes for example, and thus must incorporate some views about the range of possible behaviours of the fickle customer. Hence microelectronic systems, if unimaginative, may seriously impede later advances. Second, if the system involves a large number of employed people whose jobs it (at best) changes or (at worst) takes away, then its introduction must be expected to be resisted if the process is conducted unimaginatively or too fast. (There may, of course, be a serious conflict here with requirements for competitiveness, whose resolution is a matter for great political sensitivity and skill.)

Some cases

(1) *Telephony.* Much attention has been given to the case of telephone switching, for what can be more certain than the mapping of a macro-network of switches by a micro-network, in Stored Program Control (SPC). Microelectronics has had a dual effect – first, the use of SPC for more conventional systems of reed switches – and then, the use of ICs for the main switch network itself. The overall effect in terms of increased speed (by finding the route "on the map" instead of "on the ground"), reliability, and elimination of expensive components, has been widely commented on, as has the effect on employment. But even in this case, the cost of the software writing is high and is well over fifty per cent of the development cost of a typical system that includes fault-finding, billing and so on.

The complexity and expense of the transition to microelectronic telephony is very importantly increased, in developed countries, by the need to "meld" the new systems with the older, still serviceable Strowger and Crossbar systems. Every country has a different heritage, and therefore a different programme of need for new software and hardware. Consequently, one may almost envy the developing country with virtually no system at all, into which microelectronic switching can be introduced with no complications. This question of the constraint of a past heritage is one which will repeatedly affect microelectronic innovation and be seen as a nuisance. It will delay radical measures and during the years of coexistence of the new and the old, may create an awkward need for maintenance staff who can cope with a wide spread of technology. To some extent this can be coped with by modular construction for repair by sectional replacement, but such matters as the disparity in requirements for power, space and cleanliness will add to the knowledge and education needed temporarily. Thus it may be quite a long time before the effects of the full simplicity of microelectronics clearly arrive: things will get "worse" before they get "better" from the viewpoint of reliability (but not of employment on the switchgear).

Similarly there will be a period during which there has to be simultaneous manufacture of the new and the old (spares constituting an increasing proportion of the latter). Moreover, the period of compromise – both in maintenance and in manufacture – can be considerably varied in length. It is very difficult to say what option would be the cheapest. A "dash for modernization" might cost more in rapid write-off of still serviceable gear, save on maintenance and training, but cut out the chance of adopting VLSI for the later phases, with various advantages apart from economy. A long-drawn-out change would give more time to change to new manning levels, avoid scrapping of still serviceable equipment, and permit more drastic innovation with benefits difficult to foresee in detail.

It is the existence of such ranges of options that creates a need for very good collaboration between those responsible for the human and the technical aspects. It is not uncommon for those who lead a new technology in the first phase to be the prisoner of their early success, so that the first-phase laggards have a chance to leapfrog during the second phase. We may well find Third World countries, by the end of the century, with telephone systems much better than those of some developed countries, policies having been truly optimal in all cases. We may even find that a particular country may lead in the creation of technology and manufacturing competitiveness, yet lag in installation behind one of its overseas customers or licensees, who has started from a primitive base. Such a situation would place a great premium on skill in technology transfer.

(2) *Automobiles.* The use of microelectronics to change the speed controls of vehicles so as to permit the use of leaner mixtures and avoid surges of unburnt fuel in the exhaust during acceleration will clearly be attractive as fuel gets dearer. Here, there will be the same problem of the coexistence of the new and the old, but for a shorter period. There will be greater penalties for equipment failure or bad setting than for the older, cruder devices, with a consequent need for new skills among maintenance garages, whatever is done about "packaging" the new

technology into boxed units. Unreliability is likely to centre on the linkages and sensors rather than on the processors: will oxygen detectors, for example, prove to be really reliable? There will be a great incentive to design for very low maintenance requirements.

Again, therefore, a "dash for modernization" might not be best, although any firm or country that took this view wrongly would suffer a serious competitive setback. So, however, would a firm that forged ahead and produced cars that created a maintenance disaster. Under conditions of free trade, there will of course be no such options for national diversity as exist for telephones. Moreover, the situation seems certain to favour those whose quality control standards in electronics and engineering are highest, such as USA, Germany and Japan. Others will have to concentrate hard on systems design, so as to stay competitive.

(3) *Others.* As already stated, the list of cases for scrutiny is a very long one, and includes the crucial area of robotics – itself comprising devices of a wide range of sophistication, capability, and learning power. Sometimes, the options for speed of introduction will be broad; sometimes narrow. Sometimes, the leader will find that the early christian faces the fiercest lion; sometimes the early bird will catch the fattest worm; sometimes there will be opportunities for leapfrogging.

Difficult though these judgements may be, they are easy compared with the judgement about the more general market and employment consequences of a particular advance, to which we must now turn.

Markets and employment

Albeda, Driehuis and Freeman are amongst those who have considered the general question of the effect of technology on employment. The "base case" is that of the USA over the period 1770–1970, during which period labour economies in one industry were always offset by new needs generated either for expansion or for new industries making new products. Hence, it was always reasonable over this period to regard human "effort" as the scarcest resource and to quote productivity in terms of man-hours rather than land-acres, kWh, or gallons of water.

Now that unemployment levels are high, rising in some countries, and superficially uncorrelated with degree of technological sophistication (see Figure 6.6), there is doubt about the basic doctrine that investment always, globally speaking, creates jobs. There is no shortage of *micro*-evidence that the immediate effect of investment in improved technology for an existing product often destroys jobs. Indeed, if existing methods are reasonably efficient on materials and energy, there can

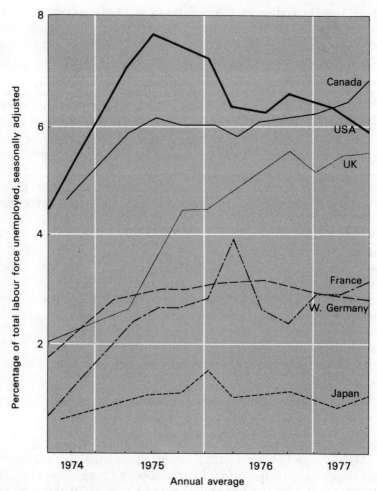

Fig. 6.6 Standardized unemployment rates in major OECD countries since 1974. (Source: *National Institute Economic Review*, May/August 1977)

often be no case for the investment unless this is so. Further, the situation over the short term is complicated by the trade cycle; it is inevitable that there should be a strong feeling during the downturn that investment destroys jobs, because output is not rising strongly. On the other hand, during upturn the same innovative investment might be welcomed by everybody, as a means for increasing output without adding to an already awkward labour shortage. But even so, there is a general feeling that across the whole trade cycle, slackening economic growth is everywhere liable to allow innovation initially to harm employment. And although there may be no limit to growth in non-resource-intensive service activities, it seems certain that escalating prices for energy and other resources must in due course strictly limit growth of dependent industries and industrial employment.

None of this, however, answers the long-term question whether cheaper, quicker and more reliable telephone switching will, overall, create more employment both in the peripherals industries and in a variety of communicating-based activities. For telephony is not resource-intensive, so that such things as Viewdata and Teletext are not likely to be energy-constrained.

To attempt an answer at this point would be pre-emptive. But it may help to consider a few propositions, and a few questions. These are as follows:

Propositions

(1) Industrial employment in operations that can employ microelectronics may, if products are price inelastic, diminish in the short term.

(2) However, the resultant economies may create new markets and jobs in downstream industries.

(3) Even if industrial jobs diminish overall, service and care jobs can be increased as long as expectations of consumption (and consequent necessary imports) can be met and paid for (including necessary exports).

(4) Proposition (3) demands that technology dependent on imports which commits us to meet any cost reductions due to microelectronics that others can make.

(5) Proposition (3) also demands that esteem for industrial jobs attracts enough able people to industry, but also that in the longer term, esteem for service and care jobs is enough to provide satisfaction and social acceptance for the majority of the workforce (perhaps greater than eighty per cent) doing such jobs.

Questions

For any microelectronic innovation:

(1) What are the options that competitiveness allows for its rate of introduction?

(2) What are the costs and benefits of delay (a) in immediate cash, (b) in opportunities for absorbing later technology, (c) in ease of human and employment adaptation?

(3) What are the immediate employment consequences of the best strategies?

(4) What can be roughly predicted (or hoped for) in terms of sustainable downstream employment in dependent industries or service/social activities?

(5) What feedback from (3) and (4) is there into the choice of options under (1)?

(6) What inflexibilities does it build in, if any? Can these, by careful systems design, be reduced?

(7) How can the attractiveness and quality of jobs be improved, and not damaged, by the innovation?

(8) How can it be used alongside other innovations, to improve national technological capability?

(9) What will be the best approach to preserve, or improve, industrial relations during the second industrial revolution?

There is no doubt that these propositions and questions are far from complete and far from adequate. But they will suffice for a start.

The Employment Consequences of Computers: A User View

W. Reay Atkinson

Not exactly a case study this, but the views of someone with twenty years' experience of the use of computers in government administration. Drawing on his experience, the author suggests ways in which mini- and microcomputers will be applied in clerical work. He emphasizes the slowness of change and is "moderately optimistic" about employment prospects. But he stresses that nothing is certain and concludes with a warning note on the treatment of people, which serves as a useful lead-in to the next chapter on industrial relations. Reay Atkinson is currently the head of the Computers, Systems and Electronics Division of the Department of Industry, London, and this (unpublished) paper was presented to a Sperry Univac seminar near Nice, France, in September 1978.

I should first identify the position from which today I am speaking within government on the employment aspects of computing. I am not speaking from my present position as Head of CSE Division in the Department of Industry with my responsibility for sponsorship and promotion of UK computer and electronics industries: my responsibility here is to help ensure the most effective indigenous industry by promoting the effective use of the technology, taking due account of both social and economic consequences. Nor do I speak for the Central Policy Review Staff or the Advisory Council for Applied Research and Development. A great deal of work is currently in progress concerning the social and economic aspects of microelectronics in the broad national context. The departments in the lead here include both Education and Employment. I speak in fact on behalf of government as a major user of computers for more than twenty years in support of the main administrative tasks of government. My concern for a number of years has been with the application of the technology in order both to promote the efficiency of administration and, supplementary to this, to promote the interests of the UK computer industry. In my talk this morning I will be considering both the potential of the technology and its problems, including the consequences which we expect to flow from large-scale application of microelectronics. In doing so, I will endeavour to identify the impact which the technology has had on our organization and institutions of government, including those responsible for introducing and operating computers within the administrative machine.

But first a few figures. Within central government alone we have now installed well over 300 large- and medium-sized computers for administrative and scientific applications and we are currently spending about £65m a year on hardware and maintenance. Over 16,000 staff are involved in data processing, almost 5000 of them as systems designers and programmers. Computers today therefore constitute an essential component in the administrative operations of more than twenty government departments including Social Security, Revenue Assessment and Collection, Banking and Accounting, Payroll and the major Defence logistics systems. Many of the tasks carried out by government would be impossible in their current form without the assistance of computers and some applications, by their very size, have had to be implemented *ab initio* on computers. Many of the systems are still massive, centralized batch processing operations but, increasingly, we are moving to on-line systems maintaining large data-bases of many hundreds of thousands of items.

The past
Against this background it might be expected that, within government, we would already have encountered on a significant scale the problems of displacement of labour, redundancy, relocation and retraining. For many applications have replaced massive clerical operations and the systems have, in the main, been justified on grounds of staff saving. But the plain fact is that we have very little in the way of hard fact to demonstrate the effect which computerization has had upon staff numbers – and, certainly, the Civil Service has gone on increasing over the years. In 1969 we made a heavily qualified estimate that some 2500 staff had been saved in the previous ten years with the expectation that a further 1000 staff would be saved over the next two years to 1971. We have also estimated that, in departments like Health and Social Security, the major pensions schemes would have required between five and six thousand staff in addition to those already employed without automation – always assuming that they could have been recruited.

There are explanations for the shortfall in achievement of savings on forecasts. The tasks for which the systems were first intended very often change during implementation: additional jobs are added and refinements built in to the system: in many cases there has been a significant volume increase in workload: in some departments the emphasis has switched from staff savings to greater efficiency. But, generally there has so far been no problem in terms of displacement of clerical labour.

This is not to say, however, that automation has not significantly affected the work of the civil servant. Such savings as have taken place have been generally among the lower clerical grades and there has been some increase in the number of higher-level staff employed. This has changed marginally the balance between the various grades in the Service: it has underlined differentials in skill and created problems in terms of pay differentials which are difficult to concede in a hierarchical and generalist service. This has caused and is continuing to cause serious problems in terms of retaining professional computer staff in a time of national shortage. The computer has eliminated some of the more tedious and repetitive clerical jobs in departments but, at the same time, has created others – for example, in data preparation. It has certainly altered the form and tempo of the work of many clerks. Regrettably, in the early stages, the tendency has been to design systems round the computer rather than to take account primarily of the requirements of staff using the machine, and of the public.

These trends – reduction of the clerical hierarchy; polarization of staff into one group of employees with low-level qualifications and predominantly mechanical work and one group of higher qualified ADP personnel, with corresponding changes in the salary structure; changes in the organization of work through adaptation of its rhythm to that of the machine – have perhaps been more muted within the Service than in other fields. Moreover, the impact has been in the main on the clerks and the lower levels of management. Only now, with the refinement of our basic operational systems, are computers being used extensively for control and genuine management purposes: only now is the machine beginning to impact significantly upon more senior management.

None the less – even without the emergence of the microprocessor and the dramatic impact which this development has had upon public thinking – significant changes are already in prospect within central government. The small computer, however defined, has transformed the work of data preparation – for example, through key to disc systems. It has marked the perhaps tentative move to word processing and office automation through the introduction initially of automated typing services. The fact that small amounts of computing power are now increasingly cost-effective has given our systems designers the flexibility to move away from large centralized systems to distributed processing systems in which the facilities are at the disposal of staff in direct contact with the public they are serving – thereby improving both the quality of response and the job satisfaction of the clerks. These developments will, over the next few years, undoubtedly move data processing into the front line of everyday administration in government and impact directly upon the work of many civil servants.

But, in my view, these changes will be gradual and will not mark the early demise of the government's large centralized batch systems. We have a significant commitment to three systems, not just in terms of programming but in terms of buildings and the clerical staff needed to support them. One inhibiting factor is that, while it is not too difficult on centralization for one or two clerks in each town to be absorbed into the local job market, the converse may not be true. Decentralization could involve the loss of several thousand jobs in one small area – often a government-designated development area – and the human and economic costs are immense. Change within government is, therefore, likely to be implemented over a longish time-scale not only because of our investment already made in large and more conventional computer-based systems but also because of several other factors:

(1) conservatism in both management and labour coupled with general lack of awareness of the potential of the microprocessor;
(2) inadequate resources in terms of skilled staff and for invest-ment, coupled with industrial uncertainty;
(3) the problems of designing effective – for example robotic – devices and of assimilating them into our administrative processes once developed.

Present position
In the light of this assessment, it would be tempting to conclude that the past, fairly leisurely rate of development is likely to continue for the future notwithstanding the advent of microelectronics, thus leaving time to plan for change on something like a five- to ten-year timetable. Tempting but, I submit, disastrous. For the technology is now advancing so fast that the time constraints for technological change are completely out of phase with those of institutions – certainly within government – responsible for the organization and administration of our operations; and indeed of society more generally. The massive reductions in cost and improvements in reliability of the computer cannot be ignored. The fact is that the total cost of a small computer system, including keyboard, memory and output device, is now less than the cost of employing a clerk. The integration of data processing activities with

those of work processing and the linking of these into networks providing such facilities as electronic mail and fund transfer must, within the next few years, impact significantly on the work of all offices, and nowhere more than in government.

For what we are now witnessing is a step increase in information technology, and information processing and handling in the widest sense – in the inclusive sense of the French term *l'informatique*. And that, above all else, is what government is about – the processing and handling of information.

At the present time the Civil Service employs more than 27,000 secretaries and typists and 198,000 clerical staff. When one sees predictions from Germany and France that between thirty and forty per cent of all clerical staff presently employed in certain offices will be made redundant by automation by 1990, one realizes the problem which we face within central government alone. The problem is complicated by the fact that the greatest concentrations of clerical and typing staff are in the large towns. The fact that the workers concerned are female and contribute significantly to family incomes could well further complicate the problems of retraining and relocation of labour. Our problem has, moreover, to be set in a wider context. Professor Freeman, for example, has predicted that, to restore full employment in the 1980s will require the creation of more than three million new jobs – nearly two million to absorb the increase in the available labour force plus a million to bring registered unemployment down to half a million. This indicates the scale of the problem with which central government has to wrestle simply as an employer. It underlines the need for urgent action.

This need for action is clearly perceived by the leaders of the Civil Service trade unions. Up till now the unions have cooperated enthusiastically in the application of computers to the work of government. They have recognized the need to improve efficiency while, increasingly, demanding that the system should be designed also to improve the working conditions and job satisfaction of their members. But this attitude is changing. This is due in part to the widespread publicity now being given to the impact of the microprocessor on society; it is due also to a genuine concern about employment prospects; about the de-skilling of jobs and the difference which this accentuates between different kinds of staff, and about the effect which automation seems increasingly likely to have both on the nature of jobs, the quality of work and the relationship between staff and management. The start position of the unions is that there should be no "technological redundancy": there must therefore be job sharing and shorter hours. More specifically, in particular departments, developments which demonstrably can lead to a reduction in staff – for instance, certain COM applications –

have been blacked. The fact that the computer has now placed the capacity for disruption in fewer hands has not been overlooked: it gives the unions significant power and muscle if they wish to exercise it.

Handling the problem

I must confess that it is easier to identify the urgency of the problem than to prescribe remedies. We are only just learning to live with this new situation in government. We are learning as we go along and our solutions seem likely to be pragmatic and, most probably, inadequate. What is clear, however, is that, in tackling our problems, we must:

> (1) consult our staff from the beginning when we consider the feasibility of new systems – for example, in the word processing field;
> (2) make it clear from our actions that the interests and require-ments of the end-user are being taken fully into account in the design of new systems;
> (3) explain as clearly and honestly as we can the consequences of these developments and plan with the staff how problems can be overcome.

This means frank recognition of the genuine interest and concern of our staff and their representatives and recognition that, while they are protective, they are certainly not Luddite.

The emphasis must be on steady and controlled progress, recognizing the all-important human aspects of the changes in prospect and the difficulty in accustoming people to new working methods. In using computers in future they will need to master new skills, such as the use of a keyboard, and become used to information appearing on a screen rather than on paper. This may be commonplace to computer profes-sionals. The stark fact is that relatively few people so far have come into contact with computers and those who have, have normally been highly motivated to accept the machine. New users may feel uneasy with the computer system and this unease will quickly turn to anger, fear and opposition. This almost certainly means that the first systems which will impact directly upon non-computer people must be simple.

In parallel, there must unquestionably be a massive effort to encour-age a generally constructive and not unnecessarily defensive attitude to the application of the new technologies. The positive aspects must be stressed – for example, the elimination of drudgery from work and the release of staff for more creative work. It is certainly more enjoyable for an officer from the DHSS to get out into the field and deal with his public on the spot than to sit behind a mass of files in a local office. In this connection, our experience to date has revealed some divergence of view between the staff actually using computers in support of their work and their staff representatives. Those actually in the field – for example, in the Departments of Education and Science and the Inland Revenue – are enthusiastic advocates of the technology: they are not minded to hold back, as are their representatives, while the wider issues of pay and grading are sorted out.

Be this as it may, it would be crass folly for Civil Service management just to sit back and wait for things to happen. The staff expect action and not just talk. But both unions and management perceive clearly that it will not be possible to solve the problems which I have identified within the Civil Service. Problems are national. The general impact on jobs; a need to retrain and perhaps to relocate staff; the creation of new jobs, for example in health, and education and in other service industries – all these matters must be tackled on a national scale. It means comprehensive planning and careful implementation. It must mean bringing in such arms of central and local government as the Manpower Services Commission and other organizations responsible for the retraining and redeployment of staff. It must certainly involve the trades unions as representatives of the workers, with a prime responsibility to preserve and enhance the quality of their members' jobs.

Within the part of government with which I have had direct responsibility we are, however, taking our own steps to meet the future. We have, for example, set up a microprocessor workshop, the main purpose of which is to familiarize other government departments with both the technology itself and its possible applications but also to consider the wider issues of planning, managing and maintaining applications. We are rethinking the organization and control of computing in government in a situation where acquisitions can no longer be completely controlled from the centre and where knowledge of the techniques involved must be spread widely among staff in general so that they can understand the potential of the new systems. The emphasis must be on advice and guidance rather than rigid central control. Finally, we are closely involved in the measures now being implemented for the more effective education of people in the broader implications of the technology and for the training of the specialists without whom effective exploitation of the technology will not be possible. This is, incidentally, at the present time possibly the biggest constraint under which we labour within central government.

Conclusion

Such is the position as I see it today from the standpoint of the government as user. On the whole I am moderately optimistic about the future course of events. The problems are certainly being identified on all sides – hopefully, just about in time. Constructive dialogue involving all parties seems to be in progress. But I am bound to say that, at the present time, what we seem to be witnessing is skirmishing around the fringes. There is a clear need to face up honestly and urgently to the fundamental problems and their implications.

For example, it is convenient but I think misleading to suggest that, given suitable retraining, the new industries which need to be developed under the influence of the advancing technology will absorb all labour displaced. This seems unlikely to be fully achieved in practice. Indeed the actual creation of new service industries is not itself likely to be "just going to happen". There can be no certainty either that any increase in productivity and profitability resulting from application of the new technology will be shared. Again, for example, do we decide that some clerical operations in part of central government and perhaps in particular areas of the country should be retained without benefit of automation in order to take up labour displaced from industries where it is imperative that the benefits from automation should be achieved? If decisions like this are to be taken and implemented, it seems probable that mechanisms of a kind not so far developed in the UK will have to be introduced. The consequences of such developments could be profound and not necessarily wholly beneficial. But without them, the whole exercise on which we are now embarked may well fail. For people are simply not going to accept the sort of change implicit in application of the latest developments in technology unless and until they can be assured that their interests are being fully considered and that they are going to get a share in whatever benefits accrue from its application.

Guide to Further Reading

Soon after the BBC television programme in March 1978, a well-documented pamphlet predicting massive unemployment also hit the headlines in Britain. Called *The "Chips" are Down* and written by Colin Hines, it was published by the pressure group Earth Resources Research.

A useful reminder of the economic facts of life facing a nation like Britain may be found in "The Challenge of Automation in Manufacturing Industry", a paper by Professor Ernest Braun of Aston University, to be published by the Institute of Mechanical Engineers.

Of course, the "classics" on this subject are:

Charles Babbage, *On the Economy of Machinery and Manufacturers* (1832).

Adam Smith, *An Inquiry into the Nature and Causes of the Wealth of Nations* (1776).

The "classics" from the 1950s include:

J. T. Diebold, *Automation: The Advent of the Automatic Factory* (Van Nostrand, Princeton, New Jersey, 1952).

L. Landon Goodman, *Man and Automation* (Pelican, Harmondsworth, 1957).

D. S. Harder and J. R. Davis, "The Automatic Factory", Paper to the American Society of Automative Engineers, Cleveland, Ohio, 1953.

F. C. Mann and L. R. Hoffman, *Automation and the Worker* (Holt Dryden, New York, 1960).

Ida R. Hoos, *Automation in the Office* (Public Affairs Press, Washington DC, 1961).

C. R. Walker, *Toward the Automatic Factory* (Yale University Press, New Haven, 1957).

Norbert Wiener, *The Human Use of Human Beings* (Houghton Mifflin, New York, 1954, and Sphere, London, 1968).

Later came two books summing up the 1950s experience:

Sir Leon Bagrit, *The Age of Automation*, the BBC Reith Lectures (Weidenfeld and Nicolson, London, 1965).

Philip Sadler, *Social Research on Automation* (Heinemann, London, 1968).

Also useful are:

353

354 *The Consequences for Employment*

Solomon Barkin, *Technical Change and Manpower Planning* (OECD, Paris, 1967).

F. Best (ed.), *The Future of Work* (Prentice-Hall, Englewood Cliffs, New Jersey, 1973).

M. D. Dunnette (ed.), *Work and Non-Work in the Year 2001* (Brooks-Cole, Monterey, California, 1973).

Paul Einzig, *The Economic Consequences of Automation* (Secker and Warburg, London, 1957).

G. Friedman, "Leisure and Technological Civilization", in *International Social Science Journal*, No. 4 (1960).

S. R. Parker, *The Future of Work and Leisure* (Paladin, London, 1972).

P. Prasow and R. Massarik, *The Impact of Automation on Individuals and Jobs. A Review of Recent Literature 1956–67* (Institute of Industrial Relations, University of California, Los Angeles, 1969).

J. Rezler, *Automation and Industrial Labour* (Random House, New York, 1969).

R. Rothwell and W. Zegveld, *Technical Change and Employment* (Frances Pinter, London, 1979).

Among the latest wave of microelectronics-inspired reflections are:

BAAS conference on Automation, various papers, published in *New Scientist*, 8 June 1978.

Peter Bennett, *Technological Change and Collective Bargaining*, an Association of Scientific, Technical and Managerial Staffs discussion document. Gives an excellent overview of the impact of microelectronics on manufacturing and in the office. Contains some interesting employment case studies.

J. Bowen, "Armageddon or Utopia? A Brief Summary of the Impact of Microelectronics on Some Sectors of the Service Industries", Occasional Paper, Technology Policy Unit, University of Aston, Birmingham, January 1980.

Philip H. Dorn, "The Automated Office: The Road to Disaster?" in *Datamation*, 15 November 1978. Reviews the British and European concern over employment and the absence of it in the US. Questions whether Americans should remain complacent and whether they can rely on free market forces to create jobs in the future.

European Trade Union Institute, *The Impact of Microelectronics on Employment in Western Europe in the 1980s* (ETUI, Brussels, November 1979).

Clive Jenkins and Barrie Sherman, *The Collapse of Work* (Eyre Methuen, 1979). Predicts UK unemployment of five million by 1990.

Sir Ieuan Maddock, "The Future of Work", paper to a symposium of the British Association for the Advancement of Science (BAAS) and the Intermediate Technology Development Group, London, November 1978.

"Microelectronics – The Impact Today", *Labour Research*, London, April 1979. Looks at a few examples of detrimental employment impact.

Simon Nora, *L'Informationisation de la Société* (Documentation Française, Paris, 1978). The famous "Nora Report".

Report on the New Technology, by Counter Information Services, London affiliate of the Transnational Institute, London, May 1979. Very pessimistic.

Tom Rowland, "Technology's Threatening Promise", *Management Today*, March 1979. An interesting survey of current thinking and a review of some case studies, on an optimistic theme.

The British government's long-awaited verdict on the relationship between employment and technology came from the Department of Employment in December 1979 in the form of an optimistic 110-page report on case studies:

Jonathan Sleigh, Brian Boatwright, Peter Irwin and Roger Stanyon, *The Manpower Implications of Microelectronic Technology* (HMSO, 1979).

A March 1979 report from a study group of the international consultants, A. D. Little Inc, headed by Jerry Wasserman, is highly optimistic – predicting that 800,000 extra jobs will be created by microelectronics in the US and Europe by the end of the decade. *The Strategic Impact of Intelligent Electronics in the US and Western Europe, 1977 to 1987*, costs £17,500 to A. D. Little clients.

A local area study of over 1000 firms in Greater Manchester, England, prepared for Tameside Borough Council by a Manchester University team, suggests that technical problems and shortages of investment funds will prevent many firms from adopting microelectronic technology for some years. Job losses will be correspondingly slow to materialize (Tameside BC, April 1980).

7 Industrial Relations Implications

What Micros Mean for Managers

Michael J. Earl

In this opener, the author reviews technical developments in micro-electronics and their application before going on to look at the employment impact. Some managers, he says, look upon the reduction of employment as wholly desirable – as one said: "One thousand employees are one thousand headaches." But the new technology will also have a profound effect on organizational structure. Micros make possible devolution into smaller units, better information flows and a higher degree of employee participation. Nothing will be achieved, however, without careful planning. Michael J. Earl is a Fellow at the Oxford Centre for Management Studies, Oxford, England, and this paper first appeared in Management Today, *December 1978.*

"Chips" have appeared more rapidly on everybody's menu than anybody could have expected. The impact of microelectronics is boosting the seminar business, attracting the media, exercising the politicians and even intruding on high-table discourse in Oxford. Microprocessing is a hot topic. The Prime Minister, initiating a Think Tank study of the social and economic implications of the microelectronics industry, suggested that this rapid technological development "... is one of the most significant opportunities of our time, and it presents the nation with a number of challenging issues. ... It will have the deepest significance in the 1980s for the way in which the skills of the British people are used, and I wish to ensure that within the present state of knowledge we are fully aware of all the ramifications in reaching our conclusions in the social and economic consequences of this technology." The Conservatives, also recognizing the importance of the new technology, have set up a new information technology committee to advise the

Shadow Cabinet on policies it should adopt if returned to power.

Meanwhile the National Enterprise Board is fostering a £50m venture into the mass production of chips, and reportedly has further plans still. The Department of Industry is spending heavily to encourage use of microprocessors in industry, while major firms, led by the General Electric Company, are planning to exploit the potential of microelectronics with considerable urgency. Thus, on the one hand, a great debate is being encouraged, and, on the other hand, a technological race is on. Less than a year ago, the topic was avant-garde; today it is mainstream.

The key element of the new technology is the microprocessor, which is founded on the silicon chip. A microprocessor can be as small as one square centimetre, is flat and is made mainly of silicon. It can contain power which twenty-five years ago would have required a roomful of computing equipment comprising extensive wiring and vacuum tubes. A short time ago microprocessors reportedly cost about £10 each to produce, more recently £5, and now, it seems, can be produced for under 50p. Until recently, if the microprocessor was to be converted to a microcomputer accepting input, having storage, producing output and (critically) having intelligence to modify its execution in response to different inputs, the manufacturer had to add external storage and input/output circuits. Now all these functions can be incorporated in the same chip. The rapid progress in miniaturization continues, and not only brings compactness, but cheapness, higher capacity and quicker processing. With the advent of bubble memory, where more than two million words can be stored on a single square inch, the horizons of microcomputing are staggeringly wide. Yet, as in previous phases of computing, the development of software is probably a constraint.

The heritage of microcomputing lies in electronics and electrical engineering per se, where engineers have used the complex assembler languages and machine codes available with microprocessors to achieve their engineering tasks of control. Commercial microcomputing now either has to relearn these basic software skills or develop higher-level programming compilers and applications software in order to realize the full potential of the new hardware. Thus software is likely to represent the major cost in extending microcomputing into commercial applications.

With this software lag in mind, several options are available to the commercial computing entrepreneur. He can develop machine code programs, where the application benefits justify the time and cost, which probably implies multiple sales or implementations of the product. He can write software in a higher-level language and then, using a mainframe computer, compile it into micro-machine code. He can employ a software house to develop his program – a growing field, but one where software skills are in short supply. Finally, he can wait until microcomputer high-level languages are available – and they may not be very far away.

One software house, CAP, is developing a language called MICROCOBOL and promises to demonstrate it very shortly. Intel, a major microcomputer manufacturer, has PL/M, a micro-answer to the general purpose language PL/1. The National Research Development Corporation is funding microsoftware with £2m, and the National Computing Centre has made available £175,000 for the development of application microprograms. With the eventual availability of operating software, utility programs and applications software for microcomputers – all of which could be programmed as hardware into the microprocessor itself – the commercial as well as engineering and scientific applications of microcomputing will explode.

The microprocessor enables a limited task to be carried out very quickly, accurately and cheaply. It is already being employed in many industries and services. Examples include process control, telephone switching systems, office products, digital watches and calculators, vending machines, robot-controlled production, controls in consumer durables, instrumentation and computer peripherals. As microcomputing becomes feasible in its fuller sense, what will follow? The indications exist now, as word processing, stock control packages, financial modelling and do-it-yourself home computing become available on a miniaturized basis. Basically microcomputers are likely to extend the trends set by minicomputers, and to make worthwhile many applications that to date have not been viable. The potential probably lies in either special-purpose applications, from controller functions at one extreme to small business systems at the other; or in replacing minicomputers and smaller mainframes, either as stand-alone machines in the office, on the shopfloor or at home; or as components of computing networks.

The trend towards distributed computing was in progress before the micros arrived. Devolving computing to local sites, using intelligent terminals and minicomputers, appealed as the costs of data communication, and its unreliability, increased. Additional advantages of flexibility, local data responsibility, simpler and quicker systems development and control of data processing by the user are becoming apparent. Microcomputers seem likely to reinforce the trend for reasons of cost and availability and, perhaps most important of all, because users can get their hands on computers once again.

Similarly, word processing has been growing in recent years, but seems likely to be boosted by microprocessing. A £5000 word processor can replace a typist. By reducing the typing task to high-speed input of raw text, with added facilities of layout design and error correction, typing productivity, it has been estimated, can be raised by 200 per cent. As microprocessors are harnessed into office functions, telecommunication, mailing, filing and retrieval and sundry other clerical tasks will be automated.

Commercial data processing and information processing are also about to be hit. Computing entrepreneurs are already developing, or have developed, interactive scheduling and stock control micro-based systems for the individual production manager. The headmaster will be able to buy a microcomputer complete with a timetabling system. The accountant can have his own modelling system on his own desk-top computer, using his own data. The schoolteacher will be able to run an educational computerized game from his table-top. Then, there is home computing. Computing has become a major hobby in the United States, where a do-it-yourself computer as powerful as the computers only the large firms possessed twelve years ago is being offered for £500. Soon a do-it-yourself computer will apparently be available for less than £150.

These are the existing applications and developments. Newspaper headlines talk of microcomputers to cook the breakfast, run the bath and do the household budget. Less frivolously, the potential for medical science should be welcome, but the upgrading of the so-called production robots perhaps less so. In the past, however, most computing forecasts have been wrong. They have predicted applications which fail to appear, and have ignored others which became commonplace. In particular, the predicted timescales go awry. Yet, suddenly, the bounds seem almost unlimited. In particular, if you have an idea for computerization, the constraints are being blown away. But where will it all lead?

For example, what effect will microprocessors have on employment – create or remove jobs, enrich or dehumanize work? Will microcomputers improve management information or add to the overload? Will the new technology radically reshape organizations or be absorbed into conventional use? Will society become technocratic or barely alter? Indeed, do microcomputers pose a major technological question which society has as yet no mechanism for answering?

In the debate so far, most noise has arisen over the possible impact on employment. More particularly, as exemplified by the Earth Resources Research report, *The "Chips" Are Down*, the focus has been on *unemployment*. With over 1.4 million unemployed, and forecasts of perhaps five million people jobless by 1990, concern about automation is hardly surprising. However, there is another side to the picture; unprecedented economic growth rates are apparently required to restore unemployment to former notions of tolerable levels; might not the arrival of a new technology conversely produce the new wealth that is so badly needed?

Opposing scenarios are postulated. The pessimists suggest that the micro-automation of manufacturing industry, and of some services, must remove untold jobs in the next few years. The optimists argue that microprocessors will create a vast range of new products, new services, and therefore new jobs. Others say that, willy-nilly, we have no option but to exploit microcomputers and endure the employment conse-quences. They argue that market competition will force industry into micro-automation; to reject or retard the new technology might create worse unemployment as markets and output decline. The decline of the traditional Swiss watch industry in the face of electronic competition is an already extant example. Nothing could have saved the mechanical watch: but its makers could have reacted far earlier.

Technologists have been heard to argue another position still. They suggest that advanced economies can regain former markets lost to the developing world by "sophisticating" products using superior technical expertise. Meanwhile, economic and social historians have pointed out that previous periods of automation have been absorbed without either economic or social turbulence. With a sense of *déjà-vu,* they hear cries of wolf; after all, employment is fifty per cent greater than twenty-five years ago. They can quote previous technical advances which in the long run have created more jobs than they destroyed. However, the rate of change occurring in microelectronics may well cause short-term havoc en route to longer-term employment growth, even though it is true that social processes of rejection, restriction and retardation have smoothed out discontinuities in the past.

Then, irrespective of employment levels, will microcomputers alter the nature of work? In one corner are heard arguments that the new automation will displace tedious, boring, dirty or unsafe jobs. In their place will be created challenging, white-collar, service or new-status jobs. Leisure will increase, the working week be reduced and retirement come earlier. In the opposite corner are those who have visions of de-skilled jobs, dehumanized workplaces and disoriented social be-haviour. And if either trend develops, there are other people who query if we will be prepared. ... Thus far, the arguments are abstract; polemics without substance. What figures and analysis are available?

Research by ASTMS (a highly interested party, as a major white-collar union) into the impact of microprocessors has predicted that 200,000 heavy engineering workers out of a present total of 475,000 will be out of work by 1995. It forecasts losses of 371,000 jobs in vehicle manufac-ture, 354,000 in textiles and 500,000 in banking and insurance. At the same time, individual firms are doing their own analysis. In a recent seminar on the subject, one major company reported the belief that 4000 of its jobs would be displaced. Another equally well-known company had apparently reached the same conclusion. The premises of their studies are not known. In contrast, one North American firm believes that just as many jobs will be created by microprocessors as will be displaced. Can we therefore speculate in general on microcomputer cause and employment effect?

The obvious applications of microprocessors, such as process control and production or machine control, seem likely to displace craftsman, assembly and engineering skills. The substitution of electronic for electromechanical functions will reduce work content. Automated testing, inspection and quality control will probably reduce the numbers of "indirect" production personnel. Manufacturing employment thus seems likely to suffer, unless new products and markets are created in compensation (some will evidently be created in the firms supplying the new equipment).

Consider the impact of word processing on the office. It seems plausible that clerical, secretarial and communication jobs will be reduced, with obvious impact on female employment. Nor are the blue-collar services insulated. Replacement of mechanical and electromechanical parts by electronic devices will probably make machines, cars, consumer durables and the like more reliable, longer-lasting and replaceable rather than reparable. How will this affect maintenance trades? (The saving grace here, of course, may be that labour in these trades is in chronically short supply.)

It does not seem at all likely that jobs may be displaced quicker than jobs are created. Yet still the impact on employment is uncertain. Forecasts are made, but there are few reported cases of major unemployment, intended or actual, to date. Furthermore, history does suggest that the lags of social and economic acceptance of automation are underestimated. Indeed, technological innovation is often oversold but it turns out that further technological advance is required before the miracles or threats materialize. Nevertheless, this time there are disturbing indicators.

First, so-called technology transfer – encouraging transfer processes of technical change – is a current fad, and perhaps a current fact. One major industrial conglomerate recently called a management conference to coordinate microprocessor technology in its diverse companies. Other firms have set up microcomputer committees, project teams and task forces. The Department of Industry is encouraging industry's use of microprocessors in both its products and production processes. If microelectronics is the key to industrial growth, this is commendable:

but is the same emphasis being placed on examining and preparing for the possible social consequences?

Second, there is some evidence that employers regard reduction of employment as a wholly desirable goal. "Labour has almost become a fixed cost and thus must not be taken on or redeployed lightly" is a common, and, of course, paradoxical, statement. A senior manager recently talked of 1000 employees representing 1000 headaches. A design engineer claimed that his role for the last few years had been "to design work out of products". If new industries rise to provide employment, these undercurrents are not so serious, but the question is whether they influence the thinking of all employers, both current and potential, to make automation still more seductive.

Third, microcomputing brings computerization to the small firm or unit. As politicians increasingly look to the small company sector to retrieve the unemployment situation, there is a strong possibility that microcomputing will provide efficiency increases which preclude job growth. Indeed, it has been suggested that even the small outposts of the Civil Service will now become computer-based. Finally, there is perhaps one important aspect that distinguishes microcomputing from previous automations. It can be almost "invisible" in its introduction and consequence. The departmental manager can acquire a microcomputer through his maintenance budget without questions being asked. Office automation is not inhibited by the same life-cycles and capital investment appraisal procedures as shop-floor automation. The design engineers can design microprocessors into products before the service employment consequences are apparent. In other words, the conventional social processes of retardation may be "spiked" before they begin – either by accident or design.

One field where no inhibitions should apply (at least in theory) is management itself. The impact of computers on organizational design and behaviour has fascinated management, computer scientists and researchers for some time. In earlier days of computing some quite spectacular claims and predictions were made; organization structures would change shape, many managerial tasks would be automated and organizational cultures would become faceless. Experience has mellowed such thoughts, and yet the relationship between computing and organization is of interest on several fronts, and microcomputing may prove to be a significant influence.

The new technology, combined with an uncertain environment, may indeed accelerate devolutionary trends. Organizational theory has long suggested that organizations combat uncertainty by at least three means. First, they employ slack resources, such as increased stocks, to absorb the uncertainty. Microcomputers could become slack resources used by local departments for irregular or less routine tasks. Second, organizations "differentiate", creating specialist functions to cope with particular or distinctive problems. Microcomputers may be employed on specialist tasks; indeed, this may be their major commercial application. Third, organizations develop their information systems especially along functional lines. Again microcomputers may be harnessed into this activity.

So microcomputing may be an aid to decentralization where the need arises. This does not necessarily mean that the larger, central or mainframe computer will die. Many data-processing tasks will still be more viable on a centralized basis. Furthermore, any increase in devolved information processing will doubtless create a need for coordinated information systems to follow. Finally, organizations may well establish networks, either within themselves, or between organizations, as a mix of central and local information processing becomes possible. Thus, while information processing and organization design are interdependent, one need not *determine* the other. A mix is possible; but the new technology also allows new organization forms to take shape. However, the issue is not quite so simple. There are the more unpredictable questions of values and power.

Distribution of information processing in turn distributes information. Information is a source of power, and thus the present power structures, tightly delineated in hierarchical organizations or concentrated in centralized structures, may be threatened. Will current management react against distributed computing to protect power balances, to preserve stability, to preserve the status quo or to avoid possible costly reversals in policy? An extreme example of this potential conflict is the group DP manager who is not sure that he welcomes his budget, influence and status being trimmed by distribution. Already people are heard to say that "distributed computing will come as and when it is necessary and without altering our present organizational structure."

When only unintelligent computer terminals were available locally, the data, the files and the data-base were centralized. Now with distributed intelligence, local data and files can be stored, maintained and created. *Alternative* information becomes possible. It always was, but perhaps not with such potency. Redistribution of managerial power is not totally impossible. Indeed, managerial prerogative may be challenged in due course. Information processing on the office and shop floor could lead to quite different notions of alternative information. Cases have been reported of managers using their own computer-based models to challenge their superiors or peers. Wider challenge becomes feasible.

Microcomputers could thus fit the trends of industrial organizations.

Their introduction could provide valuable opportunities for employee participation. Standing in the way of participative approaches to micro-computing are values. Technology can be said to be neutral, yet it can be biased, cruel or unforgiving in impact. The computer professionals themselves are not necessarily neutral in this debate. There is research evidence to show that their human understanding as expressed in computer system design is lacking. Microprocessor-mad engineers could be similar. It often seems that DP specialists, in their desire to develop and apply the latest technology, are unconcerned about mana-gerial relevance or behavioural factors. Already the professionals are raising doubts about microcomputing, often for valid reasons, but sometimes, one suspects, out of fear. Thus, even in the apparently unemotional area of management information, anxiety and controversy arise.

The uncomfortable question keeps on reappearing – will society be altered for the better? Technologists, sociologists, journalists and others have begun to sound alarm bells. In reality, most even of the alarmists do not wish to halt technological advance; they are not natural Luddites. However, in the Western world at least, a point may have been reached where people prefer to have faith in a new technology, before becoming committed to it. They want the medical scanner, but not thalidomide. Equally, before accepting a new technology, they would like to ensure choice, for example, in routing Concorde, and would wish to ensure care in application – for instance, avoiding the horrors of indiscriminate DDT spraying.

Microcomputing probably contains no *inherent* terrors. Rather the concern is about choice and care, particularly because of two worrisome factors. First, there is the rapid rate of technological change, so rapid that people might prefer to slow it down. Yet the second factor – microcomputing's "invisibility", the explosion of use in untold areas by unknown hands – may prevent any such dampening. The decision to employ microcomputers is not one decision, but the amalgam of many independent decisions by different groups using the new technology. Thus it seems that the world cannot stop microcomputing; its advance is inevitable. All that can be done is to ensure that microcomputing is acceptable, by preserving choice and exercising care. This really means both planning and controlling technology. With microcomputers, a prerequisite may be research, education and debate.

If employment changes, then so does society. Then, if organizations change shape, adopt new control philosophies and redistribute preroga-tives, society is further influenced. With more available information processing and better communication, political processes may alter. New forms of influence become possible, as pressure groups grow more potent and alternatives can be analysed more thoroughly – or perhaps instant referenda through miniaturized home terminals become possible. Or, in contrast, perhaps new constraints on information access and processing will be brought in. Indeed, data privacy, already a sensitive issue, would become more crucial as non-authorized parties can exploit new and cheap technology. At a more mundane level, consumers could become bombarded and pressurized in the home by more "advanced" forms of viewdata. In all these matters, there is choice, but choices can easily be brushed aside both by the pace of technology and by apathy.

For example, the exercise of choice and care, because of the invisibility or pervasiveness of microcomputers, will often rest on individuals or small groups. Thus the need for "computer literacy" in society is a priority. Currently the computer is still a mystery to many people. The fear or antipathy which can result may drive out the curiosity, invention and support needed to exploit microcomputing's full potential. Conversely fear, ignorance and computing could lead to minimum choice and care being applied. Perhaps the simplicity of microcomputers will remove much of the mystique which surrounds computing. Yet because the young, the confident, the skilled and the more intelligent populace may be better equipped to "survive" or exploit microcomputing, a dangerous generation gap, or knowledge, could result.

Microcomputing could pose, not for the first time, an important political question. Can democracy tackle technological challenges, or are technocratic or meritocratic forms of government more appropriate? Perhaps this in part explains why members of both the government and opposition have suddenly entered the microcomputing debate. Like most of us (presumably), they have no wish to abrogate major social and economic responsibilities to the technocrats, yet desperately need their contribution. Furthermore, the potential impact of microcomputing – on employment, information, organization and society – raises questions of values, equity and power. In short, it is a political matter.

However, the politicians may get in the way. It is not unusual for inadequate policies to be formulated through lack of understanding. It seems to be quite usual for legislation to be introduced in a panic only to achieve the opposite of what is intended. Equally, when action is needed, there is frequently no urgency – the government's handling of computer privacy is a case in point. The threats posed by computers to privacy of personal information were obvious in the 1960s. It was 1975 before a White Paper was published promising a data protection authority. Final recommendations, never mind the legislation, are still awaited.

Perhaps this time, politicians are responding in a more timely manner, as evidenced by their speeches, their party committees and the

Think Tank study. It is not clear, however, that they are employing the different streams of advice – economic, social and technical – which are required. A Royal Commission is an obvious mechanism, although people point out that it could take too long, could be given inappropriate terms of reference and could be inadequately populated. On the other hand, a Royal Commission is flexible. If it were given a sufficiently open remit, were asked to report quickly, were composed of multi-disciplinary members and given adequate research facilities, it could at least identify key issues, suggest any immediate policies required, and influence and shape a continuing debate.

Another prerequisite for planning and control of technology is education. H. G. Wells stated that "human history becomes more and more a race between education and catastrophe." If only a few of the predicted impacts of microcomputing actually materialize, smooth absorption by society will require education and learning. For example, in the field of employment, if new skills, new careers and new work ethics are required, then training, retraining and post-experience education are essential. Education is needed to maintain the people's common sense and their opportunity and ability to make judgements about how their lives should be run. Finally, just as users of technology must learn something about technology, so the providers must develop their social skills and understanding. Governments have a responsibility to understand and influence the consequences of new technologies; so have the technologists.

In an attempt to modify the "inevitability" and "determinism" of technology, commentators, politicians, pressure groups and the media are prone to indulge in sensationalism, unreasoned argument, rhetoric, and ill-judged action. So far the public dialogue on microcomputing has been more promising. Even the managing director of a major computer entity – Eddie Nixon of IBM (UK) – has called for public debate on the effect of the new technologies.

For all that, the ultimate impact of microcomputing may in years to come turn out to be minor. In the meantime, however, some discomfort and disturbance seem quite likely, and it is the duty of society's leaders to smooth the passage. Microcomputing can be used as an opportunity to learn how to plan and control technology, how to preserve choice and exercise care. Research is required to analyse what happens. Education is required to protect and involve all members of society. Debate is required to ensure that all threads of the problem – economic, technical and social – are explained. Will microcomputing bring revolution or evolution? Most people prefer evolution, but if evolution is too rapid it is tantamount to revolution. In the end, it depends not on "them", but on us – the impact on society will be what society chooses.

Unemployment and Technology: A Trade Union View

Barry Sherman

The author, who is Director of Research with the major British white-collar union, the Association of Scientific, Technical and Managerial Staffs, has been particularly outspoken on the subject of microelectronic technology. In this paper, delivered to a London conference in November 1978, he examines the relationship between unemployment and technology and predicts that the way things are going, "anyone over fifty years is unlikely ever to work again." The trade union attitude to the new technology will be largely determined, he says, by the government response to it, set against this background of rising unemployment. Trade unions will defend jobs even to the extent of opposing the new technology if the wider social changes they desire are not forthcoming.

Technological displacement of jobs has occurred and still occurs – to argue otherwise would be silly, given the almost total absence of wagon wheel trimmers and quill pen repairers. It has been argued that in Keynesian terms technological redundancies are unnecessary; public spending can create jobs and fill the vacuum as it were, but although this may be theoretically true it does cover a multitude of political difficulties. If the forecasts of growing unemployment due to the take-up of new technologies, especially those including microprocessors, are correct, then the problem itself becomes essentially political in both party and philosophical terms.

We are now undergoing a quantum leap in technology. The microprocessor, silicon chip, solid-state electronics, integrated circuitry or semiconductor technology (it trades under all these names) is the spearhead. It is, however, not the only example. Nuclear energy, molecular biology, genetic engineering and charge-coupled devices are all starting to bear the fruits of their development and these too will have impacts on work and society. The silicon chip is nevertheless the main problem, not for what it is, but what it can be used for. It should not be looked upon mainly as a computer – the uses can be far wider. Indeed it is difficult to think of many industrial processes, either batch or continuous track, commercial processes or clerical and administrative processes, that will not be affected. All jobs with repetitive elements or which are totally repetitive and where individual discretion is at a minimum are at risk to either massive job changes or job loss.

This effect of the silicon chip is not new. Since the 1939–45 war the world economy, including the UK's, has evolved in two distinct phases. The 1940s, 1950s and early 1960s were a period of almost unparalleled boom; growth rates were high, real incomes rose, and in retrospect there were consequent social changes. Granted that in this period there were short upturns and downturns, but the general effect was of a steady two decades of upturn. The first was postwar reconstruction allied to Marshall Plan funding which allowed for high investment without the painful process of internally accumulating the necessary capital. The second was the range of new products for new markets, products which had to some extent been researched and developed in the war years, and these were marketed widely because the normal inequitable income distribution was alleviated because of outside capital assistance.

The postwar engines of growth, the car and lorry industry, petro-chemicals, electronics, consumer durables, artificial fibres and plastics and synthetic materials all exhibited very high growth, for some periods as high as fifteen to twenty per cent per annum. This "You have never had it so good" period was seen as the final taming of the system. From 1965/6 onwards, however, growth rates started to slow. By the early 1970s the postwar dynamic industries were growing at around five to six per cent per year and investment was falling; it is important to realize that these symptoms were more or less worldwide, not only in the UK. It is even more important to recognize that this slowdown was well in evidence prior to the 1973 oil price rise; this has *reinforced but not caused* the current position. The result is that unemployment in the UK is over 1.6 million and in the EEC over six million, both sets of figures referring to registered unemployment only, an almost certain under-statement.

In the UK registered unemployment is generally acknowledged to understate the real position by at least 600,000, mainly because some women do not register as unemployed. The OECD when adjusting national unemployment data for international comparison purposes agrees with this proposition. The OECD *Economic Outlook* for July 1978 shows the first quarter unemployment rate in the UK as 5.8 per cent as against 6.6 per cent adjusted, and this is the lowest *gap* over the past twenty-four months. It is clear, though impossible to prove, that much of this unemployment springs from an internationally wide lack of effective demand, a lack often deliberately induced by government policies, notably in France, the UK and the USA. However, where short-term, demand-deficient and induced unemployment finishes and structural unemployment starts is not clear. For example, much of the UK unemployment in the shipbuilding industry can be put down to a global lack of demand for new ships, but if this miraculously reversed itself would employment rise in Britain? The answer, although unknown, is probably that in the absence of preferential ordering the Japanese and South Korean yards, both very capital intensive and automated, would take the lion's share of a renewed market – in other words it is probably structural unemployment.

The UK itself has employment problems both qualitatively and quantitatively different from those of its competitors. Since 1945, indeed earlier, the balance of payments has been the major concern of government policy. In order to maintain its balance we have had nineteen different incomes policies, a steady series of reductions in demand and both dramatic and slower devaluations. Each downturn in the cycle depressed output and choked off investment intentions. When the upturn came we were less able to respond – imports were dragged in, the consequent downturn was thus sooner and more severe than the previous one and so the UK drifted into its familiar vicious circle of decline. Policies have been short-term, management reaction has been short-term and trade union pressure has been short-term at precisely the time when medium-long-term planning and actions were needed. Entire industries have all but disappeared, others have greatly diminished in size, output and market shares. Productivity is low, basically reflecting the lack of investment in new processes and capital equipment. This all means that import penetration is at such a high level that increases in the growth rate to three per cent per annum could not be sustained for more than twelve months before the balance of payments again became a major constraint.

Both the Cambridge Economic Policy Group and the University of Sussex have produced forecasts for unemployment, on present policies, of around five million by the turn of the century. The Sussex study assumes low growth rates allied to the growth in the labour force; the CEPG study goes somewhat further in that it suggests that high growth is not sustainable in the absence of import controls. Thus in the absence of growth, unemployment is predicted to rise. But what happens if we do grow? What happens if services, goods and processes suddenly become competitive on an international basis? The only way that it seems likely that this could possibly happen is to adopt and totally embrace the entire range of microprocessor technology, not necessarily just on the manufacturing side but on the applications side.

It is clear that at present Japan, South Korea and to a lesser extent the USA and Germany are using this technology and that in a world system where the notion, if not the practice, of free trade is sacrosanct, other countries will have to follow. They will have to do so for two reasons. The first is that by and large the productive processes based on either robotics or other microprocessor applications are cheaper, more reliable and can be worked more intensively and thus while price can be held down quality can be enhanced. The second reason is that the microprocessors are being incorporated into the product itself. At present this is mainly in the electronic and electromechanical products themselves but within twelve months the US and Japanese car industries will be heavy users. This in turn will add reliability, reduce price and add durability to products and to compete the UK will have to use this technology. It must be clear that partial or temporary import constraints are not sufficient to deal with this. Either a full and permanent closed economy is maintained (à la Comecon allowing for certain exceptions) or trade is accepted.

However you look at it, jobs will go. Clearly the more automated a production line or the more efficiently it is run the fewer the people needed to man it. However, the more important job impact is on the component side. Reduce the number of components and you reduce the number of people needed to manufacture them, store them, move them, assemble them, install them and service them. Given that in the UK less than ten per cent of employees are now directly working on a productive process, it is clear that this factor, acting as it does on indirect production workers, is the major one.

Until microprocessor technology the cost of automating or sub-automating production lines constrained the speed of high technology to large processes. One major feature of the new technology is its relative cheapness and it can now be applied on a cost-effective basis to medium- and *small-scale* line and batch processes. The job impact is thus moving down the scale and thus potentially affecting more people. An example of its potential is manifestly clear in colour TV manufacture and assembly. In Japan the number of integrated circuits has doubled, the number of transistors halved and there has been an eighty per cent reduction in the number of other components. In all the Top Seven manufacturers *cut* their labour force by almost 100 per cent from 1972 to 1976 while increasing the output of sets by twenty-five per cent and improving their reliability and quality and reducing the need for servicing and running costs. In the UK Thorn Electrical Industries have just had to do the same thing or go out of this business altogether (in the absence of import restrictions).

The advent of the microprocessor has variously been described as heralding the second, or third, industrial revolution or, more accurately, the information revolution. Its effect on telecommunications is, at the primitive levels of System X, well documented as regards the system itself and the manufacture of the new equipment. It is however only a start. The ability of this type of system to link into a full information system using mini- and microcomputers and their data-bases, electronic typewriters and filing and the large commercial data bases, is almost limitless. These changes are now starting in the USA and to some extent in the United Kingdom, Germany and France. Siemens, the giant German firm, have, in an internal report, suggested that in West Germany forty per cent of clerical jobs will disappear within ten years – two million in all. Word processors, with and without visual displays, are now being used by the larger UK-based companies, viz. Unilever and Shell, and developments by IBM on internal company communications systems have reached the commercial exploitation stage.

Microprocessor technology thus has the ability to displace labour in the manufacturing and process sectors and the clerical and administrative sectors. However it does have other displacement functions, most of which apply to repetitive jobs or jobs with major repetitive contents. Certain services, notably the retail trade, and concomitantly, stock control and warehousing, are very much at risk and although the UK is unlikely to go as far as the US in developing totally automated supermarkets (for social reasons), developments by Tesco and other chains are clearly moving in this direction. Banks, insurance companies and other financial institutions are also stacked full of employees doing rote tasks, many of whom are replaceable even *without* the move to electronic banking or insurance provisions. One area of jobs at risk not previously considered is the managerial sector. Both as regards rote jobs which many managers perform and because if the production process is truncated the need for managers is lessened, there will be a reduction in the number of managerial jobs.

Over the past thirty years there has been a marked shift in the employment patterns in the United Kingdom. As Bacon and Eltis* have demonstrated, the decrease in the number of workers in the manufacturing sector is balanced by the increase in the numbers in the public and private sector services – *yet it is precisely in this area that jobs will disappear.* This will all occur against a background of a labour force that

---

* Robert Bacon and Walter Eltis, *Britain's Economic Problem: Too Few Producers* (Macmillan, London, 1976).

is projected to increase by 1.5 million in 1985, at which point it levels off.

A Department of Industry survey into the intentions of manufacturers in the UK showed that fifty per cent of those surveyed had no intention of using the new technology in the foreseeable future. This would accord with an internal ASTMS survey where all groups have approached management on the same question. As an indicator of the lack of awareness and imagination of British senior and middle management it could hardly be bettered, but it foreshadows an impending disaster.

There are only three major alternatives, and I would argue only really two possible alternatives in the short-middle-term run. We can ignore the technology, fulfil the Cambridge/Sussex predictions and have mass unemployment coupled with low growth, low productivity and low wages. Alternatively we can embrace the technology, have mass unemployment coupled with high growth, high wages, high profits and very high productivity. The third alternative is far more radical and is to change the entire pattern of society's expectations, both political and material, and this would almost certainly involve not only changes in ownership and control but either a permanently closed economy or having other nation states follow the same political route.

There is of course no reason for there to be an inevitable rise in unemployment even given the second of the options. There is clearly unmet demand for goods and services both in the UK and the world in general, and whilst this might argue for a change in income distribution for it to be met, it is feasible. Equally there is a mass of unfulfilled need within the UK. Health services, education, social services and public transport and a rethink on housing are all capable of almost infinite resources being applied. Whilst it is fanciful to suppose that retraining of those displaced will be possible (even if the money were made available) it needs to start now.

Work in itself appears to have an intrinsic value in the UK and many of our competitor countries. Whether this work ethic is a natural state of the human race is open to doubt – usefulness yes, work perhaps no. People have a schizophrenic approach to work: it is disliked and more importantly, the actual act of preparing for and travelling to work is heartily disliked; yet at the same time people believe that they need to work. In a situation where less work will be available this dichotomy will have to be resolved. Clearly the amount of work that people do can be reduced, preferably by reducing the number of trips to work rather than the number of hours in the same number of days, although care will have to be taken to ensure that antisocial shift patterns etc, do not emerge as a side effect.

It would, however, seem strange to run a society in which work that perhaps did not need to be done was forced upon people when patently there are so many unfulfilled needs and demands. In this respect while a shorter working week can be seen as a desirable aim in itself it should not be seen as a panacea for unemployment problems – it is a second-best solution.

There is one further factor. Although from the point of view of society the new technologies, especially microprocessors, open up a vision of increased leisure with the same or even greater levels of goods and services, such a vision will not automatically manifest itself. Indeed, if British economic policy were to remain unchanged profits would rise, overseas investment would rise and unemployment would rise. To enable the distribution of the fruits of these new technologies there will have to be a series of positive interventionist policies – the market if left to itself will only exacerbate social problems rather than alleviate them. However, the new technologies have to be used and there are two reasons why this will come late to Britain. The first reason is that British management, with some notable, but rare, exceptions have not yet realized the potential of microprocessors and this has been confirmed by a Department of Industry survey. The second reason is more fundamental and has to do with trade union responses.

Despite the fact that most unions realize the possible benefits from the introduction of the new technologies in the macroeconomic sense, each redundancy will come at the level of the enterprise concerned. No union, however persuaded they may be as to the ultimate final desirability, can allow the sacrifice of its members in the present situation. Anyone over fifty is unlikely ever to work again, especially in the north of England. In order not to resist redundancies, unions must not only be persuaded that the long-term future is secure but that in the short term their members will be disadvantaged as little as possible. This will involve a change of attitudes to unemployment benefits, to education, to retraining and to the social view of unemployment. Without these changes, and they must be government-inspired, the trade union movement will be forced into the position of resistance.

A Trade Union Strategy for the New Technology

APEX

The following statement comes from a pamphlet issued in March, 1979 by the British office workers union, the Association of Professional, Executive, Clerical and Computer Staff. Called Office Technology: The Trade Union Response, *the pamphlet gives an excellent account of word processing and its effect on job content, design and skills, as well as the health hazards. Here,* APEX *outlines a trade union strategy in the light of likely job losses.*

The most important factor for trade unionists faced with new technology is its effects on the number of jobs available and therefore on the level of unemployment. The reason why most trade unionists view new technology with suspicion – even hostility – is concern not about technology itself, but about in whose hands the technology is used. Word processing can, we believe, make possible substantial improvements in productivity for office workers. Whether that improvement results in greater unemployment will depend on the attitudes of government, employers and trade unions. The central problem is a lack of knowledge about the options available and the problems, and ignorance always encourages fear. This chapter is designed to help to extend the knowledge, and hence the power, of trade unionists over the technology which is likely to affect them in the next five to ten years.

Economic background

There can be no doubt about the genuine concern which is felt, in the UK and elsewhere, about the current level of unemployment. A major feature of the UK labour market over the last decade has been a steady decline in the number of people employed in manufacturing industry, particularly in manual jobs, and a steady rise in employment in non-manual jobs in the service sectors. Between 1971 and 1976, employment in manufacturing fell by over 8 per cent, while in services it rose by 10 per cent. This trend has been accompanied by a change in the structure of the labour force, most notably by increasing numbers of women entering employment. This is demonstrated by the following table.

Table 7.1   Employment trends 1968–1978

All employees			
1968		1978	
Men	*Women*	*Men*	*Women*
14,080,000	8,480,000	13,058,000	9,149,000
Clerical employees			
Men	*Women*	*Men*	*Women*
1,126,400	2,552,500	979,400	3,083,200

Source: Department of Employment

The table shows that the number of men in employment fell by 7.3 per cent (clerical jobs 13.1 per cent); and the number of women rose by 7.9 per cent (20.8 per cent in clerical jobs) while total employment in the sectors covered fell by 353,000, and clerical jobs increased by 383,000.

Although unemployment amongst clerical workers has traditionally been lower than for unskilled manual workers, over the past few years the pattern has been changing. Between June 1975 and June 1978, unemployment among clerical and related workers grew by 68 per cent, among manual workers by 32 per cent, and among all workers by 33 per cent.

The impact of technology on office jobs over the next five to ten years is of particular economic and social importance for two major reasons:

Office jobs have been the main area of expansion during the "deindustrialization" of the last ten years. Any factor which even limited the capacity of office employment to continue expanding would have serious implications for unemployment if, as seems likely, there is a continuing loss of jobs in traditional areas of manufacturing industry.

Clerical and secretarial jobs are vital to women's employment. In 1977, 33.7 per cent of all working women were in secretarial and clerical jobs compared to 7.5 per cent of men. Any restriction in clerical employment in the future will therefore particularly affect women, who are frequently less well organized into trade unions and open to the false charge that they are working for "pin money".

Over 50 per cent of APEX's membership are women, and as a union we have consistently taken a lead in advancing the interests of women at work through campaigning for equal pay and against sex discrimination. We therefore feel it crucial to emphasize the danger that word processing could force many women to leave the labour market altogether. Women are usually considered a "soft option" for cutting jobs because they tend to be second income earners, and because they tend not to register as unemployed and so do not show up in the official figures. Such an option is however totally unacceptable. Around 30 per cent of working women with children are the sole household earner; married women with second incomes keep many families of low paid men out of poverty; and the freedom which employment opportunities give to women is fundamental to the achievement of full equality. Thus any tendency for office technology to turn back the clock on women's employment would be a profoundly disturbing social development.

The magnitude of the general unemployment problem is reinforced by the continuing increase in the numbers of *young people* coming on to the labour markets – another 800,000 by 1982, by which time advanced technology could be having a very profound effect on the economy. The Manpower Services Commission has calculated that even to reduce unemployment to one million by 1982 will require the creation of 1.2 million new jobs. But this "job gap" figure explicitly "takes no account of the fact that some jobs currently in existence may disappear by 1982; the jobs that do disappear will add to the job gap" (MSC Review and Plan 1978).

Job losses

The major reason advanced by employers and manufacturers for word processing is that it will improve productivity in the drafting, editing and processing of textual material. A number of employers who have already introduced word processing systems have cut total job numbers as a result while others have clearly set out plans to do so in the future. This raises a fundamental question for trade unions. Put simply, the question is: 'What should our attitude be to new technological developments which increase productivity?' On the one hand, productivity increases mean that the same output can be produced with fewer people, but on the other, a policy of opposition to productivity would still have us producing cloth on cottage industry spinning wheels. The argument for increasing productivity, on the factory floor and in the office, is that it provides the ability to produce more from the same resources and hence to expand the total production of the economy.

The following table shows the close historical relationship which exists between high rates of productivity growth and high rates of economic growth.

Table 7.2 Output and productivity growth

	1922–29		1929–37		1951–73	
	Prod.	Output	Prod.	Output	Prod.	Output
Japan	5.9	6.5	2.4	3.6	8.0	9.5
Sweden	3.3	3.9	1.9	2.3	n.a.	n.a.
United States	2.1	4.8	0.4	0.1	2.0	3.7
Canada	2.1	5.1	−0.9	−0.3	2.2	4.6
Denmark	2.1	3.6	1.1	2.0	3.3	4.2
Norway	3.1	3.9	2.0	2.5	3.9	4.2
France	5.8	5.8	−1.3	−2.1	4.8	5.0
Germany	6.0	5.7	2.1	2.8	4.7	5.7
Italy	2.2	2.3	1.6	1.9	4.6	5.1
United Kingdom	1.6	4.0	0.3	0.2	4.0	5.0
Netherlands	2.0	4.0	0.3	0.2	4.0	5.0

Source: TUC

A similar, although less striking, relationship exists between productivity growth and employment growth. For this reason, to adopt a policy of resisting technological change and the improved productivity which it makes possible, would be a recipe for general impoverishment, low growth and high unemployment. Improving the productive capacity of industry and the economy in general should be a major priority for all trade unionists since it is from the production of real goods and services that the ability to improve real wages and create new jobs comes.

It is not automatic, however, that improved productivity leads to higher living standards and more employment. How productivity relates to employment depends on labour supply, including hours of work, and on the overall performance of the economy, which is affected by many factors: world market growth; investment policies; energy resources; public expenditure policies, etc. It is difficult, if not impossible, to make accurate forecasts about these factors over the next few years. Yet without such forecasts, any assumptions about numbers of job losses from technology are bound to be wrong. This report does not therefore attempt authoritative estimates of the total level of unemployment likely to arise from developments in WP, but identifies a number of clearly discernible trends about the effects of WP on office jobs from which it is possible to extrapolate to office employment in general. A number of important 'case studies' have already been made and more are under way within APEX as well as by government departments, academics and other bodies.

The importance of the case studies is in relation to the likelihood of recent trends in the occupational distribution of employment being continued. One estimate recently made by Warwick University forecasts an increase in clerical and secretarial workers of less than 200,000 in the six years 1976 to 1982 compared with over 300,000 in the five years 1971 to 1976. The more general occupational trends which the study demonstrates are also of interest and are reproduced in Table 7.3.

Table 7.3   Occupational employment (selected occupations) (thousands)

	1971	1976	71–76 % change	1982 (forecast)	76–82 % change
Administrators and managers	939	1075	+14.5	1257	+16.9
Scientists, engineers	399	472	+18.3	543	+15.0
Technicians and draughtsmen	360	402	+11.7	480	+19.4
Clerical and secretarial	3481	3795	+ 9.0	3976	+ 4.8
Skilled manual trades: engineering	2389	2324	− 2.7	2365	+ 1.8
Skilled non transferable	2127	1791	−15.8	1646	− 8.1
All non-manual	10736	11822	+10.1	12620	+ 6.8
All manual	13540	12799	− 5.5	12557	− 1.9
Whole economy	24217	24824	+ 1.4	25175	+ 2.2

Source: Warwick University Manpower Research Group

It should be pointed out that the above estimates, which together with the MSC figures referred to earlier, imply a substantial increase in unemployment to around 2 million by 1982, do not take account of significant new developments in labour saving technology.

Information sources
The major reason for quoting case studies is that we believe that they are representative of office jobs in general. The most obvious way of obtaining estimates for the economy as a whole would be to "extrapolate" the effects from the case studies across all clerical and secretarial employment. Thus if we found a 20 per cent cut in labour on average in our case studies, we could assume that the overall effect would be to cut clerical jobs by 20 per cent. Such an approach would be wrong for a number of reasons:

"Static" analyses of the economy can be very misleading. Unless the less visible "dynamic" effects of the changes which we are discussing on new industries, processes and products and on occupations and skills, are considered, a very distorted picture of the UK economy will be obtained;

Improvements in productivity which are technically feasible from WP are not necessarily realized in practice because of organizational inefficiencies: an unwillingness to lose skilled labour; or the high cost of redundancy;

It is difficult to predict with any certainty the speed with which WP will be adopted in the UK. The present number of UK installed units is the equivalent of something like 2 per cent of that of the USA. Germany has around seven times as many WP terminals as the UK. Both the tendency of UK companies to hold back on investment generally, and their traditional lack of concern about the office will limit the impact of WP in the UK in the next few years;

Case studies, unlike laboratory experiments, cannot hold external factors constant. It is not impossible to draw definite conclusions about the effects of the introduction of WP on jobs in a particular case without being aware of other factors (e.g. demand) which might have also been affecting employment.

Evidence produced by members of our working party and by outside consultants suggests that a shared facility word processor, properly installed and utilized can, over a wide spread of applications, achieve productivity improvements on average of 100 per cent – that is to say each terminal permits twice as much to be done as could be done on a conventional electric typewriter. A more detailed assessment is that a "stand alone" WP can achieve productivity improvements of between 1.3 and 1.8 times a conventional typist's performance, and a shared facility machine between two and three times (per terminal).

It should be borne in mind that a good WP operator is not necessarily the best typist since speed is the essence rather than accuracy. As a result, direct comparisons of the same person are not always the best way of measuring changes. A further relevant point is that "productivity" in the office is not usefully defined as the volume of paper work per typist/clerk employed. The existence of a WP may make it possible to redraft a document five times rather than twice – but it is still one document. If increased productivity (in terms of key depressions) leads to more management time on checking drafts or rewriting them, the net use of resources could be worse than at the start. It is always possible that decreases in typing staff have been made up, unnoticed, elsewhere.

A number of important cases are cited below (where organizations are named the information is available from published sources):

Bradford Metropolitan Council
Shared logic system. Highly centralized. Workload estimated to have increased 19 per cent. Formerly 44 staff, now 22.

A Nationalised Industry Office (APEX source)
Staff reduced from 20 to 14.

Halifax Building Society
Workload trebled with existing staffing unchanged.

Civil Service (Pilot Project)
Shared logic system. Productivity improvements fluctuating between 20 per cent and 70 per cent of control group.

Large Pharmaceutical Company
Shared logic system. Productivity improvements of 127 per cent achieved.

A Large Management Consultants
Using varied equipment, measured an increase of 25 per cent in workload with a reduction in staff from 80 to 39.

In addition to these case studies, information is available on projects within Government where detailed estimates have been made of workload and future staffing requirements arising from the introduction of WP and other computerized technology. This overcomes the difficulty of compensating for other changes in labour demand, although it is subject to some uncertainty. One such case is set out below:

Table 7.4 A government department: projected staff 1979/80–1990/91

	Executive	Clerical	Typing	DP	Manager	Other	Total
1979/80	1193	2461	490	21	166	676	5007
1990/91 (manual)	1486	3393	662	28	226	950	6745
1990/1991 (computerized)	1458	2492	20	172	174	875	5191

Source: TUC Employment/Technology Group

Overseas studies on office employment have produced some disturbing predictions. A report by Siemens in Germany has suggested that by 1990 40 per cent of present office work could be carried out by automated equipment, producing perhaps two million unemployed clerks and typists. In France, a report on the financial sector suggests that a cut in office jobs of 30 per cent could be achieved in the next ten years. These reports tend to support the conclusions of a study undertaken for the Department of Industry last year which forecast a total displacement of labour in the UK of 16 per cent arising from microelectronic technology.

The effects on office jobs

It is very likely that, as a result of the increasing use of advanced office technology over the next five to ten years, there will be a very substantial increase in the productivity of office workers. This will be most immediate and noticeable for secretarial, typing and clerk/typist jobs. At present it is estimated that the capital stock per shop floor worker is about £5000 in the UK, whereas the investment available to back up the office worker is nearer £500. More resources will, in our view, be devoted in the future to office investment and to the analysis and redesign of office systems. The impact on the number of office jobs will depend on four factors: the technological capacity of WP and associated equipment and its effective installation and use; the extent to which it is assimilated throughout industry; the overall performance of the UK and world economy (including our competitors); and the extent to which the dynamism of the economy produces new jobs in new areas. It will also, of course, depend on the strength and effectiveness of trade unions.

Technology

There can be little doubt about the capabilities of the technology. The results from experiments may not always match those achieved in "ordinary" circumstances, but the ability of systems – particularly using advanced displays, high capacity storage media, and remote printing, combined with increasingly powerful logic – to replace typists at least on a one for one basis seems virtually indisputable.

Assimilation

The question of assimilation into offices is more difficult. There are around 1 million office typewriters in the UK of which only about 50 per cent are electric.In most sizeable organizations, however, IBM or similar golfball machines are generally in use – costing upwards of £700. Cost is a major factor in purchasing decisions, and the rapidly falling cost of WP systems, likely on most estimates to continue, will help to accelerate assimilation. The cost of systems has halved in the last two years and will probably do so again in the next two to three years. A major factor keeping UK prices up is the high cost of selling equipment due to low volume, and this itself will fall once high volume sales become common. Frequently cited in WP advertising is the comparison between the annual cost of a typist and the price of a WP machine. The gap, which is small already, is likely to close still further. A shared facility machine which replaces one typist will pay for itself in one to two years, or in less time in Central London where wages and associated employment costs are higher. Figure 7.1 gives a rough indication of this trend.

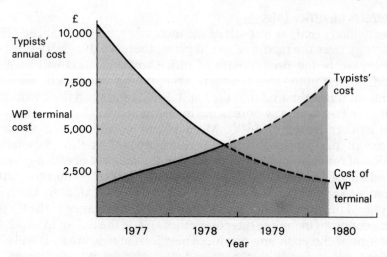

Fig. 7.1   Relative expense of typist and word processor terminal

A doubling of UK sales by 1982, forecast by some consultants, would still only result in a relatively small number of machines compared to the total office population. It will be necessary to make plans to cope with a much more rapid expansion in WP, if unions are not to be caught unawares. The pressure to expand WP may well be greater in the public sector than in the private, due to a combination of cost pressures arising from public spending constraints, increasing workload, and relatively easy internal spread of information. In the private sector, the most quickly affected firms will be small: solicitors, estate agents, and small manufacturing firms. In such areas, trade union organization is traditionally low and there will be little to prevent employers from taking the easy way out and using WP to reduce jobs.

The economy
There must be significant doubt whether the world economy will recover sufficiently in the next two to three years to take up the spare labour which automation will make available. One area which will need to be examined by industrialized governments is the position of the developing countries where there are massive unsatisfied demands to be met given sufficient purchasing power to meet them. On the home front, the possibility of expanding manufacturing employment must be fairly slim on any set of assumptions, and there will be a need for a continuing programme of expanded public expenditure on education, health and social services. The idea that Britain is a society in which all needs are satisfied and there remains nothing to be done must, after all, be a

hollow joke to those people in need of decent housing, medical care or simply living in poverty and deprivation.

New products and industries

Finally, there can be no doubt that new industries and products will expand in the next few years. Many can already be seen in the electronics sector. A constraint on effective growth in new sectors will, however, be the shortage of trained and skilled manpower. This is particularly true in the area of computer skills where there are at least 30,000 unfilled vacancies at present. The steady convergence of word processing, data processing and other technology will make more effects felt on DP staff: reducing the demands for data preparation staff; changing the skills required by programmers; and the jobs and status of operators. For the "dynamic" view of the economy to be effective in creating new jobs, sufficient attention and resources must be given to the question of training, retraining and labour mobility.

Manpower forecasts

The evidence in this chapter points to substantially reduced numbers of typing and secretarial jobs; of clerks; and of document and letter authors. To put figures on this is, as has already been pointed out, extremely difficult. There is no value in spreading "scare stories" about unemployment which have no foundation in fact. In offices where WP is properly implemented it can produce amongst typing and secretarial staff a productivity improvement of 100 per cent. If it is assumed that this effect will be halved when the impact on related groups of clerical and administrative staff is considered, then an assimilation into one-fifth of all UK offices by 1983 would mean, unless output increased to compensate, a fall in office jobs of a quarter of a million. Such a fall, viewed alongside the MSC "job gap" of 1.2 million referred to earlier, would be very serious indeed.

Conclusions

Unless adequate action is taken in conjunction with government and employers there is every likelihood of large scale unemployment amongst office workers over the next decade. This impact will vary with industry, occupation and the size of employer. Jobs could be at risk from the implementation of WP technology, but they may well be more at risk from a refusal to use it. Countries such as the USA, Germany and Japan are already well in advance of the UK in controlling their overhead costs using advanced technology, and this could continue. In many sectors, the increase in the availability of information for decision making which WP and minicomputers will make possible, will provide the possibility of expanding output and jobs.

WP provides the potential to substantially reduce the number of man hours required to do a given amount of work in the office. It could mean a better, more skilled, more satisfying, shorter and less arduous working life for the office worker. It need not lead to unemployment and indeed it should not. But in order to achieve the positive benefits of WP technology, a carefully defined strategy must be followed by APEX members, whenever necessary in cooperation with other trade unionists, and with the support and assistance of government. Employers will be the main target of this strategy but they should also bear in mind in their own interests, the futility of attempting to increase business and profits by throwing people out of work.

A trade union strategy for new technology

The major responsibility for ensuring that the effects of WP are not to raise unemployment must lie with local union negotiators. The working party therefore recommend a strategy to be followed by staff representatives and officials in coming to terms with proposals to introduce WP. (See Fig. 7.2.) Sometimes there will be difficulties in following this strategy through. It will be easiest where trade union organization is strong. As trade unionists, however, we have a substantial bargaining card with which to ensure that managements cooperate in achieving our objectives. If they do not, the equipment need not be operated by our members.

The strategy recommended by the working party has a number of elements and is set out in diagrammatic form.

What is planned?

The first step to be taken is to discover whether the employer has any moves towards automated office technology and in particular word processing in mind. If he has, the implications should be discussed in detail with the union representatives *at the earliest possible stage.* If no plans are in existence, APEX representatives should nevertheless insist on discussing the general economic situation facing the company. If it has not modernized and invested – both on the shop floor and in the office – there may well be a long term threat to job security from competitors at home and overseas who have. Representatives should not be reluctant to raise the question of increasing office investment themselves. If they do, of course, they have the initiative from the beginning and can more easily influence ensuing developments in the interests of the workforce.

What are the reasons?

If word processing etc, is under consideration, employers should be asked: what is the major reason for it? They may cite questions of

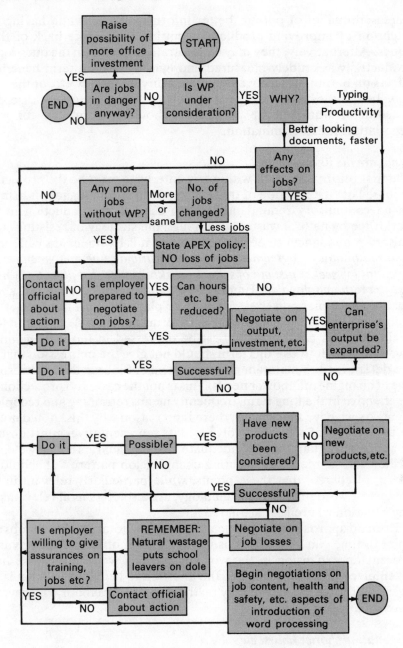

Fig. 7.2 Strategy for the introduction of word processing and other office automation

increased quality of output, better information etc, while having the intention of improving productivity/cutting jobs in the back of their minds. Alternatively, they may concentrate to excess on the question of productivity as crudely measured and ignore the long term beneficial effects on output of improvements in quality, reliability etc, or the cash flow benefits of such things as faster invoicing. In either case, the question of what effects are desired should be a matter for joint negotiation and determination.

What are the likely effects?

The first priority of APEX within any enterprise must be the protection of jobs. The first reaction of trade unionists in protecting jobs is to insist on no compulsory redundancy and to achieve any reduction in the workforce by natural wastage. Although the strategy of resisting compulsory redundancy is necessary however, it is by no means sufficient. *"No redundancy" agreements simply redistribute unemployment to the potential job seeker just out of school – making him or her potentially more and more unemployable.* Employers should therefore be asked about the long term manpower effects of their plans, not just in terms of the individuals currently employed, but in terms of the total number of jobs available. This can normally best be expressed in terms of manning levels, although to use this term should not give the impression that we are determined to maintain a particular mix of jobs and skills irrespective of changing manpower needs. This is not the case. Job protection, to be effective in the long term, frequently means retraining and redeployment. As we have made clear, there is no reason why this should not be to the benefit of all staff involved. Staff representatives must ensure, however, that guarantees of adequate training, guaranteed pay etc, are written into agreements covering changing job patterns. It should be noted, of course, that these points, while particularly relevant in the context of word processing technology, are also of general relevance to any situation where jobs are at risk.

Even an approach which concentrates on the total number of jobs at a point in time can be dangerous if the effect of office technology is to prevent an expansion in the workforce which would otherwise have taken place. In such situations, the question to be asked is: what is the overall effect of the technology on the demand for labour which would have occurred in its absence?

Negotiating shorter hours, etc

If the answers to any of these questions are less than satisfactory, APEX representatives will need to consider the correct strategy for expanding the total number of job opportunities made available by the enterprise.

High on the list of priorities in doing this should be efforts to make the distribution of work more equitable.

One area in which this should be done is to enforce the reduction of systematic overtime and insist on jobs being created to do the extra work. However, it should be remembered that some staff work overtime because their basic rates are inadequate to provide a satisfactory income. Where this is the case, basic rates will need to be raised so as to prevent financial hardship. More fundamental "worksharing" options will also need to be considered, including: reducing the standard working week without loss of pay (to the TUC target of 35 hours or the longer term APEX objective of 30 hours); increased annual holiday entitlement (to the minimum acceptable standard of 4 weeks if not already attained and further to 5 weeks or more); earlier retirement (voluntary and with full pension entitlement); and periods of paid educational leave or long service leave periodically throughout working life. Developments in many of these areas will only be possible as a part of the campaign by the wider trade union movement to reduce unemployment. In determining their collective bargaining priorities, however, negotiators will need more and more to give attention to measures such as these designed to expand job opportunities.

Bargaining on output
In conjunction with "worksharing" measures or, where they are difficult to achieve or inappropriate, the question of *output bargaining* should be raised. Productivity, which we are in favour of improving, is the ratio of output to employment. A common reaction of companies in the private sector is to treat output as fixed and concentrate on cutting labour, using any savings achieved to boost profits. This ignores the possibility of expanding total sales which is particularly important given the potential cost savings and price reductions which the introduction of WP could produce.

"Output bargaining" is simply a term which can be used to describe greater trade union involvement in the activities and policies of the enterprise. It involves discussions on investment levels and plans, product design, marketing etc, as well as on "manpower" issues. In all of these subjects the aim should be to get management to produce plans to expand output and increase jobs rather than maintain it and reduce jobs. Other terms for similar developments are "Industrial Democracy" or "Industrial Strategy", but what it is called is perhaps less important than whether it is achieved. Moves towards greater industrial democracy can be spurred very effectively by discussions which start from the basis of the solution of concrete problems such as those posed by new technology.

Negotiations at this level will normally involve at least two departures from the traditional procedures for bargaining. First, it is the enterprise (usually the company) which is the appropriate level for contact rather than the plant. This is so since decisions to expand or contract production of particular products are rarely taken at plant level by large conglomerate companies, a point which is even more obvious in the context of multinationals. Second, the involvement of all trade unions in the company – staff and manual – becomes absolutely essential. Discussions about jobs cannot be based on isolated occupational groups, and arguments about the overall company policy must be conducted by representatives of all unions affected. Since problems may exist with establishing a legislative basis for industrial democracy in the near future, the spur of planning for job expansion may be an important level in achieving progress in the shorter term.

Diversification
In some circumstances, market or other economic factors will limit the potential for expansion in existing product lines. In this case, management should be made to examine the scope for diversification into new activities. The argument that new products expand as existing ones decline is no consolation for someone made redundant by an existing company and ignored by any new ones. Employers should be made to shoulder more of the responsibility for retraining and training labour for new expanding product areas. Examples of such a policy abound overseas (the Fairchild Camera Co. in the USA is one of the foremost microprocessor manufacturers today and no camera has passed through it for many years). While a policy of diversification may involve high short term investment and low short term declared profits, it can be enormously to the benefit of the long term health of a company. The necessity is to make British management with its traditionally short time horizon realize this. Discussions on diversification involve all the industrial democracy implications discussed above.

Manpower policies
If the potential for job creation in all these areas is limited, negotiators may, as a last resort, need to consider how to handle a reduction in jobs. Here, as stressed earlier, the emphasis should be on the total number of jobs rather than on those in post at a particular time. Natural wastage should be regarded not as a solution to the problem, but as one of a number of alternative policy options which may be suitable. Natural wastage policies can be to the long term damage of other jobs within an enterprise or even to its ultimate destruction, if the result is to encourage the younger members of the workforce to leave. It can produce a

"bunching" effect as far as older workers are concerned and, eventually, a severe shortage of skilled and experienced staff when those older workers retire.

Employers should be pressed to give guarantees of training, incomes and jobs to those people genuinely surplus to its requirements. Decisions on planning and handling programmes to achieve this should be on a joint union-management basis. Employers should bear the financial responsibility for giving adequate and suitable retraining *while the worker remains on the company's books*. They should bear the responsibility for liaising with the Manpower Services Commission, local employers' associations and other employers to find new jobs appropriate to the skills and abilities of those displaced. This should all be done as early as possible as part of a long term and humane approach towards labour displacement. Changes in MSC training regulations to facilitate this should be considered by the government.

Redundancy provisions
During this period and in addition to it, employers should be made more financially responsible for the continuing employment of their employees. To aid this, some changes may be necessary in the Redundancy Payments Act, in addition to what is achievable through collective bargaining. The best approach to redundancy is one which concentrates on ensuring new jobs for those affected and putting disincentives on employers to stop them cutting jobs. The present system which can be best categorized as "lump sum and forget them" does not fully meet these objectives.

We believe that the government should consider allowing representatives of recognized trade unions to exercise an option at local level to replace service based lump sum redundancy payments by an earnings guarantee – to last as long as the worker is unemployed or is in a job at a lower wage than that which he/she has left. This should ideally be set at or near 100 per cent. of original earnings (subject to a modest deduction for employment costs and for tax) and should be uprated in line with average earnings. This would do much to solve two major problems which have been observed with the present redundancy payments scheme:

The people who benefit most from it are often the highly paid, highly skilled who can easily get other jobs. The payment is therefore not related to need but to service length and in many ways is socially unjust. . . .
Not only does the system provide little real incentive for employers to keep people on but there is also a strong element of "buying jobs". This can frequently be seen where voluntary redundancy is desired by large

numbers of workers who are more aware of the immediate prospect of a sizeable tax free sum than of the diminishing likelihood of future employment.

Some progress towards this state of affairs can be made now through collective bargaining, but in the longer term, government action will be needed to integrate the Redundancy Payments Scheme with individual arrangements in the manner proposed. The TUC should also take particular account of these points in its own general review of the redundancy payments system being undertaken as a result of motions to the 1978 Congress.

How to Fight the New Technology

Chris Harman

In contrast to the moderation of APEX, *the (British) Socialist Workers Party calls for all-out opposition to microelectronic technology. Union leaders who are prepared to accept job losses, says* SWP *spokesman Chris Harman, are "collaborators". Management should be given no assistance in boosting productivity and profitability when ownership remains in capitalist hands. In this excerpt from an* SWP *pamphlet,* New Technology and the Struggle for Socialism, *published early in 1979, the author provides rank-and-file activists with a step-by-step guide to blacking new technology.*

You might expect the union leaders to be much more worried about the new technology than the government. After all, it is the membership of their unions whose lives are going to be turned upside down. Unfortunately, however, it cannot be said that things are working out like that. We have already referred to the enthusiasm for the new technology displayed by Eric Hammond of the EETPU executive and by the APEX research department. These people are not alone in embracing measures which will destroy their members' jobs. The overall attitude of union officials is one of extreme complacency.

Even where there is some awareness of the problem, it is usually smothered by a general attitude which makes it impossible to deal with the causes of the problem. This was clearly shown in the debate on the new technology at the 1978 TUC. A motion was carried unanimously which was supposed to register concern at the threat to jobs. But there was not a mention of *action*, at the national or local level, to protect jobs. Instead, there was a vague and placid call for the government, "to declare publicly their concern at the prospect of the resulting unemploy-

391

Fig. 7.3 Who wins?

ment and support moves towards a shorter working week, month, year or lifetime, with no deterioration in living standards" and to "carry out as a high priority a comprehensive study of the employment and social consequences of advances in the new technology." At the same time, the TUC *supported* all the measures the government has carried out so far which are going to have the effect of *destroying* jobs: "Congress supports the NEB action in creating a new microelectronic company..."

There were some more "radical" elements at the TUC Congress. These went so far as to demand "... that the government appoint a Royal Commission into the new technology"! They seem to have forgotten that only a couple of years ago there was a Royal Commission into the new technology for one specific industry – the press. *Its conclusion was to advise the great newspaper companies to cut their workforces by half!* If the policy of such union leaders is followed we will have a repeat performance, with another gang of highly paid parasites telling the rest of us to surrender half our jobs.

Millions of working people need advice from their unions *now* on how to cope as word processing machines and robots, computer terminals and optical fibres, VDUs and System X, threaten their jobs. The TUC, it seems, is quite incapable of giving that advice. Like the government, its message is "grin and bear it". The reason lies in the basic philosophy accepted by all the union leaders, whether they see themselves as being on the "left" or the "right" of the movement. They all accept that the way forward for their members is through collaboration with the employers. Of course, many of them see the need for occasional industrial action to "bring the employers to their senses" – but once the industrial action is over, they again preach agreement and collaboration. If the employer follows a policy detrimental to the interests of the workers, this is said to be a "mistake" on his part – not something which is inevitable in a system based on competition between rival profit makers.

It is this approach which enables those who regard themselves as "left of centre" to expect the problem of the new technology to be dealt with by a Royal Commission made up of employers' as well as union representatives. The philosophy of class collaboration has sunk very deep into the British trade union movement. Even quite a way to the left you hear calls for "an alternative economic strategy" which will "revive British industry". What this ignores is that British industry is *capitalist* industry. Eighty per cent of the private sector is in the hands of just one per cent of the population. Even the nationalized industries are run by boards of directors drawn from this one per cent, and pay out interest payments to them.

The demand for British industry to be "more efficient", and "more competitive", is a demand for it to be more efficient and more competitive in producing profits for this one per cent. The demand for "industrial expansion" through "increased productivity" is a demand for the wealth in the hands of this one per cent to grow, without any corresponding increase in the number of workers employed.

Those who accept the basic idea of class collaboration, the idea that we should all work together to make "British industry more efficient", forget that British industry is not *our* industry. It is the industry of a very small and very privileged class of people whose interests are diametrically opposed to those of the majority of the population, a minority who have already put $1\frac{1}{2}$ million people on the dole because it is profitable to have shut down factories standing next to unemployed workers. Does anyone really believe that this minority will baulk at putting another three million on the dole, if this is the way to introduce the new technology "profitably"?

What will happen if workers follow the TUC *policy of collaboration in the introduction of the technology?*

Firstly, there will be a massive loss of jobs as microprocessors replace workers in industry after industry. Then there *might* be an increase in the sales of British companies abroad because their goods were "more competitive" than those of foreign countries. This *might* mean that the job loss through the new technology is *slightly less* than it would otherwise have been. It *would not* stop there being an overall job loss.

Finally, it would mean that companies abroad (including British companies operating overseas, and multinationals also operating in this country) would say to their workers: "We cannot sell our goods because our factories are overmanned compared to those in Britain." Workers in these countries would be subject to the same pressure to "save" their jobs by allowing the workforce to be cut. If they accepted the advice of their own TUC-type leaders, before long their employers' factories would be more competitive than factories in Britain, and the whole process would start again. The workers of each country would be involved in a Dutch auction against each other for jobs, from which the employers of *all* countries would benefit.

Another version of the collaborationist argument is found within individual enterprises in this country. Workers are told that they must accept a job loss if their firm is going to defend itself against its rivals. A good example of this is in Post Office Telecommunications. The main union, the POEU, has for many years followed a policy of urging upon management massive new investments in technological advance, so as to ensure that the Post Office prospers rather than the various British and foreign telecommunications firms. This, it tells its workers, is the only way to "defend the Post Office monopoly" and to ensure that "Post Office jobs" are protected.

It is a policy that cannot save jobs in the long run. Investment in new technology means investment in System X, in optical fibre systems, in "modular" telephone receivers – all of which will mean far fewer jobs for POEU members. Adoption of new technology on this scale may ensure the "defence of the Post Office" against its private enterprise rivals – but the mass of the workforce will not be around to enjoy the fruits of such a victory. *Maybe,* if the Post Office develops the new technology before Plessey, GEC or ITT, a handful of jobs will be saved for POEU members which might otherwise have gone to workers in one of these three companies. But that will be no more a consolation for a much greater number of Post Office workers whose jobs will have been destroyed, than it will be for the Plessey, GEC and ITT workers who will be standing alongside them in the dole queues.

In fact, the policy is a great *disadvantage* to POEU members. It leads to a situation every time someone suggests industrial action in defence of jobs, where they are told: "You will weaken the Post Office and play into hands of the private enterprise vultures." Once you accept that policy, you have to sit back and watch jobs disappear. The only real meaning for a worker of the slogan "Defend the Post Office" should be: defence of the jobs and working conditions of those people employed by the Post Office. That cannot be done by collaboration. It requires militant action.

If it is said that such action will push costs in the Post Office above those of its competitors, then the answer is to take steps to ensure that such action is also developing against the competitors, by building links between *all* telecommunications workers, in both the public and the private sector. In the same way, if it is said that protecting jobs in this country against the impact of the new technology will destroy the "competitiveness" of British industry, the answer is not to stop protecting jobs. It is to encourage workers in other countries to take similar action in defence of their jobs.

This does not mean, as some union leaders are pretending, that nothing can be done until there is some international agreement on the shorter working week. You will never get such an agreement if you wait for employers or government to make it. You will only get it when the action of workers in one country in protecting their jobs inspires workers in other countries to do the same. *The inspiration is there.* Already workers in Belgium have been striking for the thirty-five-hour week. In Ruhr steel towns there has been the first great strike since 1928, over the same issue. In this country, there has been the struggle for the same goal by the Post Office engineers. Together they begin to show a clearer way forward than all the resolutions of the TUC put together.

How not to fight

Plans to computerize offices and experiment with word processing have been given the green light at the Ford Motor Company following a national agreement with the staff unions. The plans were held up for three months because three unions were blacking all computer applications. A ten clause agreement published last week will provide a framework for upcoming local negotiations.... The agreement ranges from a pledge of no redundancies for the 11,500 Ford workers covered, to health and safety effects of working with Visual Display Units... TASS led the three staff unions in the negotiations.... John Tuchfield, a TASS national organizer, said this week the agreement was an example to others. The agreement provides that increased productivity through the introduction of computers will be reflected in improved salaries.... (*Computing*, 26 October 1978)

This agreement sums up the attitude of a whole section of trade union officialdom to the new technology. They see it as providing an opportunity to bargain with the management over *money*, usually after insisting on a "no redundancy" (or at least a "no *compulsory* redundancy") clause and certain minimal conditions for health and safety. But at the same time management are allowed to prepare to increase the total workload and to run down the total workforce.

In local government, this means that NALGO allows in word processors providing a £50 a year "special allowance" is paid to the typists who operate them. In the Civil Service the first reaction of the CPSA leadership to the introduction of word processors was not to see them as any threat at all, but simply to treat them as electric typewriters. It was only after protests by rank-and-file members and by some of the left wing on the executive that a moratorium was imposed on the introduction of word processors while a few "trials" with them took place in selected offices. But even now there are great dangers. Some activists who regard themselves as being on the left on the union say they will allow in word processors under "union control". By union control they do not mean with controls to prevent job loss, but merely a no redundancy pledge and increased special allowances. Management are left free to run down the workforce through "natural wastage", or to increase workloads by shifting work from one department to another. In an occupation like typing where there is a very high turnover of the workforce, a "no redundancy" pledge cannot by itself stop the destruction of jobs.

In the print industry, the tradition of selling jobs for money is an old one. Between 1967 and 1976, 63,000 jobs disappeared out of a total of 159,000. The general secretaries of *all* the print unions put their names to a scandalous report, *Programme for Action*, in November 1976, which would have given the Fleet Street employers carte blanche to introduce the new technology in exchange for payments to those who accepted redundancy. Fortunately, the members of the unions rejected the recommendation in a ballot. But that has not prevented the tendency for unions to be prepared to sell jobs. The result has been a rapid decline in the number of those who can enter the industry from the ranks of the school leavers and the unemployed.

In Post Office telecommunications, the POEU leadership officially welcomed the new technology, not even demanding special payments for operating it, and opposing calls for industrial action over the shorter working week, until it was finally forced by a June 1978 conference decision to struggle for a thirty-five-hour week. Even then the executive eventually suggested in private meetings with a government enquiry the terms for settling the claim on the basis of a 37½ hour week – which was to be paid for on a "nil cost" basis out of *future* productivity – a move which has been explicitly ruled out by the conference resolution (*Resistance*, journal of North London Internal POEU branch, special issue August 1978; see also the McCarthy Report).

Unfortunately, the attitude of selling jobs does not only apply to the national officers. It filters right down to many branch officers and conveners. They are often effectively full-time and they themselves do not face the dole or increased workloads when they agree to sell jobs for special payments. They are the lowest and least privileged part – but still part – of that layer of people who play a key role within the trade union movement but who are not on the receiving end of any deterioration in conditions. All this layer have felt increasingly under pressure over the question of wages over the last two or three years. Incomes policy has made it harder for their members to make ends meet. Selling jobs is an easy way to get rid of this pressure without getting involved in bitter conflicts with the employers.

Yet, for the bulk of the membership this is a tactic that is completely counterproductive. As we have seen, it means an increase in the level of managerial control and in the tedium of work. But it also means something else. Workers who grow accustomed to getting wage increases by collaborating with management to get rid of jobs, soon lose their sense of solidarity and their tradition of common struggle. They also lose to management control over key areas of work which give them bargaining power. The pioneering productivity deal, in which workers gave up control over work practices, was signed at the Esso oil refinery at Fawley, near Southampton, in 1960. The deal made Fawley wages among the highest in the country. But in evidence to the Donovan Commission on trade unions six years later it emerged that these refinery workers were by then among the lowest paid in the country.

A book on Fleet Street by a former functionary for the newspaper bosses' organization, the Newspaper Proprietors' Association, makes the same point: "If chapels... did seek to maximize their members' earnings by agreeing to reduce the number of jobs, then they were not nearly as successful as chapels... which did not" (Keith Sissons, *Industrial Relations in Fleet Street*, p. 111).

Workers who sell jobs are worse off than those who refuse to in every respect after a very little time: they have worse conditions, they receive lower wages, and more of them end up on the dole. These points are particularly important when the new technology is introduced. Management are not daft. They know that they will encounter resistance if they push up workloads the moment a new device appears. It is much more likely that they will introduce the device and only run down the workforce and then increase the workload over a period of time.

A Fleet Street worker who has already had some of the new technology introduced into his office tells how it happens:

You find management and trade union bureaucrats collaborating to let things drift up on you, letting you drift into a situation where, imperceptibly, workloads increase. . . . The new machinery comes in. You don't notice much of a difference to start with, and then you find after a year or two the workload has doubled or trebled and no extra staff has been taken on.

A group of workers who have already sacrificed jobs and control over the work process for higher pay are not likely to be in much shape to prevent such pressure. What happens was shown at the first national paper to accept the new technology – the *Daily Mirror* – as a large number of Fleet Street NATSOPA members explained in a petition they submitted calling for a special branch delegate meeting:

> The Mirror deal produced for our members wage levels which are good relative to many other Fleet Street chapels. The price that has been paid by the chapel is a heavy one, and there is much worse to come. The Mirror deal envisaged a job loss of a hundred jobs in a chapel of 600. At the time that the deal was being voted on, the members were being assured that this job loss wouldn't really happen. Already over fifty jobs have gone. Now the chapel members are beginning to feel the sting in the tail. You can only hope to apply successfully for an internal vacancy at the Mirror if you won't be replaced when you leave your current job. The management have put a block on hiring new staff. In department after department, the pressure of working is building up and our members now have no protection. . . .

The debilitating effects on shop floor organization that come from selling jobs have added importance, because the first battle over new technology is rarely the last one. Remember, few firms are going to fork out the huge sums of money required to install new technology all along the line all at once. They begin with a few devices only, located at so-called "bottlenecks" in the work process (usually, those points where the workers have most control over the speed at which they toil). Then they use the rapidity at which these devices operate to speed up everyone else whose work feeds into or is fed from the device.

At a later stage, management will claim that only by automating out further jobs can the existing electronic devices be fully utilized. Already this is happening in giant offices that were designed ten or twenty years ago around old computer systems that are now being updated. For example, the National Giro Centre was built in Bootle, near Liverpool, some years back, allegedly so as to provide jobs in an area of higher than average unemployment. But now a new microprocessor computer

Trade unionists march in London in protest at the closure of *The Times* in November 1978. The dispute centred on the introduction of new technology. *Photo by Andrew Wiard*, Report *(London)*

In the same year, British Post Office engineers struck for a 35-hour week – their response to the revolution in telecommunications technology. They got 37½ hours.
Photo by John Sturrock, Report *(London)*

system is being introduced which will destroy 1016 of these jobs (typically, the CPSA union negotiators tried to keep this full figure a secret from their own members). At the Post Office Computer Centre, a new system TOLD was recently introduced which destroyed 600 key operators' jobs. The union accepted it for a miserable pittance of £44 a year for the rest of the workforce.

In newspapers, there are three clear stages in new technology introduction. In the first stage, linotype machines, which require skilled operators, are replaced by computer typesetting, which requires little more skill than ordinary typing. In the second stage, this typing is no longer done by printers at all, but by journalists and personnel who take ads over the telephone. In the third stage the journalists' work itself is revolutionized, as the layout of the newspaper is done on a VDU. And it need not be done on a VDU in the same office, since it is becoming possible for the Press Association in London to lay out by computer and to wire through whole pages for immediate printing by local presses. At each stage in the process, a new group of workers bears the burden of the technological change. And a group of workers who have sat back and sold the jobs of a previous group for money, are not going to be in a position to fight when it is their turn to be threatened.

What to fight for
There are two mistaken reactions to the new technology that are widely found. One we have already dealt with – the claim that technology as such is a good thing, which will make "Britain" more competitive and everyone better off. Those who hold this view believe any discussion on the new technology is closed before it starts by the assertion: "We're not Luddites, are we?" They forget that the Luddites were a group of workers suffering from miserably low wages and facing a destruction of their jobs by new working methods. Their attempts to fight back by destroying machines may not have been successful (although they did succeed in holding down a bigger army than the Duke of Wellington had in the same years to fight his war against the French in Spain). But the result of their failure was not something good. It was grinding desperate poverty for hundreds of thousands of people, enduring for a whole generation.

The second approach is to be struck dumb with horror at what the technology can do. People think of all the jobs it can take over, all the workers it can throw on to the dole, and feel impotent in the face of it. They would like to fight it – indeed, often they are opposed to the very idea of new technology – but feel that the task is just too great. They forget that the new technology cannot be introduced in one go, over-night, but will be introduced piecemeal over many years in most industries. Above all, they forget that *it is very rarely indeed that new technology can be introduced without some cooperation from the existing workforce.*

Even in the US newspaper industry, where the new technology was often brought in by using scabs to do the work of skilled compositors, this was only possible because other sections of the old workforce (those on the presses) continued to work normally. In the same way, the Civil Service cannot introduce word processors without some cooperation from existing typists; local government cannot transfer all information currently in old-style filing cabinets to discs or magnetic tape without the help of those who understand the present filing systems; robots cannot be introduced on one part of the assembly line unless workers on other parts of the assembly line are prepared to work with them.

Workers of one sort or another have the power to impede the introduction of the new technology. The employing class cannot work it without us.
Does that mean we should simply say "No" to the new technology?

The flat "No" to technology comes from some of the most far sighted rank-and-file trade unionists. They see that the technology means a loss of jobs and a loss of control over the work process. It is a far healthier attitude than that of those union officials who talk of "union control", meaning the selling of jobs for money.

Nevertheless, the flat "No" is a gospel of despair. It means that instead of going on to the offensive and showing fellow workers how advances in technology could really be used to create a world without poverty and toil, if only society were run differently, we are stuck on the defensive, defending the unpleasant and often outrageous working conditions that exist at present. This is not an attitude that is going to unite different sorts of workers for a fight over new technology that will stretch over many years.

Every time management introduce new technology they claim to their workers that it is going to make work easier, as well as more productive. It is necessary to argue against these claims, especially since the technology is nearly always designed to make people work harder and to increase managerial control. But those arguments will often not be accepted by people who have the "glories" of the technology pumped into their brains by slick management brochures and fast talking reps from the computer companies. Unfortunately, there are many, many workers who do not immediately recognize management's interests as the opposite of their own. They will easily fall for the management's line, especially in those cases when the new technology does in fact get rid of some unpleasant tasks (even though it may well replace these by other equally unpleasant ones).

If we simply say to our fellow workers: "We don't want it" their attitude may well be: "Well, your peculiar desire for unpleasant tasks is not going to stop the rest of us opting for something which is clearly going to make our jobs easier." The new technology will be brought into use, jobs will be destroyed, managerial control increased – and then, if later we are seen by the other workers to be correct, it may well be too late.

It is important to remember that the first area to be hit really hard by the new technology (after the print) will be office work, and that most offices have very weak levels of trade union organization. Even in the Civil Service and local government, many of the typists are non-union temps. It is going to be very difficult to get these workers to say a flat "No" to a special payment for operating a machine that does not seem that different from an electric typewriter.

Our response has to start from the same suspicion of the way the new technology is being used that motivates those who simply say "No". We are on the same side as the Luddites, not against them. *But we cannot give the impression we are against technology as such. We are for it, provided it is used to enable human beings to create more wealth and to lead happier, freer, fuller lives. After all, it is technology that enables us to envisage the coming reality of the age-old dream of a society without misery and drudgery.*

What we are against is the use of new technology to destroy jobs and to make the remaining jobs more repetitive and more subject to control from above. What we are challenging is not technology but the control over technology by managements committed to profit making.

When the employers say that technology will make life easier for the workers, we have to show other workers that they are lying. We have to say, in effect: "OK, prove it. Guarantee us *in advance* that there will be no reduction in the total workforce; show us *in advance* that our working conditions are going to improve by cutting the working week; give us a written agreement *now* that our individual work loads will not increase. Until you do that, we will not work the new technology."

To get this argument across it will be necessary to draw up a list of demands, adapted to the particular needs of each industrial and office situation.

The sorts of things that have to be argued for are:

Blacking of new technology. Until you get a guarantee that any saving in worktime will be translated into a

Shorter working week. This should not be a demand to be half-sacrificed in negotiations, as wage demands invariably are. Its fulfilment should be a precondition for acceptance of the new technology at all. After all, if you knew that a new machine would cause a fatal injury to one worker in four, you would not work it. In the same way, you should refuse to work any machinery until management guarantee that it will not destroy the jobs of one worker in four.

No reduction in the total workforce. Some groups of workers have already begun to fight for this demand. For instance in Post Office telecommunications, where in the past workers accepted the destruction of whole jobs with new technology, they are faced with introduction of new equipment, called MOST, into exchanges which will destroy an average of one job per exchange; they are now saying they will not allow the introduction of MOST unless there is a guarantee that the workforce in the exchanges remains as at present.

Again in the Charity Commission of the Civil Service, management introduced an IBM machine without a VDU, claiming it was *not* a word processor. They also claimed it would not cause any redundancies. So union activists argued to (1) accept introduction of the machine if there were no redundancies; (2) demand special allowances for working it; (3) after a given period to black the machine if there was reduction in the total workforce.

In this case, it would have been better to have got a written management guarantee of no cut in the total workforce *in advance*.

The demand for no reduction in the total workforce does not just mean no redundancies, it also means:

No voluntary redundancies. Management must not be allowed to lure unsuspecting workers with the offer of apparently large sums of money. Every job that goes through voluntary redundancy is another job no longer available for the unemployed – including the unemployed children of existing workers who have just left school. The sums of money provided to those who accept voluntary redundancy may seem big – but they will not seem all that large after a long period on the dole.

And remember, the working lives of those left behind in the factory or office are likely to become more tedious.

No "natural wastage"; the filling of every post that is made vacant when people leave. "Natural wastage" is an even better option for management than voluntary redundancy. They do not have to fork out any money to get it. Once they decide they want to run down a particular section, it is easy for them to do so if there is a natural wastage agreement that prevents a filling of vacancies as people leave. For instance, management can simply put the most unpleasant of their supervisors in charge of it, and make life so miserable that people are glad to get out. Or they can hold down wages and deny promotion within the section, again encouraging people to look for better jobs elsewhere.

No blurring of old demarcation lines. This is an old trick by which the management get workers to accept a reduction in the workforce. For instance, they install a word processor and tell typists that it means no reduction in their number. But what the word processor will do, through its "floppy disc", is destroy the jobs of filing clerks. If the typists are going to keep their jobs, it will be because they are going to have their time taken up even more than before hitting keys, not only for typing but also for ensuring the fulfilment by the machine of filing tasks.

In the same way, the most advanced versions of the new technology in the print mean not only that journalists and tele-ad personnel take over the jobs of compositors; they also mean the destruction of jobs for office workers who invoice firms and check up on their credit, since the computer does these jobs automatically.

Only a cut in the working day which keeps the *whole* workforce intact, not just those directly working the new machines, can stop the wholesale destruction of jobs.

The involvement in discussions of all workers affected by technological changes, indirectly as well as directly. A device that might make the job of one worker easier can make more difficult the job of the worker next to him or her in the work process. For example, a word processor increases the speed at which material is typed: it is likely therefore to increase the speed at which someone who feeds work to the typist is expected to work. In the same way, the most unfortunate person in a factory may not be the individual who presses a button to start and stop a robot, but the next worker along who is expected to keep up with the robot's speed. The new technology will *revolutionize* the work of everyone in a particular workplace. Every group of workers must have the right to discuss and veto the introduction of detrimental work practices.

A written guarantee from management that they will not introduce new technology without the prior agreement of the union membership. There is story after story of new devices simply appearing one day in the office or on the factory floor, without any warning. In one Civil Service office, for example, it was purely by accident that union activists found a computer terminal being worked as a word processor by a non-union superintendent.

Written management guarantees that management will not use the new machines to get information on the workspeed or accuracy of individual workers, that is that they will not use them as electronic time-and-motion men. The written guarantee by itself will not stop management trying to do so. But it will mean that even the least trade union conscious worker knows in advance that management *should not* be doing that, and will feel some commitment to support any worker who is picked upon on the basis of data from the computer. At the same time, rank-and-file activists should establish contacts with the members of other unions who are working the computers to make sure that management is not breaking its agreement.

Full health-and-safety precautions and no increase in mental strain. Management always assume with any new machine or material that it is safe until it is proved otherwise. Look how they lied about asbestos for so many years. Our assumption should be the opposite – we should not take any risks with the health and safety of ourselves or our fellow workers.

That means:

(1) As a minimum a fifteen-minute break for every hour on a VDU and no more than 180 minutes a day on VDU work.

(2) Regular safety checks, at management expense, but with trade union nominated doctors.

(3) Management to pay for any special clothing or equipment workers need to work new machines (such as special glasses to work on VDUs).

(4) A guarantee against the sacking of anyone because their health or their eyesight does not allow them to work on the new technology.

(5) The workers involved to have the right to veto work on equipment which they think is unsafe or which causes too much mental strain.

No increase in shift working. The new technology is coming in so fast that a machine that costs £1000 today may cost only £500 in a couple of years' time. Management will therefore try to recover the cost of the machine as quickly as possible, so as to be able to invest in still newer technology in the not too distant future. That means they will try to impose shift working simply in order to increase their own profitability. But for workers that means being forced to lead a miserable social life, to suffer from increased mental stress, and to suffer a host of minor health disorders (stomach upsets and so on).

No victimization of workers who cannot adjust to the new technology. Many older workers may find difficulty in adjusting to the work involved with the new technology. As the official NUJ report on the new technology notes:

> Agreements in other industries have specified that no one over a certain age (forty and forty-five usually) may use VDUs. Apart from the health aspect, a well documented fact of age is the slowing down in reaction from visual signals to manual response. So the journalist as technician must be young, and have good vision; so working and potential journalists could find themselves excluded from the industry for reasons quite unconnected with journalistic ability.

What applies to journalists also applies to typists etc in the Civil Service, local government and so on. We must resist any attempt to throw people out of work just because they are too old (at forty!) to adjust to a new machine.

Final decisions to be taken by rank-and-file workers involved, not simply by branch officials or by conveners. Union branch officials and conveners who do not work on the shop or office floor will often be tempted to buy off jobs for wage increases. At the same time, it is not possible to wage a successful fight against management's plans for the new technology unless the whole of the rank and file are involved. In the last resort, it is they who will have to black machines and so on.

Experience shows that explaining the dangers posed by management's use of the new technology can get workers involved in the union who have previously been at best passive members. Precisely because *their* jobs and *their* working lives are threatened, they can become more militant over the issues than old-established union activists.

Decisions over whether mental strain is increasing, or over whether workers over forty are being pressurized to leave should be taken by those who know the truth – those whose lives are being hit by the change in the work process.

Management Resistance to the New Technology

Nuala Swords-Isherwood and Peter Senker

So far we have mainly been concerned with trade union responses to the new technology, with the implied assumption that it is to the unions that we should look for resistance. But not many unions and workforces have taken the advice of the Socialist Workers Party, according to this account of a study of twelve engineering firms in Britain and West Germany, specially written for this volume by two researchers at the Science Policy Research Unit, Sussex University. Ironically, the main source of resistance to the introduction of new technology was found to be ignorant and backward management. And the main source of job loss was the failure to adopt new techniques to meet the international competition.

Numerically controlled machining of batches of components (NC) has probably been the most important form of automation in the engineering industry for many years. NC became important even when electronic components much less powerful than microprocessors were available. But the advent of cheap microprocessors will facilitate the development of more sophisticated and powerful NC systems. In 1971, the number of numerically controlled machine tools installed in Britain was estimated at around 4000. The number installed increased rapidly to around 10,000 by 1976 and it is certain to be much higher now. The increased use of NC has been particularly important in the electrical engineering, instruments and mechanical engineering industries. Their use in aerospace, motor vehicles, tractors and shipbuilding has not increased as fast, although in Britain – as in the US – the aircraft industry was the first major user of NC.

Although the UK has not yet advanced far beyond the first stage of independent numerically controlled machine tools, the National Engineering Laboratory believe that other industrial nations, particularly the Japanese, are gaining valuable experience from their investments in automated batch production and are planning their first steps towards "the unmanned factory", as the Japanese describe their goal. Awareness of these trends led the Mechanical Engineering and Machine Tools Requirements Board of the Department of Industry to fund a project with the National Engineering Laboratory during 1977. The project's aims were to study and report on the UK and international activity in automated small-batch production (ASP).

As a contribution to this project, we undertook a study focused on understanding the social and economic barriers which need to be overcome before advanced systems gain wide acceptance in Britain. In this study, we compared the attitudes of managers in machine shops in the UK and in West Germany. This also formed part of a larger study sponsored by the Engineering Industry Training Board designed to assess the impact of technological change on the number and skills of the workforce.

The ASP fully automated batch production system cannot come into use for many years. Before any such system is widely adopted, it will be necessary for companies to take many intermediate steps involving increasing automation of all the processes of machine shop batch production. As any assessment of the social implications of a system which has not yet been designed would inevitably be hypothetical and unrealistic, the research reported in this chapter was undertaken in order to identify and evaluate barriers to taking essential intermediate steps. The research was, therefore, concerned to identify factors which might hinder the wider diffusion and more effective use of numerically controlled machine tools already commercially available.

We compared management, worker and union attitudes to automation. We tried to assess whether differences between the qualifications or training of German and British managers could affect their ability to evaluate new equipment purchases or to get the most out of it once installed. We tried to assess the significance of worker resistance: do differences in worker attitudes, or differences in the extent to which unions and workers were involved in equipment purchase decisions affect the rate of acceptance of new technology?

Our study method was based on a series of detailed in-depth interviews in a sample of six machine shops in Britain, matched as closely as possible by size and industry with six machine shops in West Germany. Machine shops making batches of components vary enormously in terms of the type and size of product made, batch quantities, precision standards and a wide variety of other variables. It was clearly impossible within the resources available for the study to interview a sample of machine shops representative in terms of all such variables. However, we consider that the sample of machine shops interviewed was reasonably representative of batch production machine shops in the two countries.

In West Germany, we found that managements had initially resisted NC. Unreliability caused problems and generated resistance among supervisors and managements in some firms, as did ignorance about NC and about its possible consequence in terms of reorganization. In one firm, the management had been worried initially about the responsibility involved in the large expenditure necessary to invest in NC. In general, managerial attitudes to NC in Britain were not quite as favourable as in West Germany. Relatively greater emphasis was given to cost rather than engineering considerations. Middle management in a machine tool firm considered that there was resistance to NC among top management. The other machine tool firm considered that it lacked sufficient managerial and engineering expertise to get the best out of NC equipment.

Managements in neither country considered that workers or trade unions had impeded the progress of NC significantly. One company in West Germany, a manufacturer of heavy industrial equipment, had encountered shop floor resistance to NC. In this company, although there had been no strikes, there had been some sabotage. The works council was not as against NC as the individual shop floor workers. While this was the only West German company in which actual shop floor resistance to NC had been encountered, NC was unpopular among skilled shop floor workers in five of the six machine shops. Skilled men felt that they had less chance of using their skills than on conventional machines. But in one company where semi-skilled workers were employed operating NC machines, they were welcomed as making jobs more interesting. These West German firms differed from several of the British firms as they had not recently experienced large-scale redundancies. However, there were fears of workforce resistance to NC in the future.

In Britain, there had been no significant resistance to the installation of NC, although in several plants there had been large redundancies. This may be because, in general, there was no direct and obvious connection between the installation of the NC machines and subsequent redundancies. There had been some initial problems with NC in some firms – described by one firm as "scepticism" about NC rather than resistance to it. In another firm, there had been difficulties in devising equitable payment schemes as there was less opportunity with NC for the worker to earn more by working harder. One firm pointed out that, although the effects of the installation of NC on industrial relations had been negligible, if acquisition of NC had not been well planned and preceded by discussions with the shop floor the effects could have been disastrous.

One of management's principal motives for installing NC machines was to maintain and increase production in the face of shortages of skilled labour. There was considerable variation in the increase of productivity achievable by installing NC machines, depending mainly on the type of applications in which they are used. However, if one takes it as a rule of thumb that an NC machine produces three times as much output as a conventional machine, then one worker operating an NC machine can produce the output which, without NC, would have required three.

In general, the installation of NC machines did not affect overall manning patterns substantially. If certain types of conventional machine had been operated traditionally by skilled labour in a particular plant, this pattern of manning was carried over to the operation of NC machines. The overall statistics confirm that there has been a gradual fall in the *proportion* of craftsmen employed in the industry as a whole.

However, the disturbing feature of Table 7.5 is the decline in *total* employment it reveals. This is very largely due to management's failure to undertake sufficient research and development and also to their failure to invest. The use of NC machine tools creates a need for new skills for maintenance and there is a shortage of such people. With the rapid recent increase in the use of NC machine tools it is no longer possible for machine shops to rely on manufacturers for maintenance. Machine tool manufacturers are taking advantage of technical developments, particularly in electronics, to try to alleviate this problem. NC also creates a demand for programmers. It also has indirect effects: for example, the increased precision made possible by the use of NC equipment reduces the requirements for skilled labour in fitting. Redesign of products is also needed to facilitate production on NC machines.

In general, managements consider that skilled workers find operation of NC machines boring, but semi-skilled workers appear to be less worried by this. The application in which the NC machine is used may be critical. For example, the operation of an NC machine in a shop where complex one-offs and very small batches are made (for example, in prototype production or precision tool making) may provide considerable job satisfaction. In some cases, skilled workers have been very keen to work on new machines. In other cases, NC may lead to jobs offering considerably reduced satisfaction where larger batches of simpler components are being made. The advent of microprocessor control systems gives management the opportunity to build in more opportunities for shop floor intervention to improve performance. Managements may be

Table 7.5 Craftworkers in UK engineering and mechanical engineering 1970–6

Employment (000s)	1970/71	1971/72	1972/73	1973/74	1974/75	1975/76
Total engineering industry	3322	3106	3127	3173	3072	2891
Craft workers:						
number	648	618	605	595	563	546
%	19.5	19.9	19.4	18.7	18.3	18.9
Mechanical engineering*	1052	951	935	947	927	883
Craft workers:						
number	280	255	247	243	237	226
%x	26.6	26.8	26.4	25.7	25.6	25.6

* The figures relate to the years 1971–6
x Estimated average of two spot dates
(*Source:* Engineering Industry Training Board)

reluctant to take advantage of this because it would lessen *their* opportunities for controlling output.

Overall, our study indicated that worker resistance is not a serious barrier to the automation of batch machining. Certain problems, such as changes in payments, need to be negotiated before NC systems can be installed and got to work satisfactorily. The formal German approach to industrial relations ensures that these problems are sorted out automatically. In Britain, provided that a company follows "enlightened management practice", it is unlikely to face serious industrial relations problems in this context. Thus, disruption resulting from a failure to consult workers and/or trade unions is always possible in British firms. The legal framework in which industrial relations are conducted in West Germany ensures that such problems are less likely to occur. But concern was expressed that fears of redundancy could cause increased shop floor resistance to automated production in both countries in the future.

Resistance to automated batch machining arises partly from management's reluctance to accept increased responsibility. This resistance is stronger in Britain. In West Germany, technical and economic assessments of new machinery are carried out in great detail in all but the smallest companies and engineering graduates play an important part in these evaluations at all levels, up to and including top management. In Britain, evaluations are not generally so thorough, and a higher proportion of part-time engineers are involved in them.

One of the main reasons for the greater unwillingness of British companies to employ engineering graduates is because these graduates often need extensive training before they can play a useful role in industry. In Germany, this is not so. German managements reckon that the graduates emerging from their technical universities can be useful very soon after they are recruited. This reflects a longstanding difference. A book published in 1890 pointed out the thorough scientific but practical basis of German education even then.

There has clearly been a trend towards the reduction of employment in the British engineering industry. Automation has played some part in causing this. But it has been the result to a greater extent of the failure of British management to invest sufficiently in research and development and production facilities, and to design and make products which would be more competitive on international markets. If new techniques such as numerically controlled machining are not adopted in Britain, but are adopted in other major industrial nations, then Britain is likely to suffer serious adverse consequences in terms of competitiveness in world markets. This is likely to lead to a reduction in employment opportunities in the British engineering industry. But the adoption of automation tends to lead to less workers being employed per unit of output. Therefore unless output is increased substantially, further redundancies are inevitable.

Microprocessors make possible the development of more sophisticated batch production systems which are likely to require less labour for their operation. It is possible, however, that manufacturers' attempts to make such systems reliable and easy to maintain may not be entirely successful, so the requirement for maintenance workers could increase. However, the research reported here gives some grounds for concern that other countries may adopt microprocessor-based automation more rapidly than Britain. If this happens, Britain could lose jobs through the effects of international competition – through, for example, the Japanese making a similar impact on world markets for mechanical engineering products as they have in the international markets for consumer electronic products. This effect could continue to exceed the job losses due to automation.

Guide to Further Reading

Sydney Paulden, "Calculating the Cost of the MPU Revolution", *Works Management,* January 1979, asks whether managements can cope with the changes on the way.

Tony Durham, "Germans Press for the Good News", *New Scientist,* 12 April 1979, describes how a West German news agency successfully went over to the new technology. Should be read by all *Times* employees.

Judy Stark, "Hold the Front Frame", *New Scientist,* 30 November 1978, is an account of what it is like to work with the new technology in newspapers. Ms Stark is the night metropolitan editor of the *Journal-Bulletin* of Providence, Rhode Island. Should also be read by all *Times* employees.

Ken Gill, "Microelectronics and Employment – A Trade Union View" in *Management Services,* vol. 22, No. 12 (December 1978), warns of the problems to come. The author is general secretary of TASS, the Technical and Supervisory Section of the Amalgamated Union of Engineering Workers (AUEW). Ian Benson, "Notes on the Economic and Social Impact of Computer Technology", in *Computer Technology and Employment* (National Computing Centre/TASS, 1979), by the National Computing Officer of TASS, is another trade union statement.

Peter Bennett, "Technological Change and Collective Bargaining", is the ASTMS discussion document referred to at the end of chapter 6. Also worth consulting is the "Action Programme" and other documents agreed at the November 1978 conference of the Geneva-based International Federation of Commercial, Clerical and Technical Employees (FIET) at Velm, Austria. Reprinted as *Computers and Work:* FIET *Action Programme* (August 1979).

Employment and Technology is an official Trades Union Congress report, published in August 1979. It gives a comprehensive rundown on microelectronics, job prospects and trade union negotiating positions, plus a review of manpower, education and training policies. It also discusses "New Technology Agreements" and provides a checklist for negotiators.

The idea of "Technology Agreements" first surfaced in Scandinavia, and details of the Norwegian experience, which essentially involves the provision for extensive consultations between employers and unions on the introduction of new technology, are provided by Kristen Nygaard in a lecture given at North Staffordshire Polytechnic, England, in July 1977. Professor Nygaard is Director of Research at the Norwegian Computing Centre, Oslo.

Readers may also find useful:

Gene Bylinsky, "EDP Managers put on Business Suits", in *Fortune*, 6 November 1978.

Christopher Lorenz, "How a Swedish Multinational Mastered the Electronics Revolution", *Financial Times*, 25 and 26 September 1979. Especially interesting on employment impact.

National Computing Centre, *The Impact of Microprocessors on British Business* (NCC, Manchester, December 1979).

The Transport and General Workers' Union, *Microelectronics: New Technology, Old Problems, New Opportunities* (TGWU, London, June 1979). The view of Britain's biggest union.

A useful summary of the situation so far, which examined eighteen British examples of new technology agreements either proposed or signed, appeared as "Microelectronics – The Trade Union Response", in *Labour Research*, June 1979.

Pre-microelectronics-era discussions of industrial relations and technological change include:

S. D. Anderman, *Trade Unions and Technical Change* (Allen and Unwin, London, 1967).

T. Burns and G. M. Stalker, *The Management of Innovation* (Tavistock, London, 1961).

J. Chadwick-Jones, *Automation and Behaviour* (Wiley, New York, 1969).

L. E. Davis and A. B. Cherns, *The Quality of Working Life* (Free Press, New York, 1975).

B. Karsh, "The Meaning of Work in an Age of Automation", *Current Economic Comment*, August 1957.

E. M. Kassalow, "Automation and Labour Relations", in S. Marcson (ed.), *Automation, Alienation and Anomie* (Harper and Row, New York, 1970).

E. Mumford and O. Banks, *The Computer and the Clerk* (Routledge, London, 1967).

H. L. Sheppard and N. Q. Herrick, *Where Have All the Robots Gone? Worker Dissatisfaction in the 1970s* (Collier-Macmillan, London, 1972).

M. A. Smith, "Process Technology and Powerlessness", *British Journal of Sociology*, vol. 19 (March 1968).

J. Steiber, *Employment Problems of Automation and Advanced Technology* (St Martins, New York, 1966).

A. Touraine, *Workers' Attitudes to Technical Change* (OECD, Paris, 1965).

D. Wedderburn and R. Crompton, *Workers' Attitudes to Technology* (Cambridge University Press, London, 1972).

J. Woodward, *Management and Technology* (HMSO, London, 1958).

PART THREE:
THE MICROELECTRONIC AGE

8 The Social Impact of Computers

What Computers Mean for Man and Society

Herbert A. Simon

Rather like the division between optimists and pessimists in the debate over the employment impact of the microprocessor, commentators on the overall impact of computers on society divide up between those who welcome, and those who fear for, our microelectronic future. The "optimists" in this instance, like Herbert Simon, the author of the following article, see a leisure society on the way. Fully automated machines with an artificial intelligence superior to the human mind will do most of the work. We can look forward to sitting back and enjoying what Daniel Bell, another "optimist", called the "Postindustrial Society".

The "pessimists" essentially knock holes in this scenario, pointing out numerous reasons why it might not come about. Another group, who might be dubbed the "romantics", say that we should forget all about high technology and instead go for self-sufficiency, cottage industries and "alternative" technologies like wind, wave and solar power. The "romantics" are perhaps best exemplified by the Small is Beautiful *man, E. F. Schumacher.*

But we start with Herbert Simon, who is Professor of Computer Science and Psychology at the Carnegie-Mellon University, Pittsburgh, Pennsylvania. This paper comes from Science, *vol. 195 (18 March 1977).*

Energy and information are two basic currencies of organic and social systems. A new technology that alters the terms on which one or the other of these is available to a system can work on it the most profound changes. At the core of the industrial revolution, which began nearly three centuries ago, lay the substitution of mechanical energy for the energy of man and animal. It was this revolution that changed a rural

419

subsistence society into an urban affluent one and touched off a chain of technological innovations that transformed not only production but also transportation, communication, warfare, the size of human populations, and the natural environment.

It is easy, by hindsight, to see how inexorably these changes followed one another, how "natural" a consequence, for example, suburbia was of cheap, privately owned transportation. It is a different question whether foresight could have predicted these chains of events or have aided in averting some of their more undesirable outcomes. The problem is not that prophets were lacking – they have been in good supply at almost all times and places. Quite the contrary, almost everything that has happened, and its opposite, has been prophesied. The problem has always been to pick and choose among the embarrassing riches of alternative projected futures; and in this, human societies have not demonstrated any large foresight. Most often we have been constrained to anticipate events just a few years before their occurrence, or even while they are happening, and to try to deal with them, as best we can, as they are engulfing us.

We are now in the early stages of a revolution in processing information that shows every sign of being as fundamental as the earlier energy revolution. Perhaps we should call it the third information revolution. (The first produced written language, and the second, the printed book.) This third revolution, which began more than a century ago, includes the computer but many other things as well. The technology of information comprises a vast range of processes for storing information, for copying it, for transmitting it from one place to another, for displaying it, and for transforming it.

Photography, the moving picture, and television gave us, in the course of a century, a whole new technology for storing and displaying pictorial information. Telegraphy, the telephone, the gramophone and radio did the same for storing and transmitting auditory information. Among all of these techniques, however, the computer is unique in its capacity for manipulating and transforming information and hence in carrying out, automatically and without human intervention, functions that had previously been performable only by the human brain.

As with the energy revolution, the consequences of the information revolution spread out in many directions. First, there are the economic consequences that follow on any innovation that increases human productivity. As we shall see, these are perhaps the easiest effects of technological change to predict. Second, there are consequences for the nature of work and of leisure – for the quality of life. Third, the computer may have special consequences for privacy and individual liberty. Fourth, there are consequences for man's view of himself, for his picture of the universe and of his place and goals in it. In each of these directions, the immediate consequences are, of course, the most readily perceived. (It was not hard to foresee that Newcomen's and Watt's engines would change the economics of mining in deep pits.) It is far more difficult to predict what indirect chains of effects these initial impacts will set off, for example, the chain that reaches from the steam engine through the internal-combustion engine to the automobile and the suburb.

Prediction is easier if we do not try to forecast in detail the time path of events and the exact dates on which particular developments are going to occur, but to focus, instead, upon the steady state towards which the system is tending.[1] Of course, we are not so much interested in what is going to happen in some vague and indefinite future as we are in what the next generation or two holds for us. Hence, a generation is the timespan with which I shall be concerned.

My discussion will be divided into five parts, the last four corresponding to domains of prediction: economics, the nature of work and leisure, social consequences, and how men and women view themselves. These essays in prediction need to be preceded, however, by some analysis of the computer itself, and particularly its capabilities and potential in the area that is usually called artificial intelligence. This subject is taken up in the next section.[2]

Computer capabilities

The computer is a device endowed with powers of utmost generality for processing symbols. It is remarkable not only for its capabilities but also for the simplicity of its underlying processes and organization. Of course, from a hardware standpoint it is not simple at all but is a highly sophisticated electronic machine. The simplicity appears at the level of the elementary information processes that the hardware enables it to perform, the organization for execution and control of those processes, and the programming languages in terms of which the control of its behaviour is expressed. A computer can read symbols from an external source, output symbols to an external destination, store symbols in one or more memories, copy symbols, rearrange symbols and structures of symbols, and react to symbols conditionally – that is, follow one course of action or another, depending on what symbols it finds in memory or in its input devices. The most general symbol-manipulating system that has been defined, the so-called Turing machine, requires no broader capabilities than these. The important limits on the powers of a computer are limits on the sizes of its memories and the speed of its elementary processes, and not on the generality of those processes.

There is great dispute among experts as to what the generality of the computer implies for its ability to behave intelligently. There is also dispute as to whether the computer, when it is behaving more or less intelligently, is using processes similar to those employed by an intelligent human being, or quite different processes. The views expressed here will reflect my own experience in research with computers and my interpretation of the scientific literature. First, no limits have been discovered to the potential scope of computer intelligence that are not also limits on human intelligence. Second, the elementary processes underlying human thinking are essentially the same as the computer's elementary information processes, although modern fast computers can execute these processes more rapidly than can the human brain.[3] In the past, computer memories, even in large computers, have probably not been as capacious as human memory, but the scale of available computer memories is increasing rapidly, to the point where memory size may not be much longer an effective limit on the capacity of computers to match human performance. Any estimate of the potential of the computer in the near or distant future depends on one's agreement or disagreement with these assumptions.

One common objection to the beliefs just expressed is that "computers can only do what you program them to do." That is correct. The behaviour of a computer at any specific moment is completely determined by the contents of its memory and the symbols that are input to it at that moment. This does not mean that the programmer must anticipate and prescribe in the program the precise course of its behaviour. A program is not a scenario; it is a strategy of action, and what actions actually transpire depend on the successive states of the machine and its inputs at each stage of the process – none of which need to be envisaged in advance either by the programmer or by the machine. A problem-solving program applied to a particular puzzle situation does not prescribe all the steps to solve that puzzle; it prescribes a selective search strategy that, when followed, may lead the computer to discover a path to a solution. But selective search, under the guidance of strategies, is also the process that people use to solve puzzles.

Of course humans, through the processes called learning, can improve their strategies by experience and instruction. By the same token, computers can be, and to some extent have been, provided with programs (strategies) for improving their own strategies. Since a computer's programs are stored in the same memories as data, it is entirely possible for programs to modify themselves – that is, to learn.

Probably the most fundamental differences between today's computers and the human information-processing system have to do with the input organs that provide the interface between the system and its environment. Simulating the capabilities of human eyes and ears has proved to be a much more difficult task than simulating the thinking processes that go on in the central nervous system. Computer capabilities in both visual and auditory domains, and particularly the former, fall far short of human capabilities.

Over the past two decades a moderate amount of work has been carried on in the field usually called artificial intelligence to explore the potentialities of the computer that have been outlined above. Some of this research has been aimed at programming computers to do things which, if done by a person, would be regarded as intelligent. Another part of the research has been directed at simulating not only the human capabilities but also the processes that human beings use in exercising these capabilities. The considerable progress that has been made in understanding the nature both of artificial and of human intelligence has hardly begun to translate itself into applications, and has been reflected to only a small degree in the actual practical uses of computers. Artificial intelligence research has had an impact upon the search algorithms that are used to solve large combinatorial problems, it is on the verge of practical application in the realm of medical diagnosis, and it has had an important influence upon certain computer programming techniques (for example, list processing). But its main significance for practical affairs lies in the future.

How, then, have computers actually been used to date? At present, computers typically spend most of their time in two main kinds of tasks, carrying out large-scale engineering and scientific calculations and keeping the financial, production and sales records of business firms and other organizations. Although precise statistics are not available, it would be safe to estimate that ninety-five per cent of all computing power is allocated to such jobs. Now these tasks belong to the horseless-carriage phase of computer development. That is to say, they consist in doing things rapidly and automatically that were being done slowly and by hand (or by desk calculator) in the pre-computer era.

Such uses of computers do not represent new functions but only new ways of performing old functions. Of course, by greatly lowering the cost of performing them, they encourage us to undertake them on a larger scale than before. The increased analytic power provided by computers has probably encouraged engineers to design more complex structures (for example, some of the very tall new office buildings that have gone up in New York and Chicago) than they would have attempted if their analytic aids were less powerful. Moreover, by permitting more sophisticated analyses to be carried out in the design process, they have also brought about significant cost reductions in the designs themselves. In the same way, the mechanization of business record-keeping processes has facilitated the introduction of improved controls over inventories and cash flows, with resulting savings in costs. Thus, the computer not only reduces the costs of the information-processing operations that it automates but also contributes to the productivity of the activities themselves.

The remaining five per cent of computer uses are more sophisticated. Let us consider two different ways in which a computer can assist an engineer in designing electric motors. On the one hand, the engineer can design the motor using conventional procedures, then employ the computer to analyse the prospective operation of the design – the operating temperature, efficiency, and so on. On the other hand, the engineer can provide the computer with the specifications for the motor, leaving to the computer the task of synthesizing a suitable design. In the second, but not the first, case the computer, using various heuristic search procedures, actually discovers, decides upon, and evaluates a suitable design. In the same way, the role of the computer in managing inventories need not be limited to record-keeping. The computer program may itself determine (on the basis of usage) when items should be reordered and how large the orders should be. In these and many other situations, computers can provide not only the information on which decisions are made but can themselves make the decisions. Process-control computers, in automated or semi-automated manufacturing operations, play a similar role in decision making. Their programs are decision strategies which, as the system's variables change from moment to moment, retain control over the ongoing process.

It is the capability of the computer for solving problems and making decisions that represents its real novelty and that poses the greatest difficulties in predicting its impact upon society. An enormous amount of research and developmental activity will have to be carried out before the full practical implications of this capability will be understood and available for use. In the single generation that modern computers have been in existence, enough basic research has been done to reveal some of the fundamental mechanisms. Although one can point to a number of applications of the computer as decision maker that are already twenty or twenty-five years old, development and application on a substantial scale have barely begun.

Economic effects of computers

The direct economic effects of introducing computers as numerical calculators and decision makers are like those of introducing any new form of capital that raises productivity and also improves the quality of the product. The computer (its hardware together with the associated system-programming costs) represents an investment in a capital-intensive, labour-saving device that has to justify itself, in competition with other possible forms of investment, through savings in clerical and other personnel costs together with the improvements it brings about in organizational decisions.

When the main motive of introducing the computer is to mechanize existing clerical operations – in the actuarial department of an insurance firm, say, or the accounting department of a manufacturing concern – then its main economic advantage stems from the reduction in clerical costs. When it is introduced to mechanize decision processes – engineering design, for example, or control of stock or cash inventories – then its direct effect shows up as some form of productivity increase in the organization's operations. In either case, there is nothing special about the computer that distinguishes it, in its economic effects, from any other capital investment. Any such investment can be expected to have a direct effect upon employment in the organizational components where it is introduced. When the accounting system is mechanized, fewer clerks and bookkeepers are needed, else there would be no economic motivation for mechanizing. Of course, if part of the motivation for the change is to improve the quality of the system's output, the operation may be expanded, and the net reduction in personnel may be smaller than would be estimated solely from the increase in efficiency. If there is sufficient elasticity of demand for the activity, personnel may actually increase.

The most important question, however, is what the reduction in personnel at the point of impact means for the total level of employment in the economy. Again, this is a general economic issue – of technological unemployment – that does not depend on any special properties of computers. They are simply one among the many labour-saving devices that have been appearing since the beginning of the industrial revolution (and before).

Both standard economic analysis and a large body of empirical evidence demonstrate that there is no relation, positive or negative, between the technological sophistication of an economy and the level of employment it maintains. From a systems standpoint, a cost reduction in any part of the system releases resources that can be employed to increase the output of goods and services elsewhere in the system. At any level of employment, from zero to a hundred per cent, the total revenue received by wage earners and owners of capital and land as wages, interest and rent is just sufficient to purchase the total bundle of goods and services that is produced. Economists sometimes disagree as to why economies do not always operate at or near full employment, but they are unanimous in agreeing that the reason is not that they produce more than they can consume. (Even Marxists agree with this proposition, although they argue that full employment cannot be maintained within the institutions of capitalism.)

An even stronger statement can be made about the systems effects of cost-saving technological innovations. We usually describe devices like computers (and most other machinery) as labour-saving because they require a lower ratio of labour to capital than the methods they displace. But if we measure savings relative to output, they are usually both labour-saving and capital-saving. That is to say, a smaller capital investment per passenger mile is required to transport people by jet plane than to transport them by ox cart. Similarly, a smaller capital investment per multiplication is required if a large modern computer is used to do the arithmetic than if it is done on a desk calculator or with a pencil and paper. (Do not forget to include the capital cost of the desk at which the clerk sits and the heated or air-conditioned room in which he or she works.) Now it is easy to show, for economic equilibrium and under reasonable assumptions about the supply of capital, that the introduction of capital-intensive, cost-saving innovations will raise the level of real wages and increase the fraction of the total revenue that goes to wages. This prediction from economic theory is amply supported by the histories of the industrialized economies over the present century. As productivity has increased (mainly as a consequence of technological innovation), real wages have steadily risen, as has labour's share in the total national product.[4]

Now the rate of technological change depends both upon the rate of discovery of new innovations and upon the availability of capital to turn them into bricks and steel (or wire and glass). In this process, computers compete with other forms of technology for the available capital. Hence, the process of computerization is simply a part, currently an important part, of the general process of technological change. It might be described, paraphrasing Clausewitz, as "a continuation of the industrial revolution by other means".[5]

In taking this very global and bird's-eye view of the economics of mechanization, we should not ignore the plight of the worker who is displaced by the computer. His plight is often genuine and serious, particularly if the economy as a whole is not operating near full employment, but even if it is. Society as a whole benefits from increased productivity, but often at the expense of imposing transient costs on a few people. But the sensible response to this problem is not to eschew the benefits of change; it is rather to take institutional steps to shift the burdens of the transition from the individual to society. Fortunately, our attitudes on these questions appear to be maturing somewhat, and our institutional practices improving, so that the widespread introduction of the computer into clerical operations over the past generation has not called forth any large-scale Ludditism. In fact, during the depression that we are currently experiencing, in contrast to some earlier ones, technology has not been accused as the villain.

Effects on the nature of work

We see that, so far as economic effects are concerned, the computer simply provides a particular path toward higher productivity through industrialization. Whatever benefits it produces, it produces in this way; whatever problems it creates, it creates as other capital-intensive innovations do. We must be careful, however, not to evaluate social change solely in terms of its impact on wages and employment. Of equal importance are the effects it may have on the workplace, and even on leisure. Today we frequently hear the claim that computers and automation dehumanize work and that dehumanization, in turn, causes alienation from work and society. These charges have been laid not only against contemporary developments in automation but against the whole process of industrialization. They were stated eloquently in the *Communist Manifesto* more than a century ago and by numerous social critics before and since. There has been a new surge of concern with the alienation issue in the past ten years.

Three questions need to be asked about alienation. First, how much alienation is there – is there evidence that alienation has been increased by computers and automation or, for that matter, by other forms of industrialization and mechanization? Second, in what ways is the nature of work, and the satisfactions derivable from it, changed by automation of the workplace? Third, as automation eliminates certain kinds of jobs in favour of others, what are the net effects upon the profile of jobs in the economy – are the jobs that are eliminated, on balance, more or less satisfying than the new ones that are created to replace them?

Objective data on national trends in job satisfaction are available only for about the last twenty years. About fifteen national surveys have been conducted since 1958 by professional polling organizations that included questions on job satisfaction. Although twenty years is a short time, it does cover almost the whole period of the introduction of computers; hence these data should help answer the question before us. The polls provide absolutely no evidence for a decrease in job satisfactions over this period. If alienation has been increased by automation, the increase somehow does not show up in answers by workers to questions about their attitudes toward their jobs.[6] Notice that the polls do not show that workers are enthusiastic about their jobs, only that they do not seem to like them less today than they did in 1958.

Unfortunately, comparable data are not available to measure the longer trends in job satisfaction over the whole past two centuries or so of industrialization. Perhaps even if computers and automation do not intensify alienation, they confirm and complete a loss of satisfactions that was produced by the rise of the factory system. The answer to that question must be mainly speculative. Clayre, however, recently threw some interesting light on it by examining the attitudes toward work expressed in preindustrial folk literature and popular ballads.[7] He finds few indications of a Golden Age in which work was generally regarded as pleasurable and satisfying. He concludes that, in general, daily work was the same burdensome necessity for peasants and craftsmen as it is for factory workers and clerks; and that life's satisfactions and pleasure were mainly sought, then as now, in leisure, not work.

Perhaps, however, we should not try to detect alienation in this indirect way but should look directly at the workplaces where computers have been introduced, in order to see how they have changed the nature of work and its environment. Sizeable differences have been found in worker satisfaction among blue-collar workers in different kinds of factories, some of the important variables being job variety and worker control over the timing of work. It is not the case, however, that the most advanced forms of industrialization and automation produce the most tedious and restrictive jobs. On the contrary, those forms of work organization that appear to have been most alienating – typified by the car assembly line or large-scale hand assembly operations – are declining in importance relative to other forms of mechanization. Blauner, for example, studied four industries in depth: printing, a traditional craft industry; textiles, a machine-tending industry; automobile assembly, highly mechanized with highly specialized jobs; and a highly automated continuous-process chemical manufacturing industry.[8] He found few indications of alienation in printing and chemicals, considerably more in textiles, and most of all in automobile assembly. The industry that best typifies modern automation – chemicals – was substantially less alienating than the two that typify older kinds of mechanization.

If we look at office automation, we see that, here too, the kinds of jobs that are displaced tend to be those that are most repetitive and restricting. Whisler, who studied about twenty companies in the insurance industry, found that computerization had produced only small and conflicting changes in the nature of clerical and supervisory jobs.[9] The new jobs placed greater demands on the employees for accuracy and reliability in performance, but they were not generally perceived as being significantly more or less pleasant or more or less boring than before. And, perhaps most important of all, whatever effects were produced were small effects. Automation and computerization do not appear to change the nature of work in a fundamental way.

Again we must look not just at immediate impact but at system effects. Factory and office automation are labour-saving technologies. The jobs they eliminate are mostly jobs that were already relatively routine. Therefore, when we look at the impact on the labour force as a whole, we expect to see automation bringing about an overall decrease in the percentage of persons engaged in routine work of these kinds. Correspondingly, there will be a larger percentage of employees than before in service occupations and probably also in technical occupations. The work-satisfaction studies discussed earlier show differences among occupational groups of precisely this kind. From these data it appears that if factory operatives and clerical workers decline as a fraction of the labour force, while service workers, sales personnel and professional and technical workers increase, there will be a net increase in reported job satisfaction – unless, of course, a compensating shift takes place in aspirations, a possibility we must not dismiss.

On all counts, then, we must acquit the computer technology of the charges that it has been and will be a cause of widespread alienation from work. Empirically, we find no signs of a downward trend in work satisfactions, and when we look at the actual impact of automation upon the workplace and the workforce, we find no reason why such a trend should be expected. On the contrary, the newer technologies may even have a modest humanizing effect on the nature of work. The notion of a Golden Age of work prior to the industrial revolution must also be dismissed as romanticism, unsupported by such evidence as has been examined.

Control and privacy

The potential of computers for increasing the control of organizations or society over their members and for invading the privacy of those members has caused considerable concern. The issues are important but are too complex to be discussed in detail here. I shall therefore restrict myself to a few comments which will serve rather to illustrate this complexity than to provide definitive answers.

A first observation is that our concern here is for competitive aspects of society, the power of one individual or group relative to others. Technologies tend to be double-edged in competitive situations, particularly when they are available to both competitors. For example, the computerization of credit information about individuals facilitates the assembly of such information from many sources, and its indefinite retention and accessibility. On the other hand, it also facilitates auditing such information to determine its sources and reliability. With appropriate legal rules of the game, an automated system can provide more reliable information than a more primitive one and can be surrounded by more effective safeguards against abuse. Some of us might prefer, for good reasons or bad, not to have our credit checked at all. But if credit checking is a function that must be performed, a strong case can be made for making it more responsible by automating it, with appropriate provision for auditing its operation.

Similarly, much has been said of the potential for embezzlement in computerized accounting systems, and cases have occurred. Embezzlement, however, was known before computers, and the computer gives auditors as well as embezzlers powerful new weapons. It is not at all clear which way the balance has been tilted.

The privacy issue has been raised most insistently with respect to the creation and maintenance of longitudinal data files that assemble information about persons from a multitude of sources. Files of this kind would be highly valuable for many kinds of economic and social research, but they are bought at too high a price if they endanger human freedom or seriously enhance the opportunities of blackmailers. While such dangers should not be ignored, it should be noted that the lack of comprehensive data files has never been the limiting barrier to the suppression of human freedom. The Watergate criminals made extensive, if unskilful, use of electronics, but no computer played a role in their conspiracy. The Nazis operated with horrifying effectiveness and thoroughness without the benefits of any kind of mechanized data processing.

Making the computer the villain in the invasion of privacy or encroachment on civil liberties simply diverts attention from the real dangers. Computer data banks can and must be given the highest degree of protection from abuse. But we must be careful, also, that we do not employ such crude methods of protection as to deprive our society of important data it needs to understand its own social processes and to analyse its problems.

Man's view of man

Perhaps the most important question of all about the computer is what it has done and will do to man's view of himself and his place in the universe. The most heated attacks on the computer are not focused on its possible economic effects, its presumed destruction of job satisfactions, or its threats to privacy and liberty, but upon the claim that it causes people to be viewed, and to view themselves, as "machines".[10]

To get at the real issues, we must first put aside one verbal confusion. All of us are familiar with a wide variety of machines, most of which predated the computer. Consequently, the word "machine" carries with it many connotations: of rigidity, of simplicity, of repetitive behaviour, and so on. If we call anything a machine, we implicitly attribute these characteristics to it. Hence, if a computer is a machine, it must behave rigidly, simply and repetitively. It follows that computers cannot be programmed to behave like human beings.

The fallacy in the argument, of course, lies in supposing that, because we have applied the term "machine" to computers, computers must behave like older forms of machines. But the central significance of the computer derives from the fact that it falsifies these earlier connotations. It can, in fact, be programmed to behave flexibly, in complex ways, and not repetitively at all. We must either get rid of the connotations of the term, or stop calling computers "machines".

There is a more fundamental question behind the verbal one. It is essentially the question that was raised by Darwinism, and by the Copernican revolution centuries earlier. The question is whether the dignity of man, his sense of worth and self-respect depend upon his being something special and unique in the universe. As I have said elsewhere (see note 2 reference, p. 27):

> The definition of man's uniqueness has always formed the kernel of his cosmological and ethical systems. With Copernicus and Galileo, he ceased to be the species located at the centre of the universe, attended by sun and stars. With Darwin, he ceased to be the species created and specially endowed by God with soul and reason. With Freud, he ceased to be the species whose behaviour was – potentially – governable by rational mind. As we begin to produce mechanisms that think and learn, he has ceased to be the species uniquely capable of complex, intelligent manipulation of his environment.

What the computer and the progress in artificial intelligence challenge is an ethic that rests on man's apartness from the rest of nature. An alternative ethic, of course, views man as a part of nature, governed by natural law, subject to the forces of gravity and the demands of his body. The debate about artificial intelligence and the simulation of man's thinking is, in considerable part, a confrontation of these two views of man's place in the universe. It is a new chapter in the vitalism-mechanism controversy.

Issues that are logically distinct sometimes become stuck together with the glue of emotion. Several such issues arise here:

To what extent can human behaviour be simulated by computer?

In what areas of work and life should the computer be programmed to augment or replace human activities?

How far should we proceed to explore the human mind by psychological research that makes use of computer simulation?

The first of these three issues will only be settled, over the years, by the success or failure of research efforts in artificial intelligence and computer simulation. Whatever our beliefs about the ultimate limits of simulation, it is clear that the current state of the art has nowhere approached those limits.

The second question will be settled anew each year by a host of individual and public decisions based on the changing computer technology, the changing economics of computer applications, and our attention to the social consequences of those applications.

The answer to the third question depends upon our attitudes towards the myths of Pandora and Prometheus. One viewpoint is that knowledge can be dangerous – there are enough historical examples – and that the attempt to arrive at a full explanation of man's ability to think might be especially dangerous. A different point of view, closer to my own, is that knowledge is power to produce new outcomes, outcomes that were not previously attainable. To what extent these outcomes will be good or bad depends on the purposes they serve, and it is not easy, in advance, to predict the good and bad uses to which any particular technology will be put. Instead, we must look back over human history and try to assess whether, on balance, man's gradual emergence from a state of ignorance about the world and about himself has been something we should celebrate or regret. To believe that knowledge is to be preferred to ignorance is to believe that the human species is capable of progress and, on balance, has progressed over the centuries. Knowledge about the human mind can make an important contribution to that progress. It is a belief of this kind that persuades researchers in artificial intelligence that their endeavour is an important and exciting chapter in man's great intellectual adventure.

Summary
From an economic standpoint, the modern computer is simply the most recent of a long line of new technologies that increase productivity and cause a gradual shift from manufacturing to service employment. The empirical evidence provides no support for the claim sometimes made that the computer "mechanizes" and "dehumanizes" work. Perhaps the greatest significance of the computer lies in its impact on Man's view of himself. No longer accepting the geocentric view of the universe, he now begins to learn that mind, too, is a phenomenon of nature, explainable in terms of simple mechanisms. Thus the computer aids him to obey, for the first time, the ancient injunction: "Know thyself."

Notes

1 A few years ago, Newell and I erred in predicting that certain specific developments in artificial intelligence were going to take place "within ten years". The fact that we were optimistic about the timescale has blinded a number of critics to the basic soundness of our characterization of the nature and directions of artificial intelligence. I shall try not to make the same mistake here of predicting that very specific things will occur at very specific times. See H. A. Simon and A. Newell, *Operations Research* 6, 1 (1958).

2 For more detailed discussions of these topics, see H. A. Simon, *The New Science of Management Decision*, 3rd edition (Prentice-Hall, Englewood Cliffs, N.J., 1977).

3 The position that computers can be programmed to simulate an indefinite range of human thinking processes is developed in detail, and a large body of supporting evidence is examined in A. Newell and H. A. Simon, *Human Problem Solving* (Prentice-Hall, Englewood Cliffs, N.J., 1972); and in J. R. Anderson and G. H. Bower, *Human Associative Memory* (Winston, Washington, DC, 1973).

4 For a fuller discussion of this evidence, see Simon, *New Science.*, chap. 4.

5 K. von Clausewitz, *On War* (Modern Library, New York, 1943), p. 596.

6 The polls under discussion were conducted by the Survey Research Centers of the Universities of Michigan and California, the National Opinion Research Center, and the Gallup Poll. For a detailed analysis of these data, see R. P. Quinn and L. J. Shepard, *The 1972–73 Quality of Employment Survey* (Institute for Social Research, University of Michigan, Ann Arbor, 1974).

7 A. Clayre, *Work and Play* (Harper & Row, New York, 1974).

8 R. Blauner, *Alienation and Freedom: The Factory Worker and His Industry* (Univ. of Chicago Press, Chicago, 1964).

9 T. L. Whisler, *The Impact of Computers on Organizations* (Praeger, New York, 1970). I. R. Hoos [in *Automation in the Office* (Public Affairs Press, Washington, D.C., 1961)] reaches more pessimistic conclusions than Whisler about the impact of the computer, but she mainly observed transient effects at the time the new technology was being introduced, and not the longer-term effects after the changes had been digested.

10 Two books that attack artificial intelligence on this ground are H. L. Dreyfus, *What Computers Can't Do* (Harper & Row, New York, 1972) and J. Weizenbaum, *Computer Power and Human Reason* (Freeman, San Francisco, 1976). The two books have little in common except a shared antipathy against the "machine" view of human thinking, and an eloquent contempt for those who hold that view. Weizenbaum's book is the technically more competent of the two, with respect to its understanding of the current state of the computer programming art.

Where are We Going?: Questions for Simon

Joe Weizenbaum

Are people unique feeling creatures or are they really just "information processing systems"? In this short note, which appeared in the US magazine Datamation *(15 November 1978), the Professor of Computer Science at the Massachusetts Institute of Technology hits back at Herbert Simon and other "unrestrained computer enthusiasts" for their "reckless and unreflective" belief in "Progress", Joe Weizenbaum is also author of* Computer Power and Human Reason *(Freeman, San Francisco, 1976).*

It is, in a way, surprising that the computer field is as nearly free of controversies as it appears to be. There are, of course, disagreements, and some of them occasionally do rise to the level of controversy. Years ago, for example, there were people who thought that floating-point arithmetic was an evil because it would encourage people to apply computers to problems before they understood enough of what they were doing to be able to predict the scaling of their variables throughout the whole course of computation.

Today there are disagreements over programming styles, computer architectures, ways of realizing computer system security, and so on. But, on the whole, such differences of opinion are just that – differences of opinion, not controversies. Observers from another field would, I think, be most impressed by an apparent unanimity of views in a field so large as the computer community. Where else are so many scientific and technical workers so much of one mind?

The unifying thread is, I believe, fervent optimism. And that optimism appears justified. Never before in the history of technology has there been a development whose every measure of technical progress

434

grew exponentially from the beginning and which has sustained that growth without interruption. Indeed, this explosive growth has created a momentum which has conferred on the field another characteristic perhaps unique to it among scientific endeavours: an orientation to the future so pervasive that it swamps all attempts to look back – especially to look back critically – or even to examine itself critically at all.

But the field's immunity from critical thinking, hence from criticism, hence from controversy, is not total. What critical assessment there is, is born of the optimism that also very nearly drowns every critical voice. This critical assessment seldom surfaces explicitly and, when it does, it is greeted either by cries that it is "philosophical" and therefore, by a curious logic, irrelevant, or it is met by a stony silence. There are, to be sure, occasional debates on university campuses, but it is rare to see a journal article by a technological optimist which attempts to state "the problem" and to answer the critics.

"The problem" is, of course, the one raised by the slogan "artificial intelligence" and by the images that slogan creates in the minds of workers in the computer field, and in those of the general public. As a sometime critical commentator on the sayings and doings of the artificial intelligence community, I was happy to see no less an authority than Dr Herbert A. Simon, surely a ranking leader in the AI field, write an article in which he at least alludes to a debate which I consider to be of the utmost importance.

Dr Simon writes that the most important question with respect to what the computer means for man and society is "what (the computer) has done and will do to man's view of himself and his place in the universe."[1] I agree with him. I must, however, quarrel with his precise formulation of that question and with his assertion that "attacks on the computer" are focused on the claim that it, the computer, "causes people to be viewed, and to view themselves, as 'machines'."

There are, to be sure, people who are critical of some of the ways the computer as an instrument and computation as a metaphor are being used in society. I am one of them. But, at least to my knowledge, no responsible critic attacks the computer as such or believes computers "cause" anything. This point may well be perceived as trivial. But it is not. The habit of speech, and it surely reflects a habit of thought, that makes instruments responsible for events, leads directly to speaking and thinking of science and technology as autonomous forces and to the idea of technological inevitability. It leads finally to the proposition that man is, after all, impotent to struggle with powerful impersonal agencies of his own making over which he has lost control, and that he is therefore justified in abdicating his responsibility for the consequences of his acts.

Dr Simon goes on to say:

> What the computer and progress in artificial intelligence challenge is an
> ethic that rests on man's apartness from the rest of nature. An alternative
> ethic, of course, views man as a part of nature, governed by natural law,
> subject to the forces of gravity and the demands of his body. The debate
> about artificial intelligence and the simulation of man's thinking is, in
> considerable part, a confrontation of these two views of man's place in the
> universe. It is a new chapter in the vitalism – mechanism controversy.

I am encouraged by this recognition of the fact that artificial intelligence
has something to do with ethics and that it raises the deepest possible
philosophical questions: questions, that is, about the place of human
beings in the universe, even though this characterization of what divides
the artificial intelligence enthusiasts from their critics is upside-down.

Artifacts are not part of nature; else everything to be found in the
universe is part of nature, and then to so label some particular thing or
being would be to say nothing. The critics to whom Dr Simon alludes
insist on distinguishing between human beings, whom they do consider
part of nature, and artifacts, such as computers, that are not part of
nature. Human beings are to be treated with respect and contemplated
with awe. Computers, too, may inspire respect and awe – but really, save
for idolatry, only as reflections on their human architects. Of course,
human beings are part of nature; of course, they are governed by natural
law, etc.

George A. Miller once lamented in an unpublished manuscript that:
"Many psychologists have come to take for granted . . . that men and
computers are merely two different species of a more abstract genus
called 'information processing systems'. The concepts that describe
abstract information processing systems must, perforce, describe any
particular examples of such systems." Psychologists were encouraged to
take such a view of human beings by the repeated assertions of such
leaders of the artificial intelligence movement as Dr Simon that, from an
information processing point of view, "the whole man" is "quite
simple"[2] and that the ability of computers to think, learn, and create will
"increase rapidly until – in the visible future – the range of problems
they can handle will be coextensive with the range to which the human
mind has been applied."[3]

The really deep controversy has nothing whatever to do with vitalism.
It is about the extent to which science, or indeed any other single
perspective, can lead to an understanding of man or, for that matter, of
any other part of nature. My own view is that human beings, as parts of
nature, are to be understood by whatever means we have for understanding nature. Science provides certain of those means. But science

must necessarily proceed by simplifying reality, and the first step in its process of simplification is abstraction. The information processing metaphor leads to particularly powerful and hitherto unattained abstract characterizations of certain aspects of man's mental functions. But they are *abstract* characterizations and they are simplifications of the reality they mirror. Dr Simon appeals to the way computers process information as a model for human cognition, for example, when he writes: "The elementary information processes underlying human thinking are *essentially* the same as the computer's elementary information processes" (my emphasis). He says, as of course he must, that the two processes he is discussing are "essentially" the same. None of us can avoid having to make value judgements about what aspects of whatever we are studying are "essential" to *our* purposes and what aspects to leave out of our consideration. But leave out some we must. Neither the computer metaphor nor any other drawn from the armamentarium of science alone yields a complete understanding of any natural phenomena, let alone of the whole man. The computer's information processes may serve as a model of more or less heuristic utility for human information processes. But every model has limitations.

Another belief that Dr Simon wrongly attributes to critics is that: ". . . knowledge can be dangerous . . . [and that] the attempt to arrive at a full explanation of man's ability to think might be especially dangerous."

Partial knowledge is dangerous when the knower believes it to be complete. It is, in my view, certainly one task of scientists (and of others as well) to humbly strive for ever more nearly complete explanations of the phenomena of the world. I say "humbly" because only humility can guard against the arrogance of believing we understand completely when, in fact, we can understand only partially. Systems of thought – one might well say "ideologies" – that have in the past arrogantly promised "full" explanations, have usually proved catastrophic to both their adherents and to innocent bystanders.

Dr Simon also bravely writes that "knowledge is better than ignorance." By asserting that, in the context of distinguishing his position from that of critics, he invites the inference that critics prefer ignorance to knowledge. I reject it, of course. Suggestions of this kind lead in the not-so-very-long run to the absurd charge that all critics of any aspect of science and technology are fundamentally anti-intellectual. Again, it seems to me, this turns the issue upside-down: It is not those of us who seek to understand the world from a number of different perspectives, including the scientific one, who prefer ignorance to knowledge. It is those who, blinded by their faith that science can yield "full" explanations, prefer to remain ignorant of whatever knowledge other ways of knowing the world have to offer.

The questions which define the controversy between unrestrained computer enthusiasts and their critics revolve about concerns over the scope of science and of scientific rationality. They are really questions about the power *and the limitations* of a variety of ways of knowing the world.

It is, in my view, unfortunate that there is not more debate on such important points in the computer community – and by debate here I mean specifically exchanges of views in the computer community's professional literature. We have seen the computer begin as a mere instrument for generating ballistic tables and grow to a force that now pervades almost every aspect of modern society. In an important sense, it has already transcended its status as a mere tool to be applied to specific tasks. It has become a symbol, indeed a source, of questions that were in earlier times asked only by theologians and philosophers but which have now, in part because of the role computers and computation play in the world, attained immediacy and urgency.

The history of science and technology of the postwar era is filled with examples of reckless and unreflective "progress" which, while beneficial or at least profitable to some in the short run, may yet devastate much life on this planet. Perhaps it is too much to hope, but I hope nonetheless that as our discipline matures our practitioners will mature also, that all of us will begin to think about what we are actually doing and ponder whether, whatever it is, it is what those who follow us would want us to have done.

Notes

1   H. A. Simon, "What Computers Mean For Man and Society", *Science*, vol. 195 (18 March 1977). See previous piece.
2   H. A. Simon, *The Science of the Artificial* (MIT Press, Cambridge, Mass., 1969).
3   H. A. Simon and A. Newell, "Heuristic Problem Solving: The Next Advance in Operations Research", *Operations Research*, vol. 6 (Jan–Feb 1958).

The Social Implications of Intelligent Machines

Margaret A. Boden

If your appetite for the artificial intelligence controversy has been whetted by the preceding two pieces, then Margaret Boden's article is a natural follow-on. The author, Professor of Philosophy and Psychology at the University of Sussex, England, provides a scholarly review of the ethical and social issues raised by the new phenomenon of machine intelligence. With intelligent machines likely to become much more widespread thanks to developments in microelectronics, the author argues that this poses a threat to the concept of self. The paper comes from The Radio and Electronic Engineer, *vol. 47, No. 8/9 (August/September 1977) and is based on chapter 15 of Professor Boden's* Artificial Intelligence and Natural Man (*Harvester Press*, Hassocks, Sussex, 1977).

Current achievements and future developments

Computer hardware gets steadily cheaper: it is predicted that by the year 2000, a 65 K-bit silicon chip capable of twenty million instructions a second will sell for one US dollar. But the social application of intelligent machines also demands advances in software, such as more powerful programming languages and improved organization and use of knowledge. Work in artificial intelligence has shown that the problems of organizing and accessing large data-bases will not be quickly solved. The early optimism in the field has waned accordingly: already by 1962, the mediocrity of chess programs was being stressed by someone who in 1957 had predicted that a computer would be world chess champion within ten years. And much current research claims to develop organizational principles whereby a knowledge-domain can be economically represented and appropriately addressed without triggering a combinational explosion.[1]

Nevertheless, professionals participating in a multistage "Delphi" forecasting exercise have predicted that within the next thirty years (in

439

many cases, within only ten or fifteen years), social applications of artificial intelligence will be widely, i.e. commercially, available.[2] In general, the prototype is expected 5 ± 2 years ahead of the commercial version. The dates I shall mention are taken from this Delphi study (although my own view is that these predictions tend to underestimate the difficulties involved).

The applications forecasts run from robot housecleaners, chauffeurs and industrial workers, through programmed gameplayers and story-tellers, to automatic teachers, physicians, legal justices, marriage coun-sellors and literary critics. In all these cases, the emphasis is on reasoned and flexible judgement on the program's part, as opposed to the storage and regurgitation of isolated facts, or the repetitive performance of a fixed sequence of discriminations and movements.

For example, the computer diagnosticians of the 1980s will not simply store lists of symptom-diagnosis pairs, or prescribe treatment in a blindly dogmatic (and apparently "objective") fashion. One current prototype is the MYCIN system, an interactive program that simulates a medical consultant specializing in infectious diseases.[3] It engages in question-and-answer conversations (lasting twenty minutes on aver-age) with doctors needing specialist help, and in seventy-five per cent of cases gives the same counsel as a human expert. The physician asks MYCIN for advice on the identification of micro-organisms and the prescription of antibiotics, and also for explanations of its advice expressed at the appropriate level of detail.

MYCIN's explanatory capacity enables physicians who disagree with specific aspects of the program's clinical rationale rationally to *reject* MYCIN's advice. It also helps nonspecialist doctors to learn more about the complexities of diagnosis and therapy in this class of diseases. And it allows human consultants to make general improvements in the prog-ram, by telling it about relevant knowledge that they realize in specific cases to be missing or inadequately stated.

A program like MYCIN involves artificial intelligence techniques. Quite apart from its (rather restricted) natural language understanding, its ability to explain itself on many different levels of detail implies a self-knowledge of its reasoning and goal-structure that are crucial to intelligent thinking. And its ability to learn by being told implies some mastery of the problem of making spontaneous inferences on the basis of input information, though admittedly only for a very limited area of discourse.

Many features of MYCIN would be embodied also in programmed legal arbiters (prototype predicted by 1988). These would not only search for relevant legal precedents in the judicial literature – a far from trivial task – but would also offer legal advice. Like MYCIN, legal arbiters will preferably be used to *augment* human judgement, rather than *replace* it. Accordingly, like MYCIN, they should when appropriate offer several (reasoned) alternative judgements, not just the one of which they are most confident. MYCIN's assessment of degrees of confidence is not a mere statistical probability measure. It takes into account psychological factors about the evidential relations of beliefs, factors that philosophers of science have considered in regard to "confirmation theory". Legal programs, too, would have to incorporate more subtle concepts of *confidence* and *evidence* than Bayesian probability, in order to avoid judicial absurdities of various types.[4]

Flexible planning, and an intelligently structured representation of knowledge, is used by the Computer-Based Consultant, a system designed to give on-the-job advice about how to assemble a machine to novice mechanics having varied levels of expertise.[5] The program uses the specific queries posed by the human novice as cues directing it to answer at one level or another. Thus it tells one mechanic simply to "Replace the pump," but advises a less experienced person first to "Remove the four mounting bolts at the base of the pump using a $\frac{3}{8}$-inch open-end wrench." When a human failure occurs because of an unexpected happening (including but not restricted to previous mistakes on the novice's part), the Consultant can question the mechanic in an intelligent fashion so as to locate the difficulty. In most cases, this will not be a simple matter of asking "What's the trouble?" since the novice usually does not know just what has gone wrong, and may claim to have followed the program's advice to the letter. Because the program's representation of the semantics of this domain includes detailed and intelligently structured knowledge, in the majority of cases it is able to spot the trouble and work out a way of putting the human worker back on the right track.

Future automatic tutors will be more sophisticated than today's computer-aided instruction systems, even those that allow differential branching of the "syllabus" according to the student's mistakes and queries. Like MYCIN and the Computer-Based Consultant, they will be able to initiate and answer questions at various levels of detail, according to the pupil's range of expertise. They will concentrate on asking probing questions enabling them to model the student's understanding of the topic, and will devise an individually tailored tutorial strategy designed to build on this understanding in fruitful ways. Such programs presuppose an intelligently structured representation of the knowledge concerned, in its various aspects and degrees. Commercial availability is forecast for 1988, and exploratory programs already exist.[6]

Public access to a powerful computer would be required for many of the predicted social applications of artificial intelligence. John

McCarthy accordingly has forecast the widespread use of video-teletype *home information terminals*, linked to a national network of timesharing computers.[7]

A speech-understanding program would allow the user to speak requests instead of typing them.[8] At present, this can be reliably done (for instance, by the HEARSAY system[9] for playing voice-chess) only by using a very small and deliberately distinct vocabulary, with unnatural pauses between the words. This is because (as in the interpretation of visual scenes) the continuous stream of normal speech has to be sensibly segmented into individual words before it can be understood – but, as artificial intelligence research has shown, it has first to be understood in order to be segmented. Even the individual sounds cannot be distinguished on purely auditory grounds, but only by reference to the wider linguistic context. However, commercial uses are forecast for 1983.

According to some forecasts, the stationary home terminal will in 1995 be supplemented by a domestic robot. It should not be necessary to clear the floor so that the robot can vacuum it: the robot itself will supposedly be able to recognize the objects littering the room and put them into their proper place – or, by default, in one corner. Current achievements suggest that a robot might fairly soon be able to recognize a waste-paper bin wrongly placed by the window, or even high up on the table, so as to reposition it by the desk.[10] But *only* if the room is otherwise unnaturally tidy, and *only* if the bin, window, table and desk are of uniform type.

Industrial and agricultural robots (forecast by 1980) are less fanciful. These would not have a fixed sensorimotor capability, like the automated machines of today. Instead, they would be flexible in operation, and could learn *new* tasks. They would learn not by being laboriously reprogrammed, but by being shown examples of (for instance) new machine parts and machine tools, and by being given an outline sketch of the desired procedure which they would then elaborate in detail. The sort of planning facilities used by the Computer-Based-Consultant, or programs like BUILD, would be crucial here. BUILD plans how to assemble brick structures which may require "creative" steps such as using a temporary scaffold, counterweight, or support.[11] Features like potential stability and steadiness of movement are continually taken into account in deciding what to do, and if a safer method can be found of constructing the desired building then that method will be used. If it turns out that the "safer" method is not safe after all, BUILD can alter course accordingly, meanwhile losing none of the information gained during the aborted attempt. Slight local difficulties can be recognized and overcome without affecting the general strategy, but graver obstacles prompt radical replanning.

There are already some mobile carrier-robots, and programmed hand-eye systems that can assemble simple machines from components they learn to recognize by being shown examples or that (like MIT's COPY-DEMO[12]) can build visually demonstrated structures out of a "warehouse" of familiar parts. Moreover, a robot linked to the Computer-Based-Consultant would be able to assemble a pump even if someone else had left the job half-finished, or had wrongly positioned some of the parts. This flexible behaviour is very different from that of current industry's computer-controlled devices, such as the Unimate, which require everything to be in the right place at the right time.

Possible effects on concepts of self and society
The potential social influence of artificial intelligence is ambiguous, for two reasons. First, specific applications (as of any science) may be used for good or evil ends, and may have unsuspected side-effects. Second, much depends on the background human context, including the general public's implicit philosophical assumptions or "image of man". I shall first discuss some possible bad effects, and then sketch potential good effects of intelligent machines.

There is a widespread suspicion of artificial intelligence among the general public, based on the common philosophical assumption that regarding man as a computational mechanism entails denying human subjectivity, individuality and moral freedom. This suspicion has been voiced by critics of urban industrialism such as Theodore Roszak and Herbert Marcuse,[13] and by psychologists in touch with laymen seeking practical help. For example, this complaint is from Rollo May, a therapeutic and counselling psychologist:[14]

> I take very seriously ... the dehumanizing dangers in our tendency in modern science to make man over into the image of the machine, into the image of the techniques by which we study him. ... A central core of modern man's "neurosis" is the undermining of his experience of himself as responsible, the sapping of his willing and decision.

May's point is that choices made without confidence in their possible relevance to eventual action are unlikely to be effective – or perhaps even to be made at all. For if a man's self-image represents himself to himself as an autonomous purposive creature capable of pursuing certain ends, then it can be used to generate choices and guide his action accordingly. Even in machines, as is evident in planning programs such as BUILD, the internal representation of the possible modes of action that are available to the system can be crucial in directing performance. But if a "depersonalization" of the self-image occurs so that the self is no longer seen as a truly purposive system, then relatively *in*human, "pathological" behaviour can be expected in consequence.

This type of degenerate self-model is encouraged by artificial intelligence in general, given the popular (though mistaken) philosophical assumption of total incompatibility between mechanism and humanism. What May calls "the undermining of one's experience of oneself as responsible" may therefore be exacerbated by the development of clever programs.

As well as having immediate consequences in one's personal life, this sapping of willpower can have widespread social implications. For example, the political institution of participatory democracy assumes an ascription of responsibility to individuals which fits ill with the dehumanized image remarked by May. Consequently, providing citizens with home terminals, with the partial aim of enabling them to vote and express their political views without leaving their fireside,[15] might subtly undermine their sense of civic responsibility. This is the reverse of the intended effect, which is to encourage individual citizens to engage more fully in democratic government, thereby lessening the common feeling of alienated helplessness with respect to the governmental process. (Of course, to *feel* less a cog is not necessarily to *be* any less a cog: the home terminal might function as a subtle form of social control, damping down dissent by contenting people with an illusory sense of political participation.)

While any intelligent program may have a dehumanizing effect on people who see an unbridgeable metaphysical gulf between themselves and machines, as many people do, some would be especially open to this criticism. For instance, the prediction that by the year 2000 automatic interviewers will be used to aid the diagnosis and treatment of psychiatric patients is a suggestion that many would spurn. Thus Joseph Weizenbaum, the creator of the early conversational program ELIZA,[16] has bitterly denounced the "obscene" idea of employing programs in clinical situations.[17]

In medical contexts dealing with basically physical illness, artificial intelligence may be more welcome. The MYCIN system has not yet been tried out in a clinical situation, though the authors report some resistance on the part of clinicians to the idea of using the program. When MYCIN has achieved a ninety per cent match with human experts, it will be introduced experimentally into a hospital; only then will its authors be able to see who uses it, how often, and what effect it has on the prescribing practices of doctors and the clinical status of their patients. But a much simpler program for the diagnosis of peptic ulcers has been used on patients, who often claim to prefer this diagnostic method.[18] Ironically, they describe the machine (with which they communicate by teletype) as more friendly, polite, relaxing and comprehensible than the average physician.

These chastening observations about the superiority of the personal habits of programs over those of human doctors can doubtless be expected also with regard to automatic lawyers, bureaucrats and teachers. While perhaps appreciated in isolated interactions of a tedious, technical or embarrassing nature, this imperturbable mode might come to be consciously spurned in human relations in general, with a consequent increased emphasis on emotional spontaneity. Alternatively, the opposite effect might result: the blandness of one's guest-computer might come to be emulated in one's own mode of expression – or that of one's children. (The possible ill effect on children was cited in the Delphi survey as a disadvantage of the domestic robot.)

In general, one has to consider the dehumanizing effects of people's becoming decreasingly dependent upon human contact for satisfaction of their needs. Many who today can do their jobs only by going to a particular place of work, might tomorrow be able to stay at home and communicate with their clients and co-workers via the home terminal. The socially isolating influence of television is as nothing to the alienation and loneliness that might result from overenthusiastic reliance on the home terminal and associated gadgetry.

Let us now ask whether social applications of artificial intelligence might have any *welcome* effects on the way people view themselves and other people.

Computational models of intelligence are in fact markedly more human than the behaviourists' models of mankind that have been widely accepted for years, because the computational approach can endorse the humanist's stress on the idiosyncrasy of people's subjective worldviews and on the directive role of the self-image. A program constructs its interpretation of the input by way of its particular epistemological scheme, or set of inner models of the world, and the same input may thus be "experienced" very differently by different programs. If this commonly unsuspected "humanizing" feature of artificial intelligence can be brought home to the general public, then many of the ill effects I have hypothesized will be allayed.

Educational methods based on the pedagogical philosophy of LOGO-turtles[19] might change ways of thinking about "failure". Instead of the passively defeatist: "I'm not good at this," the child would say: "How can I make myself better at it?" This attitude is encouraged by the computational way of thinking about thinking, with its emphasis on the creative interrelation of many different procedures, and on the unintended effects of specifiable bugs in basically well-conceived attempts to achieve one's goal. By contrast, constructive self-criticism is not encouraged by a conception of intelligence that views it as the product of a number of mysterious monolithic "talents" or abilities, which one either has or lacks, willy-nilly. (An increase in the use of programming in schools may also help to avert the growth of a socially divisive "computer elite", a small group of people whose members are the only ones to understand computation and so the only ones not to feel alienated in the computerized society of the future.)

Publicly available programs are unlikely to be rendered "emotional", even assuming this to be in principle possible, since there would be little point in doing so. If people still felt a need to draw a line between themselves and "machines", their valuation of the emotional life would probably increase, with corresponding effects on cultural mores. Incorporated in the self-image of most Westerners is the Protestant ethic that only hard work is a really serious activity. And "work" is implicitly defined as paid, as done in one's employer's time rather than in one's own "leisure" time, and at the employer's behest rather than for one's own purposes. Consequently, massive unemployment could be more soul-destroying than the most repetitive of factory jobs, causing men destructively to see themselves as social parasites. This is less likely to happen to women, who enjoy an internalized acceptance of emotional values that enables them to derive greater fulfilment from personal relations and the expression of emotions outside the immediate family circle. If automation increases men's opportunities for human interaction, with friends as well as family, we may expect radical changes in the social definitions of sexual roles (for emotionality at present is seen as secondary to the masculine role). These changes would be due primarily to economic shifts in working hours and the sexual division of labour, but they could be reinforced by a general increase in evaluation of the emotional life deriving from the "emotionless" nature of programs.

Precautionary measures in writing and presenting programs
Sometimes things will go wrong, so that a program needs to be adjusted. Programmers who wish to know what is going on, and what needs to be stopped should anything go amiss, must take steps beforehand to allow for this. Their programs should be intelligible and explicit, so that "what is going on" is not buried in the code or implicitly embodied in procedures whose aim and effect are obscure.

Programs should be generously commented, so that what a procedure is *supposed* to be doing (and *why*) is readily visible. The importance of this for aiding debugging (whether by a human or an automatic programmer) is evident from the program-writing program, HACKER.[20] HACKER writes programs to perform tasks such as stacking bricks in specified ways, and is able to correct its own mistakes – and to avoid similar mistakes in future tasks of a generally similar nature – by way of its understanding of the purposive structure of task and program alike. HACKER uses the intention-coding comments it attaches to each line of its "first draft" programs in amending these programs later. Only because it has such a good idea of what it is trying to do, and how it is trying to do it, is it able self-critically to modify its own procedures.

Intelligibility and explicitness are to some extent opposed, and programs get less readable as they approach the machine code level. What counts as "machine code" is likely to become rather more intelligible to human beings, since instructions that now have to be programmed may be "hardwired" into the electronics of the machine.

To economize on computation time, the next best thing to hardwiring is compiling. It would in general be advantageous to have the possibility of switching from compiled to interpreted mode if necessary, so as intelligently to guide the giving of detailed instructions to the machine in the light of current circumstances, and the programmer should specify the sorts of contexts in which this switch might be advisable. The learning program HACKER, when in doubt (and when running a new program for the first time), can switch into a slower "careful" mode in which every step is carefully examined before it is taken.

It is easier to see what is going on if sub-routines are written so that they can easily be "got out" from the program as a whole. This principle of modular programming is exemplified in programs like BUILD. The understanding and improvement of BUILD are facilitated by the clear distinction between the intercommunicating "expert" subroutines. Modular programming will be required also in writing programs that cannot possibly be spied on or maliciously altered. For unless it is small, a program cannot be proved to perform *exactly* the functions required by the designer *and no other functions whatever.* The only way to make unauthorized access absolutely unfeasible would be to build the system around individually proved modules, or "security kernels". Modular programming also helps to counter the conservatism inherent in widespread applications of very complex systems, for if faults can be adjusted without necessitating widespread tinkering with the system then programmers will be better able to face the task of improving a large-scale system.

If programmers are able to see what is going on, they should not use programming techniques which – while making for readable programs – render the control structure obscure. For example, use of the programming language PLANNER tends to produce readable programs in which one cannot tell what is going on by examining the code.[21] PLANNER programs are legible because it is a "goal-directed" language in which routines can be indirectly invoked by way of general "goal-patterns" matching the index of the routines in question. Specific advice to try one routine before another can be included by the programmer. But the language embodies an automatic backtrack facility which tags on to the end of the specific advice (if any) the instruction to USE ANYTHING that might work: that is, any routine whose index-pattern matches the goal currently being sought. This strategy might lead to some nasty situations: a distraught parent in squalid surroundings may try anything to stop the baby screaming – and succeed appallingly well. A human has to be distraught to disregard the side-effects of "effective" measures, but a program may not even know about them.

Moreover, in the PLANNER automatic backtrack situation, the program simply tries out the first method that seems apt, since it has no way of comparing all possibilities beforehand. The knowlege that hitting may hurt the baby could be buried inside the relevant procedure, to be found only when this way of making the baby quiet was run. Only if the programmer had specifically included the advice never to hit the baby, would a PLANNER program refuse even to consider it. The programming language CONNIVER (which was developed largely in response to the difficulties involved in PLANNER backtracking) by contrast does allow for the potential choices to be listed for higher-level criticism.[22] (BUILD uses this facility in deciding on the safest way to build a brick house.) If a CONNIVER program knew that hitting hurts, and was able to access this knowledge when needed, it would be able to control itself long enough to find an alternative way of quieting the baby, or to decide to abandon this goal as not legally achievable.

This example makes it clear that a flexibly intelligent control structure is only useful if the program embodies sensible criteria of what effects are "undesirable". Some "sensible" criteria are culture-specific, and one may expect much moral-political disagreement about what precautions regarding artificial intelligence are worthwhile. Isaac Asimov's well-known "Three Laws of Robotics" each assume that we know (and have communicated to the robot's program) what is to be counted as "harm".

Should we, for instance, regard it as harmful to lie? (We commonly say it is immoral, and utilitarians argue that it is socially harmful.) But if so, we may be landed with a teletyping program that is forbidden to tell tactful white lies. One of the reasons people often have for lying is precisely to *avoid* harming others. The more "personal" the program, the more likely that lying (or a tell-tale silence?) might be in order. Some people would even claim that for social-political reasons – such as preventing dissent, disorder or panic – certain "impersonal facts" should be kept from the general public. On this view, should all home terminal programs (particularly those notionally contributing to participatory government) be kept ignorant of them also, or should they be able intelligently to take account of them while "protectively" keeping them to themselves, if necessary lying in order to do so?

The ethical ambiguity of lying is only one of many difficult cases. One may therefore experience some reserve about recommendations of a new profession of value-impact forecasters: ethical experts armed with scientific tools for making cost-benefit judgements.[23] Roszak has sourly commented: "What these ethical engineers will know of 'value' (Old Style: the meaning of life) may of course be only a computer simulation of a statistical illusion gleaned from questionnaires whose unreality crudely approximates a moral imbecile's conception of an ethical decision."[24]

Roszak regards the use of psychological terms in psychological contexts, and artificial intelligence research in general, as inescapably dehumanizing for the culture that admits them. He would urge programmers not merely to refuse to write obviously exploitative programs, but to re-examine the philosophical assumptions of their whole enterprise. In view of the discussion in the second section above, "Possible Effects . . .", this is surely not too much to ask. Psychological theories in general are not purely *descriptive*, but are largely *constitutive* of social reality, and computational theories are no exception. If the public believes – rightly or wrongly – that science regards people as "nothing but clockwork", then clockwork people we may tend to become. This is why computer scientists should stress the basic philosophical compatibility of "humanist" and computational views.

In this connection, perhaps programs for public use should include explicit reminders of some of the differences between computers and people. This is done (for utilitarian reasons) in the peptic ulcer program[18] previously described: it continually reminds patients that they are on-line to a machine. The reminder helps to avoid mystification of the patients, stressing that they are merely "filling in a form" by teletype rather than engaging in flexible communication, still less participating in a human relationship. "Plausibility tricks" are sometimes included in language-using programs. For instance, the CAI programs currently used in schools take care to address the children from time to time by their first names, so as to put them at their ease. In view of the dehumanizing potential of computer applications (quite apart from the possible results of an overgenerous misunderstanding by the person), it may be that the limits of individual programs should be made as clear as possible to users, and plausibility tricks used sparingly – if at all.

On one point, however, even Roszak presumably would agree that the *similarity* between people and programs should be deliberately stressed. One of his objections to the social use of computers in an advisory capacity is that the machine may be seen by the public (including the politicians) as purely *objective*, and therefore not to be argued with. Accordingly, the inescapable subjectivity of a program's judgements should be made clear to its users. We saw that this is done implicitly in the MYCIN medical consultant: MYCIN not only offers alternative judgements when it perceives several possibilities of diagnosis or treatment, but gives its reasons for each so that physicians can rationally reject its advice if they see fit. In general, it would be worthwhile somehow to remind the user that programs function within their own subjective cognitive worlds, just as we do. Any differences between the two are matter for epistemological debate, not for servile capitulation on the part of the person.

Conclusions

Increasingly intelligent machines are likely to become socially available, whether for use by the general public or by political and administrative institutions.

Many of the potential ill-effects depend on the common (though mistaken) view that mechanism is incompatible with "human" qualities. If the public assume that science offers an image of man that is irreconcilable with humanism, they must either deny their humanity – with socially destructive results – or else forfeit a scientific understanding of mankind.

So in addition to writing programs in a sensible fashion (so that the control structure is perspicuous and alteration is facilitated), professionals involved in artificial intelligence should take pains to see that this choice is not regarded by the public as unavoidable. For example, they should avoid "plausibility tricks" in programs that might lead to unnecessary mystification of the users, and they should point out that a program's data and inference procedures may always be questioned in principle, just as a person's can be.

Recognition of these issues by the profession considered as a social institution (as opposed to isolated individuals within it) will be necessary if they are to be adequately faced. In so far as the profession succeeds in reassuring the public that mechanism (of sufficient complexity) is in principle capable of generating the distinctively human characteristics of subjectivity, purpose and choice, the increasing social use of intelligent machines will present less of a threat to humane conceptions of self and society.

Notes

1 The "chess champion" forecast was made and withdrawn by H. A. Simon, one of the programmers of the General Problem Solver (GPS). For a discussion of the organization of large amounts of knowledge, see, e.g., M. L. Minsky, "A framework for representing knowledge", in P. H. Winston (ed.), *The Psychology of Computer Vision* (McGraw-Hill, New York, 1975), pp. 221–77.

2 O. Firschein, M. A. Fischler, L. S. Coles, and J. M. Tenenbaum, "Forecasting and assessing the impact of artificial intelligence on society", Third Int. Joint. Conf. on Artificial Intelligence (1973), pp. 105–20.

3 E. H. Shortliffe, S. G. Axline, B. G. Buchanan, J. C. Merigan and N. S. Cohen, "An artificial intelligence program to advise physicians regarding anti-microbial therapy", *Computers and Biomedical Research*, 6, (1973), pp. 544–60; E. H. Shortcliffe, R. Davis, S. G. Axline, B. G. Buchanan, C. C. Green, and N. S. Cohen, "Computer-based consultations in clinical therapeutics: explanation and rule acquisition capabilities of the MYCIN System", *Computers and Biomedical Research*, 8 (1975), pp. 303–20.

4 E. H. Shortliffe and B. G. Buchanan, "A model of inexact reasoning in medicine", *Mathematical Biosciences*, 23 (1975), pp. 351–79.

5 P. E. Hart, "Progress on a computer based consultant", Fourth Int. Joint Conf. on Artificial Intelligence (1975), pp. 831–41.

6 For current attempts to base CAI on the flexible representation of knowledge, see: A. Collins, "Process in acquiring knowledge", in R. C. Anderson, R. J. Spiro, and W. E. Montague (eds.), *Schooling and the Acquisition of Knowledge* (Erlbaum, Hillsdale, N.J., in press); J. Seely-Brown and R. R. Burton, "Multiple representations of knowledge for tutorial reasoning", in D. G. Bobrow and A. Collins (eds.), *Representation and Understanding: Studies in Cognitive Science* (Academic Press, New York, 1975), pp. 311–50.

7 J. McCarthy, "The home information terminal", "Man and Computer", Proc. Int. Conf. Bordeaux 1970 (Karger, Basel, 1972), pp. 48–57.

8 M. J. Underwood, "Machines that understand speech", *The Radio and Electronic Engineer*, 47, No. 8/9, (August/September 1977), pp. 368–76.

9 D. R. Reddy, L. D. Erman, R. D. Fennell, and R. B. Neely, "The HEARSAY speech understanding system", Proc. Third Int. Joint Conf. on Artificial Intelligence (1973), pp. 185–93; D. R. Reddy, and A. Newell, "Knowledge and its representation in a speech understanding system", in W. L. Gregg (ed.), *Knowledge and Cognition* (Erlbaum, Baltimore, 1974), pp. 253–86.

10 J. M. Tenenbaum, and S. Weyl, "A region-analysis subsystem for interactive scene analysis", Fourth Int. Joint Conf. on Artificial Intelligence (1975), pp. 682–7.

11 S. E. Fahlman, "A planning system for robot construction tasks", *Artificial Intelligence*, 5 (1974), pp. 1–50.

12 P. H. Winston, "The MIT robot", in B. Meltzer and D. Michie (eds.), *Machine Intelligence 7* (Edinburgh University Press, 1972), pp. 465–80.

13 T. Roszak, *Where the Wasteland Ends: Politics and Transcendence in Post Industrial Society* (Doubleday, New York, 1972); H. Marcuse, *One Dimensional Man: The Ideology of Industrial Society* (Routledge, Kegan Paul, London, 1964).

14 R. May (ed.), *Existential Psychology* (Random House, New York, 1961), p. 20.

15 The technical aspects of "tele-voting" were discussed in 1959 by Dr Vladimir. K. Zworykin in the Institution's 4th Clerk Maxwell Memorial Lecture: "The Human Aspect of Engineering Progress", *J. Brit. Instn Radio Engnrs*, 19, No. 9 (September 1959), pp. 529–44 (see pp. 541–4).

16 J. Weizenbaum, "Contextual understanding by computers", *Comm. Ass. Computing Machinery*, 10 (1967), pp. 474–80.
17 J. Weizenbaum, *Computer Power and Human Reason: From Judgment to Calculation* (Freeman, San Francisco, 1976).
18 W. I. Card, M. Nicholson, G. P. Crean, G. Watkinson, C. R. Evans, J. Wilson, and D. Russell, "A comparison of doctor and computer interrogation of patients", *Int. J. Biomedical Computing*, 5 (1974), pp. 175–87.
19 S. Papert, "Teaching children to be mathematicians versus teaching about mathematics", *Int. J. Educ. Sci. Technol.*, 3 (1972), pp. 249–62.
20 G. J. Sussman, *A Computer Model of Skill Acquisition* (American Elsevier, New York, 1975).
21 C. Hewitt, "PLANNER: a language for proving theorems in robots", First Int. Joint Conf. on Artificial Intelligence (1969), pp. 295–301; C. Hewitt, "Procedural embedding of knowledge in PLANNER", Second Int. Joint Conf. on Artificial Intelligence (1971), pp. 167–84.
22 G. J. Sussman, and D. V. McDermott, "Why Conniving is Better than Planning", AI Memo 255a, MIT AI Lab., 1972.
23 A. Toffler, *Future Shock* (Random House, New York, 1970).
24 T. Roszak, loc. cit., p. 69.

The Political Impact of Information Technology

Theodore J. Lowi

One of the earliest – and still one of the most valuable – discussions of the political implications of developments in microelectronics-based information technology is this paper which appeared in the IEEE Transactions On Communications *(vol. COM-23, No. 10) in October 1975. The author shows that the advances in information technology are two-edged, as is the case with most social innovation. Either the new telecommunications systems will spread information more widely and thus enhance the power of the individual, or they will greatly increase man's susceptibility to manipulation. It is up to us. Choices also have to be made on the issues of government secrecy, the centralization of state power, and individual privacy. The author, who is Professor of American Institutions at Cornell University, Ithaca, points out that technological change – "The Xerox and magnetic tape explosion" – figured prominently in the Pentagon Papers and Watergate scandals. Heaven knows what microelectronics might bring.*

"That's very good, what you said about the Second Industrial Revolution," she said.

"Old, old stuff."

"It seemed very fresh to me – I mean that part where you say how the First Industrial Revolution devalued muscle work, then the second one devalued routine mental work. I was fascinated."

"Norbert Wiener said all that way back in the nineteen-forties. It's fresh to you because you're too young to know anything but the way things are now. . . ."

"Do you suppose there will be a Third Industrial Revolution?"

He paused in his office doorway. "A third one? What would that be like?"

"I don't know exactly. The first and second ones must have been sort of inconceivable at one time."

"To the people who were going to be replaced by machines, maybe. A third one, eh? In a way, I guess the third one's been going on for some time, if you mean thinking machines. That would be the third revolution, I guess – machines that devaluate human thinking. Some of the big computers like EPICAC do that all right in specialized fields."

"Uh-huh," she said thoughtfully. She rattled a pencil between her teeth. "First, the muscle work, then the routine work, and then, maybe, the real brain work."

"I hope I'm not around long enough to see that final step. . . ."

Kurt Vonnegut, Jr, *Player Piano*

There can no longer be any question that the industrial nations of the world are producing another technological revolution of historic importance. It may well emerge as the single most important influence in the development of a postindustrial society. The trigger is the revolution in information technology. The changes are so sizeable that they cannot fail to produce a discontinuous spurt in man's capacity to manipulate his environment. The question is whether the ramifications of this technological spurt will be comparable to those of the first and second industrial revolutions. Another question is whether we will be able to shape these ramifications to our own liking, or whether we will simply have to witness the changes and adapt to them.

This paper seeks to assess the impact of the information revolution on political institutions. The governing proposition is that, *as a result of information technology, man's power over his environment will increase greatly and his susceptibility to manipulation will rise proportionately.* These are coexisting tendencies to which societies adjust through cultural and institutional adaptation. The tension manifests itself at every level, from the single individual to the all-encompassing governmental structures. Information technology can contribute to an open or a secret society. The top elites in governments and major corporations are making policies today that will, cumulatively, determine the outcome. No new invention or institution was ever more directly related to the prospects of an open or a secret society.

Information as a resource: The problem of definition
Information can be most productively linked to the political process by defining it as a resource. Almost anything can be a political resource, as long as people value it highly. But resources differ in that some convert into effective political power more readily than others.

The emergence of any new resource can significantly alter the political structure. Expansion of the suffrage, for instance, transformed people into political resources, whereas before they had been no more than economic resources.

The composition of the political elites, or top power groups, was altered still further with each successive influx of social or skill types, who were identified primarily by the new resources they commanded. In recent generations we have witnessed an influx of such new elite members as the technical personnel (whose resources are specialized knowledge or expertise), the technological personnel (whose resources are mechanisms), the bureaucratic personnel (whose resources are organizational), and the technocratic or technetronic personnel (whose resources are the information that passes through mechanisms and organizations).

As a resource, information bears a superficial similarity to energy. Fast, large, timeshared computers with universally distributed, small receiving sets bear some resemblance to large generators distributing energy to users, from big industries to small household appliances. Information also resembles electricity in that it probably works best when massed and distributed in large supply – that is, both are highly sensitive to economies of scale. This suggests the emergence of a number of large information utilities operating on community franchised machines and delivery systems such as cable television (CATV).

If the resemblance to energy were close, this pattern suggests that information technology is but another industry, and that its impact would mean nothing more than expanded wealth, a change in the skills requirements, and a new group of influential corporate executives. If the resemblance were close, then the membership in decision-making elites might change, but not their character or function. But the resemblances between energy and information begin to weaken very quickly, and the political implications are interesting.

Information resources, unlike any other, *are not used up while being used*. This changes the very meanings of the words "resource" and "use", because information resources do not follow the law of conservation of energy. Only symbols, not physical units or energies, are removed; and symbols are being fed in even as they are being taken out. All of this means that, even though it will cost money to use, there will be far fewer constraints on the use of this resource than on any that we have used before. Problems such as cleaning and maintaining data, communicating it and protecting proprietary interests and confidence are on their way to being solved. In short, with fewer constraints on use, the information revolution promises to expand human powers by a factor larger than electricity.

One other distinguishing characteristic of the information resource helps to mark how different the societal impact of a large-scale expansion of information is likely to be. Information is a heterogeneous resource; it has many forms. In contrast, energies are homogeneous resources. Many important differences follow from this fact. Since individuals with special needs can draw on information pools in different ways and for peculiar purposes, the power to the individual is enhanced far more significantly compared to what a sudden expansion of energy resources would do for him.

But this great selectivity can only be provided by development and constant maintenance of information storage and retrieval systems. Information must be kept up to date and credible, and currency and credibility require continual surveillance, occasional housecleaning, regular validity checks. These are not technical matters to be dealt with by formulas. For example, uniform cost-of-living indicators affect wage and price scales, yet are themselves affected by change in taste and consumer patterns. New devices and methods of sampling attitudes alter the very definition of what decision makers will accept as information for purposes of television programming, consumer production or public policy making.

Ominously, one feature information has in common with natural resources is that deliberate restriction – as in the recent case of the international oil-producer cartel – greatly enhances prices and profits. But the information resource is still more sensitive. Not only prices can be manipulated by restriction. Restriction of information means secrecy, a deprivation of something more important, presumably, than physical comfort or efficiency. Information surpasses natural resources in another sense, too obvious, yet so easily overlooked: there is no objective way to distinguish the real McCoy from the bogus. Thus, the greater the secrecy and the greater the value and price of information, the greater the likelihood of falsification, since in the short run, lies serve as well as the truth.

Information, interdependence and the distribution of power

All of these requirements for developing and maintaining the information resources suggest that the prospects for a decentralized system are not likely, even where the desire for decentralization is strong. Moreover, the tendency toward centralization around these resources is joined by a propensity for stratification in our society. Perhaps we should call it "user stratification", but its potential effects on our political and social structure are very broad. It is based on the prospect that while the cost of information is going to drop precipitously, the cost of *being informed* will not. As use of the new technology spreads from entertainment, home economics and voting, to planning, analysis and decision making, the value to most users will change little, but the value to a few other users will increase – and the value to them will go up much faster than the cost. There is great potential here for stratification, yet it is only in small part related to ability to pay. It is related to intellectual preparation and functional responsibility. These will be the elements behind new forms of general social and political stratification.

But stratification is not the only tendency encouraged by the information resource. The same factors that produce a tendency toward stratification also produce interdependence. That is to say, information enhances individual power through interaction rather than action. When a farmer gets a tractor he gets a tool, and the tool gives him autonomy. He must depend on others to provide parts and fuel, but beyond that he has the tool and his use of it depends almost exclusively upon his decisions. Information in this sense is not a tool, nor is it fuel. Information is a process; it means little except in terms of regular interaction.

These two characteristics – stratification and interdependence (of users and their relationships to each other) – suggest the special significance of changes taking place in information technologies. The consequences for political power cannot be anything but enormous. Many will *know how*, yet few will *know*. Those who know will be setting the agenda for – i.e., programming – those who only know how. This means a potentially extreme centralization of power to set the fact and value premises of all action. If a government or any other elite comes to monopolize this function, social control itself comes to be monopolized.

Information and individual political behaviour
The earliest and most direct impact of the information revolution is probably on the individual's conceptual apparatus – his way of thinking. If these resources are to have any value at all to the individual, he must become adept at analysis and abstract thought. He must use this valuable commodity in special forms and through special kinds of procedures and technology. Already we see successive generations of schoolchildren brought up on thoughtways compatible with the computer.

Once the individual becomes adept in these matters, his power over his environment must increase. He can actually begin to plan rationally by systematically weighing alternatives, costs and consequences. But he will relate to his environment largely through concepts, theories and methods not of his own making and not examined by him for hidden premises before use. This is why it was no paradox to propose at the outset that the power of the individual and his increased susceptibility to manipulation will go up proportionately. A homely but important example of this is the contemporary graduate student in any one of the social sciences whose analytic powers have increased but whose theoretical perspectives are largely the unquestioned commitments of the persons who designed the canned programs.

The impact of formalized approaches and conventionalized concepts goes beyond acceptance of unexamined premises. These factors also tend to remove the individual further from direct experience of his environment. Information technology will be extremely flexible, but the experience gained through such processes will be indirect. Systematic use of experience requires that it be translated into indicators of experience. Indicators are measures of experience, i.e., price of goods as a measure of "cost of living" or savings and investment as a measure of "prosperity". People must agree widely as to what are the proper and reliable indicators of experience. As a consequence we shall be able to "tell about" nature and the "real world" far better than we can sense it. When knowledge is redefined as information, there is a gain in the power of analysis and a great risk of sensory deprivation. Among the problems to look for in this development is the susceptibility of the individual to mass mobilization; and that should not be looked upon as necessarily pathological. As we shall see, it has its good side as well as its bad.

At least since the birth of modern polling, mass attitudes have seemed to distribute themselves around a central tendency. Some attitudes are polarized; some are dispersed into several different kinds of concentrations. But by and large, the tendency is towards a centre, consensus, moderation. (Statistically, the distribution of most attitude samples has a single, central mode, like the classic bell-shaped curve.)

This central tendency is in part natural. Mass communications media homogenize values. Mass programming and appeals tend to reduce extremes of feeling even as they raise expectations. But part of the phenomenon is artificial. Sample surveys structure responses to questions in such a manner that some intensities of feeling are eliminated or averaged out, and many intense but peculiarly individual responses go unclassified. In either event, the central tendency has been important in shaping the strategies of business and government decision makers. It is rational for them to assume the central tendency, and their strategies make it a reality and reinforce it.

The revolution in information technology could change this quite considerably. An explosion in the number of media of all types is inevitable, and this explosion is going to have some broader effects. For example, the multiplication and specialization of television channels will ease the pressure to maximize single Neilson ratings, and this alone will introduce some degree of heterogeneity. Cable TV will use a lot of canned material in visual and data transmission, but it also makes possible a much larger variety of specialized services to particular audiences.

This is a move from broadcasting to "narrow-casting", and it involves a massive diversification of cues; that is, there will be a multiplication, even an explosion, in ideas, values, images. Almost nothing is more likely to fragment real attitudes; and improvement in two-way communication is likely to facilitate the expression and the counting of these attitudes, thereby producing entirely different data for decision makers. It will become more and more rational for merchandisers and politicians to differentiate their products and to appeal to differences rather than only similarities.

All of these factors promise significant changes in the politically relevant aspects of behaviour. First, political sophistication and participation will expand. Specialized appeals are more informative, and the technology will make further inquiries so easy and inexpensive that the average citizen will be able to do a little research on issues and candidates for himself. Introduction of electronic voting apparatus in every household could revolutionize the size of the active electorate. The reduced cost of access to communications media is likely to increase the amount of serious political communication and could significantly reduce economic differences among candidates and parties. The contribution of CATV in large cities will be immediate and significant merely in making television available on a strictly neighbourhood basis, whereas today it is uneconomical even for congressional candidates to use metropolitan television or newspapers.

All of this will contribute to a far looser political situation than any we have known in the twentieth century. Traditional party loyalties are likely to weaken. Given the referendum potential of the new media, politics for the average citizen is likely to be good deal more issue-oriented. Still more significantly, the lag between the emergence of new interests and their recognition as public issues will be drastically reduced. Distance will no longer limit the discovery of common interests.

From fragmentation to mobilization
But even if these potentialities are realized to the fullest, it is entirely possible that the political system at the level of institutions might remain unchanged. Here we begin to face quite concretely the discontinuity between microscopic and macroscopic reality. The loosening and spreading of politically relevant mass attitudes will produce two distinct tendencies at the macro level, interacting but quite contradictory: (1) the heterogeneity of attitudes, coupled with increasing participation, will tend to reaffirm and strengthen the party system – along more or

less traditional lines; (2) with access to political institutions still limited, however, ease of communication and heightening of expectations will intensify the tendency towards direct political action through social movements and special interest groups. These tendencies will manifest themselves in changing power relations, institutional patterns, and governmental policies.

(1) Paradoxical as it may sound, growing heterogeneity coupled with increasing political participation could reaffirm and strengthen the party system along more or less traditional lines. History backs that contention. Prior to the advent of efficient national communications, attitude distributions in the United States were decentralized and complex. They made fertile soil for political parties, and party politics became essential to well-functioning state and local government. Between 1832 and 1896, a period of great attitudinal diversity in this country, the party system was vigorous in every state and at the national level. Except for the 1860s it held true even for the South (and in the South it was the very uniformity of salient attitudes that hampered parties during the Confederate period). After 1896, beginning in New England and the South, opinions began to grow closer and closer towards national norms, and party structures seemed to loosen as a direct consequence.

Even when greater diversity of attitudes is accompanied by increased participation and weaker party loyalties, party institutions do not necessarily weaken. As elections come to be based on clearer policy alternatives, greater efforts have to be made to establish agenda on which meaningful ayes and nays can be expressed. Parties set agenda. And although parties may continue to avoid taking clear positions on some of the issues, the party role in setting the agenda – the simple agreements on what to disagree about – could become more important. And so long as there are presidents to elect and congresses and bureaucracies to control, some localized factions will continue to coalesce into larger aggregates with a regional and national focus.

(2) Persistence of this older structure does not, however, close off emergence of other, newer forms of mass organization. The trend is likely to be towards increased direct action through social movements. Ease of communication and rising expectations, as well as an easing of access to political institutions, will on the whole increase the "movement capacity" of the country. People will find it easier to discover and to communicate with others who share their irritations and aspirations. Physical proximity – in the past essential for the creation of social movements – will count for little; in fact, men of like mind will be able to organize without ever coming together under one roof. The new information base will help directly: the availability of seventy or eighty

local television channels could eliminate a good deal of bias in information, could in fact reach viewers with a wide variety of information in "odd lots" no longer filtered through a city editor or a national news network producer.

United States history shows ample precedents for the notion that a change in information technology will help spawn new social movements. The Populist movement of the late nineteenth century would have been impossible without the mass newspapers of the time. And what the press did for geographically dispersed social classes then, television seems to be doing for (or to) races and classes in concentrated areas today, as a producer of images that strengthen weak identifications and create aspirations where there were none before.

The two major tendencies then – re-emergence of party and multiplication of social movements – could combine to instil in the United States a new political vigour.

A third side development is also likely. This is the likely increase of withdrawal movements. These arise out of a felt inability to pierce established institutions or a genuine distrust of the available information flow. Easy access to information resources facilitates permanent withdrawal into tribes and communities, and conventional new towns. These withdrawal movements, almost by definition, are not necessarily of any significance to the political order. They become politically significant mainly when withdrawals are so numerous that they raise serious questions about the legitimacy of society and government.

These three trends are already in evidence. But the development and availability of new communications systems will multiply their potential political impacts and the speed with which any one of them may shape events in the future.

These trends can produce a healthy and reinvigorated society, but only if the various possibilities are allowed to take place. The most serious problem lies with whether the regime will be able to accept the social movements that arise and appear to challenge the system. Social movements will always be seen as producers of social disorder, and the tendency is for elites to declare disorder unlawful. If movements are defined as a threat to the social fabric, then the tendency will be to foster or allow only those political parties and communications media that can be used as instruments of social control. This was true even when there was only an army and inefficient governmental capacity to manipulate the news. In the future the potential for peaceful control through manipulation of information will go up at a rate even faster than the potential for individuals and movements to use the media for their own purposes.

Social control operates through consensus, in fact through privately organized consensus. But social control is also a deliberate function of public policy through the coercion of military, police and other regulatory agencies. The new technology offers still newer and more potent means of social control though "manipulated consensus".

There was always some capacity for manipulated consensus: witness the effectiveness of anti-Japanese propaganda movies during World War Two. The new integrated information system presents new potentials, in the extent to which it can provide the individual with an altered set of fact premises on which to base his opinions; or it can provide him with new and well-developed sets of value premises that could alter his opinions as well as his treatment of the facts. "Bi-Polar Worlds", "Containment", or before that, "Manifest Destiny" and "Yellow Peril", made for tremendously effective propaganda because they are literally systems of analysis. Once such generalized views are internalized in a people, the influence is *within* rather than *on* the individual.

Opportunities for distributing such canned programs most certainly will increase in the next twenty years, and with it will grow the capacity of decision centres to manipulate the fact and value environment of the individual. This is the means by which the healthy interplay between parties and mass movements could be weakened, resulting in a very tightly knit society indeed.

Impact on interest groups

Social scientists generally believe that the problem of mass mobilization is in part, if not altogether, solved by the presence of an intermediate stratum, that is, by private groups that intervene between the isolated, "atomized" person and the central authorities. It is taken as a fact as well as a necessity that to be free a society must be plural.

It seems quite clear that the information revolution will spectacularly expand the resources available to groups, that it will make possible much more effective control of the environment by smaller and smaller groups. Groups may ultimately come to mean a large aggregate of persons coordinated by a tiny number of brilliant people. Groups have, of course, always been shaped most fundamentally by problems of communication. The development of small computing and communications apparatus, and access on a shared-time basis to immense computer systems, will virtually obviate the difficulty of communicating in groups of all sizes.

This is bound to have some important political meaning. A large number of more efficiently operating groups will lead to cleaner and sharper distinctions in society, thus greater potential for constructive conflict. However, the changes will not be distributed evenly. Computerized access to vast information pools is far more likely to enhance the capacity of old groups to persist than of new groups to form. We already know, in the field of professional societies, the extent to which medical and legal associations control both the number of practitioners and a great deal of their behaviour. Generalizing this pattern, the result could be a kind of functional feudalism rather than a vigorous system of group competition. Because of the severe statistical limits on the number of persons who can create new trade associations and pressure groups, one of the probable and fearful consequences of a revolutionary spread of information technology is tighter, rather than looser, organizational structure among all groups, large or small, old or new.

This presents a certain and severe dilemma to the individual and to sincere decision makers. The choice is not a simple one between centralization and decentralization of power. The emergence of a computer-based group system is a very important third scenario; it involves a great deal of pluralism – and that means decentralization in a certain sense – but it also involves a great deal of mobilization, i.e., centralization inside groups rather than inside movements (as in mass society) or within a tightly bureaucratized governmental system (as in totalitarian regimes). Given a sufficient amount of technology, private groups can in effect become "private governments".

In short, there are three possible extremes all of which are unacceptable: (1) a so-called decentralized system with minimal structure, which runs the danger of anarchy followed by mass mobilization; (2) a centralized system; and (3) as described immediately above, a system which some might call a midpoint between centralized and decentralized but which can itself be tyrannical if public policy is nothing more than a policy of sponsoring group government of its own members, e.g., state professional societies, trade associations, labour unions.

The third tendency already seems the most pronounced. This means tighter rather than looser social structure, despite greater pluralism. In such a context, social movements may eventually appear to be the only means for loosening up. The primary sources of politics in such a society could be conflicts between old and new groups rather than orderly competition between political parties or between established groups on opposite sides of the market. This kind of process, where new groups must fight for a place, is almost certain to be defined as disorder, and this gives established elites additional incentive to use information as a means of social control.

Information, power, and society – emergence of the separate management component

What, in sum, is the most likely set of outcomes for the political structure at the *macro* level? There is ample basis in history to expect broad changes in power structures and policies following changes in technology and resources. There is, in fact, no reason to expect otherwise from changes as significant as those centring on the information revolution. Indeed these political changes seem already well under way and may already be too far advanced to be shaped by public policy. The following is a very inadequate sketch.

Large governments as well as corporate organizations have begun to move away from hierarchical control. External supervision through span of control, formal hierarchies of authority and narrow definitions of jobs are being supplemented and may in the long run be replaced by other principles of organization, including professionalization, lower-level decision making, network patterns rather than simple vertical patterns of communication. Narrow job classification is already being defended more by unions than by management. Much bureaucracy will still be left, but there are definite signs of broadening the notion of jobs, and of ensuring uniform behaviour by setting "decision rules" rather than by direction, inspection and review.

All of these trends seem to point towards one central development – the emergence of a separate management component, where management will in fact be an information process. Control and coordination in virtually all organizations will be carried on through the self-conscious manipulation of the information environment. This is what is most likely to replace hierarchy.

Modern management works through what we have already called "the fact and value premises". To put it in the extreme, lower-line administrators need have no contact at all with the outside world. Decision making can be handled on the basis of careful modelling of real-world situations and proper manipulation of the model, depending upon a person's responsibilities.

Management becomes, then, a process that can be factored out and placed in a separate control unit, as budgeting, personnel and finance were once separated out to auxiliary units. But management is more. It means control over those other auxiliary units; they become auxiliary to management rather than to administration.

Management also becomes a function that is interchangeable among organizations. The subject matter may change, but many of the functional requirements do not. As a direct consequence, interchange among large organizations becomes a way of life. C. Wright Mills recognized this interchange already in the 1940s. The universalizing of organizational principles and the development of a profession of management is making the interchange possible, and it is affecting power relations in the society.

One can disagree with Mills in his contention that the regular interchanges among corporate, military, and civil government elites proved the existence of a single, national "power elite". But it would be difficult, perhaps unwise, to deny that such interchanges could come to constitute such an elite. Management is a political phenomenon at the macro level; it is merely a name for the effective use of information as a power source.

Such a development would no doubt bring great gains to society. It would inevitably lead to more rationality and efficiency, in so far as leadership was based upon knowledge and command of the machinery of rational calculation and control. Even the loosening of old hierarchies could be considered again.

But there are also likely to be some fundamental costs, and while gains might be immediate, the costs are cumulative and difficult to assess for the purpose of formulating public policies designed to control costs. By costs we mean power developments that could be contrary to basic American values.

One of the most profound costs of this change in the distribution of power is its very subtlety. When conduct is influenced by manipulating the environment of conduct rather than conduct itself, it is most difficult to judge the manipulation, to criticize it, to oppose it, to plug different values into it. The use of management methods of decision making in the Vietnam conflict may very well explain why there was a slow but unstoppable escalation despite the fact that, as a number of people reported after leaving office, they and others opposed the expansion of the war. Once a process is set in train it is very difficult to step back from it and criticize it. Small steps based on *a priori* analysis can literally demoralize the opposition and never be perceived, until too late, as a large commitment.

That, in turn, may lead to magnification of error. Large computers will be able to check against error if it occurs to someone that the model of the outside world devised by management might be in error. But, as in Vietnam, or with the introduction of a new product that fails, unexpected events might not be perceived as shortcomings in the model.

Another likely political development that can be treated as a cost is loss of the legitimacy of elected political people in relation to management in the competition for responsible control of the upper echelons of decision making. There has always been a tendency for the elected amateur to lose out to the professional in any direct confrontation. The legitimacy of management, based as it is on talent as well as higher education, may prove to be the most effective adversary ever to face electoral and party-based power.

But perhaps the most fundamental and insidious cost of the rise of management could be the blurring of the distinction between public and private spheres. Interchange among top management personnel is both a measure and a cause of this obfuscation. That is to say, the notion of a public could be blurred by the simple continuity of management once it is established as a separate function with its own highly legitimate access to all decision centres. Government authority, whether directed by political personnel, capitalists or managers, has very traditional roots. Management, in public agencies and the military, is an essential part of effective government. But the emerging power holders and the emerging structures of authority depend little for their claim to control on traditional roots that are grounded in sovereignty, citizenship and loyalty. This transformation could easily reduce government to a position of mere power based on superior resources and more elaborate management techniques.

We begin to appreciate the costs of this kind of transformation when we ponder the social choices we may have to make in order to cope with the information revolution. A *1984*-type scenario will be the most likely outcome if things are let go at the present rate and no attention is paid to the information revolution. Yet it is also widely assumed that a redirection of these trends towards more decentralized and individualized patterns requires some significant types of governmental intervention in the near future.

This means that "freedom scenarios" are demanding independent government at a time when it may be losing its independence. There was never any reason to expect that politics and government would be immune to change. Indeed, the information revolution could alter the very process of governing. Politics and government could turn into one continuous process of management, and if that came to pass there would be left little capacity for planning actions outside the process itself. Democratic theory in the West is predicated upon some type of "mixed regime", that is, government made up of institutions whose powers are based upon different constituencies. A society integrated around a system of information and controlled by even the most responsible of managers could eliminate the mixed regime, making all institutions, public and private, responsive in the same way to the same challenges.

Government and social choice
Within this immense and diffuse context it does not seem highly probable that the individual will improve his own life tremendously. The new technologies do make incremental improvement possible, but improvement is based upon three related assumptions: (1) that the revolution itself will and should go on relatively unabated; (2) that society can and should be left to cope with the costs, if it is to enjoy the

benefits; (3) that society has a government and a well-organized political process capable of maximizing gains over costs and of equitably distributing the costs.

It is the third assumption that is so questionable. And though philosophic in tone, the blurring of the distinction between public and private spheres may be the single most important political development during the next generation. Governments show little sign of developing greater capacity for acting as an independent force, a counterpoise to private forces.

NASA and COMSAT are good examples. In both instances government proved itself capable of acting forcefully only in consonance with and in support of existing private interests. Neither programme brought into question the monopolistic tendencies of any cooperating company or carrier. Both programmes have been effective in so far as they were efforts to work with the grain of history. In NASA, change amounted to acceleration but no appreciable change of direction. COMSAT has essentially been an effort to ensure that no disruptive change will take place at all. It is hard in either case to know where public ends and private begins.

Where government is still clearly independent there is serious doubt about its capacity. In antitrust, government lawyers tend to be outnumbered and outclassed. In the drug and cosmetic field and in the ecology areas, government agencies have usually been one step behind in protecting the public. Yet in almost all areas, the most important social choices depend upon government's being *ahead* of the private sector. This would be particularly true in the esoteric skills. Extensive government use of contracting powers with universities and corporations, plus government programmes of subsidizing research and training centres will continue to put government in arrears.

Added to this is the fact that governments have increasingly been organized along lines parallel to and indistinguishable from private organization. There is, thus, no basis for expecting that governments will act in any way contrary to tendencies already in train in the economy at large.

Current ideology actually supports the parallels. Republicans talk about "partnership", Democrats about "creative federalism", old liberals about pluralism and responsibility through bargaining, the New Left intellectuals about decentralization, power to the people, etc. In all these instances the sum total is government indistinguishable from, and indeed collaborative with, private interests. Effective regulation of monopolies by government requires an independence that we have no basis for expecting.

The fusing of public and private administrative processes also tends to derange presidential and legislative power. Reorganization of both branches around the improved decision-making technology could improve the capacities of both, but meanwhile the field within which they are to exercise their power could become unrecognizably different. Traditionally there has been competition between the branches for the central position in controlling economy and individuals. In the nineteenth century the edge went to Congress, and during most of the twentieth century the President has enjoyed the advantage. But the twenty-first, or long before, could be a century in which the two may be collaborating for control over administration.

To be able to use the new mechanisms of decision making, administrators have subscribed to the myth that they need practically unlimited delegations of power from the political authorities. And ever since the 1930s, the political authorities have been so obliging that already they spend more time in committee oversight and budget supervision so that the amount of direct legislative control over citizens is diminishing. Like Jacob's Ladder, traditional political institutions could be further severed at top and bottom. The exasperation of President and Congress in coping with undeclared wars could become a more regular exasperation with being accused regularly of introducing irregularities into social management.

These are some of the reasons why the blurring and weakening of the public–private dichotomy could be the most important political development in the coming decades. Society may never become totally mobilized. There will be upward mobility, and even outward mobility will probably be tolerated. What is really more likely is the building of a Hell of Administrative Boredom. That is already the current of industrial organization. Unless appropriate initiatives are taken now, the information revolution may simply turn the current into a rapids.

Conclusion

The most agonizing problem about the Hell of Administrative Boredom is that all information is proprietary. Open access to lower members and nonmembers too readily deranges the authority structure and the delicate balance of interdependence of all the parts in a well-run organization. Secrecy as a policy is forced upon people not otherwise so inclined. "Executive privilege" claimed against demands for information did not begin with President Nixon. Moreover, every claim to executive privilege, except where allegations of a crime are involved, will be upheld. The Supreme Court in *U.S. v. Nixon* has affirmed this position for the Chief Executive, and the Chief can affirm it for every subordinate whose files or computers or sound equipment need protection from the public. Under present law, the Chief Executive does not even have to claim national security.

Government by a separate management component is almost inevitably and by definition a politics of secrecy – until such point that no one is aware of any secrets to demand.

Education would be the one system capable of resolving the various tendencies in favour of open society, open politics, and the autonomous individual. But the educational institutions are also uniquely capable of programming the individual for a full life of comfort within the Hell of Administrative Boredom. Here indeed is an area where deliberate policy choices are going to determine the actual shape of the future.

The most important dimension of impact here will be on social stratification – in a new and more severe form: while many will learn to use the new apparatus, only a few will understand it. As observed earlier many will *know how*; some will *know*. This may be the new version of "many are called, few are chosen."

Those who *know how* will use the technology to their own benefit and to that of mankind. Who could ever oppose greater productivity? But those who *know* the new technology become the inventors, the innovators, the critics. This will be the basis for elites in a restratified society. How many will know? Will it be one per cent? Or ten per cent? Whatever the figure, we can be certain it will be limited – a pyramid of intelligence, but of what kind and with what values?

Institutions of higher education are already becoming technocratized. More and more frequently do we find university curricula being judged by criteria of "relevance". Regents, educators and students disagree with each other on the definition of relevance, but their disagreements may be settled when it becomes clear that technocratic training provides access to a neutral or "value-free" apparatus rather than merely to a specific position in a specific organization. Such an education would not be free of dependence on some kind of regime. It might not be a regime of present governmental and corporate power holders, but it would be a regime just the same. The education process could be universalized and totally egalitarian, but that would not prevent it from serving as a channel through which regime-supporting talent would be recruited. In fact, use of the general education process as a universal pool from which to recruit elites would be a strong legitimizing force for the whole regime of the Third Revolution.

For the elite, education would be continuous and cumulative; for all others it would probably concentrate on the practical arts and problem-solving. Problem-solving would, of course, involve analysis at a level more advanced than today's, but it would be advanced only in terms of programmes made available by elites. This means that the whole present middle class of professions and skills could be converted into a mere middle-income proletariat.

The outcome could of course be otherwise, since education could shape as well as be shaped by the Third Revolution. The following is an informed list of questions that must be asked if present elites, fearful of the future, are to head it off in accord with democratic-liberal values.

(1) Can the new mass education be tailored to fit more closely the peculiarities of each individual? Could the new apparatus provide an antidote to bureaucratized teaching by reducing the fund of human knowledge to human scale? Individuality is the only ultimate defence against *any* large establishment. Can education of self be combined with education about the outside world?

(2) Can we instruct for real literacy in the new information process, or are we doomed to teaching utilization, cookbook-style? Public schools never succeeded in any vast expansion of foreign language literacy. Is information technology, because of its more immediate utility, going to be easier to convey to the casual student?

(3) Can education be combined with training? That is, can data banks be coupled with a rich historical and cultural context independent of but always associated with the specific items of data to be retrieved? Such a soft, or humane, overlay to hard data would be another check against tacit submission to someone else's conceptual framework.

(4) Can *political* education be combined with training? Will the citizen be able to make rational and effective use of the new levels of participation available to him? Will he have superior means of cutting through political propaganda, or will the citizen be free only to withdraw or to support the regime more vigorously than today?

(5) Will the education system in fact equip the individual to withdraw if he wishes, or will his increased power be conditional upon use within prescribed technical boundaries and procedures? The questions above had to do with intellectual and psychological self-reliance. Here is a question of sheer physical self-reliance: will new educational systems militate against or facilitate formation of tribes and communal groups?

Heading off the future
The chances of adequate attention, let alone answers, to these questions are extremely slight, precisely because education serves the Third Revolution so well and education is so responsive to where the money is. But the chances of heading off the future are not entirely gone until the questions cannot be asked at all. The chances have disappeared only when no demands for autonomy and no complaints against secrecy are voiced.

The two most recent "information crises" in the US actually offer a solid basis for modest optimism. These were the Pentagon Papers and Watergate. Both indicate the enormous political value of information and information technology. Both indicate the immense degree to which government controls all information of concern to itself and the tremendous power of government to keep secrets and to manipulate in its own favour what does leak out. But both indicate also that when the public becomes aware of existing information, especially in relation to criminal activity, there is almost no way to prevent revelation. The Xerox and magnetic tape explosion have worked both ways, and as long as information (as news) is a very valuable commercial item, the decline towards a secret society can be slowed.

But can it be stopped? Not unless present governments take action now to ensure the capacity of private citizens and groups. Here are, in conclusion, a few policy choices that could become some sort of agenda.

(1) Head off the centralization of production capacity of information technology. Unlike the automobile or electrical utilities industries, the computer and related industries could involve centralized use as well as centralized production. Once information retrieval and analysis capacity is centralized, it will be extremely difficult to decentralize it. All talk of heterogeneity and checks and balances would be useless. However, once this capacity were widely distributed, it would in fact be impossible for later regimes, desirous of concentrated power and secrecy, to centralize the information process. Antitrust in this area is more important than in any other industry.

(2) Head off government legal rights to secrecy regarding its policy plans or activities. The Supreme Court decision on executive privilege helps some, but not nearly enough. In one respect the cause of government secrecy was strengthened by the holding, inasmuch as a demand for secret information can only be sustained where a criminal indictment against some government official has first been secured. Of far greater value would be establishment of the legal right of citizens to bring civil suits against any government agency where there is reasonable ground for believing that the agency is exceeding its statutory power. Then a court order could obtain otherwise secret data.

(3) Head off government legal rights to secrecy in regard to information it holds on individuals. This has rightly been described as the development of *habeas data* law, and it should of course apply to private (e.g., credit bureaus) as well as public data archives. The citizen cannot have the right to deprive government or many private agencies of information on himself; social control would be rendered impossible. But now that information on all citizens can be acquired, stored, retrieved and used at relatively low cost, each citizen must have access

to his own file to contest what exists in it, and at least to add more to, if not subtract from, the fund of information.

These make only a beginning. And indeed they would not work at all unless the culture and the institutions of education produce a true citizen, a person who demands knowledge of the world around him.

The Impact of Microelectronics on Town Planning

Bruno Lefèvre

From the intangible distribution of political power, we move on to the geographical distribution of economic and social activity. Once again, the author, who is now an independent planning consultant based in Paris, emphasizes the potential of the new telecommunications technology and the need to make choices. In this case the decentralization of social activity made possible by developments in microelectronics could mop up regional unemployment and greatly improve accessibility to education. It could also lead to a dramatic reduction in travel time and transport costs and reduce the pressures on cities. This paper first appeared in Impact of Science on Society, vol. 27, No. 2 (1977).

It is perhaps exaggerated to say that cities were created to facilitate communication between individuals. It is, however, generally accepted that the need to travel, trade and associate has been among the most important factors affecting man's physical and social environment.[1] The acute conditions prevailing in cities today may thus partly be explained by the fact that despite the exponential growth in the exchange of goods and information (characteristic of the development of industrial and postindustrial societies), direct contact between individuals has remained at once the most effective means of communication between people and the principal limitation on the spatial organization of society.

For the first time in history, this limitation has been partially removed by the widespread introduction of different forms of communication technology. Since the invention of the electric telegraph followed by that of the telephone one hundred years ago, a more complete and sophisticated range of systems has been developed which makes it possible, at the present time, to satisfy almost any communication need provided it is correctly identified.

The gradual introduction of these techniques into our social processes was previously considered to be nothing more than a marginal contribution to their functioning. The overwhelming importance assumed by these forms of technology over the past ten years has changed this situation, particularly in the industrialized world. The investments made, both in the use of these systems and in research, are probably leading to a veritable mutation of society, thus radically transforming our relationships with our fellow citizens, our economies and our ways of living, as well as the relationships maintained by every nation with the rest of the world.

On this hypothesis it can be taken for granted that the organization of urban and regional space will be substantially modified, not to say turned completely upside-down. It is our intention here to take a general and rapid look at the development of telecommunications. After first examining the social and economic environment in which this development took place, we shall try to identify the use made of these forms of communication in the major sectors of activity. Finally, we shall try to envisage the possible influences of the services described on the organization of society and on urban and regional planning.

The social and economic context
The role of telecommunications was ignored until recently but is gradually being acknowledged. This change of heart seems to be attributable to a certain number of differing but complementary objective factors such as the availability of communication techniques, the growing importance of the information sector in the economy and a changing economic situation favourable to the development of this sector.

The availability of different forms of technology
Progress in modern telecommunication techniques, which began with the invention of the transistor, integrated circuits, computers and satellites, has led to the development of handy, powerful and competitive methods of information processing and telecommunication. This process is bound to be accelerated by the latest techniques such as optical fibres, waveguides, miniaturization (large-scale integration [LSI] and, soon, super LSI circuits), minicomputers and the development of increasingly simple, diversified and low-cost terminals, and, finally, fourth-generation computers.

The great reduction in the unit costs of information goods and services has itself led to an increased demand for both, not only as objects of consumption in themselves but as the necessary means for the more effective production of other goods and services. This reduction in unit costs has thus actually led to a growth in the total sums allocated to information.

Growth of the information sector in the economy
The second factor which explains the development of telecommunications is the importance assumed by information handling and processing and by communication in the economies of industrialized countries. Thus, for example, Marc Porat has examined the distribution of employment by sector of economic activity in the United States.[2] Using data based on statistics for the 1960s (provided by the Bureau of Labor Statistics), he showed that about fifty per cent of the working population were engaged in activities connected with information. The trend is representative of the development of the economies of Europe and Japan.

The causes of this phenomenon were discussed by E. Parker at a conference organized by the Organization for Economic Cooperation and Development,[3] the main ones being those we are discussing. Besides the availability of telecommunication techniques, an initial reason for this growth is the fact that basic individual and social needs are today satisfied and demand is now directed (1) towards products which carry more subtle messages to do with such things as style, social status and atmosphere, and (2) towards an increased consumption of communication goods (colour television, FM radio, hi-fi, cassettes and home video sets) and services like those of doctors, teachers, lawyers and intermediary institutions of all kinds such as banks, insurance companies and travel agencies.

A second reason for the expansion of the information sector in the economy is probably the growing awareness of the importance of information in production itself. We thus find that efforts are made to recruit an educated labour force, that there is a regular increase in the funds allotted to research or development, and that a growing proportion of the value-added element in new goods and services tends to be connected with information. Parker finally notes the part played by the inefficiency of market mechanisms in encouraging the use of communication services, and mentions advertising as an example.

Factors associated with the economic situation
It would seem that the development of telecommunications will be encouraged by a certain number of events connected with changes in the world economic situation such as the increased cost of raw materials and energy, the recession, and the demand for an improvement in the quality of living. The general rise in the cost of raw materials appears

likely to encourage the development of telecommunications as compared with other sectors of activity and to modify the kinds of technology used in that sector itself. It seems logical to assume that, faced with a regular increase in the cost of raw materials, the industrialized nations will reconsider the use they make of them.

Where national economies are concerned, a policy of this kind will imply transfer of demand to goods and services whose raw material cost is as small as possible and whose value added will be as great as possible. Changes of this kind will be to the advantage of communication goods and services. It remains to be seen to what extent such a policy can be implemented. Will it, for example, be possible to educate public taste so that people derive as much satisfaction from reading a book or a good magazine as from the purchase of new goods? Will knowledge and mental balance become status symbols, like a good address or an expensive motor car today?

The increased cost of raw materials has also led to detailed research into ways of making more rational use of existing transmission networks (multiplex and modulation transmission techniques) and the development of completely new forms of technology which can take the place of present techniques at less cost and with less dependence. This increase in cost has also made it more profitable to substitute some materials for others, such as aluminium for copper.[4] In addition, the rise in petroleum prices has provided an opportunity for expanding current research into the possible role of telecommunications in an energy conservation policy.[5]

It should be added that the recent recession has accentuated the search for increased productivity. If this can be achieved, it will certainly come from a rationalization of activities in this information sector, whether in the public or the private field.[6] We should finally mention that the use of telecommunications could modify relationships between individuals and between people and their environment in order to satisfy the growing demand for an improvement in the quality of life.[7] It is this possibility which we are going to consider next.

New services

For each key social function, we shall try to identify new services (or families of services currently being tried out) which could lead to profound changes in the way things are done and the distribution of power in society over the next thirty years. We shall try to indicate the kinds of influence that these services could have on regional and urban planning, dividing them for this purpose into three sectors: public services, business services and local services.

Public services
Under this heading we shall examine three kinds of services: (1) the provision for the public of a new collective infrastructure in the form of data transmission networks; (2) the provision of services of a general nature such as transfers of money and electronic mail; and (3) the application of telecommunication techniques to sectors traditionally considered as public services, taking education as an example.

Data transmission networks. The design of the networks is important for our study since these form the infrastructure vital to a large number of new services. Data transmission was originally a service provided by the telephone system over special lines, but it has gradually become a distinct sector of telecommunications, and one of the most profitable. In addition to very rapid growth in the overall volume of information transmitted, this development has been stimulated by a gradual increase in the specifications of these services – timesharing, long periods of line utilization, long silence during transmissions – as well as by the availability of technologies capable of satisfying these needs more effectively.

The typical networks essential for the expected development of data transmission, and necessary for almost all the services envisaged here, will have the following characteristics. They will permit the sending of digital data on a timesharing basis; they will include back-up channels and procedures for correcting errors introduced by the network during transmission; and they will use the packet-switched system which means that messages are automatically cut up and transmitted over the network as and when there is room.

These networks, which, in their present form, are used chiefly by government departments, large businesses and multinational corporations for the centralized processing of substantial quantities of data (stock management, book-keeping, records management), could be an ideal vehicle for such new services as are thought desirable. Everything will depend on the policies adopted with regard to them. If each new service had to finance its own network, only a small number of really profitable services could be set up. On the other hand a single network, or the linking of several networks, would enable every user to benefit from the investment and make it possible to provide services at an acceptable cost.

The ownership and control of the networks are thus key issues in the widespread use of these facilities, as is the problem of access to the network by various users (access which is affected by the complexity of the agreements concerning entry to the network and by the pricing policy applied). Freedom of access to the network must be preserved in the general interest and in the interests of justice. It would be desirable, in addition, to envisage a guaranteed right to information processing for every user so that all the capabilities of computers are accessible to everyone. This is perhaps what is most at stake in the coming reorganization of society.

General services. There are two things fundamental to the smooth running of the business of modern society, these being the circulation of money and the circulation of information. Telecommunications are on the way to effecting a radical transformation of the methods used. We shall consider transfers of money by electronic means and then look at electronic mail.

The electronic transfer of funds (EFT). The term "electronic transfer of funds" in fact covers all transactions using electronic impulses produced or processed by computers in order to credit or debit accounts in real time.[8] These could equally well be (1) large transfers of funds between banks or branches and the withdrawal of small sums by individuals at banknote dispensers or (2) commercial transactions recorded at sales points when payment is not made either in cash or by credit card or cheque but by direct and immediate transfer of the cost of the purchases from the purchaser's account to that of the store.

The development of EFT raises various legal and social problems. The machinery established for it could allow almost total surveillance of users and hence a dangerous sort of social control. In addition, changing over from the present system to EFT assumes a reorganization to which few of the parties involved (the state, the banks and the insurance companies) are yet ready to adapt. There is, however, no doubt that machinery of this kind is being established and that the trend is bound to accelerate.[9]

If EFT systems were introduced, the banks would be freed from existing limitations imposed by security and by the manual processing of transactions and would probably tend to set up service terminals at places most adapted to the public's needs, such as in factories, markets and blocks of flats.[10] It is also possible that in combination with stock management and accountancy systems, EFT could make it possible for small traders to set up again in residential areas and offer their customers prices and services at least competitive with those of the supermarket. Bringing shops close to the home would mean that people would not have to travel so far when making individual purchases.

Electronic mail.[11] Equipment exists today for long-distance facsimile transmission. With such equipment, it is possible to transmit a standard 21cm×29.7cm document from one place to another in from four to six minutes. There are also new experimental systems which will make it possible to carry out the same operation in a few seconds.

The post offices in most countries of the world (particularly the industrialized countries) are incurring increasing deficits, and for this reason research has been going on for many years on the problems of applying data processing techniques to postal problems as a whole.

Even a very perfunctory analysis of the kind of material carried through the post each day shows the large variety of matter entrusted to the postal service, e.g. personal letters, inland letters to government departments and firms, invoices, financial documents and cheques, newspapers and printed publications and, finally, advertising matter. Each of these types of mail presents its own particular problem.

We have already spoken about how the postal transmission of invoices and remittances could be replaced by EFT services. Tyler is of the opinion that thirty per cent of all mail could be replaced in this way.[12] The possible applications of telecommunications to the press are, furthermore, manifold and their impact on the volume of postal traffic not inconsiderable. One solution to the problem of newspaper distribution is to bring the presses closer to existing markets. Each issue of a daily paper would thus be prepared and composed in one locality and then sent by facsimile to presses in various places for printing and distribution. The edition of the *International Herald Tribune* for the United Kingdom and the Nordic countries is produced in this way from the paper's headquarters in Paris. The system has the advantage of reducing the quantity of newspapers to be carried over large distances.

Another method for distributing newspapers is currently being tried out in the new town of Tama in Japan. This involves the installation of a teleprinter in the home. The present state of development of the necessary networks, the space taken up by the terminals in modest-sized flats and the total cost seem to suggest that this system will not be used for many years yet.

The transmission of single or personal documents is possible via two kinds of electronic system. The first is a hybrid system in which the message is passed to a central office where it is coded and retransmitted to the office closest to the address given. It is then distributed by traditional means. The second system is an integrated one making transmission possible from one home to another without any intermediate stages.

In general, the volume of research and development activities devoted to the various services gives grounds for thinking that postal systems will undergo profound changes between now and the year 2000.

Telecommunications and public services; applications in education
Probably the most intensive studies have been made on the application
to education of telecommunication techniques such as remote data
processing, sound and visual methods. The reasons for this interest are
connected with the importance of this sector in the economy as a
determinant of a country's economic future, as a major employment
sector and as an important source of inflation. Current work thus covers
(1) the social organization which would be needed for available technical systems, and practical trials of these systems; (2) the conditions
under which the services envisaged would be economically viable;
(3) comparative studies of these systems and an assessment of their
impact.

One of the most longstanding uses of radio and television is for
education, and most countries are making greater and greater use of
educational broadcasts. The Ivory Coast and Niger may be cited as
examples. One of the most advanced applications in Europe is to be
found in connection with the Open University in the United Kingdom.
This combines the use of radio and television with written material sent
through the post and seminars held at various points throughout the
country. The Open University is also financing research on the development of techniques for directing studies over a distance by means of
telephone. The services offered by the university are available throughout the country and to people in all walks of life.

Whereas the Open University uses the normal broadcasting
capabilities of existing radio and television channels with their inherent
restrictions, particularly as regards broadcasting times, closed circuit
television systems are used over a smaller area but are constructed
specifically for educational purposes. There is no doubt that one of the
biggest educational networks of this kind belongs to the Inner London
Education Authority. This links more than a thousand classes, relaying
sound and visual educational material from a central video library to the
classrooms involved. It can also televise lessons from one classroom to
all classes interested. The teacher in each class then uses the broadcast
received as a basis for his own lessons, expanding the topics touched on
in the programme and answering questions.

Another line in research in recent years has been computer-assisted
instruction. Using a specialized terminal (PLATO system),[13] a telephone
linked to a television screeen (as in the TICCIT system)[14] or in some cases
a typewriter, the pupil calls up the computer with which he remains in
dialogue throughout the lesson. The program he uses is made up of a
series of multiple-choice questions. The question which the pupil has to
answer depends on the reply he selects to the preceding question. This
system permits, among other things, pupils to follow lessons at their own
speed.

Despite their difficulties such as high cost and disputed educational effectiveness, these methods are the subject of sustained research. The particular features of the technology they employ, as well as current research, hold out the promise of a substantial reduction in the cost of certain kinds of university education with no loss of quality. The introduction of these systems, however, is coming up against considerable social opposition. But once they are introduced, the new tele-education services envisaged will have an important impact on urban and regional planning. It is possible, for example, to envisage smaller institutions spaced at regular intervals throughout a country. The introduction of systems like those we have described would also encourage the continuous training of adults.

Business services
Business management will make increasing use of all telecommunication techniques. In addition to those mentioned above, two major groups of services seem particularly capable of modifying business relationships.

Teleconferences. This term covers any situation in which more than two people are in simultaneous communication by means of an electric communication system. A distinction is made between audio and video conference systems on the one hand and teleconferences by computer on the other. Each of these systems has its own characteristics and each can be combined with the others and with other complementary systems (e.g. telephone and facsimile apparatus).[15]

Although two-directional video links were thought to be indispensable for this kind of meeting, research has shown that use of narrow-band networks (telephone circuits) and audio and facsimile communication can, without impairing the quality of the discussions, take the place of forty per cent of all business meetings. A rough estimate made on the basis of American statistics shows that these methods could reduce business travel between towns by thirty to fifty per cent.[16]

This would have consequences on the income of airlines (business travel being the most lucrative part), on the building or enlargement of airports, and on rail and road traffic. Aeronautical requirements would probably be affected (such as vertical take-off and landing aircraft, and the Concorde or Tupolev-144 transport craft). The spread of meetings by teleconference, combined with automated office procedures, will also have second-order consequences of various kinds.

The automation of office work.[17] Initial research in this field has aimed at the automation of all simple office jobs, particularly the repetitive ones. Certain techniques making this possible and developed over the last ten years are now on the market. Some are connected with the concept of word processing. The logical capability of computers makes possible the typing of documents and their transmission to specific addresses in digital form (message switching).

In addition to these new methods are the facsimile transmission techniques (already mentioned) which are developing rapidly, and the application of the whole range of computer services to all branches of management.

Work at home. With all these new methods, it is possible to envisage working away from factory or office: at home, for example. Work at home offers considerable opportunities, particularly by giving a chance of employment to the housebound, for example the elderly, or those looking after children or handicapped people. Preliminary research nevertheless seems to indicate that work at home raises many psychological problems (for example, the tension created by the almost permanent presence of all members of the family), economic problems (the cost of the necessary terminals), and architectural problems (the unsuitability of homes for working purposes).[18]

Other possibilities have accordingly been thought up. The most significant is the establishment of non-institutional office centres,[19] or a kind of electronic office park along the lines of the already existing industrial estates. Centres of this kind would provide common premises equipped with suitable terminals enabling any worker to contact the government department or firm where he works. If procedures of this kind were introduced generally, they would lead to considerable savings in the energy now used for transport and to significant changes in the way towns were organized.[20]

Local services
Local services are in a category apart from the two previous ones and form a homogeneous entity comprising a large number of new services. In developed countries, homes are served, or can be served, in a systematic way by two networks, these being the telephone and broadcasting. A third network seems to be on the point of assuming increasing importance at home and in local life, this being cable television.[21] This was invented in the United States twenty-five years ago and was, to begin with, a simple community antenna to relay television broadcasts to villages or districts normally unable to receive them.

As it offered the advantage of better reception, avoided the eyesore of rooftop aerials and made it possible to envisage a whole host of potential new programmes, the system grew very rapidly in the United States and Canada where there was no nationwide television coverage. What has attracted attention, however, is the capacity of cable television networks, their architecture and their interplay.[22]

Readers interested in the possibilities of community antenna television for their own localities can go into the matter further by reading the bibliographical supplement to this article.

The impact of electronic communications

We have tried gradually to show that whatever the field of activity, telecommunications will have far-reaching consequences. So far as we know, no systematic studies have been carried out trying to give a composite picture of the kinds of future possible and the choices they imply. A certain amount of work has nevertheless been done which gives us a general idea of the situation.

The consequences for society

The influence of telecommunications will be felt in all the workings of society (and not only in urban and regional planning). As we have stressed, telecommunications and accessory electronic technology are strengthening the existing trend towards a gradual rationalization of the information sector in the economy in order to increase its productivity.

This development will have important consequences both in the kind of employment open in this sector and in the kind of curricula for education and continuous training to be followed. It will also affect the electronics and telecommunications industries. These have already grown more rapidly than any other industrial sectors. This trend will continue and the equipment they manufacture will pass into general use, thus giving electronics a key role in the economy.

On the social level, research in all branches stresses the role of electronic communications as a means of redistributing power in society. One analyst notes, for example, that since electronic transfers of funds would lead to a reduction in the volume of mail, the postal services will probably seek to play a role in organizing and supervising these transfer networks.[23]

Influence on regional and urban planning

The biggest changes to be made in existing patterns of urban and regional planning will be caused by the effects of telecommunications on the siting of economic and social activities. It is very important to remember that telecommunications are only one of the factors involved in the success or failure of the decentralization policies being followed in most developed countries, and the impact of the communications infrastructure could be neutralized by the others.

With regard to the positioning of employment, Pye and Goddard[24] have concluded that telecommunications seem to accelerate the decentralization of employment in metropolitan areas but not necessarily to lead to any transfer of activities to other urban centres. An experiment has been carried out in the State of Connecticut in the United States, as part of the New Rural Society project, to dispose economic activities in a rural environment through the use of telecommunications. Goldmark[25] has considered how communications could be used and what methods should be adopted to improve living conditions and establish "urban" employment in country districts. Other studies are examining this problem.[26]

One of the subjects most intensively studied is that of the effect of telecommunications on transport, itself linked with the problem of the siting of employment. The first two of the following four kinds of travel have been studied most: the journey from home to work, business travel, shopping journeys, and recreational or cultural travel. In the first two cases, Harkness and Pye[27] concluded that telecommunications could take the place of transport to a large extent. Business travel represents fifty per cent of air traffic but only eight per cent of the road traffic in the United States.

A survey carried out by the British Post Office came to the conclusion that about forty-five per cent of business meetings in the United Kingdom could be held using an audio conference system together with a document transmission system. Expressed in more concrete terms, two people travelling about 600 kilometres by air for a meeting which will last three hours will use an average of 2500 kWh of energy. The same meeting organized as an audio conference represents an energy output of 2 kWh. The saving is therefore substantial. In a roughly similar way, the journey from home to work could be replaced by electronic communications.[28]

Where other kinds of journey are concerned, studies so far carried out appear to show that telecommunications will supplement transactions requiring travel more than they will replace them. This is true of travel made necessary by continuous training and by the state social services. Possible substitutions for these will be few in number. Some facts and figures even tend to prove that the new services could increase the need for transport in certain fields.

The new places of communication

The introduction of the telecommunication systems and services mentioned above will transform the role and the form of places of communication in economic and social activities or will call for the establishment of new ones. At home, the telephone will become a terminal the use of which will gradually widen until the point is reached where connections to the network are built into new premises at the time of construction. It is also possible to envisage that connections to collective aerials and community or teledistribution antennae will also be provided in this way, as they already are in certain new urban areas or new towns in Europe.

The possibility of using the telephone network for a growing number of services and of combining its use with use of the television networks seems likely to encourage the installation of terminals specific to these networks in one and the same place. The need thus emerges to plan a communication area in the home, adapted to the different ways in which these terminals can be used. This area would have its own characteristics and would be more important the more business was conducted from it. It would, for example, be of special importance should it be used for working from home. What would then need to be reconsidered is probably the planning of the dwelling unit as a whole.

The possibility of working away from factory or office and the limitations which seem to exist with regard to work at home have, as we saw above, led to the idea of establishing groups of electronic offices in different places. The office space and equipment available would then be shared by employees of different firms living in the vicinity. In the New Rural Society, Goldmark had thought of combining in a community communication centre the equipment needed for the tele-services of the health and education departments, the social services, leisure and culture, business services and commercial services in general. The same concept has been developed in several studies and seems to be a reasonable and promising research hypothesis.

The introduction of teleconference networks will also lead to the provision of more space for business and public services. Public services and teleconferences have been tried out continuously in the United Kingdom for the past ten years, mostly under the Confravision system, and for one year in France. New intercity communication focal points called telecentres have thus been established at regional level.

The development of audiovisual techniques and, frequently, the development of teledistribution have finally encouraged the setting up of experimental resource centres at local and regional levels, the aim of these being to accustom the public to the production in the broad sense (and to the criticism) of audiovisual programmes. These centres lend production equipment to interested members of the public so that they can produce their own broadcasts. The centres also have video-recording libraries where available videotapes can be consulted.

The most famous of these centres is probably the Videograph at Montreal in Canada which was really the first of its kind. In the development of this concept, the importance of the video production centres of the public broadcasting networks should nevertheless be noted, for example Channel Ten in New York and Channel Forty at Milton Keynes in the United Kingdom. As designed in France, these

centres make provision under one roof for production documentation
(What programme is available? How can one get hold of it?), broadcasting and, chiefly, the education of the public by means of training
courses, actual handling of the equipment and production work. This
type of centre has been tried out at St Quentin-en-Yvelines (France)
and will gradually be introduced in Grenoble and in new towns when it
meets a clear need.

Conclusion
Telecommunications, electronic techniques and audiovisual media will
thus have an increasing role to play in the economic and social activities
of the societies of tomorrow, whether these are developed or developing. Their influence in every sector of activity is potentially very
important. The current state of research nevertheless does not make it
possible either to quantify this importance with any accuracy or to
forecast how these forms of technology can be expected to make their
influence particularly felt. The information we possess and the knowledge we have acquired concerning other systems nevertheless allow us
to see how important and urgent it is to carry out thorough studies in this
field. They further emphasize the need for the accurate planning of
communications and telecommunications as an integral part of national
planning, based on clearly defined social aims and following processes
open to public scrutiny and guaranteed by law.

Under any other condition, telecommunications could become tomorrow the tool for manipulation by an elite and an unprecedented
instrument of social coercion instead of being what we might expect
today, the means for the development and redistribution in space of
economic and social activity.

It is therefore vital, here and now, to take the necessary steps to
ensure the development of telecommunications in the interest of all. If
this is not done, Orwell's *1984* could well be the pattern of our society.
In a few years from now.

1 R. Meier, *A Communication Theory of Urban Growth* (MIT Press, Cambridge,
   Mass., 1962). See also L. Mumford, *The City in History* (Harcourt, Brace & World,
   New York, N.Y., 1961).
2 M. Porat, *The Information Economy* (Stanford University, Institute for Communication Research, Stanford, Calif., 1974), monograph.
3 E. Parker, *Social Implications of Computer Telecommunications Systems.* Paper
   submitted to the Conference on Computer/Telecommunications Policy. (Organization for Economic Co-operation and Development, Paris, 1975).
4 M. Tyler, B. Cartweight, O. Bookless and G. Bush, *Long Range Economic
   Forecasts, Long Term Materials Scarcities* (Post Office Telecommunications Headquarters, Cambridge, 1975).
5 "The Contribution of Telecommunications to the Conservation of Energy" (OECD,
   Paris, 1976), doc. DSTI/CUD/76.

6 The National Science Foundation in the United States is running an important programme of research in this field.

7 *The Coming Society and the Role of Telecommunications,* report in English (Research Institute of Telecommunications and Economics, Tokyo, 1975).

8 cf. J. Rule, "Value Choices in Electronic Funds Transfer Policy", *Compendium of Papers Supplementing the Hearings on Telecommunications Research and Policy Development* (House Sub-Committee on Communications, Washington, DC, 1976).

9 T. Horan, *Electronic Funds Transfer Systems* (Stanford Research Institute, Menlo Park, Calif., 1976); Rule, op. cit.

10 The Washington State Mutual Savings Bank has installed a system which enables bills to be paid from home by means of a keyboard telephone.

11 The National Research Council/National Academy of Engineering recently did a study for the United States Postal Service, entitled *Electronic Message Systems.* Both this and a similar study, *Metropolitan Communications Near-term Needs and Opportunities (1976–1980)* have been published (Washington, DC, 1977).

12 M. Tyler, *Innovation and Development in Telecommunications: the Implications for Transport* (Post Office Telecommunications Headquarters, Cambridge, 1975).

13 Research on this system is financed by the National Science Foundation and is being conducted at the University of Illinois (United States).

14 Mitre Corporation, *Revolutionizing Home Communications* (Washington, DC, 1972).

15 One of the phases of an exhaustive study of available systems and current testing was concluded in 1976 for the National Science Foundation. cf. R. Hough and R. Panko, *Teleconferencing Systems: a State of the Art Survey and Preliminary Analysis* (Stanford Research Institute, Menlo Park, Calif., 1976).

16 See the paper by R. Harkness in *Selected Results from a Technology Assessment of Telecommunications and Transportation Interactions,* presented to the Conference of the Institute of Electrical and Electronics Engineers, June 1976.

17 cf. for example A. Purchase and C. Glover, *Office of the Future* (Stanford Research Institute, Menlo Park, Calif., 1976).

18 J. Glover, *Long Range Social Forecasts: Working from Home* (Post Office Headquarters, Cambridge, 1974).

19 A. Custerson, "Telecommunications: The Office Mode", *Built Environment,* November 1973.

20 M. Edwards, *Service Provision via Local Communications Centres,* report (Department of the Environment, London, 1975).

21 Sloan Commission on Cable Communications, *On the Cable, the Television of Abundance* (McGraw-Hill, New York, N.Y., 1971).

22 cf. bibliographies published in the journal *Communications.*

23 Horan, op. cit.

24 R. Pye and J. Goddard, report (*Telecommunications and Office Location,* London, Department of the Environment, 1975).

25 P. Goldmark, *The 1972/1973 New Rural Society Project* (Fairfield University, Fairfield, Conn., 1973).

26 *The Possibility and Value of Broadband Communication in Rural Areas,* report (Office of Technology Assessment, Washington, DC, 1976). A comparable effort is currently under way in Canada.

27 R. Harkness and R. Pye, *Technology Assessment of Telecommunications Interactions with Travel,* report (National Academy of Engineering, Washington, DC, 1976).

28 ibid.

Micro is Beautiful

John Garrett and Geoff Wright

Following on from the thoughts of Theodore J. Lowi and Bruno Lefèvre, the authors of this article, which comes from the British alternative technology magazine Undercurrents, *No. 27 (1978), go one stage further on the road to decentralization. They represent the "romantic" school referred to at the beginning of this chapter. Yet they say the romantics of the radical technology movement have concentrated too much on wind-mills and solar panels and have ignored other technologies with an equally liberating potential – like microelectronics. The new telecommunications technology, they argue, makes possible a decentralized, self-managed anarchist utopia.*

During the current recession, many industries have been technologically stagnant, owing to lack of new investment and cutbacks in research and development. But the computer industry has been in a state of frantic excitement – almost bewilderment – over the technology it has created.

Here was an industry which only five years ago was quietly expanding, putting its main efforts into improving reliability and in giving the chiefs of commerce and industry the increased central control they wanted through the provision of suitable management information. All it was seeking to do was to run the status quo a little more efficiently. The market was dominated by one major company, IBM, with its competitors realizing that to survive, they would have to follow the leader and start making IBM-compatible equipment. The trend in the use of computing power seemed to be towards large computers handling large corporate data-bases in centralized data processing departments.

The hierarchical nature of the machine architecture, the data-base software, and most importantly, the data processing departments themselves, seemed to mirror exactly the cumbersome, inflexible, bureaucratic organizations they were servicing.

Five years on, this trend is still continuing. But strangely, a new contrary tendency is beginning to upset the steady progress towards a computerized 1984, a tendency towards *distributed processing*. This has been made practical by the introduction of low-cost commercial minicomputer systems, in 1966, and even lower-cost commercial micro-computers, in 1972.

Distributed processing is the decentralizing of computing power around a network of computers, instead of all computing power residing in one, usually large, central computer. Advances in communications technology, particularly the British Post Office Viewdata system, suggest an unlimited access to any such networks. George Cogar, President of Singer Machines in the US, has said that in twenty years' time the present phase of computer technology will be seen as the end of centralized data processing activity.

What perhaps set the seal on the changed direction in the industry was a decision made by IBM in February 1975 to abandon its next range of even more powerful data-base handling computers, called Future Series (FS). IBM had found itself threatened, not by its old familiar rivals but by the midgets of the industry, the minicomputer manufacturers, and even by the semiconductor suppliers who had started to assemble their own microcomputers. In a major turnabout, IBM have developed a minicomputer – which incidentally came out of what IBM's other branches termed the "toys division", who made office equipment. It adopted the radically new philosophy of distributed processing in its SNA (Systems Network Architecture). In addition, IBM have invested heavily in the communications industry, taking a thirty per cent stake in Satellite Business Systems, who are developing communications satellites for intercomputer transmissions across the globe.

Let us examine more closely some new products and ideas in the three rapidly merging industries in this field: electronics, computers and communications. In particular, we want to look closely at four developments which could be of great potential significance for the creation of a fundamentally changed society.

(1) The emergence of the cheap programmable microprocessor.
(2) The "domestication" of computers, i.e. the use of standard household devices for input, storage and power supply.
(3) The development of computer networks.
(4) the decline of the idea of centralized computer power.

The Microprocessor

1977, it has been said, was the year of the microprocessor. It was certainly the year in which the computer industry began to wake up to some of its implications. The microprocessor has a similar architecture to the mini- or larger computers, but its central processor can be contained on one, two or three semiconductor chips which can cost as little as £12. A complete microprocessor system with memory, buffers, interfaces, power supply and a simple input/output device can cost from £400 to £1000 – or even less in kit form.

Microprocessors can contain two types of memory, Read-Only Memory (ROM) and Random Access Memory (RAM). Programs stored in ROM are *permanent* and most can only be changed by substituting another ROM chip. Processors containing ROM only are mainly used in "dedicated" systems, where there is a single application, such as controlling traffic lights or lifts.

More interesting from a radical technology viewpoint are micro-processors with Random Access Memory, as these are readily repro-grammable without any need to change the hardware. In addition they can *modify themselves* by altering their own programming to respond to external changes. Their main advantage is that when incorporated into machinery such as numerical control (NC) or process control equip-ment, they allow far greater flexibility. The replacement of hardware by software enables the same machine to perform a greater variety of tasks. One machine can do the work of many, thus reducing the installation costs for a manufacturing requirement. In addition programs can be made "conversational", i.e. the machine will ask the operator what it should do and respond accordingly. Conversational programs allow the operator greater control over the machine and also enable mistakes to be rectified quickly. All these characteristics make them eminently suitable for small workshops or factories producing small batches of many different components, under workers' control.

Microprocessors could also be used to control the heating or cooling of dwellings – for example, heat sources could be quickly switched from solar to standard energy supplies in response to changed external conditions. They could also be used in controlling the light, heat, watering, ventilation and humidity in greenhouses – perhaps with a different program written for each variety of plant. (The new alchemists are exploring this idea in their "Arte" on Prince Edward Island in Canada.)

Predictably, micros have been attacked by many of the proponents of centralized computing as meaning a "twenty-five-year leap back". They are relatively slow, unsophisticated and have fewer software aids than larger computers. But in most computing applications, there is little need for speed and their basic nature makes them both flexible and, moreover, fun to use. These qualities, as well as their low cost, make them ideal for a democratic, small-scale industry.

The domestication of computers

Perhaps the most striking demonstration of this occurred in September 1977 when the French firm RZE brought out the Microl V computer. The "V" stands for valise or suitcase. In one standard suitcase is a Zilog Z80 processor containing a 32K main memory, a 150K floppy disc drive, a forty-character plasma display and a thermal printer. It can be programmed in Fortran and Basic and for its power supply it can be plugged into the cigarette lighter socket of a car.

Computers have got smaller, but more importantly, are using familiar household equipment. Data can now be read from and written to conventional audiocassettes and transmitted using the telephone network, via a "modem" which superimposes the pulses of digital data onto a carrier wave. Data can be entered using ordinary handwriting using the Quest Automation "Datapad" in which the machine can be taught to recognize individual styles. Speech input and output are also being developed so one will soon be able to hold a conversation with a computer. The television set has become a computer output device which with a teletext decoder can receive the teletext services Ceefax (BBC) and Oracle (ITV).

Moreover, from the moment when the remarkable Post Office service, Viewdata, commences its pilot scheme, the television set will become both an output and an input device, linked by telephone line to Post Office computers.* Viewdata, unlike the teletext services, is *interactive*, allowing a subscriber to receive *and* transmit information. Subscribers can use a "keypad" to communicate with the Post Office data-base.

Prices of Viewdata-equipped TV sets will initially be an artificially high £200–£250 above the cost of a normal colour television, but the difference is soon expected to fall to well below £100. In this society, it will probably be used by supermarket chains to give their stores instant updates of prices. A free society should be able to do much more with it.

The significant aspects of Viewdata for us are twofold:

It provides potentially unlimited access to information from all kinds of data-bases linked into the system.

It also provides a potentially unlimited medium of communication. Homes equipped with Viewdata television could use it to communicate

* Prestel service begun mid-1979.

with each other, as well as with any data-bases in the system. The system would be ideally suited for democratic decision-making. (If the Post Office restricts its use to isolated subscribers on line to a Post Office data-base, it will be a political rather than a technical decision.)

What the domestication of computers really means is that the computer is rapidly becoming available and comprehensible to the ordinary person.

Computer networks

The development of computer *networks* is perhaps the most significant of the four changes in political terms. Such networks have been operating for many years, but previously consisted of central computers with remote terminals on which data could be sent to the computer, and output received back. In recent years, however, terminals (often with the aid of microprocessors) have become "intelligent", i.e. the terminals themselves can carry out simple programming locally.

The trend has not stopped there. There are now full intercomputer networks, with minicomputers in place of terminals. Each site can now have its own local computing facilities, and also the added advantage of shared data-base. Communication is commonly via the telephone service but in future it is likely to be via high-speed computer "grids" (the Post Office is currently developing one for the UK) or via communications satellites.

Computer networks were originally developed for the defence of state communications in the event of nuclear attack, enabling the administration to survive the destruction of its key computer centres. In the event of parts of the system not operating, the network will "reconfigure" itself to branch around them. Ironically, what was designed for the defence of the state could become the communications structure of a decentralized society. Communes, farms, workshops and factories in a region, each with a computer in the network, would be able to do their own computing to link to others or to update and use shared data-bases. The ability to reconfigure round nonfunctioning units means that the system would still be able to operate even if half the communes could not get up in the morning!

Trading between units could be achieved by each inputting the goods and services they had available, and those they required. Economic coordination would be helped by consumers giving advance warning of what they desired and producers outlining what they intended to produce.

A decentralized society needs a very fast and efficient decision-making system, involving all those who might be affected. The traditional democratic method of delegate conference, as many have experienced, can end up being slower and more hidebound by rules than central direction. Communication networks should allow decision making to be faster, more responsive to events, and theoretically enable *all* members of a unit to be consulted rather than just one delegate. Politics could become the day-to-day occupation of the many rather than the personal gamesmanship of the few. Care, however, must be taken to avoid control of any computer network or control of information in the network being in any one unit's hands. To prevent this, data-bases themselves can be decentralized round the network. All that is strictly required of any central computers is to route transmissions to their appropriate destinations like a telephone exchange. Even that role can be reduced with more cross-connections – though obviously the more links, the greater the cost of the system.

Decline in the idea of centralized computing power

The present generation of large computers have central processors which, however powerful, can only handle one instruction at a time. But some of the newer "supercomputers", such as the Cray 1 or Control Data Star 100, have replaced the one central processor by sets of "functional processors", each specializing in specific processing tasks – so that one processor handles instruction fetching, others handle various different arithmetic and logical functions, and others store the results in memory. In computers like these, what is left of a "central" processor is thus changed to that of *coordinating* a series of functional processors.

As well as changes inside the machine, there have been changes in the storage and handling of data. The new types of "Data-Base Management System" (DBMS) have shifted away from "hierarchical" structures and towards "relational" structures. In a hierarchical DBMS, retrieving data requires searching through many levels of indexes or pointers for each item, which often proved to be slow and inefficient. In a relational DBMS, different kinds of data are held in different independent structures with no links assumed. Access to data can be more direct.

In a purely practical sense, the architecture of a machine or a piece of software is irrelevant. Hierarchically organized structures may be the most efficient for one particular task, relational structures for another. However, what is significant philosophically is that designers are no longer automatically thinking in terms of "hierarchical" or "tree" structures when creating either hardware or software. They are using concepts such as "parallel" structures, "ring" structures or "switched systems", all of which imply either no central control or that of coordination only.

The technology of a society is more than its tools. Because it is concrete, we use it to describe abstractions. If technical systems are hierarchically structured, then we will tend to see social systems in those terms. By the same token, the results of having distributed intelligence in machines or computer networks may have an impact in popular social ideas far greater than their physical uses.

One is tempted to compare the emergence of these products and ideas in the centralized bureaucratic societies of the industrialized world with the development of power-driven machinery at the end of the Middle Ages. The social class that had produced it, the guild craftsmen, were not capable of exploiting it. It took the rise of capitalism and the introduction of factories to utilize fully the productive forces the craftsmen had created. We believe we have now at our disposal a technology that is not capable of being fully exploited in the industrial societies we live in, and which points the way towards a new kind of decentralized future.

We have concentrated on developments which should increase an individual's control over what he or she produces and the way he or she does it. Equally, however, there have been developments which displace human beings entirely from the productive process – in particular the introduction of robots into assembly line work and the idea of an automated factory. We feel one of the debates in the RT movement must be to weigh up the advantages of humanless mass production as against small workshops using their infinitely flexible programmable machine tools to produce a wealth of small-scale and nonstandard variety. Perhaps some products are more suitable for the one and others for the other. If so, what kind of mix?

Let us now look at the political aspects of the crisis. Automation is likely to continue for very good economic reasons. Not only does it improve efficiency and productivity, it also has a future cost advantage. While the cost of automated equipment is becoming cheaper, workers' efforts to improve their standard of living are pushing up the cost of labour. In addition, recent legislation to improve job security has led to an increase in workers' power which is considered a threat by those who own and control industry. Recent CBI surveys have shown a general desire to automate, even among quite small firms, rather than employ more labour. This is even more true in countries with higher wages than our own. In Japan, there are even state subsidies to replace workers with robots. The Japanese Ministry of International Trade and Industry has started designing an automatic metal-working factory in which the production section is *completely unmanned*. The promise of an investment boom which will mop up unemployment will not be fulfilled. Any investment boom will be directed to capital rather than labour.

But there are limits to this process. One is the social danger of a growing class of permanently unemployed. A second is that governments have to finance unemployment. Even if a government were willing to tolerate a high level of unemployment, with all the social dangers, a point would be reached where the financial burden would be crippling. A third is that unless the unemployed were paid generously, the amount of purchasing power among consumers would not be sufficient to buy the increased production. This would apply throughout Western Europe, Japan and North America, so the only expanding market would be the Third World and Communist countries. But the Third World countries are also industrializing and it is likely that they will enact further legislation to protect their new industries.

Potential unemployment is therefore likely to be substantial. As far back as 1967 the British Institute of Management estimated that there were eight million people unnecessarily employed by British industry. This was well before a lot of new equipment was developed. The top ninety British companies are planning up to a thirty per cent reduction in their labour force. In the last five years the print industry unions have lost fifty per cent of their members and accept that in the next five years they will have to accept a further forty per cent reduction.

Our main point is that through the development of mainstream technology, the present social and economic system is producing a structural crisis. At the moment the politicians are saying things will go on in the same way as before and those who want to find alternatives to traditional forms of work are a lazy bunch of parasites. But the traditional Puritan work ethic becomes a nonsense in a situation where more can be produced using less people. The fact is that the politicians are wrong and the hippies were right, even if the hippies failed to analyse the reasons. We are reaching the point where the restructuring of industry and work must be the concern of everybody, not just the minority groups.

Future possibilities
It is not our task to produce a utopian blueprint but we can indicate some possibilities, suggested by the development of technology, in three main areas: *democracy, economic management*, and *decentralization of population and industry*.

There is no point in talking about extending democracy without extending the availability of information. At the moment both government and the controllers of industry hog information to help them maintain control. Information and communication have always been organized hierarchically in harmony with bureaucratic control. With recent developments in computer networks, decentralized control with no loss of efficiency is possible. All homes and workplaces in the country could be networked via the Viewdata system. If all available economic, social and political information were in the system, it would then be available to every citizen. Such a system makes possible decentralized, democratic, economic management on the feedback principle. People feed their needs into the system and the information is directly available to the producers who can gear their output accordingly.

Whether such a system is created is a political decision. The technical means are available. Other political decisions are whether to use automation to free people to participate in new creative industries. Shall we have a guaranteed minimum income in terms of goods and services? Shall we decentralize both population and industry by taking over large farms and estates to establish new communities and industries? What about worksharing of necessary but unpleasant work?

We believe that it is the job of the RT movement to examine these possibilities and the technical and political means of achieving them. The present "ecology" movement has little appeal to most people. Its public image suggests a preparation for the impending collapse of civilization and a return to a preindustrial society: hardly something to make people dance in the streets.

We disagree with this whole approach, and say a Golden Age is quite possible. Instead of predicting gloom and despair we should inspire people with a vision of the next stage of social evolution. If people have a clear idea of what is possible then the political means of achievement can be created. It is those of us who are young now who will consign the present system to the history books. It is up to us to start the debate.

Guide to Further Reading

F. J. M. Laver, "Some Social Consequences of Using Computers", in *National Electronics Review*, vol. 12, No. 3 (May/June 1976), has an annotated list of twenty-five key areas where the increased use of computers is likely to cause problems.

Central Policy Review Staff, *Social and Employment Implications of Microelectronics* (Cabinet Office, Whitehall, London, November 1978), was the British government response to speculation about the impact of the microprocessor. A slender document, and complacent in tone, it was roundly condemned for not taking the issue seriously. The response by the white-collar union APEX, in a paper issued in January 1979, was the best critique.

The Lowi paper reprinted above is taken from an extremely important symposium, *IEEE Transactions on Communications*, vol. COM-23, No. 10 (October 1975), on the social implications of telecommunications, ably introduced by Mischa Schwartz. Contributors discuss the possible impacts of interactive TV, electronic funds transfer, the videotelephone and the role of telecommunications in the Third World. More optimistic than Lowi, Francoise Gallouedec-Genuys, "The Effects of Computerization on the Relationship between Public Administration and the Community", in *Impact of Science on Society*, vol. 28, No. 3 (1978), sees greater political participation resulting from the new technology.

The *Proceedings of OECD Conference on Computer/Telecommunications Policy* (OECD Informatics Studies, No. 11, 1976) has a background paper by E. Parker and M. Porat on social implications and a useful summary of the session by D. Parkhill and H. Novotny.

The Commission of the European Communities has produced a typical Euro-report: *European Society faced with the Challenge of New Information Technologies: A Community Response* (Brussels, November 1979).

James Martin has written no less than twelve books on developments in telecommunications, most notable of which are (with A. R. D. Norman) *The*

497

Computerized Society (Prentice-Hall, Englewood Cliffs, New Jersey, 1977) and a real blockbuster, *Future Developments in Telecommunications*, 2nd Edition (Prentice-Hall, 1977). What is really a more popular version of this book is *The Wired Society* (Prentice-Hall, 1978), which sketches a science fiction scenario of life in 1984 or thereabouts.

Bruce Abell, "A Technology Assessment: The Social Consequences of Far Less Cash and Checks", in *Computers and People* (February 1977), is a brief look at such issues as crime and electronic funds transfer.

Peter Marsh, "Who Gains From the Great Data Boom?", *New Scientist*, 25 January 1979, looks at electronic mail and data networks.

Hesh Weiner, "Computers and the Future of America", in *Computer Decisions* (January 1977) contains an interview with futurologist Herman Kahn, founder of the Hudson Institute of Croton, New York. Kahn suggests that computerization may lead to totalitarianism.

In response to these sorts of fears, a new journal, *Information and Privacy*, appeared in 1979.

The promised yet slow progress of electronic funds transfer (EFT) is featured in four lively articles:

Sanford Rose, "More Bang for the Buck: The Magic of Electronic Banking", in *Fortune*, May 1977 and by the same author, "Checkless Banking is Bound to Come", *Fortune*, June 1977.

A more sceptical appraisal had already appeared as "Electronic Banking: A Retreat from the Cashless Society", in *Business Week*, 18 April 1977, and Sanford Rose came back with another, more gloomy report on EFT in "The Unexpected Fallout from Electronic Banking", *Fortune*, 27 March 1978.

The British Post Office's path-finding viewdata service, *Prestel*, is ably explained in a special feature in the magazine, *Director*, September 1979.

Other discussion papers include:

Tony Benn, "The Democratic Control of Science and Technology", Presidential Address to the inaugural meeting of the Science, Technology and Society Association at Imperial College, London, 3 February 1979.

Murray Laver, "Microprocessors, Side Effects and Society", in *Microprocessors*, vol. 1, No. 5 (June 1977).

M. Eugene Merchant, "Social Effects of Automation in Manufacturing: Trends and Perspectives", in *Proceedings of the American Society of Mechanical Engineers, Joint Automatic Control Conference*, West Lafayette, Indiana, July 1976.

F. Webster and K. Robins, "Mass Communications and 'Information Technology'", in *Socialist Register 1979* (Merlin Press, London, 1979).

Earlier contributions are:

William E. Akin, *Technocracy and the American Dream* (University of California Press, 1977).

F. E. Emery and E. L. Trist, "Socio-Technical Systems", in F. E. Emery (ed.), *Systems Thinking* (Penguin, Harmondsworth, 1969).

S. Lilley, *Automation and Social Progress* (Lawrence and Wishart, London, 1957).

E. G. Mesthene, *Technological Change: Its Impact on Man and Society* (Harvard University Press, Cambridge, Mass., 1970).

P. K. Piele, T. L. Eidell and S. C. Smith, *Social and Technological Change: Implications for Education* (Eugene, Oregon, 1970).

Philip Sadler, "The Social Implications of Automation", in *Proceedings of the Institute of Mechanical Engineers*, vol. 186 (London, 1972).

9 The Information Society

The Social Framework of the Information Society

Daniel Bell

The author of this paper is Professor of Sociology at Harvard University. He is a prolific writer and is especially well-known for coining the term "Post-Industrial Society" – a notion that found particular expression in The Coming of Post-Industrial Society *(New York, 1973). Now Professor Bell has developed his ideas further in the light of the microelectronic revolution, and here he describes the coming "Information Society" based upon the production and processing of knowledge. This essay also appears in Michael L. Dertouzos and Joel Moses (eds.),* The Computer Age: A Twenty-Year View (The MIT Press, Cambridge, Mass, 1979).

> The endless cycle of idea and action,
> Endless invention, endless experiment,
> Brings knowledge of motion, but not of stillness. . . .
> Where is the Life we have lost in living?
> Where is the wisdom we have lost in knowledge?
> Where is the knowledge we have lost in information?
>
> *T. S. Eliot: Choruses from "The Rock"*

Information and telecommunications in the postindustrial society

In the coming century, the emergence of a new social framework based on telecommunications may be decisive for the way in which economic and social exchanges are conducted, the way knowledge is created and retrieved, and the character of the occupations and work in which men engage. This revolution in the organization and processing of information and knowledge, in which the computer plays a central role, has as its context the development of what I have called the postindustrial

500

society.[1] Three dimensions of the postindustrial society are relevant to the discussion of telecommunications:

(1) The change from a goods-producing to a service society.
(2) The centrality of the codification of theoretical knowledge for innovation in technology.
(3) The creation of a new "intellectual technology" as a key tool of systems analysis and decision theory.

The change from a goods-producing to a service society can be indicated briefly. In the United States in 1970, sixty-five out of every hundred persons in the labour force were engaged in services, about thirty per cent in the production of goods and construction, and under five per cent in agriculture. The word *services* of course covers a large multitude of activities. In preindustrial societies a sizeable proportion of the labour force is engaged in household or domestic service. (In England until the 1870s the single largest occupational class was servants.) In an industrial society services are auxiliary to the production of goods, such as transportation (rail and truck), utilities (power and light), banking, and factoring. Postindustrial services are of a different kind. They are human services and professional services. The human services are teaching, health, and the large array of social services; professional services are those of systems analysis and design and the programming and processing of information. In the last two decades, the net new growth in employment has been entirely in the area of postindustrial services, and while the rate of growth has slowed (particularly because of the financial costs of education and the cutbacks in social services in urban communities), the general trend continues.

The axial principle of the postindustrial society, however, is the centrality of theoretical knowledge and its new role, when codified, as the director of social change. Every society has functioned on the basis of knowledge but only in the last half of the century have we seen a fusion of science and engineering that has begun to transform the character of technology itself. As Cyril Stanley Smith, the distinguished metallurgist, has observed: "In only a small part of history has industry been helped by science. The development of a suitable science began when chemists put into rational order facts that had been discovered long before by people who enjoyed empirical diverse experiment."[2]

The industries that still dominate society – steel, motor, electricity, telephone, aviation – are all "nineteenth-century" industries (though steel began in the eighteenth century with the coking process of Abraham Darby, and aviation in the twentieth with the Wright Brothers) in that they were created by "talented tinkerers" who worked independently of or were ignorant of contemporary science. Alexander Graham Bell, who invented the telephone about one hundred years ago (though the actual fact is in some dispute), was an elocution teacher who was looking for some means to amplify sound in order to help the deaf. Bessemer, who created the open-hearth process (to win a prize offered by Napoleon III for a better means of casting cannon), did not know the scientific work of Henry Clifton Sorby on metallurgical processes. And Thomas Alva Edison, who was probably the most prolific and talented of these tinkerers (he invented, among other things, the electric light bulb, the phonograph, and the motion picture), was a mathematical illiterate who knew little and cared less about the theoretical equations of Clerk-Maxwell on electromagnetic properties.

Nineteenth-century inventing was trial-and-error empiricism, often guided by brilliant intuitions. But the nature of advanced technology is its intimate relations with science, where the primary interest is not in the product itself but in the diverse properties of materials together with the underlying principles of order that allow for combination, substitution or transmutation. According to Cyril Smith:

> All materials came to be seen in competition, with the emphasis only on the properties that were needed. Thereafter every new development in advanced technology – radar, nuclear reactors, jet aircraft, computers and satellite communications to name a few – has served to break the earlier close association of materials research with a single type of manufacture, and the modern materials engineer has emerged.

The nature of this change, in technology and in science, has been to enlarge the "field of relation" and the range of theory so as to permit a systematic synergism in the discovery and extension of new products and theories. A science, at bottom, is a set of axioms linked topologically to form a unified scheme. But as Bronowski has observed: "A new theory changes the system of axioms and sets up new connections at the joints which changes the topology. And when two sciences are linked to form one (electricity and magnetism, for instance, or evolution with genetics), the new network is richer in its articulation than the sum of its two parts."[3]

While modern science, like almost all human activities, has moved towards a greater degree of specialization in its pursuit of more detailed knowledge, the more important and crucial outcome of its association with technology is the integration of diverse fields or observations into single conceptual and theoretical frameworks offering much greater explanatory power. Norbert Wiener, in his autobiographical *I Am a Mathematician*, points out that his first mathematical papers were on Brownian motion and that at the same time electrical engineering work was being done on the so-called shot effects, or the movement of electric current through a wire. The two topics were unrelated; yet twenty years later the situation had changed dramatically.

> In 1920 very little electrical apparatus was loaded to the point at which the shot effect became critical. However the later development – first of broadcasting and then of radar and television – brought shot effect to the point where it became the immediate concern of every communications engineer. The shot effect was not only similar in origin to the Brownian movement, for it was a result of the discreteness of the universe, but had essentially the same mathematical theory. Thus, my work on the Brownian motion became some twenty years later a vital tool for the electrical engineer.[4]

Wiener's theory of cybernetics joins a variety of fields in the common framework of statistical information theory. "The development of ideas on the structure of synthetic polymers," Cyril Smith writes, "eventually came to bridge the gap between the nineteenth-century chemist's molecule and the early twentieth-century crystal, so paving the way for the unified structural view of all materials which we see taking shape today."[5] The development of solid-state physics, which is the foundation of the electronic revolution, arose out of the work of metallurgists and physicists on the structure of conductor devices.

The methodological promise of the second half of the twentieth century is the management of organized complexity: the complexity of theories with a large number of variables and the complexity of large organizations and systems which involve the coordination of hundreds of thousands and even millions of persons. Since 1940 there has been a remarkable efflorescence of new fields and methods whose concern is with the problems of organized complexity: information theory, cybernetics, decision theory, game theory, utility theory, stochastic processes. From these have come specific techniques such as linear programming, statistical decision theory, Markov chain applications, Monte Carlo randomizing, and minimax strategies, which allow for sampling from large numbers, alternative optimal outcomes of different choices, or definitions of rational action under conditions of uncertainty.

Since technology is the instrumental mode of rational action, I have called this new development "intellectual technology", for these methods seek to substitute an algorithm (i.e., decisions rules) for intuitive judgements. These algorithms may be embodied in an automatic machine or a computer program, or a set of instructions based on some statistical or mathematical formula, and represent a "formalization" of judgements and their routine application to many varied

Table 9.1 The postindustrial society: a comparative schema

Mode of production	Preindustrial extractive
Economic sector	*Primary*
	Agriculture
	Mining
	Fishing
	Timber
	Oil and gas
Transforming resource	*Natural power*
	Wind, water, draft animal, human muscle
Strategic resource	Raw materials
Technology	Craft
Skill base	Artisan, manual worker, farmer
Methodology	Common sense, trial and error; experience
Time perspective	Orientation to the past
Design	Game against nature
Axial principle	Traditionalism

situations. To the extent that intellectual technology is becoming predominant in the management of organizations and enterprises, one can say that it is as central a feature of postindustrial society as machine technology is in industrial society.

A knowledge theory of value. If one compares the formal properties of postindustrial society with those of industrial and preindustrial society (see Table 9.1), the crucial variables of the postindustrial society are information and knowledge.

By information I mean data processing in the broadest sense; the storage, retrieval, and processing of data become the essential resource

Industrial – Fabrication	Postindustrial – Processing; Recycling	
Secondary	Services	
Goods-producing	*Tertiary*	*Quaternary*
Manufacturing	Transportation	Trade
Durables	Utilities	Finance
Nondurables		Insurance
Heavy construction	*Quinary*	Real estate
	Health, Education	
	Research, Government,	
	Recreation	
Created energy	*Information*	
Electricity – oil, gas, coal, nuclear power	Computer and data-transmission systems	
Financial capital	Knowledge	
Machine technology	Intellectual technology	
Engineer, semiskilled worker	Scientist, technical and professional occupations	
Empiricism, experimentation	Abstract theory, models, simulations, decision theory, systems analysis	
Ad hoc adaptiveness, experimentation	Future orientation: forecasting and planning	
Game against fabricated future	Game between persons	
Economic growth	Codification of theoretical knowledge	

for all economic and social exchanges. These include:

(1) Data processing of records: payrolls, government benefits (e.g. social security), bank clearances, credit clearances, and the like. Data processing for scheduling: airline reservations, production scheduling, inventory analysis, product-mix information, and the like.
(3) Data-bases: characteristics of populations as shown by census data, market research, opinion surveys, election data, and the like.

By knowledge, I mean an organized set of statements of fact or ideas, presenting a reasoned judgement or an experimental result, which is transmitted to others through some communication medium in some systematic form. Thus, I distinguished knowledge from news or entertainment. Knowledge consists of new judgements (research and scholarship) or presentations of older judgements (textbooks, teaching, and library and archive materials).

In the "production of knowledge", what is produced is an intellectual property, attached to a name or a group of names and certified by copyright or some other form of social recognition (like publication). This knowledge is paid for – in the time spent in writing and research, in the monetary compensation by the communications and educational media. The response of the market, along with administrative and political decisions of superiors or peers, judge the worth of the result and any further claim on social resources that might be made in its behalf. In this sense, knowledge is part of social overhead. More than that, when knowledge becomes involved in some systematic form in the applied transformation of resources (through invention or social design), then one can say that knowledge, not labour, is the source of value.

Economists in their formal schemes to explain production and exchange, use as key variables "land, labour and capital", though institutionally-minded economists such as Werner Sombart and Joseph Schumpeter added the notion of an acquisitive spirit or entrepreneurial initiative. The analytical mode used by economists, the "production function", sets forth the economic mix only as capital and labour – a system that lends itself easily to a labour theory of value, with surplus labour value as congealed capital, but neglects almost entirely the role of knowledge or of organizational innovation and management. Yet with the shortening of labour time and the diminution of the production worker (who in Marxist theory is the source of value, since most services are classified as nonproductive labour), it becomes clear that knowledge and its applications replace labour as the source of "added value" in the national product. In that sense, just as capital and labour have been the central variables of industrial society, so information and knowledge are the crucial variables of postindustrial society.

Intellectual foundations of the revolution in communications
For Goethe, the basis of the human community was communication. Decades before other persons spoke of such projects, he envisaged a Panama Canal, a Suez Canal, and a canal between the Rhine and the Danube as the means by which the human community might become more closely intertwined. But it was the Canadian economic historian Harold Innis, more than any other person, who saw changes in the modes of communication, rather than production and property rela-

tions, as the key to transitions from one stage of society to another.

> Western civilization has been profoundly influenced by communication
> ... [and can be] divided into the following periods in relation to media of
> communication: clay, the stylus and cuneiform script from the beginnings
> of civilization in Mesopotamia; papyrus, the brush and hieroglyphics and
> hieratic to the Graeco-Roman period, and the reed pen and the alphabet
> to the retreat of the Empire from the west; parchment and pen to the
> tenth century of the dark ages; and overlapping with paper, the latter
> becoming more important with the invention of printing; paper and the
> brush in China, and paper and the pen in Europe before the invention of
> printing or the Renaissance; paper and the printing press under handi-
> craft methods to the beginning of the nineteenth century, or from the
> Reformation to the French Revolution; paper produced by machinery
> and the application of power to the printing press since the beginning of
> the nineteenth century to paper manufactured from wood in the second
> half of the century; celluloid in the growth of the cinema; and finally the
> radio in the second quarter of the present century. In each period I have
> attempted to trace the implications of the media of communication for
> the character of knowledge and to suggest that a monopoly or an
> oligopoly of knowledge is built up to the point that equilibrium is
> disturbed.[6]

Innis was a technological determinist. He thought that the technology of
communication was basic to all other technology, for if tool technology
was an extension of man's physical powers, communication technology,
as the extension of perception and knowledge, was the enlargement of
consciousness. He argued not only that each stage of Western civilization was dominated by a particular medium of communication but that
the rise of a new mode was invariably followed by cultural disturbances.[7]

One can say that the new media of communication today are television or the computer, or the variant modes of storage, retrieval and
transmission that will arise through the "fusing" of technologies. But
the core of the present communications revolution is not a specific
technology but the set of concepts represented by the term *information
theory.*

The statistics of language. Information theory arose from the work of
Claude Shannon on switching circuits to increase "channel capacity",
the design for which he derived from the algebra of logic. The algebra of
logic is an algebra of choice and deals with the range of choices in a
determinate sequence of alternative possibilities in the routing of a
message. The parlour game of "Twenty Questions" is often taken as a
conventional illustration of how one narrows a range of possibilities by
asking a series of yes or no questions. As Shannon points out in the
article on information theory that he wrote for the *Encyclopaedia*

Britannica: "The writing of English sentences can be thought of as a process of choice: choosing a first word from possible first words with various probabilities; then a second with probabilities depending on the first; etc. This kind of statistical process is called a stochastic process, and information sources are thought of, in information theory, as stochastic processes."

The information rate of written English can be translated into bits (*bi*nary digi*ts* 1 and 0), so that if each letter occurred with equal frequency, there would be 4.76 bits per letter. But since the frequencies are unequal (*E* is common, *Z*, *Q*, and *X* are not), the actual rate is one bit per letter. Technically, English is said to be eighty per cent "redundant", a fact that one can immediately ascertain by "deciphering" a sentence from which various vowels or consonants have been deleted. By knowing the statistical structure of a language, one can derive a general formula that determines the rate at which information can be produced statistically and create huge savings in transmission time. But though transmission was the impetus to the formulation of information theory, the heart of the concept is the idea of coding. Messages have to go through "channels"; inevitably, they are distorted by "noise" and other forms of "resistance" that arise from the physical properties of the channel. What Shannon found was that it is possible to encode a message that can be accurately transmitted even if the channel of communication is faulty, so long as there is enough capacity in that channel.

Shannon's mathematical theory had immediate application to industry. The theoretical and statistical underpinnings seemed to confirm the more general theory of Wiener's *Cybernetics*, a work that had been commissioned by an obscure publisher in France after the war and became an immediate bestseller on its publication by Wiley in 1948. What Shannon's and Wiener's work seemed to promise was the move toward some general unified theory of physics and human behaviour (at least in physiology, psychology and linguistics) through the concept of information. As Shannon himself wrote in his *Britannica* essay:

> A basic idea in communication theory is that information can be treated very much like a physical quantity such as mass or energy.... The formula for the amount of information is identical in form with equations representing entropy in statistical mechanics, and suggests that there may be deep-lying connections between thermodynamics and information theory. Some scientists believe that a proper statement of the second law of thermodynamics requires a term relating to information. These connections with physics, however, do not have to be considered in the engineering and other applications of information theory.[8]

But this is a confusion of realms – compounded by the facile use of the word *entropy* to equate the degree of disorder or noise (i.e., the loss of accuracy) in communication with the loss of heat or energy in transformational activities in physics. As Wiener put it in his *Cybernetics*, resisting the easy comparisons of living with mechanical organisms: "Information is information, not matter or energy. No materialism which does not admit this can survive at the present day."[9]

However true it may be as a statistical concept that information is a quantity, in its broadest sense – to distinguish between information and fabrication – information is a pattern or design that rearranges data for instrumental purposes, while knowledge is the set of reasoned judgements that evaluates the adequacy of the pattern for the purposes for which the information is designed. Information is thus pattern recognition, subject to reorganization by the knower, in accordance with specified purposes. What is common to this and to all intellectual enterprises is the concept of relevant structure. This concept is what underlies the shift, in the works of Cyril Stanley Smith, from "matter to materials", from the classificatory and even combinational arrangements of elementary properties of matter that began with the pre-Socratics to our present-day understanding of the structural relations of the properties of materials.

These structural relations – in science, as in the economy – fall into two separate domains. The first is the transformation of matter and energy, from one material form into another. The second is the transformation of information from one pattern into another. As Anthony Oettinger puts it in an aphorism: "Without matter there is nothing; without energy matter is inert; and without information, matter and energy are disorganized, hence useless."

The use of models. Technological revolutions, even if intellectual in their foundations, become symbolized if not embodied in some tangible "thing", and in the postindustrial society that "thing" is the computer. If, as Paul Valéry said, electricity was the agent that transformed the second half of the nineteenth century, in a similar vein the computer has been the "analytical engine" that has transformed the second half of the twentieth century. What electricity did – as the source of light, power and communication – was to create "mass society"; that is, to extend the range of social ties and the interaction between persons and so magnify what Durkheim called the social density of society. In that respect, the computer is a tool for managing the mass society, since it is the mechanism that orders and processes the transactions whose huge number has been mounting almost exponentially because of the increase in social interactions.

The major sociopolitical question facing the mass society is whether we can manage the economy effectively enough to achieve our social goals. The development of computers has allowed us to construct detailed models of the economy. Wassily Leontieff recently described the extraordinary expansion of the input-output system:

> The first input-output tables describing the flow of goods and services between the different sectors of the American economy in census years 1919 through 1929 were published in 1936. They were based on a rather gross segregation of all economic activities in 44 sectors. Because of the lack of computing facilities, these had to be further grouped into only 10 sectors, for the purposes of actual analytic calculations.
>
> The data base, the computing facilities, and the analytical techniques have advanced much further than could have been anticipated forty years ago. National input-output tables containing up to 700 distinct sectors are being compiled on a current basis, as are tables for individual, regional, state and metropolitan areas. Private enterprise has now entered the input-output business. For a fee one can now purchase a single row of a table showing the deliveries of a particular product, say, coated laminated fabrics or farming machine tools, not only to different industries but to individual plants within each industry segregated by zip code areas.[10]

Though it is clear that economists are able to model the economy and do computer simulations of alternative policies to test their consequences, it is much less clear whether such models allow us to manage the economy. The critical point is that the crucial decisions for any society are the political ones, and these are not derivative from economic factors.

Can one model a society? One immediate problem is that we do not have any persuasive theories of how a society hangs together, though paradoxically, because of our understanding of technology, we have a better idea of how societies change. One can only model a closed or finite system; the econometric models operate within a closed system. Yet society is increasingly open and indeterminate, and as men become more conscious of goals there is greater debate about decisions. Decisions on social policy become more and more a matter within the purview of the political system rather than of aggregate market decisions, and this, too, weakens our ability to model a society.

Beyond this there may be reasons intrinsic to the structure of "large numbers" that could prevent the computer from becoming the instrument for the modelling and prediction of any complex system. John von Neumann, one of the pioneers in the development of the theory of electronic computing, thought that the prediction of weather would be possible once computers became sophisticated enough to handle all the numerous interacting variables in the atmosphere. Yet as Tjalling

Koopmans and others have pointed out, beyond a certain threshold introducing added complexity results in answers that are less and less reliable. Thus, the effort to optimize an objective by seeking for complete information may be self-defeating. The social world is not a Laplacean universe where one can plot, from the initial values, the determinate rates of change of other phenomena. If so many parts of the physical world now require us to deal with a calculus of possibility rather than determined regularities, this is even more true in a social world where men are less and less willing passively to accept existing arrangements but instead work actively to remake them. By letting us know the risks and probabilities, the computer has become a powerful tool for exploring the permutations and combinations of different choices for calculating their consequences, the odds of success or failure. The computer does this by using a binary code that with the speed of light can answer a question with a yes or a no. What it cannot do, obviously, is to decide like a roulette wheel whether to stop on the yes or on the no.

The economics of information. Information is central to all economic transactions – indeed, perfect information is the indispensable condition for perfect competition in general equilibrium theory. Yet we have no economic theory of information, and the character of information, as distinct from the character of goods, poses some novel problems for economic theorists.

In a price and market economy, the condition for efficiency, or optimal use of resources, is complete information among buyers and sellers, so that one can obtain the "best" price for one's goods or services. But with the widening of markets and the reduction of distances by transportation and communication – which also enlarges the sphere of competition – efficiency increasingly demands not only a knowledge of contemporary alternatives but of the likely future ones as well, since political decisions or new technologies may radically alter prices. A political embargo may cut off the supplies of a resource. A tax cut or a tax rise will affect the level of spending. New technologies may sharply cut the price of a product (witness the extraordinary changes in two years in the price of small electronic calculators), leaving firms with large inventories or committed to older production techniques at a great disadvantage.

Information, as Kenneth Arrow puts it, reduces uncertainty.[11] The random-walk theory that one cannot "beat the stock market" is based on the assumption that stock prices reflect new information about companies so quickly that investors have little chance to earn better-than-average returns on their money. Therefore the wiser strategy is to place one's money in an index fund that reflects the average prices of the market as a whole. The job search in the labour market is enhanced by access to a wider pool of information. Accurate crop reporting controls the vagaries of the futures market in commodities. One can multiply the illustrations indefinitely.

But information is not a commodity, at least not in the way the term is used in neoclassical economics or understood in industrial society. Industrial commodities are produced in discrete, identifiable units, exchanged and sold, consumed and used up, like a loaf of bread or an automobile. One buys the product from a seller and takes physical possession of it; the exchange is governed by legal rules of contract. In the manufacture of industrial goods, one can set up a "production function" (i.e., the relative proportions of capital and labour to be employed) and determine the appropriate mix relative to the costs of each factor.

Information, or knowledge, even when it is sold, remains with the producer. It is a "collective good" in that once it has been created, it is by its nature available to all.[12] In fact, the character of science itself, as a cooperative venture of knowledge, depends on the open and complete transmission of all new experiments and discoveries to others in the field. Multiple discoveries of the same theory or experimental result or technique, which Robert Merton argues is a more dominant pattern in science than the image of the lonely genius or scholar, are one result of this openness and the rapid spread of knowledge.[13]

If knowledge is a collective good there is little incentive for any individual enterprise to pay for the search for such knowledge, unless it can obtain a proprietary advantage, such as a patent or a copyright. But increasingly, patents no longer guarantee exclusiveness, and many firms lose out in spending money on research only to find that a competitor (particularly one overseas) can quickly modify the product and circumvent the patent; similarly, the question of copyright becomes increasingly difficult to police when individuals or libraries can Xerox whatever pages they need from technical journals or books or when individuals and schools can tape music off the air or record a television performance on video discs. But more generally, the results of investing in information (i.e., doing research), are themselves uncertain. Because firms are averse to risk, they tend to undervalue such investments from the social point of view, and this leads to underinvestment in private research and development.

If there is less and less incentive for individual persons or private enterprises to produce knowledge without particular gain, then the need and effort fall increasingly on some social unit, be it university or government, to underwrite the costs. And since there is no ready market test (how does one estimate the value of basic research?), it is a challenge for economic theory to design a socially optimal policy of investment in knowledge (including how much money should be spent for basic research; what allocations should be made for education, and for what fields; in what areas of health do we obtain the "better returns"; and so on) and to determine how to "price" information and knowledge to users.[14]

The merging of technologies. Through the nineteenth and up to the mid-twentieth century, communication could be divided roughly into two distinct realms. One was mail, newspapers, magazines and books, printed on paper and delivered by physical transport or stored in libraries. The other was telegraph, telephone, radio and television, coded message image or voice sent by radio signals or through cables from person to person. Technology, which once made for separate industries, is now erasing these distinctions, so that a variety of new alternatives are now available to information users, posing, for that very reason, a major set of policy decisions for the lawmakers of the country.

Inevitably, large vested interests are involved. Just as the substitution of oil for coal and energy and the competition of truck, pipeline, and railroad in transportation created vast dislocations in corporate power, occupational structures, trade unions, geographical concentrations and the like, so the huge changes taking place in communications technology will affect the major industries that are involved in the communications arena.

Broadly, there are five major problem areas:

(1) The meshing of the telephone and computer systems, of telecommunications and teleprocessing, into a single mode. A corollary problem is whether transmission will be primarily over telephone-controlled wires or whether there will be independent data-transmission systems. Equally, there is the question of the relative use of microwave relay, satellite transmission and coaxial cables as transmission systems.

(2) The substitution of electronic media for paper processing. This includes electronic banking to eliminate the use of cheques; the electronic delivery of mail; the delivery of newspapers or magazines by facsimile rather than by physical transport; and the long-distance copying of documents.

(3) The expansion of television through cable systems, to allow for multiple channels and specialized services, and the linkage to home terminals for direct response to the consumer or home from local or central stations. A corollary is the substitution of telecommunication for transportation through videophone, closed-circuit television and the like.

(4) The reorganization of information storage and retrieval systems

based on the computer to allow for interactive network communication in team research and direct retrieval from data banks to library or home terminals.

(5) The expansion of the education system through computer-aided instruction, the use of satellite communications systems in rural areas, especially in the underdeveloped countries, and the use of video discs both for entertainment and instruction in the home.[15]

Technologically, telecommunications and teleprocessing are merging in a mode that Anthony Oettinger has called "compunications" (see Fig. 9.1). As computers come increasingly to be used as switching devices in communications networks and electronic communications facilities become intrinsic elements in computer data processing services, the distinction between processing and communication becomes indistinguishable. The major questions are legal and economic. Should the industry be regulated or competitive? Should it be dominated, in effect, by AT&T or by IBM?*

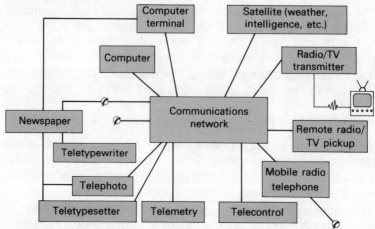

Fig. 9.1 The changing telecommunications network. As of 1974, the 144 million plain old telephones still predominated, but many other devices are now attached to a network that has become an infrastructure basic to most social functions, including many that reach directly into the home. As computers and computer terminals have become increasingly pervasive over the last two decades, the network has developed towards an integrated computer communications or "compunications" network. From Paul J. Berman and Anthony G. Oettinger, *The Medium and the Telephone: The Politics of Information Resources*, Working Paper 75-8, 15 December 1975, Harvard Program on Information Technologies and Public Policy, Cambridge, Mass.

* In 1976, AT&T introduced a bill in Congress to allow it to buy out its microwave competitors, and it wants Congress to require anyone plugging specialized services into its lines to buy a connecting device from the phone company. IBM has entered into a direct challenge to AT&T by setting up the Satellite Business Systems Company jointly with Aetna Insurance and Comsat General to operate a satellite communications service that would transmit the full range of "compunications" by 1979.

The entry of specialized carriers into the business field, undercutting AT&T prices, threatens its consumer rate structure as well, and would create large political unheavals. Yet the "computer" proponents have argued that technological innovation in the telephone field has been stodgy, whereas the energetic and bustling computer field has demonstrated its ability to innovate rapidly and reduce costs and prices, so that competition in transmission, in the end, would serve the country as a whole.

The questions I have been raising about the fusion of communications technologies – the rise of compunications – are not only technological and economic but, most important, political. Information is power. Control over communications services is a source of power. Access to communication is a condition of freedom. There are legal questions that derive directly from this. The electronic media, such as television, are regulated, with explicit rules about "fairness" in the presentation of views, access to reply to editorials, and the like. But ultimately the power is governmental. Decisions about the station's future lie with the Federal Communications Commission. The telephone industry is regulated on its rates and conditions of service. The computer industry is unregulated and operates in an open market. The print media are unregulated, and their rights on free speech are zealously guarded by the First Amendment and the courts. Libraries have largely been private or locally controlled; now great data banks are being assembled by government agencies and by private corporations. Are they to be under government supervision or unregulated? All of these are major questions for the future of the free society and bear on the problem of a national information policy.

The quantitative dimensions of the information society
In 1940, Colin Clark, the Australian economist, wrote his pathbreaking *Conditions of Economic Progress*, in which he divided economic activity into three sectors, primary (principally extractive), secondary (primarily manufacturing), and tertiary (services). Any economy is a mixture of all three sectors, but their relative weights are a function of the degree of productivity (output per capita) in each sector. Economic progress is defined as the rate of transfer of labour from one sector to another, as a function of differential productivity. As national incomes rise, the expansion of the manufacturing sector is followed by a greater demand for services and a further corresponding shift in the slope of employment. In this fashion, Clark was able to chart the rate of change from a preindustrial into an industrial society and then into a service society.

The difficulty remains the definition of services. In classical economics, beginning with Adam Smith, services were thought of as unproductive labour. Marx, accepting that distinction, had based one of his theories on the crisis of capitalism, that of the falling rate of profit, on the proposition that as a higher proportion of output shifted from "variable capital" (productive labour) to "constant capital" (machinery, for example), the rate of profit would fall since the base on which surplus value was produced would be shrinking (unless overcome by more intensive exploitation, such as lengthening the working day or speeding up the pace of work). As the notion that services were unproductive became increasingly dubious, economists were faced with a double problem of redefinition: first, determining which services were unproductive (e.g., domestic servants) and which were productive (e.g., education, by increasing the skill of labour, or medicine, by making persons healthier or prolonging working life); second, developing a more adequate set of distinctions within the services category. Some writers sought to restrict the tertiary sector to auxiliary blue-collar work, such as transportation, utilities, repair (e.g., motor mechanics), and personal services (laundry, barbers, and so on), and to define a *quaternary* sector made up essentially of the white-collar industries, such as banking, insurance and real estate, and a *quinary* sector, made up of knowledge activities like scientific and technical research, education and medicine. While such distinctions are useful for indicating the complexity of occupational distributions, with them one loses the thrust implicit in the original Colin Clark scheme, with its emphasis on differential productivity as the mechanism for the transition from one type of society to another.

Without pretending to be exhaustive, I have adopted a scheme for the postindustrial society of classifying economic sectors as extractive, fabrication and information activities. The underlying sociological rationale is that it seeks to look at the character of work as a shaper of the character of individuals. The scheme is based on the distinction that some societies are primarily engaged in games against nature, others in games against fabricated nature (things), and others in games between persons. It also derives from the propositions I have put forward regarding the centrality of knowledge in the postindustrial society, the primacy of a knowledge theory of value as against a labour theory of value, and the growth of information processing within the traditional sectors, such as agriculture, manufacture and services, which is beginning to transform the character of those sectors as well.

The measurement of knowledge. In 1958, Fritz Machlup, then at Princeton University, made the first efforts to measure the production and distribution of knowledge. The definition of knowledge was somewhat unsatisfactory, for Machlup rejected "an objective interpretation according to *what* is known", as against a subjective interpretation derived from what a knower designates as being known.[16] And Machlup worked from the standard national accounts, although in important details he varied from standard usages.[17]

Still, Machlup's painstaking work was crucial. In his accounting scheme, he grouped thirty industries into five major classes of knowledge production, processing, and distribution: (1) education, (2) research and development, (3) media of communication, (4) information machines, and (5) information services. The categories were broad. Education, for example, included education in the home, job and church as well as in school. Communications media included all commercial printing, stationery and office supplies. Information machines included musical instruments, signalling devices, and typewriters. Information services included money spent for securities brokers, real-estate agents and the like.

Machlup estimated that $136,436m was spent for knowledge, or twenty-nine per cent of gross national product (GNP),[18] and that thirty-one per cent of the labour force was engaged in that sector. Of equal importance, he estimated that between 1947 and 1958, the knowledge industries expanded at a compound growth rate of 10.6 per cent a year, which was double that of the GNP itself during the same period. In 1963, Gilbert Burck, an editor of *Fortune*, replicated Machlup's estimates and calculated that in that year knowledge produced a value added of $159 billion, or thirty-three per cent of the GNP.[19] Five years later, Professor Jacob Marschak, one of the most eminent economists in the United States, in computations made in 1968, said that the knowledge industries would approach forty per cent of the GNP in the 1970s.[20]

The last decade has in fact seen enormous growth in the "information economy", which includes various fields. In education, while the rate of growth of college education has slowed down, there has been a continuing increase in adult education, which in fact has maintained its rise. In health, the expansion of health services continues, particularly with the multiplication of federal legislation. Information and data processing continue to rise, particularly as the volume of transactions and record keeping increases. Telecommunications finds its major area of growth in international communications, particularly with the launching of new satellites. Television is on the threshold of a number of major changes with the growth of both cable television and video discs.

Still, if one wanted to measure the actual economic magnitudes of the information economy, the difficulty is that there is no comprehensive conceptual scheme that can divide the sector logically into neatly distinct units, making it possible to measure the trends in each unit over time. A logical set of categories might consist of the following: knowledge (which would include situses – locations or social positions – such as education, research and development, libraries and occupations that apply knowledge, such as lawyers, doctors and accountants); entertainment (which would include motion pictures, television, the music industry); economic transactions and records (banking, insurance, brokerage); and infrastructure services (telecommunications, computers and programs, and so on).

Two somewhat different approaches have been adopted. Anthony Oettinger and his colleagues have taken the "information industries" from the Standard Industrial Classification used by the US Census and listed their gross revenues in order to provide some crude baselines to measure changes. The difficulty here is that merging technologies and double counting defeat such efforts. The second approach, a more difficult and pioneering effort, is that of Marc Porat, which is to use the National Income Accounts to define a primary sector, the direct sale of information services (like education, banking, advertising) to consumers, and then to define a secondary sector – the planning, programming and information activities of private and public bureaucracies in enterprises and government – and impute the value added by such activities to the national product and national income.

The information economy. Marc Porat has broken down the National Income Accounts for 1967 in order to see what portions may be attributable, directly and indirectly, to information activities. In doing this, he has used three measures to compute gross national product. One is "final demand" (which eliminates the intermediate transactions that would add up to double counting), the second is "value added", which is the actual value added by a specific industry or component of an industry to the product, and the third is the income or compensation received by those who create these goods and services. Theoretically, the totals of all three figures should be equal; in fact, for statistical reasons, in part owing to different methods of collection, the figures do not always dovetail exactly. But the virtue of using all three is that one can make different analytical distinctions. For my purposes, the most important measure is that of value added, for with it one can seek to determine the actual services provided by information activities and then check these figures against the income or compensations received by those engaged in providing the services.

Porat's work is the first empirical demonstration of the scope of information activities since Machlup, but it goes far beyond Machlup's work, not only because it uses finer categories and makes three different kinds of estimations, but also because it seeks to establish an input-output matrix that would permit, once the accounts were complete, an estimation of the impact on other parts of the economy of a change, say, from a "paper economy" to an "electronic transmission" economy or from books to video discs as modes of instruction, along with hundreds of similar questions. Here, however, I am interested primarily in Porat's findings on the value of information activities in the economy.[21]

Porat sets up a six-sector economy. There is a primary information sector which includes all industries that produce information machines or market information services as a commodity. (This includes the private sector, which contributes about ninety per cent of the primary information products and services, and the government, which accounts for the remaining ten per cent.) There is a secondary information sector with two segments, the public bureaucracy and those private bureaucracies whose activities are not directly counted in the national accounts as information services – such as the planning, programming, scheduling and marketing of goods or services – yet who are actually engaged in information and knowledge work. The value of these activities has to be imputed (for example, by factoring out the income or compensation of those persons within a manufacturing firm who are engaged in such work). The three remaining sectors consist of the private productive sector, producing goods; the public productive sectors (building roads, dams, and so on); and the household sector.

The primary information sector is the one that is most easily measurable, since it sells its products in a market. It includes industries and activities as diverse as computer manufacturing and services, telecommunications, printing, media, advertising, accounting and education; it is the productive locus of an information-based economy.* In 1967, sales of information goods and services in the primary information sector to the four major sectors of final demand amounted to $174.6 billion, or 21.9 per cent of GNP. In other words, seventeen cents of every consumer dollar represented direct purchase of information goods and services. If one looks at the income side, in 1967 nearly twenty-seven

---

* Porat divides the sector into eight major classes of industries: (1) the knowledge production and inventive industries; (2) information distribution and communication industries; (3) risk-management industries, including components of finance and insurance; (4) search and coordination industries, including all market information and advertising vendors; (5) information processing and transmission services, both electronic and nonelectronic; (6) informations goods industries, including information machines; (7) selected government activities that have direct market analogs in the primary information sector, including Postal Service and education; and (8) support facilities such as office and education buildings.

These eight major groups are further subdivided into 116 industries, which can be located in the Standard Industrial Classification; the monetary figures can be located in the National Income Accounts.

per cent of all income originated with information goods and services. The civilian government was the most information-intensive – almost forty-three per cent of all federal, state and local wages were paid to federal primary information-creating personnel such as Postal Service workers or education workers.

Strikingly, as Porat points out, over forty-three per cent of all corporate profits originated with the primary information industries. All corporations in the United States earned some $79.3 billion in profits in 1967; the primary information industries earned $33.7 billion. After removing the government's share of the primary information sector's national income ($37.2 billion), the information industries alone accounted for twenty-one per cent of national income but forty-two per cent of corporate profits. Each dollar of employee compensation generated thirty-four cents in profits, as against a ratio in the overall economy of twenty-one cents – a difference that Porat attributes to the large profits earned by the telephone and banking industries with their high profit-to-labour ratios. Calculating value added, about twenty-five per cent of total GNP originated in the primary information industries. In all, over $200 billion of the total GNP of $795.4 billion originated in information goods and services.

The most interesting and novel aspect of Porat's work is the definition and measurement of the secondary information sector, a sector that Porat derives from Galbraith's notion of the "technostructure". This is the section of an industry that is directly engaged in information work but whose activities are not measured as such, for while the goods produced may be sold in the market (and thus are reflected in the GNP as manufactured goods like automobiles or transportation activities like airline flights), the information components in those enterprises – the planning, scheduling, and marketing activities in automobiles; the computerized reservation processes in airline flights – are not counted directly in the GNP.

The secondary information sector expands for several reasons. One is the inherent tendency for bureaucracies to grow, which while true is a quite simple-minded explanation since there are always constraints of costs. A second, more serious reason is the multiplication of technical activities that comes with size, complexity and advanced technology – such as research, planning, quality control, marketing, and the like. And third is the fact that firms integrate or coordinate to economize on information costs. Thus a group of independent, high-quality hotels in different cities recently banded together to create a common reservation service as a means of competing with the large hotel chains by saving on communications costs. In fact, as Porat points out, there are quasi-industries hidden within the secondary sector that under some circumstances could become independent, primary (i.e., directly measurable) industries. One is the hypothetical "reservations industry". This "industry" sells its services to airlines, trains, hotels, theatre box offices and automobile rental companies through computerized data networks. In actual fact, each of the industries or firms maintains its own reservations systems, so the information costs are counted within the product cost. Yet if a single company created an efficient reservations network that it could sell to all these industries to replace the in-house services they maintain themselves, then these information activities would be measured in the "final demand" of GNP.

Other than these quasi-information industries, the bulk of the secondary information sector consists of planning and financial control, the administrative superstructure that organizes and manages the activities of firms or government agencies – in short, the private and public bureaucracies. In 1967, according to Porat, twenty-one per cent of GNP originated in the secondary information sector – 18.8 per cent in the private bureaucracies and 2.4 per cent in the public bureaucracies. Of the $168.1 billion in value added, some eighty-three per cent ($139.4 billion) originated in compensation to information workers, some 3.5 per cent ($5.8 billion) represented depreciation charges on information machines, and the balance was earned by proprietors performing information tasks. In sum, nearly fifty per cent of GNP, and more than fifty per cent of wages and salaries, derive from the production, processing and distribution of information goods and services. It is in that sense that we have become an information economy.

The growth of the secondary sector is, of course, the growth of the

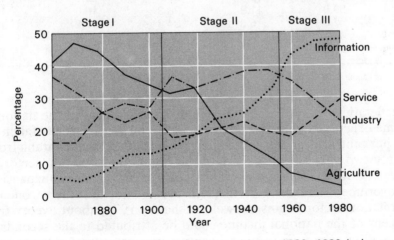

Fig. 9.2 Four-sector aggregation of the US workforce, 1860–1980 (using median estimates of information workers). [See also Fig. 6.2]

Table 9.2   Four-sector aggregation of the US labour force (median definition)

| | Experienced civilian workforce | | | | |
Year	Information sector	Agriculture sector	Industry sector	Service sector	Total
1860	480,604	3,364,230	3,065,024	1,375,525	8,286,283
1870	601,018	5,884,971	4,006,789	2,028,438	12,521,216
1880	1,131,415	7,606,590	4,386,409	4,281,970	17,406,384
1890	2,821,500	8,464,500	6,393,883	5,074,149	22,754,032
1900	3,732,371	10,293,179	7,814,652	7,318,947	29,159,149
1910	5,930,193	12,377,785	14,447,382	7,044,592	39,799,952
1920	8,016,054	14,718,742	14,492,300	8,061,342	45,288,438
1930	12,508,959	10,415,623	18,023,113	10,109,284	51,056,979
1940	13,337,958	8,233,624	19,928,422	12,082,376	53,582,380
1950	17,815,978	6,883,446	22,154,285	10,990,378	57,844,087
1960	28,478,317	4,068,511	23,597,364	11,661,326	67,805,518
1970	37,167,513	2,466,883	22,925,095	17,511,639	80,071,130
1980[a]	44,650,721	2,012,157	21,558,824	27,595,297	95,816,999

Percentages

1860	5.8	40.6	37.0	16.6	100
1870	4.8	47.0	32.0	16.2	100
1880	6.5	43.7	25.2	24.6	100
1890	12.4	37.2	28.1	22.3	100
1900	12.8	35.3	26.8	25.1	100
1910	14.9	31.1	36.3	17.7	100
1920	17.7	32.5	32.0	17.8	100
1930	24.5	20.4	35.3	19.8	100
1940	24.9	15.4	37.2	22.5	100
1950	30.8	11.9	38.3	19.0	100
1960	42.0	6.0	34.8	17.2	100
1970	46.4	3.1	28.6	21.9	100
1980[a]	46.6	2.1	22.5	28.8	100

[a] Bureau of Labour Statistics projection.

bureaucratic society. In 1929, some thirteen per cent of the national income originated in the secondary sector, but by 1933 it had fallen to nine per cent. During the depression, the secondary sector shrank from seventy-two per cent of the size of the primary information sector to forty per cent. But it is in the war and postwar years, with the expansion of government and the growth of corporate size, that the secondary information sector begins to swell, so that by 1974, about twenty-five per cent of the national income could be attributed to the secondary information sector and about twenty-nine per cent of the national income to the primary sector.

Table 9.3 Two-sector aggregation of the US labour force

| | Experienced civilian workforce | | | | |
| | Inclusive definition | | Restrictive definition | | |
Year	Information workers	Non-information workers	Information workers	Non-information workers	Total
1860	580,040	7,706,243	372,883	7,913,400	8,286,283
1870	788,837	11,732,379	500,849	12,020,367	12,521,216
1880	1,340,292	16,066,092	887,726	16,518,658	17,406,384
1890	2,980,778	19,773,254	2,480,189	20,273,843	22,754,032
1900	4,286,395	24,872,754	3,120,029	26,039,120	29,159,149
1910	7,283,391	32,516,561	4,537,196	35,262,756	39,799,952
1920	9,963,456	35,324,982	6,023,362	39,265,076	45,288,438
1930	16,031,889	35,025,090	8,883,914	42,173,065	51,056,979
1940	16,470,313	37,112,067	9,883,428	43,698,952	53,582,380
1950	21,691,532	36,152,555	13,940,424	43,903,663	57,844,087
1960	30,851,510	36,954,008	19,256,767	48,548,751	67,805,518
1970	40,529,588	39,541,542	29,464,497	50,606,633	80,071,130
1980[a]	49,154,120	46,662,879	39,955,688	55,861,311	95,816,999

Percentages

1860	7.0	93.0	4.5	95.5	100
1870	6.3	93.7	4.0	96.0	100
1880	7.7	92.3	5.1	94.9	100
1890	13.1	86.9	10.9	89.1	100
1900	14.7	85.3	10.7	89.3	100
1910	18.3	81.7	11.4	88.6	100
1920	22.0	78.0	13.3	86.7	100
1930	31.4	68.6	17.4	82.6	100
1940	30.7	69.3	18.4	81.6	100
1950	37.5	62.5	24.1	75.9	100
1960	45.5	54.5	28.4	71.6	100
1970	50.6	49.4	36.8	63.2	100
1980[a]	51.3	48.7	41.7	58.3	100

[a] Bureau of Labour Statistics projection.

The final necessary component is the change in the composition of the workforce itself over time. From 1860 to about 1906, the largest single group in the workforce was in agriculture. In the next period, until about 1954, the predominant group was industrial. Currently, the predominant group consists of information workers. By 1975, the information workers had surpassed the noninformation group as a whole. On the basis of income received, the crossover came earlier, since those in information occupations, on the average, earn a higher income. By

1967, some fifty-three per cent of the total compensation was paid to information workers.

The accompanying graph (Fig. 9.2) and Tables 9.2 and 9.3 illustrate the change. In 1930, there were twelve million workers in the information sector, almost 10.5 million in agriculture, eighteen million in industry, and ten million in services. By 1970, there were thirty-seven million in the information sector, less than 2.5 million in agriculture, 22.9 million in industry, and 17.5 million in services. In percentage terms, the labour force in the information sector today is over forty-six per cent; in agriculture, three per cent, in industry 28.6 per cent, and in services 21.9 per cent.

What of the future? Extrapolations can be deceptive. The information sector has grown hugely in the last decade and a half, but that has been a result of both the rapid introduction of new technology in computers and telecommunications and the economic growth rate that financed it. In many sectors, such as education, public policy is the decisive variable. Although the cohort of younger people will begin to shrink – in absolute numbers it is still growing, but the rate is slowing rapidly – there is an evident desire on the part of many in the adult population to undertake continuing education. Thus many community colleges are finding themselves transformed into adult schools. Whether or not society can afford these costs or wants to pay them is a different question. But aside from issues of public policy the expansion of the information economy will largely depend on two developments. One is automation – in industry and in the white-collar occupations. The second is the growth of information and its retrieval – data-bases, scientific information networks, and the explosion of international communications.

Future problems: the retrieval of information

In his *Sartor Resartus*, Thomas Carlyle wrote ironically: "He who first shortened the labour of the Copyists by the device of movable type was disbanding hired Armies . . ." He was, of course, referring to Johann Gutenberg (and praising him as well for "cashiering most Kings and Senates and creating a whole new Democratic world: he had invented the art of printing"). Yet such "technological" displacement, characteristically, had contradictory results. While old-fashioned calligraphers no longer could practise their skill and thus were relegated to the artisan scrap heap, more jobs were created by the increased demand for printed materials, and newer, less artistic but differently skilled men found employment.

And yet initially the pace of change was not so abrupt and rapid as to create wholesale turnovers in the print trade of the time. The printing press of the eighteenth century was little different from that used by Gutenberg three hundred years before. It was a wooden handpress on which a flat plate was laid upon a flat piece of paper with pressure created by the tightening of screws. Wood was eventually replaced by metal and the screw by a double lever, which allowed the speed of printing to be increased by half. By 1800 a radically new method of printing using a rotating cylinder – the basis of the modern press until the development of photographic technologies – was invented and with its greater speed began gradually to displace the flat press. The double rotary cylinder, developed for newspapers in the 1850s, made it possible to print two sides of a piece of paper at once. By 1893, the *New York World*'s octuple rotary press was printing 96,000 copies of eight pages in a single hour, whereas seventy years before the average was 2500 pages an hour.[22]

Such developments, understandably, went hand in hand with complementary technologies. The Linotype, developed by Mergenthaler in 1868, replaced monotype by selecting and casting type by keyboard, reducing composition costs by half while quintupling the speed of typesetting. The paper industry, which until the early nineteenth century was a time-consuming hand process using rags, was transformed in the middle of the century by the Fourdrinier process which mechanized the production of paper with the use of wire webs and cylinders. At the same time the development of wood pulp and a practical pulping process displaced rags, so that paper which had cost almost $350 a ton at the mid-century had come down to $36 a ton by the end of the century. Each of these developments was sped by new sources of energy. Printing presses, originally turned by hand and briefly even by horse (in America at least), became powered by steam and then by electricity. Papermaking, dependent initially on waterpower, came to use hydraulic power accelerated by electric turbines.

But what is so striking is how long it took, from the time of Gutenberg, for all this to develop. It is only in the twentieth century that one finds the mass production of newspapers (with millions of copies of a single issue printed overnight), magazines (set and printed in widely dispersed places using common tapes), and books. And now, with the revolution in communications, all this will change. The information explosion is a set of reciprocal relations between the expansion of science, the hitching of that science to a new technology, and the growing demand for news, entertainment and instrumental knowledge, all in the context of a rapidly increasing population, more literate and more educated, living in a vastly enlarged world that is now tied together, almost in real time, by cable, telephone and international satellite, whose inhabitants are made aware of each other by the vivid pictorial imagery of television, and that has at its disposal large data banks of computerized information.

Given this huge explosion in news, statistical data and information, it is almost impossible to provide any set of measurements to chart its growth. Yet there is one area – the growth of scientific information – where some reconstruction of historical trends has been carried out, and I will use that as a baseline for understanding the problems of the next twenty years.

The historical picture of the knowledge explosion was first formulated statistically by Derek de Solla Price in 1963, in his work *Little Science, Big Science*. The first two scientific journals appeared in the mid-seventeenth century, the *Journal des savants* in Paris and the *Philosophical Transactions of the Royal Society* in London. By the middle of the eighteenth century, there were only ten scientific journals, by 1800 about 100, by 1850 perhaps 1000. Today? There are no exact statistics on the number of scientific journals being published in the world. Estimates range between 30,000 and 100,000, which itself is an indication of both the difficulty of definition and the difficulty of keeping track of new and disappearing journals. In 1963, Price estimated that 50,000 journals had been founded, of which 30,000 were still surviving. A UNESCO report in 1971 put the figure at between 50,000 and 70,000. *Ulrich's International Periodicals Directory* (a standard library source) in 1971-72 listed 56,000 titles in 220 subjects, of which more than half were in the sciences, medicine and technology; but these were only of periodicals in the Latin script and excluded most Slavic, Arabic, Oriental and African languages.

Perhaps the most directly measurable indicators are university library holdings. The Johns Hopkins University in 1900 had 100,000 books and ranked tenth among American university libraries. By 1970, it had over $1\frac{1}{2}$ million volumes, a growth of 3.9 per cent per year, although it had dropped to twentieth place. In the same period, the eighty-five major American universities were doubling the number of books in their libraries every seventeen years, for an annual growth rate of 4.1 per cent. (The difference between 3.9 and 4.1 per cent may seem slight, yet it relegated the Johns Hopkins Library to the bottom of the second decile.)

A 1973 OECD survey of all the extant studies of the growth in scientific knowledge came to the following conclusions.

(1) In all the case studies, growth follows a geometric progression, the curve being exponential.

(2) However, the growth rates varied considerably, the lowest one being 3.5 per cent yearly, the highest 14.4 per cent.

(3) The lowest growth rates are shown by the number of scientific periodicals published, covering a 300-year period, and the number of specialized bibliographical periodicals involved in indexing and abstracting over a 140-year period. In the case of scientific journals, the annual growth rate has been 3.5, 3.7 or 3.9 per cent, depending whether the number published in 1972 is taken as 30,000, 50,000, or 100,000. The growth rate for indexing and abstracting organizations has been 5.5 per cent a year. In 1972 there were 1800 such services in science.

(4) A recent series reporting the number of articles by engineers in civil engineering journals (from 3000 pages of technical articles in three specialized periodicals in 1946 to 30,000 pages in forty-two specialized periodicals in 1966) shows growth rates of 12.3 per cent a year.

(5) The growth rate in the number of international scientific and technical congresses increased almost fourfold in twenty years, rising from 1000 in 1950 to over 3500 in 1968.[23]

The multiplication in the number of scientific reports and documents has naturally led to the conclusion that such progression cannot continue indefinitely, that at some point a slowdown would take place, probably in the form of a logistic curve that would symmetrically match the exponential rise of the ascent. The crucial question has been to identify the point of inflection where the reverse trend would begin. Derek de Solla Price argued in 1963 that "at some time, undetermined as yet but probably during the 1940s or 1950s, we passed through the mid-period in general logistic curve of science's body politic." In fact, he concluded, saturation may have already arrived.[24]

Yet as Anderla noted in his study for the OECD: "Today it is absolutely certain that these forecasts, repeated without number and echoed almost universally, have failed to materialize, at any rate so far." As evidence, he assembled the number of abstracts published between 1957 and 1971 for nineteen scientific disciplines and demonstrated that between 1957 and 1967 the output increased by nearly two and a half times, for an annual growth rate of 9.5 per cent. Over the fourteen years from 1957 to 1971, the volume increased more than fourfold, for a growth rate of 10.6 per cent, so that there was an escalation in growth rather than the predicted reverse.[25]

The major reason for this continued escalation is the tendency for science to generate more and more subspecialities, each of which creates its own journals and research reports system. At the same time, cross-disciplinary movements arise to bridge some of the subspecialities, extending the proliferation process even further.

What then of the future? The production of scientific literature is determined in the first instance, by the projected rate of increase in the

scientific population. It is calculated that in 1970 the scientific population represented about two per cent of the total labour force. The rate of
increase has been estimated variously at between 4.7 and 7.2 per cent a
year (a fifteen-year and a ten-year doubling time, respectively), although certain categories, such as computer scientists, have been increasing by more than ten per cent annually. Taking 1970 as a base, one
can estimate the likely size of the scientific population in 1985 by
making three assumptions: an unyielding exponential increase to the
horizon year of 1985; a break occurring in 1980, with the logistic curve
beginning to slow down at that time; or the point of inflection coming as
early as 1975. Given these assumptions, the number of scientists,
engineers and other technicians in 1985 could account for a low of 3.8
per cent to a high of 7.2 per cent of the total labour force. If one takes
the midpoints, between four per cent and 5.7 per cent of the total
working population would be scientists and engineers in 1985.

In order to project the volume of information that is likely to be
produced, we can take as a base a survey of the US National Academy of
Science which revealed that in the early 1970s about 2,000,000 scientific writings of all kinds were issued each year, or between 6000 and
7000 articles and reports each working day. For an internally consistent
time series, the most reliable indicators are the statistics of abstracts of
articles in the leading specialized reviews, which from 1957 to 1971
increased exponentially at a rate of more than ten per cent a year. As
with the growth rates in the number of scientists, one can assume breaks
in the logistic curves at 1975, 1980 or 1985 and then take a median
figure. According to these computations, there is every indication that
projections to within a year or two of the 1985 horizon might well lie
within the index range of some 300 to 400. In other words, the number
of scientific and technical abstracts would be three or four times the
present number.

The End of the Alexandrian Library. Clearly, if the explosion in information continues, it cannot be handled by present means. If by 1985 the
volume of information is four (low estimate) or seven times (high
estimate) that of 1970, then some other ways must be found to organize
this onslaught of babel. In one of these pleasant exercises that statisti-
cians like to undertake, it is estimated that under present projections,
the Yale University Library would need a permanent staff of 6000
persons in the year 2040 to cope with the books and research reports
that would be coming annually into the library. (Such projections
recall earlier ones that if the US telephone system had to handle the
current volume of calls solely through operator-assisted methods,
then every female in the labour force – a sexist remark obviously

made before women's lib – would now be working for AT&T.)

Obviously, the information explosion can only be handled through the expansion of computerized and subsequently automated information systems. The major advance to date has been the computerization of abstracting and indexing services. Most of the printed abstract index bulletins in research libraries are prepared from computer tape. The Chemical Abstract Service (CAS), the largest in the field, is a case in point. Before computerization, it took the CAS about twenty months to produce an annual index; these are now available twice a year, while the unit costs for indexing have decreased from $18.50 to $10.54. Moreover, as the new substances are recorded in the Chemical Registry System – there are now 3,000,000 items in the files – it is possible to store, recreate and display structure diagrams on video terminals from the computer-readable structure records stored in the system. A further development is the rise of computer-based searching services, drawn from the tape initially used to expedite the printing of indexes. Two American firms, the Systems Development Corporation and Lockheed Information Systems, provide on-line searching to over thirty bibliographic data-bases. Together they provide immediate access to over fifteen million citations, with an annual increase of approximately 3.5 million citations.[26]

The logic of all this is that the range of the Alexandrian Library – the single building like the Bibliothèque Nationale, the British Museum or the Library of Congress – where all the world's recorded knowledge is housed in one building may become a sad monument of the printed past. Data-based stores of information, especially in the scientific and technical field, will come from specialized information centres, transmitted through computer printouts, facsimile, or video display to the user, who will have consulted an index through on-line searching to locate items of interest and then order them on demand.

All this supposes two things. One, the creation of large-scale networks in which a national system is built through the linkage of specialized centres. And two, the automation of data banks so that basic scientific and technical data, from industrial patents to detailed medical information, can be retrieved directly from computers and transmitted to the user. But both suppositions raise two very different problems. One is the intellectual question of the distinction between programming a data-base, and constructing a program for use as a knowledge base. Retrieving some census items from a data-base is a simple matter; but finding kindred and analogous conceptual terms – the handling of ideas – raises all the problems that were first encountered, and never successfully solved, in the effort to achieve sophisticated machine translation of languages.

As early as the pre-Socratics, when philosophy was first becoming self-conscious, there was an awareness of the ambiguities of language and the hope, as with the Pythagoreans, that certainty could be expressed through mathematical relations. Descartes, in creating his analytical geometry, thought he could substitute the "universal language of logic" for the messy imprecisions of ordinary language, as Spinoza felt he could create a "moral geometry" to deal with ethical questions. In each generation that hope has arisen anew. In 1661 a Scotsman, George Dalgarno, published his *Ars Signorum* in which he proposed to group all human knowledge into seventeen sections (such as "politics" and "natural objects") and to label each with a Latin consonant. Vowels would be used to label the subsections into which each section was to be divided, and the process of subdivision was to be continued with consonants and vowels alternating. In this way, any item of knowledge would have a specific reference and identification.[27]

In the twentieth century we have had the effort of Whitehead and Russell to formalize all logic using a mathematical notation, the effort of the logical positivists such as Carnap to construct (in theory) a language that would avoid the ambiguities of ordinary discourse and to propose (in practice) a verifiability principle that would specify which propositions were testable and could be held to "make sense", as against those that were (pejoratively) metaphysical, emotive or theological and could not, given the nature of language, be "proved". And most recently, in the *Britannica* 1, Mortimer Adler has proposed a new scholastic ordering of knowledge, the *Propaedia*, that would guide encyclopedia users to interrelated sets of relevant terms, as his earlier *Synopticon* sought to be an intellectual index to the 101 major "ideas" of human thought.

The attempts to discipline human knowledge and create a vast and unified edifice, as Dalgarno and even Leibniz sought to do, were bound to fail. The effort to formalize knowledge or construct artificial languages has proved inadequate. The scholastic orderings of Mortimer Adler may help an individual to trace the bibliographic cross-relationships of ideas, but if the purpose of a library, or a knowledge-based computer program, is to help a historian to assemble evidence or a scholar to "re-order" ideas, then the ambiguity of language itself must be confronted. Terms necessarily vary in different contexts and lend themselves to different interpretations, and historical usages shift over time (consider the problem of defining an intellectual, or the nature of ideology), making the problem of designing a "knowledge" program quite different from designing an "information" program.

The process of creating new knowledge (reasoned judgements) proceeds by what Léon Walras, the great mathematical economist, called *tâtonnement*, trial-and-error tapping, by taking fragments of intellectual mosaics whose larger shapes cannot be predicted in advance and fitting them together in different ways or by regarding large conceptual structures from a new angle, which opens up wholly new prisms of selection and focus. A sophisticated reader, studying a philosophical text, may make use of the existing index at the back of the book, but if he is to absorb and use the ideas in a fruitful way, he has necessarily to create his own index by regrouping and recategorizing the terms that are employed. As John Dewey pointed out in *Art as Experience*, the nature of creativity is to rearrange perceptions, experiences and ideas into new shapes and modes of consciousness. In this process, no mechanical ordering, no exhaustive set of permutations and combinations, can do the task. Descartes once thought that the geometer with a compass could draw a circle more exactly than an artist could freehand. But a perfect circle, or even a set of interlocking circles, is not art without some larger conceptual context that "redesigns" an older or different way of arranging shapes. Art, and thought, as modes of exploration, remain primarily heuristic.

A more mundane yet sociologically important problem is the lack of a national information policy on science and technical information, let alone on library resources generally. Should there be a national scientific and technical computer network? Should there be a government corporation or utility with direct responsibility to scientific and technical users or simply a major, governmentally organized data-base (like the census) made available to commercial services that meet specific consumer needs? Such questions have been raised since the creation of the Office of Science Information within the National Science Foundation in 1958, and they have been asked over and over again in a number of governmental and National Academy of Science studies in subsequent years. No answers have been forthcoming; no policy exists. Yet if science information is the end product of the $35 billion annual investment that the nation makes in research and development, and information, broadly defined, accounts for almost fifty per cent of the gross national product, then some coherent national policy is in order.

The policy questions of the information society
My basic premise has been that knowledge and information are becoming the strategic resource and transforming agent of the postindustrial society. Inevitably, the onset of far-reaching social changes, especially when they proceed, as these do, through the medium of specific technologies, confronts a society with major policy questions. Here I can only schematically indicate some of the questions society will face in the next two decades.

The new infrastructure. Every society is connected by diverse channels that permit trade and discourse between its members. These modes, or infrastructures, have usually been the responsibility of government – as builder, financier, maintainer or regulator. The first infrastructure was transportation – roads, canals, railroads, airways – which breaks down the segmentation of society and allows for the movement of people and goods. Caravans and trade routes formed the social framework of older human societies. The second infrastructure has been the energy utilities – waterpower, steam pipes, gas, electricity, oil pipelines – for the transmission of power. By mobilizing technological rather than natural sources of energy and linking them into power grids, not only have we transformed the lives of cities through lighting, but we have provided power for the fabrication of goods and the use of consumer appliances. The third infrastructure has been communications – first the mails and newspapers, then telegraph and telephone, now radio and television – as media for the mounting explosion of messages, the bombardment of sensory experiences, and the increased degree of social and psychic interaction between persons that is now accelerating exponentially.

In the next two decades, there is little likelihood of any major developments in the first infrastructure, that of transportation. The adoption of the Concorde or other supersonic airplanes, if it comes, may halve the time for crossing the ocean, but the effect will be minor compared to the reduction in the time needed to cross the Atlantic in the last hundred years, from several weeks by steamship to six days by fast boat, to sixteen hours by propeller plane, to seven hours by jet. Mass transit in the cities, if it returns, is unlikely to replace the automobile or other modes of personal movement unless fuel prices rise so high as to overthrow the hedonistic way of life that has become entrenched in advanced industrial societies. The rising demand for personal transportation in the newer developing countries and increases in congestion may lead to new combinations of taxis, leasing and motor utilities (in which one shares in a common pool). But much of the vaunted experimental innovations, such as monorails or automated elevated speedways or even hovercraft, have proved to be either uneconomic or technologically too complicated.

In the second infrastructure, energy, there are clearly major new developments requiring large capital expenditures, involving conservation (insulating housing), better extractive techniques for coal and its gasification, potential uses of nuclear energy, research in tapping solar sources of energy, and more efficient modes of electricity transmission, such as superconductivity. These efforts, if made, will stimulate a huge expansion in the areas of research and development (and of engineers and technically trained personnel), and, if successful, will establish new energy grids that will supply a steady source of renewable power and once again bring down the price of energy relative to other goods. But such changes, large as they may be, are primarily substitutes for existing energy sources and modes of transmission. They do not presage huge upheavals in the role energy plays in the society.

The really major social change of the next two decades will come in the third major infrastructure, as the merging technologies of telephone, computer, facsimile, cable television and video discs lead to a vast reorganization in the modes of communication between persons; the transmission of data; the reduction if not the elimination of paper in transactions and exchanges; new modes of transmitting news, entertainment and knowledge; and the reorganization of learning that may follow the expansion of computer-assisted instruction and the spread of video discs.

One may be sceptical, as I am, about extravagant claims regarding the quantum leaps in level of education that computer-assisted instruction and video discs will bring. Learning, as I think we have learned, is a function of both the ability to learn and the cultural milieu; any technology is only instrumental, and its impact depends on other social and cultural factors. But in the realm of data transmission (especially in the world of business) and in the development of knowledge networks (particularly in science and research), what Anthony Oettinger has called compunications certainly will stimulate vast social changes.

This upheaval in telecommunications and knowledge poses two economic-political policy problems, one structural, the other intellectual. The structural question is what kind of technical-economic organization is best designed to be efficient, meet consumer (i.e., industrial, commercial, financial, scientific, library) use, and remain flexible enough to allow for continuing technological development. One proposal is for a single computer utility that would centralize and provide a single source for information and transmission of data for consumer use, either government-owned (as are the telephone and broadcasting systems in many European countries) or privately owned but government-regulated, like AT&T and the major broadcast networks in the United States. Among different versions of the computer utility idea, there is a proposal for diverse sources of information (i.e., different data banks operated publicly or privately) based on a single transmitting system (such as the present telephone quasi-monopoly) or, conversely, a centralized set of data-bases with diverse means of transmission. Against these are the proposals for a completely unregulated, competitive market system, in which different "producers" would be free to set up diverse informational services and transmission would be through cable, microwave, or satellite communication operated by different combines, each competing for the business. These are the issues whose economic aspects Noll has addressed *

It has been argued that a single national computing service, interconnecting all user terminals from geographically dispersed data banks, would achieve vast economies of scale, and if run as a government utility (like TVA) would avoid the concentration of vast power in the hands of a single private enterprise. Against this, as Noll points out, computer systems sell not merely computational power or data processing but "information", and the large and varied needs of thousands of different kinds of users for different kinds of information – medical, technical, economic, marketing – would best be served by specific firms that would be responsive, in the way efficient markets can be, to the diverse needs of consumers. Others have argued that government control could be as dangerous, if not more so, than private concentration since it could be more easily misused for political purposes. And there is the further question of whether a competitive decentralized system would not be more flexible technologically, and more innovative, than a large monopoly system, either public or private. The record so far, in the instance of the computer versus the telephone, would indicate that technological innovation has come more rapidly and more responsively in an unregulated and competitive atmosphere than in the government-regulated sphere.

On the traditional grounds of economic efficiency and technological responsiveness, it seems to me that Noll makes a convincing case for the primacy of the market and for a market system. Yet he also points out that regulators tend to see prices as taxes to be levied according to some calculus of social worth, favouring one group over another, rather than seeing prices as signal-covering information about costs that induce buyers to make economically efficient decisions. He is, I believe, right in his observation. Yet is the policy itself so wrong? Where markets are open and competitive, the allocation of resources does respond most efficiently to the preferences and demands of consumers, and this is the justifiable defence, theoretically, of the market as the arbiter of economic activity. Yet if in the institutional world income distribution is grossly distorted, or various social groups are discriminated against, then redress through subsidy may be one means of achieving equity, even if sometimes at the expense of efficiency. Also, there is the growing realization that markets do not often reflect the larger range of social costs that are generated in the process, and these may be unfairly distributed. As Arthur Okun has pointed out, the trade-off between efficiency and equity presents a real problem. The point is not to

* Roger G. Noll, "Regulation and Computer Services" in Dertouzos and Moses, op. cit.

disguise the issue but to make it as explicit as possible, so that one knows the relative gains and losses in equity and efficiency that result from market and regulatory decisions.

The second problem posed by the upheaval in telecommunications is intellectual rather than structural and concerns the question of a national information policy, particularly the dissemination of science and technical information. The government is obviously committed to the furtherance of research and development. Increases in productivity depend increasingly on the more efficient distribution of necessary knowledge, but so far there is no unified government policy or an organized system to bring scientific and technical information to diverse users, to speed the process of innovation, and shorten the time of development and diffusion.

After Sputnik, there was a flurry of sides reviewing the problem. A report by William C. Baker of Bell Laboratories stated the unexceptionable principle that the flow of scientific information was necessary. A second report in 1962 by J. H. Crawford for the president's Office of Science and Technology recommended that each agency of government set up a specific office to produce scientific information, and these were created in the Department of Defence, the Atomic Energy Commission, and the National Aeronautic and Space Agency. In 1963, a report by Alvin Weinberg of the Oak Ridge National Laboratory argued that the government had the further responsiblity to organize the dissemination of research information in order to avoid costly duplication of effort. The government did create a coordinating body called COASTI (Committee on Scientific and Technical Information) to implement this effort.

Yet the odd if not surprising fact is that little has been done. During the Nixon administration, COASTI, the Office of Science and Technology, and the Science Information Council were dismantled. Inevitably the number of hortatory studies multiplied. In 1969, the National Academy of Sciences and the National Academy of Engineering brought forth the SATCOM (Committee on Scientific and Technical Communication) report, which involved more than 200 scientists, calling for a national policy-making body to deal with information policy. In 1972, the Federal Council on Science and Technology and the National Science Foundation commissioned yet another report, by Dr Martin Greenberger of Johns Hopkins University, which concluded, unsurprisingly, that the government was not well organized to deal with the problems of scientific and technical information facing the country.

It still is not. Meanwhile, the number of scientific papers and the volume of scientific information continue to rise. There is a growing trend towards cross-disciplinary information which the single-disciplinary systems (such as abstracting and indexing) are not equipped to handle. The proliferation of diverse types of material, stored in different ways from books, films, computer tapes, video tapes and so on, makes it difficult to keep track of everything. And finally, the number of users continues to increase.

All trends pose a large variety of policy issues. Should there be, as Fernbach suggests,* a national Library of Data, like the Library of Congress, to store all basic data and programs in giant memories? Should this library – if such a Library of Babel as Jorge Luis Borges envisaged ever comes about – also concern itself with the dissemination of data, as the government's Medlars system does for medical information, or should it be available for private companies, such as Lockheed or Systems Development Corporation or the *New York Times*, to provide specialized services for subscribers through proprietary communications and terminal systems?

The growth of shared communications systems and on-line terminals makes a national scientific and technical information network a tangible possibility. Denicoff describes the development of the interactive computer network invented in 1968 by Dr L. G. Roberts for the Advanced Research Projects Agency (ARPA), which was first employed by the Defence Communications Agency in 1976.† Its most valued result, according to Denicoff, was the emergence of a "user community". The operational reality of such a community, he writes, is the proof of the gains we have made in scientific cooperation. In the same vein, Joseph Becker has argued that:

> a national scientific and technical information network implies the inter-connection of discipline-oriented and mission-oriented information systems for remote use through standard communications. Unless cohesive development takes place, the separate systems will remain insulated from one another and from their users. But, if maximum communication can be established among them, the array can be converted into a national resource of immense value to America's scientific enterprise.[28]

H. G. Wells, in one of his megalomaniacal visions of the future, proposed a "world brain" that like a vast computer would bring together in one place all organized scientific knowledge and make it available through communication networks to the "new samurai", the coming scientific elite of the world. Is such a technological phantasmagoria feasible (as some computer scientists claim it is) or desirable (as others do), or is it simply one of those marvellously simple visions (like

---

* Sidney Fernbach, "Scientific Use of Computers", in Dertouzos and Moses, op. cit.
† Marvin Denicoff, "Sophisticated Software: The Road to Science and Utopia", in Dertouzos and Moses, op. cit.

that of Sidney Webb) of tidily and neatly organized bundles of knowledge that can be separated and reassembled by pressing the right button? If the last, it is a deceptive vision, which misunderstands the way the mind actually works, and which makes the sociological error of assuming that some central knowledge system can function better than the decentralized, self-organizing system in which demand specifies the organizational and market response to the needs of the users. This is an issue that should remain open to extended debate, for it is too serious and too costly to be settled on purely ideological grounds.

And finally, on a more mundane level, there is the legal and economic question of what is an "intellectual property" – at least where the intellectual product is clearly defined (such as a book or a journal article), let alone where the boundaries are blurred, as in the instance of a computer program. How does one balance the rights of fair use as demanded by libraries against the economic rights of authors and publishers? As books become stored in computer memories and can be retrieved on tapes and printed by attached photocopying devices, who is to pay for what? Should Xerox and IBM receive financial returns while the intellectual producers gain only the psychic satisfaction of the widespread reproduction of their words?

The courts and the Congress have been struggling with these questions for years. Clearly no solution will completely satisfy those who press for the widest possible dissemination of intellectual material under some fair-use and information-need concept, or those who demand payment for any use of copyright material. But we need a clarification of the legal and philosophical issues at stake.

Social and economic transformations
The major determinant of policy issues, as I have indicated, is the question of what kind of infrastructure will be created out of the merging technologies of computers and communications. Inevitably this will give rise to more diffuse policy issues deriving from the economic and social transformations that may come in their wake. I will conclude by examining five central issues of this kind.

(1) The location of cities
Historically, all cities were formed at the crossroads of overland caravan routes, at the strategic confluence of rivers, or at large, protected ports on seaways and oceans as entrepôts and trading centres. Almost all the major cities in the world have been located on rivers, lakes, and oceans since transportation – and particularly waterways for heavy barge loads – tied areas together in the first infrastructure.

In the industrial age, cities were located near major resource bases, such as coal and iron, as one sees in the English Midlands or the German Ruhr and most strikingly in the great industrial heartland of the United States, where the great iron-ore resources of the Mesabi Range in upper Minnesota were connected to the great coal regions in southern Illinois and western Pennsylvania through a network of lakes and rivers. In this way the great industrial cities of Chicago, Detroit, Cleveland, Buffalo and Pittsburgh were intricately linked in one huge complex.

In the transition to a service economy, the metropolitan cities became the major financial centres and headquarters for the great enterprises. The histories of New York and London form striking parallels. Both began as port cities through which goods could be sent overseas or transported inland. New York was a large, ice-free port, protected by two great bays, yet connected through the Hudson River and the Erie Canal system to the midwestern Great Lakes complex. As trade increased, banking, factoring and insurance arose as auxiliary services to commerce; later, with the rise of industry, they became nerve centres for financial and stock transactions. In its third phase, New York became a large headquarters city, where the major corporations located their head offices to take advantage of the external economies offered by the concentration of banking, legal, publishing, and communications services.

In economic geography, the resource base was the decisive locational factor up to the last forty years, when all this began to change. In the United States in the postwar years, the economic map of the country was reworked largely through politics, since the new large aircraft, space and missile companies were created entirely by government contracts, and the decisions to locate them in areas like the Pacific Northwest, southern California and southwest Texas were made on political grounds. With the rise of air cargo, we have witnessed a phenomenon in which new "airplane cities", such as Dallas–Fort Worth, Houston, Denver and Atlanta, rather than water and rail cities, serve as regional hubs for industrial and commercial spokes. And now, as the increasing spread (and cheapness) of telecommunications reduces the former external economies of physical proximity, we see the dispersal of corporate headquarters and major white-collar concentrations like the insurance industry from the decaying central cities to the suburbs. The location of research laboratories, new universities, and large hospital complexes is less dependent on the traditional factors of economic geography and more influenced by the nearness of educational facilities, easier lifestyles, and political factors. Phenomena like the development of "Silicon Valley" in California – the electronics and computer firms around San Jose – and Route 128 around Boston were a response to the availability of university research facilities, plus more pleasant space for the smaller-sized physical plants and offices than the industrial areas could provide.

C. A. Doxiades has envisaged the growth of linear cities without the older focal piazzas and market centres of the classical European towns. B. F. Skinner has suggested that in an age of advanced communication, networks of towns will replace the large, increasingly ungovernable cities. The question of whether these apocalyptic visions will be realized is moot; the life and death of cities is a long historical process. But what is changing is the concept of "urbanism" itself. Thirty years ago Louis Wirth wrote a famous essay entitled "Urbanism as a Way of Life", in which he summed up the characteristics of urbanism as a highly interactive, heavily mobile, culturally and politically attentive mode, as against the older small-town and rural patterns centred on the church and the family. What is happening today is that the entire nation (if not large parts of the world) is becoming urbanized in the psychological sense, though increasingly more dispersed geographically.

The changes in the character and pattern of telecommunications pose problems of national land use, of the social costs of dispersions and concentrations, the management of the decay of old cities, and the control of the sprawl of new ones. Inevitably, the decisions will reflect the interplay of market and political forces, since neither one can be decisive in itself. But it is the exact mix of the two that remains as the interesting sociological question for the next decades.

(2) The possibilities of national planning

Leon Trotsky once said that a capitalist society is one where each man thinks for himself and no one thinks for all. That a single "one" can think for "all" is probably impossible and, if so, would be monstrous, since the "one" would be some giant bureaucracy and the "all" a putative single interest equally applicable to all citizens in the society. As Alan Altshuler of MIT has remarked:

> Those who contend that comprehensive planning should play a large role in the future evolution of societies must argue that the common interests of society's members are their most important interests and constitute a large proportion of all their interests. They must assert that conflicts of interests in society are illusory, that they are about minor matters, or that they can be foreseen and resolved in advance by just arbiters [planners] who understand the total interest of all the parties.

In this respect, Altshuler is probably correct, yet such a view unduly restricts the meaning of planning in all its possible varieties. The different kinds of planning can be arrayed in a simple logical ladder:

(a) Coordinated information. Almost all major enterprises make five- and even ten-year plans (for product development, capital needs,

manpower requirements, new plants) as a necessary component of their own planning. And various services, such as the McGraw-Hill survey of capital spending budgets or the federally financed University of Michigan surveys of consumer intentions, seek to provide more comprehensive information for firms about these trends to aid them in their planning. A national computerized information service, through the Bureau of the Census or some similar government body, could bring together all such relevant information – just as the various econometric models now in use make forecasts of the annual GNP and its major components, which become the basis of both governmental and private policies. To this extent, the idea of a coordinated information system is simply an extension of the planning process that is now so extensive in the corporate and governmental sectors.[29]

(b) *Modelling and simulation.* Using an input-output matrix, such as that developed by Wassily Leontieff, one could test alternative economic policies in order to weigh the effects of different government policies on different sectors of the economy. In a more radical version, the Russian economist Leonid Kantorovich has argued that a national computerized economic system, registering the different prices and allocations of items, could spot items that deviate from planned or targeted goals or the disproportionate use of resources in various sectors.

(c) *Indicative planning.* In this model, which is used by the French Commissariat du Plan, several thousand industry committees coordinate their plans regarding economic activities, and these plans become the basis of governmental decisions to stimulate or inhibit certain sectors, largely by easier credit facilities or credit restrictions.

(d) *National goals.* In this scheme, the government would stipulate certain major goals – the expansion of housing or levels of economic growth – and monitor the economy to see whether such goals were being achieved as a guide to which further measures (tax cuts, investment credits, credit allocations, preferred sections such as housing) might be necessary to achieve them.

(e) *Mobilized targets.* This is, in effect, a "war economy", such as that exemplified by the War Production Board in the United States during World War Two or the British Ministry of Supply; in practice, it is the actual nature of Soviet "planning". In this system, certain key targets are specified (level of steel output, kind of machine tools, number of tanks and aircraft, and so on), and the government physically allocates, by a priority system, the key materials and manpower to designated factories. In this respect, the entire economy is not planned, but key sectors are controlled.

These different modes of planning range from direct controls and policing at one end to "simple" information coordination at the other. Which kind of planning society will adopt is a political question. Given the degree of interdependence and the spillover effects of various individual decisions, some larger degree of planning – analogous to the rise of environmental monitoring and regulation planning – than we now have is probably inevitable. The computer and the large-scale information systems that are being developed will make it feasible; but how one reconciles planning with various kinds of individual freedom is a very different and more difficult question.

(3) Centralization and privacy

Police and political surveillance of individuals is much more possible and pervasive because of sophisticated advances in the information process. In a survey of federal agencies' use of computerized data banks, former Senator Sam Ervin wrote in the preface to a report by the Senate Judiciary Committee's Subcommittee on Constitutional Rights:

> The subcommittee has discovered numerous instances of agencies starting out with a worthy purpose but going so far beyond what was needed in the way of information that the individual's privacy and right to due process of law are threatened by the very existence of files. . . . The most significant finding is that there are immense numbers of government data banks, cluttered with diverse information on just about every citizen in the country. The 54 agencies surveyed were willing to report 858 [data banks] containing more than $1\frac{1}{4}$ billion records on individuals.

Government demand for information can be highly costly to enterprises and institutions. Derek Bok, the president of Harvard, reported that the demand of the governmental agency enforcing the affirmative action programme for detailed information on every aspect of employment practices and the need to keep records of all job searches for applicants to teaching and other positions cost the university over a million dollars a year. What information is necessary and what is not is a difficult question to decide, particularly in the abstract. Yet the tendency of almost every bureaucracy, reflecting an aspect of Parkinson's Law, is to enlarge its demands on the principle that (a) "all" information might conceivably be necessary; and (b) it is easier to ask for everything than to make discriminations.

The simple point, for it is one of the oldest and most important truisms of politics, is that there is an inherent potential for abuse when any agency with power sets up bureaucratic rules and proceeds without restraint to enforce them. The other, equally simple, point is that control over information lends itself more readily to abuse – from withholding information at one end to unlawful disclosure at the other, both processes exemplified by Watergate – and that institutional re-

straints are necessary, particularly in the area of information, to check
such abuses.

(4) Elite and mass

Every society we have known has been divided, on one axis or another,
into elite and mass. On a different axis, a society may be designated as
open or closed. In the past, most societies have been elite and closed in
that aristocracies have been hereditary. Even when there has been an
examination system for choosing mandarins, as in Imperial China, the
selection process has been limited to a small class of persons.

In the West the major elites have traditionally been landed and
propertied elites. Even in an occupation like the military, which requires some technical skill, until about a hundred years ago (in Britain,
for example) commissions could be purchased. The older ladders of
social mobility were "the red and the black", the army and the church.
Modern capitalist and industrial society began to break open those
moulds. In business, there was the rise of the entrepreneur, the engineer
and the manager. With the succeeding breakdown of "family capitalism", the managerial elites were no longer children of previous owners
but men who earned their way up by technical competence. In government, there was the expansion of the administrative bureaucracy, in
which top positions were achieved, as in France, through a rigorous
selection system by rites of passage through the *grandes écoles*, or by
patronage, as was usual in the United States.

Modern societies, in contrast with the past, have become more open
societies, but at the same time, as knowledge and technical competence
have become the requirement for elite positions, the selection process
has fallen more and more on to the educational system as the sluicegates
that determine who shall get ahead. The result has been increasing
pressure on the educational system to provide "credentials" for those
who want to move up the escalator of social mobility. In the postindustrial society, the technical elite is a knowledge elite. Such an elite has
power within intellectual institutions – research organizations, hospital
complexes, universities and the like – but only influence in the larger
world in which policy is made. Inasmuch as political questions become
more and more intricately meshed with technical issues (from military
technology to economic policy), the knowledge elites can define the
problems, initiate new questions, and provide the technical bases for
answers; but they do not have the power to say yes or no. That is a
political power that belongs, inevitably, to the politician rather than to
the scientist or economist. In this sense, the idea that the knowledge
elite will become a new power elite seems to me to be exaggerated.

But what is equally true is that in contemporary society there is a growing egalitarianism fostered in large measure by sectors of the knowledge elite, especially the younger ones, and given the most vocal support by those in marginal positions and marginal occupations in the knowledge sector. Within institutions, this has taken the form of attacks on "authority" and "professionalism" as elitist and demands that all groups have some share in the decision-making power. In certain European universities, for example, even the nonprofessional staffs are given a voice and representation in university affairs, while on academic issues, from curriculum to tenure decisions, the three "estates" of students, junior faculty and senior faculty have equal corporate rights. How far this egalitarianism will go remains to be seen.

The fear that a knowledge elite could become the technocratic rulers of the society is quite far-fetched and expresses more an ideological thrust by radical groups against the growing influence of technical personnel in decision making. Nor is it likely, at least in the foreseeable future, that the knowledge elites will become a cohesive "class" with common class interests, on the model of the bourgeoisie rising out of the ruins of feudalism to become the dominant class in industrial society. The knowledge class is too large and diffuse, and there seems little likelihood, either in economic or status terms, that a set of corporate interests could develop so as to fuse this stratum into a new class. What is more likely to happen, as I have argued previously, is that the different situses in which the knowledge elites are located will become the units of corporate action. One can identify functional situses, such as scientific, technological (applied skills like engineering, medicine and economics), administrative, and cultural, as well as institutional situses, such as economic enterprises, government bureaux, universities, research organizations, social service complexes (like hospitals), and the military. The competition for money and influence will be between these various situses, just as in the communist world the major political units are not classes but situses such as the party, the government machine, the central planners, factory managers, collective farms, research institutes, cultural organizations and the like.

What one sees in contemporary society is the multiplication of constituencies and consequently the multiplication of elites; and the problem of coordinating these elites and their coalitions becomes increasingly complex.

(5) International organization

The problems of creating a new infrastructure for telecommunications (or compunications) on a national scale are magnified when the questions are projected on the international scene. Just as within the last thirty years the United States has become a "national society", so in the next thirty years we will have an international society – not as a political order, but at least within the space-time framework of communications. Here not only is the scale enormously larger, but more importantly there is no common political framework for legislating and organizing the creation of a worldwide infrastructure.

International telephone traffic, for example, has been growing by about twenty per cent a year, and international communications are handled by Intelstat, an international commercial satellite organization with ninety-odd member countries. Yet Intelstat has been largely dependent on one American aerospace company (Hughes Aircraft) to build the satellites and on the American space agency to launch its satellites into orbit. The day-to-day financial and technical management of Intelstat has been in the hands of an American corporation, Comsat, whose ownership is distributed half among ordinary shareholders and half by the large communications companies, among which AT&T has a prominent voice. The question of such dominance is bound to become more and more of an international political issue in the next decades.

On a different level, the creation of worldwide knowledge data banks and services becomes an important issue as more and more countries and their scientific, technical and medical organizations seek to share in the enlarged computerized systems and on-line networks that are being developed in the advanced industrial societies.

And finally – although this is only a sampling of the international issues that will play a role in the transformation of contemporary society – there is the question of the spread of computers, specifically the sharing of advanced computer knowledge and the creation of international computer data-transmission systems. In the period before World War One, steel production was the chief index of the strength of nations, and when Germany began to overtake Great Britain and France as a steel producer, it was a tangible sign of the growth of her economic and military power. A few years ago, the Soviet Union overtook the United States in steel output, a fact that received only passing mention in the back pages of the *New York Times*. Yet the Soviet Union is far behind the United States in the production of computers and their degree of sophistication. The export of computers – to the Soviet Union and to China – is still a political, not commercial, question, for one of the chief uses of computers has been for military planning, the design of military hardware, and most importantly the creation of guided missiles and "smart" bombs.

Turning points and promises
I have been arguing that information and theoretical knowledge are the

strategic resources of the postindustrial society, just as the combination of energy, resources and machine technology were the transforming agencies of industrial society. In addition – is the claim extravagant? – they represent turning points in modern history.

D. S. L. Cardwell has identified four major turning points in the rise of scientific technology.[30] One was the era of invention at the close of the late Middle Ages, signalled by the development of the clock and the printing press. The second, the scientific revolution, was symbolized by Galileo, with his emphasis on quantitative measurement and his technical analyses of the strength of materials and the structure of machines (for example, the square-cube law on the nature of size and growth). The third, the industrial revolution of Newcomen and Watt, was the effort to realize a Baconian programme for the social benefits of science. The fourth is represented in the work of Carnot and Faraday, not only because it produced new conceptions of thermodynamics and field theory but also because it provided the bridge to a more integral relationship between science and technology.

The new turning points are of two kinds. One lies in the changing character of science. The transmutation of materials made possible by knowledge of the underlying structure of the properties of matter and the reorganization of information into different patterns through the use of the new communication technologies, particularly the computer, are transforming the social organization of science. On the one hand they create Big Science and on the other enhanced communication through on-line networks, cooperative ventures in the discovery of new knowledge and the experimental testing of results. Science as a "collective good" has become the major productive force in society.

The second turning point is the freeing of technology from its "imperative" character to become almost entirely instrumental. It was – and remains – a fear of humanists that technology would more and more "determine" social organization because the standardization of production or the interdependence of skills or the nature of engineering design forces the acceptance of one, and only one, "best" way of doing things – a theme that itself was fostered by prophets of the industrial age like Frederick W. Taylor. But the nature of modern technology frees location from resource site and opens the way to alternative modes of achieving individuality and variety within a vastly increased output of goods. This is the promise – the fateful question is whether that promise will be realized.

Notes

1 For an elaboration of this concept, see my book, *The Coming of Post-Industrial Society* (Basic Books, New York, 1973). A paperback edition with a new introduction appeared in 1976 (Harper & Row, Colophon Books, New York).

2   Cyril Stanley Smith, "Metallurgy as a Human Experience", *Metallurgical Transactions A*, 64, No. 4 (April 1975), p. 604. Professor Smith adds: "As an undergraduate (a half century ago) I had to decide whether to enrol as a ferrous or a non-ferrous metallurgist; I heard little about ceramics and nothing whatever about polymers. The curriculum, though refined in detail, had pretty much the same aim as the eighteenth century courses in the mining academy in Frieberg and the Ecole de Mines in Paris." (ibid., p. 604.)

3   Jacob Bronowski, "Humanism and the Growth of Knowledge", in Paul A. Schlipp (ed.), *The Philosophy of Karl Popper* (Open Court Publishing Company, LaSalle, Ill, 1974), p. 628.

4   Norbert Wiener, *I Am a Mathematician* (MIT Press, Cambridge, Mass., 1970), p. 40. (The book was first published in 1956 by Doubleday, New York.)

5   Smith, loc. cit., pp. 620–1.

6   Harold A. Innis, "Minerva's Owl", in *The Bias of Communication* (University of Toronto Press, Toronto, 1951), p. 3, given as the presidential address to the Royal Society of Canada in 1947.

7   For example:

   The use of clay favored a dominant role for the temples with an emphasis on priesthood and religion. Libraries were built up in Babylon and Nineveh to strengthen the power of monarchy. Papyrus and a simplified form of writing in the alphabet supported the growth of democratic organization, literature, and philosophy in Greece. Following Alexander, empires returned with centres at Alexandria and elsewhere and libraries continued as sources of strength to monarchies. Rome extended the political organization of Greece in its emphasis on law and eventually on empire. Establishment of a new capital at Constantinople was followed by imperial organization on the oriental model particularly after official recognition of Christianity. Improvement of scripts and wider dissemination of knowledge enabled the Jews to survive by emphasis on the scriptures and the book. In turn Christianity exploited the advantages of parchment and the codex in the Bible. With access to paper the Mohammedans at Baghdad and later in Spain and Sicily provided a medium for the transmission of Greek science to the Western world. Greek science and paper with the encouragement of writing in the vernacular provided the wedge between the temporal and the spiritual power and destroyed the Holy Roman Empire. The decline of Constantinople meant a stimulus to Greek literature and philosophy as the decline of Mohammedanism had meant a stimulus to science. Printing brought renewed emphasis on the book and the rise of the Reformation. In turn new methods of communication weakened the worship of the book and opened the way for new ideologies. Monopolies or oligopolies of knowledge have been built up in relation to the demands of force chiefly on the defensive, but improved technology has strengthened the position of force on the offensive and compelled realignments favoring the vernacular. (ibid., pp. 31–2.)

   Marshall McLuhan, as is evident, was a disciple of Harold Innis (he wrote the introduction to the paperback edition of *The Bias of Communication*) and derived most of his major ideas from him. But McLuhan not only "hyped up" and vulgarized Innis's ideas, he also reversed the thrust of his argument, for Innis feared that the tendency of new media was to extend centralization and concentrate power, while McLuhan, though propagating the notion of a "global village", argued that the newer media would encourage decentralization and participation.

8   *Encyclopedia Britannica* (1970 ed.), s.v. "information theory".

9   Norbert Wiener, *Cybernetics* (Wiley, New York, 1948), p. 155.
10   Wassily Leontieff, "National Economic Planning: Methods and Problems", *Challenge*, July–August 1976, pp. 7–8.
      Referring to the further consequences of this new capacity, Leontieff writes:
      Such systematic information proves to be most useful in assessing structural – in this particular instance technological – relationships between the input requirements on the one hand, and the levels of output of various industries on the other. In the case of households these relationships would be between total consumers' outlay and spending on each particular type of goods. Stocks of equipment, buildings and inventories, their accumulation, their maintenance and their occasional reduction are described and analyzed in their mutual dependence with the flows of all kinds of goods and services throughout the entire system. Detailed, as contrasted with aggregative, description and analysis of economic structures and relationships can indeed provide a suitable framework for a concrete, instead of a purely symbolic description of alternative methods of production, and the realistic delineation of alternative paths of technological change. (ibid., p. 8.)
11   Indeed information is merely the negative measure of uncertainty, so to speak. Let me say immediately that I am not going to propose a quantitative measure. In particular, the well-known Shannon measure which has been so useful in communications engineering is not in general appropriate for economic analysis, for it gives no weight to the value of the information. If beforehand a large manufacturer regards it as equally likely whether the price of his product will go up or down, then learning which is true conveys no more information, in the Shannon sense, than observing of the toss of a fair coin.
      Kenneth J. Arrow, *Information and Economic Behavior*, Office of Naval Research Technical Report No. 14 (Washington, DC), pp. 4–5.
12   As Arrow remarks:
      The presumption that free markets will lead to an efficient allocation of resources is not valid in this case. If nothing else, there are at least two salient characteristics of information which prevent it from being fully identified as one of the commodities represented in our abstract models of general equilibrium: (1) it is by definition indivisible in its use, and (2) it is very difficult to appropriate. (ibid., p. 11.)
13   Robert K. Merton, "Singletons and Multiples in Science", in Norman W. Storer (ed.), *The Sociology of Science*, the papers of Merton (University of Chicago Press, Chicago, 1900), p. 356.
14   The problem is that economists have no direct measures of such "inputs" and treat them as "residuals", not accounted for by direct increases in the productivity of capital or labour. As Michael Spence writes:
      The difficulty in measuring information has hampered research concerned with the effects of information on [economic] growth. It is common practice to estimate the effect of education and knowledge on growth in GNP by first estimating the impact of real factors like the increase in capital stock, the labour force, and so on. One then attributes the growth that is not explained in these real factors to increases in knowledge.
15   There is a huge and growing literature on all these questions. I have drawn largely on the reports of the Harvard Programme on Information Technology and Policy for the material in this section.
16   See Fritz Machlup, *The Production and Distribution of Knowledge in the United States* (Princeton University Press, Princeton, 1962). For a detailed discussion of

Machlup's types of knowledge in comparison with those of Max Scheler and my own, see Bell, *The Coming of Post-Industrial Society*, pp. 174–7. Since, for me, the heart of the postindustrial society is the new ways in which knowledge becomes instrumental for science and social policy, I have attempted an "objective definition" that would allow a researcher to plot the growth and use of knowledge.

17 Marc Porat has reformulated the 1967 National Income Accounts to make them consistent with accepted practices, and despite some admitted deficiencies, he has hewed to the standard usages. As Porat points out,

> Machlup's accounting scheme innovated rather liberally on the National Income Accounts and practices whereas this study does not. . . . His work includes an admixture of "primary" and "secondary" type activities, whereas this study keeps them distinct. Third, a variant of *final demand* is used by Machlup as a measure of knowledge industry size, whereas this study uses primarily the value added approach but reports both sets of figures. . . .

"The Information Economy" (Ph.D. diss., Stanford University, 1976), vol. 1, pp. 81–2.

18 Machlup's key data can be presented in tabular form:

Distribution of proportion of Gross National Product spent on knowledge, 1958

Type of knowledge and source of expenditures	Amount in millions of dollars	Percentage of total
Education	60,194	44.1
Research and development	10,090	8.1
Communication media	38,369	28.1
Information machines	8,922	6.5
Information services (incomplete)	17,961	13.2
Totals	136,436	100.0
Expenditures made by:		
Government	37,968	27.8
Business	42,198	30.9
Consumers	56,270	41.3
Totals	136,436	100.0

(*Source:* Machlup, *Production and Distribution of Knowledge*, pp. 360–1. Arranged in tabular form by permission.)

19 Gilbert Burck, "Knowledge, the Biggest Growth Industry of Them All", *Fortune*, November 1964.

20 Jacob Marschak, "Economics of Inquiring, Communicating, Deciding", *American Economic Review*, 58, No. 2 (1968), pp. 1–8.

21 The statistics and tables here, except where noted, are taken from Porat, "The Information Economy", vol. 1. The page citations refer to that volume. The figures on trends in the workforce are from a briefing packet that Mr Porat had prepared for presentation at an OECD conference. I am grateful to him for making these materials available to me, and for his correspondence in clarifying some of my questions. His revised work is scheduled to be published by Basic Books.

22 I am indebted for this technological information to a research paper by Paul DiMaggio, a graduate student of sociology at Harvard.

23 Georges Anderla, *Information in 1985. A Forecasting Study of Information Needs and Resources* (OECD, Paris, 1973), pp. 15–16.

24 D. de Solla Price, *Little Science, Big Science* (Columbia University Press, New

York, 1963), p. 31. For a critical discussion of the use of logistic curves and some questions about Price's various starting points, see my *The Coming of Post-Industrial Society*, chap. 2. "The Measurement of Knowledge and Technology", pp. 177–85.

25 Anderla, *Information in 1985*, p. 21. The major specialist journals were: *Chemical Abstracts* and *Biological Abstracts* (which between them accounted for more than 550,000 items, more than half of the one million produced in 1971), *Engineering Index Monthly*, *Metals Abstracts*, *Physics Abstracts*, *Psychological Abstracts*, and a Geology Index Service.

26 The figures are taken from a paper by Lee Burchinal of the National Science Foundation, "National Scientific and Technical Information Systems", presented to an international conference in Tunis, 26 April 1976. I am grateful to Dr Burchinal for the reprint.

27 Cited by Colin Cherry, "The Spreading Word of Science", *Times Literary Supplement*, 22 March 1974, p. 301.

28 Remarks made at the Science Information Policy Workshop, National Science Foundation, Washington, DC, 17 December 1974.

29 One major difficulty is the inadequacy of our statistics. As Peter H. Schuck remarks:

What is perhaps more disturbing, given the imminence of national economic planning, is the abject poverty of our economic statistical base, upon which a good theory must be grounded. In recent years the inadequacy and inaccuracy of a broad spectrum of economic indices – including the wholesale price index, the consumer price index, the unemployment rate, and business inventory levels – have become quite evident. The wholesale price index, for example, reflects only list prices rather than actual transaction prices (which are often lower) and uses anachronistic seasonal adjustment factors; yet it is considered a bellwether statistic in economic forecasting.

("National Economic Planning: A Slogan without Substance", *The Public Interest*, Fall 1976, p. 72.)

30 D. S. L. Cardwell, *Turning Points in Western Technology* (Science History Publications, New York, 1972).

Once More, the Computer Revolution

Joe Weizenbaum

In another broadside, Professor Weizenbaum expresses great scepticism about the microelectronic revolution and in particular he attacks Daniel Bell's belief that developments in computer technology will transform our society into an "Information Society". He questions the abilities of computers and raises a number of ethical issues concerning their use. The author is Professor of Computer Science at the Massachusetts Institute of Technology.

Both the cost and the physical size of computer hardware are decreasing at an exponential rate. It follows from this that the very measures by which computers are classified as micro, mini, small, large and very large are also consistently being readjusted. Today's so-called minis are functionally equivalent, at least roughly, to the most powerful large computers of only a decade ago, yet almost all their physical indices – for example, their bulk and power consumption – are a very small fraction of the corresponding indices of their ancestors, and so is their cost. It is almost as if the cost of computers as a function of their weight is a constant of nature – if, it must be added, the cost of much of their necessary peripheral gear is neglected. Another effect of this ongoing process is that computers of the size of the older large computers have many times as many components packed into them and are therefore functionally much more powerful while being no more expensive than their recent predecessors. This phenomenon is, of course, also reflected on the software side: the measures according to which programs are ranged from small to large are changing similarly. Programs that only a few years ago would have been classified as rather large are now shoehorned into mini- and even microcomputers, while on the other end of the scale, programs of hitherto unimagined size and complexity are developed for the newer giant computer systems.

One need have only ordinary, decent, American respect for the genius of the free market system in order to share the belief that these dramatic technological developments must inevitably induce a veritable flooding of the marketplace with computers. In the not too distant future computers will be as pervasive on the American scene as, for example, fractional horsepower electric motors are today. The analogy to these small engines underscores, by the way, not only the magnitude of the expected flood but the fact that many of these computers will be, as are many of the motors currently in use in homes, unobtrusive parts of a wide variety of household gadgets.

The widely shared belief in technological inevitability, especially as it applies to computers, is translated by scholars and the popular media alike into the announcement of still another computer revolution. (It will be remembered that the past two decades have, according to these same sources, already witnessed one or two such revolutions.) This time, the much-heralded revolution will transform society to its very core, and a new form of society will emerge: the information society.

A question that appears to be asked only rarely is what pressing problems this inundation of technological fixes is supposed to attack. Certain problem areas *are* often identified, to be sure. There is, for example, some discussion of the drabness of modern society. This is seen by some computer scientists to be owing in large part to the deadly uniformity of most consumer goods. This monotony could, it is argued, be relieved by "individualizing" products through the use of versatile manufacturing robots. Education is also raised as a problem area. Here it is occasionally argued that the visions of such thinkers as Dewey, Montessori and Neill "fail in practice *for lack of a technological basis*. The computer now provides it."* But it is clear in these and other cases that the discussion is carried out in a mode of thought that has become altogether too traditional, especially among computer technologists: it begins with a great many solutions and then looks for problems. One consequence of this way of thinking is that it obscures real problems. The aimlessness of everyday life experienced by millions in modern society has deep roots in the individual's alienation from nature, from work, and from other human beings. As long as that is not understood and dealt with there can be no relief. To give everyone who can afford it a pair of shoes different from everyone else's and then advertise that achievement as a step towards the amelioration of some of society's deepest ills is not revolutionary; it is absurd. Similarly, the real problems

* My emphasis. Seymour A. Papert, "Computers and Learning" in Dertouzos and Moses, op. cit.

to which people like Neill and Montessori actually addressed themselves are not functions of some "technological base", except perhaps in
the contrary sense; that is, they might not be so stubborn were it not that
schools exist in an already overly technological society. No fix, technological or otherwise, of the American education system that does not
recognize that American schools are rapidly becoming America's principal juvenile minimum security prisons can be expected to have socially
therapeutic effects. Giving children computers to play with, while not
necessarily bad in itself, cannot touch this or any other real problem.

The home computer
Enthusiasts for the home computer struggle with problems that could
arise only as consequences of the triumph of the kind of mass-marketing
techniques that gave us, for example, the multimillion-dollar deodorant
industry. The product to be marketed is invented simultaneously with
the dysfunction it is designed to cure. It is simply assumed that, what
with the lowering of prices to below any conceivable threshold of
consumer resistance, virtually every household will have a programmable computer. The "problem", then, is created by the solution itself;
what are people to do with this appliance; what is it to be applied *to*? The
electric carving knife, whatever its faults, at least answered that question for itself.

A typical essay on the home computer begins by assuming that there
are computers in the home and then addresses the question of what they
may be used for. The home computers foreseen are miniature versions
of the kinds of computers that exist in the world at large, including, for
example, freestanding computers on which anything at all may be
programmed, computers equipped with prepackaged systems, and
process-control computers. The issues that emerge from considerations
of the computer in the home are much the same as those arising from the
presence of the computer in modern society generally. Chief among
these are what social – that is, political, cultural, educational, and so on –
needs computers help satisfy today and what roles they are likely to play
tomorrow.

Perhaps the first question to ask is just what fraction of American
homes will have the kinds of computing machines typically envisioned.
A standard analogy is to television. It is certainly true that essentially all
American dwellings that could conceivably be called homes have at
least one television set now. It appears to be true that many of the
dwellings of the poor and even of the very poor have, whatever else they
lack, a television set. Television, then, is an example of a technological
gadget that has vindicated the marketeers who think in terms of
consumer resistance thresholds below which it is possible to duck

absolutely. It has to be noted, however, that the television sets of the poor are often purchased at a cost that is outrageous when measured in terms of what elementary necessities are given up.

Will the home computer be as pervasive as today's television sets? The answer must almost certainly be no. The picture of the home that emerges implicitly from the accounts of advocates for the home computer (it appears to be derived from television's own tedious so-called family dramas) is one of a middle-class, even an upper-middle-class, home. The wall-to-wall carpeting needs to be cleaned by a robot; roasts are in the oven; the family is united by its preoccupation with toys, games, sports; the computer helps "the mother" pay the telephone bill; and so on. B. O. Evans, another computer scientist, imagines the same kind of home when he addresses himself to the home computer. He writes:

> For home use, terminals have potential for catalogue ordering, activity planning, home library and education, and family health, including histories, diagnoses, doctors' speciality lists, and emergency procedures; family recreation, including music selection and games; career guidance, tax records and returns; home safety and property maintenance, including house plan retrieval, maintenance schedules, electrical and other physical facility layouts, and energy management; and budgeting and banking.

What and whose needs will be satisfied by the functions described here and by the ongoing proliferation of computers and computer controlled systems? What will be the indirect effects on a society that increasingly, possibly irreversibly, commits itself to being monitored and controlled by systems that even its own technostructure ill understands?

We may recall the euphoric dreams articulated by then Secretary of Commerce Herbert Hoover at the dawn of commercial radio broadcasting and again by others when mass television broadcasting was about to become a reality. It was foreseen that these media would exert an enormously beneficial influence on the shaping of American culture. Americans of every class, most particularly children, would, many for the first time, be exposed to the correctly spoken word, to great literature, great drama, to America's most excellent teachers, and so on. We are all witnesses to what actually happened. The technological dream was more than realized. Scratchy low-bandwidth radio was replaced by high-fidelity FM, then by stereo broadcasting of the finest sound quality. The tiny black-and-white television screen grew to impressive size and was painted in "living colour". Satellite communication systems made it possible to display almost any event taking place, even in outer space, on television screens in homes anywhere on Earth. But the cultural dream was cruelly mocked in *its* realization. This

magnificent technology, more than Wagnerian in its proportions, combining as it does the technology of precise guidance of rockets, of space
flight, of the cleverest and most intricate electronics, of photography,
and so on, this exquisitely refined combination of some of the human
species' highest intellectual achievements, what does it deliver to the
masses? An occasional gem buried in immense avalanches of the ordure
of everything that is most banal and insipid or pathological in our
civilization.

We are beginning to see this same calamitous script reenacted in
terms of the home computer. Again we have the euphoric dream. But
the heralds of its transmutation to disaster are already obvious: the
market is inundated with computer games in which the players' main
objective is to kill, crush and destroy. We have spacewar, battleship,
tank battles, and so on. I overheard an MIT graduate student who was
deeply engaged in a game of spacewar with his fellow students say to
them: "We ought to get more points for killing than for merely
surviving." That statement seemed perfectly reasonable to all concerned. It may well be prophetic in a deeper sense than anyone present
realized.

The home computer is in its current form merely a miniature version
of the freestanding computers that today can be found in countless
laboratories, business offices and other enterprises. However, just as
many of these computers are increasingly being interconnected to one
another to form computer networks, so, according to most authorities,
will home computers become, in effect, satellites of a variety of large
computer networks. Only in this way would the home computers be able
to access the large data-bases needed for the tasks B. O. Evans
visualized their function to be; for example, banking and catalogue
ordering. Indeed, many authorities believe that home computers that
function in part as nodes of extensive computer networks will play a
crucial part in the process of transforming our society into what Daniel
Bell, professor of sociology at Harvard University, calls an *information
society*.

The information society
Bell is perhaps the foremost American social scientist to have written
extensively on the information society. He sees it already: a child of the
marriage between modern communication and computer technologies,
of which existing computer networks are but the first issue.

Certainly, one foundation of the information society is knowledge.
This Bell defines above as:

> . . . an organized set of statements of facts or ideas, presenting a reasoned
> judgement or an experimental result, which is transmitted to others

through some communication medium in some systematic form. Thus, I distinguish knowledge from news or entertainment. Knowledge consists of new judgements (research and scholarship) or presentations of older judgements (textbooks, teaching, and library and archive materials).

Elsewhere in the chapter he characterizes this definition as an attempt at an "'objective definition' that would allow a researcher to plot the growth and use of knowledge." The inner quotes are, to his credit, Bell's.

What renders Bell's definition of knowledge nearly useless for the present purpose is that it is fatally (again, for the present purpose) circular and incomplete. What "facts", "experimental results", and "reasoned judgements" *are* is itself determined by the observer's organizing principles. This, the observer's Weltanschauung, is itself "knowledge", but a knowledge that is largely tacit and one that almost entirely escapes Bell's categories. Bell's definition is incomplete also in that it systematically excludes almost everything called knowledge in everyday life. People know a great many things that are neither products of research and scholarship nor materials in textbooks or archives, for example. They know what pleases people they see every day and what offends them. They know their way about their cities and what detours to take when the usual paths are blocked. (In fact, that kind of knowledge is closely analogous to a mathematician's knowledge of a special mathematical domain; mathematicians see shortcuts in the construction of proofs of theorems, for example, that they do not deduce logically but at which they arrive as a consequence of their deep general understanding of their domains. Taxi drivers in big cities know their domains similarly.)

Bell's perhaps unconscious willingness to exclude this kind of knowledge from consideration betrays, it seems to me, precisely the kind of parochialism that afflicts almost the entire intelligentsia, especially when it turns its attention to large-scale social problems. It betrays what for the intelligentsia is to count not only as knowledge but as fact. Bell himself gives a broad hint as to what these determinants are, and what they are not:

[The] upheaval in telecommunications and knowledge poses two economic-political policy problems, one structural, the other intellectual. The structural question is what kind of technical-economic organization is best designed to be efficient, meet consumer (*i.e., industrial, commercial, financial, scientific, library*) use, and remain flexible enough to *allow for continuing technological development.*
The second policy problem . . . is . . . the question of a national information policy, *particularly the dissemination of science [sic] and technical information.* [My emphases.]

For Bell, "the crucial variables of the postindustrial society are information and knowledge."

> ... recoding is an extremely powerful weapon for increasing the amount of information that we can deal with. In one form or another we use recoding constantly in our daily behaviour. ...
>
> Our language is tremendously useful for repackaging material into a few chunks rich in information. ... the kind of linguistic recoding people do seems to me to be the very lifeblood of the thought process.*

I agree entirely.

What Miller had in mind when he spoke of "chunking" is the phenomenon that permits us to recall, say, the telephone area code of New York, not as the sequence of the three separate integers "2" and "1" and "2" but as the single number "212". Even more important from the standpoint of daily life, words like *mother, enemy,* and so on are not remembered merely as words, that is, letters chunked into aggregates, but as chunks that engage huge, often conflicting conceptual structures laden with emotional meanings. And of course these meanings come into play when human beings talk and otherwise communicate with one another in ordinary language. A welfare computer system may very well be able to dip into its data bank and calculate that, say, five people occupy a particular household; it cannot understand what difference it makes in reality whether those five people are merely roomers who happen to share the rent burden, or a family. It may very well be able to deduce (from their last names, for example) that they are a family and jump, as computer specialists say, to a subroutine that treats them as a unit, in that sense chunking its data. Still, what it means in human terms to be a family cannot be part of the computed chunk.

Computer-based information systems *necessarily* induce recoding of data into information-rich chunks of precisely the sort Miller is talking about. But the recoding required for the computer, some of which computers commonly do by themselves, is such as to denude the original data of the nuances and subtleties that accompanied them and that determined their meanings while they were still cast in ordinary language. The "richness" of chunks created either by or for the computer is of a different, that is, a lower, order than their sources. As Bell himself says:

> ... if the purpose of a library, or a knowledge-based computer program, is to help a historian to assemble evidence or a scholar to "reorder" ideas, then the ambiguity of language itself must be confronted. Terms necessarily vary in different contexts and lend themselves to different interpre-

---

* This passage is from a longer version of Professor Bell's essay, to be published separately.

tations, and historical usages shift over time (consider the problem of defining an intellectual, or the nature of ideology), making the problem of designing a "knowledge" program quite different from designing an "information" program. .... A sophisticated reader, studying a philosophical text, may make use of the existing index at the back of the book, but if he is to absorb and use the ideas in a fruitful way, he has necessarily to create his own index by regrouping and recategorizing the terms that are employed. ... *In this process, no mechanical ordering, no exhaustive set of permutations and combinations, can do the task.* [My emphasis.]

I believe Bell intended this passage to voice his conviction that there are limits to what computers can do, particularly that artificial intelligence cannot bring forth an artifact that exhibits the entire range of human creativity. After all, every computation is fundamentally a "mechanical ordering" based on permuting and combining its data. If that is his assessment, then I agree with it wholeheartedly. However, Bell seems to see this boundary as being relevant to only the most extreme fantasies of the leadership of the artificial intelligence community (the artificial intelligentsia), hence irrelevant to hard-nosed, practical current concerns. This is where he and I disagree.

Some hard questions

The use of large-scale computer-based information systems induces an epistemology within which reigns an extremely poverty-stricken notion of what constitutes knowledge and what is to count as fact. Unfortunately, this same notion – a kind of pragmatic positivism bordering on scientism – dominates much of the thinking of modern intellectuals and political leaders. It has also, in my view, profoundly infected the thought of ordinary people. It has no *necessary* relationship to the computer; it existed, after all, long before there were computers. But the computer is its starkest symbolic manifestation. It is the instrument that, more than any other force, reifies it.

To see its influence one may turn to Bell's own examples.

Consider first the report of the Club of Rome, the *Limits to Growth* study, about which Bell writes:

What gave the Club of Rome study a degree of authority was the announcement that the authors had succeeded in modelling the world economy and carrying out a computer simulation that traced out the interconnections of four basic variables: resources, population, industrial production and pollution.*

---

* This passage and the remarks in the paragraph that follows are from the longer version of Bell's essay.

Bell goes on to remark that the *Limits to Growth* study has been largely discredited. Nevertheless, the study had and continues to have "authority". But not every announcement of the completion of a study immediately lends that study the kind of great and far-reaching authority that the *Limits to Growth* immediately came to enjoy. It was not the announcement that lent authority to the study; it was the fact that the study was conducted by insiders of that very temple of high science and technology, MIT (which proudly characterizes itself as being "polarized around science and technology"), *and* that the model being announced was done on a computer. Interestingly enough, Bell claims the *Limits to Growth* model to be discredited by the "unreliability of [its] initial data" and by "its simplified assumption of a linear, extrapolative growth". He never hints that this or any other model's difficulties might be more fundamental, located for example, in their epistemological foundations. But then he appears to share their basic assumptions.

Professor Jay Forrester, the main driving force behind this and similar models, has repeatedly revealed his models' epistemological foundations. For example:

> ... the human mind is not adapted to interpreting how social systems behave.... until recently there has been no way to estimate the behaviour of social systems except by contemplation, discussion, argument, and guesswork.
>
> The great uncertainty with mental models is the inability to anticipate consequences of interactions between parts of a system. This uncertainty is *totally* eliminated in computer models. Given a stated set of assumptions, the computer traces the resulting consequences without doubt or error.... Furthermore, any concept or relationship that can be clearly stated in ordinary language can be translated into computer model language.[1]

It is the widely shared belief in the epistemology expressed by these words that is, in my view, chiefly responsible for the acceptance of Forrester's and similar models.

Consider the impact of Forrester's words on the members of the US Congress, to whom they were addressed, or on any other group of people who have no training in or intuition for formal systems. They hear that the basis of their thinking, mental models, leads to uncertainty, whereas Forrester-like computer models totally eliminate this uncertainty and all doubt or error. That is what they hear; it is not precisely what Forrester said. For he said only that given a system of well-formed equations, their solutions (if they exist) are unambiguously determined. And with that one cannot quarrel. But the word "doubt" is curiously out of place in this context. It is a word out of psychology, not out of mathematics or logic. Clearly, what Forrester really means to communicate is that because of the uncertainty inherent in them, one must doubt conclusions reached from mere thinking. Conclusions derived from computer models are valid beyond doubt.

The "stated assumptions" to which Forrester refers may be correct or they may be incorrect, but they must necessarily be incomplete. And their necessary incompleteness derives from exactly the same source as the incompleteness of the set of knowledge Bell is willing to admit into his calculus. The last sentence of the quotation reinforces this thesis; it implies that anything worth saying at all, hence worth knowing in Bell's sense, can be "clearly stated in ordinary language", hence "translated into computer model language".* It is on precisely this epistemological foundation that Bell rests his vision of the coming (or already present?) information society. For "the crucial variables of the postindustrial society", Bell argues, "are information and knowledge. By information I mean data processing in the broadest sense; the storage, retrieval and processing of data become the essential resource for all economic and social exchanges." Of course he envisages an extension of what is already true, namely the widespread use of computers to do the data processing in the information and knowledge society. Furthermore, almost all the processing will be done on data-bases also stored in computer systems. These Bell characterizes as characteristics of populations: census data, market research, opinion surveys, election data, etc. But what about these data bases? Bell himself quotes Peter H. Schuck:

> What is ... disturbing, given the imminence of national economic planning, is the abject poverty of our economic statistical base, upon which a good theory must be grounded. In recent years inadequacy and inaccuracy of a broad spectrum of economic indices – including the wholesale price index, the consumer price index, the unemployment rate, and business inventory levels – have become quite evident. †

The trouble is that the computer induces confidence (as in the Club of Rome report) and that it usually magnifies errors and their consequences enormously.

Another classic example comes from the much-touted command and control system in operation during the Vietnam war. "The mechanisms of [this system] were so complete," Bell says, "that basic tactical decisions (on military targets to bomb, or harbours to blockade) were controlled by political centres in the White House, ten thousand miles away, but transmitted in 'real time'." However "complete" this system

---

* In these circumstances one needs to recall Ionesco's remark: "Not everything is unsayable in words – only the living truth."
† The Schuck quote and Bell's comment on Vietnam are from the longer version of Bell's essay.

may have been, Admiral Moorer, then chairman of the Joint Chiefs of Staff, testified to the US Senate Armed Services Committee that specially programmed computers in the field systematically lied to the Pentagon's computers with respect to the secret bombing of Cambodia. It was of course not some computer in the Pentagon that was misled by such lies – computers process information, not meanings – it was the policy maker who relied, or claimed to rely, on "what the computer says" whose decisions were gravely affected. As Admiral Moorer complained at the time: "It is unfortunate that we had to become slaves to these damned computers."[2]

It is instructive to note just how the US Air Force computers in Vietnam, whose function it was to maintain records of sorties flown, ordnance and fuel expended and so on, were made to lie to the Pentagon's computers in Washington. Computers in the field were programmed automatically to convert the geographical coordinates of targets struck by US planes in Cambodia to coordinates of "legitimate" targets in Vietnam. Tapes of these allegedly raw though actually "cleansed" data were then forwarded to Washington to be entered into the Pentagon's computers. Highly placed Washington insiders who were permitted to see the summaries produced by Pentagon computers wrongly believed themselves to be gaining a privileged insight into what was actually happening in the field. Thus did the military create a textbook example of Orwell's Ministry of Truth: thus did it create history.

From a military point of view, this procedure raises serious questions of command and control. It raises even more general questions of responsibility and accountability in a highly technologized information society. Clearly, the technically relatively simple task of writing the coordinate conversion programs had to be assigned by someone to someone. Perhaps the programmers who actually did the job were given their assignment in purely abstract form, without being told, that is, what the ultimate function of their product was to be; they may have been given merely a specification of a black box that was to exhibit certain input-output behaviour. If so, then the programmers could deny responsibility for the consequences of their handiwork on the ground that they didn't know what they were doing. But should they not have inquired? On the other hand, perhaps they knew what they were doing but being in the military thought it their duty to follow orders – more importantly, perhaps they felt that duty removed all responsibility from their shoulders. Just what are the responsibilities of the mere technicians, or of engineers or scientists, in the information society?

Decisions crucially affecting people's lives are made with the aid of computer systems contaminated by a "broad spectrum of inadequate and inaccurate economic indices" and by systematic lies. If the programmers of these systems – and by extension their professional managers, systems analysts, and so on – are not responsible for the consequences of actions based on what these computer systems tell policy makers, and if policy makers are excused from responsibility on the ground that they merely relied on "what the computer said", then who is responsible?

This question poses what is at bottom a special case of the problem of individual responsibility and accountability that has been with us ever since human beings organized themselves into large social units. In modern times, it has manifested itself symbolically and actually most egregiously in the form of an Adolf Eichmann's claim of personal innocence based on the plea that he was "merely following orders" – as indeed were US Air Force computer programmers in Vietnam – when he supervised the transportation of millions of human beings to death camps. Is there any *moral* difference between Eichmann's failure to confront what he was actually doing and the Air Force programmers' identical failure? We Americans puzzle over the circumstance that neither General Westmoreland nor Lieutenant Calley is responsible, nor is anyone else along the chain of command that unites them, for the men and women and babies Calley shot and killed with his own hand. Nor have any committees of the US Congress nor anyone else been able to find any individuals in the US military's chain of command who acknowledge accountability for implementing the disinformation machinery, to borrow a truly Orwellian term from the world's intelligence agencies, that systematically deceived at least some policy makers. In another sector of our affairs, we wonder how it can be that neither the workers on the assembly line nor the executives nor anyone in between is responsible when General Motors installs cheap Chevrolet engines in high-priced Oldsmobiles. Some of us can still be astonished by the spectacle of an American secretary of state publicly grieving over "the tragedy that has *befallen*" the Watergate criminals.[3] There appear to be no actors on stage, only anonymous events. We are, I believe, entitled to be at least a little sceptical of Admiral Moorer's characterization of the Joint Chiefs as victims of computers in the sense he apparently intended. Or are we to believe that the bombing of Cambodia was a secret even from them? More likely, Admiral Moorer was in this instance using the computer as an instrument to help create and preserve, in the picturesque phrase coined by the White House, plausible deniability.

The institutionalization on the most fundamental social and political levels of a systematic retreat from responsibility and accountability has no necessary relation to computers. However, the computer, and particularly the role advocated for it by many social scientists and computer intellectuals, amplifies and intensifies the problem and exacerbates its effects. Computer intellectuals are aware of this and sometimes give voice to their concern, but usually in ways that are oddly detached from present-day reality. For example, Professor Alan Perlis, head of Yale University's Computer Science Department, like most thoughtful computer scientists sees the computer as "having a day-to-day effect on man and his society", as causing an "ecological transformation".* He sees computer science as studying the nature and consequences of "the phenomena arising around, and because of, computers." Yet what will surely prove to be by far the most important of these phenomena, the transformations in man and society induced by the computer, are strangely absent from his and, I would say, the actual agenda of frontier research in computer science. It isn't that Perlis is totally unaware of some social and political problems that are sharpened by the application of certain computer technologies. For example he acknowledges, again as would many computer scientists, that "research on speech understanding [by computers] can lead to programs that eavesdrop or deny us human contact in some telephone-regulated transactions." (Indeed, the current press gives us abundant evidence that governments are already using computers to sort "interesting" communications from the mass of those they illegally monitor.) But then he dismisses the crucial problems raised by this development, such as the problem of responsibility and control, by saying: "It is not up to the programs themselves either to exploit or correct our social deficiencies." I suppose this is intended to absolve *programs* from any responsibility for any harm that may come from their use, just as bullets are not responsible for the people they kill. But not a word about the responsibilities of the researchers who put such tools at the disposal of a morally "deficient" society.

Professor Marvin Minsky of MIT, to give another example, confesses that he is:

> inclined to fear most the HAL scenario [He is here referring to the computer on board the spaceship in Arthur C. Clarke's *2001*. The computer eventually wrested control from the ship's astronauts.] The first AI system of large capability will have many layers of poorly understood control structure and obscurely encoded "knowledge". There are serious problems about such a machine's goal structure: if it cannot edit its high-level intentions, it may not be smart enough to be useful, but if it can, how can the designers anticipate the machine it evolves into? In a word, I would expect the first self-improving AI machines to become "psychotic" in many ways, and it may take many generations . . . to "stabilize" them.

* Alan J. Perlis, "Current Research Frontiers in Computer Science" in Dertouzos and Moses, op. cit.

> The problem could become serious if economic incentives to use the unreliable early systems are large – unfortunately there are too many ways a dumb system with a huge data-base can be useful.

Minsky believes himself to be talking about machines of the future, a future in which some of the most ambitious goals of artificial intelligence will have been very nearly realized. His "fear" is therefore abstract and has little if any influence on what he believes he or currently active workers with or designers of computer systems ought to worry about today. But if we, as we should, conceive of computer systems as including the people who manage and maintain them, then it becomes clear that the "unreliable early systems" Minsky rightly fears are already very much with us and that the economic incentives to use them are, for many organizations, already insuperably large. And millions of people would probably agree that our self-improving "machines" – where that word is taken in the large sense – have already become psychotic. But do we have the many generations' time to "stabilize" them? Are these, indeed, the systems we want stabilized?

It is simply a matter of fact that almost all very large computer systems in use today *have* "many layers of poorly understood control structure and obscurely encoded knowledge". It is simply no longer possible for these systems' designers – or for anyone else – to understand what these systems *have* "evolved into", let alone to anticipate into what they *will* evolve.

Large computer systems typically are not designed in the ordinary sense of the word *design*. To be sure, they begin with an idea – a design, if you will – which is then implemented. But they soon begin to undergo a steady process of modification, of accretion to both their control structures and their data-bases, which changes and continues to change them fundamentally. Typically too, this sort of surgery is carried out not by the original programmers but by people who come and go from and to other assignments. As a result, there are, again typically, no individuals or teams of people who understand the large systems to which they have contributed their labours. Modern large-scale systems have no authors; they have, in Minsky's words, simply *evolved into* whatever they have become. Robert Jastrow, director of NASA's Goddard Institute for Space Studies, boasts of systems of precisely this sort, in complete disregard of the dangers inherent in their use, when he asserts: "Computers match people in some roles, and when fast decisions are needed in a crisis, they often outclass them."[4]

Professor Minsky long ago absolved *programmers* of credit and responsibility for whatever effects may issue from the incomprehensible systems they may create on precisely the ground that their systems *are* incomprehensible:

[The] argument, based on the fact that reliable computers do only that which they are instructed to do, has a basic flaw; it does not follow that the programmer therefore has full knowledge (and therefore full responsibility and credit) for what will ensue. For certainly the programmer may set up an evolutionary system whose limitations are to him unclear and possibly incomprehensible.[5]

What does it mean to understand a computer system at all? Minsky correctly points out that "'understand' ... implies ... some sort of schematization and getting at the basic principles rather than attending equally to all details, however small. In that sense, 'understanding' means understanding an idealized model of something rather than the thing itself." Minsky comes very near to saying here that to understand something complex is to have an economical theory of the thing – and in this I would agree with him. To know every line of the code that constitutes a large computer program is not necessarily and not even probably to understand the program. A theory of what the program is supposed to do is required in order to be able to tell, for example, when the program is malfunctioning; in other words, to understand it. But it is precisely this form of understanding that is rendered impossible by the very way large computer systems are constructed – unless, that is, the computer systems in question are based on robust theories from their inception to their current state of evolution. There are very few such computer systems outside the domain of scientific computing. We are thus in precisely the situation Minsky fears: designers cannot anticipate what their machines will evolve into. And that is, as Minsky observes, a "serious problem". Once one understands the seriousness of the problem, one must surely be led to wonder what Bell had in mind when he wrote: "Obviously, the information explosion can only be handled through the expansion of computerized and subsequently automated information systems." Perhaps a better course would be to attempt to contain the information explosion. Programmers can make a contribution and in the process gain a sense of responsibility and dignity by refusing to add to systems whose purposes and theories of operation cannot be explained to them. How else, by the way, could programmers possibly be sure that they are not working on systems to whose ultimate purposes they could not reconcile their consciences?

Are there technical solutions to the problem presented by essentially incomprehensible computer systems? It seems to me there are not. Clearly, to accept one's responsibilities is a moral matter. It requires, above all, recognition and acceptance of one's own limitations and the limitations of one's tools. Unfortunately, the temptations to do exactly the opposite are very large. It is true, as Minsky observes, that even dumb systems can be of considerable use. Their uses are encouraged when, in the short run, they benefit their users, while the harm they cause to others is remote and largely invisible. Moreover, architects of systems that initially appear to function well are usually richly rewarded until and often even long after their systems' faults have become obvious and the harm they have done has become irreversible. This last observation holds true even for systems that have nothing directly to do with computers: witness, for example, the fate of the coterie of American "statesmen" who led America into the Vietnam war.

On the other hand, the impressive number of comprehensible though large computer systems that exist in the scientific domain, in chemistry, physics, mathematics and astronomy, teach us that incomprehensibility is not a necessary property of even huge computer systems. The secret of their comprehensibility is that these systems are models of very robust theories. One can tell when they go wrong, for example, because the errors they then produce result in behaviour that contradicts their theories. What this should teach us is that the construction of reliable computer systems in the social and political sphere awaits not so much the results of research in computer science as a deeper theoretical understanding of the human condition. The limit, then, of the extent to which computers can help us deal with the world of human affairs is determined by the same thing that has always determined such limits: our ability to assess our situation honestly, and our ability to know ourselves.

Artificial intelligence

No discussion of the role computers are to play in the emergent information society would be complete without an appraisal of the state of and the hopes for artificial intelligence (AI). This must be because the ethos of so much of the rest of the computer practicum is now pervaded by the spirit – and by what little substance there is – of AI. There is talk not simply of robots but of intelligent robots, not simply of home computers but of intelligent home computers; kids in school will have AI at their disposal and even help create more of it. Dr Sidney Fernbach, previous head of the Lawrence Livermore Laboratory's Computation Centre, one of the world's largest computation facilities, invokes an absurd vision of AI's potential use in science and in education that gives an idea of what leading computer managers expect from their instruments:

> The scientist experiences and learns to understand physical phenomena throughout his entire life, but his most active years for thought are relatively few. The experiences of large numbers of scientists can be put into the data banks of computer systems, and *the computers can then be*

programmed to sort through all this information and come up with "original" ideas ... Thus far I have provided for bookkeeping functions, data retrieval, problem solving in both numeric and analytic bases, and a *reasoning system stocked with all the scientific knowledge in the world.* This latter system should not be restricted to science alone. Our educational facilities in general need to have the information in the Library of Congress at the fingertips of teachers and students. This could be the greatest educational tool in the world. [Emphases mine.]

Artificial intelligence, much like real intelligence, has been extraordinarily resistant to attempts to define it with precision. But there seems to be general agreement that however else intelligence manifests itself and whatever else it may be, a necessary property of it is that it must be able, to use Fernbach's words, to "come up with 'original' ideas". There is also a widespread consensus that the production of original ideas has much to do with the application of analogies and metaphors. As Minsky says: ". . . in analogy lies the secret of really useful learning, a way to apply something learned in one situation to a problem in a quite different area." Minsky then goes on to discuss a program written by Thomas Evans, then one of his students, "that proposed solutions to geometric analogy IQ test problems and achieved performances resembling those of teenagers – although, of course, only in this restricted microworld." Obviously, Minsky thinks this program to be of very great importance to AI. I know of few papers or books Minsky has written or talks he has given since this program was written (1964) in which he has not emphasized its importance.

This is not the place to discuss the Evans program in detail. Suffice it to say here that the program is given descriptions of two geometric figures A and B, the source figures, and a small set of target figures, say C, D, E and F. The problem is to select one of the figures D, E, or F such that C is to the selected figure as A is to B. A and B may be related in that, for example, some subfigure of A, A1, is *above* another subfigure of A, A2, while in B the corresponding subfigure B1 is to the *right* of B2. The possible relations between the subfigures of A are above, left, and inside. A2 may also be smaller or larger than A1, or it may be rotated or reflected or be some combination of these relationships. Given that the set of possible relationships of subfigures to one another is very small, it is possible to specify rules that govern how source figures are transformed. The program's problem then becomes to find a rule that transforms C into one of the target figures, such that that rule most closely resembles the rule that transformed A1 into A2 in the original problem statement.

A metaphor is fundamentally a borrowing between and intercourse of thoughts, a transaction between contexts.[6] The extent of the creative analogical reach of a metaphor is always surprising. Its power to yield new insights depends largely on the richness of the contextual frameworks it fuses, on the potential mutual resonance of disparate frameworks. Newton fused the contextual framework consisting of the behaviour of everyday objects in the material world, like apples falling to the ground, with that of the solar system, and produced the remarkable idea that the moon is falling to Earth.

Do the processes embodied in Evan's program have much to do with whatever processes may exist for coming up with original ideas by the use of analogy and metaphor? This is an extraordinarily important question in view of the stress Minsky places on Evans's program, for in effect Minsky claims that Evans's program and those that have followed the general methods it pioneered are achievements in a progression that terminates in the realization of true computer creativity. We recognize that the firecracker of the ancient Chinese was such an achievement in the progression of technologies that led to the moon landings, but that mountain climbing, no matter how much nearer it brings the climber to the moon, can never be such a step. The question then is whether the kind of analogy programs on which Minsky appears to be betting so heavily are more like firecrackers than like mountain climbing.

The answer seems to me to be obvious. Truly creative thought, to the extent that it is based on analogical and metaphorical reasoning – and it is a very large extent – gains its power from the combination of hitherto disparate contexts. The act of creation is that of selecting from among the infinitude of similarities shared by every pair of concepts precisely those two frameworks that shed the maximum illumination on one or both of them. The A1 community will readily agree that the analogical reasoning programs A1 has produced so far are *given* the relevant criteria of similarity they need – that is, the two frameworks that are to be fused. This is not to criticize the quite clever programs produced to date; it is rather to illustrate on what profoundly and fundamentally misguided bases some of the most crucial concepts of A1 are built.

Conclusion

The computer in its modern form was born from the womb of the military. As with so much other modern technology of the same parentage, almost every technological advance in the computer field, including those motivated by the demands of the military, has had its residual payoff – fallout – in the civilian sector. Still, computers were first constructed in order to enable efficient calculations of how most precisely and effectively to drop artillery shells in order to kill people. It is probably a fair guess, although no one could possibly know, that a very considerable fraction of computers devoted to a single purpose today are still those dedicated to cheaper, more nearly certain ways to kill ever larger numbers of human beings.

What then *can* we expect from this strange fruit of the human genius? We can expect the kind of euphoric forecasting and assessment with which the popular and some of the scientific literature is so abundantly filled. This has nothing to do with computers per se. It seems rather to be characteristic of a peculiarly American tradition of thought. We have seen many other examples of it, and these may be instructive. Americans thought that universal schooling – not to use the term education – would lift the masses by their bootstraps and ensure a happy, prosperous, democratically governed society. This dream was realized in substance; that is, almost all American youngsters are today forced to attend school during the whole of their adolescence. But the American primary and secondary school has become not a centre of learning, not even a centre where elementary reading and writing can be taught. It has become, as I noted earlier, a minimum security prison in which millions of children and adolescents are contained for a considerable fraction of each of their days. Government reports document that America's young people are largely functionally illiterate. As a university professor, I can testify that not many youngsters recruited from among the best and the brightest can compose a single paragraph of standard English prose. As for democratic governance, a recent Health, Education and Welfare Department study revealed that nearly half the sampled high school graduates did not know that their representatives in the Congress were elected, let alone who they are or what terms of office they serve. Other examples of dreams that have been realized in a technical sense but have spawned disasters in place of the social bounties they foretold can be cited from medicine, urban planning and architecture, mass transportation, and so on.

We can also expect that the very intellectuals to whom we might reasonably look for lucid analysis and understanding of the impact of the computer on our world, the computer scientists and other scholars who claim to have made themselves authorities in this area, will, on the whole, see the emperor's new clothes more vividly than anyone else. They will shout their description in the most euphoric terms. Some of us will find their accounts unrealistic, not because of mere differences of opinion but because their accounts are plainly silly. For example, the distinguished Princeton professor of public and international affairs Robert Gilpin writes:

> ... in order to exercise power, a nation must be able to process vast amounts of data. The classic case in point is the Arab petroleum boycott against the West following the October 1973 Arab-Israeli war. Without sophisticated data-processing capabilities, the Arab oil producers *could*

not have kept track of Western oil tankers, refinery output, and all the other information needed to enforce the embargo. Moreover, given the complexity of the oil industry and the potential for cheating by Cartel members, it is doubtful if the Organization of Petroleum Exporting Countries (OPEC) would remain intact without the benefit of electronic data processing. [Emphasis mine.]

Oil tankers spend weeks at sea. An old-fashioned clerk with a quill pen could keep track of them on the back of a few large envelopes. And there have been effective cartels since at least the rise of modern capitalism, long before there were any electronic computers.

It is not necessary to credit computers for accomplishments with which they have nothing to do. They can be realistically credited with having made possible some easing of the lives of some people. Modern airline reservation systems, for example, have made it easier for me to travel. Herbert Simon believes that computers are raising the level of expertness in decision making on complex matters. I would suggest, however, the Admiral Moorer might be asked his opinion on that point. There is no question that computers have helped enormously to extend our vision of our corner and even the farther corners of the universe: I have in mind both that computers have radically transformed many aspects of astronomy and that without computers spaceflight, hence the dramatically symbolic picture of the earth floating in space, would have been impossible. Many other examples could be given of how and in what ways the computer has done some good. But some questions are almost never asked, such as: Who is the beneficiary of our much-advertised technological progress and who are its victims? What limits ought we, the people generally and scientists and engineers particularly, to impose on the application of computation to human affairs? What is the impact of the computer, not only on the economies of the world or on the war potential of nations and so on, but on the self-image of human beings and on human dignity? What irreversible forces is our worship of high technology, symbolized most starkly by the computer, bringing into play? Will our children be able to live with the world we are here and now constructing? Much depends on answers to these questions.

Notes

1 United States Congress, House Committee on Banking and Currency. Hearings before the Subcommittee on Urban Growth, 7 October 1970, 91st Congress, 2nd session, pp. 205–65.
2 *New York Times*, 10 August 1973.
3 "The Wide World of Watergate", *Newsweek*, 20 August 1973, p. 13.
4 "Toward an Intelligence beyond Man's", *Time*, 20 February 1978, p. 59.

5 "Steps toward Artificial Intelligence", in Edward A. Feigenbaum and Julian Feldman (eds), *Computers and Thought* (McGraw-Hill, New York, 1963), p. 447.
6 I. A. Richards, *The Philosophy of Rhetoric* (Oxford University Press, Oxford, 1936), p. 93.

A Reply to Weizenbaum

Daniel Bell

To invoke an old Russian proverb, Mr Weizenbaum is knocking down an open door. He sets up a confrontation between the "technologist" and the "humanist" and, having recently made the crossover, he is angry and harsh with those who seemingly do not share his new enthusiasm. More regrettably, he adopts the tactic and even the tone of the heresy hunter to sniff out – usually by pouncing on statements taken out of context – technological hubris and to berate this attitude as being morally blind. That is a pity. Since I share many of Mr Weizenbaum's concerns, I wish he had written with a pen, not a large paintbrush.

In his thick strokes, Mr Weizenbaum fails to make some necessary distinctions. The first centres on the understanding of the word *knowledge*. Mr Weizenbaum, like any tyro in epistemology, begins with the statement that "acts", "experimental results", and "reasoned judgements" are themselves determined by the observer's organizing principles. He seems to think that such a statement necessarily disproves the idea of objective knowledge. But this is to confuse the source of knowledge with its validity. Would he have us believe that all knowledge is completely relative? That there is *no* basis for deciding which knowledge is better than other knowledge? He points out, quite understandably, that much knowledge is tacit knowledge. But the scientist-philosopher who did most to establish the idea, Michael Polanyi, then went on to assert most emphatically that tacit knowledge becomes translated into public knowledge by the process of open discourse – debate, testing and evaluating – which is the very process of science, what Polanyi has called "the republic of science".

Since Mr Weizenbaum does not follow through with the logic of his own argument, it is not clear what he is driving at. He would seem to be saying that what everyone knows may be knowledge, and it is only the parochialism of the "intelligentsia" that would rule out the knowledge that the "masses" (i.e., the taxi drivers) possess. This is the kind of populism that would lead us to abolish all schools in favour of the street knowledge that the tough minds pick up so readily as "street smarts".

If I can make sense of his remarks, let me distinguish between two issues. First, Mr Weizenbaum, in coming close to the argument that there is probably no objective knowledge, is seemingly (I have to make these qualifications, for none of his arguments are fully stated) equating objective knowledge with fixed or absolute knowledge. But clearly this would be an absurdity. The stoutest defender of the idea of objective knowledge in the contemporary philosophy of science, Sir Karl Popper, is also the strongest proponent of the argument that all knowledge is tentative, conjectural, hypothetical, exploratory, incomplete. In fact, in dealing with Hume's challenge to inductivism, Popper admits that no theory can ever be accepted as true. Then what is objective knowledge? It is knowledge that is *testable* by its ability to set up some criterion by which it could be falsified. As Popper has said:

> Ad hoc explanations are explanations which are not independently testable; independently, that is, of the effect to be explained ... the testability of a theory increases and decreases with its *informative content* and therefore with its *improbability* (in the sense of the calculus of probability) ... a man of practical action has always to *choose* between some more or less definite alternatives, since even *inaction is a kind of action*. Which theory shall a man of action choose? Is there such a thing as *rational* choice? ... there is no "absolute reliance"; [yet] since we *have* to choose, it will be "rational" to choose the best-tested theory.[1]

The controlling term for both Polanyi and Popper (though the two differ in many significant respects) is critical rationalism. That is the basis for "objective knowledge".

The second issue Weizenbaum raises is why, in my definition of knowledge, I excluded such street knowledge as the taxi driver's or the intuitive knowledge of a mathematician regarding proofs of a theorem. The simple point is that a definition is related to a purpose. I was not giving an absolute definition of knowledge. The purpose was instrumental, namely, what kinds of knowledge could be measured, stored readily, retrieved, and used within an instrument that could be designed for that purpose. I do believe, as is evident in my paper, that judgemental knowledge and evaluative knowledge cannot be ordered in the form that some computer scientists believe. Mr Weizenbaum, who is apparently so fearful of any concessions to the computer, italicizes a phrase of mine to indicate that I am making only "limited" concessions to the "most extreme fantasies". Mr Weizenbaum is simply pushing harder on the open door.

If Mr Weizenbaum is a cognitive relativist in one realm, he is a moral absolutist in the other, and as simplistic in the latter as he is in the former. Leaving aside the heavy-handed analogy between Eichmann and the Air Force programmers – another use of a paintbrush rather than a pen – there are two distinctions that arise in the relation of technology to society and technology to moral problems. The first is the point that technology is not a "reified thing" or some abstract "logical imperative" but is embedded in a social support system, and it is the support system, not the technology, that determines its use. One can, with the same technology, design totally different outcomes by designing different social support systems. To take the example of the automobile, one can have a system of complete private ownership and the large degree of personal mobility it affords yet suffer a large social cost in the amount of garage space needed or pollution of the air. But another system deploys automobiles as a public utility; one takes an automobile from widely dispersed pools or stations throughout a city, uses it as needed, and leaves it at another station near one's destination. The technology is the same, yet the pattern of use is highly dissimilar. The crucial decisions are sociological, not technological.

The second problem, however, arises from that very fact. It is often said: "We have been able to go to the moon, why can't we build better houses, or design a better curriculum or assure a better health system?" The point is that getting to the moon is largely a technical problem, but the other, social, questions frequently involve a difference if not a clash of values. We may say that individuals have a right to determine the decisions that affect their lives, yet if a community insists that busing its children to schools outside the neighbourhood disrupts its own community patterns, the problem is compounded because we have a conflict here between community decisions and racial integration. Or if we say that places in a medical school should be allocated on the basis of cultural disadvantage to a stipulated number of minority persons, even at the expense of the merit principle, it is not a matter of right versus wrong but of right versus right. This is what makes moral decisions so difficult. And these are the hard questions.

I fear that Mr Weizenbaum, with his highly focused tunnel vision, has misread my essay. In my work on postindustrial society, I have reiterated the point that a change in the techno-economic order (and that is the realm of information) does not *determine* changes in the political and cultural realms of society but poses questions to which society must respond. In the Commission on the Year 2000, which I chaired for a decade, the insistent point of the enterprise was that the effort to plot alternative futures or the likely outcome of the present is not to stipulate the future but to widen the sphere of moral choices. In my essay – and it is a single essay, not the world – I have sought to deal with the way in which a change in the infrastructure of a society – in this instance, the expansion of a communications system – begins to have societal effects whose consequences must be understood in order for a society to make intelligent policy choices.

I can understand Mr Weizenbaum's moral concerns, but he puts these forward with the hyperbolic fervour of a convert, and in this case I fear that his sermon is misdirected. Many years ago, Norbert Wiener wrote a book with the fetching title *God and Golem*. Mr Weizenbaum fears that the computer may be a Golem, a clay monster into whom life has been breathed. That may well be, though I doubt it. In any event, fearing the Golem, one should not try to play God, or his prophet. The secular tasks of the world are difficult enough.

Notes

1 Karl R. Popper, *Objective Knowledge* (Clarendon Press, Oxford, 1972), pp. 15–16, 17, 21–2.

Guide to Further Reading

Daniel Bell, *The Coming of Post-Industrial Society* (Basic Books, New York, 1973 and Harper and Row, New York, 1976; Heinemann, London, 1974).

Jay W. Forrester, Testimonies before Subcommittee on Urban Growth, 7 October 1970, and Subcommittee on Government, 20 December 1973, US Congress, Washington DC.

Jonathan I. Gershuny, "Post-Industrial Society: The Myth of the Service Economy", in *Futures*, vol. 10, No. 2 (April 1977). A critique of Bell's notion of the 'postindustrial society' which examines in detail the growth and potential growth of the service sector.

After Industrial Society? (Macmillan, London, 1978). A longer version of the previous article, in this book the author demonstrates the growth of the "Self-service Economy" or the "Informal Economy" based upon capital investment in domestic consumer goods.

A. W. Gouldner, *Ideology and Technology* (Heinemann, London, 1976).

D. F. Harris and F. J. Taylor, *The Service Sector: Its Changing Role as a Source of Employment* (Centre for Environmental Studies, London, 1978).

Fred Hirsch, *The Social Limits to Growth* (Routledge, London, 1977).

Krishan Kumar, *Prophecy and Progress: The Sociology of Industrial and Post-Industrial Society* (Pelican, Harmondsworth, 1978).

Dennis L. Meadows *et al.*, *The Limits to Growth* (Potomac Associates, Washington DC, 1972).

David Reisman, "Leisure and Work in Post-Industrial Society", in S. D. Douglas (ed.), *The Technological Threat* (Prentice-Hall, Englewood Cliffs, New Jersey, 1971).

G. Ross, "The Second Coming of Daniel Bell", in *Socialist Register 1974* (Merlin Press, London, 1974).

Theodore Roszak, *Where the Wasteland Ends: Politics and Transcendance in Post-Industrial Society* (Doubleday, New York, 1972).

Fred J. Shafer, "Social Effects of Automation in Manufacturing – The Relationships Among People, Materials and Technology", in *Proceedings of the American Society of Engineers, Joint Automatic Control Conference*, West Lafayette, Indiana (July 1976).

Tom Stonier, "A Profile of the Post-Industrial Society", in R. Page (ed.), *Strategies for Change in a Technological Society* (Bath University, 1977).
"Education for the Post-Industrial Society", paper to conference on "The Future of Work", Manchester Polytechnic, 21 March 1978.

Alvin Toffler, *Future Shock* (Random House, New York, 1970).

E. Trist, "Toward a Post-Industrial Culture", in R. Dubin (ed.), *A Handbook of Work, Organisation and Society* (Rand McNally, New York, 1976).

Glossary of Terms

AI Artificial Intelligence.

Algol A computer language used in programming for many technical and scientific applications of the computer.

Alphanumeric Ordering or ordered by both letters and numbers.

Analog or Analogue Sometimes referred to as linear. A system in which the output signal bears a continuous relationship to the input signal. Thus an analogue computer uses physical properties analogous to the properties being studied (as a slide rule uses length as analogous to a number) and is most commonly used in continuous process control. Opposite of *digital* systems which are discontinuous.

Basic A computer language, resembling natural English, used in programming for simple calculations.

Binary A digital system where only two types of signal are used, usually just On/Off or Yes/No.

Bipolar Refers to semiconductor devices in which a gain is obtained by the interaction of positive and negative charges.

Bit The basic unit of information in a digital computer and an acronym of BInary digiT. 1024 bits go to make up a Kilobit or K. Thus a 64K RAM device, for example, contains $64 \times 1024 = 65,536$ bits of information.

Byte A byte is a group of bits taken together and treated as a unit.

CAD Computer Aided Design.

CCD or Charged Couple Device A device in which information is stored by means of packets of minute electrical charges.

Chip or silicon chip A small, square piece of pure silicon, layers of which have been etched away and doped with impurities so as to form alternate insulators and conductors which together make up the pattern of a complete integrated circuit, equivalent to thousands of transistors. Chips are normally a fragment sliced from a much larger wafer of silicon. The chip is not ready for use until packaged.

Cobol Acronym from COmmon Business Orientated Language. A computer language used in programming for most commercial applications of the computer.

Computer   An electronic device used for processing information received in a prescribed and acceptable form according to a predetermined sequence of instructions.

Console   The control panel or terminal, usually a keyboard plus a VDU and other readout mechanisms, used for communicating with the CPU of a computer.

CPU   The Central Processing Unit is the main part of a computer and comprises a logic unit, an arithmetic unit and a control unit.

CRT   Cathode-Ray Tube.

Data   One of the two classes of information fed to a computer. The other is the program.

Diffusion   A process by which selected chemicals, called dopants, are implanted in semiconductor materials like silicon to enable them to conduct or not conduct electricity.

Digital and Digital Computer   A system or computer system that handles information coded as numbers and transformed into electrical pulses. Digital computers handle large numbers of numbers at very high speeds with great accuracy.

Discrete device   A single function component, such as a transistor or a diode.

DMOS   Short channel high performance devices with precise channel length determined by double diffusion rather than photolithography. Originally developed for microwave oven applications.

EDP   Electronic Data Processing. The use of digital computers for manipulating information.

Emf   Electromotive force.

FET   Field Effect Transistor. A transistor controlled by voltage rather than current.

Flip flop or half-shift register   Device in which the two inputs correspond to two stable states. Widely used for counting and storage.

Floppy disc   A flexible magnetic disc resembling a 45 rpm record on which information is stored.

Fortran   FORmula TRANslation. A computer language used for programming many technical and scientific applications of the computer.

Hardware   The mechanical, electronic, magnetic and electrical parts of a computer system. Opposite of software.

IC   See Integrated Circuit.

Input   The information fed into a computer either in the form of data or the program.

Integrated circuit   A semiconductor device containing circuit elements which are made from a single piece of material and which are indivisibly connected.

LCD display   A type of display utilizing liquid crystals. The standard seven-segment numerical display on pocket calculators uses liquid crystal technology, as do many digital readout displays.

LED display   A type of display utilizing Light-Emitting Diodes. Especially useful for low-voltage devices, such as digital watches.

LSI Large-Scale Integration. A term usually applied to integrated circuits containing from 100 to 5000 logic gates or 1000 to 16,000 memory bits. Cf. SSI, MSI and VLSI.

Mainframe Mainframe computers are the large "traditional" computers. Now the term refers more specifically to "third generation" computers built since the mid-1960s which use microcircuits. They are extremely expensive but also very sophisticated, with a wide range of peripherals. "First generation" computers were the machines of the 1950s and the early 1960s which used valves. "Second generation" computers were the machines of the early and mid-1960s in which transistors had replaced valves. The slice of the total computer market held by mainframe computers is declining rapidly.

Mask A mask is the photographic plate, used in the construction of a wafer of chips, on which the integrated circuit pattern required is printed. Different masks are used for each step in the process of building up the wafer.

Memory A device which stores information used by a computer. Memory can be immediately accessible or it can be in back-up form, such as magnetic floppy discs.

Microelectronics The study, design and use of devices that depend on the conduction of electricity through semiconductors and which are made to extremely small dimensions.

Microcomputer A CPU chip and storage chips mounted on a board – for use, for example, as the complete control unit in an automatic machine tool – constitute a microcomputer. The single-chip microcomputer is a CPU with memory storage and other facilities all on the same chip. See minicomputer.

Microprocessor or MPU The microprocessor is simply a CPU on a chip. In other words, it is the entire central processing unit of a computer in the form of an LSI circuit built up from a single piece of silicon. It can interpret and execute instructions just like a traditional mainframe computer.

Minicomputer The border between a minicomputer and a microcomputer is not clear, since the term minicomputer is often used to describe any board-mounted array of a CPU and other packaged chips. If the term microcomputer was reserved solely for the single-chip microcomputer things would be a lot easier.

MIP Million Instructions Per second.

MNOS Metal-Nitride-Oxide-Semiconductor.

Modem modulator – demodulator. A device used to convert signals from one type of equipment into a form suitable for input into another type.

MOS Metal-Oxide-Semiconductor. The name of the technology based on insulated-gate field-effect transistors which is used in large-scale integrated (LSI) circuits.

MPU Microprocessor Unit. See Microprocessor.

MSI Medium-Scale Integration. Cf. SSI, LSI and VLSI.

Multi-access A system whereby several users may tap in to the same computer from their own terminals.

Nanosecond A measure of time in computing. It is one thousandth of a microsecond, or expressed mathematically, 10^{-9} seconds.

NC Numerically Controlled. Usually refers to machine tools which are run automatically by a program, usually on a punched tape.

N-channel   A type of field-effect transistor in which the conducting channel is *n*-type (negative) semiconductor material. *N*-channel devices operate at a higher speed than *p*-type (positive) devices.

OCR   Optical Character Reader. An OCR will read printed and even hand-written characters. An important new technology that is rapidly increasing in sophistication.

Output   The information that emerges from a computer.

Peripheral   A terminal or piece of equipment attached to a CPU to form a usable computer system. The term covers all backing store units, keyboards, VDUs and printouts.

Prestel   The British Post Office's computer-based information system launched early in 1979. It links the user's TV to a central computer by using the telephone wires.

Program   A sequence of instructions to be obeyed by a computer, written by a programmer.

PROM   Programmable Read-Only Memory. A memory device into which information can be written after it has been manufactured, but thereafter cannot be altered.

RAM   Random Access Memory. A memory device in which information can be entered into or retrieved from any storage position, rather like a pigeonhole system.

Remote Terminal   A terminal sited to be convenient to the user rather than next to the computer. Linked up through telecommunications.

ROM   Read-Only Memory. A memory device into which information is written during the manufacturing process and which thereafter cannot be altered.

Semiconductor   A material, such as silicon, which can be arranged to conduct or insulate from electricity. It has a crystal structure whose atomic bonds allow the conduction of current by either positive or negative carriers when the appropriate dopants are added.

Shared Logic Facility   A computer or, say, word processor system with geographically dispersed terminals, all of which have access to one CPU and its storage devices.

SIC   Silicon Integrated Circuit. See Integrated Circuit.

Silicone   Synthetic substance, sometimes used to increase size of female breasts. Not to be confused with silicon, which comes from common sand.

Software   General term to describe computer programs, that is, the set of instructions given to a computer. Cf. hardware.

Solid-state   The area of physics which deals with materials in their solid form. All silicon semiconductors are solid-state devices.

SSI   Small-Scale Integration. Cf. MSI, LSI and VLSI.

Stand-alone   Term used to describe complete computer installation in one place.

Systems analyst   Someone who analyses a function (for example, of an office or department) and devises a computer system that will perform the same functions. This usually includes preparing a brief from which a programmer writes the necessary software.

Teletext System for conveying written information from broadcaster to user's TV screen. For example, the BBC's *Ceefax* service and ITN's *Oracle* service in Britain. Because it uses the airwaves, *Teletext* is more limited than *Viewdata/Prestel* in the amount of information it can carry.

Terminal Station for inputting or retrieving information from a computer system. Usually a keyboard or VDU but also can be a teleprinter, an OCR, a paper tape punch or reader, or a card punch or reader.

Transistor An active semiconductor device with three electrodes (emitter, base and collector). Can be used as a switch or an amplifier.

TTL Transistor–Transistor Logic. A family of high speed integrated circuits. Largely supplanted by MOS logic circuits which can be packed more tightly and consume less power.

UDR Universal Document Reader. A peripheral that scans each sheet in a stack of printed forms, recognizes special marks, and feeds the information back to the CPU.

UNIMATE The name of a make of industrial robot usually used for welding.

Viewdata Earlier name for *Prestel*.

VHSIC Very High Speed Integrated Circuit.

VLSI Very Large-Scale Integration. A term usually applied to integrated circuits containing a minimum of 5000 logic gates or more than 16,000 memory bits. The manufacturing technology needed to produce VLSI devices involves electron beams or X-rays to etch the minute patterns on the chips. Cf. SSI, MSI and LSI.

VDU Visual Display Unit. A television-like terminal, consisting of a cathode-ray tube on which may be displayed script or line diagrams generated by computer.

VMOS MOS circuits fabricated using the V-groove technique.

Wafer A round, thin disc of semiconductor material, usually about four inches in diameter and usually silicon, on which many devices can be built up at the same time. When the fabrication process is completed, the devices are separated for packaging and use.

Yield A measure of the efficiency of the chip production process which shows the proportion of devices completed in working order.

Index